P9-CDX-764

MR. WRIGLEY'S BALL CLUB

MR. WRIGLEY'S BALL CLUB

CHICAGO & THE CUBS DURING THE JAZZ AGE

Roberts Ehrgott

University of Nebraska Press | Lincoln and London

Library of Congress Cataloging-in-Publication Data
Ehrgott, Roberts, 1951–
Mr. Wrigley's ball club: Chicago and the Cubs during
the jazz age / Roberts Ehrgott.
p. cm.
Includes bibliographical references and index.
ISBN 978-0-8032-6478-6 (cloth: alk. paper) 1. Chicago
Cubs (Baseball team)—History. 2. Chicago (Ill.)—
History—20th century. 3. Chicago (Ill.)—Social life
and customs. I. Title.
GV875.C6E37 2013
796.357'640977311—dc23   2012039457

Set in Fournier MT Pro by Laura Wellington.
Designed by A. Shahan.

This book is dedicated to Susan Malone
Ehrgott, a lifelong resident of Chicago's
North Side and a Ladies Day veteran who
took me to my first Major League game.

CONTENTS

ACKNOWLEDGMENTS

The following individuals were all willing to help freely with information and advice: Bob Allen, George Brace, Michael Emmerich, Col. John P. Fitzgerald, Nolan Gottlieb, Stephen S. Gottlieb, Sharon Hankinson, Charles E. Herman, Sheila Hartnett Hornof, Mark Jacob, John Kiesewetter, Dr. H. Hoffman Groskloss, Frederick A. Krehbiel, Forrest Docenus Jensen, Edward Linn, Leonard R. Merullo, Joseph G. Moore, Andy Pafko, Clyde Partin, Daniel J. J. Ross, Robert C. Root, E. R. "Salty" Saltwell, Marla L. Sayers, Riggs Stephenson II, Riggs Stephenson III, Barbara Strangeman, Jeffrey R. Twyman, and Mike Veeck.

The Chicago Historical Society, the Chicago National League Ball Club, the *Chicago Sun-Times*, the National Baseball Hall of Fame and Museum, the *Sporting News*, and the Wells Library at Indiana University–Bloomington all furnished me with outstanding service and cooperation.

Special thanks go to the University of Nebraska Press and staff and to my agents, Lukas Ortiz and Philip Spitzer, two men I cannot thank enough.

Finally, I must acknowledge the extraordinary patience and understanding of Lynne and Nicholas Ehrgott.

1 | The Capital of Baseball

Chicago's bid for grandeur has failed. . . . [Chicago], it now seems certain, will never be first. —A. J. Liebling, *Chicago: The Second City*, 1952

"Chicago is still the second city." —John Lindsay, mayor of New York, 1969

The bases were loaded with two outs in the home eleventh inning at Wrigley Field on September 13, 1931, while the crowd roared for the sacrifice of the solitary youngster standing at the center of the diamond. The threats to that forlorn figure, Boston pitcher Bruce Cunningham, had mounted batter by batter: a one-out double, an intentional walk, then a desperate lunge by the second baseman to stop a sharp drive and hold the Cubs' lead runner at third base. The right-handed Cunningham intentionally walked the next batter through the inning, filling the last available base. Cunningham now had to record an out, any out, by strikes, force, fly, or tag to preserve the 7–7 tie. Cunningham in particular needed this stop. The howling of the Wrigley mob may have been only a vicarious release, but Cunningham, 3-11 on the year after three unremarkable seasons in the big leagues, might soon need to find another livelihood, and there weren't many of those available in late 1931.

The opposing teams on this bright September afternoon were a collective fifty games or so from first place; only the Cubs' need to remain in the first division to share in World Series proceeds provided any plausible suspense, yet thirty-three thousand Chicagoans howled as if the pennant were on the line. The third-place Cubs—17½ games from first place and mathematically eliminated from contention, and the perennially downtrodden Braves, 7-24 in the last month—nonetheless faced a crowd whose size the 1930 World Series had not matched. Cunningham and the sixth-place Braves were fortunate if they saw so many Boston fans in a full week. In fact, that afternoon in Boston, the two Sox teams were playing before seven thousand; Redland Field in Cincinnati had attracted just eight thousand fans. New York City could claim more fans for the day, but with two mostly empty venues: ten thousand at Brooklyn's Ebbets Field, and twenty-five thousand at Yankee Stadium, supposedly more than seventy thousand in capacity.

Seven other major league parks with empty seats and blasé late-season customers, yet young Cunningham had to pitch in the epicenter of a sports madhouse, before a hoarse rabble in full cry for the 143rd game of a home team also-ran. Still, in the capital of baseball a half-dozen radio stations and their hundreds of thousands of listeners were following each pitch and every play of the Cubs' eleventh—the one-out double by Les Bell, two intentional walks, the second baseman's marvelous stop.[1]

Across the sprawling city the announcers' voices squawked through windows and doors still open in the warm late-summer afternoon, down quiet side streets and alleys, inside stores and barbershops and the ice cream parlors that fronted for the ready availability of beer. No other program—no music, no comedy, no soap opera, no news—aired during the Cub game. The flat Midwestern deliveries of the play-by-play men were the common denominator of a city where sociologists had recorded the presence of at least twenty-eight spoken tongues. The broadcasts reached not just the 7 million residents of "Chicagoland"—the city and its suburbs—but an audience of millions more in a six-state swatch of the upper Midwest. Cub games had created the world's first electronic village, a daily monopoly of the airwaves rivaled at first only by the World Series, heavyweight title fights, presidential inaugurations, and appearances of Charles Lindbergh.[2]

Confounding the scoffers who predicted that this total broadcast immersion would cripple the ball club's attendance, the Cubs' radio coverage had touched off the greatest boom since the arrival of Babe Ruth in New York more than a decade earlier. By 1931 the capital of baseball had outdrawn the "House That Ruth Built" four summers running. Two years earlier, in the last halcyon summer of the Roaring Twenties, Mr. Wrigley's turnstiles had recorded 1.5 million visits, more than the major leagues would see until the Depression and World War II had run their course. Despite the ever-deepening Depression and the club's unexpected fall from contention, Wrigley Field's 1931 attendance count handily exceeded, at 974,688, anything most teams had dreamt of in the fattest years of the Jazz Age. Each year in this new capital of baseball, one of every four National League customers passed through Mr. Wrigley's turnstiles.[3]

The crowds of this boom time might storm the gates and even the field in midgame; express disgust or jubilation by littering the field with pop bottles, fruit, or straw hats; and watch the rise and fall of fabled careers and batting records. Friend or foe found himself razzed or cheered according to standards that shifted as quickly as the breezes off Lake Michigan, a few blocks to the east. But at any moment a hero or a villain could turn things around with a lovely wind-blown drive into the right-field bleachers, a county fair–style structure of scaffolding and planks whose first row met the playing field behind a cyclone fence only 320 feet from home plate, the famous ivy-clad walls yet unforeseen. After Labor Day, especially in the heat of a pennant race, a decisive home run signaled a seasonal ritual: flinging the passing summer's straw hats—"skimmers"—onto the field with a flick of the wrist, a Jazz Age Frisbee toss that jumbled the field with mounds of hats and halted games while the ground crew hauled them off.[4]

The noise could reach its highest decibels in the bedlam of the Cubs' unprecedented Ladies Day carnivals, when the complimentary admission of women left proportionately many fewer men on hand. Wrigley Field's female fans were the most numerous and enthusiastic assortment of sportswomen yet witnessed in the modern world. Reaching numbers of twenty thousand and higher, their riotous Friday afternoon presence often dwarfed the day's paid attendance in any other major league park. The women poured into the ballpark every Friday the Cubs played at home, applauded foul balls enthusiastically, adopted and discarded favorites, and hounded the chosen ones for autographs; the boldest flappers forwarded their phone numbers to the dugouts. Massing in the streets outside the park, willing to charge the gates if necessary, Chicago's womenfolk had forced management to adopt an elaborate advance distribution system to cope with the onrush.

Saturdays and Sundays brought yet more women, this time paying customers who had learned baseball on Friday afternoons or by listening to the broadcasts during household chores and now attended with spouses and families. Aided by the female reinforcements, the park sold out frequently on weekends, and latecomers, in their Sunday best, might have to settle for standing-room-only admission, lining up behind ropes that Andy Frain's resplendent, paramilitary ushers stretched deep in the outfield, sweltering under the summer sun—up to four thousand souls, a typical weekday figure in several other major league parks.

While the bleachers and the overflow teemed with the humble and the late arriving, the grandstands held a cross-section of Jazz Age Chicago. Amid a sea of straw hats, the inevitable flask of moonshine liquor, perhaps produced by a snappy dresser wearing spats, emerged, and from time to time knots of hard-faced men in snap-brimmed panamas invaded the box seats, the kingpin of the moment safely in their midst.[5]

Most games though, the inhabitant of another box, just behind the Cubs' dugout along the third-base line, commanded attention. There, three or four days each week during the club's lengthy home stands and his own visits to his privately owned 58,000-acre Pacific island, sat the team's chief cheerleader, a double-chinned older gentleman clad in bowtie, three-piece suit, and expensive skimmer: William Wrigley Jr.—"Bill" only to the public, never to his face—a free-spending overachiever, dreamt of owning the greatest baseball team in the world. A perfectionist, he monitored the condition of his plant in minute detail, ever vigilant for the signs of dirt or disorder, insistant that even his team's uniforms were the pride of the major leagues. Not shy about leaping to his feet for an exciting play or proudly passing out cigars after a home run, he monitored his prized athletic thoroughbreds up close, pampered them, encouraged them. In the six years since Mr. Wrigley had retired from active control of his eponymous company, the world's premier seller of chewing gum, Mr. Wrigley's ball club and the great surge in attendance had caught the baseball world by surprise, complete with the Ladies Day crowds SRO and sellouts, not to mention frequent hurling of hats and fruit. Wrigley, in close alliance with his trusted baseball man, William Veeck Sr., snapped up athletes as he had his semitropical island—Santa Catalina Island, floating like a cloud off the southern California coast, where he presided while his players trained each February and March, the lord of an estate inspecting his chattel, feeding and sheltering them, sponsoring their honeymoons, providing them entertainment and introductions to Hollywood's stars, starlets, producers, and agents.[6]

Wrigley made sure no payroll in the National League exceeded his and that his expensive player acquisitions made a splash in the newspapers. After years of extravagant offers and dealings, his top sluggers earned as much as Lou Gehrig (though not Babe Ruth himself). Wrigley's charges owned large stretches of the record book untrod by even the Bambino of New York. Mr. Wrigley openly hankered to own the greatest ball club in the world, and he would see that they played in its baseball capital.[7]

By September 1931 Wrigley's promotions, his ambitions, his hirings and firings, his dissatisfaction with ordinary definitions of success, had created a participatory baseball democracy in which the humblest fan expected a say and a ball club that occupied a central place in the national conversation. The shirt-sleeved folk booing in Mr. Wrigley's ballpark were a cloud on the horizon, harbingers of change—soon to become foot soldiers in something called the New Deal, when the culture would turn on Bill Wrigley's chums and allies—Hoover, Coolidge, Big Bill Thompson, Samuel Insull, Andrew Mellon. The voters would eject them from the seats of power, and an army of business regulators and prosecutors would treat them much as they did the murderous Al Capone, going to trial downtown in a few weeks. Wrigley's death, only four months off, would spare him this spectacle. His son and successor, the reticent, cautious Philip, would personify a new business paradigm, conserving as well as acquiring, stepping carefully, avoiding flamboyant risk-taking and braggadocio.

In September 1931, none of that was obvious, or inevitable. Depression or not, pennant race or not, Wrigley's customers were out in force on a warmish Sunday afternoon, on the edge of their seats, still following every twist of their team's fortunes and its politics. That said, the wild pennant races of the past three Septembers had not repeated themselves in 1931; the streets around the ballpark were no longer blocked with ticket seekers, no temporary bleachers were going up for a World Series, and the more recent losses and disappointments and controversies were yet fresh in the minds of Cubs' fans. That itself was not necessarily good news for Wrigley and his favorite Cub.

Pat Pieper, the Cubs' field announcer, was surprised to see the Cubs' player-manager, Rogers Hornsby, calling his on-deck batter back to the dugout. It seemed an odd move: the scheduled batter was a capable hitter and a favorite of Hornsby's—why not let him face the right-handed Cunningham?

Pieper had been at his job ever since the Cubs moved into the park in 1916. His main tool was a green, fourteen-pound megaphone that measured some three feet long and eighteen inches across at the bell; an assistant helped him tote it down each foul line and bellow the lineup changes to the grandstands and box seats. The bleacher customers, not to mention the reporters in the press box, had to cup their ears or rely on word of mouth to keep track of changes. Trying to read the back of a player's uniform was no help, for the Cubs had not yet adopted numbered jerseys.[8]

Yet before Pieper could reach his first station, even the bleacher dwellers recognized who had swaggered from the dugout, swinging two bats over his head. For Cunningham, high on the mound, it was a disconcerting sight: wielding the bats was Mr. Wrigley's prize superstar, the Cubs' leading RBI man, their player-manager, and by most lights, the greatest right-handed hitter who had ever stepped into a major league box. As the club's player-manager, Hornsby was the self-same party who had decided that in this instance baseball's lefty-righty rule need not apply.[9]

Little that Cunningham and the Braves had experienced prepared them to see thousands of angry customers leaping to their feet as one, shaking fists and jeering; then came a spirited reply loudly approving the manager's choice. Cunningham might have harked back to the ancient history lessons still taught in that day, Blues and Greens demonstrating in the imperial Circus, factions that could turn on their fellow citizens—or upon the imperial box itself. Civil war had broken out in the capital of baseball. While Pieper tried to announce the expensive pinch hitter through his cone, the great Rajah, taking no heed of the commotion, strode to the batter's box, stepped in, and cooly awaited Cunningham's first delivery.[10]

With the bases full, Cunningham was free to take his full windup again. Hornsby let the first pitch go by, a called strike. He did not complain; umpire baiting was not among his faults, and for someone of his stature in the business, star and umpire more or less collaborated on the scope of the strike zone. The stone-faced Texan presented Cunningham and all pitchers with unique problems. Thrice a .400 hitter, owner of one of the highest career batting averages ever, he had done the most, aside from Ruth himself, to launch baseball's Golden Age, the era of the lively ball. But unlike Ruth and others of the new breed, he represented the old order in both his attitudes and his play; off the field, he was surly and cold— "wintry-souled," in the words of one historian—to rivals and teammates alike, though assuredly not to Mr. Wrigley. Disciplined and relentless, the Rajah never overswung or forced himself to pull the ball for distance; at all times he was willing to take pitches to the opposite field. "There's only one batting rule," he said. "Keep your eye on the ball."[11]

As long as a warm lakeward breeze cooperated, the dimensions of Wrigley Field, with its right-field bleachers some 320 feet off, favored an opposite-field hitter like Hornsby. On a pleasant day like September 13, 1931, any overgrown fly ball could reach those bleachers.

Chicago in 1931 was still a turbulent boomtown, the country's most diverse in the years after World War I. After the startling half-century of growth that followed the great fire of 1871, its population had mushroomed another 25 percent in the 1920s. Those born abroad and their children made up two-thirds of the city's population: "the largest Lithuanian city in the world" or "the third largest Irish city in the world," depending on who was counting. Many other inhabitants hailed from farms or small towns in the hinterlands of the Midwest and the South. Chicagoans, said one who knew them well, were the type who "eat with a knife instead of a fork, who take a bath on Saturday night, who play an occasional game of pinochle, and who cuss at the traffic cop who doesn't let them park in the Loop." Many lived in apartments or shotgun-style cold-water flats; even those with hot water might bathe no more than once or twice a week. Après bath, even the best-scrubbed fan had only perfume or cologne for further defense: deodorants and antiperspirants were not yet in widespread use— making the sights and smells of Wrigley Field's bleachers, to consider one example, even more problematic.[12]

Chicagoans of that description filled the right-field bleachers, and the similar, if much smaller "jury box" in left-center field; physically and socially the bleacherites resided far from William Wrigley's box seat. Between the two bleacher sections loomed the scoreboard, topped by the only advertising Wrigley allowed in the park: the Wrigley Doublemint twins. A space on the bleacher planks cost 50 cents (about $5 in today's money); for those not within walking distance, it took another 7 cents' streetcar fare or 10 cents to take the Northwestern El to the Addison Street stop.[13]

It was a trek the West Siders made willingly and cheerfully. For their first forty years the Cubs were a team of the Central and West Side districts, at the old Lakefront Stadium and the West Side Grounds. The team moved to the more affluent North Side only in 1916, after the renegade Federal League folded and the late, unlamented Chicago Whales franchise left behind a brand-new ballpark that proved much superior to its roster. Baseball on the North Side was a new experience for many Cub fans, quite a few of whom, in typical big-city fashion, seldom ventured so far outside their own tight-knit ethnic quarters, making transfers on the trolleys or the El. Ring Lardner of the *Chicago Tribune,* himself a North Sider, tried to describe the strange new land for his readership when the Whales opened for business in 1914: the new park, he explained, lay in a neighborhood "largely inhabited by Caucasians, otherwise it is very similar to ourselves." In particular, he noted, the familiar smell of the stockyards was missing.[14]

More than two decades earlier, in the glory days of the Tinker, Evers, and Chance infield, the Cubs had played south and west of the north branch of the Chicago River, another world from the North Side or the lakefront's glittering "City of the Future." There were scenes of startling squalor and grimness, rows of tottering wooden slum dwellings, crumbling nineteenth-century structures of cheap brick and stone, lots filled with debris.

> At times all Chicagoans grow weary of the almost universal ugliness of Chicago and everyone sags. One feels it in the street, in the stores, in the homes. The bodies of the people sag and a cry seems to go up out of a million throats,—"we are set down here in this continual noise, dirt and ugliness. Why did you ever put us down here? There is no rest. We are always being hurried about from place to place, to no end. Millions of us live on the vast Chicago West Side, where all streets are equally ugly and where the streets go on and on forever, out of nowhere into nothing."[15]

It might be added that in these environs, the Volstead Act, the law of the land that enforced alcohol prohibition, was anathema, and the city's

The Capital of Baseball

gangsters found the bulk of their recruits. To the south lay the neighbor-hoods of the Irish and the city's latest arrivals, blacks from the South. West were Bohemians, Jews, and more Irish; north and west, Polish, Swedish, and Germans. They bickered and fought, violated the Volstead Act, and bet on the horses. Gangs of young men, often fronting as athletic clubs, were dominated by members of each ethnic group. The Ragen Colts, an Irish sports club on the South Side, had led the horrific race riots of 1919. On the West Side, the Bohemians of Pilsen and the Jews of Lawndale squared off year after year, sometimes on the streets, sometimes on the playing field or the boxing ring.

Baseball, fights, and anything else sporting supported a bookmaking industry that flourished throughout the city. Betting was open in Wrigley Field's bleachers. It was in Chicago, after all, that professional gamblers had nearly brought baseball down by conspiring to throw the 1919 World Series, and that Judge Kenesaw Mountain Landis had begun his reign in 1921 by banning eight Chicago White Sox from baseball for their involve-ment in the scheme.[16]

Landis, himself a Progressive, good-government Republican like Wrig-ley, watched the developing Chicago scene of the 1920s without enthusi-asm. The politicians of the 1920s, from the mayor and the state's attorney on down, aided and abetted—and in turn were aided and abetted by—a welter of booze-running, numbers-running, brothel-operating gangs. Mindful that a Chicago jury had found the Black Sox not guilty, Landis had no intention of letting this zeitgeist infect the sport he commanded. His harsh treatment of the Black Sox was proof of that. From his head-quarters on Michigan Avenue, he tried to extend baseball's rules over the most likely connection to gamblers: horse-track betting. Many a ballplayer liked to spend his day off at the track; a few others—most conspicuously, Rogers Hornsby—could not resist laying their bets at the "handbooks" of Uptown, just to the north of the ballpark. The word on the street had it that Hornsby relayed his bets to the bookies while running his ball club from the dugout.[17]

For the time being Landis was limited to hectoring Hornsby about his bad habits and scheming against the evils of racetrack betting. But sports or betting had little to do with Chicago's most notorious law breaking. Nowhere had the inhabitants of a city more enthusiastically and frequently defied Volstead Act enforcement. The results were the most spectacular of the Prohibition era. If Chicago did not pioneer bootlegging, speakeasies, illegal breweries, organized home stills, distribution networks, beer-truck smuggling, gang wars, police payoffs, and judicial corruption, the metropolis certainly became a showcase for these and a host of other symbols of the age. Chicago police estimated that hardly a block in the city lacked its two or three stills; the city harbored perhaps twenty thousand speakeasies. After the final out of each Cub game, the voice of Wrigley Field, Pat Pieper, strolled over to a neighborhood establishment where he moonlighted as a bartender.[18]

The bleacherites, a solid block of "wets" if ever there was one, had little use for the teetotaler William Wrigley had placed in charge of the Cubs: Rogers Hornsby. In addition, the transplanted Texan's reputed membership in the Ku Klux Klan was no recommendation to ethnics or their sons and daughters. The Rajah held himself up as a nondrinking, nonsmoking role model—and then signed on as the national spokesman for a brand of cigarettes. The fans had also heard how the Rajah, who judged others in the harshest ways, welshed on his gambling debts.[19]

No, long before William Wrigley had brought the Rajah into his baseball paradise, the bleacher folk had adopted a very different Cub as their hero. The people's choice was no teetotaler, no pedestal climber, but all too human, lusty, short, exuberant, always ready to solve problems with his fists or a home run. He was Hack Wilson, the working-class idol of Chicago in the Roaring Twenties, the rough-and-ready, self-made embodiment of the blue-collar success story.[20]

On the afternoon of September 13, 1931, though, Wilson was absent from the park he had so often held in his thrall. The week before, Hornsby had stripped him of his Cub uniform and suspended him for the season and closed the clubhouse to him. Now the Hacker was making the long drive back to his home in the panhandle of West Virginia. Hack Wilson would never again wear a Cub uniform in the ballpark he had thrilled and generally captivated for half a decade, and that was the real problem as Hornsby stepped into the batter's box to face Bruce Cunningham.

Almost exactly a year before Wilson's departure, the bleacher residents, and most other Cub fans, had protested another drastic management order, the sacking of Hornsby's predecessor, Joe McCarthy. That hard-drinking

Irishman, Wilson's mentor and faithful ally, had committed the sin of standing in Rogers Hornsby's career path. Now, the fans thought, fun-loving Hack was gone for the sin of being himself—being like them.[21]

The stands were still in an uproar. Cunningham delivered his 0-1 pitch, which came in on the outside corner of the plate. True to his maxims, the Rajah swung cleanly and met the ball with the end of his bat. With a sharp crack of contact, it soared toward right field above Wes Schulmerich, the Braves' stocky right fielder, who retreated to the high wire-mesh fence that separated the field from the bleachers, turned, and leaped as high as he could, in vain. The ball sailed untouched into the bleacher crowd, a grand slam, the 294th home run of Hornsby's storied career, and surely the most contested. The Cubs' starter, Charlie Root, would get credit for the 11–7 victory, an eleven-inning complete game. Not much more than a year later, Babe Ruth would deal with him as Hornsby had Cunningham. At least Root could look forward to another decade of paychecks from one of the wealthiest teams in the major leagues; Bruce Cunningham, two weeks shy of his twenty-sixth birthday and toiling for one of the neediest teams in the league, had incurred his 12th loss of the year, against 3 victories. Less than a year remained in his major league career.[22]

Hornsby had emphatically finished both the game and the game within the game. The Rajah circled the bases briskly, while his crestfallen foes slumped, one by one, against their seatbacks. The Hornsby faction among the crowd, emboldened, flung a small blizzard of straw hats near the plate.[23] The base runners Hornsby had plated waited to congratulate their boss. Hornsby accepted their handshakes matter-of-factly. Then, picking his way through the boaters scattered about, he headed for the open gangway under the stands that connected the dugout to the clubhouse. Well-wishers might try without luck to intercept him on the way. There was a second game to be played that day, and Hornsby had to tend to his pregame routine. Among other matters, he decided that his game-winning pinch hitter was done for the day.[24]

Hornsby had crushed the revolt for the time being, but the days that a gimpy thirty-five-year-old could quell a mob with his heroics were growing short, no matter the batting records. If the obvious dislike of so many fans bothered Hornsby, he had given no sign of it throughout the difficult 1931 season. He had the unqualified support, even the adulation, of William Wrigley, who had called Hornsby "the smartest manager and baseball player that ever lived." Even Bill Veeck, the team's urbane and unflappable president, seemed to be in his corner.[25]

Wrigley and Veeck had chosen Hornsby as manager to rid the club of the excesses of the McCarthy era, the days of the fatted calf, the giddy 1920s: veterans setting their own hours and their own training rules, sometimes spending the night in jail, miring themselves in litigation with their exploits, and then taking the field overconfident, nonchalant—and often hung over. Such men and such habits, Hornsby and Wrigley believed, had cost the club the 1929 World Series, certainly the 1930 pennant, and the hangover was holding the club down again in 1931. After years of success the club had become ridden with autograph hounds and publicity seekers: Wilson posing with all manner of admirers, he and his teammates pursued by the crowds of small boys or the female Chicagoans who swamped the park, or even gangsters.[26]

Hornsby had spent the summer alternately benching and platooning Wilson and other McCarthy favorites. He even set about restructuring the free-swinging batting style of Wilson, who had set the single-season National League home run and the major league RBI marks the year before. In the second half of 1931 Hornsby began playing his own, younger men at the positions veterans like Wilson and Gabby Hartnett had claimed for so long.[27]

The situation had come to a head several weeks earlier, in late August, with the latest in a series of Hornsby-Wilson run-ins, this one at the Polo Grounds in New York. In the locker room, Hornsby forced a tearful Wilson, hung over and dejected, to promise the team that he would never flout Hornsby's rules again. The Chicago public had heard little about that scene at the time, nor that Wrigley, Veeck, and Hornsby had reached a decision on Wilson's future.

Veeck had been cryptic about Wilson's future. "Never discuss these things in advance," he said.

"In advance of what?" asked a reporter.

"In advance of his signing or going elsewhere," replied Veeck, ambiguously.

William Wrigley finally confirmed Wilson's fall, adding, "You can't be a sport at night and a ballplayer the next day."[28]

There was still no official decision from the club, but in Cincinnati a few days later the Cubs found themselves short-handed in the outfield. While the National League's reigning home run champion remained on the bench, Hornsby wrote out a lineup with a pitcher playing the outfield in Wilson's place. Hornsby explained, "Hack knows he is through as a Cub, so it would hardly be fair either to himself or the team to play him." Besides, he observed forthrightly, Wilson's replacement, Bud Teachout, wasn't much of a pitcher anyway; what harm was there in trying him out in a new spot?[29]

At the end of the series the Cubs gathered at Cincinnati's union depot for the return trip to Chicago. A six-game losing streak and Wilson's troubles had soured the atmosphere. The Cubs, in recent years the league's powerhouse, were only three games over .500 and fading. They lost again that afternoon, their sixth setback in succession. Wilson, who had probably been drinking on his way to the station, cornered a couple of sportswriters in one of the Pullmans and began griping about how they had covered his difficulties that summer. (Actually, the Chicago press had treated Wilson's troubles sympathetically for the most part.) While Wilson warmed up to his subject, Pat Malone, star pitcher and Wilson confrere, joined the group. Malone had also probably been drinking, probably with Wilson.

"Hello, Pat," said Harold Johnson of the *Chicago American*. "I've just been talking to one of the four greatest pitchers of all time," he said with a smirk; Johnson was evidently referring to the old-time Cub great Mordecai "Three-Finger" Brown, who had just appeared in an old-timers' game that afternoon. The reporter and the two-hundred-pound player were at close quarters in the cramped train car. Malone's reply was a quick right jab to Johnson's jaw, and then another, and a third. Wayne Otto of the *Chicago Herald and Examiner* tried to push Malone away. Malone turned on him. With more operating room this time, he landed a roundhouse that bloodied Otto and loosened several front teeth. Wilson, himself a renowned brawler, stood by while several Cubs and the team's traveling secretary, Bob Lewis, pulled Malone away. When Hornsby pushed his way to the scene, Wilson turned loose a barrage of insults on the manager—"everything I could think of," he admitted later.[30]

The train rolled into the night, Chicago-bound. Hornsby caught up with Wilson when it pulled into the station the next morning. "Report to Mr. Veeck at noon today. He wants to see you," he told Wilson. The Cubs' most popular player since Grover Cleveland Alexander made his way across the Loop to the Wrigley building, situated on the jog that Michigan Avenue makes as it crosses the Chicago River. Even today it is the city's most superb vantage point—to the south the panorama of Grant Park and its Grecian museum temples; to the east, at the bend of the Chicago River, the mammoth white bulk of the Merchandise Mart; to the north, the Magnificent Mile, climaxed at its extremity by the Palmolive Building, a giant new lighthouse topped with the Lindbergh Beacon in 1931, a midcontinental guide for air travelers approaching across the expanse of Lake Michigan, shimmering to the east.[31]

The son of the western Pennsylvania mills, though, was not a sightseer as he stepped from the cab. Newspapermen mobbed him as he entered the lobby and asked the elevator attendant for the ninth floor, a moot request, because the elevator man certainly recognized Wilson on sight and knew exactly which floor he wanted. There was also no doubt in the mind of anyone present that Wilson was about to share the fate of Grover Alexander, another franchise icon who had made this same trip five years earlier.

Wilson was ushered into room 936, where Veeck and Hornsby awaited. Veeck pulled out a sheaf of reports from private and hotel detectives who had shadowed Wilson and Pat Malone each night in Cincinnati. Hornsby broke in to add that Wilson had insulted both Veeck and Mr. Wrigley himself in his profane outburst the night before. Wilson hotly denied mocking the owner or the club president. Hornsby was lying, he protested. Veeck, unmoved, told Wilson he was suspended.[32]

Wilson left the room with his head down, brushing by the press. Then Veeck called in Malone, who had arrived and taken a seat in the anteroom. After a briefer conference, Malone too left wordlessly. Veeck emerged to issue a short statement: Malone had been fined $500 for assaulting the reporters. Wilson, the onlooker, if not the innocent in the fracas, was suspended without pay "for infraction of training rules." He would lose approximately one-sixth of his $33,000 salary—more than $5,000—the price of a new Lincoln or Cadillac. It was clear that Wilson had been banished from the Cubs not just for the season, but forever. At thirty-one, the steelmaker's son could never again hope to earn as much as he had for William Wrigley, even if he recovered his batting touch with another franchise.

Wilson brought his wife to the ballpark the next afternoon to watch the Cubs begin a series with the Cardinals. He seemed relaxed, even jaunty, onlookers thought. The crush of well-wishers, male and female, young and old, grew so great that ushers had to escort the Wilsons away. After the game, demanding autographs, the fans held Wilson hostage for another quarter hour. Then, buoyed by the affections of his public, he made his way to the Cub clubhouse to clean out his locker.[33]

Hornsby was absent, and Wilson's friends were free to gather round, console him, offer their best wishes. Hornsby learned soon enough, and even though Wilson's locker was bare, and Wilson was packing for the trip back to the Potomac valley, he officially banned Wilson from entering the clubhouse again. But nothing Hornsby did, inside the clubhouse or out, could erase the memories of the grinning little fellow who had stirred Chicago's Prohibition drink for so long.

Later that week the Cubs traveled crosstown to Comiskey Park to play the White Sox in a benefit game for the city's unemployed, an idea broached first on the *Chicago Tribune*'s sports page by Arch Ward (also soon to propose and promote baseball's first midsummer All-Star game). By some estimates, up to half the men in Chicago were out of work. The parks were filled with them during the day, and at night the lower deck of the acclaimed Michigan Avenue Bridge, hard by Mr. Wrigley's splendid terra-cotta skyscraper, was theirs. In "Bronzeville," the ghetto not far from Comiskey Park, families evicted for back rent were holing up by the thousands in condemned buildings; in the vacant lots of the near West Side, plainly visible from the skyscrapers of the Loop, the homeless were constructing their "Hoovervilles" of plywood, cardboard, anything that warded off the wind and the rain.[34]

Newly elected mayor Anton Cermak, other high-ranking politicians of both parties, and more than forty thousand fans turned out for the Cubs-Sox benefit contest. Commissioner Landis, with his little granddaughter, made his way to his box seat and settled his chin on the railing in the pose he had made famous at so many World Series. In another box, Wilson sat with his wife, once again drawing applause and good wishes as they took their seats; on the field a shower of spoiled lemons and tomatoes greeted Hornsby as soon as he emerged from the dugout. For once, Cubs and Sox fans were speaking in unison.[35]

With Hornsby on hand to make a list, only one of Wilson's well-wishing teammates from the day before had the brass to acknowledge the presence of Wilson a few feet away: Gabby Hartnett. The Cubs' regular catcher since 1923 may have been motivated by courage or simple bravado—or, after spending much of the summer sharing the Hornsby doghouse with Wilson, he may have wanted his own ticket out of town.

In 1931 Hartnett, who would carve out his own niche in the Hall of Fame, had nothing like the national celebrity of either Hornsby or Wilson. What happened next, though, lives on in pop culture, beyond the technicalities of Hornsby's .424 batting average in 1924 or Wilson's 191 RBI in 1930. Perhaps Hartnett was simply careless when he heard a call from a nearby box—it could have been "Machine Gun Jack" McGurn, or someone else in the entourage surrounding Al Capone in his box seat, even Capone himself. But there the Big Fellow sat, whiling away the days before the income-tax-evasion trial that by the end of the month would end his own career.[36]

Hartnett might have thought that Hornsby wanted to banish him from the roster; perhaps he was even trying to bait Hornsby into action—after all, it was obvious that the intolerable Rajah had a virtual lifetime contract with William Wrigley. It could have been mere bravado: Hartnett, plainspoken, a man's man, a natural leader, was yet a man of nearly thirty-one with a family. Whatever the overture, Hartnett approached Capone, leaned over the retaining wall among the ward-heelers and fedora-topped bodyguards, and signed a baseball for Capone's son, who sat on his father's right. A man and his boy at the ballpark on a late-summer day—what could be more American? Signing a baseball was something the gregarious catcher would do for any lad who asked, whether that lad had goons with him or not. If Hartnett really did want Hornsby to fire him, there were plenty of photographers on hand to capture the moment.[37]

Then the game got under way. The fans seemed most interested in booing Hornsby, and the heckling redoubled when he was caught off base in the middle innings. Showers of lemons and tomatoes dogged him wherever he went. Yet no one remembers the day for Charlie Root's shutout of the Sox, or the $45,000 raised for the unemployed that afternoon. The message sent by the photo—that a gangster could summon a major league ballplayer for small talk on the grounds where the Black Sox had thrown the World Series to the underworld—caught the nation's eye.[38]

According to baseball tradition, Landis summons Hartnett for a conference, where Hartnett supposedly unleashes an immortal riposte: "I go to his place of business, Judge; why shouldn't he come to mine?" True or not, the National League soon instituted a rule prohibiting player-fan interaction at the ballpark. Hartnett somehow survived the displeasure of both Landis and his manager. He would snap back from his off season, outlast Hornsby, resume his role as starting catcher, lead the Cubs to three more pennants, manage the team, stroke a famed, pennant-sealing home run ("The Homer in the Gloamin'"), and join the Hall of Fame.[39]

Capone had no such future. Within weeks he made the news again by attending a sports event—this time a football game at Northwestern University's Dyche Stadium. The dark lord of Chicago had to abandon his seat after the first half with the crowd jeering him, and not long thereafter a jury of his Illinois peers bravely decided that he was guilty of tax evasion. By the next spring he had had entered the federal penitentiary system, the effective end to his career and power. Somehow, though, Capone entered baseball history identified with the Cubs. Eventually old-timers would specify Wrigley Field as the place where Hartnett and Capone met. Some said that Scarface was a regular patron at Cubs Park, and that fans crowded around him for his autograph, just as they would for Wilson's or Hartnett's. By the end of the century, an establishment in Uptown, deep in the old O'Banion-Weiss-Moran territory on the North Side, staked out a claim as Al Capone's favorite speakeasy.

Capone's sudden fall did not mean that the boobirds had forgotten about a more important bad guy, Rogers Hornsby. The Cub manager escaped from Comiskey Park after the Thursday afternoon charity exhibition and headed back to the North Side for the last weeks of the 1931 season. Suddenly, Rogers Hornsby's own future was on the line, his inaugural season as Cub manager not proceeding according to plan. A nine-game losing streak had left the team only three games above .500—territory that no

Cub team had entered so late in years, certainly none since McCarthy's arrival in 1926. Fortunately, a couple of second-division contingents were coming to town—first the Phillies, then the Braves, for a five-game series, capped by a doubleheader on Sunday the 13th.

Hartnett and Capone entered history on Thursday, September 9. By Sunday the 13th, as Bruce Cunningham and Rogers Hornsby faced off, Hack Wilson was somewhere on the way to Martinsburg, West Virginia, his off-season residence about seventy-five miles northwest of Washington DC. Unlike the previous autumn, no band blared when the Wilsons and their son, Bobby, finally pulled into Martinsburg, no committee awaited to present another new Buick.[40]

Wilson pulled last year's model up to the white clapboard two-story at 512 John Street. The maples on the block were beginning to turn, and there was the early-autumn feel that comes to the Alleghenies in September. Inside the house, the Wilsons looked around as people will when they have been gone a long while. Wilson passed through the living room, where in winters past reporters had sat reverently, asking the home run king about which ballparks he liked best, his latest plans for vaudeville, or his projected boxing career. They had wanted to know how he trained, how he chose his bats, his favorite food, his pastimes.

At some point Wilson reached the basement. He could convert the area into a little gym, he decided, with a punching bag and an exercise bicycle and some other fitness equipment. His comeback would have to begin here.[41]

He had faced worse before. His unmarried mother had died when he was seven. By the time he finished sixth grade at age fourteen, it was time to go to work. Playing for company teams led to semipro ball, then the minor leagues, and finally John McGraw's New York Giants and a starting assignment in the 1924 World Series. However great it was to be young and a Giant, though, Wilson lost his batting eye, just as in 1931, or overdid his roistering, or both. Then Joe McCarthy picked him up. Wilson and McCarthy, joining the Cubs the same week in 1925, formed the foundation stones of Mr. Wrigley's ball club. Hack had been McCarthy's special project, a carefree, unbuttoned sort who threw bats and fists, and thought about it later. In the Wilson-McCarthy partnership, thinking was McCarthy's job; all Wilson had to do was show up at game time and batter the ball unmercifully. He did that often for the next five seasons, leading the league in home runs four times and in RBI twice; for the period he averaged 35 home runs, double figures better than any rival in the league. Odd-looking, hot-headed, hitting and fielding unconventionally, Wilson became the National League's "draw," its most-booed member, his neck reddening as the fans jeered the frequent Wilsonian strikeout, the long black bat slamming to the ground or skittering across the field, the answering shower of lemons from the stands, or the likewise not-infrequent error—followed, almost inevitably, by the crash of a base-clearing drive, often into the seats. He tossed bats, beat up spectators and other ballplayers, and drew a police escort.[42]

Wilson's 1930 season stamped him as one of the extraordinary players in the game: 56 home runs, a National League record that lasted nearly seventy years, and a major league mark of 191 RBI that lasted into the next century. Toward the end of the desperate 1930 pennant race, an Atlas in a patchwork lineup, he singlehandedly shouldered his team's drive toward a league championship. Day after day, there was a new personal high, a new league record, a new major league mark.

It had not been enough. Wilson's ally and mentor, Joe McCarthy, paid the price for disappointing the ownership with a second-place finish, immediately following a World Series loss the previous year. In McCarthy's place, the Cubs chose Rogers Hornsby—driven, acid-tongued, intolerant, among the greatest of the great players, and the manager of a world champion by age thirty. To many, especially and most crucially William Wrigley, Hornsby seemed to represent everything that McCarthy was not. New York, the Gotham City that Chicago had dreamed of over-taking, quickly obtained McCarthy's services, and there he would be good for another eight major league pennants and seven world championships, seven more than Mr. Wrigley and the son who inherited his ball club would claim. Nearly fifteen years McCarthy reigned in New York; Hornsby could not last another year with the Cubs before being banished to a lifetime of losing ball clubs and a descent into the minor leagues, even some low comedy in the Mexican League. Hornsby was outside the winner's circle for good—in both baseball and his chosen hobby of horse-track wagering.

Despite Mac's departure from Chicago, Wilson could console himself with his 1931 contract, at well above thirty thousand dollars, a level that only Ruth and probably Hornsby had ever exceeded. A product endorser and even, for a short time, a vaudevillian,[43] he spent the off-season relaxing in Martinsburg with his family and his numerous lodge brothers. Wilson seemed to be living the American dream, his lifestyle assured and his team poised to contend indefinitely for NL supremacy.

In truth Wilson was only a few ballgames from a downfall almost unparalleled in American sport. From September 1930 to September 1931, Wilson virtually undid a lifetime's work, his long journey to overcome poverty and illiteracy, his hard-won status as one of America's best-paid men, his ascendancy as the quasi-Ruth.

McCarthy and then Wilson, the favorites of the era that had drawn the largest crowds and the most excitement in baseball, had left the scene less than twelve months apart. By the time Wilson departed, the Depression had come to stay, and the raucous beat of the 1920s that Chicago symbolized in so many ways was ebbing. Capone, that gangster of gangsters, was going down. Chicago's eager claims to national and even world leadership, not just in baseball but in industry and commerce, architecture, public works, even corruption and notoriety, slowly faded. The Century of Progress lakefront exhibition of 1933–34 never dominated the popular imagination like the Columbian Exposition of 1893; New York's exposition of 1939 instead became the gateway to the future. Chicago had been the birthplace of the skyscraper, but new construction on its skyline, having thrust above the long lakefront in decade after decade of innovation, would stagnate into the 1950s. By that time the term "Second City" had become popular—coined by a New Yorker who concluded with much truth, "Chicago's bid for grandeur has failed."[44]

Neither would Mr. Wrigley's ball club ever fulfill its owner's extravagant vision. Time and again they would fall short of the prize—twice, in humiliating fashion, to New York—a number 2 team in the number 2 city. But that lay far in the future. Perhaps the booing and jeering Cub fans of September 1931 dimly realized that the exits of McCarthy and then Wilson meant the end of the sweet Wrigley Field madness of the late 1920s, when the fans stormed the gates and even the field in midgame, when Wilson invaded enemy dugouts and friendly stands to prove his manhood, when fans toured the neighborhood speakeasies of the toddling town with their favorite, Wilson, heckled and booed and cheered wherever he went.

But the story did not quite end with Wilson's downfall, and Mr. Wrigley's dream had always embraced more than the exploits of one hard-drinking, if superb, slugger. It had begun in another day, really another age, before Chicagoans had ever heard of Joe McCarthy and Hack Wilson.

2 | Samples of Baseball

Come and show me another city with lifted head singing so proud to be alive.
. . . [H]ere is a tall bold slugger set vivid against the little soft cities. . . .
—Carl Sandburg, "Chicago" (1916)

Chicago is . . . the Wrigley Building.—Jimmy Van Heusen and Sammy Cahn,
"My Kind of Town"

The tragedy of Hack Wilson was many years in the making. To begin
with, there was the drinking. There had been other famous drinkers in
baseball and there would be more, but none of their careers matched the
time and place so well as Wilson's: Chicago, Prohibition, speakeasies—the
bender that became a hangover in a few years.

He was an illegitimate, orphaned son of Pennsylvania's industrial back-
waters. His mother was dead before he turned eight; his father, an alcoholic,
drifted in and out of his life, leaving him in foster care much of the time.
Father-son togetherness, when it happened, was sharing a beer at the
neighborhood tavern. Wilson's schooling ended in the sixth grade, and
he took on a series of blue-collar jobs: printer's devil, riveter, sledgeham-
mer wielder, riveter again. By his teens he was an unusual, spectacular
physical specimen: 5'6" tall, nearly 200 pounds, with a size 18 neck, broad
shoulders, and the forearms of a blacksmith. This massive physique rested
upon an ordinary pair of legs and size 6 feet.[1]

Like so many ballplayers of that era, he began his baseball career playing semipro ball while working his blue-collar jobs, in his case just outside
Philadelphia. Soon, in another typical progression, he was recommended
to the minor league team and signed to a professional contract.

The early 1920s were a good time for a two-hundred-pound strongman
starting out in organized baseball. The inside baseball that had ruled the
sport for a quarter century was going the way of the horse and buggy and

22

gentlemen's calling cards. Out went the dead ball and intricate strategies that acquired runs with painstaking economy; in came Babe Ruth's new style of swinging from the heels, and Wilson adopted it eagerly. No longer the base-at-a-time guessing game of frugal, middle-aged men, baseball had become a wide-open sport for free-spending capitalists.

In 1923 a scout for John McGraw's world champion New York Giants noticed Wilson slugging for Portsmouth of the Virginia League. Even though the Giants were in the middle of an unprecedented four-year run of pennants, just across the Harlem River from their Polo Grounds rose the house that Ruth built—Yankee Stadium, a monument to the popularity of the new game's supreme evangelist.

Power potential and the threat that Ruth represented promoted Wilson directly to the major leagues without further seasoning. At Coogan's Bluff, he joined a distinguished group of Giant prospects that included Fred Lindstrom and Bill Terry. At season's end he joined a barnstorming group, and one day to his delight he became "Babe Ruth's legs" as substitute for the superstar in the late innings.

After a successful rookie season in 1924, Wilson faded at bat the next year. Even in a slump, though, the youngster could still turn heads: on July 1, he became the second player since 1900 to hit two home runs in one inning. But a few weeks later, after his batting average had sunk to .239, McGraw returned him to the minors, sending him to the Giants' highest minor league affiliate, Toledo of the American Association. Wilson was more vocal than most youngsters in that situation would be, especially with a manager of McGraw's repute. "I may not be good enough to play on your ballclub," Wilson told McGraw, "but I'll be back and playing on a better club someday." One who had survived the ruthless McGraw's scrutiny, Ross Youngs, exclaimed to a sportswriter, "Bill, they let go the best outfielder I ever played alongside, and they're going to regret it."[2]

McGraw later suggested that Wilson had been ill when demoted. The suspicion, considering the outfielder's later struggles with another authoritarian manager, is that McGraw had seen enough of Wilson's freewheeling ways. Or McGraw may have had in mind only a bit of seasoning in the high minors for Wilson. One of the renowned talent evaluators in baseball history, he once called Wilson "the greatest judge of fly balls since Tris

Speaker." Remaining under the Giants' control, Wilson might have eventually replaced the team's outfielder Ross Youngs, a brilliant all-around talent who was struck down at a young age by a fatal illness. Or like so many talented figures of the 1920s and 1930s—Lefty Grove, Buzz Arlett, Joe Hauser, Frank Sigafoos, or the memorably dubbed Bunny Brief—Wilson might have spent his prime wowing folks in Baltimore, Rochester, Minneapolis, Seattle, or one of the other medium-sized cities where they played a reasonable facsimile of major league ball. After a few years of that, getting past thirty, Wilson would be either too old or too expensive to interest another major league club. It was still nice work to get. The high minors could pay decently; the fans were enthusiastic and loyal in the days before mass media became all-powerful. The attendance, and hence revenues, might approach that of the smaller major league cities.[3]

The American Association that Wilson joined had a long-time manager in a similar bind. After finishing up a journeyman's career as a minor league infielder, Joe McCarthy had been managing the association's Louisville entry for the better part of a decade; pushing forty, he appeared comfortable, and trapped, at his level of competence. By now McCarthy knew quite a few people in the business, including Wilson's new manager with the Toledo Mud Hens, Jimmy Burke, who had once managed a young ballplayer named McCarthy.

To the baseball establishment, smart fellows in the big cities, McCarthy, if they even knew his name, was just another nonentity who'd never even sipped his cup of coffee in the big show. Then again, these supposed sharpies were dependent on a certain element of predictability, and for years the establishment had been overtaken by events more than once—the Federal League, the Black Sox, Babe Ruth's very transformation of the basic game itself. They knew all the angles except the unknown.

Joe McCarthy, no fast talker or wise guy, was every bit their equal, even if he did divide his time between provincial Louisville and his off-season home in Buffalo. He just had to find a way to get out of Louisville and prove it. As he directed the Colonels to yet another AA pennant, he would have sized up Jimmy Burke's latest outfielder over the half-dozen contests Louisville and Toledo played the second half of 1925. Now there was a fellow who would fit right in in the system McCarthy was devising.[4]

Then came Wilson's break, a chain of events that unfolded outside the established routines of scouting, farm teams, and personnel evaluations.

In the chilly, overcast twilight of October 7, 1925, thirty-nine-year-old Grover Cleveland Alexander of the Chicago Cubs ambled off the mound of Comiskey Park and to the visitors' dugout. Old Alex had just finished up his nineteenth inning of work in the opening game of the Chicago City Series, a best-of-seven event held each October neither the Cubs nor the White Sox played in the World Series—in other words, an annual event post-1919.[5]

Alex had squared things up himself at 2–2 in the fifth inning with a sacrifice fly, driving in his fellow alcoholic and ex-manager Rabbit Maranville. That had been the last time either team scored. The Sox starter, Ted Blankenship, was fifteen years and nine hits better than Alex, but the older man paced himself through the Sox's twenty hits with frequent rubdowns from the Cubs' rough-and-ready trainer, Andy Lotshaw. He let the leadoff man on base each inning from the twelfth through the nineteenth; in the thirteenth he thwarted a double, two singles, and a walk. The closest the Sox came to scoring again was on Ray Schalk's foul, just inches wide, with a man on third and two outs in the eighteenth.

Alexander must have thrown more than two hundred pitches that day—perhaps closer to three hundred. That was the way they had done it in his heyday before World War I, when he and the other pitching giants who had dominated the "modern" (post-1900) era—Mathewson, Young, and Johnson—loomed over the major league diamond. Big men, large figures, they pitched three to four hundred innings a year, winning twenty-five or thirty games a year almost as a matter of course. In grainy photos they appear in a kind of perpetual twilight, towering above the field and the ordinary men who were forced to confront them at the plate.[6]

Another member of the great foursome, Walter Johnson, had taken the mound the same afternoon that Alexander was holding the Sox at bay in Comiskey Park: Johnson shut out the Pittsburgh Pirates in the opening game of the 1925 World Series. The very day of Alexander and Johnson's postseason heroics, Christy Mathewson died in a Saranac Lake, New York, sanatorium. Mathewson, seven years Johnson and Alexander's senior, had been in his magnificent prime when the two younger men broke into the big leagues. World War I, as with Alex, had ruined his health. The only man to pitch three shutouts in a single World Series, Mathewson had won more games in National League history than anyone except Alexander.

By the seventeenth inning, darkness was falling on Comiskey Park. But the umpires, huddling frequently, kept the players on the field. After Alexander got the last out in the bottom of the nineteenth, they called the game at last. One hundred fourteen putouts, 31 hits, 6 walks, and a couple of blunders afield had taken no longer to complete than a routine game of the twenty-first century: 3:03.

An anticorruption rule instituted after the 1919 World Series—"thrown" on the diamond the Cubs and the Sox were using—excluded the revenue from tie games when calculating player shares for postseason series. October 7's 19 innings of work thus earned the contestants not a cent—but winners' shares as high as a thousand dollars still awaited the winners, a real reward for young men who might not earn five thousand in a year, especially true if the players' club qualified for a portion of World Series revenue by finishing in the first division. (To forestall such thoughts and focus players on winning the pennant, the Cubs in 1934 announced that they would not play in the City Series regardless of how the pennant race turned out.)

A protocol surrounded scheduling the series: the team first eliminated from the pennant race had to make the challenge. These Cubs-Sox showdowns had traditionally featured displays of red, white, and blue bunting; parades with bands playing; and, at least earlier in the century, demonstrations by rooters' clubs. The series was played under World Series rules, with extra umpires and the host league for the opening game corresponding with that of the World Series. In 1925, though, City Series attendance was scanty; after all, the fifth-place Sox were playing the National League's cellar dweller. Chicago's major league teams, like Alex, seemed past their prime, in contrast to the Sox and Cub powerhouses of the century's first two decades. In the 1920s neither Chicago franchise ever seemed to threaten the league leaders past June.[7]

Chicago's City Series peaked in 1928, when 184,000 souls turned out for the seven games. For days on end, the city was divided; lemon throwers turned out in force to bombard the Cubs' new star, Hack Wilson, and Cub fans returned the favor when the Sox visited Wrigley Field. By the 1928

City Series, though, Chicago had hosted a different postseason baseball series, one in which neither the Cubs nor the Sox would ever participate, because of their skin color. More than a few of the team's rosters might not have made the cut. A third major league franchise, largely unpublicized but well-known to baseball buffs, played in Chicago; indeed, its Chicago edition, the Chicago American Giants of the Negro National League, was the foundation stone of its league. In 1926 and 1927 the American Giants were the self-proclaimed champions of the world—a brash claim, Chicagoan in its audacity, but plausible, and therefore also Chicagoan.

The new champions, winners of the Negro National League World Series of 1926 and 1927, played just a few blocks south of the old frame Comiskey Park at 39th and Wentworth, now renamed Schorling's Park after Comiskey's son-in-law. The park had hosted the Sox's home games in the first few City Series, as well as three games of the 1906 World Series. The memorable sixth game in 1906, when the Sox's Hitless Wonders pounded Mordecai Brown and Orval Overall for 14 hits in an 8–3 rout that ruined the Cubs' historic 116-victory season, had been played at the site.[8]

Now a team called the American Giants called Schorling's Park home. The Giants' owner, Rube Foster, a native of a country called Texas where his kind was unappreciated, had migrated, like so many Chicagoans, from the country's interior to the city by the lake. He was a self-made man, a genius of organization: like Charles Comiskey, a former star player; like William Wrigley of the Cubs, a sound businessman; like Judge Landis, the commissioner and arbiter of a league—the Negro National League, which he had organized and largely financed. Foster's business partner, John Schorling, was Charles Comiskey's brother-in-law.

Many years earlier, Foster had become "Rube" by outpitching another dead-ball great, Rube Waddell. After facing Foster, Honus Wagner had called him "the smartest pitcher I have ever seen." And much like the Sox's Hitless Wonders of 1906, Foster had battled Christy Mathewson's main National League rival, the Cubs' Three-Finger Brown, on equal terms in postseason matchups. In fact, he was said to have taught Mathewson how to throw the screwball.[9]

Foster's original barnstorming club competed frequently in Chicago's thriving semipro scene before World War I. The market for such entertainment began to dwindle in the twenties, crowded out by radio, movies, and Sunday drives in the auto, but for Foster it was an opportunity to move beyond the haphazard semipro life. He saw a special, growing market in his segregated part of town: "Bronzeville," the area east of Wentworth. Migration from the segregated South had swollen the population of the neighborhood from thirty thousand in 1910 to sixty thousand in 1920; by 1930 it would more than double again.[10]

One Sunday in the mid-1920s Foster's Giants drew twelve thousand spectators to Schorling's Park; the same afternoon only a few thousand more turned out at Comiskey's cavernous stadium down the street to see Ty Cobb's Detroit Tigers. Foster encouraged an entrepreneurial attitude practically moribund in the baseball establishment. By the end of the decade the Giants' autumn face-offs with Earle Mack's all-American League ballclubs were playing under the lights—starting time 8:30 p.m.—and often drawing as many white as black spectators. There were other promotions like Ladies Nights.

Connie Mack had first met Foster during spring training in 1899 and praised the young pitcher; Foster's only son was named "Earl Mack Foster." William Wrigley had surely encountered Foster in the first decade of the century, when both men had operated in Chicago's semipro prairie leagues. From the Macks to John McGraw to the White Sox's trainer, Bill Buckner, whose brother, Harry, had been one of Foster's pitching rivals in the early Negro leagues, Foster had made friends and contacts throughout baseball. Foster kept other franchises afloat by serving as the league's central banker, even sharing players if needed. Foster's own half-brother, Willie, was the rock of his franchise, an acknowledged equal of the best major league pitchers.[11]

The men of the NNL played a game that was at once the past and the future of baseball, even if that future was a few decades off. At Schorling's Park, spikes flew and pitchers doctored the ball in the finest dead-ball tradition, but the home run and the bases-clearing double were welcome too.

Willie Foster and his teammates could have been the honest, genuine black Sox Comiskey needed, men who could have made up for the loss of Comiskey's superb 1919 aggregation, blessed his old age, sent him into history with another championship and, better yet, a legacy as baseball's great emancipator. A three-way City Series could have demonstrated to the world just what the NNL's top team could do against major leaguers, and there were years in the 1920s they might well have taken the city crown. It was not to be, could not be; neither on the South nor the North sides of Chicago, nor in Landis's Loop offices, were such ideas entertained, not even for a business associate of Charles Comiskey's brother-in-law. Landis, the man whose harsh and decisive ban of the Black Sox simultaneously ruined Comiskey's franchise and refurbished the image of the national pastime, was a frank bigot; and there was no guarantee that anybody but the egotistical, bombastic judge could have pulled it off. Then again, in the absence of Landis's reforms, the ruination of the professional baseball monopoly might have opened up new opportunities for Foster's men. Whatever the case, year after year, only blocks from Comiskey's withering empire, a parade of talent passed through his old ballpark, as untouchable as the despised Black Sox of 1919 themselves.

Since 1905, and through all the vicissitudes of his franchise, Comiskey had employed Bill Buckner, a black man, as the White Sox trainer. The owner notorious for his financial pettiness with the Black Sox employed dozens of other workers from Bronzeville (one of them the renowned jazz pianist Jimmy Yancey, a groundskeeper at Sox Park), and the Old Roman was respected and even admired in that quarter of town. Even so, Comiskey was still participating in a conspiracy to deny the Negro League players their best means of maximizing their talents.

The physical closeness of the two South Side franchises only deepened the irony. Upon Comiskey's death in 1931, an editorial in the *Defender,* a publication not liberal in complimenting members of the white establishment, eulogized the Old Roman, to whom "color did not constitute the major qualifications of a major league ballplayer." Comiskey had "never said no to a Race charity," the paper also remembered. The man detested by many of his own players was esteemed by second-class citizens who considered him an ally and a friend. Perhaps he had done all he could.[12]

In 1925 the Sox had had their best season in years and set a new attendance record, even if they finished in fifth place, only four games above .500. While Rube Foster's franchise won titles down the street, Comiskey undertook a vast expansion of his fifteen-year-old ballpark; soon it was second in seating capacity only to Yankee Stadium in all of professional baseball. Denied access to trade opportunities—it was said that the rest of the American League was boycotting him for his mismanagement of the Black Sox debacle—Comiskey spent huge sums on tyros, few of whom panned out. One modestly successful third baseman cost him $100,000; Comiskey dropped an even larger sum, $125,000, for a Pacific Coast League shortstop who became a discipline problem before he ended his unremarkable major league career elsewhere.[13]

And more trouble came Comiskey's way: his North Side competitor for the majority of the white fan base was a man with both deeper pockets and a willingness, like Foster, to explore new ideas and take chances. William Wrigley, whose closest nonwhite associate was a houseman named Walter, was about to complicate Comiskey's problems.

For the Chicago National League ball club's aging, free-spending owner, baseball life was just beginning. In contrast to Comiskey and Foster, who had both started out as players, Wrigley had not become involved in organized baseball until he was nearly sixty. (His first recorded baseball experience came at the turn of the century, when he sponsored a team in the prairie leagues, where blacks and whites were allowed to face off. The young Rube Foster could have pitched at some point against the "Wrigley Nips.") "Nothing great was ever achieved without enthusiasm," read a sign in Wrigley's office on Michigan Avenue, and he had pursued success enthusiastically, starting out on a shoestring, going broke at least three times in his telling, all the while honing his back-clapping style and his belief in ubiquitous, unending advertising and promotion. Wrigley had built empires in all sorts of situations: starting the William Wrigley Co., the world's largest purveyor of chewing gum; acquiring and reengineering a semitropical island of romance; and launching assorted other ventures with fellow entrepreneurs. To supervise his realms, he maintained residences at Catalina, Pasadena, Phoenix, Wisconsin's Lake Geneva, and the Gold Coast of Chicago—the last his legal address, a twenty-two-room duplex at 1500 Lake Shore Drive.[14]

Wrigley's idol was Teddy Roosevelt, and like T.R. he believed in the strenuous life: bustling about, constantly phoning, telegraphing, reading the ticker tape from his private machine; playing ruthless games of tennis, golf, and medicine ball at his Lake Geneva, Wisconsin, estate; and in his younger years, breaking in his more restive polo ponies. This Bull Mooser's patience was a sometime thing. "How was the golf game?" an associate might inquire. "Fine—I finished in an hour and twenty minutes," Wrigley would reply. He snapped his fingers to make multimillion-dollar deals, stalking away if the parties were late—or if his newfound favorite pastime beckoned. "The hell with it today!" he cried before the scheduled signing of a million-dollar advertising contract. "The Giants are in town!"[15]

Reaching the impetuous tycoon with a business proposal could test one's mettle. Andy Frain, a go-getter who had grown up the sixteenth of seventeen children in a shack in the South Side's infamous Back of the Yards, had spent his boyhood picking up bottles and selling cushions to help the family. By the mid-twenties he ran a small business that ushered prizefights and the occasional event at the Chicago Coliseum. Once Wrigley and Bill Veeck began attracting sellout crowds to their ballpark, Mr. Wrigley's burgeoning baseball business was his best opportunity—seventy-seven well-attended home dates a year. Increased attendance had created problems for the Cubs. Traditionally, the first hundred volunteers who showed up at the park each day were handed red-visored caps and assigned to act as ushers. Dependent on tips for their pay, the temporary ushers awarded seats to the highest bidders (or themselves) regardless of what the ticket read, expectorated without bothering to check the direction of the breeze, and picked pockets as the opportunities arose.[16]

Eventually, as the team's record and attendance improved apace, the crowds often threatened to become unmanageable. One part of the problem was the size of Cubs Park, never more than two-thirds that of Yankee Stadium even as the Cubs' turnouts began to rival those of the Yankees. Compounding the problem, weekends accounted for a disproportionate amount of the club's business. The result was that though seats were readily available Monday through Friday, when the club was lucky to attract ten thousand customers for any single weekday game, Saturday and Sunday crowds could easily exceed thirty thousand in a park that was still single-decked. Wrigley and Veeck were being punished by success, like any businesspeople faced with a rapid, uncontrollable upsurge in customer demand. The plant had to be enlarged—that was certain—but in the meantime they needed to cope with the chaos.

Frain tried repeatedly to crash Wrigley's office and residence to pitch his idea for a professional ushering service, and each time, Wrigley's manservant, Walter, informed him: "Mr. Wrigley isn't in." One turbulent Sunday afternoon at the ballpark Veeck sent bad news down to Wrigley's box: the ticket offices, it seemed, were under siege by disgruntled patrons who had paid for seats, only to find a stranger occupying them. Wrigley stewed. His pockets were deep enough for a few refunds, but it was no way to run the world's greatest ballpark. The master advertiser knew that you had to finish the sale by delivering the product.

No doubt himself bribing an usher to get near the owner's box, Frain stole up, tapped the magnate's shoulder, and immediately made his pitch in his best stockyard accent. "Give me a crack at organizing the ushers out here, Mr. Wrigley," he pleaded.

Wrigley, temporarily short of bonhomie, frowned at the interruption. "Who are you?" he snapped. "My name's Frain, and I've been trying to see you for weeks," the young man explained. "Those ushers of yours are cuttin' in on your racket. They only make half-a-buck per and they're seatin' the buck-ten customers in the [buck sixty-five] seats for a dime drag. It's hurtin' business."

Wrigley, sweltering in his three-piece suit, frustrated by the chaos over-taking his property, peered closer at this importunate fellow. He sounded like a Sox fan, but he talked and acted like a Wrigley man.

"All right, the job's yours," Wrigley told his brand-new business partner without further ceremony.[17]

To start out, Frain began culling the few keepers from among the rough-necks who showed up at the park each day—"fellows with dirty shirts and a chew of tobacco in their mouths," Frain recalled. That meant daily personal rejections, and more than once fisticuffs with the rejects. Frain would turn up bloodied, clothes torn, at the Cubs' clubhouse door and ask Ed Froelich, the young attendant, "Can I use the shower, kid?" Soon, impressed with Frain's initial progress at ridding the premises of the toughs, Wrigley staked the brash youngster with loans. Frain concocted an eye-catching blue-and-gold uniform for his crew. His spit-and-polish "Andy Frains," all young men of above-average height and all working their way through school, would eventually become fixtures not only at Wrigley Field and then Comiskey Park but across much of the city and the country: the Kentucky Derby, prizefights, World Series, and Democratic and Republican national conventions. The discipline was military: a retired

World War I major oversaw the training, and Frain men who violated the rules had their gold epaulets stripped before being drummed out of the corps.[18]

Wrigley, himself a political convention-goer, played an influential role in national politics. He supposedly had turned down the Republican vice-presidential nomination in 1920 when it was bartered in the famous smoke-filled room at Chicago's Blackstone Hotel, and in 1924, the story was, he had to discourage another vice-presidential boomlet vetted by Mayor Bill Thompson—another T.R.-inspired outdoorsman, a cowboy, in fact. Calvin Coolidge, the chief beneficiary of these decisions, received Wrigley's hospitality at Catalina Island; Herbert Hoover, too, would also come calling at the Magic Isle.[19]

In 1920 the gum king crossed the Chicago River for the first down payment on Michigan Avenue's "Magnificent Mile": a rococo, terra-cotta-sided company headquarters he called "an expression of my personal faith in the future of Chicago." The building rose, starkly pristine, amid a warren of low-rise brick warehouses. Because the site occupied a slight jog in Michigan Avenue, pedestrians far to the south could always check the time by looking toward the huge timepiece atop the building's tower. Wrigley ordered floodlights installed at the base of the building, so that after dark his building would gleam up and down the avenue and far out into the lake. The illumination, it was said, raised his electric bill by $1 million a year. Nearly a century later, the building endures as a symbol of Chicago.[20]

Wrigley's new skyscraper and the opening of the Michigan Avenue Bridge across the Chicago River created the Magnificent Mile north of the river. Just across the street Colonel Robert McCormick soon built the Tribune Tower, which housed the self-proclaimed "World's Greatest Newspaper." Each day McCormick's editorial page renewed its pledge to make "Make Chicago the First City in the World." Boosters were quick to explain that the city held the world's greatest hotel (the Stevens), the world's greatest department store (Marshall Field's), and the world's greatest medical center, not to mention its two best ballparks. When a new zoo was planned on land donated by Edith Rockefeller McCormick, nothing less than "the greatest zoo in the world" would do. By the end of the decade the city's boosters announced that the Michigan Avenue Bridge outside the Wrigley Building carried more traffic each day than the intersection of 42nd Street and Fifth Avenue in Manhattan. (Where this finding left "the world's busiest corner," the intersection of State and Madison, was left unexplained.) By then Chicago had added or was adding the world's largest commercial structure (the Merchandise Mart) plus a museum triangle of classical buildings—the Field Museum of Natural History, the Shedd Aquarium, and the Adler Planetarium—that some locals compared to the Acropolis.[21]

Along Michigan Avenue and inward toward the south branch of the Chicago River soared the newest generation of limestone-faced skyscrapers, streamlined masterpieces that expressed the modernism of Eliel Saarinen's runner-up—and rejected—design for the Tribune Tower. All over the Loop and north of the river they rose: 333 North Michigan, the Board of Trade, the Carbon and Carbide, the La Salle–Wacker, the Palmolive with its Lindbergh-welcoming beacon, the Medinah Shrine.[22]

In mid-1930 came the announcement that the new census figures made Chicago the world's fourth-largest city. Flags unfurled in the Loop, factory whistles blew, classrooms burst into song, and cheering broke out at business meetings. Colonel Robert Randolph, the president of the chamber of commerce, predicted that Chicago would be in first place in a few decades. "New York is slipping," he concluded.[23]

As absurd as all that sounds in the twenty-first century, it was plausible, straight-line thinking: in barely a half-century, the city whose central section burned to the ground in 1871 had overtaken scores of competitors to reach fourth place in the world. What could stop such a juggernaut? More than that, Chicago had become a diverse laboratory that even the metropolises of the East Coast could not replicate. The city's growth had come not just from the waves of immigrants from central and southern Europe who filled the Eastern cities—Chicago had those aplenty—but from the farms and small towns of the interior, streaming to the city's midcontinental location. No comparable cross-section of America existed in comparable numbers and proximity: WASP, Catholic, Jewish, and eastern, central, northern, and southern European, and more recently, migrations both from Appalachia and, in huge numbers, from the Mississippi Delta. There were enough Chinese to populate a thriving Chinatown near the Loop.

It was only natural in this atmosphere that William Wrigley, a master marketer and overachieving optimist in the worst of times, and an internal immigrant himself, should have utter faith in his adopted city's destiny. He might go a bit over the top, too. Early on, he had settled on one of his most famous dictums: "Baseball is too much of a sport to be a business and too much of a business to be a sport." Now this sportsman resolved to transform his second-division baseball team into the greatest in the world. In early 1925 he turned over day-to-day control of the gum company to his son, Philip. Not coincidentally, and notwithstanding the Cubs' poor season, the pace within the Cub organization began to quicken. Early in June, William bought out the advertising genius Albert Lasker, a dissenting minority shareholder. Now the owner of an estimated 75 percent of the club's stock, Wrigley was free to impose his dynamic vision on the venerable franchise, and the world.[24]

Enthusiasm notwithstanding, Cub policies were open to question in 1925. For the first half-dozen years of Wrigley's control, the team had appeared to be little more than another diversion for him—additional publicity for, say, chewing gum or Santa Catalina development. Who exactly owned what, and when, is unclear, and that may explain the franchise's often muddled state in the early 1920s. Wrigley's story was that he originally bought into the Cubs to reclaim the franchise from out-of-town ownership (the Taft family of Cincinnati owned the club during the Federal League era), but his original shares were apparently obtained as collateral for a loan to Charles Weeghman, the owner of the Federal League Chicago Whales and then the Cubs. It was Weeghman who built the ballpark that still stands at Addison and Clark. Wrigley was one member in a consortium of Chicago potentate-investors, and Albert Lasker may have retained the actual majority of shares until June 1925. Whatever the case, by that time Wrigley had been bustling about as the front man of the franchise for several years, and it was now irrevocably Mr. Wrigley's ball club.[25]

In 1919, Wrigley's first major decision as putative full owner was to install his own man, a Chicago sportswriter named Bill Veeck, as the club's president. Wrigley and Veeck spent the next several years learning the business, which early on basically meant aping Comiskey's ill-fated attempts at rebuilding. The Cubs' management trainees bought and sold players frequently and unsuccessfully, and in the process they became known as easy marks. "[W]henever a rival club owner had a fading or spavined athlete to dispose of at top prices, Wrigley was the gentleman to see," one of Veeck's former sportswriting colleagues recalled. The search for an adequate third baseman occupied the better part of a decade and some four hundred thousand dollars of 1920s money; Wrigley lay in his grave before the solution, Stan Hack, eventually emerged. Like Comiskey, Wrigley also undertook extensive enhancements of the Cubs' facility. Where Comiskey billed his park as "The Baseball Palace of the World," Wrigley and Veeck proclaimed of their still-single-decked facility: "In All the World, No Park Like This."[26]

The reality was more down to earth. Wrigley Field, as Andy Frain knew, tended to attract an uncouth clientele that included gamblers, pickpockets, and rowdies who often doubled as ushers, awarding seats to the highest bidder. Fans might try to crash the gates, and once inside wander the aisles, steal seats, and then stand in them at crucial moments. Calls that went against the home team could touch off showers of pop bottles. Wrigley later claimed that the better elements of society avoided the place. The main tangible asset Wrigley and his group had acquired with the initial purchase, besides the three-year-old ballpark, was Grover Alexander, already acclaimed as one of the great pitchers of all time but either shell-shocked, partly deafened, or epileptic when he returned from World War I to begin pitching for Wrigley.[27]

It was said that Alex was often physically unable to take his turn on the mound; once, between starts, he toppled from the bench in mid-inning in full view of onlookers. Alexander had likely suffered an epileptic seizure, but his heavy drinking and the social attitudes of the day led to more judgmental conclusions.[28]

Regardless, Alexander continued to outpitch men who had been children when he started out. He won twenty-seven games for the Cubs in 1920 and twenty-two in 1923. He outlasted the Cubs' fence-moving experiment that began in 1923 with a forgettable slugger named "Hack" Miller in mind. In 1925, his thirty-ninth year, he led the last-place Cubs in victories, complete games, and innings pitched. He finished in the top ten in the league in all three categories. As Alex reached his late thirties, his position and fame in Chicago seemed secure. His longtime teammate and battery mate, Bill Killefer, was field manager. His protégé was the team's best young player, a catcher named Gabby Hartnett.

In 1925 young Hartnett, a right-handed hitter, discovered how to exploit the newly inviting left-field fence and smashed a one-season team-record twenty-two home runs (and moreover, the major league's venerable single-season mark for catchers) by midseason, then slumped badly in the second half after Veeck removed most of the left-field bleachers, beginning at the foul line. By then the club was on its second of three managers for the year and trapped deep in the second division. On the final day of the season, the Cubs had one last shot at escaping the cellar, but Hartnett committed two errors before five thousand chilled, unhappy spectators. The second error, a muff of a strike from the outfield, let in the lead runs for St. Louis, and the Cubs had earned their first last-place finish in a full half-century of business.[29]

A few days later, Alexander and Ted Blankenship opened the City Series with their pitching marathon. It turned out to be Alex's last appearance for the year. His teammates defeated the White Sox in four of the next five games. The old master's services wouldn't be needed again until the next spring.

Alexander's performance, though, had served notice that he would be a major leaguer—and, one would think, a Cub—for as long as he could play. But Chicagoans, and especially Grover Cleveland Alexander, were in for a surprise. Grover Alexander's world was about to enter the Roaring Twenties.

Daily broadcasting of Cubs games, the first such effort in baseball, had begun earlier in 1925, but no sportscaster was on hand to describe the heroics of Alexander and Blankenship, or any other game of the 1925 City Series. In fact, a year earlier, WGN, the official radio arm of the *Chicago Tribune*, had broadcast all six games of the 1924 City Series. For the opening game, October 1, 1924, "Sen" Kaney, WGN's program director, took a seat atop the roof of Cubs Park's single deck to describe the 10–7 complete game thrown by Grover Alexander. Alex started for the Cubs and let the Sox lineup play catch-up all afternoon, shifting back to his big league stuff when things threatened to get out of hand. Alex won his next start, too, but the Sox took all four games in which Alex didn't pitch for their tenth city championship in thirteen tries. Sen Kaney was on hand each day to describe it for an indeterminate number of listeners in his Chicago radio audience.[30]

WGN was by no means the first station in the nation to broadcast a major league baseball game. In 1921 KDKA in Pittsburgh had carried a game live during the Pirates' exciting pennant race with the Giants; a Cincinnati radio station broadcast the Reds' opening day in 1924; and several World Series broadcasts had already originated from the East Coast. In the latter, Graham McNamee emerged as the first national radio star, supplanting the original choice for the job, the preeminent sportswriter Grantland Rice. In the midst of the 1923 classic, the wordsmith found himself tongue-tied and out of place in the strange new world of the wireless. The theatrical McNamee took up the slack, improvising a technique we now take for granted—man-in-the-street excitement over a thrilling play, supplemented by patter and colorful descriptions to fill the routine stretches. Much like the Cubs' future television superstar Harry Caray, McNamee tended to misidentify interview subjects and invented many or most of his background facts. Then too, in the early days the broadcasters, if not sent to the roof, were housed in the press box, which meant that the cream of the nation's sportswriters witnessed McNamee's idiosyncrasies at close quarters. During one World Series game in Pittsburgh the most famous and talented among them, Ring Lardner, announced that he was heading back to the hotel: "It is asking too much to keep track of two games, the one I am seeing out on the field and the one I am hearing."[31]

WGN was again on hand for the Cubs' 1925 season opener, April 14. Grover Alexander once again took the mound, tossing the first pitch at 3:00 p.m. For the new season, Sen Kaney had benched himself for a new starter, a brisk, mustachioed young fellow named Quin Ryan. Upon reaching the roof of the grandstand, however, the new WGN man and a technician found themselves face-to-face with a brand-new broadcasting team from rival station WMAQ, owned and operated by the *Chicago Daily News*. This second broadcasting team's lineup included an authentic big leaguer of a few years back, Artie Hofman (nicknamed "Circus Solly" for his defensive prowess). When the Giants' unfortunate Fred Merkle forgot to touch second base in late September 1908, it was Hofman who fielded Al Bridwell's single and earned the most important assist of his career for Johnny Evers's ferociously contested putout of Merkle at second.[32]

Sports broadcasting immediately faced a dilemma that would continue through the Harry Caray era and beyond: announcer, or athlete? The thrill of victory, or expert analysis? Ryan, an energetic Northwestern University dropout who had spent much of his boyhood near movie stars, was probably unfazed by the presence of a retired professional ballplayer. At twenty-six, he had all the prestige of the *Chicago Tribune* and its ten-month-old commitment to its new station behind him. Soon he would interview Gloria Swanson and then oversee the first broadcast of the Kentucky Derby. In the mid- to late 1920s, at least, Ryan may have reached more listeners, pioneered more formats, and spent more sheer time on the air than anyone in the business. Football, baseball, boxing, celebrity interviews, political conventions, circus openings, the Kentucky Derby, the Indianapolis 500, comic strips read to children on Sunday mornings, and a weekly column in the *Tribune*: Ryan may not have been the first or the most outstanding at any of those assignments, but he had to be among the leaders in this new league. As he reflected later in the decade: "In the first three years we never had a day off. There was a time when we handled all the broadcast from nine in the morning until after midnight. And many's the night we slept in the studio."[33]

The previous autumn, Ryan had broadcast the most brilliant performance of Red Grange's (perhaps anyone's) career, when the Illini's "Galloping Ghost" scored four touchdowns in the first quarter against Michigan. Ryan, who would become noted for a "gee whiz" style reminiscent of McNamee's approach, was no doubt in full cry as the Galloping Ghost repeatedly crashed into the end zone.[34]

Amid the crush of his many duties, Ryan might understandably have underestimated the significance of his latest assignment. That summer, his station would invest a thousand dollars a day renting phone lines from Dayton, Tennessee, all so that the station's youthful broadcaster could cover the Scopes evolution trial. That extravaganza was an unforgettable cultural watershed of the decade, science versus religion, the citified Clarence Darrow versus the good old boy William Jennings Bryan, but radio's presence also created a curious precedent: a callow if intelligent dropout from Chicago was reaching countless more citizens, at least in the short term, than H. L. Mencken, the famed journalist, critic, and scholar who had arrived in Dayton to write a syndicated column on the trial and its ramifications. Several times Ryan and the noted iconoclast found themselves perched together on a windowsill overlooking the jammed courtroom in the atrocious midsummer heat. Exploring the small county seat suddenly swamped with out-of-towners, Ryan also chatted with Bryan and mixed with dozens of prominent writers and editors.[35]

Mencken abruptly left Dayton before Darrow's surprise decision to put Bryan on the witness stand—a celebrated event evidently captured by Ryan's microphone and carried to WGN's transmitter in Chicago—but Ryan's assignment required him to remain in Dayton to trial's end, the big microphone labeled "WGN" always prominent, even after the judge moved the proceedings from the sweltering courtroom to the courthouse lawn. A young Irish Catholic Chicagoan, transported to a remote area of the Bible Belt, broadcasting under conditions never before attempted, had delivered a historic event with efficient panache to a large swath of the country.[36]

The size of Ryan's audience for the Scopes trial was indeterminate because of various factors, not the least of which was that the broadcasts traveled only as far as the direct WGN signal would carry through the air in the daytime. Even more of the nation, though, would soon hear Ryan's voice in an entirely different kind of production: the opening game of that year's World Series, carried over a network that reached both coasts. It had been just two years since McNamee had taken over the 1923 classic for Grantland Rice and phone wires had carried the series to transmitters in far-flung cities, first up and down the East Coast, then pushing farther and farther into the nation's heartland.

Although Ryan's baseball-announcing experience consisted of the two Saturday Cub games he had called for WGN the previous April, he was selected (by Judge Landis, probably at the behest of Ryan's employer, Colonel McCormick) to alternate with none other than McNamee of station WEAF in New York, the anchor station of the nascent NBC network. McNamee's handling of the 1924 national political conventions and World Series, then President Coolidge's inauguration in March 1925, had made him a national name, radio's first national figure. The plan was that New Yorker and Chicagoan share their chores game by game, rather than swap time during each contest. Whichever man broadcast on a particular day, the shotgun pair apparently shared their makeshift workplace each day all through the rain-plagued series, elevating their feet in the flooded ground-level press box at Forbes Field and peering desperately between the shoulders of the print reporters to guess the names of dozens of players in their numeral-free uniforms. McNamee evidently had control of the mike for the momentous seventh game, when the Pirates' second-year man Kiki Cuyler settled things in the bottom of the eighth by doubling with the bases loaded off Walter Johnson, Grover Alexander's last active peer.[37]

Although McNamee was and remained the superstar of the pair, at least one listener agreed with Ring Lardner's assessment of his approach: "You failed in 1924, but, my God, you get worse as you get older. Stick to music and weather reports, but let the Chicago man handle the large events for the good of us all." McNamee's star was such that he didn't need to hide that message from his bosses, but he and Ryan were never paired for a sports event again. In fact, for the 1927 Dempsey-Tunney rematch in Chicago, McNamee had the NBC microphone to himself while both Ryan and Hal Totten of WMAQ broadcast their own independent accounts. Both men were frank about their difficulties, working as they were without training and under extreme pressure before millions. "Sorry I didn't get to see you after the fight," Ryan wrote the New Yorker in an open letter he placed in his Sunday column a few days later. "They tell me we both got so excited that we said, 'Gene shoots a left to Tunney's body' and 'Dempsey has Dempsey pinned to the rails a few times,' but they knew what we meant, anyway."[38]

McNamee proved to be only one of Ryan's many on-air partners and interview subjects, a list that expanded to include Barney Oldfield, Eddie Rickenbacker, and at least one head of state: Eamon de Valera of the Irish Free State. In the WGN studio, Ryan conducted the first radio interview with Gertrude Ederle after her conquest of the English Channel. Gloria Swanson made her inaugural appearance on radio when Ryan interviewed her in April 1925, while the astonished Ryan watched classic signs of stage fright: "She fled into another room and was actually shaking. . . . All through our radio-interview she frantically fingered the handle of the table drawer, and it wasn't till the end of our half-hour chat on the air that she recovered her real voice."[39]

It was a measure of radio's dizzying trajectory that in April 1925, with his *annus mirabilus* just beginning, Ryan was still wrapping himself in an overcoat like a vagabond on Wrigley's Field's roof (covering just a single deck at that point) to broadcast the opener of a team that hadn't threatened anyone in years. The rival broadcasting crews headed by Ryan and Hofman took up their stations atop the roof and watched a crowd throng of 38,000, ten thousand above capacity, fill the park and part of the playing field, and then described how Alexander and the Cubs smashed the Pirates, 8–2. Afterward, WGN's listeners flooded the station's mailbox with approving messages; WMAQ had already promised to broadcast every game that week.[40] But a week later, when Ryan climbed the catwalk to the roof for WGN's second Cub broadcast, Solly Hofman and crew were nowhere in evidence. According to the schedule published that day, the Cubs had been preempted by the opening of the Women's World Fair at the Furniture Mart; President Coolidge was scheduled to open the event with a long-distance talk from Washington DC, and the station's programs would emanate from the Furniture Mart until 8:00 that night. Nonetheless, baseball updates were scheduled every quarter hour, even at 4:00, when Eva Gordon Horodesky, "well-known concert contralto," was scheduled to perform.

TODAY'S WMAQ PROGRAM

[*Chicago Daily News*, Saturday, April 18, 1925]

12:30 p.m.—President Coolidge, opening the Women's World's Fair in Chicago with a talk by sealed wire from Washington, D.C.

2:00 p.m.—Cyrena Van Gordon, soprano of the Chicago Civic Opera Association

2:15 p.m.—Talk by Mrs. Joseph T. Bowen, "The Women's World's Fair"

2:20 p.m.—Talk by Dr. Julia Holmes Smith, "The Board of Managers of the Chicago World's Fair, 1893"

2:30 p.m.—Mme. Sturkow-Ryder, pianist

2:45 p.m.—Talk by Mrs. John T. Sherman, president, General Federation of Women's Clubs

3:15 p.m.—Baseball scores

3:30 p.m.—Baseball scores

3:45 p.m.—Baseball scores

4:00 p.m.—Baseball scores

4:00 p.m.—Eva Gordon Horodesky, contralto

4:15 p.m.—Baseball scores

4:30 p.m.—Baseball scores

4:35 p.m.—Donna Dettmers, harpist

5:00 p.m.—Baseball scores

5:15 p.m.—Opera in English quartet[41]

However the schedule conflict with Madame Horodesky was resolved, listeners would have learned by 5:00 that the Cardinals (Rogers Hornsby, 3 for 3 with five runs scored; Jim Bottomley, 6 RBI) were well on their way to a 20–5 thrashing of the home team and five of its pitchers. WMAQ was off the air the next day, Sunday, April 19, but WMAQ scheduled another broadcast—Artie Hofman unmentioned—to cover the last game of the Cubs' home stand on Tuesday. That game was postponed, and on Wednesday afternoon at Comiskey Park the Sox held their own home opener, an event aired by neither station.[42]

WGN and WMAQ, then, each had baseball broadcasting to its credit for 1925. It was the first time (excepting the Reds' 1924 opener) that anyone had broadcast games that counted toward the season's standings, but for all anyone knew, broadcasting baseball live from the ballpark was just another experiment like broadcasting the circus, or carrying live stage performances from Loop theaters—and Ryan and Hofman might have to find other ways to earn a living. For the next six weeks, talks and live music, mixed with occasional dead time, filled WGN's and WMAQ's schedules.

Besides live, stilted music, radio carried a lot of talk. Most stations' schedules resembled that of WMAQ (and to a startling degree, contemporary public radio): *Items of Interest to Women, Household Talks*, farm bureau talk, book talk, and travel talk, not to mention Shakespearean drama and University of Chicago talks. Classical and "potted palm" orchestral music occupied most of the remaining broadcast hours, which could be irregular. Stations frequently signed off the air, sometimes in favor of "frequency partners," sometimes simply to leave the air until the next act began.[43]

At first, no one seemed to have contemplated advertising as a revenue source; many of the larger stations had been launched more or less to enhance the prestige of a sponsoring newspaper or store, rather like a corporation establishing a website in later decades. No soap operas had yet been developed, no Jack Benny or Fred Allen or Gracie Burns, no Green Hornet or Lone Ranger. Downscale material—in particular, any music that might be construed as "popular"—aired late at night or on weekends: each Saturday evening, for instance, WMAQ featured "the men with a thousand and one songs," a comedy-song team of a future baseball announcer, Russell Pratt, and his partner, Fred Daw, sporting tastes unknown. The same night, WLS hosted a country music show.[44]

Extravaganzas such as renting hundreds of miles of phone lines were quite beyond the budget of Judith Waller, the WMAQ program director. Her station was owned by Chicago's afternoon *Daily News*—a respectable, well-established, but fairly distant runner-up to the mighty and influential *Tribune*, the self-proclaimed "World's Greatest Newspaper" (hence its station's call letters), Colonel Robert McCormick, proprietor. The thirty-six-year-old Waller, then, would have to battle the overwhelming monetary resources of WGN and its parent *Tribune* with verve and initiative. Over the winter of 1924–25, casting about for something with more potential than live theater or the circus for her afternoon programming, Waller decided to contact one of the few men in Chicago not overawed by Colonel McCormick: William Wrigley. (In fact, McCormick's new Tribune Tower had just opened for business across the street from the Wrigley Building.) The petite Waller, a clear-thinking sort who could also flash a disarming smile, had managed WMAQ's station since its beginnings three years before. A physician's daughter from the well-to-do suburb of Oak Park, she had a background in advertising, including stints with the J. Walter Thompson agency in both Chicago and New York. Waller had never heard of a radio station, much less listened to one, so she was flummoxed one day early in the decade when the business manager of the *Daily News*, an old friend, approached her about the WMAQ job. Her ignorance was understandable: WMAQ, a *Daily News* property, was the only station operating in Chicago in early 1922. "We don't know what it is either, but we have just decided to start one," her friend replied. "Come on in and we'll talk about it."[45]

Soon Waller, starting out with a staff of one engineer, set about figuring out what "it" was. She began by scheduling opera, classical music, and book reviews. With virtually no budget to spend on programming, Waller hustled for performers and commentators by offering free publicity: write-ups in the *Daily News*. Editors from the parent newspaper also appeared gratis, with book reviews and specialty commentary (including the program *Items of Interest to Women*). Still, Waller found it difficult to fill the broadcast day, so the station periodically went off the air. Sometimes she ad-libbed, or filled in on the drums herself. The celebrities Waller did recruit for appearances were often disoriented by the experience. "This only went over to the Daily News Building, didn't it?" asked Sir Gilbert Parker after the Canadian novelist had declaimed into Waller's microphone. Equipment broke down frequently in the middle of broadcasts. No popular music was aired, by decree of Victor Lawson, the *Daily News*'s publisher, nor was Sunday broadcasting allowed.[46]

It was a respectable product, at least by comparison with the early years of the World Wide Web seven decades later. By spring 1925, after three years of struggle, Waller had established a well-regarded radio station, but this genteel executive was about to jump start radio as a mass medium. Radio ownership in the United States had grown tenfold—from 400,000 to 4 million—since Waller first joined wMAQ and there was no sign of a letup. Wider audiences beckoned.

Early in 1925, Waller heard from the mother of a disabled boy. Broadcast accounts of major league ballgames, she wrote, would be a wonderful diversion for her son, who was unable to attend games in person, the woman wrote Waller. The woman's letter prompted Waller to consider the market that might exist beyond shut-ins. By 1925 Chicago was full of women with more leisure time than ever before, thanks to labor-saving devices, increased discretionary income, lack of career opportunities, and the general prosperity. There were perhaps a million women at home in Chicago and its suburbs each afternoon, most of them with husbands at work, and many with access to one of the several hundred thousand radio sets in Chicago. Radio's infant years of wet- and dry-cell batteries, technical problems, and crystal-set jargon—heterodyne frequencies, rheostats, millihertz, headsets—were rapidly giving way to user-friendly models with speakers. In the Loop, shoppers could find them in elegant Louis Quinze cabinets at Lyon and Healy, the faithful sponsor of Waller's midday chamber concerts. Most important to Waller's plan, at 3 p.m. each afternoon hundreds of thousands of Chicago women could listen to a speaker-equipped set while engaged in, or taking a break from, their household chores.[47]

Waller gained entrance to William Wrigley's office high in his white-clad tower—with considerably less trouble, apparently, than had the equally enthusiastic but working-class Andy Frain—and promptly proposed the next logical step in daytime radio: regular broadcasting of home baseball games. WMAQ faced little downside. The stage and the cast would already be provided, and the quantity of radios now in use within the city limits almost guaranteed that a ballgame broadcast might prove as popular as household hints or the random music recital. The risks would be all Wrigley's.[48]

The gum king, stubbing one of his omnipresent cigars into the ashtray on his huge triangular desk, thought the matter over. "Baseball is too much of a business to be a sport, and too much of a sport to be a business," he would explain in the *Saturday Evening Post* a few years later. It wasn't a question of baseball's popularity—Judge Landis had successfully dubbed the sport a "national institution" and Babe Ruth had finished the job with his bat—and the sport had also recently acquired its unique antitrust exemption. Yet the typical major league ballpark was seldom filled, and Cubs Park was no exception. Weekday baseball crowds, even in so huge a city as Chicago, seldom reached five figures. Saturday attendance was limited by the half days that most people in the 1920s still worked each Saturday morning. Sundays and doubleheaders were the only real crack at capacity crowds that Wrigley and his fellow owners had—"capacity" meaning 25,000 or 30,000 in most ballparks of that era, including the Cubs Park of 1925. A Sunday afternoon thunderstorm could ruin a ball club's take for the week. A banner attendance year was half a million fans; only Gotham's Yankees and Giants possessed the seating and the customer base to make the turnstiles revolve more frequently than that.[49]

Now Waller offered to make a live account of each game available free to Wrigley's millions of potential cash customers. It could be that no one would bother to go to a game anymore if the game were available free on radio—a scenario that would daunt other baseball magnates until well into the 1940s, but William Wrigley heard Waller out. "Whether he was intrigued by the fact that a woman was asking him for this privilege, or just because the whole venture was so new, I don't know," Waller recalled years later. Not every male executive Waller pitched would prove so understanding. "I think you'd better go back to Chicago. It's very plain to see that you know nothing about radio," a CBS network executive told Waller a couple of years later after she proposed taking a daily WMAQ comedy show coast to coast. The show in question was *Amos 'n' Andy,* which eventually became one of the most popular, if racially insensitive, radio programs ever—on NBC.[50]

Wrigley promised only to think it over. Cub president Bill Veeck already had several special projects in the works. Veeck was recruiting a minor league manager, Joe McCarthy of the Louisville Colonels, to join the Cub coaching staff, the opening step in replacing the current Cub manager, Grover Alexander's longtime battery mate Bill Killefer. The National League's fiftieth jubilee would be celebrated at Cubs Park in June. Wrigley himself was in the midst of building the first official "Wrigley Field," a $1 million edifice in Los Angeles that he hoped to open before the end of the season.[51]

Wrigley and Veeck huddled over Waller's proposal. Veeck, a former newspaperman, and Wrigley, the master promoter who had built a five-mile-long stretch of billboards and sent gum samples to every telephone customer in the United States, well appreciated the uses of publicity. Probably, Wrigley sensed the boost that radio could provide the Cubs' semi-dormant Ladies Day promotion, which had drawn a lively crowd of twenty thousand early in 1924 but then slipped back into the doldrums. Whatever his reasons, Wrigley gave Waller the go-ahead to test the concept. How WGN also became involved is not as well documented, but one way or another, both the WMAQ and WGN crews were on hand Opening Day to describe Grover Alexander's 8–2 victory over the Pirates. Only WGN broadcast an additional game before the Cubs went on the road for five weeks. In late May the team returned and settled in for a monthlong home stand that might repair its dismal 16–25 record to date.[52]

On June 1, a small item on the *Daily News* radio page informed readers that Russell Pratt would announce that afternoon's Cub game. Pratt, "one of WMAQ's 'men of one thousand and one songs'" (referencing his song-and-dance show that aired live on WMAQ each Saturday night) and a "baseball enthusiast," would be assisted, not by his fellow crooner Fred Daw, but by "Hal"—almost certainly Hal Totten, a *Daily News* rewrite man who had already broadcast college football for WMAQ the previous autumn. Artie Hofman's name was again absent—Hofman, it seems, had succumbed to the same sportscasting phobias that had driven Grantland Rice from the World Series broadcasting and opened the door to Graham McNamee's fabulous success.[53]

That June afternoon Pratt and Hal described what would prove a rare victory that year for the young Guy Bush, tossing a single inning in relief of Grover Alexander.

The 1925 edition of the Cubs was already 11½ games from first, and the June home stand did little to improve things. Attendance was slipping noticeably from the previous year, and a less-stalwart owner could have made radio the scapegoat. Wrigley, though, had made his name and his millions by sticking to his hunches, and that no doubt gave Judith Waller maneuvering room as she experimented with her project that summer.

An experiment it certainly was, as Waller improvised on her shoestring budget while WGN busied itself writing checks to rent hundreds of miles of phone lines to carry the Scopes trial. Waller's substitution of Pratt for Artie Hofman (who had evidently been suggested by William Wrigley) seemed to model itself on the successful World Series broadcasts of Graham McNamee, likewise a singer by trade. For Pratt, the arrangement was a twofer: his Saturday-night musical show received a free plug, and in the bargain he could spend a couple of hours at the ballpark free each day. He was probably already under contract to WMAQ, and if not, was unlikely to charge extra for his time. Hal, already a *Daily News* employee, likewise added little overhead.

Mid-June brought more of Waller's economical tinkering: guest shots by performers from current theater productions in the Loop: Berta Donn of *June Days*, Wanda Lyon of *The Lady Next Door*, and Shirley Ward of *Just Married* all joined Pratt on various afternoons. Odd as importing glamorous women to the world of the ballpark might seem, Waller, Veeck, and Wrigley didn't need to cater to the core of male Cub fans; upgrading the ball club would solve that problem, so they ignored the fear that broadcasting ballgames would discourage attendance, especially among the fair-weather fans. Instead, the trio were staking their bet on actually expanding the market of baseball patrons. Coinciding with the first WMAQ broadcasts, Wrigley and Veeck renewed their Ladies Day promotion with smartly illustrated display advertising in the *Tribune*: "The Chicago National League Club wants every woman to acquaint herself with the joys and thrills of baseball." (Later ads made sure everyone understood a key point: "YOU DON'T NEED AN ESCORT.")[54]

The actresses' radio careers proved as short-lived as Artie Hofman's, and for that matter, *Monday Night Baseball* of the 1970s (one evening featuring Danny Kaye's repeated evocation "BOCC-a-BELL-a! BOCC-a-BELL-a!" whenever the Montreal Expos' journeyman catcher entered the picture). Neither was the career of the world's first daily play-by-play man, Russell Pratt, destined for a long run. Through the dog days of July and August, Pratt's name showed up only intermittently; the station might mention a generic "announcer," or even "the game will be reported from Cubs Park."[55]

Pratt's unnamed announcing substitute was no doubt Hal Totten, for several reasons, chief among them his previous identification with the initial June broadcasts and our hindsight knowledge that the pudgy, bespectacled Totten was setting out as history's first full-time professional sportscaster. By 1929 WMAQ was referring to him as "the dean of baseball broadcasters," and he would keep at it into the 1940s before he eventually became an executive in the minor leagues.[56]

In 1925, though, Totten was still a novice journalist whose bosses were constantly shuffling his duties. Broadcasting baseball would have provided fairly steady work that summer and a welcome opportunity for a twenty-four-year-old to head for the ballpark, at least most of the afternoons the Cubs were in town. (The exceptions were Sundays, per Victor Lawson's policy, and White Sox games; Charles Comiskey had declined Waller's suggestion that he try an arrangement similar to the Cub deal.) When the Cubs left town, WMAQ reported baseball scores every fifteen minutes or so from the studio—once again, without attribution, the mild-mannered Totten is the logical candidate for the announcer.[57]

WMAQ stayed with its brave new baseball programming all the way through the Cubs' historically difficult season: lengthy losing spells, Rabbit Maranville's two-month managerial fiasco, all the way to the uninspiring season's end, when the Cubs finally settled into last place; then Totten was swiftly assigned to the next University of Chicago football game, while radio ignored the City Series. Thus Totten—indubitably the most-experienced baseball broadcaster in the land after covering all or parts of several Cub home stands in recent months—was nowhere in sight when Graham McNamee and Totten's Chicagoan rival, Quin Ryan, began broadcasting the Pittsburgh-Washington World Series that week. McNamee and Totten did cross paths at one point in the early days of the medium, probably when the New Yorker visited Chicago for the Dempsey-Tunney rematch in 1927, and the new superstar advised the Chicagoan not to abandon newspapering. "Only the World Series will interest real baseball fans," he mentored his young colleague in a knowledgeable baritone.[58]

The feminine emphasis was not at odds with Veeck and Wrigley's plans. The Cub impresarios were looking for ways to encourage that other Cub giveaway, Ladies Day, which in the mid-1920s might attract an extra five thousand fans or so. Veeck and Waller sent out questionnaires for listener reactions. They came back in volume. Veeck and Waller learned that their production was a hit in "Chicagoland," the *Tribune*'s name for the multi-state region centered on lower Lake Michigan. Baseball parks had traditionally been filled by those within walking distance of the park, along with those who could hop the El to the Addison Street station, plus the more fortunate fans who drove their own automobiles. But now, Veeck learned, millions of out-of-towners, in addition to Chicago's homemakers, were learning about Cubs baseball in a way not possible before. "Don't stop it," wrote one farmer from somewhere in Chicagoland. "I have a radio in the field with me. I plow one turn, sit down for a cool drink out of the jug and listen to the score. It's grand." (Battery-powered radios were not uncommon in radio's early years.) A dentist said he used the broadcasts to keep his patients calm.[59]

The stands were often filled with obvious country folk—"You could spot 'em by the haircuts," the *Tribune* commented one day. Entire families might show up at the gate at 7 a.m. after driving all night. Within a few years observers were estimating that radio had tripled the number of baseball fans in the hinterlands. One newspaperman sitting down in a small-town lunch counter in downstate Illinois found a dozen men gathered around the radio, "intent upon every word of the broadcast," analyzing statistics and debating strategy like urbanites gathered at Broadway and Lawrence to place a bet or two.[60]

Within a few years the Cubs, radio coverage and all, were outdrawing even Babe Ruth and his New York Yankees. Veeck, gazing on the 1927 opening-day crowd, muttered, "They keep coming faster than we can build." That year the Cubs became the first National League team to draw a million customers. (The Yankees had done so for several seasons already.) By 1929, the Chicago National League Ball Club set a major league season record, just shy of 1.5 million. Nearly one of three National League customers was a Wrigley Field patron. Baseball's booming 1920s had reached high tide.[61]

The national pastime, Chicago, and popular culture would never be the same. Veeck and Wrigley evidently took care to avoid an exclusive agreement with WMAQ, because in 1926 WGN and Quin Ryan resumed broadcasting the Cubs, initially just home games on weekends and later, as the Cubs stormed into contention, every home date. The station's early-season weekend broadcasts featured an abortive twist on WMAQ's "guest shot" experiment of 1925: Ryan received broadcast "help" from WGN's "Sam 'n' Henry" act—Freeman Gosden and Charles Correll, who would later become better-known as Amos 'n' Andy; the act's announcer, Bill Hay, also substituted for Ryan later in the season, evidently independent of Gosden and Correll.[62]

Charles Comiskey, noting the stampede of ball fans to the North Side, decided to allow WMAQ and WGN into Comiskey Park after all. By the end of the decade, at least five stations were simultaneously broadcasting home games of the Cubs and the Sox. A unique and long-lasting link was being forged between baseball and the mass market. Initially WMAQ's Totten, then WGN's Ryan and Bob Elson, WBBM's Pat Flanagan, and yet others became team ambassadors, more familiar to the average fan than William Wrigley, Bill Veeck, and even many ballplayers. Eventually every major league franchise would introduce itself to its fans with its own Totten or Ryan and utilize their salesmanship to create a sense of excitement about the ball club. The dramatic ups and downs the Cubs encountered in the coming seasons would have an immediacy that no fans anywhere had ever experienced.[63]

Radio would never be the same, either. The Cub broadcasts were the first permanent daily intrusion in the once-refined world of radio programming. Even at their brisk 1920s pace, ballgames occupied a larger swatch of time than any radio show yet conceived, and took it more often. The national sport gained its foothold in the new medium, which itself was about to begin a frank pursuit of ratings, advertising dollars, nightly situation comedy shows, and all the other mass-culture phenomena we live with today. By the late 1920s some Cub broadcasts, now aired by other stations as well, had become so commercial that a writer visiting from New York satirized the most blatant abuses:

[The base runner] has reached home—hooray—and is now going into the Chicago dugout midst a tremendous ovation. Just imagine, folks, how Kiki Cuyler would appreciate a drink of Cola Coki while resting in the shady retreat of the dugout on this sweltering day.[64]

Baseball traditionalists greeted radio broadcasting with the same enthusiasm they would accord to night baseball and racial integration. No matter that the Cubs' attendance leaped 140 percent from 1925 to 1929 (from 623,000 to 1,485,000): the game seemed less "inspirational" over the airwaves. People listening at home would be deprived of fresh air, and national morale might be adversely affected! True, the White Sox's embrace of broadcasting produced no legions of new fans, but on the other hand, their attendance didn't suffer, either, despite the team's prolonged residence in the second division.

The old guard, convinced that the Cubs' record attendance in the late twenties was all about their improved record, continued to shun radio coverage for years. Even late in the 1930 season, after years of unprecedented attendance success in radio-dominated Chicago, only two other cities—and three stations total—were airing live home games for their fans. The general attendance decline of the early 1930s triggered a new wave of disparagement, as if the Depression had nothing to do with empty seats. The Cubs kept up their defiance of the conventional consensus even after Wrigley, Veeck, and the anti-radio American League president, Ban Johnson, were gone and Waller had taken her talents elsewhere. (She became an NBC executive and later, in 1946, wrote the standard textbook for college broadcasting courses.) Not until the end of the 1930s were all major league clubs broadcasting their teams' home games.[65]

In the 1920s and early 1930s, moreover, the Cubs' ballpark also welcomed hundreds of thousands of unpaid visitors each year—numbers that probably exceeded some teams' paid attendance. "Ladies' Day Today," the Cubs would proclaim in the newspapers, accompanied by sketches of chic matrons converging en masse on Cubs Park.

LADIES' DAY

Mothers

Daughters

Sisters

Wives

Grandmothers

You are again to be the invited guests of the Chicago National League Ball Club. It's official Ladies' Day at the prettiest baseball grounds in the world. . . .

ADMISSION FREE[66]

As with radio broadcasting, Bill Veeck was not the natural father of Ladies Day, but he adopted it in childhood. There had been in various cities ladies days since before the turn of the century, and for several years the Cubs and the White Sox had both been admitting women into their ballparks free on Fridays. It had been a desultory promotion, producing no great shifts in allegiance or attendance. A few thousand women at a ballgame, after all, could easily double the size of the usual weekday crowd.[67]

But the Cubs' decision to flood the airwaves with free baseball broadcasts and to promote Ladies Day more vigorously—not to mention a vastly improved product stocked with charismatic, muscular fellows—soon transformed Fridays at the North Side ballpark into a circus seldom witnessed outside dramatic pennant races and the World Series. One Friday afternoon in 1928, an unprecedented 17,000 women thronged to the park. Soon Fridays at the park had become a happening. The afternoon of June 20, 1929, the Cubs recorded 19,021 free female admissions. That record lasted six weeks, until the memorable pandemonium of August 6, when more than 25,000 women stormed the park. When a contender was in town, the women could find themselves jostling with an equal number of paid male customers—a few thousand, at least, no doubt peeved at the sudden shortage of good seating, but also quite a few pleased to bring a spouse or a date at no cost. The twelve Ladies Days held in 1930 drew 240,000 female guests, a figure that compared favorably, for instance, to the Pittsburgh Pirates' total paid attendance of 260,392 and the Cincinnati Reds' 263,316, and incomparably greater than the 179,126 souls the American League's St. Louis Browns drew to Sportsman's Park that year—notwithstanding ten dates featuring Babe Ruth, complete with a Sunday doubleheader—a rare Browns sweep—staged before a corporal's guard of 5,000.[68]

Chicago's new fans, invading a bastion of masculinity in force, were willing to stand in hat, dress, and heels in the outfield, enduring the blazing summer sun just as the men had always been willing to do during sellouts. They could completely fill the niche in left field to the west of the jury box; before them, extending in a semicircle all the way around to the right-field foul line, were the front rows of standees, at least five to six deep. Thousands more, disappointed and angry, might fill the streets outside. More than once, they overwhelmed the security forces and took their objective. Everyone seemed to agree that Hack Wilson and the Cubs were the best show in town. "I am 61 years old, and this is my first ball game," said Mrs. Fred Lumpp of Niles Center in August 1930, after watching a heart-stopping, thirteen-inning Cub victory in the heat of a pennant race. "It was the most exciting sport I have watched in all my life. I am going to attend the games from now on as often as possible." At the same game were Mrs. Gustav Brunke, a resident of Sycamore, a small town fifty miles west of Chicago; Alice McMahon, who liked to play baseball herself at the Emmet playground off Milwaukee Avenue; and Mrs. Herbert Barth of North Kenmore Avenue, who said she followed the team on the radio when she couldn't attend. Mrs. Barth allowed that she had enjoyed herself at the game, but the lack of color in the Cubs' uniforms troubled her. Gustave Brunke probably spoke best for the restless Friday afternoon multitudes: "If I didn't have a family," she said, "I'd follow the Cubs all over. Personally, I don't believe I'll ever see enough baseball games."[69]

The folkways of the park changed. A foul ball into the stands now meant screams and dozens of well-manicured hands stretching fearlessly for the ball, bracelets and necklaces flying. During a rain shower, brightly colored parasols popped up in the midst of the once-drab crowds. Hoarse cheering was replaced by a distinctly higher pitch. Remarkable plays received a round of hand clapping, as if the spectators had just witnessed something pleasing at the theater. There was also, at first, an obvious and palpable ignorance about the basic rules of the game. But radio exposure provided day-to-day experience in the game's niceties, and by the end of the decade the Chicago sportswoman rated as a reasonably savvy baseball fan. More important, Veeck estimated that up to 35 percent of his burgeoning, and paying, Sunday crowds were now women.[70]

Particular ballplayers were singled out as the ladies' favorites—and not necessarily due to their skill or statistical prowess. Women besieged the clubhouses before and after the ballgames; autograph sessions became opportunities to present one's phone number to an athlete. One resourceful visiting player—a married man—found he could make some headway through the crush by hobbling from the clubhouse on a crutch.[71]

To handle the surge Veeck constructed the big leagues' first two ladies restrooms, furnished with davenports, divans, chairs, and that necessity for the late-twenties flapper, ashtrays. Wrigley explained the business logic of Ladies Day this way: "I spend $1.5 million a year for advertising. I manufacture chewing gum and give away samples to the public. I own a ballclub in the National League and I give away samples of baseball." The number of women willing to pay extra to upgrade to a reserved seat itself paid for the program.[72]

Wrigley and Veeck, commanding a franchise headed for the cellar, one that had never drawn more than 721,000 in a season, had caught the wide-open spirit of the age. In a city where women were smoking, frequenting speakeasies, and wearing form-fitting outfits at the Oak Street Beach, hollering at the ballpark was no longer an unladylike thing to do.[73]

Now all Veeck needed was a new star, a league-leading headliner, to keep 'em coming. He added that to his to-do list.

On October 13, 1925, a small middle-aged man with a prominent jaw sat by William Wrigley in the Comiskey Park boxes to watch the deciding game of the City Series. It had been a great day all around, but Wrigley's guest, a career baseball man, must have felt a twinge of disappointment after the final out. He had seldom been able to see Alexander the Great pitch, and now the series had concluded before the Cubs could call on Alec's services again.[74]

Wrigley's guest had lived in the Philadelphia area in the earliest years of Alexander's career, but he had rarely been in Philly in the summertime as Alexander began to accumulate his brilliant record. For most of the past twenty summers he had been playing or managing baseball at less-glamorous levels than Old Pete's, in such locales as Wilmington, Delaware; Franklin, Pennsylvania; Toledo; Wilkes-Barre, Pennsylvania; and finally Louisville, where he had spent a decade as player, player-manager, and bench manager, in leagues named Peach, Tri-State, the "outlaw" Interstate, New York State, International, and American Association. Mr. Wrigley's guest was the definition of a career minor leaguer, a "busher"—for baseball aristocrats like Alexander, a term of contempt.[75]

That was unfortunate, for this particular busher, whose name was Joseph McCarthy, had just signed a contract to manage Alexander and the Cubs the next season. Bill Veeck had been after him since the spring, first offering him twelve thousand dollars to coach with the Cubs—an impressive amount of money for a coaching position, in those days generally a low-paid afterthought for ex-ballplayers. Nonetheless, McCarthy had demurred. He was well established in Louisville, where he had managed the American Association Colonels since 1919. His 1921 club had won the Little World Series, upsetting a twenty-one-year-old named Lefty Grove and the mighty Baltimore Orioles. The 1925 season brought another pennant to Louisville, and the fans even put on a little "day" for McCarthy, with a sizable check, floral tributes, and speeches. And whatever Louisville was, it was a step or two up from the likes of Wilmington, Franklin, and Wilkes-Barre.[76]

By early September, McCarthy's Colonels had his third AA pennant wrapped up, and their skipper heard from Veeck again. By this time the Cubs were on their third manager for the year. Veeck said he wanted to discuss the Cubs' head job. The salary, Veeck added, would be twenty thousand dollars.

McCarthy decided to consider the new offer more seriously. Twenty thousand dollars a year was significant money in 1925—some two hundred thousand in our dollars, and more than just about anyone in baseball other than Babe Ruth and Rogers Hornsby earned. And few major league teams had ever hired someone with McCarthy's lack of big league experience. A thirty-nine-year-old with his background might never get such a chance again. McCarthy accepted Veeck's invitation to meet and talk things over further. Within a few days, McCarthy and Veeck were huddling in French Lick, Indiana, a remote mineral springs resort some fifty miles northwest of Louisville, just off the main line to Chicago. It was actually an undercover gambling mecca with few bothersome reporters, or lawmen, for that matter, as publicity-averse visitors like Al Capone well knew.

Veeck, likewise, needed no extra publicity at the moment. He had run the Cubs for seven years, and hiring five managers and finishing last for the first time in the franchise's fifty years of operation were all he had to show for it. The franchise was a laughingstock among baseball insiders for its eagerness to buy over-the-hill ballplayers at premium prices. The 1925 season threatened to finish off Veeck's reputation. Hiring Rabbit Maranville in July started out as a disastrous farce and declined from there. Maranville, whose madcap ways masked his playing excellence, was a confirmed alcoholic. Within days of his promotion, the new manager and two of his players were arrested for brawling with a New York cabdriver; that incident, and dousing everyone in the Cubs' train with the contents of an ice bucket, or possibly a spittoon, compose the main body of Maranville-Cub lore. After two crazy months Veeck, with the team sinking fast in the standings, aborted the Maranville experiment and appointed an interim manager to finish out the season.[77]

Now Veeck was violating unwritten baseball rules by negotiating with a career minor leaguer.[78] Late-summer sunshine bathed the pillared veranda of the French Lick Springs Hotel while McCarthy huddled with Veeck. McCarthy, known then and throughout his life for economy of speech, listened carefully to Veeck's pitch. McCarthy finally told Veeck he would think it over and let him know after the Colonels finished the Little World Series, where, as in 1921, his men would face Baltimore's Orioles.

Despite Veeck's precautions, rumors of his offer to McCarthy were circulating in Chicago by the time Alexander and Blankenship opened the 1925 Chicago City Series. Louisville, after gaining a three-games-to-two advantage in the best-of-nine series, dropped the next three contests to the Baltimore Orioles in early October. Within hours McCarthy fired off a telegram of acceptance to Veeck.[79]

William Wrigley celebrated by announcing that he had bought four "leading hitters in the National League" for his new manager; he would "shoot a million to put the Cubs over the top in 1926." When McCarthy arrived in the Wrigley Building the next morning, Wrigley was still talking big. The Cubs would win the pennant in 1926, he said, "if Bill Veeck and I have got to get into the lineup ourselves. . . . [W]e are going to give Chicago a winner if we have to spend one million dollars for 40 new men." The identity of the four leading hitters of the National League, and how much of the million dollars had been spent on them, was left hanging.[80]

McCarthy signed his contract, then quietly offered that "the first thing I will do is get another pitcher." The new Cub troika, joined by Mrs. McCarthy, headed for Comiskey Park to watch the sixth game of the City Series, which the Cubs led three games to one. Wrigley and Veeck took McCarthy to the clubhouse to meet the Cubs, including Old Alex. Then McCarthy and his new bosses watched the Cubs pile up a 4–0 lead on the Sox behind Lefty Cooper.

McCarthy's arrival marked the fourth head man the Cubs' bosses had shaken hands with that year. And if Wrigley's words were to be believed, at least four players wouldn't return the next year. Grover Alexander, the survivor of fourteen major league campaigns, plus an all-too-real one in the military, was probably the least concerned of anyone. He had witnessed lots of fresh starts and vows of renewal in his day, and few of them had come to anything. Come spring and another trip to balmy Santa Catalina Island, he would size up this busher. Then he would languidly shuffle to the mound at Cubs Park every few days the next season, his too-small cap perched precariously on his shock of red hair. What choice would the new skipper have?

One new Cub had already been selected before McCarthy even showed up in Chicago. Though by no means one of the promised "leading hitters in the National League," to that point anyway, the newcomer would transform the venerable Chicago National League Ball Club like no one else before or since.

After verbally committing to the Cub post, McCarthy had contacted an old friend and boss from the minors, Jimmy Burke, about serving as his number 1 assistant. Burke had just been let out as the manager of the New York Giants' top minor league club, the Toledo Mud Hens, so McCarthy's offer to coach in the Big Show was a godsend. From Burke, McCarthy also obtained some valuable information: the Giants had omitted a Toledo outfielder from the protected list in the upcoming major league draft. One of the top minor leaguers in the country, only twenty-five though he had accumulated more than six hundred at-bats in the big leagues, he would be available almost gratis to the team with the first pick in the postseason minor league draft.[81]

Courtesy of Gabby Hartnett's two errors in the final game of the regular season, the Cubs had claimed last place in the league and, consequently, the first pick in the annual draft of minor league players. On October 10, 1925, a full three days ahead of McCarthy's official signing, the fine print in the sports pages listed the Cubs' selection: "Outfielder Lewis Wilson, from Toledo, O."[82]

The Second City had just fleeced Gotham. Lewis "Hack" Wilson would return to his rightful place in the major leagues, and baseball history would be the richer. The man and the moment were united. Prohibition Chicago and all its burgeoning, quarreling, fractious elements had their bellwether—husky, brawling, broad-shouldered, and frequently drunk.

3 | The Age of Wilson Begins

You can get a lot farther with a smile and a gun than you can with a smile.
—Attributed to Al Capone

It was May 8, 1926. Hundreds of boys and young men raced through the crowd exiting Cubs Park and charged down the runways to the Bruins' clubhouse. Grover Alexander had just completed a 6–4 victory over the New York Giants that beautiful early May afternoon—yet the lads wore anxious looks. And there was no question that a crisis was at hand. Hack Wilson had sprained his ankle!

Underneath the grandstand, the youths snaked around the support beams and began jostling for position, necks craning, near the staircase that led up to the clubhouse. Could Hack, their new idol, even walk? Was it a fracture? How long could the ball club function without its center fielder and cleanup man, the hero of the North Side for some two weeks now, the indispensable Cub, the talk of baseball?

Soon Wilson appeared, limping slightly on his way down the flight of stairs. At the foot of the steps, the crowd pressed around him with congratulations and questions about his injury. Then a white-haired figure on the edge of the crowd called out Wilson's name, and the ranks of the crowd parted for the newcomer: the commissioner of baseball himself, Kenesaw Mountain Landis.

Landis's appearance among the masses may have been more than a courtesy call. In the seventh year of the lively ball era, the National League lacked any gate attraction who could stir the kind of excitement that followed Babe Ruth everywhere, only Rogers Hornsby's icy brilliance, and where better to begin than in the nation's second-largest metropolis? More than one hundred thousand souls had attended the first three games of the series with New York. Wilson was outdrawing the gangland funerals.

The hallway mobbed with hundreds of young men and boys was testament to that.

"It's nothing, Judge," the stocky athlete, who was not much taller than his young fans, assured the lord high commissioner as they shook hands. "Just twisted my ankle a bit, but I'll be in there in a few days."[1]

Landis and Wilson went their separate ways at the nearest gate. Dozens of the youngsters left the most powerful man in baseball by himself and followed Wilson out of sight into the young evening.

Hack Wilson's career and the arrival of sports broadcasting in Chicago were nearly simultaneous; each one made the other. By the time Wilson first appeared in a Cub uniform in April 1926, the original broadcasting experiment Judith Waller and William Wrigley had embarked upon a year earlier had faltered over an outcome neither executive had foreseen: the club's first last-place finish in 1925, after fifty years of NL combat. Through the last two-thirds of the 1925 season Waller had gamely sent her announcers out to the park day after day to describe the action while the team's record sank from a passable 26-31 in mid-June to the final cellar-clinching 68-86. Cub attendance had fallen from 716,000 in 1924 to 622,000, but free radio broadcasts could hardly be blamed.

The beta test of baseball broadcasting, then, had been something less than decisive. Waller had to decide whether a team rebuilding with recycled AA players and an unknown new manager would draw more interest than *Items of Interest to Women*. Over in the Wrigley Building, Wrigley and Veeck could be forgiven if they noticed in turn that full radio coverage had coincided with an attendance drop of 13 percent.

The technology, the concentration of population, and the sporting public were already available to marry baseball and radio, but no law of inevitability said the breakthrough had to materialize in Chicago, in the mid-1920s, with the Cubs. As it was, New Yorkers wouldn't hear their teams' games for nearly fifteen years in the future. As the 1926 season got under way, moreover, it seemed as though the Cubs, WMAQ, or both might have given up on the whole idea. April 1926 came and went without any return of Totten and his WMAQ microphone to Wrigley Field; any audience that had developed for the 1925 broadcasts was abandoned. Only two Cub games were broadcast in April 1926, both by Quin Ryan and WGN: the

Cubs' home opener and a game the following Saturday. It seemed to indicate that the Cubs, at least, were the party most interested in keeping the broadcasting initiative alive.

Through Wednesday, April 28, nothing much happened with the new Joe McCarthy edition of the Cubs to convince anyone that the 1926 team, 6-7 so far, was any real improvement over the woebegone 1925 club. The home team had just dropped three straight home contests to Pittsburgh, and the club's perennial mainstay, Alexander, despite pitching well, was 1-2; in a May 2 start he would hear the unthinkable: "Take him out!" On April 29 the Cardinals arrived, and one of the newcomers on the roster, Lewis Wilson, smashed his second home run of the season to help the Cubs break their losing streak with a 6–5 win.[2]

No one issued a press release announcing that the National League's next big star had been born, but that day proved to be Hack Wilson's coming out. In the next three games he hit safely in 7 of 14 official appearances; more important, five of his hits were doubles and another his third home run before 36,000, the largest crowd in the history of the park. The Cubs had scored twenty-seven runs from Friday through Sunday and swept the Cardinals four straight. Wilson was suddenly hitting a man-size .364.

A layoff prevented the Cubs from going back to work until Thursday, May 6, but then things began moving fast; the sleepy ballpark was awakening to the roar of the 1920s. The Cubs took the field Thursday afternoon to discover a nigh-unprecedented weekday crowd of twenty thousand in the grandstand; more significant, if not as obvious to those present, Hal Totten and his WMAQ engineer had returned. Never again would radio ignore a Cub home game; from now on, baseball and radio would be one and inseparable. The Cubs were back on the air, Hack Wilson was terrorizing pitchers, and everyone was going to have a good time. The Cubs lost that Thursday, a 2–1 heartbreaker for Wilson's fellow newcomer Charlie Root, but the Cubs stroked three more doubles, including another by Wilson. After each game, throngs of boys and young men mobbed the clubhouse, cheering and calling for Wilson, then trailed him out of the ballpark. Wilson, like many of the Cubs in those days, walked from his apartment to the ballpark and back every day. The Lakeview and Uptown neighborhoods in the park vicinity contained probably dozens of speakeasies. The field announcer, Pat Pieper, who likewise lived close enough to the ballpark to walk to work, tended bar in the evenings at one. The legend of Hack Wilson was about to begin its off-the-field phase.[3]

Wilson disappointed his newfound followers with a hitless Friday, then reversed course by upstaging Alexander's next start, Saturday the 8th, with three hits, including two more doubles, against the Giants. On his final double he sprained his ankle going into second. Teammates had to carry him to the clubhouse, whence he emerged for his postgame rendezvous with Judge Landis and friends. On Sunday the largest crowd ever at the ballpark, more than thirty-six thousand, turned out for the finale of the Giant series. Somewhere between five and ten thousand customers were turned away; another throng of standees filled the outfield. With the score tied in the ninth, Wilson hobbled out to pinch hit. John McGraw, knowing Wilson's game as well as anyone, ordered his outfielders to swing around to the right, while his pitcher worked Wilson inside. But Wilson rammed an inside 2-2 pitch into the left-field overflow for another ground-rule double. He limped off the field for a pinch runner while the throng roared. After the Cubs sent Wilson's pinch runner home with the game winner, the postgame gang met Wilson at the clubhouse door and followed him out of the park.[4]

By Wednesday Wilson was back in the regular lineup. He managed only one single, but the next game his three hits and three RBI led to a 6–3 triumph over the Phils. On Sunday, May 15, there was another huge turnout, which Bill Veeck kept off the field this time, but the grandstand was packed with standing-room-only customers. Wilson hit another double and his fourth homer to drive in four more runs; the Cubs beat the Phils again, 10–9. The great era of Chicago fandom was well under way, the object of hero worship established. But first Chicagoans would have to pay tribute to yesterday's hero.

Saturday, May 22, 1926, brought the kind of chill that can overtake the lakefront well into June, prompting fans and ballplayers to don sweaters and jackets. Grover Alexander, who had suffered through injury and illness all spring, was scheduled to pitch, but before he could undertake his duties there was the matter of Grover Cleveland Alexander Day to deal with.[5]

Jack Bramhall's band, a fixture at Cub ceremonies since the West Side days of the 1890s, tried to strike up a cheery pregame note for the shivering fans. Then the entire Cub team, joined by the visiting Boston Braves, paraded around the field in tribute to the famed veteran. They ended up at home plate, where speeches, baskets of flowers, and a brand-new maroon Lincoln awaited the veteran hurler. The five-thousand-dollar auto was the kind that gangsters might covet. In fact, just outside the city limits almost exactly a month earlier, the Capone organization had riddled a rival's Lincoln (and four rivals) with a withering round of submachine-gun fire.

Alexander climbed in the passenger compartment for a brief inspection and then emerged to lean jauntily on the car, one foot up on the running board and a slight smile marring his usual poker face. He was surrounded by several stout, beaming North Side business owners, well insulated from the cold by Homburgs and overcoats. They had organized the event and raised the money for the car. The chairman of the event, one Charles Brebner, gave a tribute to Alexander. No one showed any inkling of how soon the shiny new motorcar would take the great pitcher from Chicago for good.

Someone moved the Lincoln off the diamond, the dignitaries retreated to the box seats, and the cheering died away. Alexander began working briskly against the Braves, who had marched in his honor only moments before. With two out in the top of the fourth a Boston triple nicked him for two runs. Another run followed in the sixth, and then three more, two of them unearned, in the eighth. The score stood at 6–1 for the visitors. Although no one was rude enough to cry, "Take him out!" when the Braves began hitting freely again in the ninth, McCarthy finally called in a reliever to end Grover Cleveland Alexander Day for Grover Alexander.

On Sunday fair skies returned to Cubs Park. In the fifth inning Wilson confirmed the new generation's takeover by smashing a thunderbolt that struck thirty feet up on the center-field scoreboard, 420 feet away.[6] It was the longest home run anyone had seen in the park since its debut more than a decade before. The Braves, impressed, knocked Wilson down in his next at-bat. Wilson threw down his bat and charged the mound. McCarthy rushed over from his post in the third-base coach's box. Reinforced by some of the Cubs, he pulled his centerfielder and cleanup man out of danger.

After the game Wilson drifted from the ballpark with the usual admirers. Some or most of this crowd, including Wilson, eventually found its way to an address on North Sheridan Road.

Recent events had demonstrated that there were really no noncombatants in Chicago's Big Thirst. Chicagoans were cheerfully defying the Volstead Act in huge numbers, racketeers had divvied up the city to supply the citizens with thousands of speakeasies, and by the mid-twenties City Hall tardily decided to enforce the law.[7]

The net effect of the crackdown was not less drinking but more shooting as the stronger gangs moved in on the territories of the weaker. And the killing was easier. The winter after Wilson was drafted, the beleaguered Chicago police met yet another demand on their competence—gangland's adoption of the Thompson machine gun as the preferred way to kill uncooperative rum runners fast, thoroughly, and indiscriminately. The murder rate in Cook County had doubled in the first four years of the decade. Ninety percent of the gang-related killings went unsolved. There had been forty-three such deaths since the beginning of the year.[8]

Wilson had been in town only a few days when a demonstration of the new weapon made the front pages. William McSwiggin, a young Cook County prosecutor, like Wilson twenty-six years old, stepped out with a few companions—racketeer companions—for a night on the town. They decided to visit Cicero, immediately southwest of Chicago, where a couple from the group were competing with Al Capone for beer distribution. The group's Lincoln pulled up in front of a tavern and its occupants stepped out. Just then a line of autos drove by in low gear. Gun barrels poked from the windows and raked the sidewalk with bullets—dozens of them, blanketing the area so quickly that three of the men from the Lincoln, including the prosecutor, were cut down almost instantly. Capone, it was thought, had pulled the lead trigger himself.[9]

Three dead mobsters was routine; a dead prosecutor was not. In the coming months, six grand juries were unable to sort out just what was up that evening in Cicero. The juries' confusion was understandable. McSwiggin's own boss, State's Attorney Robert Crowe, was a notorious crony of mobsters. Crowe's record since assuming office included failing to convict the Black Sox in 1921, losing to the famed Clarence Darrow in the Leopold and Loeb murder case, and in one year, 1923, modifying or dropping nearly 24,000 cases while convicting less than one-tenth that number.[10]

McSwiggin, for his part, had investigated Capone for at least two murders, first in November 1924: the Dion O'Banion killing, the first in the feud that would climax on February 14, 1929. Looking into O'Banion's death, McSwiggin hauled in the galaxy of Chicago's star mobsters for interrogation, first the relatively unknown "Al Brown—real name Alphonse Caponi" and the rest of the thugs who had taken over the city's streets—Torrio, Weiss, Drucci, Alterie. He continued through the night, joined in the third degree by John Sbarbaro, who had cracked the Leopold and Loeb murder case earlier that year with Loeb's confession. By dawn McSwiggin and Sbarbaro emerged with the gladsome news that Capone and every other hoodlum they had questioned were exonerated. Meanwhile, the coroner had set up shop at Sbarbaro & Co., a family-owned mortuary business four blocks toward the lake on North Wells (Sbarbaro's apartment was upstairs), and examined the six wounds on the corpse. When Sbarbaro's law-enforcement duties had concluded, he went to work making the funeral arrangements for the man Capone hadn't killed. The day of the funeral, gawkers swarmed in the streets and on the rooftops as long lines, predominantly of middle-aged women, filed past O'Banion's ten-thousand-dollar casket, and ten thousand mourners and twenty-six truckloads of flowers followed a cortege of limousines. It was the kind of send-off that movie idols like Rudolph Valentino might earn.[11]

All the world could see the status that racketeers had purchased in Chicago. But there was no reprimand from Sbarbaro's boss, State's Attorney Crowe. Although the firm would never top its O'Banion production, Sbarbaro & Co. continued to handle a succession of mob funerals; the next year Schemer Drucci, one of O'Banion's main henchmen, was ambushed on the sidewalk below the Standard Oil Building, where Sbarbaro was visiting the office of a municipal official. Many people were quick to assume that the thirteen thousand dollars in Drucci's pocket (he was unhurt) was intended for a transaction in the office Sbarbaro was visiting. Several months later, Drucci's boss, Hymie Weiss, was assassinated; one of the cars in the funeral cortege displayed a "Sbarbaro for Municipal Judge" banner. Sbarbaro duly won his judgeship the next spring—the same day that Drucci was shot by a policeman. Once again, Sbarbaro & Co. handled the funeral.[12]

Sbarbaro's colleague McSwiggin, too, was in regular touch with the underworld. In 1925 Capone publicly executed a small-time hood in a tavern on the South Side. No charges were filed, even after Capone was questioned—by McSwiggin. The two stayed in touch. Later, Capone sent the young prosecutor a bottle of Scotch. After McSwiggin and friends were killed, Capone left Chicago for a few months, then returned in July to face the press and the police. "Of course I didn't kill him," Capone told them. "Why should I? I liked the kid."[13]

Many Chicagoans besides McSwiggin and Sbarbaro were leading double lives. Robert Crowe had worked closely in the Black Sox case with Alfred Austrian, an attorney who simultaneously represented both Charles Comiskey and Arnold Rothstein, the consensus choice as fixer of the 1919 series. Austrian's firm also did legal work for William Wrigley, whose chief lieutenant, William Veeck, had originally triggered the Black Sox investigation when he publicized an attempt to fix a Cub game.[14]

Veeck himself, before catching Wrigley's eye, was a sportswriter for several Chicago newspapers. He ended up on the staff of Hearst's afternoon paper, the *Evening American*. Hearst's morning *Herald and Examiner* employed Jake Lingle as a crime reporter. Both reporters had a taste for the good life, three-piece suits, and luxury automobiles. But where Veeck hooked up with the ultrarespectable William Wrigley, Lingle began moonlighting in the rackets, possibly after he left Hearst's employ to work for the *Tribune*. When he was shot down in the middle of a crowded underpass outside the Illinois Central railroad terminal at Michigan and Randolph in June 1930, he was wearing a diamond-studded belt, the gift of Al Capone himself.[15]

The *Tribune*'s publisher, Robert McCormick, announced that he was shocked to learn about Lingle's associations, but he too had walked on the wild side. A few years earlier the *Tribune* had hired a private army of "sluggers" to get its papers to the newsstand. Several of Chicago's leading racketeers got their start during the ensuing mayhem, which McCormick later estimated had caused more than two dozen deaths. By one account, McCormick once himself entered a meeting called to deal with a labor dispute and found himself making small talk with Scarface Al himself.[16]

Bill Veeck, who worked directly across the street from the *Tribune*, may have been acquainted with Capone too—at least his son would later claim to have known the Big Fellow from his visits to the ballpark his dad ran. Veeck, like Lingle, was partial to pricey suits—preferring vests, often with a bow tie—and as a Cub executive, he could now afford the five-thousand-dollar autos that were beyond a reporter's means.[17]

His second career, big league baseball, was certainly a cut above Lingle's, but still not quite the acme of respectability. Baseball in general was rife with rumors of fixed games and gambling in the late teens, when William Wrigley first invested in the club and hired Veeck. Rowdies and small-time criminals lined up each day to serve as ushers.[18] Open gambling was common. After gaining majority control, Wrigley and Veeck did what they could on the franchise level by improving the facilities and courting female fans. They also moved decisively in the wake of the Black Sox scandal. With baseball's future at stake, Cub management proposed creating the post of Major League Commissioner and lobbied for Judge Landis's appointment.

Yet the atmosphere outside the park kept intruding despite Wrigley's and Veeck's best efforts. The Cubs' own immaculate, clean-cut ushers, the elite Andy Frains, paid union dues into a mob-controlled fund. Gambling still went on in the bleachers, hip flasks made it impossible to keep booze out of the ballpark, and Cub ballplayers were just as likely to violate the Volstead Act as any other Chicagoan—if not more so.[19]

On the evening of April 24, the Cubs' triumphant new center fielder, fresh from his scoreboard-hitting feat, and his postgame companions made their way to the Sheridan Road flat of Michael and Lottie Frain, a few blocks north of the ballpark. The Frains were having the neighbors over for some postgame drinks. Hack and his entourage entered the flat, where they received what must have been a huge welcome from the partygoers. The newcomers found beer available from either a bucket or bottles.

It had been exactly one month since William McSwiggin had headed out on the town for the last time. Ever since then Chicago had been under siege by its own law enforcement agencies, angered and embarrassed at the cold-blooded killing of a law-enforcement official.[20] Police soon showed up at the Frains'. The apartment erupted in confusion as the police charged in. Defending her dwelling, Mrs. Frain aimed a bronze bookend, an ashtray, or both, at Detective Sergeant Patrick Burke's forehead. Wilson headed out the rear entrance, but the police had covered that escape route with guns drawn. Wilson then tried a rear window—possibly the bathroom window, because when the officers caught up with him, it was said, Wilson had immobilized himself, wedging his muscular torso in the window frame.[21]

Once free, Wilson, full of beer and adrenaline, and now flushed with embarrassment, suggested that the officers put their weapons down and settle things man to man. The officers drew their pistols instead, and the young Cub reconsidered, full of alcohol and far from his manager though he was. Soon Wilson and ten other partygoers, including three women, were herded into two paddy wagons. Hundreds of gawkers, evidently having heard that the Cubs' new star was in trouble, backed up traffic for blocks on Sheridan Road. The police motorcade proceeded to the Town Hall station, where the eleven were booked for disorderly conduct. Wilson gave his name as "Thomas Murtaugh," but no one was fooled. The news showed up in the morning papers anyway.[22]

An attorney appeared for Wilson at a hearing Monday morning. The police produced a beer bucket and bottles as proof of the Frains' lawbreaking. The defendants insisted that it was just a friendly neighborhood get-together—nothing to violate the Volstead Act. The judge heard out the policemen about the bookend—or was it an ashtray? Then he addressed the defendant: "Frain, as a philanthropist you have it all over John D. Rockefeller." The court fined Frain one hundred dollars and costs and ordered the other defendants to give a dollar each to the Aged and Adult Charities Tag Day fund. Such were the wages of sin in Jazz Age Chicago.

McCarthy put Wilson back into the lineup without delay that afternoon, and Hack crashed a loud double the first time he came to bat. It was a pattern that would become familiar to Chicagoans over and over in the next five years.

After only a few weeks in town, Wilson had established a persona on field and off, but Joe McCarthy was still a mystery to fans and media alike. At spring training in Catalina newsmen had watched McCarthy oversee practices, speaking only to give orders or playing tips. "Well, the boys look pretty good" was the only preseason forecast that newsmen could get out of him as the Cubs broke camp.[23]

The change from the team's last spring training was unmistakable. Bill Killefer had celebrated April Fool's Day 1925 by tossing a pitcher of ice water on Gabby Hartnett while the youngster slept. Killefer enjoyed kidding and bantering with his ballplayers in general. He allowed betting on poker, pinochle, and bridge during the long train rides. A young pitcher named Guy Bush first attracted notice as a rookie by winning four hundred dollars at dollar-stake poker with a knot of veterans.[24]

One of McCarthy's first orders of business in 1926 was to ban the open gambling. Some of the veterans suddenly found themselves nostalgic for the good old eighth-place days. The busher manager, they suspected, was "high hat." McCarthy was certainly not going out of his way to ingratiate himself with them. At Catalina, Alexander twisted an ankle, and x-rays seemed to reveal a fracture. A specialist decided that the x-rays showed an old fracture, not a new break. When the team moved over to the mainland for exhibition games, McCarthy made Alexander hobble along on his crutches.[25]

William Wrigley learned for himself that the new man played no favorites. The owner had arranged to have a surprise waiting at Catalina for his new manager: a pitcher-turned-outfielder named Frank O'Doul, who had gone 16 for 17 in the Pacific Coast League while Wrigley was visiting California the year before. Although Veeck was supposed to be overseeing player evaluation and acquisition, fellows who could hit .942 for the better part of a week were hard to find, and after the PCL season Wrigley personally acquired O'Doul's contract—his only documented contribution toward the proposed million-dollar rebuilding plan. Truth be told, Wrigley had done quite well as amateur talent scouting went, considering that Frank O'Doul, whom we remember fondly today as the inimitable "Lefty," turned out to be a .349 lifetime hitter. In 1926, however, the novice outfielder's glovework did not impress McCarthy, and his training habits seemed to be more Killefer's style, not a plus with the new boss. McCarthy lost little time in turning the ex-pitcher over to Hollywood of the PCL.[26]

Eventually O'Doul would fight his way back to the big leagues, acquiring a couple of National League batting titles on the way. The matter festered with Wrigley for years. "O'Doul, my O'Doul," Wrigley would moan while watching Lefty rough up McCarthy's pitching staff, often with calamitous consequences.[27]

McCarthy began to cultivate another left-handed hitting outfielder, Joe Munson, for the cleanup spot. The previous autumn's draftee, Wilson, made the cut, too, without publicity. Cliff Heathcote, a holdover and a stellar gloveman, held the third outfield spot. In early April the club finished up its exhibition schedule on the West Coast and made its way back to the Midwest, stopping for exhibition games along the way. The veterans were complaining openly about the card ban, and grumbling without attribution about the new regime in general. The club's best veteran southpaw, Wilbur Cooper, had been complaining about his sore elbow. McCarthy, as usual, said little.[28]

Probably things came to a head at Kansas City, the Cubs' last stop before the season opened. The story has been told many times and in many ways. Evidently Alexander, perhaps hung over, walked in late or fell asleep during one of McCarthy's skull sessions and defied him with some sort of impertinence. McCarthy calmly went on with the meeting, but soon Alex was on an airplane for Chicago while the team left by train for the opener in Cincinnati. Again, McCarthy kept mum.[29]

Cooper, his elbow restored to health, opened the regular season in Cincinnati in place of Alexander. The lefty veteran did well enough as the Cubs lost in extra innings; the next day Alexander, back from Chicago without ado, took the mound and lost another tight duel. The season's first win did not come until the next day, and it was a hint of things to come: the starter and winner was Charlie Root, a stocky newcomer from the Cubs' Los Angeles farm team. A St. Louis Browns reject, he had won 25 games for Los Angeles in 1925 with a newfound curveball.

After trips to Cincinnati and St. Louis, McCarthy brought his Cubs into Chicago for the first time. For all of Wrigley's bravado, the roster was little changed. A journeyman, Jimmy Cooney, had taken Maranville's spot at shortstop; Wilson, the bargain pickup who had shown some surprisingly agile defensive play in Cincinnati and St. Louis, took over the cleanup spot, where Cub stars seldom tread. Wildfire Schulte had been the only twentieth-century Bruin who had driven in over 100 runs in a season, with 107 in 1911.

Wilson did not bash his first homer at Cubs Park until the end of the month, when he drove the ball into the left-field "jury box." On May 2, he took the Cards' Bill Sherdel even deeper, completely over the wall and into Waveland Avenue. Even before then the word had been going around the North Side that something new and exciting was finally happening at Cubs Park. McCarthy's men were near the top of the league. A few days of pleasant weather arrived, and the grandstands began to fill up in Mr. Wrigley's ballpark.

For weeks Grover Alexander had been complaining about soreness in his pitching arm. He had almost missed his turn on Alexander Day. His battering at the hands of the Braves, then, should have been less than a surprise.[30]

By the last week of May the Cubs were back on the road. A few days later Alexander sat with the rest of the Cubs on the bench at Pittsburgh's Forbes Field when Bob Osborn, the Cubs' starting pitcher, stroked an apparent extra-base hit past the outfielders. After rounding first on the dead run, Osborn suddenly collapsed, writhing and clutching his ankle. All eyes followed Andy Lotshaw, the Cub trainer, who sprinted out to help Osborn.

But another commotion broke out in the dugout as Lotshaw headed for the stricken Osborn. In full view of everyone, Alexander had toppled from the bench onto the hard floor of the dugout. He lay there several minutes until he could be revived; then the Cubs' veteran reserve catcher, Mike Gonzalez, helped him to the clubhouse, where Lotshaw was working on Osborn. Soon Alexander was on the way back to Chicago—to have his sore arm treated again, for all anyone knew.

The Cubs left Pittsburgh for St. Louis, then reversed course to Pittsburgh and on to the East Coast. On the Pullman and in the hotel rooms, Alexander's collapse probably reopened the issue of his indispensability. In 1926 managers—successful ones, at any rate—were considered "masterminds" who played chess with their counterparts across the diamond. Wrigley had even awarded a novice mastermind a contract that paid better than the club's renowned and beloved staff ace. By late May 1926 McCarthy had revived the ball club's élan, earned an avalanche of good press, and had Mr. Wrigley's turnstiles clicking again—all without much help from

Alex, 3-3 on the season. McCarthy now represented the team's future; Alex, a slightly dreary past. Then too, the exact state of Alexander's health can only be surmised, perhaps some interrelated combination of alcoholism and epilepsy. The best minds of the day were baffled by both conditions; antiepileptic drug treatment was decades away, and Alcoholics Anonymous did not appear until the next decade. Joe McCarthy's main concerns were his team and his career, and Grover Alexander, unbeknownst to the veteran or the public, was a steadily diminishing factor in the equation.[31]

With Alexander unavailable again, the form chart would have made Lefty Cooper, McCarthy's Opening Day pitcher, the staff ace. A four-time twenty-game winner in his days with the Pirates, he had been known for his quick-order duels with Alexander in the early 1920s, classics of the fading dead-ball style. But age and a sour attitude about the new manager swiftly ended his stay in the limelight. On June 8 Veeck packed Cooper off to the Detroit Tigers on waivers. Only May 10, he had shut out the Dodgers 9–0 at Cubs Park, his 216th and final victory in the big leagues, but only 13⅔ innings remained before his career ended the next month. This, too, was a warning that Grover Alexander ignored.[32]

The roster was churning in advance of the mid-June trading deadline. Up from the high minors came Riggs Stephenson, a former American League second baseman, in exchange for two reserves. Like Lefty O'Doul, he'd had to return to the minor leagues to try to learn how to play the outfield. Unlike O'Doul, McCarthy had looked him over in the American Association the year before. He installed Stephenson in left field without delay.

Alexander rejoined the team in Philadelphia about the same time, but he saw no action. Alex seemed to be in no hurry to show up for the games, at least in a condition McCarthy would accept. Whether out of friendship, pity, or awe, other managers had always worked around Alexander's comings and goings. Alexander Day had seemed to confirm that life would go on as it had, even with the busher around.[33]

But the new man from Louisville wasn't a member of the old major league club—as Alexander himself had taken trouble to let him know. One morning a reporter passed by McCarthy in the hotel lobby and asked casually, "Any news?"

"Nothing much," McCarthy replied evenly, "except that Alexander is suspended."[34]

Quickly the big news flashed back to Chicago on the reporter's wire, then spread around Philadelphia itself and all over baseball. Alexander had misjudged his man. Although the papers usually referred to Alexander's "breaking training," the usual euphemism for drunkenness, the busher used plain talk: "No man can drink and get away with it if he isn't winning." For six of the past ten days, he added, Alexander couldn't be found at ten in the morning. The pitcher announced that he would return to Chicago and take up his case with President Veeck. There, Alexander promised Veeck he would get back in shape by working out daily at the ballpark. But Veeck was cool and reserved. McCarthy's way would be the only way, he said.[35]

On the 22nd of June—one month to the day after Grover Alexander Day—came the final announcement. After nearly eight years of more or less faithful service to the Chicago National League Ball Club, Alexander was placed on waivers like any common journeyman. Two more outfielders were likewise disposed of. McCarthy had turned over nearly 25 percent of the roster in just over two weeks, and what's more, he had let the baseball world know that résumé or reputation wouldn't intimidate this busher. Not so long before, the Cubs had spurned a reputed hundred-thousand-dollar offer for Alexander. But once he was cut William Wrigley sent McCarthy a telegram: "Congratulations. For years I've been looking for a manager who had the nerve to do this."[36]

In Chicago, Alexander returned to the rooming house he and his wife, Aimee, shared on Addison, just west of the ballpark. He parked the new Lincoln at the curb and walked up the steps where on summer nights he liked to come out and tell the neighborhood boys about his days playing against Honus Wagner and Christy Mathewson, Three-Finger Brown and Rube Marquard. Alexander teared up when he tried to speak to Aimee. He was an undisputed baseball demigod: a thirty-game winner three years straight, bearer of the Phillies' only winning pennant, the consummate control artist, a standard by which others were measured. He had once pitched and won both games of a doubleheader—the second game in fifty-eight minutes flat—not to mention his nineteen-inning day in the City Series. Now a busher had disposed of him.[37]

The league's second-division clubs all passed on the chance to obtain Alexander, but within twenty-four hours the fourth-place St. Louis Cardinals, where Bill Killefer had caught on as a coach, picked up baseball's most famous refugee for the waiver minimum, four thousand dollars. By the calculus of the marketplace, the all-time great's playing services fetched about what the new Lincoln was worth. Two days later the Cubs made a reciprocal waiver deal for a St. Louis journeyman named Walt Huntziger.[38]

Rogers Hornsby, the brusque superstar the Cards had made playing manager the year before, met Alexander with the first positive words Alex must have heard since Grover Alexander Day: "Glad to have you on board. Think you can help us. Just follow the curfew like the other guys."[39] Despite all their accomplishments, their peak experience lay just ahead. And no one could imagine in June 1926 that one day Hornsby would take over for the little fellow who had just fired the great hurler, or that the same bush leaguer would one day take his place alongside the Rajah and Alex in baseball annals.

It took Hornsby only four days to throw Alexander into action, and it was against the McCarthymen in the first game of a doubleheader at Sportsman's Park. The grudge match produced a raucous turnout, the largest in St. Louis baseball history to that point. "Hello, batboy," St. Louis fans screamed at McCarthy each time he trudged out to his third-base coaching box. "Make him like it, Alec," yelled a group in one section of the stands. Alexander, once more the great, delighted his new followers with a ten-inning four-hitter for a 3–2 St. Louis victory. After the game, Alexander passed by the Cub dugout, where McCarthy sat, brooding over the loss. Alexander tipped his cap and strolled on.[40]

With the Cubs leading 5–0 in the second game, an interference call that went their way in the ninth inning generated a rain of pop bottles and cushions. The players on the field had to retreat to the middle of the field. It took fifteen minutes for the groundskeepers to clear the debris so that the Cubs could complete their win and a split of the doubleheader.

The Cubs returned to a North Side still in shock over Alexander's departure. The team's best player since the Tinker, Evers, and Chance era had been jettisoned without warning, and many thought without justification. Meanwhile, the club's 9-16 performance on the monthlong road trip had returned them to .500. The pitching was shorthanded, the result of sore arms and McCarthy's ruthless roster changes. Veeck and Wrigley's gamble on the busher seemed to be in jeopardy.[41]

The day following Alexander's release, Charlie Root, a twenty-seven-year-old rookie who would earn the name of "Chinski" with the pitching style that had attracted McCarthy's favor at Catalina, beaned Dolph Luque of the Reds. The Cuban promptly retaliated by hitting Root with the first pitch his next time up. The tough Root laughed it off as he trotted down to first base, but in the third-base coaching box, McCarthy stewed. Now that he had jettisoned the veteran stars of Killefer's pitching staff, Root was left as the linchpin to the rebuilding program. The National League would have to think twice about trifling with this valuable asset, and the quiet man decided to speak loudly. From the coaching box, he baited Luque, who dropped the ball and his glove and headed in McCarthy's direction. Somehow players from both squads were able to get between the two before any damage was done. This day may have been the origin of the story, recounted years later, of how Root informed the Reds that their entire lineup would have to hit the dirt to set things right. In the telling, the home plate umpire patiently watched all nine Reds go down. Then he informed Root that the fun was over for the afternoon.[42]

The Cubs eventually pulled things out for Root in the tenth. His steady excellence was one reason that the McCarthy experiment did not go awry, but it was the talented, insecure Wilson who, after less than half a season, established himself as the team's superstar and box office draw. No longer shackled by McGraw's heavy hand, he was playing exuberantly, exhibit A for the McCarthy way: no browbeating, no spur-of-the-moment humiliation. McCarthy criticized mistakes, not the men who made them, often preferring closed doors, or at least a cooling-down time. Then he provided an explanation and instruction instead of criticism, and preferably in private. In place of a potential enemy, McCarthy very often earned another convert to his system.

Misbehavior, on the other hand, was a threat to operations that called for punishment. During one game early in his Cub tenure, McCarthy noticed that an outfielder had taken to stopping at the bullpen instead of returning to the dugout when the Cubs came to bat. He sent Ed Froelich, his favored batboy, out to bring the fellow back to the dugout. Once the miscreant arrived, McCarthy unceremoniously told him to report to the showers. After the game McCarthy called the team together for a rare speech: "[So and so] took off his uniform today because he didn't come into the bench. You fellows aren't going to learn my methods while you're sitting along the fence. You may learn something on the bench."[43] McCarthy was a bridge builder when he saw potential. One of his most important projects was establishing rapport with young Leo "Gabby" Hartnett. Leo had been close to Grover Alexander ever since the young catcher first arrived on the scene at Catalina in 1922, a twenty-two-year-old with just one year of experience in the Eastern League. Hartnett had been signed on the recommendation of Bill Veeck's grizzled head scout, Jack Doyle, an old teammate and rival of John McGraw's from the 1890s. Doyle had bestowed his highest compliment on the young catcher: "He has a strong puss."[44]

The next spring Leo, who had probably never been west of the Berkshires, joined the Cubs' train to Catalina, where Veeck and Wrigley had just decided to establish the world's first offshore training camp. (The Cubs had played a few games there in the spring of 1921 while training in Pasadena.) Hartnett, the oldest of a working-class family of fourteen, was so quiet on the trip that a newspaperman took to calling him "Gabby," and the name caught on with the team's veterans. They had no way of knowing that their ribbing would become the trademark of one of the sport's most boisterous personalities.[45]

At the end of the long trip west lay the Wilmington harbor, whence Wrigley's steamship embarked across the San Pedro Channel. The three-hour crossing left Hartnett nearly prostrate—an ordeal he would endure annually for the next eighteen seasons. But Hartnett's real obstacle lay on Catalina in the person of Bill Killefer, an expert on catching: he had caught most of Grover Alexander's major league victories, which at the time numbered some 250. Killefer, who already had one of the best catchers in baseball on his roster, Bob O'Farrell, made ready to cut Hartnett after a perfunctory look-over. But Doyle insisted that Killefer first let Hartnett catch a game with Grover Alexander before cutting his prospect.

It was the making of Hartnett. After pitching to the youngster for nine innings, Alexander walked over to Killefer and told him in his laconic style, "Bill, the kid is all right." One great had recognized another. Within a few weeks, Hartnett was catching the immortal one on Opening Day in

Cincinnati. Before the game, a sportswriter asked the rookie if he'd ever played in a big league game before. Hartnett replied, "Hell, it's the first big league game I ever saw." He caught Alexander all nine innings: seven hits, one walk, a 7–3 triumph. Gabby went oh-for-two, Alex one-for-three. Babe Pinelli fanned for the last out. Hartnett kept the ball and hung on to it for the rest of his life.[46]

As the years went by, a milestone of some sort was set almost every time Alex went to the mound. In 1924 Hartnett caught the master's 300th win. In 1925 Hartnett was behind the plate for all nineteen innings of Alex's epic City Series duel with Ted Blankenship.

By then Hartnett was Chicago's first matinee idol of the Roaring Twenties—the only figure on the team with even a trace of Alexander's star appeal. Bill Veeck was paying him a princely ten thousand dollars a year. Still boyishly slender, the once-shy rookie had become a high-living bachelor, a lover of big new autos and expensive clothing. The lady folk were dazzled by his ballfield feats, beginning with his flashy snap throws to first base. A newspaperwoman contrasted him favorably with Red Grange, who was considered "pesky and unmanageable"; Gabby, however, was "everything he should be—young, good-looking, unmarried, and not averse to feminine wiles." The youngster's laughing presence could create a hubbub in a once-quiet hotel lobby. This celebrity proved expensive, however: at the end of one season Hartnett had to borrow two hundred dollars to make his way back to Massachusetts.[47]

For all the flash, though, Leo was what Chicagoans called "an old-neighborhood guy." Anybody could go up to Gabby and ask him over for dinner with the folks. Many a Chicago neighborhood would remember the night Gabby came to dinner as the highlight of its history. The future Mrs. Hartnett entered his life as a result of one dinner invitation.[48]

The old-neighborhood guy went down to the South Side one day to watch a high school baseball squad practice at St. Cyril High School, where he knew the football coach. Soon he shucked his jacket and began hitting flies to the high schoolers. One of them, the future novelist James Farrell, later wrote and invited Hartnett to visit the school's inaugural prom as a kind of guest of honor. When the dance took place a few weeks later, Farrell and his date spied the young Cub catcher and a teammate lurking shyly on the sidelines of the ballroom. Hartnett had a folded ten-dollar bill ready to slip to the youngster to pay for his date. Through the years Hartnett would continue to haunt the rubber-chicken dinners and the youth testimonials. He was a year-round Cub resident of Chicago, its unofficial ambassador, the first "Mr. Cub"—including on the South Side, where his Irish Catholicism was no drawback. Many years later Bill Gleason, a Chicago sportswriter of the postwar era, remembered the impact Hartnett made on a roomful of boys when he visited Holy Rosary Hall in the 1930s: "Hartnett had this great face that looked like a sunrise over Lake Calumet. And he was so big. We had heard about how big he was and we had heard Pat Flanagan [wBBM radio's baseball announcer] yammer about his size, but having been brought up on White Sox catchers, we expected a really large receiver to be 5'9"."[49]

In 1925 Hartnett put on the greatest power surge that a catcher had displayed in decades. Assisted greatly by left-field bleachers not much more than three hundred feet away, he hit six homers in his first seven games. By the end of July he had accumulated a stunning 22 home runs, a record for big league catchers and a potential threat to break Cy Williams's single-season National League record of 41, set just two years earlier. But the opposition was aiming in the same direction too, and in early August Veeck had the bleachers from the left-field foul line over to left-center ripped out. (A stub of the left-field bleachers, the "jury box," remained just to the left of the scoreboard.) Hartnett hit no more home runs the rest of the year, and the Cubs entered the freefall that resulted in Joe McCarthy's hiring that fall.[50]

Hartnett did eventually adjust to the park's new dimensions and become the first power-hitting catcher of the live-ball era—and of course late in his career he would author the celebrated "Homer in the Gloamin'"—but his legacy ultimately rested on leadership and magnificent defense. At 6' 1" a large man for the time, and gradually filling out from the lanky appearance of his rookie days, Hartnett dominated the field physically as few players could. There were two Hartnetts, though—the affable, perpetually grinning Irishman who met his worshipful public before and after contests, and the intense on-field competitor who wielded his force of personality as another weapon. His voice, with its broad New England "A," boomed unceasingly over the crowd noise and the dugout chatter as he directed his eight teammates and the crowd, the noise oft-accompanied by a defiant fist waved over his head. A pitcher foolish enough to lose his concentration would find a sizzling missile returning to him from behind the plate. Ever alert for pitchouts and double steals, Hartnett was the master at calling the pitchout. And there was no question about it—it was Hartnett who decided what the next pitch would be, at least while Joe McCarthy ran things.[51]

Hartnett was startlingly quick for his 6'1" frame, but his greatest physical asset was a remarkable throwing arm. He was known to wave his pitchers off when they tried to hold runners on base. "Let 'em run, let 'em run," he would yell at a Cub pitcher who was paying too much attention to a runner. "I'll pick 'em off." And quite often he did. Contemporaries agreed that his arm was the best they had ever seen, at least since the turn of the century; both Bill Killefer and John McGraw, than whom there were no greater authorities, considered him the class of the league. Harry Hooper, the great Red Sox outfielder of the teens, remembered being picked off base only once in his career—by Hartnett, in the 1923 City Series.[52] Five years later, another noted base runner decided to test the fabulous arm:

> Gabby Hartnett don't miss many fellows trying to steal second on him. It makes no difference how fast the runner is and how much of a lead he obtains. Max Carey will attest to this. He endeavored to purloin the keystone in the fifth, but Hartnett's bullet-like heave had him [by] several feet.[53]

In July 1927 Hartnett used Wilson as a prop in perhaps his most spectacular throwing demonstration. The Cardinals' Billy Southworth, who had reached first on an error, lit out for second base during the next at-bat. Hartnett, rushing to get rid of the ball after taking in Hal Carlson's slowball, cut loose. Wilson, backing up the play in center field, saw the throw sailing out of the infield and over his head. Wilson wheeled about, dashed back, and ran the ball down on the fly in deep right-center, but by the time he could return the ball to the infield, Southworth had circled the bases.[54]

By then, helped by the stability of the McCarthy regime, Hartnett was already a complete ballplayer. "The greatest catcher in the game," McCarthy called him—and his opinion hadn't changed two decades later, even after eight Yankee pennants caught by Bill Dickey. Hartnett, they said, made McCarthy's case in the clubhouse when the veterans were making it hard on the busher. He may have welcomed McCarthy's brisk competence after the lackluster Killefer years. For the close-mouthed McCarthy, Hartnett's ebullience and his baseball acumen would have made him a welcome ally.[55]

Ebullience; Irishness; baseball acumen. For McCarthy's other veteran ally, Karl Johann Grimm, it was one of three. Karl, or Charlie, was a now-extinct German ethnic: one of the jolly men who far past their youth liked to sing and hoist steins in dark, but jolly, cellars while wearing shorts, suspenders, and feathered caps. No one knew exactly how old Grimm was; by the birthdate he furnished, he was still sixteen when he appeared in his first major league game in 1916. (Current records have pushed his year of birth back a year to 1898.)

By 1920, either twenty-one or twenty-two years old depending on the means of reckoning, Grimm had won a major league starting job as a dependable, slick-fielding first baseman on the Pittsburgh Pirate contenders that faded in the stretch run. Grimm and his merry companions, who included Cotton Tierney and Rabbit Maranville, became noted for their lighthearted approach to major league ball. In the clubhouse, win or lose, they liked to break into song. Grimm, singing tenor himself, provided the accompaniment on a tenor banjo. During one spring training Ignace Paderewski took a room in the Pirates' hotel, just above Grimm's. The famed pianist sent word through management that he would appreciate musical silence during Grimm's stay. Sure, Grimm replied; and, oh—could Mr. Paderewski please hold the noise down on the piano?[56]

Revelry was all well and good as long as the Pirates were winning, but their owner, Barney Dreyfuss, soured on the trio after the Pirates came up short once too often. "I got rid of my banjo players," he confided with some satisfaction after jettisoning Grimm and Maranville from the Pirate ship.[57] The Pirates quickly acquired two pennants in their first three years minus the pranksters.

Thus Grimm, the man destined to participate in or direct no fewer than five Chicago pennants, boarded ship for Catalina in early 1925 with a reputation as a cut-up and even a malcontent.[58] The fun had only begun for the man they called the "Joker Wild." For starters, he was accompanied by Maranville—the real object of the trade, still a star shortstop at age thirty-three. Then, at midseason, Veeck fired Bill Killefer and turned to none other than the Rabbit as a replacement.

The appointment was only weeks old when Maranville and three other Cubs—not, for once, including Grimm—beat up their taxi driver in Manhattan after the poor fellow complained about the size of the tip. The new manager spent a few hours in jail before being bailed out. For a few hours, Grimm himself was technically the ball club's temporary manager: Maranville had already appointed his fellow music maker as team captain. After getting out of jail, Maranville lasted only another six weeks as Cub manager, time enough to add to his already detailed list of hijinks. George Gibson—the one-time manager of the "banjo players," whom Dreyfuss had likewise cut loose—took over as interim manager for the last month. Maranville continued to play shortstop.[59]

When Joe McCarthy convened the Cubs in Catalina the next spring, Maranville and Gibson were both gone, but Grimm was still at first base— and still captain. Joe McCarthy had another gregarious ally who could help make sense of surly veterans and uncertain youngsters.[60]

So Charlie Grimm joined the establishment, no longer just the Joker Wild but "Der Kaptink." Except for two memorable tours of duty in Milwaukee in the 1940s and 1950s, he spent most of the rest of his life working for the Wrigleys one way or another. Artist, musician, vaudevillian, broadcaster, magician, mimic, acrobat, he was a renaissance man with a grade school education, and Cubs Park was his stage. After he died in 1983, his ashes were scattered around the ballpark.[61]

On Catalina Island, on the train, in the hotel first thing in the morning or after the ballgame, Grimm's impromptu concerts were a fact of Cub life. His teammates could hear German-language versions of "Maryland, My Maryland" or "Shine On, Harvest Moon" sung in Grimm's fine tenor as Der Kaptink accompanied himself on his custom-made, $450 left-handed banjo—a cool lager preferably nearby to soothe his throat. Soon he was auditioning teammates for trios and quartets—no knowledge of German required. He celebrated the good days with joyous noise in 4/4 time and after defeats, tried to soothe morale with a mellower sound. During his second spring training with the Cubs he took his playing to the southern California airwaves on KFWO, Los Angeles; listeners swamped the station with letters from the station's twenty-five-state range, demanding, "Give us more of Grimm." Fans who had taken up the twenties fad for banjos, only to give up their lessons in frustration, were said to celebrate the occasional Grimm home run with a present of their orphaned banjos. Most of these donated instruments were, naturally, strung right-handed. No matter—the left-handed Grimm amazed even professional musicians by playing the instruments unmodified.[62]

William Wrigley commissioned Grimm to paint him in oil, and Grimm's rendition of Wrigley Field hung for years in the Wrigley Building. A talented and ambidextrous woodworker, he had invested thousands of dollars in a home woodworking shop, where he hoped to design custom furniture. He, like McCarthy, also liked doing magic tricks, so Grimm had acquired an elaborate collection of magician's equipment, including a silk hat intended to turn water into wine. He was not Mac's equal in such diversions, however, and that perhaps was a clue William Veeck should have noted for future reference.[63]

No one ever claimed that Karl Johann had a great baseball mind. Henry Aaron, who broke into the majors under Grimm in the 1950s, later referred to him as "just an entertainer," still playing the banjo a lot after all those seasons—observations that the affable Charlie would probably not have objected to strenuously. One of the stalwarts for his winning 1930s ball clubs observed, "He turned a lot of the game over to us," and Andy Pafko, a star on Grimm's 1945 NL pennant winner, said simply, "He sure wasn't any x's and o's guy." There was much more to Grimm than bluster and clowning, though. A sobersides like McCarthy wouldn't have warmed to him otherwise, and Grimm would repay that.[64]

Grimm's antics became a regular sideshow: he might curse an umpire in German, or trick him into calling a balk with his own melodramatic flourishes. They called him the "Happy Warrior of the Diamond," "cocky," "double-jointed," a clown who "swaggered" onto the field. In the on-deck circle he might brandish two bats in an imitation of a butcher sharpening his knives. He and Hartnett liked to play "burnout" in front of the fans, advancing up the line and firing the ball toward each other at closer and closer quarters. To the roars of the crowd, he might mimic an umpire's walk behind his back—an act that at least once earned him an ejection as a manager.[65] Twenty years later, coaching third base as a nonplaying manager, he seemed remarkably unchanged from his ballplaying days: "[Grimm] cups his big paws and joyously bellows out the count after each pitch. He wiggles and waddles back and forth, lets out an occasional piercing whistle, mimics rival pitchers." Grimm also enjoyed brushing off third base for any Cub who homered and collapsed in a mock faint when a pitcher did so.[66]

One item the younger Grimm could contribute was spectacular in-game acrobatics. Once, it was said, he leaped upon the box railing at the Polo Grounds in pursuit of a foul fly. The laws of physics now dictated that his bulk and momentum should hurl him sprawling into the spectators' laps; instead, Grimm somehow braced himself atop the rail. Teetering there, he doffed his cap and bowed dramatically to the patrons. It wasn't just showmanship, though, and it could produce results under the spotlight: in game 2 of the 1929 World Series, he twisted himself into a pretzel to grab a low throw from the infield, then executed a graceful, slow-motion somersault. The umpire, convinced that Grimm had his foot on the base at the right moment, signaled an out, and not a murmur was heard from the ordinarily raucous bench of Connie Mack's Athletics.[67]

McCarthy's mix of fairness and sternness had made many a friend before he arrived in Chicago. They called his Louisville Colonels "a big, happy family," and it seemed to be more than just talk. The weekend of Alexander's first start with the Cardinals, a delegation of minor leaguers trooped over to the Cubs' hotel in St. Louis. They were members of McCarthy's old Louisville squad, passing through town on the way to Kansas City, and they just wanted to say hello to their old boss.[68]

Today McCarthy seems to be remembered as the cold, world-conquering leader of the Yankees. The "Mac" of Louisville and then Chicago, the overseer of the merry Jazz Age circus taking shape in Chicago, hardly computes with the unlovable "Marse Joe" who directed the relentless conquests of the Yankee corporation. Chicago's Mac was a familiar and beloved figure who strode out to the third-base coaching box each day and visibly involved himself in his men's successes and failures, but by the time he reached the shadows of the cavernous Yankee Stadium, he had abandoned that job to his assistants. His public persona in Chicago was of a Mack—Connie Mack: that is, quiet, intelligent, observant, fatherly.

McCarthy had in fact grown up just outside Philadelphia, in Mack's sphere, during the first glory years of the Athletics.

Despite Chicagoans' evident fondness for McCarthy, his brooding, lonely alcoholism became more noticeable as the seasons passed, and word of it must have eventually reached ownership's ears. Then too, inevitably, four or five years of success would alter the original equation. Mac had begun with a virtual startup, a motley, last-place club of dead-end kids and banjo players. He had cleared out the timeservers and malcontents like Cooper and Alexander, but one day the youngsters he had taken in and raised would themselves be hard-drinking, defiant veterans. And by then others had arrived, new faces, men who owed little to Mac.

One thing was undisputed: on any given day, McCarthy was one of the brightest fellows in the ballpark. On June 30, 1926, at Cubs Park, he strolled to the plate in the eighth inning after an RBI single by the Reds' Bubbles Hargrave. Hargrave, McCarthy calmly told Cy Rigler, was batting out of turn. Rigler, surprised, pulled out his lineup card. Could this be right? Hargrave had been hitting in that position all afternoon—four times in all. But it was true, and Rigler had to call Hargrave out. The rally was over. McCarthy had been watching and waiting for Hargrave to do something productive—then he would bring the matter up. No batboy he.[69]

The Cubs, now truly McCarthy's outfit, managed to right themselves in July after the long June road trip that had featured Alexander's dismissal. On July 1, Wilson ended a slump and a ballgame with an eleventh-inning drive into the right-center-field bleachers. Hack's army—hundreds of cap-clad boys, and even grown men in suits and boaters—hopped out of the stands and converged on home plate with congratulations. Wilson had to touch home plate hurriedly and take off on a dead run for the clubhouse to escape.[70]

The new outfielder from Indianapolis, Stephenson, had already established himself as an important part of McCarthy's offense and an all-around hustler to boot. It was a blow when he went out of the lineup for several days with a minor injury. A strong July home stand with Wilson and Stephenson both in the lineup improved the young Cubs' record enough that they briefly considered themselves contenders once again.[71]

The next road trip quickly ended that fantasy. But the squad kept itself in the first division, and the crowds kept coming: the team's attendance was the league's best. Wilson stayed out of further trouble with the police and drove toward the National League home run crown, something no Cub had taken since Heinie Zimmerman in 1912. Whether homering or not, Wilson, his emotions, his batting stance, his hustle, his perpetually dirty uniform, crystallized the new attitude that McCarthy had brought to the club. He attracted attention from the moment he stepped into the batter's box. A heavy perspirer, he incessantly scooped up dirt to keep his hands dry, then wiped the excess onto his uniform. The process went on all day. Wilson was the lone player with a gray home uniform; no amount of laundering seemed to help.[72]

Hands now dry and uniform dirty, Hack would step in and wave his bat ominously. It was a specially constructed, Ruthian-inspired model that Wilson had begun using in his semipro days. Nearly as long as its owner and, at some 42 ounces, as heavy as traditional bats, it was by contrast thin-handled to concentrate the weight at the business end. With it Wilson struck more home runs than any other National Leaguer of his time.[73]

Then too, Wilson struck out more than any contemporary, in numbers that in a given year could exceed home runs by a factor of three. They were titanic affairs conducted with a vicious swing of the long, black bat, gripped right on the nub. A called third strike could trigger another Wilson trademark: rage. Home and away, booing and baiting broke out when his neck flushed a deep red after a call he didn't care for. The big, black bat might go flying across the field, or fly high in the air. Beans Reardon, umpiring at home plate in the Polo Grounds, once watched Wilson launch his bat after a called third strike. As the bat sailed skyward, Reardon warned, "If that bat hits the ground, you're out of the game."[74]

In 1926 Wilson's reputation had already preceded him. "Give him a high ball," yelled a patron at Forbes Field after Hack crashed a tremendous triple on July 5. Earlier in the day Wilson had flung his bat off the dugout concrete after popping up; still seething, he kicked at Hartnett's shin guards lying in his path. That display did not earn ejection, but the next day, an umpire ruled his long fly down the line a foul ball. Wilson, certain he had hit a home run, disagreed profanely; he was swiftly tossed.[75]

As long as Wilson was in the lineup, McCarthy and the Cubs felt they were contenders. The Cubs' last, fading hopes for 1926 were quashed by a September road trip and Wilson's beaning by his future teammate Hal Carlson at Philadelphia's Baker Bowl. The short mound of muscle tumbled to the ground and lay motionless for five minutes; then he wobbled to his feet and collapsed again. Some muscular Cubs carried him back to the clubhouse, where the Phillies' team physician examined him and diagnosed a slight concussion.[76]

Wilson did not reenter the lineup until the final game of the regular season, two weeks later. By that time the Cubs had settled comfortably into fourth place, a finish that disappointed almost no one except the Alexander loyalists. Wilson's 21 home runs led the league.

Once again, the Cubs and Sox would square off in the traditional City Series played in pennantless years. Wilson was caught off guard by the intensity of the crosstown rivalry, and even more by his own notoriety after a tumultuous, highly publicized season. "The south-side fans were 'on' us," he told a reporter, "and for some unknown reason, especially 'on' me, right from the start." Not until the series' fifth game, though, did Wilson learn just how just how tough a house Comiskey Park could be. In the sixth inning he flattened the Sox's beloved catcher Ray Schalk in a play at the plate. Schalk, giving forty pounds to Wilson, hung bravely on to the ball, and after some dithering, the home ump reversed his initial call and ruled Wilson out. The favorable ruling didn't stop the booing, which kept up the rest of the day.

The following day, the Comiskeyites saluted Wilson's first at-bat with an unprecedented avalanche of fruit—mostly lemons, but also oranges, tomatoes, onions, and squash. "Most of them were unfit for other than throwing purposes," Wilson remembered. "They kept it up all afternoon," he added plaintively. But he was unfazed, collecting three hits that day as the Cubs evened the series, three games to three.[77] Ted Blankenship's seventh-game shutout wrapped up the 1926 city championship for the Sox. The two clubs split a forty-thousand-dollar pot and went home for the winter.

The Sox fans had started something. "Ever since that day, I have been the target of lemon tossers," according to Wilson. Although the Sox fans would always be Wilson's nemesis, Cub fans soon joined in the fun. Starting the next spring, fans on their way to Wrigley Field began to stop at the corner grocery. They would pick up a few mildewed lemons and stuff them in their coat pockets. After hopping on the El or a trolley headed for Addison and Clark, they waited for their moment—one of Wilson's outlandish and frequent strikeouts—and hurled the missiles Wilsonward. There was no dearth of opportunities. Each year, as Wilson's offensive totals improved, his strikeout totals swelled to levels the National League had never seen—70, 94, 83, 84. Sometimes, he out-fanned the lords of baseball themselves: Babe Ruth, Lou Gehrig, Tony Lazzeri. Lemons, Hack Wilson, and controversy would be part of the story as long as the little slugger played in the big leagues.

While the Cubs and the Sox played for the championship of the Windy City, Grover Alexander, of all people, was playing for the championship of the baseball world. The alcoholic has-been of June had become the inspiration of the Cardinals' stretch drive, the man held in highest confidence by Rogers Hornsby and his young St. Louis club. The Cardinals returned to Cubs Park in the midst of their stretch run in early September. A standing-room-only crowd turned out to see the old hero pitch again in Chicago, his first appearance since Grover Alexander Day just over three months earlier. Alex methodically went about his business, ignoring both the boos and the even louder clapping from the crowded stands. Unfazed, the master worked in typical Alexandrian time, an hour and half, to finish off Charlie Root and the Cubs with a three-hitter, 2–0. No base runner got past first all day. When it was over, the last batter, Charlie Grimm, joined Alexander and his new teammates to congratulate him. Then Alexander made his only nonpitching gesture of the day. He looked up to the stands and tipped his cap.[78]

Alexander and the Cardinals kept it up over the next weeks as the Cardinals drove on to their very first World Series appearance. In New York, Alexander started game 2 after the Yankees' victory in the opener. Awed observers watched the dead-ball ace use his hopping fastball and trademark pinpoint control to master the mighty Yankees of Ruth and Gehrig. In the first inning Ruth walked away from the plate in disgust after Alexander sliced a screwball over for a called strike 3. Three innings later Alexander struck out the side—Gehrig, Lazzeri, and Dugan—with a rapid-fire combination of fastballs and curves. The Yankee Stadium fans rose to give him an ovation. The game ended 6–2 for the Cardinals, knotting the Series at one game apiece.[79]

Alexander tied up the Series again in game 6 with another complete game, a 10–2 laugher. It appeared to be all that one middle-aged pitcher could do for his club in one series. But it was to be game 7 that secured the Alexander legend for all time, a final coming-together of Alexander's renowned skills and equally renowned personal problems. Jesse Haines, who had loaded the bases with two out and the Cardinals still leading, 3–2, signaled that he was through—he had split his finger. Hung over, by both legend and by eyewitness account, after nine victorious innings the day before, a lanky figure emerged from a far corner of the chilly stadium when Haines (with Hornsby standing nearby) beckoned. The Yanks' announcer ran along the grandstand, stopping periodically to bark through his megaphone, "Alexander now pitching for St. Louis." The bases were loaded. Alexander threw Lazzeri a ball, followed by a called strike. He got the next pitch inside and Lazzeri pounded it far and deep into the left-field corner; the 38,000 fans had to watch the umpire's signal to learn that it had hooked foul. Alexander, coolly going back to work, gave Lazzeri his specialty, a low curve on the outside corner. Lazzeri lunged awkwardly and missed. The Yankees' greatest threat was over, and a walk to Ruth with two outs in the last of the ninth was the only other blemish on Alexander's afternoon. Ruth went out stealing. The world championship belonged to St. Louis.

In a series full of sterling pitching performances—the Cardinals' Jesse Haines, the Yankees' Waite Hoyt and Herb Pennock—Alexander was the star of stars. In 20 innings, he had allowed the mighty Yankees only 12 hits, while striking out 17. His cumulative ERA was 1.33. By game's end, the crowd had forgotten the Yankees, and the champion Cardinals, for that matter. They were on their feet for the man of the hour, chanting, "Alec! Yeah, Alec!"[80] Alexander, who knew more than most men about the intensity and duration of fan worship, hustled quickly off the field, a calm man surrounded by ecstatic teammates. The New York fans lingered in the stands for nearly an hour, still calling out Alexander's name. In the tumultuous Cardinal dressing room, Alexander went through his next duty, the postgame interview. "Pressure?" he repeated after another question about how he had handled Lazzeri. "There was no pressure on me.

He was the one who had to hit the ball." The World Series antihero might have had his mind on the winner's cut of the series money. Or perhaps he was thinking of the busher in Chicago, the one who had just managed his club to a City Series defeat against the White Sox.

So Alexander had his World Series ring, the only one of his career. But there was still left one more "world title" for 1926 that hadn't been decided.

On Thursday, October 14, just before the dinner hour on the South Side, Sandy Thompson of the Chicago American Giants banged a one-out single in the bottom of the ninth at Schorling's Park. Jelly Gardner, representing the winning run, rounded third base and headed for home at full gallop. He scored standing to give the Giants a 1–0 victory, their fifth in the best-of-nine series against the Atlantic City Bacharachs. Willie Foster, Rube's left-handed brother, was the winning pitcher. The crowd poured from the stands in jubilation. Their team had taken what they called, without irony, the world championship.[81]

Missing from the celebration was Rube Foster, the Negro National League's combination Judge Landis and Joe McCarthy. He had left the team suddenly three months earlier: a "vacation," they said. The disappearance of the league's founder threw the whole season into doubt. Foster was ill, it was announced. The NNL directors held an emergency meeting in Chicago. They decided to finish the season and go ahead with the playoffs.[82]

In spite of dismal attendance in Atlantic City, where the final round of the playoffs began, the directors' decision proved wise, in the short term, at least. Foster's league, which he had patiently kept alive with constant transfusions of money, players, and leadership, was proving it could function without its founder. Foster, it turned out, had suffered a mental breakdown. Soon he was confined at a state facility in downstate Kankakee, where he would live the last four years of his life.[83]

But he had left his mark. Black baseball would have its ups and downs, but it was established for good. And Chicago had a champion, even if it was one that the *Tribune* buried on the inside pages of the sports section with a brief item about the "colored world series."

On the North Side, Cubs Park stayed open for business even after all the world series and city series had run their course. Now the sport was football, with the gridiron crammed into the park north-south, one end zone only a few feet from the first-base dugout. The Cubs' football equivalent, the Bears of the new National Football League, were the featured attraction; the year before, they had astounded everyone by signing the great collegian Red Grange and then selling out Cubs Park for his debut. By 1926 Grange had left to start his own league, but such Chicagoans as Grover Alexander, who was still on the Bears' complimentary pass list, could come out to watch George Halas, George Trafton, Paddy Driscoll, and other primitives of early professional football.[84]

On Sunday, October 17, at Cubs Park, the Bears held the football version of the recently concluded City Series, taking on Chicago's other NFL entry, the Chicago Cardinals. Into one of the box seats slipped a young North Sider. Wearing glasses and a snap-brim fedora, he looked altogether unlike the rum runner, extortionist, and murderer he really was. He was Vincent "Schemer" Drucci, a participant in the Michigan Avenue shootout, and he was the brand-new head of the city's anti-Capone coalition.[85]

Drucci had held his new post only a few days, since the spectacular demise of his predecessor and mentor, Hymie Weiss. That unlucky fellow and some friends had been jaywalking one afternoon across State Street, not far north of the river, when at least two Thompson guns had punished their infraction by opening up on them from apartment windows. Weiss and his companion fell in a heap on the sidewalk, stone dead. An attorney they had just stopped to meet was severely wounded; from his hospital bed he told police that he was on his way to meet his wife when he met up with Weiss. That may have been so, but the barrister had also been in court that morning, defending Frankie McErlane, a killer notorious even on the mean streets of Chicago. McErlane, who was Capone's main competition south of the river, was charged with murdering a witness who had been planning to identify him as a . . . murderer.

To deepen the mystery, inside Weiss's pockets the police found a list of all the jurors and witnesses for McErlane's trial. Giddy at finally getting a hoodlum, even a dead one, to talk, the police swooped into Cubs Park that weekend and collared Schemer Drucci, who had been taking in the Bears' domination of the Cardinals. Taken downtown for questioning, Drucci appeared blasé about the development, but his companion, "Potatoes" Kaufman, seemed upset. "I'm a decent potato seller and live with my wife and children at 4709 Ellis Avenue," he snapped. "I'll show you can't be always arresting me. I've got constitutional rights."

The Bears, minus any support from Drucci and company, managed to finish off the Cardinals 16–0. The next morning Drucci was back on the street for the last six months of his short life. The police had learned nothing for their efforts, and Weiss's killer was never identified.

In early December, the Cubs announced that their ballpark would reopen in 1927 as "Wrigley Field," which the Cubs would enlarge with an ambitious program of double-decking the stands. It was time for a change; in most people's minds "Cubs Park" meant the place where Grover Alexander worked, and that would never happen again. William Wrigley, always an astute reader of the marketplace, could see that it was finally the right time to associate his name with a winner.[86]

4 | The McCarthymen Take the Stage

Get a horn and blow loud for Chicago. . . . Put on a big party! Let the jazz band play! Let's show 'em we're all live ones! —Mayor William Hale Thompson

Alexander the Great spent his forty-first summer, that of 1927, spotting his fastball and curve as required and, one last time, winning twenty games. Up in Chicago, the man who had fired him was busy shuffling his overachieving roster, including a young and erratic Cub pitching staff and an "American Association infield," as his ragtag collection of inexperienced infielders became known around the league. McCarthy auditioned a half-dozen men at third base, even Stephenson, who had already logged several forgettable big league seasons as a second baseman. At short McCarthy alternated a veteran who wasn't hitting and a high-priced twenty-year-old, Elwood English, an agile, strong-armed rookie who soon proved he could consistently reach the first-base stands with his throws.[1]

On the mound Charlie Root sopped up the innings that in previous years had gone Alexander's way—309 by season's end. He pitched in 48 of his team's 154 games, 36 as a starter, ending up with an Alexander-like 26-15 won-lost record. He worked fast in Alexandrian time, the way Root had seen the old master do it for two springs at Catalina: no peering for signals or rubbing the ball. Root kept hitters off stride with an odd-looking, deceptive motion, pitching quickly after each return from Hartnett. His sidearm delivery took advantage of the shirtsleeves in the left-center field jury-box bleachers. In command of a ballgame he was a brisk, nonchalant workman, confident, methodical. He liked to work the batters inside, a crucial tactic when the home run dominated all. Root's style earned him the name of "Chinski." "Can I help it if I'm a little wild?" he responded when one umpire warned him to quit throwing at the hitters.[2]

The short, quiet Root became the short, quiet McCarthy's pitcher of choice for the opening games of seasons, City Series, and eventually, the World Series. In the manager's words, "Charlie is calm and knows what it's all about." But by the end of 1927, the faithful little soldier was exhausted by all the starting and relieving that his young manager had given him. He still labored on uncomplainingly, remembering all too well, like Stephenson and Wilson, what it was like to go back down to the minor leagues. That wouldn't happen again until 1942, when Root had reached the age Grover Alexander was in 1927. By that time, Root had long since earned his own special place in baseball history, if not quite the one he would have chosen.[3]

By the June trading deadline Bill Veeck got Root some help by acquiring a veteran starter, Hal Carlson, the Phillie pitcher who had beaned Wilson near the end of 1926. The team began a serious midseason move. In late July the Cubs, behind the pitching of Root and Carlson and the slugging of Wilson and Stephenson, overtook the teams that had dominated recent seasons—Alexander's defending 1926 champion Cardinals, the 1925 champion Pirates, and John McGraw's 1921–24 champion Giants—charged into first place, and began to build their lead. Root threw a one-hitter in July and won his 20th game on August 7—another relief appearance. By that time, McCarthy's minor league rejects were the country's underdog darlings. "The Cubs are in," they said in Pittsburgh, where a new manager and a star outfielder, Kiki Cuyler, were at loggerheads in the midst of a losing streak. In Chicago, the fans had their first opportunity to watch a real pennant race since the breakup of the Black Sox. They flocked in ever-greater numbers to the renamed and enlarged Wrigley Field, now sporting a partially finished upper deck along the Clark Street side. Attendance leaped by another quarter million: the total by the end of 1927, at 1.59 million, was nearly 200,000 greater than the National League's previous high, the Giants' 973,000 of 1921.[4]

The outpouring could not be measured by paid admissions alone. Ladies Day, once a success if five thousand women showed up, could attract double that number or more each Friday the Cubs played at home. Adding in the growing number of women who paid their way, the Cubs' female customers alone outnumbered the total season attendance that any one of several major league franchises could draw. Mere logic was insufficient to explain the sheer numbers of female customers: Ladies Day had been around since the late teens, and the Cubs began promoting it with display ads in 1922, with indifferent results for several years. The winning record of the McCarthymen and especially Wilson's stardom had something to do with it, no doubt; so, unarguably, did the radio coverage, but perhaps most of all, a growing acceptance and embrace of women's new freedoms.

Feeding this land rush, and confounding the doubters, was the audience pool created by ever-expanding radio coverage. Although WMAQ had decisively committed to broadcasting the Cubs by May 1926, Wrigley and Veeck had never given Judith Waller an exclusive arrangement. In August 1926, with the Wilson phenomenon in full swing, WGN began broadcasting every home game, and for the 1927 opener both Quin Ryan and Hal Totten had seats in the Wrigley Field press box to describe Charlie Root and Grover Alexander duel to a tie before 42,000, another record crowd—a record that lasted four days, until 45,000 poured into the park the next Sunday.[5]

By mid-1929 most major Chicago stations had made Cub home games their staple, effectively eliminating afternoon alternatives from Chicago airwaves seventy-seven afternoons a year. As the broadcasts became part of the sports culture, the play-by-play men emerged as personalities in their own right, no longer the afterthoughts they had been in the early days. Totten—or was it Ryan? Elson?—pioneered the on-the-field interview; soon there was sponsorship and advertising. Some of the new radio headliners seemed unlikely candidates for baseball fame; they might be termed battlefield promotions. By 1927 an early trend confirmed the lesson of the Artie Hofman fiasco: the glib and even the articulate received preference over the professional athlete. WGN's Quin Ryan, who had actually broadcast games from Wrigley Field some two months before WMAQ's Hal Totten, had already made his name in WGN's innovative coverage of the Scopes trial in the summer of 1925. He, like Totten, had been chosen from the reporting ranks, and again like Totten, by the station's owner (in Ryan's case, the *Chicago Tribune*). The son of a Chicago judge, Ryan hardly looked or acted the part of a baseball buff. As a young man, he had served as an extra at the famed Essanay studios in Uptown, where future Hollywood stars like Chaplin and Swanson began their careers before World War I. After the studios relocated to the West Coast, Ryan entered Northwestern University and eventually caught on at the *Tribune*. Ryan was considered enough of a writer that he began contributing his own radio column for the *Tribune*. In addition to his other duties, he also played the beloved "Uncle Walter" on a children's show, *Skeezix Time*. Urbane, an acerbic critic of many of the trends in radio's development, Ryan sported a mustache that no respectable ballplayer would consider. He devoted one of his columns to detailing his painstaking methods of preparing for a broadcast—interviews, note-taking, scrapbooks, all followed by hours of intensive study—others to his whimsical observations of the radio and show-business personalities he had met.[6] He also confirmed what Veeck and Waller had learned from their experience: the Cubs' broadcasts were creating, or at least intensifying, an unprecedented level of interest level among women in general, and particularly among major league followers in the small-town Midwest, who gathered in gas stations, hotel lobbies, and shops to listen. Ryan observed, "[M]any a person writes to report that Grandma is rapidly learning the lingo of the diamond and is daily found shouting, 'Come on, Hack,' when the slugging Wilson comes to bat."[7]

Although Ryan would witness the great early days of the McCarthy years, he spent just three full seasons covering the Cubs, and he was not destined to be remembered as a baseball announcer—or for much else, despite his early, intense exposure to the national and especially the Midwest public. One of his downstate listeners, a future baseball announcer named Ronald Reagan, later referred to Ryan as "the father of sportscasting. It was Quin who got the idea that you could describe a baseball game and make someone else see it. In just a few years Quin had created a profession." Today, though, Ryan is mentioned, if at all, for his role in the Scopes trial—more often than not with his first name misspelled "Quinn." By 1930 Bob Elson, probably with the blessing of Ryan, who had moved into management, took over WGN's baseball announcing. Ryan's reputation was still strong enough in 1935 that he was invited to work on the NBC World Series broadcast team. Years later, Red Barber remembered his astonishment at what he considered Ryan's casual approach to his assigned duties as the broadcast's "color" man: "[Ryan] never went to the dugouts or to the field—he just came to the booth and read from some newspaper stories." In fact, after the second game of the series, Barber was promoted to the role of "color man," and then Elson took over the role for the remainder of the Series.[8]

In contrast, Hal Totten of WMAQ was prepared to make sports, particularly baseball, his life. Lacking Ryan's style and flash, he was a plumpish, bespectacled ex–copy editor who dispensed with the flamboyance of Ryan or Graham McNamee and tried to be like no one but himself. "Stephenson is at bat. The first pitch is wide for ball one," he would intone with Stephenson at bat and Kiki Cuyler on second; the Cubs were down three in the ninth inning of an important game in a Wrigley Field stuffed to the rafters with screaming fans. Then silence from Totten. "Stevie hits the next one. It is a long wallop down the right-field line, but it is going foul and lands back in the very end of the right-field stand for strike one." More silence. "Stevie hits the ball hard out into the left center for a base hit. Cuyler rounds third and swings on his way home, and Stephenson pulls up at first."[9]

This foursquare, unapologetic way of doing things caught on with the long-term fans. Totten also contributed features to the *Daily News* sports page. His measured approach and calm analysis set a standard for the brand-new field. In the short run, at least, Totten's approach won out. Bob Elson, the young man who replaced Ryan as WGN's primary baseball broadcaster, was another announcer who cultivated a dry, understated approach, and his career would last even longer. With Wrigley and Veeck welcoming any interested radio station into Wrigley Field, rival stations tried to keep pace by trotting out their own strong on-the-air rivals for their own broadcasts. Pat Flanagan of WBBM, a Silver Star recipient from the Great War and a dropout from chiropractic school, would become the probable inventor and acknowledged master of re-creating road games, and Johnny O'Hara of WJJD became the first announcer to champion the White Sox. WLS, a latecomer to the burgeoning Cub market, countered by replaying WMAQ's Artie Hofman experiment of 1925 with a true baseball immortal: Tris Speaker, a baseball titan whose presence hurt the infant medium not a bit. Speaker, a former player-manager, anticipated plays and strategy so well, it was said, that both teams kept an ear to his broadcasts for his ideas about what would develop next.[10]

The White Sox, notwithstanding the emptiness at their newly enlarged stadium, admitted defeat in 1927 and authorized regular radio coverage of their own home games—still one of the first American League franchises to do so. The Sox attendance remained in the doldrums anyway in the face of the phenomenon taking place on the North Side, and soon the Sox's tattered dignity suffered another blow: by mid-August, the Cubs having suddenly climbed atop the league, Totten and Ryan began interspersing their Sox broadcasts with telegraphed updates from Cub road games.[11]

Ryan's replacement by Elson may have been a sign that the industry was maturing, developing specialists; symbolically, it was another sign that the shrill enthusiasms of radio's early days had run their course. Ryan's more-celebrated New York counterpart, Graham McNamee, who had likewise found himself thrown into every conceivable broadcasting situation, found his career ebbing as the 1930s wore on. McNamee was not yet fifty-three when he died in 1942, but already he was a figure from a distant age: In "Mr. Radio Is Dead," a Cleveland newspaper saw fit to editorialize on the passing of "Mr. Radio" in words that could have applied to his onetime colleague Quin Ryan (who lived on, respected but largely forgotten, until 1978): "McNamee's job had been . . . not to interpret but to transmit ebullition from the ring side and the bleachers to the fireside and the corner store. . . . We are glad radio and the radio audience have put on long pants and gained something of adult sophistication, but we wouldn't want to have missed the Graham McNamee period of radio any more than we would want to have skipped over our own childhood."[12]

The coming of Wilson and Stephenson and radio and female fans meant that the new Wrigley Field, its upper deck boosting seating capacity from 28,000 to the mid-30,000s by 1927 and near 40,000 by 1928, still couldn't accommodate the weekend crowds. If enough SRO tickets were sold, the only thing to do was to herd the folks into the outfield behind ropes, held by uniformed policemen and ushers ready to quell any possible uprisings. If the crowd outside grew unruly, Bill Veeck could call on mounted police to keep order in the streets.[13]

The Cubs who played in these shrunken outfields—Riggs Stephenson in left, Hack Wilson in center, and a platoon of Cliff Heathcote and Earl Webb in right—spent much of their time almost shoulder-to-shoulder with the fans. It was personal-scale stardom, unfeasible in New York's vast stadia and infrequent in smaller cities: fans standing just behind the outfielders, watching the pitcher's wind-up and the batter's swing at field level, tracking the small white ball rocketing toward their sector as their favorites judged its flight and tore off in pursuit. The fans could banter with the outfielders and even coach them—over here, Stevie!—and, by taking control of the restraining ropes from the ushers, enhance the home park advantage. Does Hack have a chance for that fly? Let's back up a few steps. Is Hartnett's ball playable? Not if we all move forward a few steps.[14]

Major league baseball had seen few flychasers like Wilson and Stephenson, who looked more like a backfield than an outfield. Lacking some of the traditional outfielder's traits, such as arm strength and grace, they compensated with hustle. Routine plays became adventures—but not disasters, because both men could track a fly ball. Wilson played a deep center field, whence he could race in for last-second catches. Long after Wilson was gone, Bill Veeck Jr. would fondly remember his teenage years, watching Wilson skid on his big belly to grab Texas leaguers and other short shots. Stephenson too, a converted infielder, stretched, rolled, dived, or tumbled any way necessary to get to the ball. His regular outpost, left field, was the primary gathering spot for Veeck's overflow; one Memorial Day, after Stevie's gymnastics had taken a hit away from the Cards' Gus Mancuso, the SRO section ribbed Stephenson: whatever the umpire, George Magerkurth, thought, they were wise to the game. Putout or not, more drama ensued after Stephenson came up with a ball: a shoulder injury from his college football days made his throwing arm less than dangerous, so young English had to range deep from shortstop to get the throw from Stephenson—and likewise with Wilson, himself not blessed with a strong arm.[15]

The results, nonetheless, were satisfactory for McCarthy, who had not acquired the young veterans for their defensive prowess. McCarthy, grasping the logic of the lively ball, believed in playing for the big inning. He refused to use that dead-ball talisman, the sacrifice bunt, until the late innings.[16] No manager had ever placed the majority of his outfield in such rough-and-ready hands for the sake of big innings, but then, few previous managers had graduated directly from the minor leagues. That logic led him to deemphasize defense, provided it was still adequate and the offensive rewards were great. Without the benefit of sabermetric models and computing tools, McCarthy played the percentages. He thought good hitting could outweigh the old virtues of defense: "[McCarthy's] explanation is that a third baseman has so few fielding chances that in the course of three or four games the difference between the star fielder and the average player will be only about two or three assists."[17]

Such thinking was made to order for the bulky Wilson and Stephenson, but it meant less for Heathcote, a superb outfielder who had been born too late: he was a classic singles hitter. Wilson was of the right time and place; his Jazz Age appeal had made him a star from his first weeks in Chicago. "Stevie," though, was entirely outside the Chicago zeitgeist. Where Wilson was a cheerful autograph signer, eager to mingle with throngs of worshipful boys, Stephenson was shy and soft-spoken. Wilson had dropped out of school after reaching sixth grade at age fourteen; Stephenson graduated from the University of Alabama with nine letters in football and baseball, and membership in the Iota Iota chapter of Sigma Chi fraternity. He had earned the nickname "The Ol' Hoss" as the Crimson Tide's fullback, and he stood for strength and dependability in baseball too. Wilson, who lost his mother at age seven, married a woman ten years older and stepped out on her; Stephenson, still a bachelor in his late twenties, used his pay from Mr. Wrigley to buy a house for his widowed mother. When Stephenson retired from baseball in the midst of the Depression, he had saved a resounding one hundred thousand dollars of his baseball earnings; in other words, his ballplaying had made him a millionaire by our lights. Wilson died broke after earning more than a quarter million dollars in his short career. There was no secret where the money went. The club's traveling secretary, Bob Lewis, remembered giving Wilson a $450 check—at least $5,000 of our dollars—one evening before dinnertime. By midnight it was all spent.[18]

After stepping in at the plate Wilson waved his huge bat like a toothpick and then flailed away murderously, his mighty strikeouts nearly as crowd-pleasing as his clouts. Although he argued constantly about called strikes, he wasn't considered a good judge of the strike zone. In contrast, Stephenson approached each at-bat cautiously, as though he dreaded the duty, even though he never finished a year hitting under .296 until the 83 at-bats of his final season at age thirty-six; and his career on-base percentage was .407. His uncanny two-strike hitting had earned him special respect: by consensus of the leading pitchers, Stevie was the one man they least wanted to face in a pinch. He used a disciplined, line-drive-producing swing;

Wilson lashed indiscriminately at anything that moved, tossed bats, and incited crowds with his tantrums. Stephenson's strongest recorded oath was "gol durn it." After a questionable strike call, he might murmur to the umpire, "Wasn't that one a little bit outside?" Within a few years, Wilson's flamboyance and outbursts made him the most controversial figure in the league; Stevie was the best-respected player of his day. "Never booed," they said of him.[19]

A church deacon back in Alabama, Stephenson carried a unique moral authority. One afternoon in the midst of the 1927 race, he briefly questioned an umpire's call during a close game. Fruit and pop bottles began flying from the stands; any call bad enough to upset the Ol' Hoss was obviously a very poor call indeed. Then there was the time Stephenson leveled his old college teammate, Hughie Critz of the Reds, with a thunderous but legal slide. Critz was knocked out of the lineup for weeks; the Cubs and the Reds undertook an ongoing battle of beanballs, spikings, brawls, and fistfights. As a result, Wilson was suspended for three days, and both teams were hauled in to testify in the office of the league president. But not a brushback or a sharpened spike seemed to come Stephenson's way.[20]

Wilson had never known anyone like Stevie. During practice one day, Hack supposedly watched a hatless young man—the era's mark of a college boy—approach Stephenson and speak to him in a strange tongue. "Hello, brother," the man said to Stephenson. "I'm the annotator, Kappa Kappa '31."

Stephenson sized up the stranger, then put out his hand and completed an awkward-looking shake. "Stephenson, Iota Iota '18," he replied.

Afterward Wilson caught up with the stranger. "You seem to know Steve pretty well," he said. "Where was you two pals?"

The young man was taken aback. "Why, sir, we are brother Greeks."

"The big stiff," Wilson supposedly exclaimed. "A hundred times he's told me he was born in Alabama!"[21]

Wilson was himself a great joiner—at one point belonging to the Elks, Eagles, Moose, Knights of Pythias, and Dokkies simultaneously—not to mention his after-hours network in the speakeasies and nightclubs, where the Hacker could always be counted on to pick up the tab. "He reminds you of the jovial, roly-poly small-town butcher," an acquaintance said. His generosity was real. When the Cubs passed through San Antonio on the way back from Catalina in the spring of 1927, it was Wilson who took up a collection for Ross Youngs, his fatally ill ex-teammate from his New York days. Summed up one sportswriter during the greatest month of Wilson's career: "When he says he'll do a thing, he does it, whether it involves visiting a bunch of sick kids in an orphanage, autographing a baseball, making an appearance at a German picnic, or any other courtesy like that."[22]

Visiting a children's hospital ward his first year with the Cubs, Wilson came upon a boy stricken with polio. He looked down at the boy's helpless form and tried to think of something positive to say. "Stick it out, kid," he said. "You'll be able to walk someday." The youngster, Maniford Harper of Washburn, Illinois, did eventually learn to walk again, with a new nickname, "Hack," and "CUBS" tattooed on his forearm in inch-high letters. He arranged to be buried in a Cub uniform; fifty years later he was still touting his one and only baseball hero, the one who had given him ten seconds of his time one Chicago evening.[23]

Out of respect, autograph hunters were less likely to approach Stephenson than Wilson. But one day a woman fan leaned over into the Cub dugout, called Stephenson over, and handed him a sheet of paper. Stephenson chivalrously obeyed, even after learning that what the woman wanted was the autograph of another Cub, probably Wilson or Hartnett. But as Stevie ambled off on his mission, the woman added one more instruction: "Don't let some other player fake that signature." Pushed beyond endurance, and to the shock of his teammates, Stephenson muttered, "Oh, hell," and handed the paper to a teammate for delivery—taking care, however, to relay the woman's instructions in detail.[24]

One day Stevie nearly went beyond uttering a bad word. In the ballplayers' habit of those days, he had left his glove on the field at the Polo Grounds while the Cubs came up to bat in an extra-inning game. Seconds after he reached the dugout, the umpires called the game on account of darkness. One of the fans pouring onto the field raced over and helped himself to Stephenson's glove. The old All-Southern back gave chase through the postgame mob. The man who had once devastated Auburn's line closed in on the youngster and brought him down with a crisp tackle. Stephenson stood and glared down at the terrified wrongdoer. Then he wagged his finger vigorously and drawled, "Don't you evah, *evah* let me catch you stealin' mah glove again." Lucky for the lad he hadn't grabbed the center fielder's glove, or things just might have turned out much differently.[25]

While Wilson and Stephenson were establishing themselves as outfield stars, the odd man out was gaining his own kind of prominence. Cliff Heathcote had been on the team longer than anyone but Hartnett. Heathcote broke into the big leagues as a teammate of Rogers Hornsby's in St. Louis, where the fans called him "Rubberhead" for getting skulled early in his career after losing a long drive in the sun.[26]

"Rubberhead" then made the history books with another non-milestone. On Decoration Day 1922, fresh from driving in the winning run in the first game of a doubleheader, he stretched out on a trunk in the Cards' clubhouse between games. He had dozed off when Branch Rickey, the Cardinals' manager, shook him awake.

"Had to have a leadoff man," Rickey informed Heathecote. "I've traded you for Max Flack. You have on the wrong uniform and you're in the wrong clubhouse."[27]

As quickly as that, the obscure Heathcote and Flack became a baseball history trivia item by exchanging uniforms in the middle of a doubleheader. The lightness of Cliff Heathcote's achievements, however, had only just begun.

In Chicago he continued to serve as a steady hitter and a fast, strong-armed outfielder under both Killefer and McCarthy. Soon after joining the club, on August 25, 1922, he went 5 for 5 with two walks and five runs scored in a 26–23 victory over Philadelphia. (Only three home runs were hit that day, none of them by Heathcote.)[28]

Jeers of "Rubberhead" were unknown in Chicago—quite the contrary. Something remarkable was happening in Chicago, where the increasing number of women turning out at the ballpark exercised their baseball vote by choosing modest, unassuming Cliff Heathcote as the most desirable fellow of them all. The "John Gilbert of baseball," some called him, even though Heathcote was clean-shaven. The ladies' letters to the *Tribune*'s sports department invariably addressed their concerns about "Heathie," whose rightful place in center field had been usurped by Wilson. Hack's many ups and downs could trigger a renewed round of calls for Heathcote's restoration, although some women such as "Honey" and "Heathie fan" were more forthright about their druthers: "I think Heathie is just about the cutest thing in his baseball unie. Don't tell me he's married or I'll just die. . . . P.S. Don't forget Heathie's picture." The idolators overlooked the Cubs' charismatic stars—Grimm, Hartnett, Wilson, Cuyler—as well as their hero's mundane off-season occupation—overseeing a dairy route back home in Pennsylvania. The end of one long Cub winning streak meant little to the twenty-five thousand women who had just set a new Ladies Day attendance record—they had spent their most of their afternoon chanting fruitlessly for Heathcote to come off the bench.[29]

In 1927 an outfielder named Earl Webb joined the club and bashed a flock of first-half home runs, nearly as many as Wilson. Heathcote's at-bats fell by half as the Cubs raced into the league lead. But after the team hit a late-season slump, second-guessing women began grumbling.[30]

Not long after that season closed, the Cubs acquired the stellar outfielder Kiki Cuyler. It became clear to any objective observer that Heathcote, who was about to turn thirty, would never be a regular again. Heathcote made friends the next spring with the newcomer, though; the two outfielders plus Charlie Grimm soon made up the Cubs' musical threesome. Heathcote and Charlie Grimm were already fast friends, road roommates, and the partners in a ukulele-banjo duo for several years. And all three musicians were said to carry a tune.[31]

Another newcomer was Hal Carlson, "the silent Swede," acquired by Veeck in the midst of the 1927 race. At thirty-five, he seemed as venerable as Alexander and, like Alex, he was a casualty of the Great War. After a respectable rookie season for Pittsburgh in 1917, he had entered military service and shipped out to the Western Front with the 76th Division. Going into action as a machine gunner, he was gassed in the Argonne. He came back home with a Distinguished Service Cross, the Croix de Guerre, and intestinal problems that would plague him for the rest of his life—a condition he concealed from teammates.[32]

Again like Alex, Carlson was able to reestablish himself in the majors, posting 14 victories for the Pirates in 1920. Then his career met with a new setback: the ban on the spitball, which went into effect at the beginning of the 1921 season. Exactly how this affected Carlson is unclear. According to one account, Carlson's "out" pitch was a spitter, and the Pirates simply forgot, or declined, to register Carlson as one of the pitchers still allowed to doctor the ball with his saliva. Or perhaps Carlson's trick pitch was some kind of shine ball or emery ball, tactics that no one, even vets, could use anymore. He seems to have developed a sore arm as well. Whatever the causes, by 1922 Carlson's once-respectable ERA had ballooned to an atrocious 5.70. Just about to turn thirty-one, he had to trudge off to the Texas League to learn all over again how to get people out—this time by working on a slow curve and a change of pace that he learned to disguise with his fastball delivery. He certainly knew how to keep the ball down, a skill that had helped him flourish at Baker Bowl: in one 1929 start against the New York Giants, he allowed only two fly balls while pitching a complete-game six-hitter.[33]

Carlson learned enough in his second apprenticeship to return to the big show by 1924. His reward was admission to right-handed-pitching hell, otherwise identified as dilapidated Baker Bowl with its tin right-field fence, 280 feet from home plate. Yet in that pitching graveyard, the stolid Carlson persevered and even prospered. In 1925 he led the National League with four shutouts; his 1926 record of 17-12 was one of the finest a Phillie recorded in the long decades between Grover Alexander and Robin Roberts.

That performance evidently convinced McCarthy that Carlson could help the Cubs in the 1927 pennant run. The very decrepitude of Baker Bowl played at least some role in Carlson's salvation. On May 14 Carlson took the hill for the Phillies against the defending world champion Cardinals. Sixteen thousand fans had turned out for a Saturday afternoon at the park. Rain beginning in the third inning had driven hundreds of fans beneath the covered portions of the first-base grandstand. Evidently the rain continued, because many of the displaced persons were still there, cheering and stamping their feet excitedly, when the Phillie lineup staged an eight-run outburst in the bottom of the sixth. Carlson returned to the mound in the top of the seventh with an outlandish 12–3 lead. After he retired the Cardinals' leadoff batter, a portion of the weakened, overloaded grandstand collapsed with a huge roar. Three hundred fans were thrown from their seats or off their feet, and in the ensuing stampede, one person died and more than fifty were injured. (The game was called, and Carlson received credit for the victory.) Three weeks later, the Phils sent their only reliable starter to the Cubs; the surmise was that the need for twenty thousand dollars of William Wrigley's cash had been more critical than the two rarely used veterans the Cubs sent the Phillies' way.[34]

Carlson's years of struggle were finally paying off. With Root, Guy Bush, and the steady, unspectacular Sheriff Blake already on hand, Carlson's presence provided McCarthy a rotation as deep as any in the league. Bringing a stiff, prewar style (and a walk ratio per nine innings that rivaled Alexander's) to Wrigley Field, Carlson won five games in his first three weeks with the club; his victory on July 7 put the Cubs into the National League lead, where they stayed for most of the next six weeks—more time in the top spot than all the Cub teams combined since the pennant-winning season of 1918. In celebration, Chicagoans poured into the ballpark during the July-August home stand, including a record 14,000 women who joined 23,000 paying male fans to see Carlson go nine innings against the Giants on July 29. He gave up 12 hits but only 1 earned run; in the tenth Root relieved him and picked up the victory when Stephenson singled home the winning run.[35]

From crumbling Baker Bowl to a virtual baseball paradise of teeming, happy crowds, generosity, and camaraderie: it was outrageous good fortune for anyone, much less the long-suffering Swede. Wrigley's elevated pay scale enabled him to begin building his wife a new house—a "shrine" to her, he called it—in his hometown of Rockford, northwest of Chicago. He also had two of the best catchers in the business to work with: Hartnett, the team's fireplug (the two eventually roomed together on the road), plus Mike Gonzalez, a savvy veteran from Cuba. Carlson was soon sampling the luxuries that a contending ball club could provide, such as the rubdown services of the Cubs' trainer, Andy Lotshaw.[36]

Lotshaw's formal qualifications as a trainer were uncertain. A star ballplayer himself in the American Association before World War I, he reputedly caught Grover Alexander's first game in the minor leagues. Several more years in the minors led to brief flirtations with the Federal League and the Cleveland Indians; an injury had impaired his fielding, if not his hitting, abilities. By the early 1920s he was a millwright playing semipro ball for the Staley Starch company of Decatur, Illinois. The team's second baseman, an ex–New York Yankee named George Halas, organized a semipro football team for the Staleys, and Lotshaw, who had played first base for the company team, enthusiastically insinuated himself into Halas's operation as the football team's trainer, notwithstanding his lack of any relevant experience whatsoever. Soon the Staleys and Andy Lotshaw's impressive new library of medical volumes moved to Chicago, where they soon became the Bears of the infant National Football League, taking an autumn lease on Cubs Park.[37]

The stories about how Lotshaw joined the Cubs differ. In the prosaic version, his hustling attitude caught the eye of Bill Veeck, who had arranged the lease to the Bears. In a more dramatic vein, Lotshaw made his name by helping Grover Alexander overcome a sore arm to pitch two complete (although losing) games in the 1921 City Series. Whatever the case, each February from the mid-twenties on, Lotshaw climbed on the Cubs' train for the West Coast in a huge cream-colored hat, a loud tie with matching socks, and his oversize set of lungs. "Windy," they called him. In his time Lotshaw would serve at least seven Cub managers and scores of players, outliving many of them and watching up close the rise and fall of William Wrigley's ball club. Lotshaw's trainer shtick seemed to combine elements of snake-oil sales and the chiropractic arts, with various ointments and diathermy treatments mixed in. Rogers Hornsby, who was later Lotshaw's boss for nearly two years, noticed that Lotshaw handled most complaints by referring to a chiropractic chart hanging in the clubhouse. "Yep, it's a pelvic nerve," the trainer would sagely observe. The fitness-obsessed Hornsby may also have looked askance at Lotshaw's role distributing cigarettes to the athletes.[38]

It was hard to argue with Lotshaw's results: the Cub pitching staffs of the twenties and thirties were among the most durable and successful in the major leagues. Before long Lotshaw was prominent enough to peddle "Lotshaw's Liniment," an ointment that took its place on the shelves of midwestern pharmacies. Lotshaw became a presence in the clubhouse and even on the bench, flourishing in competition with extroverts like Hartnett and Grimm, a kind of a coach without portfolio for McCarthy and other Cub managers.

Lotshaw and his mouth would one day help incite Babe Ruth to hit one of the most famous home runs in Cub (and baseball) history, but usually a pitcher named Pat Malone served as his foil. During an exhibition game against Seattle of the Pacific Coast League, Malone decided to spoof the name of the opposing manager, Jack Lelivelt, and Lotshaw warned Malone,

"You'd better find out what his name is, because that's the club you're going to be with next season." A few years later, hearing that Malone, a well-known carouser, considered flying over the San Pedro Channel to the new airport Mr. Wrigley had constructed at Catalina, Lotshaw quipped that he had already seen Malone up in the air many times without the help of a plane. Malone eventually wearied of hearing Lotshaw brag about his minor league hitting feats, particularly the time during the Great War when he had supposedly escaped federal prosecution after one of his drives had nearly killed two soldiers. He dared him to a batting practice duel. The fiftyish Lotshaw crashed the ball over the wall on his first swing, then quickly lit out for the clubhouse, pursued by the maddened, cursing Malone.[39]

Lotshaw's bombast had other victims. One spring on the West Coast the trainer umpired a charity game between the Cubs and team of Hollywood stars and crew put together by the comedian Joe E. Brown. Harry Ruby, a songwriter whose claim to fame was "Three Little Words," came to bat and struck out. "Three little words," roared Lotshaw. "You . . . are . . . out!" No one could call him sensitive. "Been pushing that banana cart too long?" he yelled at an Italian-American Cub of the 1940s. And any ballplayers who thought it was good sport to heckle the old man were silenced by dark references to the "embalming fluid" he might be forced to use sometime on an injured player.[40]

Lotshaw's difficulties with names and language—"he was dressed in the nude"—were fabled. Once a bystander tapped on his shoulder outside the clubhouse. "I remember the face—tell me your name," said Lotshaw. It was a brother he hadn't seen for several years. One autumn someone taunted Lotshaw that he couldn't remember the names of the Bears' players. "Sure I can," Lotshaw shot back. "Bronko Nagurski."[41]

Soon after joining the club, Hal Carlson became Lotshaw's steadiest customer since perhaps Grover Alexander. The day came when Carlson rushed into the clubhouse, planted himself on the rubbing table, and asked for a quick massage—it seemed that McCarthy had just asked him on short notice to start in that day's doubleheader. Lotshaw, who had been sipping on a bottle of Coca-Cola, told Carlson "some new stuff" might help him and promptly began rubbing Carlson down with the unconsumed portion of his soft drink; Carlson pitched successfully; and for the rest of

Carlson's abbreviated life, Lotshaw continued his therapy without ever letting on.[42]

But Carlson's real physical woes were beyond the ingenuity of a midwestern medicine man.

Even among the Cubs' thousands of new female fans, Evangeline Hurley stood out. A devoted follower of the team for several years, she had attended every Cub home game in 1927, and she considered herself just as qualified to hold forth on the Cubs' prospects as any of the men she knew.

Even when the team was riding high with a six-game lead in August, Hurley predicted that the Cubs would be lucky to finish third. Her male friends reacted scornfully, but she refused to back down, citing "woman's intuition and three cents' worth of intelligence."[43]

By early September, Hurley's lonely stance had been vindicated. Woody English and the other members of the American Association infield were choking in tight road games.[44] Root, who had won his twenty-fourth game on August 28, was near collapse. The Cubs wobbled for a couple of weeks, then swiftly fell from first place in early September. On the 4th, back in Wrigley Field before another overflow crowd, Wilson and Stephenson capped the follies by running themselves into a triple play against the Cardinals.

Even Hurley was surprised by the suddenness of the collapse. In early September, after listening to a special "re-created" broadcast of a 5–0 defeat in Cincinnati, she revised her forecast. The Cubs, she announced, would end up no better than fifth in the league. By now no one was arguing with her. The crowds grew edgy. The day of the triple play, one fan heckled Grover Alexander so badly that the old fellow emerged from the Cardinals' dugout and tried to climb into the stands after him. The fan retreated to safety a few rows up while Bill Klem and a group of players tried to restrain the one-time idol of Chicago, who took some swings at the good Samaritans (including Klem) before he disappeared, screaming, under the stands. On September 9, with the Cubs still only 2½ games back, the home umpire, Ernie Quigley, called ball 4 while the Giants' batter stood outside the batter's box. A barrage of pop bottles and lemons came sailing from the stands, one bottle barely missing Quigley. The Cubs beat the Giants the next two days, but on the 12th, the Cubs found themselves down 7–5 to open the bottom of the ninth. Stephenson rolled to Rogers Hornsby, the Giants' second baseman, and the mild-mannered Stephenson briefly questioned Cy Pfirman whether he had beaten the throw. A wave of pop bottles promptly flew from the stands, first targeting Pfirman, then the Giants' right fielder, George Harper. After a delay to clear the field of the debris, the last two Cubs of the afternoon went down, and the barrage renewed itself. After one bottle hit Pfirman on his ankle, the New Yorkers surrounded him and moved him safely into the dugout. In the box seats, Judge Landis sat and watched quietly.[45]

Whatever Landis was thinking, William Wrigley and Bill Veeck were unfazed by their ball club's quick exit from the pennant race—or thoughts of what Alexander's 21 victories might have meant. The smallest crowd during the slide still exceeded thirty thousand; Wrigley's franchise was about to become the National League's first to top 1 million for a season. A desperate fan phoned Wrigley one day to plead for tickets. "They told you the truth at the park," Wrigley said crisply. "I couldn't buy a ticket for my own folks if I wanted to. Sorry and good-bye." Then he turned to Veeck, who was in the room. "And now, Bill," he continued. "You've got to build that ballpark bigger. I don't like to be telling folks I can't get tickets."[46]

The White Sox had already enlarged their park, but it hadn't helped. Charles Comiskey's newly remodeled stadium, now the major leagues' second largest, had drawn just 610,000 customers for the year. Comiskey could have blamed the decline on Hal Totten's and Quin Ryan's broadcasts of Sox home games, which the American League had only allowed for the first time that year, but the Sox's 70-83 record probably had more to do with it. The Sox had a rival to Charlie Root's Herculean performance, the 22-14 record of Ted Lyons, and the league's second-best team ERA, but their batting average was among the league's lowest; their leading home run hitter had 9 to Hack Wilson's eventual National League–leading 30.

Any excitement on the South Side was all with the franchise operating in Comiskey's old wooden-decked ballpark. Even in the absence of Rube Foster and their outfield mainstay Jelly Gardner (Gardner through a contract dispute), Foster's player-manager, Dave Malarcher, marched the American Giants to another title. It was once again Chicago versus Atlantic

The McCarthymen Take the Stage

City in the "World Series," as the NNL and the Eastern League proudly called it. With Mayor "Big Bill" Thompson in the crowd at one of the games in Schorling's Park, the Giants charged out to a four-game lead; by October 13 they had sewn up the series in Atlantic City, 11-4.[47]

It was the end of the NNL's first full season without Rube Foster's omnicompetence. Attendance was down: there had been bad weekend weather, and signs that the roaring economy of the 1920s had faltered enough to affect the Giants' heavily blue-collar clientele. Umpire baiting, with cursing and threatening gestures, had become more frequent. Pitchers took more and more time between pitches, and some of the players had begun walking casually to and from their fielding positions between innings. Many games were taking an unheard-of three hours from start to finish.[48]

There were still hopes that Foster would be able to return and take charge once again. But he was confined to the state hospital in downstate Kankakee, helpless to affect the anarchy that was slowly overtaking his life's work. His ball club had won its last NNL pennant, and he would never get out of the hospital.

A week after the battle of the bottles, with the Cubs hopelessly out of the race, the Cubs' brass rewarded McCarthy with a bit of the profits he had helped generate. They signed him to a three-year, $25,000-a-year contract—a figure better than most big league stars could negotiate; certainly more than the needy St. Louis ownership could afford for Grover Alexander. The deal done, Wrigley told Mac and all the Cubs that he'd bought everyone ringside seats to the Jack Dempsey–Gene Tunney heavyweight championship rematch in Soldier Field a few days later.[49]

Thirty-one Cubs and coaches, plus Lotshaw and the traveling secretary, Bob Lewis, accompanied Wrigley and Veeck to the huge new arena. Like most fight fans—meaning most sentient American males—Mr. Wrigley's ballplayers were pulling for Dempsey, the "Manassa Brawler," the scowling representative of a still-undereducated nation. Not for them the sophistication of Tunney, the current heavyweight champion, a college-educated, thinking man's boxer. The Cubs' leading men numbered just one, Stephenson, with a bachelor's degree. Heathcote had accumulated two years of credit at Penn State College—an unusual amount of education for the day. McCarthy, too, had finished two years at Niagara College, on a base-ball scholarship.

Hartnett and Bush, who had both finished high school, were aspiring businessmen, so Tunney's polished approach might have appealed to them; likewise Hartnett's backup, Mike Gonzalez, a future baseball franchise owner in Cuba. Neither Grimm nor Wilson, though, had even attended high school. Root, along with the ball club's permanent nonplaying pres-ence, Lotshaw, was a refugee from millwork. Earl Webb, the home run hero of the season's early months, had followed his father into the coal mines. Excepting Gonzalez, Mr. Wrigley's ball club was a representative swatch of Caucasian, northern European Americans, in ethnic composi-tion and social class a mirror of organized baseball the year that Ruth hit 60, Lindbergh crossed the Atlantic, and Dempsey fought Tunney.

The Cubs joined a throng that dwarfed Wrigley Field's recent sellouts or anything Yankee Stadium could handle: 140,000 spectators pouring into the lakefront's new Soldier Field. The Cubs entered the stadium jaun-tily, fedoras pulled over their eyebrows and sharp creases in their slacks; after all, they were among the best-paid players in organized baseball, and all but the very poorest Americans put on their Sunday finest for public outings. Veeck and Wrigley would have kept to their bow ties, vested suits, and Homburgs, so too probably the dignified Hal Carlson, a man who seemed closer to his employers' generation than the young men who had come of age in the 1920s.[50] Wrigley and his employees were watching the ultimate sporting event of the 1920s, the most storied prizefight of them all. Thirty thousand of the spectators occupying the most expensive seats had arrived in Chicago on special trains or private cars attached to regularly scheduled trains. Princess Xenia of Greece came in from the municipal airport, where she had landed in a Fokker.

A furniture retailer from Toledo found himself contesting a space with an elderly fellow who wore a bowtie. A policeman stepped in to handle the standoff. "Move along, me lad," he ordered the older man. "Yes, sir, right away," William Wrigley replied.[51] Wrigley, the Cubs, and the fur-niture man took their seats near dukes, barons, Astors, and Vanderbilts; the heads of General Motors, General Electric, and Bethlehem Steel; Rob-ert Peary of North Pole fame; and celebrities—Swanson, Sharkey, Chaplin, Cohan, Lloyd, Ziegfeld, Baruch, Fairbanks. Al Capone, a great sports fan, was there too. The fight's promoter, Tex Rickard, turned to a companion and said, "I've got in those ten rows all the world's wealth, all the world's big men, all the world's brains and production talent. Just in them ten rows, kid. And you and me never seed anything like it."[52]

Capone's political allies, State's Attorney Robert Crowe (the late Bill McSwiggin's old boss) and Mayor "Big Bill" Thompson, stood at the intersection of several-score floodlight beams and welcomed the fighters to the ring. Graham McNamee prepared to call the action for the NBC network; his former partner, Quin Ryan, controlled the WGN mike and Hal Totten held WMAQ's. Then the punching began.

Through the early going Tunney steadily outpointed Dempsey, but round after round the crowd continued roaring encouragement to the ex-champ. In the seventh round, Dempsey finally caught Tunney with two left hooks followed by a right cross. McNamee was nearly delirious: "And now Tunney is DOWN! Tunney is DOWN from a barrage of lefts and rights to the jaw and the head. The count is going on. Tunney is still down. Dempsey is on the other side of the ring now. Eight . . . nine. Tunney is up. And now they are at it again!"[53]

The champ was down for the famed "long count." He struggled to his feet slowly, so slowly that much of the crowd wondered why the ten-count had hardly begun. At the end of the scheduled ten rounds, Tunney was on his feet, still the champion of the world.

Twelve individuals were said to have perished while listening to McNamee's account. His words had been illegally recorded, thereby becoming one of the earliest and surely the greatest of the early radio archives, although McNamee's ever-growing body of critics faulted his explanation of the long count. No deaths were reported as a result of Ryan's or Totten's narration.

Mr. Wrigley's ball club filed out with the rest of the huge crowd, still abuzz over the great and puzzling drama. Woody English was sure Dempsey had been shortchanged, and the Tunney bloc among his teammates probably kept silent. They were part of a Wrigley family now: the showmen—Hartnett, Grimm, Wilson, Bush—and the quiet ones—Stephenson, Root, English, Carlson. To the end of their days their names would be linked, the Cubs of the Roaring Twenties. They would carouse, hunt, honeymoon on Wrigley's island, try show business, testify, manage the team, coach, captain. Their wives would attend Mrs. Veeck's tea parties. They would celebrate championships, fight with spectators, cover up a felony, bury their dead, fall out among themselves. One of them would not live to age forty, and several wouldn't see age fifty, alcoholics and teetotalers alike. They would fall short of the world's title, in peculiarly humiliating ways. One of the longest-lived among them would have his ashes scattered over Wrigley Field, almost sixty years later, long after most Chicagoans had forgotten about William Wrigley and William Veeck.

5 | My Dad the Sportswriter

They was trying to beat Bill with the better-element vote. The trouble with Chicago is that there ain't much better element. —Will Rogers, 1927

Vote early and vote often. —Attributed to Capone's protégé, Murray "The Hump" Humphreys

Mayor Bill Thompson had visited Schorling's Park for the American Giants' World Series in October 1927. The next April he was out at Wrigley Field for the Cubs' 1928 home opener. But in those six months the mayor's world had changed for good.

A record throng of 46,000 booed a ballyhooed new Cub, Kiki Cuyler, for striking out his first time up. Thompson showed up in the fourth inning with George Getz, a coal-mining heir who, besides hunting lions, had helped to bring the Dempsey-Tunney fight to Chicago. They later saw Cuyler smash a home run into a strong headwind off the lake, and the boos promptly turned to cheers.[1]

Thompson knew a thing or two about the fickleness of crowds. Many a time he might have upstaged Bill Veeck's baseballers all by himself: dressing up in cowboy regalia and riding his horse down Michigan Boulevard or wherever the latest parade happened to be, appearing in the rodeo at Soldier Field, inviting horsemen to ride into the City Hall council chamber. When he visited other cities, cheering crowds had gathered below his hotel window; admirers lined up to shake his hand, and he dreamt of succeeding Calvin Coolidge as president. In fact, after his election to a third term in 1927 he set out on a seven thousand-mile railroad trip through the American heartland: Omaha, Kansas City, Denver, Cheyenne, Los Angeles, and San Francisco, where 1,200 gathered to hear him speak at a luncheon hosted by the Chamber of Commerce. His entourage distributed copies of a booklet with a red, white, and blue cover and his four main proposals for the Mississippi River Valley—"the backbone of the nation." In California, William Randolph Hearst entertained Thompson's party at San Simeon; in San Francisco, Thompson boasted that he would control 80 percent of the Illinois delegation at the upcoming national convention. As one contemporary observed, if Thompson was not a candidate for the Republican presidential nomination in 1928, he was doing a fine job of fooling everyone.[2]

More than a showman, Thompson was the ribbon cutter for Chicago's monumental neoclassical lakefront development, the vast Lake Shore and Wacker drive projects, and the whole new mini-city of the Magnificent Mile. His huge "shovel ready" projects created jobs for the working class. He was one Republican who knew how to court the Chicagoans of the Saturday night bath. His stage play rallies featured what he called "stockyard rats" as stand-ins for his opponents—not the optimum way to reach the supposed better elements of the city.

During Thompson's tenure the Prince of Wales, studying the itinerary for his upcoming visit to Canada, expressed a particular royal interest in visiting the United States' renowned Windy City; in most cities such an honor—a visit from royalty—would spark an outpouring of civic pride and an elaborate welcoming ceremony hosted by the mayor. Not in Chicago, though, where Thompson instead threatened to "punch King George in the snoot" if he met him face-to-face (political objective: the Irish and German vote, as well as everyone else disillusioned with the results of World War I). Thompson identified strongly with Lincoln (a nod to the rapidly growing black community) and T.R. (aiming at big-government Republicans; like Roosevelt, Thompson had actually worked as a cowpuncher), and he made sure to be seen not only at Wrigley Field and Comiskey Park (a cross-section of every social class) but at Schorling's Park too (where not only blacks but also numerous comparatively unbigoted whites attended). Ever since the World War, "America First!" had been Thompson's rallying cry (appealing to anyone who didn't like Woodrow Wilson's internationalism). Above all, Thompson mocked and derided Prohibition (a nod to nearly every non-Anglo-Saxon ethnicity, and most of the Anglo-Saxons too), and that stance inevitably made him the tacit if not formal ally of the greatest bootlegger of them all, Capone. However unfair the assumption, Thompson died in the 1940s with some $1.5 million in cash and jewels in his safe-deposit boxes.[3]

For good or ill, Chicago was Big Bill's city. His regime was the fountainhead of payoffs, boodle, and quasi-alliances with the underworld. Murders were up, prosecutions down, convictions for gang murders nonexistent. The *Tribune* ran a "Hands of Death" column on its front page, with three categories: deaths by automobiles, alcohol consumption, and shootings. In the winter following the Thompson-hosted Tunney-Dempsey bout, the lawlessness spread with an outbreak of bombings throughout the city—more than sixty from autumn into the first months of the year.[4]

Bombs, usually exploding in the night without injury or death, were a Chicago tradition that predated submachine guns, a means of silencing and intimidating. Soon after the Cubs set out for Catalina in mid-February, a bombing on the Near North Side intensified the national fascination with Chicago's violence. Late in the evening of the 17th, the soft silence of a snowfall was shattered by an explosion that rocked the apartment of a municipal court judge, John Sbarbaro, who lived upstairs from the family-owned Sbarbaro & Co. mortuary, founded in 1882. This old prosecuting comrade of Bill McSwiggin's had acquired much attention for juggling investigation and funeral profit on the same homicide.[5]

The force of the explosion threw the judge and his wife, who were asleep in their third-floor bedroom, to the floor. Other than the scare, the couple were unharmed, and their tastefully furnished quarters survived intact, although the mortuary's first-floor chapel was virtually ruined and twenty-five square feet of the garage wall demolished. (The *New York Times* noted drily that the garage was "long known to police and government agents as a rendezvous for alcohol peddlers and gangsters." God save the mark!) It made three times since January that a prominent politician's residence had been targeted with a bomb, and later that night, a couple of miles north of the Sbarbaro & Co. premises, two more bombs went off at two other dubious establishments, one the smoke shop of Louis Barsotti, considered a "close friend" of Sbarbaro's. (Barsotti's business evidently doubled as a gambling operation.) As the Spring 1928 primary drew near, other politicians had been targeted with bombings, and one, a gangster ward-heeler who in a typical muddle had aligned with the reformers, was gunned down. Although civic leaders normally celebrated the elimination of hoodlums, with or without due process, as "removing vermin from Chicago's streets," the timing of this particular death only made the Thompson administration look even more corrupt.

Chicagoans began wondering out loud why their ambitious, flamboyant mayor couldn't govern. The anti-Thompson faction cried, "What do we get? Pineapples!" (The reference was to World War I hand grenades.) In the campaign for April's "Pineapple Primary," as it became known, no proprieties were observed. The mayor had "the carcass of a rhinoceros and the brains of a baboon," one of his opponents proclaimed. The voters rejected Thompson's slate by a landslide; the mayor's major ally (and Sbarbaro's old boss), Robert Crowe, lost by nearly a hundred thousand votes countywide.[6]

It was the first real rejection the electorate had ever delivered to Big Bill. After his appearance at the Cubs' home opener eight days later—most likely a belated effort at placating William Wrigley—he seldom went to the office. Amid rumors of a nervous breakdown, he left town for a long vacation in Wisconsin's north woods, not to return until September. By then, that summer's Republican National Convention had nominated Herbert Hoover by acclamation. William Wrigley, Thompson's friend since their younger days, first tried to withdraw his support for Thompson's nomination, and soon he publicly allied himself with an anti-Thompson good-government group. Wrigley, it seemed, supported the good-government, middle-class progressives after all.[7]

John Sbarbaro, an incumbent who had not appeared on the April ballot, somehow avoided both the bombs' early light and the decline of the Thompson regime. He stayed in town and went about his judging, as he would (with a six-year interruption) for more than thirty years to come—a remarkable feat for a mob-connected Republican in a city that was about to turn permanently Democratic. Or was that no surprise in Chicago?

Sbarbaro would be one of several judges to play roles in the Cubs' future. In the meantime, the prospects of the Cubs looked very bright, and nearly as colorful and entertaining as Big Bill's performances.

Just after four on midsummer's afternoon, June 21, 1928, thirty-seven-year-old Edward Young, a resident of Ainslie Street in the Uptown neigh-

My Dad the Sportswriter

borhood, just off the lake and a few blocks north of Wrigley Field, slipped from his grandstand seat and headed for an empty box seat he had spied behind the Cubs' dugout. It was the bottom of the ninth, and Young had something he very much wanted to tell Hack Wilson. In fact, he had been trying to tell him all day, but he wasn't sure that Hack had heard him from the grandstand.[8]

By trade, Young was a milkman—more precisely, a milk wagon driver. For some fifty dollars a week he drove a team of horses around the North Side while he delivered his milk to delicatessens, corner groceries, and private residences. (The ice to keep the milk cold came in a separate delivery, also horse-drawn: refrigerators were a novelty most people couldn't afford.) Children would emerge from alleys and doorways to feed the horses apples during deliveries. Mothers made especially sure their children learned to hold their thumbs tight against their hands while feeding the animals.[9]

Young belonged to the milk wagon drivers' union. As long as he paid his dues, union committeemen wouldn't bother him with blunt instruments or worse. Young, said to have played rough-and-ready minor league ball in the Dakotas twenty years earlier, probably considered himself more qualified than most to critique the play of Mr. Wrigley's ball club—as loudly and often as he liked.[10]

Young would have hurried through his deliveries on June 21 to make the one o'clock starting time for the Cubs-Cardinals doubleheader scheduled that day. Wrigley Field was only a mile or so south of his usual habitat. On the way to the ballpark, he stopped for a nondairy drink. By the second game his persistent heckling had already earned him scrutiny from the Cub dugout, especially Wilson and Hartnett. In the bottom of the ninth, with the home team trailing 4–1, the box seat patrons began to thin out, and Young opportunistically upgraded his seating. Now he was almost as close to the action as in his ballplaying days.[11]

The 17½ innings the Cubs and the Cardinals had played, plus the break between games, had taken just over three hours. Sheriff Blake, the Cubs' unsung fourth starter, had two-hit St. Louis in the first game. Much of the scoring for the afternoon had come via unearned runs, all of them in the first inning. With one out in the ninth, Hack Wilson, the Cubs' cleanup hitter and the National League's home run leader, came to the plate. He was having, for Hack, an unexciting game: a single and a walk in three plate appearances, after going 1 for 3 in the first game. Defensively, Wilson had committed none of the Cubs' three errors, which for Hack was a solid accomplishment.

Sylvester Johnson, who had allowed the Cubs only three hits, went to work on Wilson. Soon Wilson topped a ground ball to the Cardinals' second baseman, Frank Frisch, who picked it up and made a routine toss to Jim Bottomley at first. Johnson had one out to go to wrap up a complete-game victory. With Johnson in complete command and the home team three runs down, not even the diehards in the crowd would have been making much noise.

In the midst of this ennui, Wilson took the well-trod route back to the Cub dugout on the third-base side while Riggs Stephenson headed to the batter's box for what might be the Cubs' final at-bat. As Wilson neared the dugout, Young intensified his commentary from his new box seat. Before Wilson reached the dugout, he abruptly peeled off his path, vaulted the low railing, and headed pell-mell in Young's direction. Wilson's cleats clattered and slid as he lit on the concrete floor of the grandstand. The exact sequence of events, which would become the subject of a lawsuit and baseball lore, became confused. The observers who spoke up agreed that Wilson and Young fell to the floor in a flurry of punching and flailing, although who was doing the most damage was disputed. Not in dispute is that within seconds Hartnett and Joe Kelly, another muscular Cub, had hustled out of the dugout and joined the action. They just wanted to pull their teammate off Young, they claimed later, although Young testified that the first responders did more damage than the original attacker. That sounds reasonable enough, for however tough a customer Young may have been, he could have been no match for three much younger professional athletes in midseason form. He could be thankful, though, that the Cubs, unlike many union sluggers, had left their bats in the dugout.[12]

The Cubs' dash into the stands signaled a much larger, and largely nonviolent, demonstration. While Young and the ballplayers tussled, some five thousand of the remaining customers—perhaps by that time a majority of the original crowd of twenty thousand—poured from the grandstand, pushed and shoved, hurdled seatbacks, and surged down the aisles onto the field. Their target did not seem to be Wilson, Young, reprobate umpires, or opposition players, only chaos, midsummer's madness.[13]

My Dad the Sportswriter

The police quickly went about shagging the revelers back into the stands. While things calmed down, Bob Lewis of the Cub staff pointed out Young, face lacerated, to the police, and the blue-coated men took him into custody for inciting a riot. As he was led away, Young shouted that he would sue Wilson.[14]

The elapsed time for the fight and the riot totaled a mere twelve minutes. The umpires resumed play; Stephenson popped up to Bottomley to send everyone home. After an elapsed three hours and thirty-nine minutes, counting all scheduled and unscheduled intermissions, the two teams retired to the locker rooms. Wilson, peeling off his jersey, noticed that Young had ripped it.[15]

After spending the night in jail, the milkman was led in the morning before the Chicago judiciary, well accustomed to punishing miscreants with severity. Judge Francis Allegretti of the Town Hall Court rebuked Young after he admitted to being under the influence of alcohol when he insulted Hack. "You are not a sportsman," said the judge. "When a man makes a good play, encourage him, and when he makes a bad play encourage him to make a good one the next time." Young, who must have known much more about professional sports than the judge, listened silently as his penalty was pronounced: a $1 fine and costs. Wilson's punishment came from the president of the National League, John Heydler, who fined him $100 without further comment. The episode seemed closed.[16]

Chicago had dealt decisively with the menace of Edward Young.

A volley of boos greeted Wilson on his first at-bat June 23, before he even had a chance to strike out or pop up. The little slugger had at least temporarily made himself as unpopular as Mayor Thompson.

Wilson ignored the critics. He hammered Flint Rhem's first pitch deep into the right-field bleachers, sending the Cubs on their way to an 8–4 victory. The next day he pounded an even longer homer, high into the last row of the centerfield bleachers. This time the stands fairly shook with the cheers.[17]

Wilson kept it up, perhaps his best stretch of slugging since he had reached Chicago. On June 30, Wilson homered twice; solo homers followed in both games on the 4th. On July 6 he roughed up Brooklyn's southpaw Jess Petty for two more, and he closed out the barrage the next day with a drive deep into the right-field bleachers, his 22nd homer of the year. He had hit ten homers in just over two weeks; his batting average for the week just concluded was .531. Then the Cubs went on the road, and Wilson went into a hitting tailspin. Late in the month came the news that Edward Young had filed suit for fifty thousand dollars—twenty thousand for a sprained back and thirty thousand for humiliation.[18]

Another member of the outfield, the heralded newcomer Kiki Cuyler, was having his own struggles. After three months in a Cub uniform, he was hitting in the mid-.200s, almost a hundred points below his lifetime batting average. He had already learned that the big-city fans, expecting in Cuyler a savior, were as quick to boo as they were to cheer—something that might trouble any ballplayer, but especially the proud Cuyler.[19]

Even in a slump, though, buying a ticket to watch Cuyler play was seldom a disappointment. A graceful all-around athlete (he had been offered a football scholarship with the then-dominant Army football program), he had averaged better than .340 for Pittsburgh his first four years in the major leagues. On two Pittsburgh pennant winners, the slender Cuyler augmented that lofty mark with superlative baserunning, fielding, and throwing. The summer he turned forty, he could still wow the hard-bitten fans of Ebbets Field with his running catches and rocket throws, their reactions similar to those of Ralph McGill, a young Southern journalist and later a famed editor and champion of civil rights, who had watched Cuyler play minor league ball in 1923. McGill had accepted his paper's sportswriting assignment reluctantly, but the sight of Cuyler day after day won him over, as Cuyler impressed him with his intelligence, fielding prowess, and baserunning artistry, finishing successfully 68 times that summer with a hook slide into the next base:

One of the pictures which will always be bright in the mind is of a sunny day at Sulphur Dell with the grass green and white clouds in the sky and Ki Ki Cuyler going way back to deep centerfield and going up high with his gloved hand and devouring the ball.[20]

Always worth the price of admission, Cuyler's major league derring-do included reaching base 14 times in a row in September 1925, with 10 straight base hits, itself part of a larger stretch in which he reached base safely in

20 of 22 plate appearances; the next month, in game 7 of the World Series, he delivered a famous double off Walter Johnson to break the game open. The players who have ever at any point merited serious comparison to Ty Cobb are few, but Cuyler's extraordinary early seasons generated such talk—not to mention dreams of racial integration. Spending most of his career in Pittsburgh and Chicago, two important Negro League locales, he was judged capable of thriving in that league's more wide-open style of play: "Our guess is that Cuyler dropped between Stearns and Rogers or Thompson would assure either outfit [i.e., the American Giants or the Cubs] just what the doctor ordered," noted Al Monroe of the *Chicago Defender* when Cuyler was well into his thirties.[21]

His peers, though, always suspected Cuyler as a "batting average player," something of a worrywart, and vainglorious to boot. In his rookie year he was called "yellow" after striking out a dozen times in one series with the Giants, despite his .354 batting average for the season. Once, in the midst of a long winning streak, he griped in the clubhouse about his hitless day. In 1927, with the Pirates fighting for the pennant they would eventually win, he and the club's new manager began clashing about where Cuyler should play in the outfield and hit in the order. His offense began to suffer after a leg injury. Things came to a head in August, when Cuyler went into second base standing on a force play. The manager, Donie Bush, fined and benched Cuyler.[22]

Bush was probably making a stand like McCarthy's with Grover Alexander, or Pirate management may have simply tired of Cuyler's proud bearing, with Cuyler's holdout in spring 1926 not forgotten. Even the sacking of Alexander, though, created no uproar like that of l'affaire Cuyler. The Pittsburgh newspapers promoted the controversy and probably aggravated it, one paper running a photo of the actual play at second with a caption inviting readers to decide, "Was Cuyler or Bush right?" Letters of protest poured in to the newspapers, and the fans continued chanting "Put Cuyler in" through the end of the season, even after the Pirates had wrapped up the NL title.[23]

This was the year that the Bronx Bombers' cannonade in batting practice before the series opened in Forbes Field supposedly cowed the Pirates into defeatism. Bush might have improved morale quickly by calling on the cavalry, at least the standout cavalryman he was holding in reserve, and the Pittsburgh fans certainly thought so: at least twice during the opening game a banner reading "We Want Cuyler" unfurled from Forbes Field's concrete bleachers. With the Pirates down one run in the bottom of the ninth and the pitcher due to lead off, the stands rocked again with cries for Cuyler, but Bush chose Fred Brickell, a twenty-year-old rookie who had batted 21 times during the season. Brickell grounded out. Lloyd Waner and Clyde Barnhart likewise went out, and the Yanks had the all-important opening win on the road.[24]

That was as close as Cuyler came to getting into the series his mates lost against the same club Grover Alexander had mastered twelve months earlier, but the pro-Cuyler demonstrations continued throughout the second game, another defeat for the Bucs. In games 3 and 4, even the Yankee Stadium crowds took up the cause by chanting for Cuyler as the Yanks finished up their four-game sweep.[25]

As if not noticing the Pirates' lineup suffered by comparison with Murderers' Row, Bush and the Pirate front office began shopping their own heaviest hitter as soon as the series ended. At the league meetings that fall, the Cubs made an appointment with Barney Dreyfuss, the Pirates' owner. An outfield of Cuyler, Stephenson, and Wilson could give the club three 100-RBI men in "the garden," something unseen since the 1890s. When Veeck and McCarthy showed up, Dreyfuss glared at them. "You want Cuyler, don't you?" he asked briskly. Veeck offered the Cubs' veteran little second baseman, Sparky Adams, a thirty-three-year-old who had blasted exactly seven home runs since breaking in in 1922. (He was good for two more by the time he retired.) Dreyfuss quickly rejected the deal but counteroffered: he also wanted Pete Scott, a twenty-nine-year-old reserve outfielder. Veeck and McCarthy looked at each other, then left the room to grin and shake hands on it. Back in Dreyfuss's lair, Veeck said, "Well, Barney, I guess I'll have to give you Scott, too. Joe seems set on Cuyler. . . . Dreyfuss accepted," remembered Veeck. "The whole affair didn't take five minutes . . . and look what we got for what we gave."[26]

Veeck and McCarthy had put the capstone on one of baseball's finest outfields for a modicum of cash and spare parts; the Pirates had added a .340 slugger to the roster. That might give Ruth (.772) and Gehrig (.765) pause at the next World Series batting practice. And the Pirates could still

My Dad the Sportswriter

claim the services of young Brickell, who would eventually power 8 home runs in 1,448 major league at-bats.[27]

The next February Cuyler reported at the Dearborn Street Station to board the Santa Fe special for the West Coast. Sporting a fedora and a well-tailored overcoat, a neatly folded newspaper under his arm, he looked more like a young executive than the auto roof installer he had been in his semipro days. Wilson, standing nearby in his own expensive ensemble, might as well have rented his outfit. He looked pudgier than ever. For the first time since Alexander's departure, the Cubs had a new rival to Wilson's star power.[28]

At Catalina, Wilson and the other Cubs found out just how different the new man was from the ordinary run of ballplayer. Cuyler smoked not; neither did he drink—or chew. His posture was faultless, as befit someone who had once started officer training at West Point. In the evenings Cuyler danced in cotillions that the Cubs sponsored in the St. Catherine's ballroom, encouraging young women from the mainland to attend. The debonair Cuyler dominated the dance contests as thoroughly as Wilson commanded the National League home run race, taking the title year after year, spending night after glamorous night on the dance floor: strengthened the ankles, he claimed. It certainly was a more civilized program than Bill Killefer's forced marches through the island's mountainous interior.[29]

Wilson cut a much less svelte figure, and his thin ankles were always tender from carrying his two-hundred-plus pounds, so his participation in the rigorous dance floor regimen went unrecorded. Wilson soon came up with an after-hours alternative. The 1928 Catalina camp also introduced McCarthy's latest import from the American Association: Perce "Pat" Malone, a beefy fellow with a large voice, a large laugh, and a picaresque past. The sportswriters soon dubbed him "The Black Knight of the Border" for a military stint with the First Cavalry at Fort Douglas, Arizona, near the Mexican border. Malone had dropped out of school at age fourteen and pitched as an adolescent on an amateur "ballclub"—probably a front for a gang. "If I couldn't strike out a guy, I'd lick him," in Malone's words. He also tried organized amateur boxing before joining the First Cavalry. After his discharge, small-college football and semipro pitching led him to the minor leagues and then to the training camp of John McGraw's New

York Giants. McGraw knew a hard-drinking troublemaker when he saw one. After two springs of trying to confine Malone to quarters, he sent the Black Knight's strong right arm and left forearm tattooed with "Ramona" back to the bushes before the 1924 season began. In the meantime, Malone had the chance to meet a talented young outfielder who was also trying to make the Giants' roster that spring: Lewis Wilson. The pair's friendship would one day make Malone more famous than anything his considerable pitching talent ever accomplished.[30]

Few minor league scouts or managers were interested in "wild man" Malone's services—McCarthy, then entrenched at Louisville, included.[31] Malone, undisciplined, uncoached, and probably discouraged, suffered through a succession of dismal seasons in the minors: 1-6, 9-21, 2-9. In 1923 he allowed 93 hits and 56 walks in 77 innings. Along the way he married, fathered a baby girl, then turned his career around with a 28-win season and an American Association–leading strikeout total in 1927. By this time Joe McCarthy, now established in the big leagues, decided he could take a chance on Malone, whose strikeout pitch had no doubt impressed Mac when the two both worked in the AA.

After all his journeys, Malone was still only twenty-six when he washed ashore in Catalina in February 1928. McCarthy, who like most managers was still acting as his own pitching coach, worked with Malone on the best grip for a curveball to complement his lusty fastball. Malone appeared in relief at the Cubs' home opener on April 18 before 46,000 filling the newly completed upper deck and spilling out on the outfield. Malone struck out four in 2⅔ innings, losing the game on an unearned run. By the end of April, the Black Knight was 0-5, all in relief appearances—yet his ERA was 2.49. Malone's fastball was obviously a major league pitch: on May 6, relieving Sheriff Blake (himself reputed to have the best "stuff" on the staff), Malone turned heads by fanning eight batters in five innings to capture his first victory. McCarthy gave him his first start a few days later, which Malone turned into a complete-game victory, followed by a shutout his next time out. By the time he lost again on May 30, a ten-inning battle in which he yielded one earned run, he was 4-6 with an ERA of 1.93 for the year. "A fellow like John McGraw would have had me back in the minors before I'd lost half that many," Malone remembered. But "Boss Joe," as Malone called him, had once again turned an American Associa-

My Dad the Sportswriter

tion has-been into a frontline contributor. Meanwhile, Malone and Wilson were becoming reacquainted.[32]

Charlie Root was doing little better after his great twenty-six-victory performance of 1927: he had reported overweight in spring training, his arm probably very tired from pitching 309 innings the year before. By the midpoint of 1928 his record was 6-11, and although few noticed that he had actually lowered his ERA from the previous year's figure, he would never be the same kind of workhorse again. Hal Carlson, the team's vital addition of 1927, was no longer a part of the rotation at all: diagnosed with what was described as a bad case of the flu in spring training, he hadn't been able to regain his strength. The problem was actually far worse, life threatening, as it happened—a result of the gassing Carlson had suffered in France a decade before. An examining physician in California, in fact, had told Carlson he had only a few months to live and sent him home to Illinois. The doctors back home were more optimistic, and by the time the Cubs opened in Chicago on April 18, Carlson was back with the team and in uniform. Nonetheless, he would be good for only 56 innings on the year with a 5.91 ERA. At age thirty-six Carlson didn't appear to have a future in professional baseball.[33]

Kiki Cuyler's woes continued to be McCarthy's biggest disappointment. The trouble originally began in one of the last spring exhibition games, when Cuyler jammed his hand while running into an outfield fence. As the season began, he was unable to raise his batting average above the .260s. The fans were booing him despite his daring leaps at the fences, whirling, bullet throws to the infield, and spectacular speed on the base-paths. (The disgruntled Chicagoans were denied the sight of Cuyler's inside-the-park home run at the Polo Grounds, where he crossed the plate before the relay man could receive the return throw from the outfield.) "Indescribably great," wrote one Chicago baseball writer after watching Cuyler turn a Frank Frisch drive into an out.[34]

But great wasn't good enough for the fans when it meant hitting well under .300. First McCarthy tried platooning Cuyler with the left-handed hitting Cliff Heathcote, but after Cuyler went 0 for 14 at-bats in June, McCarthy decided to sit him down for a few days. A year after the run-in with Bush, Cuyler was on the bench again. He hit no better after McCarthy reinserted him in the lineup a few days later.[35]

Wilson was in his red-hot post-fight phase. But then he too abruptly slumped when the Cubs went on the road in July. At the Polo Grounds late in the month, Wilson played to his growing reputation. Bill Klem, the dean of umpires, called him out on strikes. Wilson hurled his bat high in the air, then somehow wrested the ball from the Giants' oversize catcher, Shanty Hogan, and drop-kicked it. Klem gave the heave-ho signal, but Wilson trotted back out to center field for the bottom half of the inning and picked up his glove as if nothing had happened. Klem waved furiously at Wilson, who started in toward the plate as if to find out what Klem wanted. "Not this way—that!" barked the old umpire, pointing toward the clubhouse beyond the outfield. McCarthy kept Wilson out of the lineup for the second game played that day.[36]

Back at Wrigley Field on August 20, Wilson hit a fifth-inning drive that bounced over the screen and into the stands in deep right center. By the rules then in effect it counted as a home run. In the bottom of the eighth, with the game still in doubt, Wilson came up with the bases loaded after Cy Pfirman had called two Cubs out on strikes. With the Cub bench, led by Malone, all over Pfirman, Wilson was called out on strikes too. The long-handled bat once again flew high in the air in protest. Pfirman ejected Wilson without delay while Malone continued his barrage of insults from the dugout. For their efforts Wilson earned his first suspension, along with the standard $100 fine, and Malone was charged $50 for his supporting role.[37] The incident marked the debut of the famous, long-running Wilson and Malone act, with all the consequences that would bring to themselves, Joe McCarthy, and the franchise.

No one took much notice at the time. Wilson returned to help the Cubs sweep Boston in an August 24 doubleheader before a crowd of 32,000 that included 16,000 women. Cuyler, his hand finally healed, was banging the ball all over the field, beating out infield hits and stretching singles into doubles. On September 8, he bashed three doubles, including the game-winner in the bottom of the fourteenth; the next day, 46,000 watched him score one run and drive in the other run as Bush shut out the Reds 2–0. That week the Cubs closed to within two games of first place. No one was booing Kiki anymore.[38]

The pennant race was so wide open that Judge Landis invited Bill Veeck to the annual September planning meeting for potential World Series participants. Facing a two-week road-trip to close the season, the Cubs, who had not been in a race this late in recent memory, were undaunted. "We'll win this thing yet, no foolin'!" burbled Wilson on the train to Boston in mid-September.[39]

Bill Veeck, the dapper president of the Chicago National League Ball Club, commuted to the Wrigley Building from the exclusive DuPage County suburb of Hinsdale, southwest of Chicago along one of the rail lines leading to the Loop. Hinsdale claimed seven hundred millionaires among its small population. Veeck, a cabinetmaker's son from a small Indiana town not far from the Ohio River, was now the president of the Hinsdale Golf Club and a parishioner of Grace Episcopal Church, amid the huge Victorian and Edwardian residences of the upper and upper-middle classes. His teen-age daughter was the belle of Hinsdale; his son and namesake a bright and devoted fourteen-year-old.[40]

As Veeck drove up Ogden Avenue toward the Loop that September morn, he could take satisfaction in another successful season, the third in a row since hiring McCarthy. The most recent home stand had turned into a box-office smash; the Cubs' attendance would mount above one million for the second straight year. It was doubtful that any major league franchise had ever pressed its seating capacity to such an extent.

The continual crush of people was taxing the old methods of crowd control beyond endurance. The traditional transient band of day-hire ushers, reinforced by the Chicago police, still directed foot traffic and steered customers to their seats. But the Wilson-Young riot, or a chaotic sellout crowd that hopelessly snarled the park one Sunday afternoon, or both, may have been the trigger that convinced Wrigley and Veeck that they should listen to the sales pitch of Andy Frain, the persistent twenty-three-year-old from the Back of the Yards neighborhood. Out went the tobacco-chewing riffraff, hired from day to day, who might pick the customers' pockets, take bribes, or help themselves to the best seats. In came Frain's men in snappy blue-and-gold uniforms that were soon a fixture at Wrigley Field, an indispensable element of the franchise that worked.[41]

The Andy Frains, 125 strong, were a spectacle unto themselves:

They are adorned in brilliant uniforms[,] and the officers are clothed even as a general in the Mexican army. They form a square around the base lines at the conclusion of the game, keeping fans off the diamond. If a spectator is overcome they quell disturbances and, in general, look after the welfare of the patrons.[42]

At the center of it, coordinating the ushers and the police, overseeing the removal of bleachers and the addition of ladies' restrooms, negotiating contracts, handling the press, was Veeck. After nearly a decade in the job, he had become the consummate baseball executive, the indispensable linchpin and intermediary between the baseball people and Wrigley. He managed to personify professionalism and authority in Wrigley's overwhelming shadow, brisk without rudeness, dignified without stuffiness.

There had been no career guide for this self-made lord of baseball. Dropping out of school before his teens, he worked successively as a "printer's devil," copy boy, and reporter. In his twenties, he moved from his hometown paper to the *Louisville Courier-Journal*, then to the Windy City, where he worked for the *Chicago Inter-Ocean* and finally the *Chicago Evening American* in the fast-developing field of sports reporting, serving the urban middle-class readers that newspapers wanted. As "Bill Bailey," he became a popular and thoughtful observer of Chicago's sporting scene. Early in his career with the *American*, he filed the front-page story on the fabled "Merkle boner" at the Polo Grounds. He also distinguished himself as a poker player in late-night combat against his fellow writers.[43]

It was a wonderful time to be young and a Chicago sportswriter. Lardner, Fullerton, Crusinberry were his sportswriting colleagues; Carl Sandburg, a newsman for the *Daily News,* was writing the lines that would capture their Chicago: "Stormy, husky, brawling / City of the Big Shoulders." When Veeck began covering baseball, Frank Chance's mighty Cubs were still the team to beat in the National League; as that aggregation aged and declined, the Federal League unleashed its threat to major league baseball's monopoly. When all the wheeling and dealing was finished, Charles Weeghman, the owner of the Federal League's Chicago Whales and builder of the ballpark that became Wrigley Field, emerged as the new owner of the Cubs, and Bill Veeck had himself an invaluable education in the business of baseball. At one point Veeck even looked into purchasing a minor league franchise. By the time of the Sox-Giants World Series of 1917, he was the Chicago representative of the Baseball Writers Associa-

My Dad the Sportswriter

tion, and his smooth handling of the press box and wire service arrangements attracted favorable notice.[44]

Weeghman, who had already shouldered the strains of the Federal League adventure and the cost of building the new park, had to sell more and more of his Cub stock to other wealthy Chicagoans to survive. William Wrigley Jr. was one of them. By the late teens, Wrigley was noticeably more involved in Cubs' affairs than the other stockholders.[45]

At some point this involvement brought Wrigley into contact with "Bill Bailey." Mr. and Mrs. Wrigley included Veeck in a group of baseball writers they invited to their Pasadena mansion for dinner during spring training in 1918. It turned out to be Bill Veeck's big break.[46]

It was a tumultuous time all over the world, and no less for baseball. The U.S. entry into World War I had placed the 1918 season in jeopardy. Many players were subject to the draft—notably the Cubs' new acquisition, thirty-game-winning Grover Alexander. The Phillies had discarded him precisely because of the draft risk.

At the Wrigleys' dinner, Veeck succinctly analyzed the franchise while ingratiating himself with Mrs. Wrigley. In Cub legend, Veeck's take induced a challenge from Wrigley to try to do better. (Charles Weeghman was still officially president, and probably the majority stockholder, until the next November.) Whatever the case, Alexander was soon thereafter drafted, but the Cubs took the pennant in a war-shortened season, winning 84 of 129 games.

Veeck's next baseball tutorial came when the Cubs and the Red Sox went on strike before game 5. The strike fizzled quickly, papered over by a compromise with the owners' representatives. Babe Ruth performed his last great pitching feat, throttling the Cubs with a 29⅔ consecutive-scoreless-inning string. Boston took the series, four games to two, but the incident was an early warning of baseball's festering labor-management problems. In due course Veeck would be involved more directly.

While the series lasted, Bill Bailey was evidently still a newspaperman. But his ability to criticize the Cubs' policies fairly having already attracted the attention of William Wrigley, a couple of months later, Wrigley's backing resulted in a career change for Veeck: he was named vice president and treasurer of the Cubs at the same time that Fred Mitchell, the Cubs' pennant-winning manager, became president. It was an unusual arrangement, a reporter and a manager running the business side of a franchise, and within days, the Cubs learned that league rules forbade a manager from attending owners' meetings. Within days, then, the brand-new baseball man Veeck was the Cub executive representing the franchise at the December 1918 baseball owners' meeting.[47]

All this time Wrigley was becoming more and more involved in Cub affairs, so it was probably the gum king's idea in early July 1919 that Veeck replace Mitchell as president of the Cubs, with Mitchell remaining field manager. The whole process was probably facilitated by the opinion of one of the Cubs' co-owners, the advertising genius Albert Lasker, who would later take credit for recruiting Wrigley to the Cubs and at that point may have been the actual majority owner of the franchise. Lasker, the man whose campaigns had virtually created the Palmolive and Sunkist brands, among others, had sized up Veeck as a "very high kind of man."[48]

One of Veeck's first problems as the head of operations was what to do with Lee Magee, a second baseman that Veeck had helped the Cubs pick up in June 1919, about a month before he became president. At some point, probably helped by the legion of contacts developed during his reporting days, Veeck learned that Magee had helped the infamous Hal Chase fix ballgames when the two ballplayers were teammates in Cincinnati the year before. Over the winter of 1919–20, Veeck rid himself of the problem by simply dropping Magee from the roster, even though he was in the middle of a two-year contract. No other club moved to pick him up.

Magee, correctly sensing that he had been blackballed, sued the Cubs for breach of contract. The trial took place in federal court in Cincinnati in June 1920. Veeck testified that Magee had confessed to him, and he also produced a canceled check Magee had made out to a gambler. John Heydler, the president of the National League, corroborated Veeck's testimony. The jury settled for the Cubs within minutes.[49]

Veeck and Heydler, acting in concert, had in effect banned Magee from baseball. (Chase, with less fanfare, likewise never played again in the big leagues.) If more baseball executives had acted as decisively when confronted with credible evidence of gambling, the sport might not have faced the crisis that now loomed. In Chicago, just ten miles to the south, the Lee Magee fiasco was about to be repeated on a scale that the sport would never forget.

My Dad the Sportswriter

Veeck had his own small but essential role in this baseball *degringolade*. In early September 1920 he received several untraceable phone calls and telegrams warning that an upcoming Cub game had been fixed by gamblers. With rumors everywhere, Veeck decided to release the hard evidence of the telegrams and pledged cooperation with the state's attorney. To throw off the oddsmakers, he had the Cub manager, Fred Mitchell, bench the next scheduled starting pitcher, a journeyman named Claude Hendrix, and start Grover Alexander in his place. Hendrix's career was terminated as surely as Lee Magee's.[50]

Charles Comiskey could have learned a thing or two from the young Cub president. As Veeck may well have expected, the Cook County state's attorney soon had a grand jury delving into all aspects of gambling and baseball in Chicago, including some fascinating information trickling out about Comiskey's White Sox. Claude Hendrix's penny ante scheme was forgotten. The rock Veeck had kicked became an avalanche of revelations and counterrevelations that fell on organized baseball like a slag heap. The Black Sox entered history.

There were few winners in the scandal; Bill Veeck was one. The American League president, Ban Johnson, and Charles Comiskey, the White Sox owner, both busily tried to undercut the other and never recovered their lost prestige. As the crisis deepened, Veeck and the Cubs led a bloc of franchises that threatened to secede from baseball unless a new and powerful post, that of commissioner of baseball, was created to forestall disasters like the Black Sox. The Lasker Plan, as it was called, had been developed by Wrigley and Veeck's influential colleague, Albert Lasker.[51]

After the opposition, outmaneuvered and outvoted, gave in, Veeck played his next card. He and the Cub owners had just the man for the job, an irascible Chicago federal judge, a Cub fan of long standing (and former Hoosier, just like Veeck). Judge Kenesaw Mountain Landis would personify the institution of baseball for a generation to come and beyond, beginning with the summer of 1921, when he electrified the world with his harsh, summary edict against the "eight men out." The new commissioner set up office on Michigan Avenue, less than a mile from the Wrigley Building, behind an office door that read "BASEBALL" in uncompromising, black letters.[52] He continued patronizing Cub games. Soon Landis, his chin resting on the box-seat rail, was a familiar figure all over the major leagues.

The debacle on the South Side did nothing to improve the North Siders, despite Alexander's return from overseas. Veeck's early Cub years involved the hiring and firing of sundry managers and the establishment of the Cubs' spring training camp at William Wrigley's Santa Catalina Island, twenty-six miles across the sea from the California coast. Fred Mitchell was the manager during the Cubs' last spring in Pasadena in spring 1920; in 1921 Johnny Evers led the athletes across the San Pedro Channel for their first tentative stay on Catalina. By 1922 Bill Killefer, Grover Alexander's old batterymate, was overseeing the island visit, which continued as an annual event for the next three decades. Thanks to William Wrigley's relentless spending, it was held in surroundings that became more and more sumptuous.

Killefer lasted 3½ seasons, usually keeping the club around .500, but by midseason 1925 he too was gone. After the brief and unsuccessful experiment with Rabbit Maranville as player-manager, Veeck rode the train in September to southern Indiana to confer with Joe McCarthy about becoming the Cub manager. McCarthy signed his Cub contract the next month, accompanied by Wrigley's promise to spend a million on the Cubs.

Soon the team, reenergized by the new Cub stars McCarthy had sized up in his American Association days, was on the rise. Veeck—despite his new status "Bill," not "William," to all—continued to represent the Cubs before the public and within the industry with his urbane, self-assured persona. A rumor would be swatted down with a brisk, knowing, "Not a chance. Not a chance." During McCarthy's first spring, a reporter was foolish enough to ask Veeck what was the matter with the Cubs. "I didn't know there was anything the matter with them," Veeck replied icily. Then he softened, giving his questioner a list of improvements that potential customers could read about the next day.[53]

During the Veeck regime there were no holdouts, no public wranglings over salaries. More than thirty years after Veeck's death, Philip Wrigley said, "If I could find another Bill Veeck I'd put him in there in a minute," and he was referring to Bill Sr. Years later, the better-known Bill Jr. was asked where he had acquired his flair for public relations. The younger Veeck replied simply, "My father was a sportswriter." Although in Rube Foster's Bronzeville neighborhood, Veeck was blamed for the segregationist attitudes of the Cubs, the frank hero worship of his son, a leader in desegregating baseball, suggests that William Sr. did not teach bigotry at home.[54]

Veeck's public relations chores shaded into administration and promotion. He brokered the deals once McCarthy or Jack Doyle, the Cubs' head scout, made their recommendations, and he handled the contractual negotiations. He administered the Cubs' sweeping innovations: the wildly popular ladies days; the open-radio policy, whereby up to five or more stations all broadcast Cub home games; the introduction of Andy Frain's corps of professional ushers; and the building of Wrigley Field's upper deck and all other physical improvements.

In the early 1930s, Arch Ward of the *Tribune* asked Veeck to pitch major league owners with Ward's proposal for the inaugural All-Star Game. "Great. Let's go through with it," said Veeck without hesitation. After the success of the first All-Star Game, Veeck also grappled with the lull in attendance during the "dog days" of summer, before the pennant races really heated up. As a solution, he proposed a scheme for interleague play. Sixty-five years went by, and the Bills *père* and *fils* were in their graves, before baseball adopted his vision.[55]

One day in the early 1920s Veeck was visited by a pair of underfinanced young businessmen who asked him how much it would cost their struggling professional football team to rent Cubs Park each Sunday in the fall. Although pro football was hardly even a minor league sport in 1921, Veeck did not laugh at the earnest young fellows or send them on their way. William Wrigley's ballpark stood empty each autumn, after all, while Amos Alonzo Stagg's University of Chicago Maroons drew vast crowds on several Saturdays. College football, in fact, was in its golden age, almost rivaling baseball in popularity, with coaches like Stagg and Knute Rockne and stars such as Notre Dame Four Horsemen and Red Grange of the Fighting Illini.

But the blue-collar class (and many others) still worked Saturdays in the days before the New Deal and unionization; a professional football team might pull them in on Sunday, their lone day off. "Fifteen percent of the gross gate receipts," Veeck said crisply. "And we keep the profits from the concessions."[56]

One of the visitors, George Halas, piped up, "But we keep the profits from the program sales." Veeck shook on the deal. In about seventy-five seconds, by Halas's estimate, pro football was established at Addison and Clark, where it would remain for another fifty years. In good time the world would know Halas's outfit as the Chicago Bears, the "Monsters of the Midway," and their league as the National Football League. Halas would perfect the split-T formation and initiate Grange, Nagurski, Luckman, Lujack, Sayers, and Butkus into football greatness at Wrigley Field— still, after all these years, the site that has hosted more NFL games than any other.

The arrangement stabilized quickly, to the point that the "skin" of the infield was sodded each fall to create a real football field. The trouble was worth it. Red Grange's Bear debut at Cubs Park in November 1925 created such intense interest that Halas was tempted to charge a one-time, special-event premium, World Series style. But after Veeck counseled the young entrepreneur to think about the long run, not a quick killing, Halas gave up on the idea. No one regretted the decision. The debut game pulled in no fewer than 38,000 fans, as large a crowd as the Cubs had attracted on Opening Day, and far more than the 5,000 or 6,000 attendance the Bears had drawn their first few seasons at the park. By arrangement with the Bears, Grange earned twelve thousand dollars from the game alone, a scoreless tie with the Cardinals of the South Side.[57]

Veeck had amply demonstrated that he could learn on the job, adjust to changing circumstances, exploit opportunities as they arose, innovate, and take daring chances. Hiring a career minor leaguer as manager had been virtually without precedent, a stroke that stole a march on the rest of the major leagues. He had seen the potential of the NFL decades before it captured the country's fascination. His team abounded with talent; the stands were full, or as near to full as anyone could have dreamed. And yet, as Veeck took up his spot looking over Michigan Avenue that morning, one could claim with some accuracy that Veeck and his boss were essentially running a storefront operation dependent on the cash infusions of its patron.

For all the hoopla and panache of the past few years, the long-term significance of the standings Veeck saw in his *Tribune* on September 14, 1928, was the name at the top of the National League column: the St. Louis Cardinals, gamely fighting off their rivals from the nation's two largest cities. After decades of futility, the Cards—a franchise with a budget and

My Dad the Sportswriter

a fan base minuscule compared to that of their principal rivals—were on the verge of taking their second pennant in three years. After their world's title in 1926, they had abruptly shed the franchise mainstay—Rogers Hornsby, a genuine superstar of the modern game—yet actually increased their wins from 89 in 1926 to 92 in 1927. Now they were back on top of the league again.

Baseball was too much of a sport to be a business: that was the first part of William Wrigley's famous aphorism, but in St. Louis, Branch Rickey and Sam Breadon were nothing but business. They were running a whole network of minor league teams, a "chain," it was called, completely bypassing the middleman—the traditional independent minor league that earned its keep by developing players and selling them to the big leagues. Rickey, his intellect honed at a private college and at the University of Michigan's law school, bought cheap, sold dear, and deployed a virtual army of scouts who scoured the land for young talent. Through rigorous, penetrating thinking, he was applying the techniques of the modern corporation to sport. The imperious Wrigley didn't seem impressed. In July 1929 he pronounced, "We have two minor league clubs now. That's plenty."[58]

Wrigley and Veeck combined had but a fraction of Rickey's education. Wrigley had founded a modern corporation that would survive into the twenty-first century, and he dreamed dreams as large as anyone's. He delegated well to Veeck—indeed, few public partnerships have lasted so long, so smoothly. Yet the Cubs' business plan seemed wedded to the traditional process of sniffing around the minors for potential bargains. Their most successful open-market transaction, the deal for Cuyler, had been a windfall, a distress sale. McCarthy and the Cubs' doughty chief scout, Jack Doyle, excelled in the old ways of procuring talent, but on their own these two authentic baseball masterminds, regardless of their widespread, long-cultivated network of contacts, could hardly keep up with Rickey's faceless corporate army of talent hunters. In fact, McCarthy's place in history would be secured when he became the "push-button manager" at the top of just such a chain—one that combined Rickey's acumen with pockets as deep as Wrigley's.

To be sure, the steps taken by Wrigley and Veeck, and their henchmen, McCarthy and Doyle, would propel the Chicago National League Ball Club through one of baseball history's longest stretches of winning baseball—fourteen consecutive first-division finishes through 1939, and five pennants through 1945, if no world title. But the Cardinals' log for the same period shows eight pennants and five World Series championships. Wrigley knew gum, and Veeck knew administration and networking, but Rickey knew baseball.

The Cardinals' 1928 showing was like a mere cloud on the distant horizons of Lake Michigan; the Cubs themselves, after all, had been down and out only three years earlier, and now they were in the hunt with two weeks to go in the race. Who could say the Cardinals' way was better? And however things turned out in the current season, Veeck and his boss were working on a plan for next year that wouldn't require putting another nickel into the farm—though many nickels would exit the club's bank account.

Veeck, the old sportswriter, unfolded his *Tribune* on September 14 to read about how his club's unexpected late-season surge was progressing in the East. The Cubs, after a successful home stand, were squarely back in the pennant race, just two games from first place.

"PHONE BILLS REVEAL RACE TIP SCANDAL," shouted the headline on the front page of the Trib's sports section. But it was the subhead that was important to Veeck: "Name Hornsby, McGraw among Turf Clients."

It was serious business, all right. Rogers Hornsby, the player-manager of the Boston Braves, and John McGraw, the manager of the New York Giants, had been singled out as parties called long distance by C. E. Allen, a jockey at Arlington Park, a horse-racing track just northwest of Chicago. The paper reproduced a photostat of Illinois Bell's letter dunning Allen for the calls—and listing McGraw and Hornsby as two Allen had been calling. The implication was that a jockey would contact well-known bettors like McGraw and Hornsby only to fix races.[59]

Veeck forgot about the pennant race for the moment. He and William Wrigley had had a longtime interest in obtaining Hornsby for the Cubs, going back at least to the fall of 1926. If the Rajah had been receiving betting information from a race jockey, he was participating in a scheme to defraud the betting public—a potential criminal matter. Even if no crime was involved, there was still Judge Landis to deal with. He had long hankered to add racetrack betting to his long list of punishable offenses. The owners—with common sense on their side for once—resisted Landis's designs. Such a rule would be no more enforceable than Prohibition, not to mention that trackside betting was legal in many locations (including the Chicago area).

Reporters scuttled over to Landis's offices to learn what he thought about the developing story. "I don't care to talk about it," the commissioner snapped. "Look it up in your rule books."

Hornsby, in Boston preparing for the Cubs-Braves series, sent a wire to Chicago. "I don't know Jockey Allen, wouldn't know him if he was to walk into this office," Hornsby's message said. "If anybody called me from Chicago, that's something I can't help."[60]

Behind Landis's focus on racetrack betting there was a sensible insight: such betting could easily become compulsive, especially among young, often single, ballplayers with large salaries and time on their hands. A debt-ridden ballplayer could be one on the way to fixing ballgames—the issue that had made Landis, and could just as easily break him. Landis and Hornsby, two individuals who disliked compromise, were fated to spend years sparring over the issue. Once, after the 1929 crash Hornsby supposedly responded to Landis's hectoring on racetrack betting by pointing out its resemblance to playing the stock market. The commissioner, a vigorous buyer and seller of stocks, lapsed into momentary silence.[61]

There matters stood as the *Tribune* muckraked through C. E. Allen's affairs. Soon it became clear that Allen had nothing to do with the calls: a professional tipster had listed the phone in Allen's name, probably to gain credibility for the racing information he wanted to sell to bettors.

Hornsby had wired, if not the whole truth, enough of the truth. At best he was a sales prospect for a shady character; at worst he was a participant in a bunko scheme. Either scenario still left him in Landis's sights under the "conduct detrimental to baseball" clause.[62] The episode was publicity that Hornsby did not need. For two years the great hitter had been at the center of one negative story after another: traded twice and unexpectedly; embroiled in an interminable squabble over whether he could own stock in one of his old teams while playing for another; sued by a bookmaker for $92,000, a daunting sum in the 1920s.

It was all disconcerting for someone who had had his run of the diamond for so long: six batting titles, 1920–25 inclusive; the highest season batting average in modern baseball history; the first forty-homer season in National League history; a world championship in his second year as a manager (with the aid of Alexander's memorable performance in game 6). But Hornsby had become the league's gypsy star. "Go on, stop your kiddin'," he protested in the fall of 1927 at the news that he—the Giants' captain, and acting manager for several weeks that summer—had been traded for the second time in twelve months. That trade took him from the well-financed, contending Giants to the penurious, lackluster Boston Braves (and away from his fellow horse player, John McGraw). Possibly that was the Giants' motive for disposing of Hornsby; a consistent string of gambling scandals and rumors of scandals was a long-standing feature of the McGraw regime. McGraw's interest in the horses was notorious, extending to a silent partnership with his employer in a Havana racetrack.[63]

In Boston, Hornsby was named Braves' manager only weeks into the season. He ignored the whispering that he had connived for the job and set out to demolish the idea that he couldn't hit and manage at the same time. (His batting average had dropped sharply while he managed the Cardinals to the pennant in 1926.) He got half of it right. His batting average for 1928 soared to .387, giving him his seventh batting title, but he couldn't duplicate the '26 Cardinals feats with the '28 Braves. In fact, they hadn't yet won their fortieth game by late August. But nobody blamed Hornsby, and in early September Judge Emil Fuchs, the Braves' president, awarded Hornsby a brand-new three-year contract that the underfinanced, underattended Braves couldn't possibly afford.

It wouldn't be the last time that Rogers Hornsby made a club owner do foolish things.

Bill Veeck shouldn't have been surprised to learn that William Wrigley, approaching age seventy, still fancied himself a baseball executive. In the early days of the century, back when he was still an up-and-coming businessman, the young entrepreneur had sponsored a team of amateurs in the city's thriving West Side Prairie Leagues. He dubbed them the "Wrigley Nips" and outfitted them in green uniforms with red lettering. This younger Wrigley, relatively poor by tycoon standards, nonetheless held court on vacant lots somewhere in the vast and relatively undeveloped tracts at the city's edge—only he sat on a box rather than in one, as one wag recalled. He knew each player's name, and he rejoiced publicly when his men did something spectacular, as when the Nips' Lefty Brabbets struck out the side with the bases loaded one day about 1906. At the seventh-inning stretch everyone in the crowd got a free sample of something called Nips, evidently a forerunner of Wrigley's eventual chewing gums.[64]

Wrigley's approach had changed little by the time he took over the Cubs in his late fifties. The big difference, besides the amount of money he had at his disposal, was that the culture of professional baseball proved a bit opaque to the master salesman. Once Wrigley overheard a player predicting that he wouldn't have any luck against that day's opposing pitcher. "I thought that a terrible offense," Wrigley recalled several years later. "I had the man released." Local legend has it that on days when the owner couldn't attend spring training practices at Catalina, he scrutinized the sessions via a telescope installed at his mountaintop mansion. Any player giving an effort deemed insufficient received a summons to explain himself. Whether the current field manager was consulted is unrecorded; one imagines that McCarthy brooked no such interference, with possible implications for the pair's future relationship.[65]

Several years of prodigious swapping and purchasing gained Wrigley the reputation among NL owners as an easy mark for dumping over-the-hill material. McCarthy's hiring in 1925 didn't end the amateur hour completely. Over the winter Wrigley purchased Lefty O'Doul's contract as a present for his new manager. But McCarthy's specialty was judging American Association talent: he preferred Hack Wilson, the burly fellow he, Jimmy Burke, and Bill Veeck had heisted from John McGraw, as his new outfielder. O'Doul was sent packing to the Hollywood Stars.[66]

On the South Side, Charles Comiskey still spent freely for prospects. In the summer of 1927 he laid out $123,000 for a young PCL shortstop. Within weeks, Wrigley announced from Los Angeles that he, too, had made a lucrative offer for a young PCL shortstop. Apparently, the Cubs' owner had appointed himself as an acting scout during one of his California stays. But once again, the gum tycoon had forgotten to check with his baseball operations first. Veeck and McCarthy already had the young shortstop they wanted, another American Association graduate, the twenty-year-old Woody English—and he cost some $40,000 less than Wrigley's choice.[67]

It was not that McCarthy, in spite of his long run of successful finds from the American Association, was an infallible judge of talent. The Cub manager had to give up on Earl Webb, a slugging outfielder who gave him a sensational half season in 1927 but little else afterward. While Webb faded from the Cub scene, Lefty O'Doul, hitting robustly, showed up in a Philadelphia Phillies uniform. Webb too, with lesser acclaim than O'Doul, was able to work his way back to the big leagues after McCarthy had axed him, even setting a major league record with 67 doubles in 1931. O'Doul, who couldn't even make Mac's spring training cut, decisively outdid Webb with two batting titles (one of them after Wrigley's death), topping out at .398 in 1929.

The position closest to Wrigley's box seat was the third baseman's spot, where McCarthy's AA contacts didn't solve the long-running sore. He spent 1928 maneuvering three light-hitting AA products around in his infield.

Wrigley watched it all up close, no telescope required. By the late 1920s his day-to-day existence basically centered on two passions, his ball club and his beautiful Pacific island. Passing out cigars after Cub home runs— his top-of-the-line twenty-dollar boater was much too valuable to toss into the heaps with the common folks' discards—he attended nearly every home game in his box seat near the Cub dugout. For his 1927 stay at Catalina, WMAQ had begun providing a special telegraphic hook-up so he could listen to Hal Totten's broadcasts, seventeen hundred miles from the station's five-hundred-watt transmitter. As the Cubs took the league lead in July 1927, the telegrapher at Avalon reported back to Chicago: "Mr. Wrigley very pleased and lately smokes box of cigars during short time of game. Must be getting excited." Wrigley visited Catalina again in July 1928, surely consuming at least as many cigars each Cub game, and when he returned in late July he was in New York to watch his team at the Polo Grounds.[68]

Wrigley had one more player transaction left in him, and it was a doozy. His fellow amateur-owner-enthusiast, Emil Fuchs, was paying the league's biggest salary—Rogers Hornsby's—for one of its most hopeless franchises. The Braves had put together one winning season in the past thirteen years, and that was back in 1921. Even the team's most stalwart fans weren't coming out to Braves Field very often.

In late August, Hornsby somehow managed to wangle his contract extension from the beleaguered Fuchs.[69] Within a few days of that, the C. E. Allen story made the superstar manager's need for a raise more plausible, and then another and another. A few days later, Bill Veeck, representing the almost unlimited wealth and ambition of William Wrigley, suddenly showed up at Braves Field.

Veeck was fresh from the World Series planning meeting in New York, where he had met with Fuchs.[70] There were phone calls back to Wrigley in Chicago, and probably the greatest row of Wrigley and Veeck's long partnership.[71] It was a crucial turning point for the Chicago National League Ball Club. Wrigley, almost seventy and still ambitious, knew that, by definition, the greatest right-handed anything was unlikely to come his way again. Veeck, a much younger man with a longer time horizon, might have been willing to search for the second- or third-greatest hitter, one without Hornsby's personal and professional shortcomings. There were words between the owner and his chief executive. Finally the tycoon won out by giving Veeck a small concession, now that he had the greatest right-handed hitter in hand: he would never try anything like this again.

Veeck arrived at Braves Field shortly before game time and immediately huddled with McCarthy. McCarthy certainly knew of Wrigley's previous attempts to acquire the Rajah, nor, after three years in the National League, was he unfamiliar with Hornsby's game. McCarthy could get positively talkative explaining the mathematics of good bats versus poor gloves (although he was never able to square theory with application at third base). In the world according to Joe McCarthy, Rogers Hornsby was a dream player: an adequate defender with batting skills that few human beings could equal.[72]

That was only the good part in the Faustian bargain the Cubs were about to make. For one thing, upon joining the Cubs Hornsby would be an ex-manager once again, an arrangement that had turned out poorly two years running. For another thing, Hornsby had won a world title with the help of McCarthy's reject Grover Cleveland Alexander, and a few months earlier he had also taken the scalp of a busher manager (actually, a former college baseball coach), who had lasted only a few weeks in Boston after Hornsby the player arrived.

While Veeck, who had just threatened to quit, and McCarthy, who probably should have, huddled, the manager of the Boston Braves strolled over to greet Veeck. Within earshot of at least one reporter, Hornsby let the Cub official know that he would enjoy playing for McCarthy.[73]

The get-together was quite irregular. Technically, Veeck was tampering with a player from another team by even participating in the conversation. Hornsby, for his part, was ultra vires. A field manager had no authority to deal with other clubs, and the Braves had a general manager, the old Cub Fred Mitchell. Officially, he was in no way a free agent eligible to offer his services to the highest bidder. Unofficially, he was a superstar with a lot of clout, and he was using it.

After making his offer, Hornsby returned to the Braves' dugout, and the ballgame got under way. In the top of the second, after Hartnett lifted a high pop into shallow right field, Veeck was able to watch another example of Hornsby's best-documented defensive weakness. Hornsby barely moved for Hartnett's ball. The Braves' right fielder, playing deep and over to the left for the pull-hitting Hartnett, had to make a desperate run for the ball, and he dropped it. The scorer, who had seen this kind of thing before, ruled it a hit.[74]

The Cubs took the game, 8–3, prolonging their pennant chances one more day. Veeck left with the Cubs that night for New York, where the pennant drive came to grief—but not before they had played spoiler to the chances of John McGraw's Giants. Wilson went 7 for 8 in three games against the manager who had given up on him. Hartnett grabbed a Giants' base runner on a crucial play and held him until the ball arrived. The man was out, and so were the Giants for the year. McGraw was said to have hung a photograph of the play on his office wall.[75]

By World Series time—this year it was the Cardinals for a quick four-and-out against the Yanks—rumors about Hornsby and the Cubs were everywhere. The implications mesmerized everyone—adding one of the biggest bats in the majors; patching the American Association infield; placing the capstone on three years of increasing success.

But that was only the half of it—the tangible half. Hornsby the superstar, already enshrined as one of the greatest ever, was every bit as controversial as Cobb or Ruth had ever been. His arrival in Chicago would mean no turning back, raising the stakes. Chicago baseball would have its first

My Dad the Sportswriter

front-runner since the doomed White Sox teams of the late teens. McCarthy's men would never again be a carefree young pickup team chasing the "haves": with Hornsby, they would become the favorites, the heavies, the booed.

Then there was Hornsby the man. Was he an "underminer," as the term of the day had it? Would he respect McCarthy, the man from the bushes? The year before, while Hornsby was running the Giants during McGraw's absence, Fred Lindstrom, himself a future Hall of Famer, had delivered a memorable put-down to his great but flawed teammate: "When you put down that bat, you're a detriment to any team." (Among other sins, Hornsby was trying to alter Lindstrom's batting stance.) Then again, not so long ago Wilson had been another refugee from McGraw's regime, and most Chicagoans seemed willing to give Hornsby and his lofty lifetime batting average another chance.[76]

The negotiations between the Cubs and the Braves dragged on through October and into November. Finally, Braves officials—including Fred Mitchell, the former Cub manager who had given up the Cubs' presidency for Veeck—traveled to McCarthy's home in Buffalo. Veeck came east from Chicago. Mitchell seemed more than willing to queer the deal. "Those players are terrible," he would say of each combination Veeck brought up, and he may have been right. Then Mitchell would counteroffer. Once Veeck replied: "I'd lose my job if I approved that deal." The haggling started all over.[77]

As Veeck recalled it, he called Wrigley back in Chicago at lunchtime to tell him the deal was in trouble. Wrigley listened and then asked, "Well, you want Hornsby, don't you?"

Veeck loyally agreed. Then Wrigley asked, "Joe wants Hornsby, doesn't he?"

"Sure, he does," Veeck replied.

"Well, I want Hornsby too," Wrigley told him. "Let's get him."[78]

Whatever Veeck's actual thoughts, an hour, five Cubs, and $150,000 of Wrigley's money later, Hornsby was in fact a Cub. The transaction dwarfed the only comparable deal in baseball history, the $137,000 the Red Sox were said to have received for Babe Ruth in 1920.[79] In 1917 Grover Alexander and Bill Killefer together had been worth just two nondescript players and $55,000. That was not to say that anyone considered Hornsby the equal of Ruth or even Alexander; it was to say his acquisition was worth it in Bill Wrigley's eyes, an insurance policy on that elusive world championship that the elderly man desired so strongly.

Within a week Hornsby, flanked by Veeck and Wrigley, was in William Wrigley's office to sign his 1929 contract. He would enjoy playing at Wrigley Field, he told everyone. The white-shirt background of the jury box had never bothered him the way it did a lot of other hitters (he might have added, anyone who couldn't hit .400). Come to think of it, he concluded, that explained why Cub pitchers were so tough at home.

Having duly informed some of his most important new teammates exactly how he judged their accomplishments, Hornsby next donned a Cub jersey and, with a big smile, posed for photographers. Then he departed for his newly purchased minifarm near St. Louis, where he planned to raise bluegrass for ballparks and golf courses. William Wrigley's name came up as a potential customer.[80]

Back in Chicago, they could talk of nothing but another "Murderers' Row," a blatant borrowing from the First City's phrase for Babe Ruth and associates. If the Cubs could claim no Ruth or even a single left-handed slugger, the sheer depth of Cuyler, Wilson, Hornsby, Stephenson, and Hartnett compared favorably with the Yankees.[81] The pennant that Hornsby predicted would come in due course, but the rest of the story would not be so pat. William Wrigley would die without his world's championship. So would Bill Veeck. McCarthy, then Wilson, and finally Hornsby would all be ordered to remove their Cub uniforms. There would be bizarre World Series humiliations, fallings-out between old comrades, immortal deeds and records, sackings, near misses, fistfights, scandal, a shooting, vaudeville, high comedy, low drama.

But first the Cubs had to prepare for spring training.

6 | To Paradise and Back

In Xanadu did Kubla Khan
A stately pleasure-dome decree.
—Samuel Taylor Coleridge, "Kubla Khan"

"Murderers' Row," a hopeful comparison of the Cubs to the Yankees of 1927, was probably a bad choice of words in a city with Chicago's reputation. Chicagoans venturing to other parts of the country and abroad learned that their city was becoming a byword for mayhem and violence. At a 1928 international disarmament conference in far-off Geneva, Switzerland, a Soviet envoy saw fit to joke about the threat "Chicago gangsters" posed to world peace.[1]

The scene on North Clark Street the frigid morning of February 14, 1929, was one that might have shocked the most hardened Bolshevik. The Cubs' pitchers, catchers, and rookies were scheduled to leave the Dearborn Street Station for Catalina early that afternoon. Hundreds of well-wishers and photographers thronged the headhouse. A major attraction was the sight of Mr. and Mrs. Leo Hartnett, a married couple of just a few days who were going to spend their honeymoon on the isle with a smile.[2]

But the news of the morning was already buzzing through the station. That morning, in a garage some blocks north of the Loop, not halfway to Wrigley Field, men in police uniforms had coolly lined up seven members of Bugs Moran's North Side crime ensemble against a wall. There they cut them down with "Chicago pianos"—Thompson machine guns—and left their riddled bodies lying for the real police to discover.

The consensus, never proven, was that Al Capone had made his endgame move to eliminate organized competition on the North Side, the last part of town still beyond his control. (A few months later, Capone was said to have personally silenced his own assassins by getting them drunk at a banquet, tying them up, and bludgeoning them to death with a baseball bat in front of several dozen witnesses. Who needed Murderers' Row?)

The massacre went down shortly after 10:00 a.m., three hours before the Cubs' Santa Fe Railroad special pulled out for the West Coast at 1:15. By then, the news must have raced through the crowd and into the Cubs' Pullman cars. The train chugged westward through the bitter cold of the upper Midwest in the coming days, and on into the Great American Desert. At each stop the players and the coaching staff could follow the reports of the grisly episode and the manhunt being flashed coast to coast.

At the first stop, though, a crowd of more than a hundred boys and men at the little downstate town of Streator called out a more urgent question as the Santa Fe train stopped in downstate Illinois: could they see Hack and Gabby? Leo—who one day would have his own brush with Capone—had to step out and explain to the lads that only the pitchers and catchers were aboard.[3]

If one Cub were likely to resent Wilson's popularity, it should have been Hartnett. Long before there was any McCarthy or Wilson, the big, hearty catcher had been the club's young star, its first real slugger, autograph target, and Ladies Day favorite, and Alexander's personal choice as receiver. Then came McCarthy, and Hartnett watched as the new man eliminated, part by part, the team he had known, not even stopping at Alex himself. By 1929 only Hartnett, Grimm, Heathcote, Blake, and Bush were left from Killefer's roster. But Hartnett's commitment, his intensity, his on-the-field generalship flourished in the new, winning environment. Grimm, still clowning, mugging, and strumming his banjo in the club-house, may have been "Der Kaptink," but it was Hartnett who strapped on his catcher's equipment each hot and exhausting day to serve as McCarthy's actual alter ego on the field. Thus McCarthy already had two understudies as potential managers, and in fact one or another of this trio would oversee every pennant the Cubs would claim through the end of the century and beyond.

Wilson, of course, could compete with no one this side of Rabbit Maranville as a future manager. But what if a star bigger than Wilson, and an heir apparent more qualified than either Hartnett or Grimm, joined the club? On February 22, several days after Hartnett and the rest of the first group reached far-off Catalina, Murderers' Row itself assembled at the

Dearborn station. The heroes of the recent past—Wilson, Cuyler, Stephenson, English—were forgotten as the fans mobbed a new idol who hadn't yet delivered a base hit for the team: the Rajah. The unlovable loner had become the focus of the sporting hopes and dreams of the world's fourth-largest city.[4]

Soon the team's second Santa Fe train rolled across the great Midwest as it did every year, on the way picking up other Cubs or would-be Cubs. Each year, Charlie Grimm, banjo in hand, hopped aboard at Kansas City. On through the Rockies the train sped. As it entered the Great Basin, the temperatures rose; the players put their winter clothing away, and, with no air conditioning available, they cracked the windows of the cars. A hot southwest wind, full of alkali dust, filled the coaches. Many aboard were getting their first view of the American continent: St. Louis was still the "West" (and hard by the Deep South) as far as major league baseball was concerned. Few of those who reached the West Coast had sailed two hours on the open sea to the tiny, Magic Isle of Catalina, hovering like a purple cloud on southern California's horizon, a place where, it was said, "unkind winds never blow, snow and frost are unknown, and the rain falls only in gentle showers."[5]

A long-departed manager, Johnny Evers, had first led the Cubs across the San Pedro Channel in 1921. Although no one was left from that squad, the rituals of the passage endured on the *S.S. Catalina*, a converted Great Lakes cruiser, or her sister the *S.S. Avalon*, a ferry custom-designed for Catalina's tourist trade. Before seasickness could even set in, veterans routinely dispatched rookies on searches for the ship's bowling alley or billiard table. But any year, the veterans were as helpless as any rookie at coping with the frequently choppy waters of the San Pedro Channel. Two hours sailing the channel could waylay the stoutest soul. One seasick rookie who had won the International League batting title the year before decided that a chance at the big leagues wasn't worth it. Glassy-eyed, he stared at a canary chirping in its cage. "Wring that damned bird's neck; then shoot me," he begged anyone within earshot. "They All Get Sick," concluded a newspaper subhead summarizing one passage.[6]

Hartnett liked to put on a brave front, although he was usually one of the first to break down. Reaching shore after one ordeal, he confessed that he hadn't been sure midway if he was dead or alive. Grimm was no stronger. "One hundred and fifty dollars for a horse and buggy right now," he groaned during one rough crossing. Nearby, Pat Malone, a tender soul who had been chortling at his teammates' misery a few minutes before, was doubled over the railing himself. It was no surprise that when William Wrigley built an airstrip on Catalina, Hartnett and Malone were two of the first volunteers to take a flight from the mainland.[7]

In February 1929 the ballplayers who were still upright could look up from the main deck to the ship's bridge, where they saw something completely new. There was William Wrigley, who had met them on the mainland. Next to him was the newest member of the team, Rogers Hornsby.

No one had ever seen a hired hand accompany Mr. Wrigley to the bridge. The message was clear to everyone on board. McCarthy, waiting ahead on the island, would find out on his own.[8]

The Catalina experience each spring began Wrigley's choreographed ritual: the Cub players departing from the frigid Chicago in mid-February, gathered like dignitaries on the platform of the Pullman car, photographers and hundreds of worshipful fans in attendance. It was another leg of William Wrigley's campaign to glamorize his ball club and his resort destination in one stroke. Although John McGraw of the New York Giants had been the first to establish a semipermanent spring training site, and other teams had already moved into Florida by the early 1920s, it was William Wrigley who created an unsurpassed spring training mix of climate, scenery, and swank surroundings.[9]

The mountainous, 48,000-acre Santa Catalina Island became Wrigley's outright in 1919, the same year he took control of the Cubs. By most accounts he struck the deal before actually visiting the island and began plotting his development schemes only after he and his wife made their first visit. Ada Wrigley looked out over the majestic view their first morning there and murmured in Victorian tones, "I should like to live here." Catalina would never be the same. The peak overlooking the harbor was named Mount Ada in Mrs. Wrigley's honor.[10]

Before Wrigley's purchase, the island's only village, Avalon, was a hamlet with serious power and water shortages. Many visitors camped out in tents. Within a few years Wrigley's millions changed all that. Hundreds of new bungalows surrounded Avalon; a greatly expanded luxury hotel, the St. Catherine, arose; and the custom-built *Catalina* joined the *Avalon* in ferrying hundreds of thousands of visitors from the mainland annually. The tourists, generally summer day-trippers, disembarked at the same pier the Cubs used each February, with much of the hoopla that greeted the Cubs every February—various musical ensembles, several hundred of the island's fifteen hundred year-round residents, and perhaps the summering Mr. Wrigley.[11]

The 1929 Cubs' first sight of little Avalon was the whitewashed walls of the nearly completed Moorish-style casino (a dance hall) standing eight stories high on a promontory, a dazzling contrast to the blue shades of the sky and the water. A band played noisily as the *Catalina* pulled alongside the pier at noon, Wrigley's carillon chimed, hydroplanes roared in welcome, and seagulls wheeled overhead. McCarthy and the coaching staff did not turn out to see the debarking of the Cubs, including a smiling and expansive Rogers Hornsby. "Which one's Hornsby?" the villagers shouted; Hornsby continued to beam, even when one woman asked him to pose for her Kodak. By consensus, Hornsby was selected to drive the ballplayers and their luggage to the St. Catherine's Hotel in a rig pulled by two draft horses borrowed from a street repair project. Hornsby and his new charges passed by the little town's nearly empty Spanish-style hotels and cafés, temporarily shuttered for the Cubs' arrival.[12]

The horses balked on the way, and the players had to jump out and make their way on foot to check in at the hotel. Then it was off to the ballfield, where McCarthy awaited. Hornsby sought out his latest manager, who met him halfway and asked, "How are you, Rog?"

"Fine."

"How do you feel?"

"Great."[13]

Hornsby made sure that he was a conspicuous volunteer in that afternoon's first practice, the first regular to take the field during batting practice. After the typically brisk and well-organized session, the players and several spouses—increasingly a common sight in Catalina in February and March—had a chance to explore the village and the rest of the island. Near Avalon, in the developed section of the twenty-mile-long island, the newcomers might stroll nearly two miles of boardwalk, shop in the Spanish-style village, or examine the construction progress at the casino, with its dance floor for five hundred directly above a 1,250-seat theater, scheduled for its grand opening in May. Just outside of town travelers could visit Wrigley's year-old aviary, which would eventually include 8,000 exotic birds in 650 varieties, or board a glass-bottomed boat to observe rainbow kelp, sea urchins, and brightly colored fish.[14]

Wrigley maintained most of Catalina's interior as a nature preserve, which his visitors could reach most easily by touring car. Just outside Avalon, the island's mountain peaks, dotted with clematis and columbine, rose steeply. Further up the slopes, there were groves of flowering manzanita and dwarf live oaks, then cactus, sagebrush, and chaparral. From a higher ridge or a peak, the views were clear for hundreds of miles, the Pacific glittering to the south, west, and north; far below, near the shoreline, the water turned aquamarine, flecked with white surf crashing against the rocks. Deep, mist-filled canyons snaked through the interior, crowned by multicolored cliffs and, here and there, a small tree. Thousands of wild goats and some two thousand boars roamed the interior; by the 1930s they were joined by two herds of bison, left behind by a motion picture company after they had worked as extras in a silent movie. Here and there, at least early in the rookie-baiting season, could also be found the occasional first-time visitor, instructed by savvy veterans to bring back a few snipe for dinner. Roy Hansen, a left-handed pitcher, went down in the record books as "Snipe" (22-45 lifetime, 5.01 ERA, although he never made the cut at Catalina) by conscientiously extending his mission until after dark.[15]

Wrigley invited the ballplayers and their families on goat hunts and horse rides, and in the evenings, barbecues at his mansion overlooking the harbor. Betrotheds like the Hartnetts set their wedding dates so they could combine a honeymoon and spring training in off-season suites that Wrigley provided. These alterations in the traditional male rites of spring might have upset an old-timer like the club's chief scout, "Dirty Jack" Doyle, a survivor of the ferocious pre-1900 Baltimore Orioles, but the irascible Doyle could take some cheer in the ongoing hazing of rookies. The honeymooning Hartnett was inhibited from leaving his trademark dead fish among the rookies' personal effects, but most of the veterans were still spring-training bachelors, and they continued to torture the youngsters, if not with fish, then perhaps by lining a newcomer's pants pocket with butter or tucking a piece of rock in a bunk. Success triggered prolonged guffaws and whetted the appetite for further merriment.[16]

Catalina's semitropical wonders were too convenient and photogenic for Hollywood to pass up. Directors used the island's semitropical landscape as the backdrop of such silent-era classics as *The Ten Commandments*; the feeding of the multitude in Cecil B. DeMille's *King of Kings* required the great director to construct a village of cabins to house the cast and crew. The same year, for *Old Ironsides*, an aging sailing ship was actually burned and scuttled at the entrance to Catalina Bay (some distance up the coast from Avalon). Successful talkies that utilized Catalina's scenery include *Treasure Island*, *Hurricane*, and *Mutiny on the Bounty*, which brought Clark Gable and Charles Laughton to the Magic Isle. Over at the bird park, Old Jack (no relation to the Cubs' Doyle), a raven who had hatched in the 1870s, was the model for the Wicked Queen's pet in Disney's *Snow White and the Seven Dwarfs*, and a penguin, a cockatoo, and a cassowary made actual film appearances. The comedian Joe E. Brown, a professional-caliber athlete, liked to sponsor exhibition ballgames between the Cubs and his theatrical friends, who at least once included Buster Keaton. The Cubs invited young women, including a few starlets, to sail over for the dance contests held for the Cubs in the Grand Casino. Other Hollywood types followed. In the 1930s, a few years after William Wrigley's death, a movie agent noticed one of the Cubs' many radio announcers, a fellow from Iowa, and asked him to sail over to Los Angeles for a screen test. The film career of Ronald Reagan was under way.[17]

Wrigley was intensely involved in all aspects of the resort's development, from the massive well-digging required to solve the island's freshwater shortage, to a new power plant (lights on the island had previously dimmed when the St. Catherine's elevator went into action), to his attempts to create a self-sufficient, year-round Santa Catalina economy. A clay soil found on the island was discovered to possess commercial potential, and mining began. Then, with considerably more fanfare, a vein of silver was discovered.[18]

Wrigley was everywhere inspecting all phases of development. He would have his chauffeur drive out high in the hills to witness the mining operations up close. One day his son, Phil, arrived to find his father smoking while a crew prepared dynamite charges for the day's blasting. Phil, a practical-minded fellow with a mechanical bent, lost no time hustling his elderly father away from the explosives. Later he asked the crew why they had allowed his father to risk everyone's lives that way. The workmen looked at the younger Wrigley in puzzlement. Who were they to tell William Wrigley he was making a mistake?[19]

The idea of a training camp and practice field for the Cubs evidently occurred to Wrigley while the resort's nine-hole golf course was under construction. A small mountainside was duly leveled in a spot that allowed the Cubs to use the clubhouse as their dressing room. By the time the first Cub contingent arrived at Catalina in 1921, the island's fame was already spreading, thanks to generous doses of the famed Wrigley advertising strategy—"tell 'em quick and tell 'em often." The Cubs' visits were part of that strategy, and Wrigley continued to generate promotions that would bring tourists to "the island of romance," the "Magic Isle," the "isle with a smile"—"in all the world, no place like this."[20]

In 1926, seeking to capitalize on Gertrude Ederle's historic swim across the English Channel, Wrigley offered to pay the now world-famous celebrity $5,000 to swim the San Pedro Channel, a similar distance. The feat had never been accomplished—the people who knew best, the area fishers, pronounced it "impossible." Their point would have seemed reasonable to the many Cubs who had contended with the choppy wintertime crossings of the channel—and the ballplayers had never coped with the sharks and barracudas that regularly visited these waters. Ederle declined Wrigley's offer, a setback that Wrigley characteristically trumped with a more ambitious marketing scheme: a cross-Channel race open to anyone, male or female, who wanted to try. The prize would be $25,000. When a leading woman swimmer protested that women were almost automatically excluded from the winner's circle, Wrigley sweetened the purse: $25,000 for any winner; if the winner was a man, the first woman to finish would receive $15,000.[21]

The entry of women proved a boon to Wrigley, generating such intriguing news blurbs as "Mrs. Schoemmell Denies She Will Wear Suit" (she planned to wear a thick coat of axle grease instead) and references to "mermaids" dotting the newspapers. A few weeks into the new year, thousands of spectators watched eighty-eight male and thirteen female swimmers, accompanied by flotillas of barges and small boats, splash into the midday surf off Catalina's northeast coast and set out for the mainland.

Wrigley followed at a distance aboard the *Avalon*, which also served as the event's aid station as well as the transmission center for the silent film comedian Harry Langdon, evidently prepping for the talkies by radioing race reports to Catalina's little radio station and on to fourteen California outlets. Many of the swimmers tore off their suits as soon as possible, counting on their coat of grease to keep them warm as they battled the chilly, treacherous waters. For sixteen hours, sustained by sucking food through tubes, they forged on in ever-diminishing numbers, many pulled onto the *Avalon* "knotted and twisted by cramps and shaking like leaves"; attendants swiftly provided rubdowns, blankets, hot drinks, and another round of massage. Only one of the contestants, a seventeen-year-old Canadian, George Young of Toronto, reached the mainland unaided. Young fought off a reverse current and a final attack by a bed of kelp to stumble ashore early the next morning. Then, remembering that he was wearing nothing but grease, he swam over to his trailing boat, where his crew wrapped him in blankets. He was five pounds lighter than he had started out, and it took a few minutes for his skin to return from blue to its normal hue. Wrigley, meanwhile, had impulsively informed the last two women that if they would stay afloat (one of them a heartbreaking mile off-shore) he would award them each $2,500—an impulse worth perhaps $40,000 in our dollars. The Amateur Athletic Union (AAU) celebrated the occasion by announcing that all participants lost their amateur status, which could take up to five years to reclaim.[22]

Even at a total cost of $75,000, the race was a sizable publicity coup for Wrigley amid the incessant hype of the 1920s. Young's victory dominated the front page of the next day's *New York Times*, and an innovative entry in the magazine field, a current-events review named *Time*, recapped the event in detail; offers of screen tests poured in for Young. Wrigley, despite his original preference for an American champion, quickly befriended the young Canadian (he had already lent Young sixty dollars just to motorcycle and, eventually, hitchhike from Toronto to the West Coast). Wrigley fended off would-be agents and other charlatans—Young was now a wealthy man by the standards of the day—and lent the services of his own lawyer to the young man, who had no close family other than his widowed mother.[23]

There was brief talk of another Channel swim, even one restricted to women only, but memories of the episode soon receded into a tiny scrapbook entry filed somewhere between Gertrude Ederle, summer of 1926, and Charles Lindbergh, spring of 1927. For Warren Brown of the *Herald and Examiner,* though, the swim would always stand out amid the crowded decade. He remembered the contestants covered with axle grease; a legless swimmer who briefly took to the surf in a two-part rubber suit; and a two-legged competitor who surrendered even earlier when the first waist-high roller splashed him. Concluded Brown, "I have covered practically every sort of sport there is in all parts of the country. I have never covered an event quite as daffy as that Channel swim."[24]

Soon things were back to wintertime normalcy on the little island. The four revenue cutters assigned by U.S. Secretary of Commerce Herbert Hoover quickly lifted their blockade and opened the channel to regular traffic, and the scores of yachts, schooners, tugs, and assorted scows that had had shadowed the swimmers returned to their routines on the California coast. Thousands of contestants, crews, helpers, searchers, reporters, and gawkers who had thronged Catalina departed for the mainland—"overtown," in island lingo—to resume everyday life.[25]

Within a few weeks, the *S.S. Avalon,* reconverted to ferry status, brought the first group of Cubs for spring training, their first without Grover Alexander. Although the islanders turned out en masse as usual to greet the ballplayers, the contrast with January's zany episode was hard to miss. Only the Chicago and Los Angeles sportswriters and the usual hangers-on came down the gangplank with the Cubs.

The 1927 team, though, turned into a bona fide pennant contender that summer, so the Cubs arrived at the island in spring 1928 already among the experts' preseason picks, and the camp marked a new record for press photographers reaching Mr. Wrigley's island—six.

Then came 1929.

Ed Burns of the *Chicago Tribune*, like Warren Brown of the a.m. rival *Herald and Examiner*, had observed more than one media spectacle in his day, beginning with Dempsey-Tunney at Soldier Field. In February 1929 he gazed at the unprecedented swarm of reporters, photographers, and newsreel crews and shook his head:

[W]e have been observing photographers for years, but never before have we seen half so many camera operators [in one area]. It already appears that the world is more interested in the Cubs than it ever has been in any other ballclub. You have no idea.

Ruth and the New York press might have disputed Burns's claim, but all this was working out exactly as Mr. Wrigley had hoped: the steady accretion of a superstar per year, megadeals, ballyhoo. The movie colony and its filmographers may have had an affinity for the club from the old days at Essanay. Across the channel lay a huge metropolitan area with its own Wrigley Field, and in the hinterland an even larger audience, the huge swatch of midcontinent that had been following the exciting pennant races of 1927 and 1928 on Chicago radio.

Burns wrote before Rogers Hornsby showed up on February 26—Hornsby the reigning batting champion, winner of seven of the last nine such titles, and twice a manager and once a world champion by age thirty-three. Wrigley had acquired his services through the biggest combination of players and dollars yet seen in a baseball transaction, and Hornsby's well-publicized differences with owners, teammates, and at least one bookmaker only added to his mystique. Burns wrote frankly that his editors had directed him to follow Hornsby and McCarthy around camp, looking for the tiniest signs of "undermining" or superstar-manager differences.[26]

Into this Wrigley-created dream world of luxury and ambition came the first real news of the season, and it was not good. Hartnett was out of action. Jokes about the honeymooning Hartnett's loss of virility aside, the fact was that the National League's best catcher couldn't throw the ball without pain.[27]

The excitement about Hornsby's arrival softened even this blow. With all eyes searching the eucalyptus-lined practice field for signs of insubordination, Hornsby strode about briskly, acknowledging even the rookies by their nicknames, arriving at practice on schedule—and not, it was noted, scouring the newspapers for parimutuel reports. He needled his former Cardinal teammate, Hartnett's backup Mike Gonzalez, about his throwing arm, and Gonzalez laughed heartily, flashing his gold tooth. And after Guy Bush fooled Hornsby badly on the first batting-practice session, he showed no irritation when Grimm ribbed him with a standard ballplayer's taunt, "There's your cousin, Rogers."[28]

Despite this riot of affability, Hornsby's teammates could see that a distinctive, aloof personality had joined their ranks. Hornsby was a kind of anti-Wilson, of strict habits—early hours, no liquor, no tobacco. After practice, back at the St. Catherine's Hotel, the Rajah turned every conversation to baseball, and he refused to participate in Wrigley's popular evening dance contests. Andy Lotshaw served as emcee each night, urging the ballplayers to take a gal onto the dance floor. "Keep the ladies happy!" he would boom. One evening Hornsby caught sight of Cuyler pirouetting on the dance floor. "Great gawd!" Hornsby exclaimed. "Don't that guy have to conserve no energy for baseball?"[29]

Soon after arriving on the island, Hornsby cornered the Cubs' traveling secretary, Bob Lewis, and dictated his requirements for a roommate: "I want a lad who goes to bed before ten o'clock at night, who doesn't stay awake reading *True Confessions*, who doesn't walk or talk in his sleep." Just the man for the job was available, and that was Hornsby's new double-play partner to boot—Woody English, still a gawky and boyish bachelor, who liked to go to bed at 8:30 after a few rounds of bridge.[30]

On March 7, to the strains of "Aloha Oe," the Cubs sailed for the mainland to play their first exhibition game of the spring in Los Angeles, in the replica Wrigley Field against the Cub-affiliated Angels. Most of the eight thousand fans present seemed to have shown up solely for their first look at the great Rajah, who had never appeared in uniform on the West Coast. McCarthy penciled Hornsby in as the cleanup hitter, bumping Wilson down a notch to fifth in the order. Hornsby, ever cool, responded by homering in his first at-bat. The next day he blasted a grand slam. When he found a good place in Los Angeles to eat his favorite meat, steak, most of his teammates showed up too on the premise that whatever Hornsby was eating, they wanted. No rash of retiring at 10:00 p.m. was reported, however, but all in all it must have seemed that the fortunes of the Chicago Cubs were going to revolve around their new superstar.[31]

Hornsby's celebrity threatened the White Sox with a near-blackout in the sport pages. That danger was averted mainly through the efforts of one Art "The Great" Shires.

Since the days when the Sox's Ted Blankenship matched pitches (actually, many fewer pitches) with Grover Alexander in their magnificent nineteen-inning 1925 City Series stand-off, White Sox fans had suffered through the obverse of Veeck and McCarthy's success on the North Side: three years of decline, managerial changes, and bad luck. It was not that Charles Comiskey had given up, aging and disillusioned though he might have been. His renovation and enlargement of Comiskey Park was completed, and his scouts were busy signing prospects to expensive bonus contracts—perhaps too many for the skills they were uncovering, and more expensive than Wrigley's. The Sox's player-development plan reached some sort of nadir when the third, and only healthy, catcher on their roster went down to injury one day in 1927. Through a miscommunication, Moe Berg, a reserve shortstop, was sent in as the new backstop. The problem was that Berg had never caught or even considered strapping on the tools of ignorance. But Berg, who had studied seven languages at Princeton and rode his bike "every morning, rain or shine, in the vicinity of 53rd and Hyde Park Boulevard," did well enough that Sox pitchers were soon requesting him as their battery mate.[32]

The Berg experiment aside, the Sox were seriously unlucky. The Black Sox's bad karma seemed to linger over the South Side. Blankenship's arm went sour. The talented Tommy Thomas tried to take his place, but he turned into a classic hard-luck case, barely over .500 even when pitching well. Ted Lyons, one of the really great pitchers of the era, was the team's only year-in, year-out mainstay; he would last more than two decades in the Calvary of South Side baseball. The Sox's center fielder, Johnny Mostil, tried to kill himself in spring 1927. He recovered, but he was never the same ballplayer again. The team's two best remaining regulars, the inseparable Bibb Falk and Willie Kamm, became dissidents—despite (or maybe because of) a series of fatherly, understanding "Clean Sox" managers Comiskey hired, reminders of better times before the great scandal.[33]

As the losses mounted, the Clean Sox went out, and so did Falk, eventually followed by his buddy Kamm. Nothing, it seemed, could break the Sox's long losing string, until Art Shires burst into the lineup in August 1928 with a 4-for-5 performance. "So this is the great American League that we hear so much about down in Texas!" exclaimed the brash new fellow after the game, earning his first and most lasting nickname. He hit .300 for the rest of the year, and then led the Sox batters in a rare City Series defeat that fall. The Sox veterans promptly tried to reduce his share of the players' cut on the grounds that he had played only part of the regular season. Shires appealed to Commissioner Landis, who upheld the rookie's case. But it was no way for the Sox to welcome their best newcomer in years.[34]

The Sox skipper for 1929 was yet another "player's manager," Lena Blackburne, better remembered today for developing (and maintaining as a trade secret) the "rubbing mud" the big leagues still use to take the sheen off baseballs. Blackburne's honeymoon with the Sox was short-lived that spring. In a disjointed series of events, the manager named Shires, not yet twenty-two, team captain but then had to suspend him for "breaking training" (i.e., getting publicly intoxicated) with a teammate. By Opening Day, Shires was back in the lineup, if no longer team captain. Within a month he and Blackburne conducted a fistfight in the White Sox clubhouse. As usual in such episodes, it was unclear who swung first or even who connected, and within a few weeks Shires was back in the lineup and hitting as well as ever.[35]

Keeping up with the galaxy of stars Wrigley and Veeck had assembled was a tough assignment for a twenty-two-year-old in his first full season, but Shires was the man for the job. He was the immediate baseball forebear of Dizzy Dean: a young, talented loudmouth from Italy, Texas, who had somehow figured out how to keep the pot stirring in the big city. In a world where the bewildered, humble rookie's traditional role was to keep silent and hope the veterans would accept him, Shires courted attention in his dress, his talk, his attitude. He showed up for his first spring training with a wardrobe of 12 suits, 5 overcoats, 2 canes, 10 scarves, 75 pairs of socks, 8 pairs of shoes, and 35 shirts. By the end of the tumultuous year this collection had grown, by one estimate, to four dozen suits, 100 hats, hundreds of neckties, 20 canes, 40 pairs of spats, a morning suit, a silk hat, and 6 tuxedos, as well as various evening, golf, riding, motoring, and yachting wear. He quickly began feuding with the Yankees' Leo Durocher, another spats-wearing, cane-carrying fashion plate, and otherwise let fans and players alike know that the Great Shires was present. "What are you squawking about? You got a good break when you came in to see me play," he shouted at a heckler in San Antonio. "What do you think? Am I better looking this year than I was last year?" he asked a writer. Soon he was comparing himself to Babe Ruth. Bravado aside, the 6'1', 195-pound Shires was in fact an able hitter who reached .300 with excellent on-base percentages every season he was healthy.[36]

Art the Great was never in any danger of rivaling the achievements of Ruth—nor those of Hornsby or Wilson. Future athlete-braggarts—Dean, Ali, Namath—generally managed to back up their big talk with big deeds. But the attention given to Shires, a smart country boy who packed the largest chaw of tobacco the majors had yet seen but only modest power, was a clue to just how corrupted the mass culture of the 1920s had become. In all the self-promotion, it was hard to tell exactly where the blue sky met the shadowy horizon. Shires regaled interviewers with tales of his college football career—enrolling at five or six small colleges, accepting money, skipping town, changing names—and his supposed stint with Hal Chase and several Black Sox in the "outlaw" leagues out West. The papers couldn't resist printing every boastful word. Shires even insinuated that he and the newspapermen were concocting some of his promotions together. It might have been true, or it might have been just one more Shires invention.[37]

Chicago's sports-celebrity scene was getting downright crowded. It was just one more challenge for Lewis Wilson, who wasn't going to let either the Great Shires or the great Hornsby spoil his day in the sun.

Wilson's approach to keeping the spotlight on himself was the straightforward response of a blue-collar kid: he would use his muscles faster, harder, and longer than anyone else. While the dispatches from Catalina and the Sox training camp in San Antonio detailed the dress, diet, and comments of Hornsby and Shires, Wilson spent his time crushing baseballs at a rate that was impressive even for a three-time home run champ. He led Murderers' Row with six homers for the spring and a .440 batting average, more than a hundred points better than Hornsby's. In a St. Patrick's Day contest at Wrigley Field in Los Angeles, he swatted three homers and went 5-6 in a 17—0 Cub victory over the Cubs' minor league team, the L.A. Angels. Soon the Cubs were rolling through the Southwest on their way back to Chicago. On April 12, with the Cubs in Kansas City for their last preseason stop, Hornsby sent an eighth-inning drive over the scoreboard. Wilson, not to be outdone, hit the next pitch for an even longer drive over the wall. "If the boys can do this act in Wrigley Field, there ought to be a riot," wired one writer back to Chicago.[38]

Two nights later the Cub party, some three dozen, boarded a Chicago & Alton train bound for Union Station in the Loop. For sleeping purposes, the players were assigned to one of two Pullman cars, a "hyena" car for the first-string players and the "semipro" car for rookies, McCarthy and his coaches, newsmen, and Bob Lewis, the traveling secretary; during waking hours, everyone intermingled freely. Each player had his own section, with a lower berth for sleeping and an upper berth for various paraphernalia—hand baggage, portable radios and Victrolas, and in Charlie Grimm's case, the unavoidable, essential banjo. Lotshaw, possessed of powerful build, pugnacious personality, and blue-collar background, delivered messages from McCarthy and Lewis to the veterans in the hyena car.

In the next six months the Cubs' Pullmans would carry them across the northeastern United States: three major excursions to the East Coast, plus several shorter jaunts ("jumps," they were called) to Cincinnati, St. Louis, and Pittsburgh. Playing low-stakes bridge, rummy, pinochle, and hearts (as ever, McCarthy forbade poker; Wilson was the informal kibitzer for all other games); reading magazines, the occasional book, and in Hornsby's case, racing forms; doing crossword puzzles; listening to the music of Grimm and Heathcote (often by request of the cardplayers) and the banter of Hartnett and Lotshaw: counting the spring-training trip to California, the group would accrue some ten thousand miles of frequent travel, enduring the sweltering months without benefit of air-conditioning. By then the 1929 National League pennant would be theirs, as Wrigley and Hornsby (but not McCarthy) had made bold to promise. That would make the Rogers Hornsby experiment a success.[39]

The two Pullmans rolled across Missouri and the Mississippi and veered northeast toward Lake Michigan. This final spring leg was like no other that a Cub team had made since they had begun patronizing the Magic Isle, or indeed any spring training since the days of Three-Finger Brown. The new Murderers' Row would arrive in Chicago as almost-unanimous favorites for the 1929 flag, and with that, they would immediately face more scrutiny than any media carnival at Catalina could generate. Aboard the lurching cars, the clickety-clack, the team's leaders settled into the roles they would play on the thousands of miles and months ahead: McCarthy, stern, patient, unflappable; Hornsby, hard-bitten and blunt; Hartnett, talkative but inwardly reserved; Wilson, ebullient, open, energetic; Grimm, a constant source of optimism and bonhomie; Root and Stephenson, strong, reserved, reliable.

Optimist or pessimist, extrovert or introvert, everyone but Hornsby looked forward to the rite that signaled the formal opening of the baseball season: Hack Wilson's annual appearance in an immaculately pressed and laundered, snow-white uniform.[40]

7 ‖ "A Sort of Frenzy"

I would like to say something extra for Lew. Here's a player who is
misunderstood. . . . Let me say that Wilson has been more sinned against than
he has sinned. —Joe McCarthy, September 14, 1929

How are the Cubs doing today? —Reputed last words of ex-Mayor William
Dever, September 3, 1929

About seven o'clock on the evening of July 1, 1929, Hack Wilson steered
his Hupmobile 8 into the All Weather Tire Co. at the southeast corner of
Ashland and Lawrence, a mile or so northwest of Wrigley Field. The
slugger's arrival climaxed the grand opening celebration of "Uptown Chicago's finest tire and battery station." All day long the station had been
providing every purchaser of gasoline, batteries, tires, tubes, or general
maintenance with a FREE! autographed photograph of Wilson, not to mention flowers for the ladies and cool beverages for all visitors (a real attraction in the days when cold drinks depended on ice delivered by a horse-
drawn wagon).

A knot of worshipful North Siders gawked as Wilson, who had just
gone 3 for 5 with a game-winning sacrifice fly that afternoon in a wild
extra-inning victory over Cincinnati, stepped out of the Hup and turned
it over to the attendants for installation of four Goodyear Double Eagles.
(A full set of 33x6's, the store's most expensive, cost $48.80.) Wilson mixed
with the clientele and signed autographs for an hour before heading off to
his next scheduled appointment, at the Main State Bank, 2452 West North.
There he, Gabby Hartnett, and WMAQ's Hal Totten would autograph baseballs for anyone opening a new savings account.[1]

Murderers' Row was doing well in the endorsement business, but as the
traditional July 4 mark drew near, their muscle had made them only fourth
in the league in runs scored, fifty-three runs behind the Giants, and seventh

in team batting average. A rival gang, the Pittsburgh Pirates, appeared completely unintimidated, trailing the Cubs by just a half-game. Five times so far the Cubs had faced Pittsburgh's Burleigh Grimes, and five times Grimes had gone the route against them, winning four and giving way to a reliever in extra innings the fifth time. On June 21 the spitballing Grimes picked up his eleventh victory of the year by beating the Cubs, 14–3.

The club's prize acquisition, Rogers Hornsby, was hitting some thirty points under his league-leading 1928 pace. His presence made McCarthy's Cubs the circuit's center of attention, but the smart money said these Cubs were a punk group, wheezing and laboring without the fiery leadership that Hartnett had always provided. Still sore-shouldered, Leo sat dejected in the dugout day after day, contributing only an occasional pinch-hit appearance. Thirty-eight-year-old Mike Gonzalez and two rookies were trying to cover for him behind the plate, but they weren't fooling anybody.[2]

Only one Cub, breaking out to an unexpected 11-1 record, was having Grimes's kind of success. Guy Bush, the "Mississippi Mudcat," was a young veteran of twenty-seven whom McCarthy liked to shift between starting and relieving at a rate unusual even in the 1920s. For a player who began the year with a lifetime record barely over .500, Bush had so far attracted his share of attention on a team of stars. He won over fans and sportswriters alike with his good-natured bravado and the ability to laugh at himself. A running joke was his fantasy about developing into a great hitter, even though his long-armed, pretzel-like swing often left him sprawled on the ground. (Years of boasting and prediction yielded no home runs but two triples.) He dressed flamboyantly, and a set of long sideburns gave him a sort of riverboat-gambler look. He was, in fact, one of the best cardplayers on the team.[3]

Bush had not always felt so comfortable about the big city. After the Cubs originally bought his minor league contract (as so often, on the recommendation of Jack Doyle), the newly minted graduate of the Tupelo Military Academy hid out for half the summer under an assumed name, playing in a couple of Deep South minor leagues. Eventually Bush worked up the nerve to call Bill Veeck on the long distance line. "Why, we've been looking for you for a month," said Veeck, who ordered the youngster to hop a train for Chicago ASAP. Bush agreed, but, fearful of being robbed while asleep, he refused to board the Pullman sleeper and instead spent the night in the depot waiting for a day coach. When he arrived in Chicago the next day, exhausted, much of his cash disappeared anyway on a cab drive that toured the Loop and parts north thoroughly before dropping him at the Wrigley Building. There, the flustered Bush signed his contract without even looking at the figures. Veeck talked him into taking a sleeper to join the team at Pittsburgh, although Bush, once aboard, tried to stretch out for the night on the bench. A porter showed him how to pull out the bed. At Pittsburgh he was put to work pitching batting practice. One of his heaves struck a batter on the hand and broke a bone. Bush's new teammates convinced him that he would have to pay a heavy fine or go to jail for this misdeed. Only then did they tell him that the hitter was no Cub, only a friend of Bill Killefer's who was working out with the team.[4]

The dark-haired, dark-complected Bush soon took a liking to the strange Northern ways, renting an apartment just off the lakefront year round. He married the graduate of an Eastern university and became a management trainee in the trust department of a bank. Still restless, he tried to cash in on the miniature golf craze, buying both an outdoor and an indoor course, and eventually operated gas stations in the Uptown and Rogers Park neighborhoods north of Wrigley Field.[5]

On the mound the fiery Mississippian was a spectacle. He fidgeted, shook, and scratched. He worked his feet like a shadow boxer. Before each windup, he hitched his trousers and bent forward as if he were a frock-coated gentleman making introductions. Then he wound up in a curious knot and let fly like a whiplash. After the pitch he ran off the mound and jumped with joy or dismay, as the result dictated. When a call didn't go his way, he liked to play the aggrieved Southern gentleman, ready to challenge the ump to a duel: "May I ask you, suh, where was that pitch you just called?"[6]

At Catalina that spring of 1929 Bush was his usual comical self, experimenting with several new deliveries. One involved reaching down so far that the knuckles of his right hand almost scraped the ground; then slowly he brought his arm overhead in a huge windmill before delivering the pitch. As Hornsby had suggested, it was difficult for a batter to see the ball against the white shirts in Wrigley Field's left-center field jury box, so for good measure Bush also worked on a sidearm and an underhand pitch, along with an experiment with a knuckleball and the screwball that Grover Alexander had first shown him, years before.[7]

By early July, Bush's contortions seemed somehow less freakish. An 11-1 record (16-1 by early August) had much to do with it; he was competing with Burleigh Grimes for the league lead in wins, on his way to a season of 50 appearances and more than 200 innings pitched, a feat only a select group of rubber-armed hurlers has registered. Charlie Root, who had just missed the 50–200 club in 1927 with 48 appearances and 306 innings, suffered for it with an ineffective 1928. He was back in form for 1929, the only other starter giving McCarthy consistent work. Pat Malone had lost velocity on his fastball; Fred Blake, the quiet West Virginian who had always been what they called a "stuff" pitcher, was having trouble finding the plate. Hal Carlson, supposedly recovered from the stomach problems that had disabled him in 1928, appeared completely washed up. McCarthy was running through all of them frequently, especially Root and Bush.[8]

Athletic mortality was also visiting Miguel Gonzalez, Hartnett's backup for the past four seasons but now suddenly the first-string catcher. Since 1914 Gonzalez had been shuttling between his native Havana and the States, playing ball year round and, more recently, managing the Cuban League's Havana Giants to a string of titles. Because Bill Veeck had banned winter play for the Cubs—after all, one of his high-priced Bruins might hurt himself—manager Gonzalez had to write player Gonzalez into the Havana lineup as "A. Suarez." No one seemed to be the wiser when Gonzalez showed up at Catalina each February in suspiciously good shape, but regardless, by spring 1929 the thirty-seven-year-old was no longer up to full-time major league duty.[9]

Mike was still a valuable man to have on the ball club. If his English was rough, he handled condescension about it with style. A brash patron once hailed him from the box seats. "Tell me, Señor, is Guy Bush a Cuban, too?" The reference was to Bush's dark hair and eyes. Gonzalez's gold tooth glistened as he smiled and replied, "No, no. Just Mississip."

More than one teammate was disconcerted to hear Gonzalez bellow, "There's one smart dummy!" after a good play, and press interviews could be an adventure. "Are you married?" a feature writer asked him in early 1929.

"Seex year," Gonzalez answered.

"How many kids, Señor?"

"Not."

"Have you ever brought the wife to the United States?"

"One season for honeymoon. She spik no English; get self-consh. Won't come back."[10]

John McGraw had once asked Gonzalez to evaluate a minor league infielder. Gonzalez tagged the light-hitting prospect—none other than the White Sox's future shortstop-turned-catcher Moe Berg—with a phrase that captured the frustrations of baseball men everywhere. "Good field, no hit," the Cuban telegrammed New York, in words that *Norteamericano* would adopt. Besides that, he was dead on about Berg's talents.[11]

Gonzalez was a trailblazer in the universal language of numbers, too, scouring the sports pages to find the batting averages of everyone in the league, and then, from the box scores, the streaks they were on and which pitchers they had faced. Relying on his knowledge of what every pitcher in the league threw, Gonzalez could project what each batter was swinging at to make his hits or his outs. Later generations of managers and coaches, armed with punch cards and computer printouts, would attempt what Gonzalez was doing in his head in the summer of 1929.[12]

One statistic couldn't be ignored: his own batting average, one of the league's lowest. Good field, no hit: Mike had scored just nine times at the season's midpoint. McCarthy had to have some production from the number 8 slot. Even though the trading deadline was past, Veeck set off looking for Don Miguel's replacement. Gonzalez had plenty of baseball ahead of him—coaching for the St. Louis Cardinal's Gashouse Gang of the 1930s; temporary stints as the Cards' manager; ownership of the Havana entry in the Cuban League; and to cap it off, a brief acknowledgment of his managing acumen in the early going of Ernest Hemingway's *The Old Man and the Sea*.

As far as a few female fans were concerned, another Cub was expendable. In early June, these dissidents began writing letters to the editor with their plan: bench Wilson and give the regular center-field job back to Heathcote. Given the chance to play every day, they were convinced in the face of all evidence to the contrary that their darling would not fail to outhit Wilson.[13]

McCarthy must have heard the complaints at the ballpark each Friday afternoon. The dour skipper was unmoved. Heathcote was still an occasional performer, getting into action in situations like that of May 25. Wilson got himself ejected in the twelfth inning by throwing his bat over a called strike 2. McCarthy called on Heathcote to step into the batter's box, where he watched strike 3 sail past.

Heathcote fans could console themselves that it would not be long until Pat Pieper once again cried out, "Replacing Wilson in center field, Heathcote." It would be a day to remember.

The Cubs showed some signs of emerging from hibernation in the July 2 game against Cincinnati. The Reds' manager was Jack Hendricks, whose unfriendly history with Hornsby went back to 1918, when Hendricks briefly managed the St. Louis Cardinals. Beginning in spring training, Hendricks poormouthed the Cubs' prospects at every turn: Hornsby would be of no help to them; their right-handed sluggers were "pop fly hitters" who would flop outside what he termed the Cubs' "little park." When that got into print, Hendricks tried to offer McCarthy an apology, which McCarthy pointedly declined to accept.[14]

Hendricks opened the series on July 2 by sending an aging left-hander, Eppa Rixey, against the almost entirely right-handed-hitting Murderers' Row. For eight innings Rixey made Hendricks look smart. He went into the bottom of the ninth with a 4–2 lead, but with no one out and a man on, Hartnett pinch-hit and bashed the ball off the left-field bricks. Minutes later a passed ball tied things at 4–4 and sent the game into extra innings.[15]

Things became interesting again in the Cubs' half of the tenth. With Stephenson on first base, Grimm rolled a ball to short. Stephenson crashed into the Reds' second baseman, Hughie Critz, 5'9" and 147 pounds, a classmate of his at Alabama and an off-season hunting companion. Stephenson's combined velocity and mass flattened Critz so thoroughly that the little fellow had to leave the game.[16]

In the eleventh the incensed Reds tried three times to spike Grimm at first. Bush in turn dusted a Reds' batter, who grabbed the ball from the catcher and threw it into the outfield. He was ejected. The Cubs pushed over a run in the bottom of the inning to give Bush another victory.

The two clubs split the next two games in routine form. On the Reds' bench, however, sat Ray "Windy" Kolp, better known for his bench jockeying than his official role, pitching. Kolp had once goaded John McGraw into calling him "Fathead," screaming that he would buy Kolp's contract and send him to the boondocks, "so far that your relatives will think you've died or left the country." Kolp replied jauntily, "Wrong again, sucker. You'd just keep me and win the pennant."[17]

A talent for embarrassing McGraw was ordinarily a plus with Hack Wilson, but on July 4 Kolp's jests were no longer amusing him. The Cubs had battered the Reds' Pete Donohue for seven runs after falling behind early, 4–0. When Wilson cracked a single to lead off the fifth inning, Hendricks decided to replace Donohue. Wilson stayed at first while the Reds brought in a new pitcher and Cuyler flied for the first out. The whole time Kolp, sitting next to Hendricks in the Reds' dugout a few feet away, bombarded Wilson with his choicest invective. Wilson later said, "He called me a ——." Later, his teammates, Joe McCarthy, and even league president John Heydler all agreed that whatever "——" was, it was a very bad word. Kolp was obviously mocking Wilson's illegitimate birth—a devastating insult to any American in 1929.

That did it. As the next hitter, Stephenson, stepped in, Wilson suddenly bolted from the bag and headed straight for the visitors' dugout on the dead run. His powerful figure charged into the sea of gray visitors' flannel harder than Stephenson ever hit the Auburn front line. All was chaos. Eppa Rixey howled with pain; someone, probably Wilson, had spiked his foot.

As the Cubs ran over to help Wilson, the fans left their seats and began streaming down the aisles for a better look. But Andy Frain's smartly dressed ushers were ready for their first big test, and there were more of them and off-duty police than usual for the holiday crowd. They held the fans in the grandstand while police broke through to Wilson and hustled him back to the Cub dugout. An umpire, Cy Rigler, pushed close enough to Wilson to tell him he was ejected.[18]

The faithful Heathcote took Wilson's place in the lineup, going hitless as the Cubs took the game, 10–5. Wilson, however, had not finished his day's work. After the game both teams hurried to Union Station, where they each had a Pullman attached to the Gotham Limited. The Reds would stop at Pittsburgh and the Cubs head on toward Boston. Chicago and Cincinnati players mingled as they passed through the gate.

The brawl had done little to soothe Wilson's feelings. (It was never clear whether Wilson had actually reached Kolp in the dugout.) He told a knot of Reds that he still wanted an apology from Kolp. Jakie May, a Cincinnati left-hander who had been shelled by the Cubs in the second game, volunteered that Kolp was already in the Reds' car.

Wilson began to redden, always a bad sign. He would enter the Reds' coach and force an apology, or else, he announced. Donohue, standing nearby, spoke up. He told Wilson with a smirk not to enter the car: he might never come out. Wilson wasn't sure if he had heard a joke or a threat. "What's that to you?" he snarled. Donohue repeated his remark with an extra touch of insolence.

Now the two were as nose to nose as practicable at 5'6" and 6'1". The ruckus had attracted the attention of scores of would-be travelers. Oblivious to their timetables, they gathered round. Wilson quickly unleashed a right that sent Donohue down on the concrete in a heap. He stumbled over some luggage trying to get to his feet, and Wilson unloaded once more to send him back down. Cubs and Reds players pushed their way in. Before a free-for-all could break out, railroad employees rushed over to separate the players. Meanwhile, all was confusion in the general vicinity. "It looked as though someone had flung a handful of dollars in the air and everyone was scrambling for them," Art Nehf recounted the next week.[19]

The fisticuffs were over, but not the fighting. Over the years the story of Hack's Fourth of July celebration has been told and retold. In one version he and Pat Malone roam through Union Station looking for helpless Reds to punch out. In another, he corners Kolp and belts him, rather than Donohue, at the station. Sometimes the action takes place at Cincinnati's union depot (where Malone did attack two reporters, inside a Pullman, two years later).

At the time, it was enough that Wilson was yet another Chicago roughneck, violent and hot-headed enough to make grown men cower in their Pullman berths. That image, especially in the hands of the newspapers, was all too believable given the time, the place, and the dead-end kid Wilson was to begin with. He had talked with his fists since he was a boy. He treated every at-bat and fly ball as an adventure and a challenge, as if he were inventing every play from scratch. He failed miserably and succeeded magnificently and there was never anything clinical or routine about it.

"I'm no Dempsey. But when anyone says I'm yellow, I'm going to try to show 'em they're wrong," cried Wilson to newsmen in Pittsburgh before hurrying on to Boston with the rest of the club. Hendricks supplied his own blow-by-blow account of the fight and warned that "there will be something doing for a certainty" when the Cubs and Reds played again in six weeks. By that time, anyway, the Cubs were going to "wilt under strong opposition," he added.[20]

McCarthy was unimpressed. "Why should I make any reply to cracks like that? Hendricks is only the manager of a tail-end ballclub, and may not be that for long," he said. Hendricks's old feud with Hornsby was the real problem, he said.[21]

The Cubs' mood changed when their train pulled into Boston the next morning. Before Wilson could finish his coffee, he learned that he had a message to call President Heydler in New York. Wilson rushed to the phone without finishing his coffee.

Heydler was interested in the details of the Kolp fight. "What did Kolp call you?" he asked Wilson.

"You just think of the vilest words you ever heard and that's what it was," Wilson replied.

"I understand," Heydler answered. But he told Wilson he was suspended for three days and fined $100. He read from a letter he had already sent to Wilson: "Your actions might easily have started a riot."[22]

"Should have had a year," the Reds grumbled when they heard the news in Pittsburgh. Hendricks returned early to Cincinnati to huddle with the Reds' ownership about filing a protest.[23]

Heydler still hadn't taken up the matter of the Pete Donohue fight. Finally he decided on an extraordinary midseason hearing. He summoned all the participants and witnesses to New York. This time, Heydler said, the possible fine was $200 and the suspension, ten days—an outcome that could neatly sink the road trip, and the Cubs' season with it.

In this dark hour, Thomas Bowler, the alderman for Wrigley Field's Lakeview neighborhood, stood tall: "I know that Mr. Donohue deserved to be struck in the mouth; otherwise Mr. Wilson would not have struck him in the mouth," he reasoned. Nor was that all. "While not a voter in

Chicago, Mr. Wilson's splendid courage is typical of the 'I Will' spirit of the greatest city in the world." Bowler and his fellow alderman Dorsey Crowe (no relation to ex–State's Attorney Robert Crowe) volunteered their services as character witnesses for Wilson. Crowe's ward was the Near North Side neighborhood that also produced Dion O'Banion and John Sbarbaro.[24]

The Cubs pasted the Braves twice during Wilson's three-game suspension, scoring 26 runs in the two victories. The Reds' prosecution of Wilson had brought the whole club alive. McCarthy became a regular chatterbox. "Riggs Stephenson and Hack Wilson are not roughnecks," he proclaimed. "You won't hear them or any of the rest of our club crying, no matter where we are in the race."[25]

When the Cubs reached New York, the skipper held a mock trial in the clubhouse for the benefit of the baseball writers. Even Hornsby chimed in. "I suppose next they'll be bringing a tea wagon out between innings and serving tea to the ballplayers, hey?" McCarthy recalled an incident earlier in the year when the Cardinals' Ernie Orsatti slid into Hornsby and "knocked 'im higher 'n a kite, didn't he, Rog?"

"Higher 'n that," agreed Hornsby.[26]

Wilson, for his part, told his story to all who would listen: "I looked at him [Donohue], thinking he was just joking. . . . I wasn't looking for trouble. When a man gets personal with me he's got to fight and I don't care who he is. And when he said that I said that went double for him, and then the fight started."[27]

The "Trial of Hack Wilson" began with the Reds' testimony in Heydler's Manhattan office on July 11; the Cubs followed the next morning. Aldermen Bowler and Crowe were not on hand. The following day Heydler issued a prepared statement. One fact had impressed him most in the midst of all the contradictory testimony. "I cannot conceive a man [*sic*] in Donohue's position," Heydler wrote, "following the passage of insults with an angry man, stooping down and looking away. . . . I can only deduct with certainty that the men had passed insults to each other. . . . Donohue in all reasonableness should have been prepared to defend himself." Heydler would mete out nothing more than a "severe reprimand" to Wilson.[28]

The Cubs received the news joyfully. They knocked Carl Hubbell out of the box in the first game at the Polo Grounds. Hal Carlson, an invalid no longer, threw his second complete game, this time a four-hitter. He cut his ERA, a career-threatening 10.80 at the end of June, to a more manageable 5.80.[29]

In these victories Carlson was throwing to the team's new first-string backstop, Zack Taylor. One day the week before, Taylor had arrived at the Boston ballpark as a Brave; his owner-manager, Emil Fuchs, intercepted him and told him to head for the visitors' clubhouse and put on a Chicago uniform. Fuchs and Veeck had just made a waiver deal for Taylor. Taylor, unbelieving, had to be convinced by McCarthy that the news was for real. McCarthy then wrote him into the starting lineup.

Taylor, a well-traveled but respected veteran, was a 100-game-a-year catcher, the benchmark for catchers in that era. His arrival ended the May-December platoon of a couple of rookies with Mike Gonzalez. The Floridian Taylor, unlike Gonzalez, spoke fluent Yankee; he had learned how to drop his drawl by listening to the tourists as a boy. The year before, when the Rajah managed the Braves, he had been Hornsby's number 1 catcher. Hornsby's opinion evidently counted for something with Veeck and McCarthy.[30]

In the leadoff spot there was more evidence of Hornsby's new influence. Norm McMillan, another infielder out of the American Association, had been working on his batting stroke with Hornsby.[31] McCarthy was sufficiently impressed to make McMillan his latest regular third baseman.

To the sporting public, though, Hack Wilson had long since become the official representative of Murderers' Row. Fans at the Polo Grounds presented him with a set of boxing gloves in a home plate ceremony.[32] Hack tried them on good-naturedly, but in Brooklyn a few days later he got an overflow crowd at Ebbets Field going by tossing his long-handled bat after a call he didn't like.[33] The Brooklynites booed him lustily the rest of the afternoon while the Cubs won twice. Wilson stretched his hitting streak to 27 games. Since arriving in New York the Cubs had closed a three-game gap between them and the Pirates and taken first place.

The next day, the Dodger fans had their revenge. Dazzy Vance got Wilson swinging four times, allowing him one foul ball all afternoon. The hitting streak, the longest in club history, had spanned two spectacular fights, a suspension, a hearing, and virtually all of a road trip, but now it was over. Wilson threw no bats while Vance shackled him, but the fans hounded him all afternoon with the special cheer named after the Yankees' home borough.[34]

Vance's ten-strikeout performance knocked the Cubs out of first place one last time. Somehow, the people of Pittsburgh decided the news meant that the pennant was theirs, and fairly won. The Pirates rolled into the station in Pittsburgh the next morning to the strains of a welcoming brass band, a caravan of limousines, a public breakfast at the William Penn Hotel, and a speech by the mayor. In July! Somehow forgotten was the loss of their spitballing ace and Cub killer, Burleigh Grimes, who had broken his hand a few days before. But the well-fed Pirates went out, tromped Brooklyn 13–3, and began taking reservations for World Series tickets.[35]

Chicago fans were nearly as giddy after their team's 11-6 road trip. A midweek turnout of 28,000 greeted the Cubs for the opening game of the new home stand. In the usual box on the third-base side sat William Wrigley, just back from his annual vacation on Catalina. From 1,800 miles away he had monitored the progress of his ball club, including Wilson's hearing, via a cable that had been laid across the San Pedro Channel for his convenience. After the game, a duel that Root won over Hubbell, 2–0, the crush around Wilson required a three-policeman escort out of the ballpark, treatment more often reserved for politicians.[36]

The next day, as a driving storm swept over the field, the Giants exploded for seven runs against Guy Bush. In the bottom of the seventh Wilson, who had earlier hit his 24th home run, stepped into the muddy batter's box to wallop number 25, climaxing a four-run answer that decided the contest for the Bruins.

A heat wave and one of the great hitting binges in baseball history struck Chicago that week, a concentrated summer fury that fulfilled all Joe McCarthy's theories and William Wrigley's hopes. Some weeks before Wilson's suspension, McCarthy had moved Hornsby into the third spot in the lineup. When Wilson returned he kept the Rajah third, keeping Wilson in his pre-Hornsby cleanup role. (Cuyler, a natural-born number 3 hitter, stayed in the fifth spot and the uncomplaining Stephenson moved to sixth.) For the week of July 25–31, Wilson was 16 for 32; Hornsby, 15 for 39. Wilson drove in 17 runs; Hornsby 12. In the three days from the 25th to the 27th,

Wilson hit 2 homers and drove in 7 runs; Hornsby added a homer and drove in 7 runs. For the three days the two were a combined 14 for 33.

Day after day the bombardment continued. It was July 31 before the Cubs lost again, dropping the first game of a doubleheader to Boston. Then they took another five in a row before bowing to Brooklyn in the closer of the home stand. A ballpark record of 50,000, 25,000 of them nonpaid Ladies Day guests, turned out for the final game. In the outfield overflow, women's hats seemed to outnumber the men's boaters. Hundreds of men had to perch on top of the brick walls running along Waveland and Sheffield. Another 10,000 would-be customers filled the streets and sidewalks outside the park. The rooftops of the three-flats across Waveland and Sheffield were filled with standing spectators—"snipers," they were called—and boys were shimmying up the lampposts outside. They saw consecutive seventh-inning hits by Wilson, Cuyler, and Stephenson send the Cubs into a lead. The Dodgers and Babe Herman stormed back for a 5–4 victory. But the second-place Pirates lost again; the Cubs' 14-2 home stand had sent them from 1½ games down to 7½ up. Bill Veeck projected that the franchise was going to draw a million and a half, enough to break the New York Yankees' single-season attendance record of 1.3 million.[37]

The seventh-place White Sox were on the road while this great exhibition of baseball's Golden Era took place at Addison and Clark. But the Sox were not yet eclipsed by their rivals, thanks almost solely to the efforts of Art "The Great" Shires, a.k.a. "Whataman."

Shires had lingered on the White Sox bench for a few weeks after winning the fight and losing the decision against Blackburne. But by mid-June the manager, his club going nowhere, had to give his attacker another chance. The Great One freely admitted his youthful mistakes. On one road trip, he and Blackburne evidently even roomed together. The repentant Shires also stressed his good relations with the league's umpires (which, it seems, was true).[38]

The new, mild-mannered Shires, though, could no more avoid controversy than he could quit bragging. Shortly after his fight with Blackburne came the news from Texas that Shires was being sued for $25,000 for wrongful death. Shortly before joining the White Sox the year before, Shires had silenced a heckler, a black man, by successfully aiming a baseball at his head. After his victim died several months later, his widow decided, plausibly, that Shires was responsible.[39]

A judgment of the size in question would be disastrous for a free-spending, oft-fined rookie. (By the end of the year he would forfeit more than a third of his eight-thousand-dollar annual salary to fines alone.)[40] But Shires seemed unfazed. Back in the lineup, he resumed his hitting ways without delay. In early July he began a hitting streak that eventually reached 22 games. For a first-year man it was commendable; on the bedraggled White Sox it was a season highlight, and Shires led the team in hitting.

Shires's hitting streak ended, the same afternoon that Dazzy Vance cut Wilson's streak short at 27 games. As the Cubs returned to Chicago for their awesome home stand, Shires and company headed east. In Philadelphia, Shires announced plans to visit the Holmesburg Prison, just outside Philadelphia—a ploy to catch everyone's attention, because Al Capone was locked up there on a gun-possession charge. Shires then scored the Sox's only run and made a dazzling fielding play as the Sox went down to the A's, 8–1.

Two days later Shires announced that he had signed his last autograph. Instead, he said, he would henceforth write poetry for admirers. His first effort read: "They is a ballplayer / He is the Great Shires / Which he can paste the old apple / Whenever he tries." Asked about the last line, he replied, "A waiter told me poetry don't have to rhyme."[41]

That doggerel was only an out-of-town warm-up for the Sox's next stop—the Big Apple. There, the Great One meditated on a 16–2 loss to the Yankees with these thoughts: "You rave about Babe / You rave about Lou / Why be so greedy? / The Great Shires is good, too." The next day he drove in the winning run in a rare Sox win and then announced plans to perform in vaudeville after the season. He would sing, lecture, perform string tricks, tell jokes—and of course, recite poetry. Any earnings, no doubt, would be applied toward his legal fees.[42]

On August 2 the Sox reached Boston, where one paper provided him a half-page of coverage. While admiring that material, he received a letter from Judge Landis turning down a claim for $4,125 of the amount the White Sox had paid for his contract the year before. The Jazz Age child was undaunted, and insouciant about his powerful elder. "Looks to me like the Jedge ran into his office between a couple of rounds of golf to give my appeal weighty consideration," he said. "When the golf season is over I'm going to appeal again."[43]

That afternoon he was 2 for 6 as the seventh-place Sox scored nine runs in the third inning, all of them unearned, in a 15–4 pummeling of the eighth-place Red Sox. The Boston fans, always a tough house, showed that Shires's act hadn't improved their mood: after the Chisox scored nine in the third inning to up the lead to 11–0, Pat Pieper's counterpart went out to announce the two teams would play again tomorrow. The crowd of 7,500 booed so vociferously that the poor man received police protection on the spot.[44]

The next day, Shires went hitless with two errors in an 8–0 defeat. As the Sox left for a three-day exhibition trip to Canada, still eight full games ahead of the Red Sox but 35½ games behind Philadelphia, Shires dashed off some more verse. The theme was liquor availability in Canada. "T'hell with the white ribbon / T'hell with the pledge / The Great Shires won't take likker / He won't get no edge," went the final verse. The literary gem of the day, however, came from the *Tribune*'s headline writer:

SOX REFUGEES LEAVE COUNTRY AFTER 8–0 LOSS

Art Shires's one-man publicity campaign faltered as the season moved into August. Not even the antics of one unusual twenty-two-year-old or his lengthy hitting streak could upstage the spectacle that the Cubs had created in the National League. The Bruin offense that had been sputtering in early July was on its way to setting a new major league record for runs scored in a season.

Everyone in baseball was hitting better, and farther, than ever before. In pregame warmups one day in August, Babe Ruth broke Ed Walsh's twenty-year-old fungo-distance record with a 447-foot wallop.[45] Walsh, the great pitcher of the Sox's Hitless Wonders, tried out a 1929 ball himself and found that he could fungo farther than the 418 feet he had managed two decades earlier.

Scientific American tested the ball. Although it appeared to be wound tighter, it performed no differently than a 1924 ball. The publication concluded, with a nod to John McGraw, that the practice of putting new balls into play more frequently was causing the batting upsurge.[46]

"A Sort of Frenzy"

The journal didn't explain why the Cubs' Murderers' Row was slugging the lively ball so much better than anyone else. One day, after trailing 7–0, they came back to win 13–10. Taking a day off with a 1–0 squeaker, they followed up with a 12–2 romp. Grabbing the league lead for good on July 24, they took fewer than ten days to build the margin over second-place Pittsburgh to 7½ games. Then it was time for another long trip to the East. Just out of Chicago, the greatest right-handed hitter in the history of baseball shared his satisfaction over the team's success as only he knew how: "If the Cubs don't win the pennant they ought to cut their throats, and my throat is included."[47]

Pittsburgh's manager, Donie Bush, the man who had pushed Kiki Cuyler out of Pittsburgh two years before, had to do something to counter the Row's onslaught. *Pour encourager les autres*, he axed a spare pitcher named Fred Fussell for "breaking training rules."[48] But even without Fussell's 8.62 ERA, the Bucs dropped 12 of 16 at one stretch in August. Meanwhile, the Cubs were storming the East Coast redoubts successfully in 12 of 16 battles. By August 21 the Pirates were 10½ back, and by the morning of August 28, the gap had reached 14½. Their only consolation was that they were still in second place.

With the Cubs coming into town for a four-game set, Bush had to do something about his team's freefall. He decided on one more firing. Without Fussell to blame anymore, he turned in his own resignation.[49]

Grover Alexander was also at a career crossroads at age forty-two. He had begun the year with a 4-2 record, but in June things began to go awry for both Alex and his St. Louis Cardinals. After he was driven from the mound several times, he gave up two first-inning homers to the Cubs on June 20, an inside-the-park job to Hornsby and a bleacher-reacher by Wilson. The Cardinals' manager, Billy Southworth, sent a new pitcher out for the bottom of the second. Alex did not appear in a game for the rest of the month. On July 1, he checked into a hospital with a reported case of lumbago.[50]

The Cardinals had nosedived from first place on June 18 to fourth ten days later. Soon after Alex rejoined the team in mid-July, their record had sunk under .500; the Cardinals fired Southworth and brought back their pennant-winning leader of the year before, Bill McKechnie. McKechnie continued using Alex in the rotation. Five days later he won again, then took a fourth-inning shellacking from the Giants on the 28th. On August 1, Alex tied Christy Mathewson's National League career victory record of 372 with a classic performance: 11 hits, no walks, 1:26 playing time. He had lowered his ERA for the year to 3.66—indisputably, quality work with the overall league ERA ballooning somewhere above 4.50. Victory number 373 followed on August 10, when he pitched four scoreless relief innings at Baker Bowl, the place he had begun his storied career. What a wonder this forty-two-year-old was!

Celebrating these milestones may have proved too much for the aging master. After getting knocked out of the box at the Polo Grounds on August 17, Alex was a no-show in the clubhouse for the next few days. On the 19th, McKechnie ordered him back to St. Louis, where the Cardinals' front office decided to send him home to Nebraska, with pay, for the rest of the season. The news there was not much better. Earlier in the year Aimee Alexander had filed a suit for divorce, and in early October it was granted. Two months later, the Cardinals traded him to the Phillies. Alex would never win another major league game.[51]

While Alex the Great was fading from the scene the Chicago Cubs were in the midst of their mighty run. It was a delicious moment for the city. The Cubs hadn't led the league by 14½ games since the days of Frank Chance and Mordecai Brown. In the Wrigley Building, William Wrigley beamed as he followed the Cubs' road games on the ticker tape machine installed in his office.[52]

One of the White Sox decided to get in on the fuss by trekking up to Wrigley Field to pay a courtesy call on the champs. Naturally, that was Art Shires—and just as he planned, he got his picture in the papers again, posing with Wilson near the Cubs' dugout. The dapper Shires, a head taller than Wilson, eyed Hack and his dirty uniform awkwardly; Wilson casually folded his hands behind his back. Neither man smiled.[53]

At least Shires had made the effort. Back at Comiskey a few days later, some of Shires's teammates were photographed listening on the clubhouse radio as the Cubs won another one. There was a smile or two on the Sox faces as they gathered round the set, but they couldn't have been happy that the already overpaid Cubs were not only going to pick up a World

Series slice, but the City Series and its lovely bonus were off too. There must be some way to bring the swaggering North Siders down to earth.[54]

But support was widespread in the city, aside from the Sox and their diehards. In a residence on Sheridan Road, not far from Wrigley Field, William Dever, the former mayor, lay dying. When it became obvious that the end was near, this foe of Bill Thompson and Al Capone received a last kiss from his wife. That accomplished, he summoned the strength to ask a pressing question: How are the Cubs doing today?[55]

Dever's passing was barely noticed. Chicago was giddy. A press-service correspondent described it for out-of-towners who had heard only about the home runs and the huge crowds at Wrigley Field: "The barber tells you about the team in the morning. The waitress expresses an opinion at lunch, and the conductor on the 5:15 takes twice his usual time to punch your ticket while he wonders if 'they'll hold that lead.'" During one rally several balls Wilson fouled into the stands went untouched: the crowd was too busy watching to see if Wilson could drive in the go-ahead runs. Cheering women were standing on their seats for a better view.[56]

Most excited of all were the hordes of boys on the North, the West—and yes, even the South Sides of Chicago. The municipal parks and the vacant lots that dotted the residential areas were full of young men playing ball. On the West Side, young Bernie Rosenberg imagined himself another Hornsby. At Lincoln Park Louis Niedringhaus executed slides in the manner of Kiki Cuyler. Capitalizing on the enthusiasm, The World's Greatest Newspaper asked in its sports page one morning, "Boys, Do You Like the Cubs? Tell Readers Why." The readers were invited to explain in detail: "What do you like best about the Cubs? What makes them a winner—what player, combination of players, or management?" The prize: World Series tickets for the six best essayists.[57]

Nearly three thousand young men and women responded over the next several weeks, and the paper printed several dozen of the essays. "A crackerjack good team," said Milton Benas of Winnemac Avenue. "Look at them even in practice. They are full of pep and act just like the slogan of Chicago, which says, 'I Will,'" he added in an echo of Alderman Bowler's rhetoric. Ellsworth Reed, writing from Cottage Grove Avenue on the far South Side, said Cub games were "filled with thrills that keep their spectators in a sort of frenzy." Fifteen-year-old Bernard Adlerblum praised the Cubs' "knack of pulling the unexpected . . . of thrilling the fans with some timely base clout or a bit of sensational fielding." Betty Pestka of Oakley Avenue reminded everyone that girls could be fans, too. "You cannot find one boy who is more interested in our dear old Cubs than I am. . . . I'll give the laurel wreath to Riggs Stephenson. Stevie doesn't knock a homer every time up, but keeps a-sluggin' every day."

The youth vote, however, went overwhelmingly to one man. "I am writing about Hack Wilson's homers," began Stuart Stockwell, a forthright thirteen-year-old from Springfield Avenue. "I listen to every one of the Cubs' games in Chicago. I have been to two of the Cubs' games, and Hack Wilson hit home runs, and they were long ones, too." That made a good case for Wilson's supremacy, but ten-year-old Robert Eils of suburban River Forest had more. "O boy, when Hack Wilson hits that pill it goes. I hope Hack will be the leading home run hitter of the National League. I saw Hack make a nose dive catch. He caught the ball sliding on his elbows." Leonard Rowe, age fifteen, of Spaulding Avenue harbored no doubts about Hack, either. "If you want the name of my favorite, he is Hack Wilson. He is on the tip of every boy's tongue I know," Rowe finished. Fred Wach of Edison Park, too, lauded "the boys' favorite, the player who has won many a boy's heart by his home runs—Hack Wilson!"[58]

Even the boys of Cincinnati, ignoring their own woebegone club, followed Wilson around the ballpark when the Cubs visited Cincinnati in late August. The bitterness of July had evaporated. Wilson spent the afternoon joking with the Cincinnati bleacherites, and afterward strolled out surrounded by new young friends. That night, he spoke over a nationwide radio hookup on the subject of youth baseball. He was for it—Cincinnati kids included.[59]

After swelling to 14½ games the lead shrank to 10½ in early September, but it was only a pause in the coronation procession. Back at Wrigley Field, merely coming to bat was a pretext for an ovation. Showers of straw hats greeted every success: a bases-loaded single by Cuyler; two home runs by Hornsby and another by Wilson in a Labor Day doubleheader. The two-game, morning-afternoon attendance that day unofficially totaled 81,000, said to be the greatest number of fans who had ever visited a major league ballpark in one day.[60]

The Cub offices in the Wrigley Building were deluged by premature World Series ticket applications, which were returned without delay. When Veeck finally began accepting applications, still a week before the official pennant clinching, some 10,000 orders arrived special delivery the first day. The two-cent first-class mail brought another 190,000 that day and the next. Veeck ordered the installation of temporary bleachers, seating an extra 8,000, that would extend halfway over Sheffield and Waveland avenues.[61]

The Cubs' chief fan after William Wrigley, a fireman named Dan Cahill, fêted the players' wives at a luncheon and presented them all with roses. The ballplayers themselves were in demand for more appearances and endorsements than ever—church suppers, lodge dinners, commercial pep talks, radio spiels, and always autographing, more autographing. Wilson and several other teammates mulled over vaudeville opportunities and offers to "write" columns during the World Series. Before the game one day, Wilson strutted with the baton of a Boy Scout fife-and-drum corps. Standing nearby, the young batonist laughed joyously.[62]

The Bruins' hit parade lasted well into September. On the morning of the 7th they equaled a record with ten consecutive hits in a 13–6 victory over Boston; in the afternoon they won again, 9–2. Hornsby closed out the week 15-26 with five home runs; Wilson was 13-28 with three homers; Cuyler was 12-30 with a homer and four doubles.

McCarthy's other heavy hitters, Riggs Stephenson and Charlie Grimm, were both out with hand injuries. The irrepressible Grimm segued smoothly into broadcasting Cub games for WENR, the radio outlet of a brand-new tabloid, the *Chicago Times*. It was great publicity for the post-season vaudeville deal he was working on, too.[63]

With Jolly Cholly venturing into media and entertainment, the Cubs lacked a captain to take the lineup out to the home plate umpire before each game. Joe McCarthy capped the era of good feelings by naming Rogers Hornsby acting captain. The sinecure paid a thousand dollars a year to whoever filled the position. Hornsby accepted McCarthy's appointment but demurred at the bonus. "I don't want the extra money," he told Veeck. "Give it to Grimm. I'm glad to help out."

"Keep it," Veeck replied evenly. "We didn't dock Grimm. It wasn't his fault he got hurt. As long as he's out both you and he will get the captain's salary."[64]

Whatever Veeck and McCarthy had thought about bringing Hornsby into the family, 1929 seemed to have removed all doubts. The Hornsby experiment had, in fact, been a success in every way imaginable. The Rajah had produced heroic statistics, he had gotten along with his mates, and his manager self-evidently liked and trusted him. "Never saw a better team player in my life," McCarthy told J. Roy Stockton of the *St. Louis Post-Dispatch*. "[Hornsby] is the first player in the clubhouse every day and the last one off the field. . . . All he does is live baseball. That's his life and that is why he has been such a successful ballplayer."[65]

The Rajah was having a hard time doing anything wrong. He continued hitting prodigiously during the Cubs' early September splurge. The batting averages of his pupils, English and Norm McMillan, reached career highs. One day Jimmy Burke, McCarthy's first lieutenant, gently corrected Hornsby's baserunning, and the Rajah accepted the coaching without a murmur. And he hadn't been seen placing a bet all summer, at least as far as McCarthy knew.[66]

Before the Cubs could officially clinch the pennant, Hornsby and Wilson's only real rival as a newsmaker took one last fling at driving the Cubs off the front page. And for a day or two, the grand climax to Art Shires's season did the trick.

On Friday, September 13, the Sox were in Philadelphia after dropping a 5–2 contest to the Athletics that moved the A's one game from clinching the pennant. The Sox's record sank to 53-81 on the year. Late that evening, according to the most widely circulated account, Lena Blackburne was strolling down the hall of the Ben Franklin Hotel when he heard the sounds of conviviality floating through the transom of Shires's room. Blackburne, throwing the door open without knocking, surprised Shires and a reserve outfielder, Doug Taitt, surrounded by a collection of empty liquor bottles. A wild look gleamed in Shires's eyes.

Blackburne, even though his days as manager were numbered, decided it was time to crack down. "Are you drunk again?" he roared. The 6'2", 190-pound Shires answered by tackling the much smaller Blackburne.

Young Taitt, who had not bargained for anything quite this serious, scrambled out to summon help. The Sox's road secretary, Lou Barbour, was the first to answer the call. (By one account he was with Blackburne.) He entered the room to find Shires on top of Blackburne, beating his head against the floor. "Stay out of this," Shires yelled. "I can lick a dozen like you and Lena."

Barbour dived in anyway and got his finger bitten for his trouble. (Shires later claimed that Blackburne did it in the confusion.) When several policeman and hotel employees arrived, they found Shires standing in front of the bed, shouting, "Come out from under the bed and I'll pound you both into jelly."

The reinforcements overpowered Shires and dragged him off to another hotel. Blackburne and Barbour felt safe to crawl out from under the bed. Blackburne had a black eye; his hat was crushed and blood stained. Barbour's hat was lying in the corner in several pieces. His finger was still bleeding. Both men declined to press charges.[67]

When Shires showed up at Shibe Park the next day, two policemen were waiting. After frisking him, they escorted him to the locker room. As they walked, Shires blustered about "stool pigeons" and "front office dicks." He was proud of the work he had done on Blackburne, he said: "I don't believe I ever gave a man such a sweet shiner. It was a masterpiece." Barbour informed him that he was no longer welcome in the team quarters and handed him a railroad ticket back to Chicago.[68]

Shires cleaned out his locker and headed back to the main gate with his escort. On the way out, he encountered Connie Mack. Even though the Athletics were about to clinch the pennant that day, the grand old manager paused to give the young man some advice: "To me, you looked like one of the best prospects in many a season, but you'll never get anywhere as long as you carry on that way." He warned Shires, "You haven't gained anything. In fact, you have two strikes on you."

"Yes," Shires replied lightly, "but that third one is the big one and you'll find me swinging when that comes." With that he marched out of the ballpark and hailed a cab that disappeared from view on Lehigh Street.[69]

Mack returned to his managing duties. His Athletics wrapped up the pennant by shutting out the Sox, 5–0, in one hour and twenty-five minutes. After that, he did something outside his usual postgame routine. He went into a meeting with a few of the White Sox veterans, less hotheaded but perhaps wilier than their departed comrade.

Charlie Grimm had been out of the Cub lineup since breaking his hand at the Polo Grounds in August. In the meantime he had been broadcasting home games for WENR, one of the four stations covering the Cubs down the stretch. The Merry Prankster was already a radio veteran, having performed on the air with his famous banjo.[70]

While Grimm dabbled in broadcasting, Hornsby took over as temporary team captain; the ball club immediately hiccupped to four straight losses at Pittsburgh in late August, but the early-September hitting binge at home swelled its record to 91-43. Then they slumped again as September wore on.[71]

Grimm struck a jaunty air in his temporary perch in the broadcasting booth, but it was apparent that the élan that had driven the club from the Fourth of July to Labor Day was eroding day by day. Bush had not won in more than six weeks; Root had strained his arm. Wilson, whose legs suffered every year from the punishment meted out by his huge upper body, could no longer take the field without elaborately taping his ankles. He limped noticeably. Nor was Hornsby, slowed by a bad heel, covering much ground at second base.[72]

The Cubs' huge lead was insurmountable, though, and the inevitable pennant was finally clinched with a loss on September 18—or rather, by the Pirates' loss the same day. Those unflagging realists, the gamblers, were quick to take note. Their odds for the upcoming series made Philadelphia, the American League champion, the consensus favorites.

8 | McCarthy's Debacle

Mr. Hoover seemed as dumbfounded as the Chicago players by this sudden turn, and that was very dumbfounded, indeed. —Damon Runyon, Game 5, 1929 World Series

One night in May 1926, when movies were still silent and Hack Wilson was an obscure young outfielder, the lights dimmed inside the Loop's newest movie palace at Randolph near State. An unseen orchestra burst into song; then under a sudden concentration of floodlights, Paul Ash and his merry musical gang rose from the basement, instruments unleashed.

It was opening night at the gaudy Oriental Theater, a landmark even among the overdecorated movie palaces of the Jazz Age. Ash and his men were borne into the theater hall on a "Magic Flying Stage" that could revolve and move up, down, or sideways. In midset, the *Tribune*'s movie critic, "Mae Tinee" (the pseudonym used by all *Tribune* movie critics) and the other 3,216 other moviegoers in attendance gasped to see the portion of the stage that supported Ash and company begin to rise; almost simultaneously, another segment, filled with dancers, moved into the space just occupied by the band, which continued making music in its new perch as the dancers stepped to the beat. Tinee's review did not address further stage acts for the evening, but a movie palace "presentation act" typically would have offered a medley of vaudeville skits and at some point an organ solo, after which a hush set in and four thousand square feet of velour curtain, depicting a maharajah's victorious return from battle, opened majestically to expose a towering movie screen. Cinematic "shorts" and coming attractions would have preceded the central attraction: *Tramp, Tramp, Tramp*, a silent film starring a comedic rival of Keaton and Chaplin named Harry Langdon, and a starlet destined for bigger roles once the talkies arrived: Joan Crawford.[1]

This multimedia extravaganza cost a Loop theatergoer the price of a bleacher ticket at Wrigley or Comiskey—50 cents a show (35 cents before 2:00 p.m.). Every sizable American city had at least one such palace. Chicago and New York had dozens of varying sizes, each built with a theme in mind—Moorish, Louis Quinze, classical, Italianate, hodge-podge: in the Oriental's case, "the spirit of the famous Indian Durbar," or carnival. The Oriental's contributions to bad taste—memorable enough to be mocked thirty years later by a character in *Auntie Mame*—included Buddha figurines guarding the drinking fountains; walls packed with carvings of East Indian drummers, tambourine players, and dozens of bare-breasted *houris*, horn-tooting dragons, winged lions, and elephant-headed seahorses; ceilings dotted with gods and goddesses; and in the remaining spaces, a profusion of filigreed leaves and stems. Riotous colors predominated throughout; the silver- and gold-leaf statuary struck Miss Tinee as especially pleasing. Giant chandeliers and elephant lamps with protruding tusks lit the way past elephant-supported chair-thrones that sat on carpeting as deep as a fist. To the tones of a grand piano, visible above the foyer through a glass ceiling, attendants in turbans and silken robes steered the clientele to one of the theater's plush, velour-covered seats.[2]

Although the Oriental, a relative latecomer among megatheaters, had half a dozen theatrical competitors within walking distance and several more scattered throughout the city, it quickly caught on as one of the city's theatrical landmarks—notably, its eight-story "Oriental" sign, topped by an onion dome silhouette that loomed over Randolph Street in the heart of the theater district. For the rest of the decade, Ash's band or an appropriate substitute rode the revolving stage up and down (by the end of the decade Duke Ellington appeared frequently), three shows a day, accompanying all the movie hits and duds and the vaudeville routines.

For the last three months of 1929, the Balaban brothers and Sam Katz drew an average of 7,813 customers a day—about 600,000 for the quarter, similar to Wrigley Field's summertime attendance figures (although B&K played at home all the time). They advertised their movies in newspapers much as theaters have done ever since, except for extra blurbs that promoted the stage acts. For instance, the week the 1929 World Series began, the Balaban & Katz firm added this notice to the advertisement for its current showing, *The Love Doctor*:

Today! Periodic Results of the Game
Cubs Vs. Athletics
Will be announced in all Balaban & Katz Theaters
during the performance.[3]

The Cub-mad public could now desert their radios and leave home even in the midst of a World Series. And once the fans were lured inside, more baseball awaited.

After Ash's music and the other live acts finished, the gigantic velour curtain draw apart. The short subjects whirred into action. Within minutes the customers were gazing at gigantic, flickering images of Charlie Grimm, Kiki Cuyler, and Cliff Heathcote—three musically inclined Cubs promoting the live act they had contracted to perform on the Oriental's revolving stage just as soon as the Cubs were done with the Athletics.[4]

On the afternoon of October 8, Bernie Rosenberg and his grade school friends gathered around the radio in his West Side home. The boys had all taken the day off from school to listen to the opening game of the World Series.

As the afternoon wore on, Mrs. Rosenberg thought she could hear sobbing coming from the living room. Investigating, she found her distraught son and his friends in tears. Something terrible had happened, something the boys of the summer of 1929 had never imagined possible. The Cubs were losing. In living rooms, kitchens, barbershops, schoolrooms, and speakeasies all across Chicagoland, listeners slumped by radios, aghast at the disaster Hal Totten and Quin Ryan were describing. Downtown, knots of dismayed pedestrians stared at the huge Playograph in front of the *Herald and Examiner* building. Baseball's highest-scoring lineup was going down on strikes to a blasé journeyman, Howard Ehmke, a sidearming, underhanding thirty-five-year-old who had not started a ballgame for Connie Mack since midsummer. In fact, exactly ten innings remained in his regular-season career.[5]

Fans and ballplayers alike had been flabbergasted, twenty minutes before the scheduled game time, to see the other Philadelphia pitchers quit warming up. Only the gangling Ehmke was left still throwing before the late-arriving crowd.[6]

"Are you going to let that guy pitch?" [Al] Simmons asked Mack, half belligerently.

"Yes, I am, Al," Connie replied quietly.

The great outfielder started to say something, but quickly thought better of it. "Well, if he's your selection, it's all right with me," he said.[7]

In the bleachers, which included temporary stands built over the streets behind the ballpark, more than 12,000 customers had been warming their plank seats since just after the doors were thrown open at 7:30 a.m. Disappointed ticket seekers still clogged the sidewalks as the 32,000 reserved seat holders began arriving early in the afternoon. Atop the apartments across Waveland and Sheffield, the rooftops were filling up, too, along with assorted telephone poles, trees, and even a chimney, where one youngster, Eugene May, had somehow perched himself. On Sheffield Avenue, running behind the right-field wall, a young woman used a telescope to provide both legitimate and bleacher customers and "outlaws" atop apartment roofs with a play-by-play description of what the tiny figures on the diamond across the street were actually doing.[8]

Seat prices for game 1, by decree of Judge Landis's office, had leaped nearly 400 percent: $5.50 for a box and $4.50 for the grandstand. Nearly 200,000 Chicagoans still applied for the tickets; Veeck and the office staff chose the lucky 32,000 by lot. In a grand affirmation of what Veeck had accomplished with Ladies Days, the first application the Cub president had pulled was that of Miss Catherine Lynch, 4320 North Kenmore Avenue. The 168,000 lottery losers and the less affluent could listen to game 1 on radio or brave the bleacher and standing-room-only lines that began at the Waveland-Sheffield gate, wound both ways around the block, and crossed themselves and doubled back several times.[9]

After one o'clock, once the ticket holders managed to make their way through the sidewalk crowds, the grandstands began to fill up. Ladies' orchids and chrysanthemums brightened the sea of spectators, a colorful tribute to the cultural revolution of Ladies Day and radio coverage. William Wrigley had made his ballpark a place to be seen socially. Take, for instance, the curious adventure of Mrs. Stanley Field, 1550 North State Parkway in the city's famed "Gold Coast." Her husband, the nephew of

Marshall Field, whose department store clock oversaw State Street, had contributed $2 million dollars to establish the Field Museum. Armed with a box seat ticket, Mrs. Field arrived outside the gate wearing a broach that had cost her some three thousand dollars—more than the average fan made in a year. In the crush Mrs. Field's jewelry was torn from her dress and lost.

Mrs. Field, minus her broach, made her way to her box seat, probably with the help of one of the 371 Andy Frain ushers patrolling the grounds. Two detectives showed up to interview her. As she described what had happened, a voice spoke up from an adjoining box; the finder of her broach had overheard her sad story. Within seconds Mrs. Field and her jewelry were reunited. Verily, how Mr. Wrigley and Mr. Veeck had transformed the landscape and culture of the traditional ballpark![10]

When Charlie Root finally threw his first pitch, about twenty minutes after the scheduled starting time, an unanticipated consequence of attracting the well-bred to the park revealed itself. The hoarse, wild cheering that had filled the park in July and August—Ladies Days included—was muted. When Root did well, the crowd applauded. When Ehmke did well, they applauded too.[11]

One reason was the mastery of both pitchers. Ehmke's delivery seemed to be coming right out of the white shirts of the jury box in left-center field—the same technique that the Cub right-handers like Alexander, Root, and Bush had relied on for years. In the second inning Cuyler lunged futilely at Ehmke's high 3-and-2 offering, and Stephenson followed up by looking at a called third strike. In the third, McMillan singled and English doubled into the right-field corner. McCarthy held McMillan at third: Hornsby and Wilson were up next. While Lefty Grove warmed up in the bullpen, Ehmke made Hornsby fish for a combination of slow curves and change-ups on the outside corner. The Rajah struck out without getting his bat on the ball. Wilson went down too with a half-hearted swing. Ehmke had struck out the side and escaped the jam. The crowd gave him a hand.[12]

Cuyler went down swinging again in the fourth. In the fifth Ehmke struck out the last two Cubs, and all three he faced in the sixth—English plus Hornsby and Wilson again. Ehmke, who had managed only 20 strikeouts in the 55 innings he had pitched that year, ambled about the mound nonchalantly, giving no hint that he might be pitching himself into history.[13]

If anything, Charlie Root was outpitching Ehmke, allowing the A's just two hits in the first six innings. But in the seventh inning, he tried to drive Jimmie Foxx off the plate with a high fastball after the powerful slugger had fouled off a couple of 0-2 pitches. Foxx, off-balance, muscled the would-be duster straight into the northeast breeze and beyond the jury box in deep left center onto Waveland Avenue—"one of the longest hits ever made in this park," Hal Totten informed his listeners.[14]

One bad pitch had Root on the hook, 1–0. But in the bottom half of the inning the Cubs put runners on second and third with only one out. McCarthy sent Heathcote to hit for Taylor, and he flied weakly to left center. Cuyler, at third, had to hold. Hartnett came up next, hitting for Root. He took two called strikes, barked at Bill Klem's pitch calling, and then waved at a tantalizing curve for strike 3 and out 3. The crowd cheered Ehmke.

The A's pushed the lead to 3–0 against Guy Bush in the ninth inning, thanks largely to two errors by English. In the bottom of the inning, Cuyler reached second with one out on Dykes's throwing error. Stephenson cracked a single to send him home, and Grimm followed with a sharp hit to right field. With only one out, the Cubs had the tying run on base. But a pinch hitter forced Grimm for the second out, and then McCarthy sent in Chick Tolson, a reserve first baseman, to hit for Bush. Tolson worked Ehmke to a 3-2 count and waved at one last curve ball for out 3. It was Ehmke's thirteenth strikeout of the day, a Series record. During the regular season he had fooled just twenty American League batters.

Ehmke finally displayed his joy, jumping into the arms of his catcher, Mickey Cochrane. Well he might celebrate one of the most famous series upsets ever. The victory burnished Connie Mack's reputation even further. The sixty-seven-year-old McGillicuddy had taken control of the World Series on the Cubs' home grounds without even expending his superlative frontline pitchers.

Mack had in fact been running a brilliant disinformation campaign against the Cubs for several months. In mid-August, he left Ehmke behind when the A's left for a "Western" swing (meaning Cleveland, Detroit, Chicago, and St. Louis). The few who noticed Ehmke's absence or cared assumed either a sore arm, or perhaps a final parting of the ways. Despite a 7-2 record, Ehmke was not well regarded by his hard-driving younger teammates, proud as they were of unseating the mighty Yankees. Earlier in the year the A's had run Ehmke out of the locker room for his seeming indifference to giving up a game-deciding home run. Ehmke also annoyed them by requesting such privileges as six days' rest between starts. There was also a story that Ehmke and Al Simmons had staged a fight in the clubhouse.[15]

It turned out that Mack had not cut Ehmke or probably even disciplined him; it was just that, with the AL flag well in hand, up-to-date information about the Cubs would prove more valuable to the A's than a few spot starts. So while the Cubs were conducting their long march through the East, Ehmke slipped into the East Coast ballparks—the Polo Grounds, Ebbets Field, Baker Bowl—and studied Murderers' Row with his veteran's eye.[16]

Mack's series preparations didn't stop there, according to the stories. Not long after counseling Art Shires at Shibe Park, Mack conferenced with four Sox—Tommy Thomas, Ted Lyons, Red Faber, and Moe Berg. In a two-hour session, they passed along the fruits of their City Series experiences with the Cubs. When John McGraw's Giants traveled to Chicago, Mack dispatched another secret agent, an ex-A's player, to record exactly where McGraw stationed his outfielders for different Cub hitters.[17]

The Cubs had scouted the A's, too, but with no attempt at secrecy. McCarthy sent Joe Tinker, the old Cub great and an ex-manager himself, to watch the A's. Tinker even introduced himself to Mack, his old foe from the 1910 World Series, when he arrived in Shibe Park. The Cubs' openness triggered another ruse from Mack. With the pennant safely in hand, the A's big hitters, Simmons and Foxx, acted out a pantomime for Tinker, swinging at pitches they normally wouldn't touch, ignoring the high fastballs they feasted on. Tinker hustled back to Chicago with the word for McCarthy: Simmons and Foxx had trouble with fast stuff high and inside.[18]

Mack's final pre-series gambit was refusing to make the traditional announcement of a starter for the opening game. The baseball writers took the bait. The sports pages were filled with story after story: would Mack would choose one of his lefties, Lefty Grove or Rube Walberg, or the right-handed George Earnshaw? When the A's train pulled into Chicago, Ty Cobb, only a year retired from the A's roster, stepped off and added a couple of new possibilities: Ehmke or Jack Quinn, another old-timer on the staff. That convinced no one, the Cubs included. Even when Ehmke began warming up on the sidelines the afternoon of the game, they refused to believe he would be the starter. Soon, Earnshaw or Grove would emerge and orthodox baseball would commence.[19]

But it was not to be. Mack, they said, had the first game of the 1929 World Series in his pocket before a pitch was thrown. Maybe Grover Alexander was right after all: McCarthy was a busher.

"I would love to play in this ballpark a couple of years!" exclaimed one of the many ballplayers-turned-reporters attending game 2. Surveying Wrigley Field from a perch in the press box, the athlete guessed that he would be able to hit seventy-five home runs a year playing for the Cubs. The correspondent, of course, was Babe Ruth, covering the A's-Cubs World Series for the Christy Walsh Syndicate.[20]

Ruth had arrived at the park clad in a topcoat. Chicago's lakefront weather, always fickle, had changed dramatically since the Indian summer of the day before; it was suddenly cloudy and cold. During batting practice, Wilson, Cuyler, Heathcote, and English huddled under a blanket, just as the stylishly clad Mrs. Clifford Connors, Mrs. George Mitchell, and Mrs. Clarence Slinging were doing up in the stands. The performance of Foxx and Simmons in the second game seemed to prove the Babe's point. In the teeth of the cold breeze blowing straight in from the outfield, they both crashed long home runs that provided all the scoring their club needed. There was much more scoring in the chilly, overcast conditions, most of it by the A's. Malone, wild and behind in the count to most batters, was knocked out in the fourth; his reliever, Carlson, was pummeled too. The Athletics dominated the Cubs with their pitching, their hitting, and their all-around aggressiveness. They were playing the way McCarthy himself favored, disdaining the sacrifice bunt, always looking for the big inning. It was a style the Cubs had seldom faced in their march through the more traditional National League.[21]

The A's never let up. The vehemence of their bench jockeying caught the Cubs by surprise and enlarged the vocabularies of many socialites in the first-base boxes. The Cubs tried returning the barrage individually, but it was the box patrons who finally took up the Cubs' cause late in the first game. The A's, unfazed, leaned out of their dugout and redirected their abuse at the fans, even though Judge Landis, sitting nearby in a box seat, was within earshot.[22]

As the Philadelphia lead mounted in the second game, the jockeying broke out again, and the Cubs began to look more and more demoralized. Hornsby struck out on three straight pitches in the first, and the crowd muttered. In the third the mutterings turned to outright boos when he struck out again—the first time the great batsman had heard the "stockyard cheer" in a Cub uniform.[23] Hornsby stalked off barking at the home plate umpire, then threw his bat angrily on the bat pile. Minutes later, Cuyler walked, but Stephenson flied out to end the inning. The Cubs went back out on the field with a beaten air about them; English soon committed his third error of the series.

The Cubs eventually managed to knock out the Athletics' starter, George Earnshaw, but that only brought on Lefty Grove, the preeminent left-handed pitcher in the universe. Although someone among the all-right-handed Murderers' Row should have welcomed the opportunity to face a fastballing, non-curving lefty, outside of Dazzy Vance the Cubs had probably not encountered anyone with Grove's kind of speed and control. Grove dominated the Cubs the rest of the way on three hits and a walk, striking out six in 4⅓ innings. Hartnett fanned again as a pinch hitter, making it four strikeouts in six attempts for Cub pinch hitters. The Cubs tied the World Series record of thirteen strikeouts they had set the day before. Cuyler had fanned five times in the two games, Hornsby four. The customers had begun heading for the exits long before the last out. More than a few stopped on their way out, turned, and booed. Baseball was finished for the decade at Addison and Clark.[24]

The Cubs boarded the train to Philadelphia that evening and raced through the night for the continuation of a series that was apparently turning into another American League sweep. On board the Cubs' special was a contingent of dazed ballplayers, newsmen, and the rest of the entourage. On the train a Cub star known for his blunt, outspoken ways buttonholed a reporter. McCarthy, he said, had been relying on bad information. Joe Tinker obviously didn't know what he was talking about with the high-and-tight stuff. How many others he spoke to about Tinker's advice is not known. Surely his comments eventually reached other ears.[25]

The A's catcher, Mickey Cochrane, sprang to his feet in the sixth inning of Saturday's fourth game and shouted furiously at the home plate umpire, Roy Van Graflan. Grimm is out! Cochrane insisted. The Cub first baseman had just beaten a perfect throw to the plate with a banzai slide under Cochrane's tag.

The Cub bench hooted merrily at the Philadelphia catcher from their dugout seats.[26] No longer the downhearted crew that had left Chicago a couple of days before, they were laughing the laugh of the fortunate, the confident. After taking game 3 the day before, they were dominating game 4. Today it was the A's pouring from their dugout in the third inning to protest a call, and Bing Miller allowing Cuyler's single through his legs and on to the wall in the fourth. Two pitches later Grimm brought Cuyler and himself home with the Cubs' first homer of the series, a screaming shot into the right-field stands. In the Cubs' dugout Guy Bush, the winner of game 3, waved a blanket in triumph as the rest of the bench erupted in joy. The Mudcat was the first National League pitcher to win a World Series game since Grover Alexander saved game 7 for Jesse Haines three years earlier, and well could he celebrate—game 3 had marked the pinnacle of his career.[27]

The Cubs kept hammering away at Connie Mack's forty-six-year-old starter, Jack Quinn, Connie Mack's candidate to repeat the Ehmke ambush. In the sixth inning Cuyler, down 0-2 after missing two straight sacrifice attempts, swung away and drove in another run. That was it for Quinn; Grimm, next up, tried to sacrifice the base runners along. The reliever promptly picked up the ball and threw it all the way to the right-field corner. Two more Cubs scored. Charlie Root went back to the mound in the bottom of the inning with a 7–0 lead. He was toying with the Philadelphia lineup.

The fifteen innings played so far in Philadelphia had almost precisely reversed the trauma in Chicago. The day before, Guy Bush had come out for game 3 high-spirited and laughing, tormenting the A's with Ehmke-style sidearm curve balls that swept away from the right-handed Simmons and Foxx.[28] Joe Tinker's scouting report had obviously been discarded.

Bush clowned his way on base in the sixth inning, refusing to unshoulder his bat until he had irritated George Earnshaw into issuing a walk. It was the opening the Cubs needed. Jimmy Dykes mishandled English's grounder, Hornsby singled Bush home, and Cuyler singled two more in.

Bush protected the Cubs' first lead of the series. After allowing two A's on base in the seventh, he retired Simmons and Foxx in succession. It was the A's last threat of the day. Bush finished a 3–1 winner—the exact score of game 1.

"Boy, that was the greatest game Ah evah won!" Bush exclaimed after hugging Grimm and Taylor and shaking hands with a lineup of his teammates. Cheering and hollering, the ballplayers poured into the clubhouse and took up a collection to rent a banjo for Grimm, who had been disheartened enough to leave his own instrument behind in Chicago. Soon Der Kaptink was playing the rented instrument "as he never played before. Sweet and loud beyond description." Joe McCarthy, too, was smiling again—and eating, too, after overcoming an attack of nervous indigestion. William Wrigley, stepping into a cab outside his hotel that night, exulted to a group of newsmen, "Boys, the Cubs can't lose!"[29]

Before game 4, someone mentioned to Wilson that Cochrane had complained about the Cubs' jockeying the day before. Wilson's wide features broke into a grin. "I'm glad they like it. They started it in Chicago and we says, 'If you want, we will give you plenty,' and that's what we're doing."[30]

The Cubs fairly gamboled onto the field, and by the fourth touched up Quinn with Grimm's homer. Then came the five-run sixth: Cub hits and Athletics' throws sailing to all parts of the field, followed by another clutch of hits in the seventh. Dykes speared Stephenson's hot one-out smash and started a lightning double play that closed out the inning, but the Cubs were the aggressors.

Root went to the mound in the bottom of the seventh with a four-hitter and an 8–0 lead. His only scare had come in the fifth, after Wilson dropped a fly ball with a man already on base. But then Taylor cut down the lead runner on a double steal attempt, and Wilson followed with the outstanding play of the series, a leaping, running catch of Jimmie Foxx's long drive for the third out. Veterans of many World Series thought it one of the great plays in the history of the classic. The Cub bench poured out to greet Root and Wilson as they came off the field. Cuyler and Grimm each gave Hack a hug.[31]

Wilson had trouble with another fly to close out the Athletics' sixth. He managed to hang on to it, but the autumn sun, hanging low in the sky, was obviously bothering him. The *Herald and Examiner*'s Wayne Otto had noticed both center fielders stabbing at fly balls as they struggled with the sun; now, in the late innings, the sunlight would be slanting directly in their eyes, especially if something were hit on the line straight at them.[32]

The Philadelphia fans were barely finished with the seventh inning stretch when Al Simmons whacked Root's third pitch onto the roof of the left-field pavilion. "Well, we won't be shut out, anyway," Dykes told Mack as Simmons trotted around the diamond.[33]

Up in the press box, the power and esprit the Cubs displayed had turned the consensus, that ever-fickle groupthink, toward the Cubs. Around the ballpark and in other points unknown, the oddsmakers, who had consistently favored the A's so far, were recalculating.[34]

The pale October sun hung almost directly over the grandstand as the bottom of the seventh got under way. The Philadelphia public, sedate even in the best of times, sat down after the seventh-inning stretch to watch Root continue work on his three-hitter. The reverie was broken on Root's third pitch to Simmons, leading off. There was a smattering of applause from the stands.

The spell had somehow been broken. Somewhere, in Valhalla or wherever these decisions are made, a decree had been issued that Charlie Root could not pitch the Chicago Cubs to a world title, that William Wrigley's lifetime of success and generosity would come to naught, that only a handful of the members of the 1929 Cubs would ever know what it was like to play on a world's champion. The ball began jumping off Philadelphia bats and finding places to fall. There were four singles in a row, then a pop out, then seven more safeties. Taylor barked at Root, the Cubs infielders huddled around him, but it was no use. History's wheel had turned, and that was all there was to it.

In the midst of the skein, Wilson staggered under an ordinary fly ball off Bing Miller's bat, and it dropped from the sun for a hit. The sun was hanging ever lower in the sky; in the stands, John McGraw watched his former player, Art Nehf, relieving Root, shielding his eyes with his hand each time Taylor tossed the ball back to him.[35] Then another drive, this one long and deep, headed for Wilson's territory in center. He drifted back, squinting into the sun, then stopped and grasped frantically with his bare hand as the ball sailed by and rolled to the fence. Three Athletics, including the batter, Mule Haas, sped around the bases while Wilson frantically chased the ball down. The score was suddenly, unbelievably, 8–7.

"What can I do?" McCarthy moaned aloud as the dream died. The answer was, Nothing. A double play ball bounced over McMillan's head at third base. After a tying single, Malone came in to relieve. He hit the first batter he faced. With the bases loaded, he worked Dykes, the next hitter, to a 2-2 count. Dykes whaled the next pitch to deep left. Stephenson, trying to keep the go-ahead runs from scoring, dived desperately, but the ball trickled off his fingers and into the left-field corner.[36]

The A's third-base coach, Eddie Collins, a forty-two-year-old still listed on the active roster, ran around in circles while Simmons and Foxx scored. Finally, delirious with joy, he threw himself into a slide in foul territory. The scoreboard attendants hastily improvised a hand-painted "10" to prop into the window for the A's seventh: ten runs across with only one out. Twelve of thirteen batters had reached base safely.[37]

Then, as suddenly as the squall had blown up, it was over. Malone went back to work and overpowered two A's batters on strikes to close out the inning.

In the vast darkness of the Oriental's giant auditorium, someone looked up at the smiling faces of the Cubs promoting their coming act and let loose with a stockyard cheer.[38] Then someone else, and quickly several more, until the unhappy crowd had had its fill. The rest of the day it went on like that in the big theater on Randolph near State: orchestra rising, skits running, shorts playing, and stockyards cheering.

In the space of a mere four October days the Chicago Cubs had managed to loosen their hold on the populace of Chicago. In fact, the fortunes of the Chicago National Ball Club for decades to come had been settled by the events of that sunny, sunny day in Philadelphia, Pennsylvania.

The sun had settled behind the grandstand as the Cubs came to bat in the eighth. A two-run deficit in the late innings had meant nothing to them in the dog days of July and August. Time and again, Murderers' Row had refused to concede any deficit, and the runs had appeared like manna.

But in July and August, the Row had faced no one resembling Lefty Grove. The Olympian left-hander, well rested after pitching just five innings three days earlier, came in to hurl thunderbolts through a shadowy diamond at mere mortals. Overmatched, the Cubs fouled Grove's fastballs weakly to the opposite side. An infield roller and two strikeouts quickly closed out the top of the eighth.

In the bottom of the inning, the A's threatened to build their lead, but Stephenson threw a runner out at the plate to cut the rally short. McMillan and English, the top of the Cubs' order, led off the ninth. Grove, never noted for his finesse, was rearing back with everything he had, and the two Cub infielders looked more than ever like overmatched glove men. They went down futilely against the overpowering Grove.

The Cubs' last hope, their megastar, the Rajah, came up. The Greatest Right-handed Hitter faced the Greatest Left-handed Pitcher; righty against lefty, ninth inning, two out. Hornsby took a ball from Grove, then two strikes, then fouled one down the right-field line.

It was 3:42 p.m. Wilson was on deck, waiting for the chance to redeem himself. Hornsby cracked Grove's fastball toward Bing Miller in right field. Miller came on and tucked the ball away easily.

The great upset was in the record books. The A's, suddenly up three games to one, charged jubilantly off the field toward the clubhouse. Several minutes later their courtly manager followed them there for a rare postgame visit. Dressed in a blue suit with an overcoat neatly tucked over one arm, he waited a moment in front of the door, listening to the bedlam of cheering, singing, and inarticulate bellowing emanating from the quarters. Then he yanked on the doorknob and walked in.

The tumult receded like the Red Sea before Moses. Mack looked around and cleared his throat. Finally, he spoke. "I'd just like to be able to express to you the things I feel. But I can't. I'll have to let it go at that." He turned on his heel and quickly left the room. The frenzied celebration resumed.[39]

Outside the press followed Mack down the hall. "I've never seen anything like that rally," he told them. "There is nothing in baseball history to compare it with. It was the greatest display of punch and fighting ability I've ever seen on a field."

The Cub locker room was full of defiance and anger. "Breaks. I'll say they got them," said Art Nehf. Asked McCarthy bitterly, "You can't beat the sun, can you?" Not far away Charlie Root sat in a daze. A writer approached him for a comment. Root answered with a stony stare. On the way back to the hotel, Andy Lotshaw was accosted by a jeering Philadelphian. The strapping Lotshaw, wordless for once, felled the man with a single punch.[40]

Wilson was tight-lipped too. Holding his three-year-old boy in his arms, he made his way through the postgame crowd and out to the team bus. Soon it pulled away for the Ben Franklin Hotel, where hundreds of onlookers, mostly supportive, filled the sidewalks around the entrance. In the lobby, there were hundreds more.

Wilson managed a smile after he stepped off the bus and entered the hotel lobby. "Couldn't see the balls," he told a knot of fans who called out to him. Root finally spoke, too. Miller's fly was the turning point, he told a Chicago reporter. Except for that, he said, he was sure he would have been strong enough to finish.[41]

The press corps covering the series, three hundred strong, who had collectively covered centuries of baseball, couldn't stop talking about what they had just witnessed. Writers strained for metaphors to explain it. "The greatest debacle, the most terrific flop, in the history of the World Series. . . . We've been looking at our score book for an hour now, thinking there must have been some horrible mistake, but ten she is, folks," Ed Burns wrote on page 1 of the World's Greatest Newspaper. John Drebinger of the *New York Times* thought back to the start of the seventh inning, when Murderers' Row was a mighty machine, moving "magnificently and in all its glistening splendor. Twenty minutes later it lay strewn all over the field, a jangled mass of junk."[42]

Newsmen found a couple of old series opponents, Johnny Evers and Ty Cobb, likewise groping for explanations of the great meltdown. The two greats surmised that Root, in the manner of old-timers like Alexander and Chief Bender, had been coasting on his big lead, then found himself unable to regain his rhythm when real trouble started.[43]

Learned diagnoses were not scarce. McCarthy had gone too long with Root, misallocated his relief pitchers, ignored the telltales of Wilson's trouble with the sun, and even forgotten that he had an excellent reserve outfielder named Cliff Heathcote.[44]

Ordinarily, the two ball clubs would have met again the next day for game 5. But this was Philadelphia, where law and tradition still forbade Sunday baseball. One wag nominated Sunday in Philadelphia as the strongest possible argument against the policy.

Early in the morning Root and Grimm stopped by Wilson's room and knocked on the door. It was just a ballgame, Root told him with a clap on the back. Wilson wasn't buying it. "That's a sweet speech, but it's a lot of baloney," he replied.[45] Root left for a round of golf; the ever-popular Grimm chose among four dinner invitations he had received around town.

Down in the lobby, Hornsby faced a swarm of reporters. "What's the use of moaning about it? That one's gone," he said.[46]

The Athletics, most still living in their summer residences, were surrounded by admirers whenever they set foot outside. Eddie Collins delivered a side of venison to the baseball writers' headquarters, the Bellevue-Stratfford, and invited all the correspondents over for a feast. He appeared unconcerned about Monday's game, announcing plans to leave Tuesday morning on a hunting trip.[47]

Mack himself even admitted that his team had the Cubs "slightly on the run." On Monday he and McCarthy were summoned to Landis's presence, where the all-high one dressed them down like a couple of schoolboys. The bench jockeying had gone far enough, Landis told them, exposing the box-seat customers to truly rough language. Landis's exact phrasing wasn't recorded, but the imminent arrival of the president of the United States at the World Series must have been his chief concern; the commissioner apparently had ignored the widespread gutter talk in Chicago. Henceforth offenders would have their World Series shares confiscated by the commissioner's office. To make sure he had both men's attention, Landis added that if he couldn't make out the exact culprit, the fine would go on the manager's tab. Whatever one thought of the judge or his methods, there was no question that he had a way of getting his point across.[48]

The Cubs' would-be vaudevillians had financial pressures of their own. While their leader, Grimm, socialized, Cuyler and Heathcote had spent their Sunday holed up at the hotel. Guessing correctly that Chicagoans would not be in the right mood to catch their act after the series, they drew up a carefully worded telegram and sent it on to the Balaban & Katz offices in Chicago.

Balaban & Katz needed no persuading. The raucous booing and hissing at the Oriental had already convinced the firm that the act would be a loser. Two B&K employees left for Philadelphia with the authority to settle with the three Cubs. They arrived Monday morning and, ignorant of the previous day's telegrams, made their way to the Cubs' hotel, where they immediately looked up Grimm and made the buyout offer authorized by management.

Grimm welcomed the envoys cordially and heard out their proposition with pleasure. B&K's payment for cancellation would nicely cover that gap between the winners' and losers' Series shares. Then Cuyler and Heathcote stopped by. The two outfielders blurted out their urgent wish to be rid of the contract. Grimm, standing behind the B&K men, gestured frantically to his teammates, but it was too late. The theater representatives quickly accepted Cuyler and Heathcote's offer and made their adieus.[49]

Grimm was beside himself. The Cubs couldn't get anything right.

Soon the ex-vaudevillians joined their teammates for the bus ride to the ballpark. This day they would play the biggest game of their lives before the still-popular President of the United States, Herbert Hoover. The presidential group arrived shortly before game time to a generally friendly reception. A few disgruntled anti-Prohibition folks shouted, "We want beer!" Decorum was restored when Mrs. Hoover was presented with a bouquet. She flashed a gracious smile, and even the wets joined in the cheering.[50]

Then the Hoovers settled into the bunting-draped presidential box, where they were joined by Attorney-General William Mitchell, Mayor Harry Mackey, and those two men's spouses. The sportswriter Damon Runyon, a wet New Yorker if ever there was one, half-jokingly noted that Hoover's hat twitched each time a call went against the Cubs. Runyon guessed that Hoover might favor the Cubs because they trained in California, the president's voting residence. That was plausible enough, but Runyon explored no further possibilities: Hoover's roots in the Midwest, his status as one of Mr. Wrigley's Catalina house guests, or Wrigley's role in what we now term "crony capitalism."[51] Hoover would have plenty of opportunities to fret. The Cubs were only 27 outs from oblivion. They marched grim-faced from the clubhouse. Pat Malone, who Saturday had at least showed that he could strike out a few Athletics, would be their standard-bearer. The Cubs soon settled one score by knocking Howard Ehmke from the box with a fourth-inning rally, keyed by Cuyler's leadoff double. Mack, seeing that Ehmke's spell over Murderers' Row was gone, rushed in Rube Walberg, the fireballing left-hander who had won the second game. Walberg began matching goose eggs with Malone, who gave the A's just one hit in the second and another in the fifth. In the seventh Walberg retired the Cubs on just three pitches.[52]

With both pitchers in command, the first 8½ innings took less than an hour and a half to complete. English and McMillan backed Malone up with brilliant plays on the left side of the infield in the early innings. In the fifth Cuyler timed a magnificent leap at the fence to rob Simmons; a couple of plays later he unleashed a powerful throw to hold an A's runner on base. President Hoover and his wife watched intently, trying hard to conceal their loyalties until Hoover arose for the visitors' seventh-inning stretch. That itself might have been a politician's show of impartiality, but before the A's at-bat in the bottom of the inning, he had stayed seated until the Philadelphians in the vicinity shamed him into rising again.[53]

The Cubs were still leading 2–0 when a pinch hitter for Walberg struck out to open the bottom of the ninth. Malone seemed to be growing stronger as the innings went by, his fastball knifing through the shadows the way Grove's had on Saturday. Soon he had little Max Bishop, next up, in a 1-2 hole. Malone was smiling broadly. He was four strikes from victory.[54]

Bishop fought off the next pitch and sliced it far down the left-field line. Stephenson came over quickly to cut the ball off and hold Bishop to a single. Malone had been working the next batter, Mule Haas, on the outside corner successfully all day. Now, still looking unconcerned, Malone went inside with his first offering. Haas caught the ball on the nose and lofted it high and deep toward right field. Cuyler flattened himself helplessly against the fence as the ball sailed overhead for a home run. The shutout was gone, the game tied.[55]

The ballpark erupted in pandemonium again. While Collins danced in the Philadelphia dugout, Mack, rolled-up scorecard still in hand, allowed that Haas's homer was "very helpful indeed, very helpful." Malone stalked toward home plate and berated Zack Taylor for the pitch he had just called. Grimm and the rest of the Cub infield rushed over, peppering Malone with questions about his arm. "Let me go. I'll get 'em," Malone assured them, and he headed back to the mound.[56]

By now the crowd was in a continuous, unrelenting uproar. In the midst of it, Runyon had the presence of mind to turn his reportorial eye back to the presidential box: "Mr. Hoover really seemed as dumbfounded as the Chicago ballplayers by this sudden run, and that was very dumbfounded, indeed. He was a little island of great calm in a boiling ocean of excitement."[57]

Returning to work, Malone quickly fell behind Mickey Cochrane 2-0 but finally got the Athletics' catcher to bounce out to Hornsby for the second out. Malone seemed to have eluded the reaper.

Unfortunately for the Black Knight's place in baseball history, the next batter was someone hitting around .360 in his still-young career: the redoubtable Al Simmons, a man every bit as tough as Malone fancied himself. He took one strike and then slapped the 0-1 off the scoreboard like a ping-pong serve. Simmons pulled into second with a standup double.

Malone's stuff had obviously deserted him, but McCarthy had no one warming up in the Cub bullpen. He ordered Foxx walked so Malone could pitch to the right-handed-hitting Bing Miller. Hornsby jogged in to say something to Malone, who got Miller to swing and miss badly on the next two pitches. Miller refused to nibble at two waste pitches, and at 2-2 Malone came in with one more fastball.

Miller cracked the pitch over Wilson's head toward the scoreboard in right center, almost the same place Simmons had hit the ball moments before. Wilson chased the ball as it rolled to the wall, but there would be no time for a play on Simmons, who rounded third, half running, half leaping, as another celebration began. "The Athletics are crazy," Hal Totten noted somberly in the press box. "They are doing a war dance all over the field in front of the clubhouse. They are world champions and are telling everybody about it."[58]

Wilson tracked the ball down by the scoreboard and stuck it in his pocket before beginning the long walk to the clubhouse. Even the Hoovers had begun cheering for the home team. Mayor Mackey hastily abandoned the presidential box to congratulate the A's. How close he got in the melee is unknown, but Hoover and his wife waited until he returned. Hoover yelled over the bedlam, "Well, Mr. Mayor, you'll give me credit for having been neutral most of the game."[59]

The president arose to depart for a political oblivion more historic than the antics of a few dozen ballplayers on a pretty autumn afternoon. Runyon reported a remarkable phenomenon considering the circumstances: the Philadelphia fans, at least those in Hoover's vicinity, remained seated until the presidential party exited. Bits of torn-up scorecards rained down everywhere, and the cries of the fans rent the air unceasingly.

Seven decades later, it is clear that the 1929 A's did not just get lucky. Lefty Grove's 300 wins, Jimmie Foxx' 534 home runs, Al Simmons's .334 lifetime batting average, Mickey Cochrane's contributions to three consecutive Philadelphia pennant winners, and two more for Detroit as a playing-manager: all are part of the baseball firmament.

But it was not as easy to understand for the Cubs who steamed out of Philadelphia late in the afternoon of October 15 on what would be remembered as the "Funeral Train."[60] The Chicagoans had often played brilliantly, even dominating their foes for considerable stretches. Except for game 2 and the two surreal innings in games 4 and 5, their pitchers had contained the Athletics' lineup. Wilson's sun blindness aside, all three Cub outfielders contributed spectacular outfield play, and English and Grimm were undeniably superior defenders to their counterparts on the Athletics. The disappointment was only sharpened by thoughts of what might have been with Hartnett in the lineup.

If it had been left at that, this might have been merely one series among many. Unfortunately, William Wrigley would not leave it at that. Wrigley was more than the benevolent grandpa who in midgame might hand a groundskeeper half a day's wages to pick up an item down the street—keep the change. The jolly man of good cheer, the ebullient deal maker and brainstormer, was a flinty taskmaster in the bargain. "Bill" Wrigley to his public, up close he was "Mr. Wrigley" or, at best, "William" to everyone but his wife. Subordinates could err—once. "Jake, don't let that happen again," was all he told an executive who had just made an expensive mistake.[61]

Now, after four years of success, one of Wrigley's baseball men had made his own very expensive mistake—several of them. Beginning with Tinker's scouting mission, McCarthy had zigged where Connie Mack had zagged. The result had been the thrashing that William Wrigley's stable of thoroughbreds had just absorbed. McCarthy's pinch hitters fizzled; his relief pitchers flopped. Murderers' Row managed one home run to the Athletics' five. Root and Malone had fed fastballs to the Athletics' bashers, with predictable results when their arms tired in the late innings. Among the scores of sportswriters and ex-players attending the series, the consensus was that McCarthy was a capable fellow who might lack the quicksilver qualities necessary for greatness. No one said "busher" out loud, but the term must have crossed more than a few minds.[62]

Past the turn of the century, we can smile at the scope of that misjudgment. McCarthy would spend most of the next two decades hunting Mack's Athletics like frightened quarry. Where Mack won acclaim for taking two more pennants and one more World Series in the next two years, McCarthy would win four straight world titles at one stretch and seven World Series total—six of the eight played from 1936 to 1943. He won so much and so often that, sometime in the 1940s, a despairing American League manager supposedly gestured at McCarthy one day and said, "Look at that guy. He doesn't have to do anything but push buttons to win." The envious critic was Jimmie Dykes, who had been repaid tenfold for that decisive double off Stephenson's outstretched glove in game 4 of the 1929 World Series.

But on October 14, 1929, McCarthy was not a Hall of Fame manager, just a losing one. "I'll be damned if I say the best team won," he croaked. "I'll never believe what my eyes saw in that bad dream Saturday.

"Wonder what time the train leaves for Chicago?"[63]

It left none too soon for the Cubs, who were taking the sleeper back west. William Wrigley, preparing to board, announced that he would not "sit around and figure what might have been." His watchword, he said, would be "strengthen," his goal still the world championship.

Even before the final game, Wrigley had reached some conclusions. After the ten-run explosion in the fourth game, he shared the hotel elevator with Irving Vaughan of the *Chicago Tribune*. Joe McCarthy had one more year on his contract, Wrigley told Vaughan, and that was all he was going to get.[64]

There were downcast faces aplenty when the Cub train pulled into Union Station Wednesday afternoon. About five hundred of the hardiest fans tried to lift their heroes' spirits. "They give me hell with their razzing when I'm going good, but now when I deserve it they give me cheers instead," Wilson said wonderingly. "You can't figure 'em." Few other Cubs were consoled. They walked away silently, most of them refusing to pose for photographs. Hornsby glumly let a cameraman take a shot. With one hand jammed in the pocket of his open overcoat, a suit and tie underneath, he could have been a young financier whose portfolio had just gone sour.[65]

In fact, Hornsby's own portfolio, and many others', was in jeopardy. Brokers' offices had become dispirited places after all the hoopla of the past few years. For many weeks, declines had been outnumbering advances on the stock market. Countless small investors had already been ruined. Ten days after the Cubs' final pratfall in Philadelphia, the New York Stock Exchange began its final slide toward disaster.[66]

It was frightening, and it would prove to be the beginning of the greatest economic crisis in modern history. But few had any understanding of the danger, and there was still a willingness to traffic in 1920s-style silliness. Two of Chicago's foremost athletes were ready to contribute to the winter of unreality, the death throes of a feckless age.

9 ‖ "I Wanted Wilson"

They didn't have fighters like that nowadays. . . . [M]ost of them were real
Irish, lads who'd bless themselves before they fought; they weren't fake Irish
like most of the present-day dagoes and wops and sheenies who took
Hibernian nicknames. —James Farrell, *Young Lonigan*

In the autumn of 1929, James Farrell's fictional Studs Lonigan would have
been not quite thirty years old, yet far along in his career of dissolution
and disillusion. Farrell's trilogy of the doomed South Side man's life portrayed the long party of the 1920s, its loss of faith and the lawless, heedless
pleasure seeking that left Chicagoans like Lonigan's old 58th Street gang
adrift in a strange, materialistic new world. They drank and caroused
while trapped in dead-end lives of manual labor or menial clerical work.

A few of them achieved marriage and lower-middle-class respectability;
others succumbed to street life, drink, prison, or worse. The neighborhood
success was Studs's brother-in-law, a numbers runner. Studs himself was
a housepainter, working with his father.

The urban culture of the 58th Street gang had adopted the modern cult
of sports, in part as an outlet for ethnic rivalries. Bohemian football "clubs"
met Jewish football clubs; Irish boxers took on black boxers. Farrell's
fictional crew played a little organized amateur football, and Studs was
good enough at it that he began to regret dropping out of school after the
eighth grade. A real-life counterpart, Ragen's Colts, a supposedly sports-
oriented South Side club, was nothing but a street gang, the provocateurs
of the gruesome 1919 race riots. In the novel, Studs and friends did their
part on the fringe of the mayhem by cornering and humiliating a small
black boy and throwing bricks through windows.[1]

When rioting or organized sports were not available, Chicago's young
men haunted Chicago's ballparks and racetracks and boxing stadiums.

There were dog races and a new sport called jai alai, all with abundant opportunities for betting thrills. But in the 1920s fewer and fewer young men visited Comiskey Park, where only the periodic visits of Babe Ruth produced any sizable turnouts.

A seedy South Side alternative to watching the Sox lose was White City, a ramshackle wooden amusement park situated at 63rd and Stony Island near the site of the 1893 Columbian Exposition. The park's name harked back to the great exposition, but none of the glamour remained. There was a roller coaster, a bowling alley, a roller rink, and two dance floors, where the young men could hunt for young women they did not want to bring home to Mother. Professional boxing matches were a regular addition to White City's bill of fare, an opportunity for crowds of young men to vent their frustrations.[2]

On December 9, 1929, an excited capacity crowd filled White City's roller rink. The fans fortunate enough to gain entrance had already sat restlessly through the first five fights on the card, the fifth of which ended mercifully in the first round with one efficient knockout punch. Now it was time for the headliners on the evening's card. The customers were jostling for position in the sold-out general-admission section; even the windowsills were full of spectators. In the front rows millionaires and bootleggers, sometimes one and the same, leaned forward in anticipation as the next pair of boxers stepped through the ropes.

The din swirled around Dan Daly, a 210-pound heavyweight boxer only a few months removed from a cement-mixing crew in Ohio. In his first professional bout, Daly would be facing another first-timer, a lanky, 190-pounder, relatively new to town himself, with an intense, businesslike air about him.

Daly's opponent came out in a flowing wine-colored robe, made of silk and trimmed in gold and black and tied with a wide satin sash instead of the usual cord. On the back of the robe, in huge scarlet letters for all to see, was the bold proclamation

ART THE GREAT SHIRES

The customers burst out booing as soon as they recognized the Great One. They hooted again when the p.a. man announced "C. Arthur Shires,"

"I Wanted Wilson"

and louder than ever when he called Shires "the pride of baseball." Shires listened intently as the referee instructed the fighters and their handlers. Then both parties returned to their corners. Shires shed his robe to reveal black silk trunks with red stripes.

When the bell rang, the men began to stalk each other. They stood about the same height, 6'2", Daly a much burlier specimen. Daly opened with a right to the jaw. Shires hit back with an identical punch. Daly quickly answered with a left hook. Shires replied in kind. For twenty seconds this continued mercilessly, one punch after another with no attempt at defense. The crowd leaped as one to its feet in full blood lust. Daly unloaded his tenth punch at twenty seconds; at twenty-one came Shires's answer, which erased the lights of White City and the noise and the grimacing face of Art Shires from Daly's consciousness. He pitched face forward onto the canvas.

It was bedlam. They were all Shires fans in White City now, shouting huzzahs as Shires retreated quickly to the farthest corner while the referee ticked off his count. Then he helped the seconds pick up Daly's fallen form and carry him over to his corner for the requisite application of smelling salts.

The fans clamored for Shires's gloves as souvenirs. Shires, silent for once, merely smiled amid the hubbub. Only three months after suspension and disgrace, the twenty-two-year-old Texas tornado had once again figured out how to get his name in the papers—and this time earn money even Wilson or Hornsby would be hard put to equal.

The Great One declined to announce further boxing plans. But Jim Mullen, his manager, was not so shy. In front of the gathered newsmen he proclaimed that his charge would square off again in White City in a week, against George Trafton of the Chicago Bears. Mullen's words cleared Shires's head faster than a pinch of smelling salts, and the Art Shires of last summer reasserted himself. "No more punk fighters get any free publicity through me," he snarled. "I want the best or none. Get Tunney out of retirement for me."[3]

In mid-December 1929 Hack Wilson said good-bye to his wife, Virginia, and little Bobby and stepped out the back door of his house in Martinsburg, West Virginia. He was wearing a small, visored cap, not unlike the one he wore for the Cubs, a denim jacket with a tunic collar, and denim pants tucked in boots that fit over his size 6 shoes. They laced around from his famously thin ankles all the way to the knee.[4]

Hack told people that he enjoyed walking through the woods with a rifle better than hitting home runs in Wrigley Field—or chasing fly balls in Shibe Park, he might have added. So he spent his winter vacation hunting turkey with his brother-in-law in the nearby Blue Ridge Mountains, duck hunting on Maryland's Eastern Shore, and at the turn of December, deer hunting in Pennsylvania. Between hunts, Wilson and his friends liked to pile in a car and take off to the big cities of the eastern seaboard for a prizefight or a football game—Army–Navy at Philadelphia, or Notre Dame–Navy at Baltimore.[5]

Back in Martinsburg, there were evenings at the Martinsburg Elks Lodge No. 778, where the brothers still called him "Stouts," the nickname Wilson had picked up in the early '20s after breaking into organized baseball with the Martinsburg Blue Sox. One evening, just after watching kings lose two straight hands at the Elks lodge, Stouts was called away from the table. A telegram addressed to him had just arrived.[6]

An ambitious sort like Art Shires naturally wanted to fight someone more famous than a lineman for the relatively obscure Chicago Bears, whose only real star was Red Grange, decidedly not heavyweight material at 5'11", 175 pounds. Besides, Grange's brother Garland, who also played for the Bears, happened to be George Trafton's fight manager.

Only two athletes in Chicago possessed fame enough to meet Shires's criteria, and they both played in Wrigley Field for William Wrigley, not George Halas. One of them, Rogers Hornsby, was a fellow Texan, good with his fists and chronically short of cash, but it was inconceivable that he would have anything to do with Shires's buffoonery.

Buffoonery would be no problem for Mr. Wrigley's other star, and he was even better known as a fighter, in a strictly amateur sense, than Shires. The symmetries were compelling: Art Shires versus Hack Wilson. South Side versus North Side, American League versus National League, short versus tall, Sox versus Cubs. The two were even facing similar-sized lawsuits from disgruntled hecklers (in Shires's case, the widow of the heckler).

"I Wanted Wilson"

So it was that Chicago's sports fans woke up one Friday in mid-December 1929 to the news that Hack Wilson had agreed to fight Shires, sometime after the first of the year in the cavernous new Chicago Stadium. Bill Veeck was said to have okayed the arrangement, and Joe McCarthy, a boxing aficionado, volunteered to serve as one of Wilson's handlers. Shires's manager predicted a two-hundred-thousand-dollar gate, ten thousand of it guaranteed to Wilson.[7]

Shires could hardly contain himself. "The fact that Hack belongs in the National League, which is really just a minor league, doesn't hurt my major league pride," the Great One began. "The worst thing that I have against Sunny Boy is that he is an outfielder, and outfielders are for the most part a worthless lot."

Shires's joy was soon blunted by bad news from the Wrigley Building. Bill Veeck had without warning changed his mind about the fight—or had a greater power situated just down Michigan Avenue changed it for him? The Cubs' president had spent much of the day making long-distance calls to Martinsburg. One of his three calls came while Wilson was out hunting ducks; Veeck took advantage of the situation to solicit Mrs. Wilson's support for his new position. Although risk of injury may have motivated Veeck's changed position, it's easy to imagine Wrigley or even Judge Landis calling Veeck to register their surprise and disapproval—oh, and Bill, please leave my name out of it.[8] The fight's promoter, unwilling to let this financial killing go, upped his offer to Wilson to fifteen thousand dollars.

Ed Burns of the *Tribune* took a train all the way to Martinsburg, where he found Wilson beset by indecision. He told Burns, "I've been undecided all along, what with wanting to grab that $15,000 and yet not wanting to offend Mr. Veeck or cross my wife." He and Burns trooped over to the local bank, where Wilson asked to see fifteen thousand dollars, first in bills and then in gold. "I was curious to run my fingers through that much dough at one time," the little fellow explained sheepishly. "I'm not one of those greedy ballplayers you read about, but thoughts of those bucks certainly caused me to break out in a rash.

"I'm a spender, as everybody knows," he told Burns. "And I need all the money I can get. Just to remind you how I am about money, I tipped a waiter in Houston a dollar during last spring's season. . . . I understand Babe Ruth once gave a waiter $1 in spring training, but I've always doubted it."

Then it was off to the lodge, where Hack shadowboxed to show his brothers exactly how he would silence the obnoxious upstart of Comiskey Park. Back at the Wilson residence, the ballplayer moved the center table in the parlor so he could continue his demonstration for Burns. But a less enthusiastic decision-maker entered the room. "I don't believe I'll allow Lewis to go to Chicago alone, and I now feel a bit indisposed," Virginia Wilson told Burns. "I may cancel the trip entirely, or at least until after the holidays."

After Virginia left the room, Wilson explained, "The poor girl is all upset because she can't decide what to get me for Christmas. I've got a couple dozen watches, a full supply of hunting equipment, and all kinds of haberdashery and golf togs and jewelry. I've even got three pairs of slippers with 'Papa' embroidered on them and five smoking jackets."[9]

Wilson's quandary was solved when the results of the Shires–Trafton meeting came over the wires later the next night. Before another raucous White City crowd, Trafton floored Shires twice in the first round, saved by the bell after the second knockdown.

Neither fighter appeared to be in shape, Trafton in particular displaying more flab than fight fans expected from a professional heavyweight. The fight dragged on for another four dreary rounds. While George Halas and his Bears screamed, "Hit him!" from their front-row seats, Shires made that difficult by clinching at every chance he got. One of the Bears delivered the most decisive punch of the night when the WBBM announcer, Pat Flanagan, said something that angered him. He promptly walloped Flanagan in the eye. While the Andy Frains dragged his attacker out the door, Flanagan collected himself and went back to his broadcasting.[10]

By the last round the spectacle of the clumsy, exhausted fighters, still doggedly pursuing each other, was creating more jeers than anger. After the final bell, the victorious Trafton looked more relieved than joyful to hear the unanimous decision in his favor. It was a reasonable reaction under the circumstances. During the run-up to the fight, Trafton had answered the phone one day to hear an ominous message from an anonymous voice: Shires must win. A few days after that Trafton and his manager, Red Grange's brother Garland, had received a visit at the gym from one of Capone's main men, Machine Jack McGurn.

"Anybody talking to you?" Al Capone's right-hand man asked without formalities. Trafton and Grange, wisely enough, told McGurn about the phone threat. "Don't you worry," the gunman answered. "There ain't going to be any trouble. I think you can whip Shires. I just wanted to make sure there wasn't going to be any trouble."[11]

There was relief in Martinsburg too. Wilson was back at the Elks lodge when the news of Shires's defeat arrived. "Well," he told Burns, "you can tell the world that there needn't be any more talk about me going to Chicago to fight Shires. . . . There's no use in me bucking the Cubs, and making my wife mad, just to floor a guy who has already been licked."

Shires heard about Wilson's decision at his room in the Pershing Hotel the next morning. He was still in bed, barely able to speak through cut lips. "How could they expect me to lick a guy weighing 40 pounds more than I did?" he asked. "I might as well have been slapping the hull of a battleship."[12]

Not all was lost. For his troubles Shires was wealthier by $1,800, an amount equal to about a quarter of his annual baseball salary. He had a new offer to do vaudeville at $1,000 a week. Al Spohrer of the Boston Braves had announced his interest in fighting Shires; so had the captain of the football team at Grange's alma mater, the University of Illinois, as well as one Ray Fitzpatrick, supposedly a friend of Edward Young, Wilson's amateur fight opponent.

When Shires felt well enough, he traveled across town to speak before an advertising men's banquet. Shires obviously had valuable know-how in their chosen field. He was in it for the money, he confessed. "When I came to Chicago I didn't have a dime. You can call me crazy, but before I leave Chicago I'm going to have a quarter of a million."[13]

He gave the ad men the lowdown on Getting Your Picture in the Papers:

Folks said, "That Art Shires is publicity crazy." I want to tell you here and now that I don't give a damn for publicity. But that photographer had two kiddies to support, and if he hadn't got that picture his managing editor would have fired him.

That's Art—thinking of the other fellow.

A lot of fellows work a year for $1,800. I worked five rounds and got it. I may be dumb, but I think the guys who paid $5 a seat to see me are dumber.

The next morning Shires kept preaching the gospel of hustle as he wolfed down his eggs, sunny side up, in his room. "I was busted when I came to Chicago. Now look at me. And I was busted after playing ball part of the year when I finished paying my fines. But I've made 4,000 bucks since then and from now on watch me go." He gestured out the window toward the South Side sprawling toward the prairie. "Now these White Sox—who ever heard of them since they were cleaned ten years ago? Nobody. But me, everybody knows me."[14]

On December 22, Hack Wilson opened his mail to find a Christmas card signed "The Great, Great Shires." In 1929 the mail could leave a West Virginia town the afternoon of December 22 and make it to Chicago before Christmas, so Wilson fired off a reply: "Why not battle it out next October in the 1930 World Series? I'll be in it, so it's up to you to carry out your end."[15]

Art Shires's boxing career had three more turbulent weeks to run. The day after Christmas, he traveled to Buffalo to knock out Bad Bill Bailey of Texas in 1:22 of the first round. Joe McCarthy, a boxing enthusiast who had just built a home in Buffalo, was looking on. On January 1 Shires went to Detroit to meet Battling Criss, but he backed out with a cold that had settled in his neck.[16]

A physician had supposedly been called in to monitor Shires's condition, but both the cold and his boxing career suddenly fell under suspicion. First, Battling Criss's manager, one Bandes, or possibly Vance, Gildersleeve, provided an affidavit in which he charged that Shires's illness had developed soon after Gildersleeve refused either to fix the fight or to back out of the contract. He quoted Shires's people as telling him, "You know that we can't lose that fight tomorrow night." Soon "Dan Daly" approached the boxing authorities and alleged that he had taken a dive for Shires in White City. In fact, he explained, his name wasn't Dan Daly, but Jim Gerry, and Shires's promoters had showered him with inducements—evidently walking-about money and new clothing as well as subtle threats—to take the fall under the assumed name they gave him. The Illinois and Michigan boxing commissions both launched investigations, and Shires's professional boxing status was swiftly suspended in thirty-two states. Shires and his manager denied the accusations, the Great One rambling,

"I Wanted Wilson"

"All I am in it for is to entertain the fans and get some money. I had to eat somehow this winter and as long as the fans want to see me fight, I'll continue."[17]

Mullen defended his operation, asking why a dishonest promoter would have allowed George Trafton to punch out his "best meal ticket." At any rate, Shires was still eligible to box for pay in sixteen states, including Minnesota, so on January 7 he traveled to St. Paul for another first-round knockout, this time of Tony Faeth, a former major league pitcher; Shires then defiantly asked the crowd if anyone thought Faeth resembled Dan Daly.[18]

Even better news came from Chicago. After listening to several witnesses, the Illinois State Athletic Commission decided that Shires and his people had been telling the truth. The decisive testimony seemed to come from the fight's referee, who had poked his finger into Daly's gut after the knockout without drawing the reaction a conscious person would show. In Michigan, the chairman of the comparable Michigan authority had already told the press that his agency had found no evidence implicating Shires personally in the Battling Criss fiasco.[19]

Shires moved on to Boston for his most ambitious date. There, on January 10, a derisive throng of more than eighteen thousand watched him TKO Al Spohrer, the bald-headed Braves catcher. After Shires decked his opponent for a nine-count in the second round, Spohrer held a defensive pose for the duration, until his handlers finally conceded in the fourth round. Although the scoring had awarded Shires a decisive advantage of 87 hits and 39 misses to Spohrer's 27 and 20, the crowd jeered the verdict. The Great One, unfazed, waved them into silence before announcing, "I didn't want Al Spohrer—I wanted Hack Wilson."[20]

Post Spohrer, Shires moved into the best suite of an expensive hotel in Back Bay. He anticipated his biggest payday yet for the huge turnout at the Spohrer match. That would mean that in the past month, he had easily surpassed the $8,200 salary Charles Comiskey paid him—shrunken as it was by some $3,000 in fines. "I already am as great an attraction as Babe Ruth," Shires boasted. "If you don't think so, compare the way the crowds razz me and razz the Babe. . . . I really am God's gift to the hard-working sportswriters."[21]

Shires also learned that he had won one on the legal side. At the very peak of Shires's earning capacity, Mrs. Ida Lawson had decided to settle for $500—about $24,500 less than she had sued for in March 1929, after Shires skulled Mr. Lawson with a baseball. A few days later more good news arrived. Wilson's "press representative," a Martinsburg sports reporter named King Larkin, announced that Hack Wilson was reconsidering: Shires's recent success, he said, had restored the Great One's fighting reputation. Learning that Shires had cleared more than five figures in the past month may have motivated the Martinsburg team as well. Wilson promised Jim Mullen that he would visit Chicago within ten days to discuss terms.[22]

Unfortunately for the dual-sport sluggers and their entourages, Judge Landis had been closely following these very public negotiations. Before Shires could do any more damage to baseball, boxing, his opponents, or himself, the commissioner summoned the sometime White Sox first baseman to his office on the Boul Mich post haste. Shires appeared one frosty January morning after arriving on the overnight train from the East. Unshaven, he sat down in the judge's anteroom to await his review. After a while Landis's shock of white hair popped out the door. Ignoring Shires, he called another party into the office.

Finally Landis beckoned Shires, who meekly entered the inner sanctum. Reporters trying to listen through the keyhole could hear almost nothing but Landis's voice. "Either baseball or boxing for you from here on out" was the only phrase that came through clearly. The few times Shires's voice became audible, the judge cut him off. The tongue-lashing was brief, of about four minutes' duration. Shires emerged, a sickly smile on his face. He declined to make a statement or to pose for photos, saying only, "I'm sorry, boys, but I'm doing what I'm told." After he left, the judge appeared and handed out a short statement he had prepared: "Hereafter, any person connected with any club of this organization who engages in professional boxing will be regarded as having permanently retired from baseball. The two activities do not mix."

Later in the day Shires formally announced his retirement from professional boxing. The totals for his six-week career: a 4-1 record with three knockouts.[23] The new decade was only three weeks old, but the high times were already over for Art Shires: no more luxury suites, no more ten-thousand-dollar months. The '20s were over, indeed. "In the Wake of the News," a *Tribune* sports column, mused the same week: "We wonder where all the market tips of August and September have gone. We haven't been handed a 'good thing' in several months."

A few weeks later Shires began a spring training holdout. At first, Shires seemed as blithe as ever after all his adventures. All that talk about his requesting $25,000 in salary from Comiskey? Bunk, said the Great One—he'd be more than happy with $15,000. By mid-March, his boxing stash evidently dwindling, he capitulated to Comiskey's offer of $7,500. Yet even that humbling amount came with another lecture from the older generation. Comiskey wired Shires that to be reinstated, he would have to know "who accused you of wrongdoing while participating in the boxing ring, who suspended you, and who produced the evidence that caused your reinstatement. Do not report to San Antonio until you have answered the foregoing questions to me." Landis could not have been more concise.[24]

Shires evidently satisfied the Old Roman's curiosity, because soon he reported to the Sox camp without incident, or, indeed much flair at all. For one thing, he didn't have Lena Blackburne to kick around any more—Comiskey had hired a new manager, Donie Bush, the very fellow who had stared down Kiki Cuyler in 1927. Jimmy Powers of the *New York Daily News* watched the new Shires in action:

> Baseball's most notorious playboy, Arthur (The Great) Shires, has reformed. He says "Yes, ma'am" to the waitresses and he nods an attentive and respectful "Yes, sir" to the diminutive Donie Bush, manager of the Chicago White Sox. Gone are the swaggering ways, the loud lobby speeches, the waxed blond mustachios, and the troupe of embellished pronouns trotted out for the benefit of gaping strangers.
>
> Art entered a Fort Worth hotel unheralded and unsung recently. He nodded politely to three members of the press who were gabbing with the red-headed cigarette girl, and asked the clerk in a surprisingly low and well-modulated voice for his key. He assisted a leather-necked old rancher into the elevator and unostentatiously withdrew to his chamber.[25]

Over the winter, Bush had promised that Shires would start out with a clean slate, and the newer, quieter Shires was the Sox's starting first baseman for the season opener, but he went out of the lineup after colliding with Cleveland's Johnny Hodapp in the season's fourth game; when he returned his batting average stalled in the .250s. On June 16, the trading deadline, he pinch-hit for Ted Lyons and singled in his final appearance in a White Sox uniform. That evening the Sox sent Shires to Washington for two serviceable veterans.

The new, more-discreet Shires arrived in the capital, still overdressed but conspicuously wearing his new, team-oriented persona. Walter Johnson, though, was managing a contending ball club whose first baseman (and the Big Train's longtime teammate), Joe Judge, had held the job since 1916. In late July the Senators brought in yet another first-baseman from Kansas City, and it became obvious that Shires, despite the .369 he hit for Johnson the rest of the way, was suddenly a third-stringer.

Maybe he had said something wrong—for instance, addressing the Big Train as "Walter" or telling him "I'm human like the rest of you and I'm glad to be winning the pennant for you." He hustled as usual on the field, his uniform screaming for attention with the number 13. At season's end the Senators asked waivers on him, but not a single American League team wanted to take on a time bomb like the Great One. Washington eventually sold him to Milwaukee of the American Association. "The best ballplayer I have ever sent back to the minors," concluded Clark Griffith, the Senators' owner.[26]

In early February, Hack Wilson finally made it into Chicago. Rather than Art Shires in the Chicago Stadium, he would be facing Edward Young in Cook County Circuit Court.

Young, testifying first, admitted to drinking beer before the game the afternoon of June 21, 1928, but insisted he was not "intoxicated." He claimed he had called Wilson nothing worse than a "tub" through the course of the game. Young's attorney then called his first witness, a physician who had treated the milkman for a bruised back and a lip that had required three stitches. That was the only witness for Young. Inexplicably—or perhaps not, considering the nearly totalitarian hold Wilson and the Cubs had established over the populace—Young could produce not one more supporter, even though numerous box seat patrons had witnessed Wilson's charge, not to mention the many news accounts, beginning with the mighty *Tribune*, that had consistently described Wilson as "thumping Mr. Young soundly": one who "slapped down Edward Young," "punched an abusive fan," and "endeavored to land several large swipes" at Young's jaw.[27]

After a recess for lunch, Wilson, nervous but unflustered, took the stand himself. Wilson's version of his charge into the stands differed greatly from the original press accounts. He admitted going into the stands after Young but explained that his spikes had made him slip and fall on the concrete. As a result, he had never laid a hand on Young, he said: on the contrary, Young had jumped on him while he was sprawled on the grandstand floor.[28]

Wilson turned argumentative only once, when Young's attorney mentioned during cross-examination that Wilson had struck out just before the incident. "I didn't strike out. I grounded to first base," Wilson corrected him quickly. "If I had struck out there would have been a lot of noise. . . . There wasn't any excitement. Everyone was quiet and Stevie was at bat." Wilson said Young had called him "a—a name." "What was it?" inquired the judge, William Fulton. Wilson, turning red, whispered the word into the judge's ear. "Hmm," commented Fulton. The jury could guess what the word was: Wilson's attorney had already informed them in his opening remarks that Young had insulted Hack's ancestry.[29]

A parade of witnesses—Gabby Hartnett, two policemen, a hotel owner, and a customs attorney—backed up Wilson's version. The jury took less than half an hour to reject Young's complaint. Hartnett and Wilson, grinning broadly, posed with a flock of admirers outside the courtroom. Hartnett stood a head taller than Wilson, who in a crowd of typical Chicagoans was nearly the height of the group as a whole. Wilson told everybody he would be back in town to leave for Catalina in a couple of weeks. As far as Hack was concerned, 1930 was shaping up as a very good year.[30]

10 | The Prime of Mr. Hack Wilson

My candle burns at both ends;
It will not last the night;
But ah, my foes, and oh, my friends—
It gives a lovely light!
—Edna St. Vincent Millay, "First Fig"

There wasn't a time that whole year that I was ever in a hotel room before 11
o'clock in the morning. —Hack Wilson, *Chicago Daily News*, August 19, 1938

High on Mount Ada, a distinguished houseguest at the Wrigley mansion
stared down glumly at Avalon Harbor from the porch. Below, he could
see the *S.S. Catalina* making landfall. At the dock, William Wrigley, a
fife-and-drum corps, and a platoon of talkie cameras were straining for a
look at the 1930 edition of the Chicago Cubs—not to mention a genuine,
if recently retired, president of the United States. The ship's orchestra was
sawing away on "Happy Days Are Here Again."

From the Wrigleys' front porch, several hundred yards away, the guest—
known the world over for his silent ways—could hear the strains of the
tune that before long would become the theme song of the Democrats'
presidential standard bearer. The diversions of the exotic locale he was
visiting, including an observation tour in a glass-bottomed boat, had failed
to capture the imagination of this close-mouthed New Englander, although
he had laughed when Mr. Wrigley's pet macaw squawked after settling
on his shoulder.[1]

To be fair, the onlooker had just survived the heavy, whitecapped seas
and stiff breezes of the wintertime passage across the Catalina channel, a
trip that had fazed more than one of Mr. Wrigley's superb athletes, including several Wrigley's guest was watching stagger off the ship. Then again,

the state of the failing U.S. economy was enough to bring anyone low—he'd heard talk all winter that his policies had brought on the crisis.

After ignoring the hubbub over the arrival of the National League champions for several more hours, the man and his wife left for the mainland, where Charles and Anne Lindbergh visited the tourist in his hotel suite. His mood remained subdued. A day or two later, still in Los Angeles, he opened an envelope to find a warning of imminent assassination. "Guess this belongs to you," said the ex-president of the United States, Calvin Coolidge, handing the letter to a bodyguard.[2]

Silent Cal's visit seemed to set the tone for the Cubs' spring training. After the gala welcome at the dock, William Wrigley began avoiding the practice diamond as stubbornly as Coolidge. Some guessed that the disappointment of the World Series still weighed heavily on the Cub owner. No one could really say. Perhaps Coolidge had shared his forebodings about what was to come for the country.[3]

Wrigley's absence meant none of the family barbecues on Mount Ada or rides around the island in his red-upholstered limousine. Not even the good news about Hartnett could lure the owner back to attend with his usual frequency. Hartnett arrived in camp proclaiming he was back to normal after having his tonsils removed. In one of the practices, McCarthy impulsively grabbed a mitt and challenged Hartnett to throw the ball to him at second base. Hartnett began rocketing throws past the old infielder. After Hartnett's third missile nearly ripped the glove from his hand, McCarthy tucked the mitt away and headed back to the dugout without a word. It was the best news for the beleaguered little man since the pennant clincher the fall before.[4]

The word was quickly flashed back to Chicago, where the regulars were gathering for the second train west. When they arrived on the island several days later, Hornsby went out to see for himself. After watching Hartnett fire the ball around the infield a few times, he grunted, "That ought to settle it"—"it" meaning, in Texan, the pennant.

But even the optimism of the most knowledgeable player Wrigley had ever met could not change the owner's mind. His absences did not mean he had forgotten about his ball club. Over the winter he and Veeck had already sent McCarthy one message by dismissing one of his coaches, Grover Land. Ray Schalk, the ex–White Sox star and manager, took his place.[5]

McCarthy and Schalk barely exchanged words while they accompanied the pitchers and catchers on the first train to Catalina. During the ride, McCarthy drew a longtime friend aside. Winning or losing wouldn't make any difference, McCarthy told him—the coming season would be his last with the Cubs. The way McCarthy put it left no doubt that he had no say in the matter. McCarthy's pessimism made sense, thought his friend. There was no forgetting Wrigley's outburst after losing the Series: "I must have a winner—anybody can finish second or third!"[6]

The Rajah was having a tough spring himself. His troubles dated back to the latter stages of the 1929 campaign, when he had slowed down noticeably in the field. Little had been made of it, even when he slumped in the World Series. Over the winter he underwent an operation to remove a bone spur from his right heel. At Catalina Hornsby's lack of vigor concerned almost no one at first; the Rajah was always allowed to pace himself in the springtime, but by late March he was hobbling about on tiptoe, unable to put any pressure on the heel. In early April, as the Cub caravan left California to begin the long exhibition swing back through the Southwest, Hornsby was on the bench, and on the 5th he returned to Chicago to be examined by a specialist. Wrigley hustled to the station to greet his star benchwarmer; beaming, the two men posed for a *Tribune* photographer.[7]

A specialist in Chicago examined the famous heel and found no permanent problem. The surgeon reexamined the star and agreed. Hornsby rejoined the lineup in Kansas City and accompanied the team to St. Louis to open the season. But he still had trouble maneuvering, and after going 2 for 4 in the season opener, he made mostly pinch-hitting appearances. By April 28 he was starting at second base again, this time vowing to play until his foot either gave out or quit bothering him. He continued to undergo some form of electric treatment on the foot.[8]

The team Hornsby returned to was 7-7 so far for the season. "What's wrong with the Cubs?" asked fans in barbershops and the "soft drink parlors"—perhaps the one where Pat Pieper moonlighted—as if the answer weren't obvious. But there were other reasons than Hornsby's absence. The pitching was in disarray: Bush, fighting an attack of boils; Malone, knocked out as regularly as Shires's palookas. A long-awaited solution to the third-base problem, Les Bell, had been out all spring with a sore arm. Bell, a teammate on Hornsby's 1926 St. Louis world champs, had come at a high price: a talented young slugger, Wally Berger, who had starred for Mr. Wrigley's Los Angeles farm club in 1929.[9]

Berger, a rookie, had 15 homers for the Boston Braves by early June, on his way to 38 for the year. For the next fifty-seven years no rookie topped the mark. Something was in the air, or rather the ball, as spring merged into summer. Joe Tinker, McCarthy's World Series scout the year before, noted how the infielders were playing back on the grass as a matter of course.[10] Not just the Cubs' pitching staff was under pressure. Scores with both teams in double digits were becoming common. John McGraw came out in favor of moving the pitching rubber back. Baseball had embarked on a season still remembered as the year of the hitter, a statistical binge that rivaled the stock market of the year before. Whole teams averaged .300 for the year, a .400 batting average the new benchmark of excellence, and a team scored 1,000 runs for the first time.

But one offensive record set in 1930 stood above them all and endured into the next millennium—owned yet by one of McCarthy's Cubs, one of the manager's favorites, a husky, brawling sort . . .

Fan frustration in early 1930 centered on the Cubs' star center fielder. "Sunny Boy," they cried when Hack Wilson went to the plate, baiting him with the name that Art Shires had used disparagingly as far back as December.[11]

Hack brushed it off. Free of Edward Young's claims, rejuvenated by his bragging battle with Shires, he had been buoyant ever since his first visit to Chicago in February. He mugged with sunglasses when photographers showed up, and when a practical joker handed him some goggles on the Catalina practice field, he was a philosopher: "I should have had them last October in Philadelphia." In the St. Catherine's restaurant he asked to have the shades drawn because, he said straight-faced, "The sun hurts my eyes."[12]

When the season got underway, Hornsby's absence from the lineup established "Hanzie Franzie" (his nickname from Grimm) as the vital center of the ball club, no matter the fans' yells. He settled one score early, on May 6. An old nemesis, the great right-hander Dazzy Vance, started against Wilson and the Cubs at Wrigley Field. Humiliating Wilson was a habit with Vance. In Hack's first year with the Cubs, he rang up a four-strikeout game against Wilson. By 1929 Vance was thirty-eight years old, but still spry enough to strike out the Hacker eight consecutive times over two contests—four times in the second game, to derail Wilson's 27-game hitting streak with emphasis. A couple of weeks later he walked Hornsby to get to Wilson, who promptly rolled out to the infield. The Dazzler's mastery obsessed Wilson. One day he jockeyed Vance so hard from the dugout that Clyde Beck, a Cub reserve, begged him to stop: "Please, Hack, I got to play today, too."[13]

In 1930 Vance was still on top, the only full-time NL starter able to hold his ERA under 3.00 that year—a full run and a quarter per nine innings less than his nearest, and much younger, competitor. (The Sunday averages didn't even record ERA.) On May 6, English cracked a lead-off triple off Vance in the first inning, but Heathcote and Hornsby both failed to get him across. Vance's craggy features broke out in a smile as Wilson walked to the plate. Vance fell behind 1-0, then 2-1. He was throwing so hard into Hank DeBerry's mitt that the pop could be heard all over the park. The 2-1 pitch fooled Wilson badly, and Hack staggered after a violent swing and a miss. From the stands came laughter mixed with boos for Sunny Boy.[14]

Vance and the doubters presumed too much. Wilson took one more mighty cut when Vance's fifth offering zoomed in. With a crack, the ball went rocketing over Vance's head and soared into center field, past Johnny Frederick, climbing until it finally crashed high off the scoreboard with a terrific clap. The boos that had filled the park faded abruptly; Vance's shoulders slumped. Wilson wagged triumphantly, jubilantly around the bases. After touching the plate, he looked over and grinned at the crestfallen Vance. Wilson had provided Fred Blake all the runs he would need that afternoon. "The rest of the game was just an encounter between eighteen men doing nothing in particular," wrote Irving Vaughan in the next morning's *Tribune*. The Cubs hung on to win, 3–1.

It was shaping up as a very good year for Hack Wilson. If Dazzy Vance couldn't handle him anymore, who could?

Pat Malone peered in irritation through the haze inside the Midnight Frolics Café, 18–20 East 22nd Street. He and his party had taken in the floor show

1. William Wrigley, the Cubs' owner and founder of the eponymous chewing gum company, failed in his ambition to create the world's greatest baseball team, but for a few short years his franchise and ballpark occupied baseball's center ring. Here Wrigley monitors the club's progress during its August 13, 1929, road win in Boston. The wall hanging behind him may depict another of his far-flung holdings, Santa Catalina Island. Courtesy National Baseball Hall of Fame Library Cooperstown NY.

2. *(above)* Wrigley, semiretired by the late 1920s, watched nearly every Cub home game from his personal box seat. Note that even the owner had to sit on a folding chair. Courtesy National Baseball Hall of Fame Library Cooperstown NY.

3. *(opposite top)* Charles Comiskey, the owner of the fading White Sox, and Cub president William Veeck Sr. confer, probably in the early 1920s. Soon Veeck's astute leadership would make the Cubs Chicago's most popular team, and Wrigley Field a showcase of baseball. Courtesy National Baseball Hall of Fame Library Cooperstown NY.

4. *(opposite bottom)* Joe McCarthy—"Mac" to Chicagoans of the 1920s—is more familiar today as the New York Yankees' formidable "Marse Joe" of the 1930s and 1940s, but he first made his name in the major leagues by building Mr. Wrigley's ball club into a force. Courtesy National Baseball Hall of Fame Library Cooperstown NY.

5. In September 1924 the beloved Grover Cleveland Alexander won his 300th major league game. The only bona fide major league star left in Chicago seemed set to finish his career as a Cub—until spring 1926, when the new boss decided that Alex had been abusing his privileges. Courtesy National Baseball Hall of Fame Library Cooperstown NY.

6. *(top)* Charles Leo "Gabby" Hartnett, shown here at the Cubs' spring training camp on Santa Catalina Island, was probably the premier all-around player on the Cubs—one of baseball's greatest defensive and offensive catchers, combined with a hearty clubhouse presence and fiery drive on the field. Courtesy National Baseball Hall of Fame Library Cooperstown NY.

7. *(bottom)* Hack Wilson, Joe McCarthy's first find and his devoted follower. Bleacher fans, women, and kids formed the core of the affable Wilson's supporters, while men and boys in the grandstands, as well as road crowds, enjoyed goading the thin-skinned slugger. One afternoon in 1928 an unfortunate milkman goaded Wilson once too often. Courtesy National Baseball Hall of Fame Library Cooperstown NY.

8. *(top)* Riggs Stephenson spoke mainly with his powerful bat, good for a .337 lifetime batting average and the affection of Chicagoans, who knew him simply as "Stevie." He followed Wilson into McCarthy's lineup a few months into the 1926 season. Courtesy National Baseball Hall of Fame Library Cooperstown NY.

9. *(bottom)* "Der Kaptink," "The Joker Wild"—few ballplayers seemed a less-promising match for Joe McCarthy than Charlie Grimm, a musician, artist, bon vivant, and confirmed prankster. Grimm, though, became the sober-sided McCarthy's confidant and trusted assistant. Courtesy National Baseball Hall of Fame Library Cooperstown NY.

10. Kiki Cuyler, the prototypical "five tool" player, unnerved opponents with his formidable power, speed, and defensive prowess before admiring Wrigley Field throngs in the late 1920s and early 1930s. Courtesy National Baseball Hall of Fame Library Cooperstown NY.

11. *(top)* The mainstay of Joe McCarthy's Cub pitching staffs, the sidearming right-hander Charlie Root won 201 career games, but he's best known for his losing duel with Babe Ruth in the 1932 World Series. Courtesy National Baseball Hall of Fame Library Cooperstown NY.

12. *(bottom)* Guy Bush dressed and pitched flamboyantly, and his entrepreneurial successes made him the target of at least one spendthrift teammate. Probably more than any other single Cub, it was Bush who goaded Babe Ruth's unforgettable retaliation in the 1932 World Series. Courtesy National Baseball Hall of Fame Library Cooperstown NY.

13. Rube Foster, a Chicago trailblazer who did it all while Wrigley and Veeck's Cubs received all the attention: an outstanding pitcher who had faced the Cubs' great "Three Finger" Brown as an equal; owner and manager of the champion Chicago American Giants; and founder of the Negro National League. Courtesy National Baseball Hall of Fame Library Cooperstown NY.

14. Hal Carlson, "the man who came back." Gassed in France during World War I and then forbidden to throw his mainstay pitch, the spitball, he eventually helped the Cubs reach the World Series before the effects of his war injuries struck him down. Courtesy National Baseball Hall of Fame Library Cooperstown NY.

15. *(top)* One of the first Cubans to enter the major leagues, Miguel Angel Gonzalez was "Mike Gonzales" to the press of the time. The Cubs' backup catcher was noted as an acute student of pitching and an author of pithy comments in his halting English. Courtesy National Baseball Hall of Fame Library Cooperstown NY.

16. *(bottom)* Pat Malone, a hard-throwing and hard-drinking companion of Hack Wilson around the Toddlin' Town, twice won twenty games for Joe McCarthy. Courtesy National Baseball Hall of Fame Library Cooperstown NY.

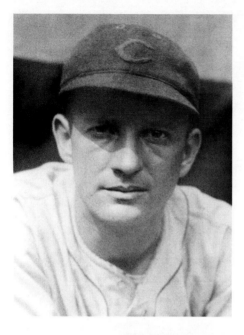

17. *(top)* The "John Gilbert of baseball"? Hack Wilson's equal? Opinions about Cliff Heathcote's precise strengths varied widely, but there's no doubt that the Cubs' backup outfielder was a favorite of both the Ladies Day crowds and his teammates, who depended on his musical talents on the long train rides. Courtesy National Baseball Hall of Fame Library Cooperstown NY.

18. *(bottom)* Art Shires, sometimes a first baseman for the White Sox, promoted his modest accomplishments incessantly; beat up his manager; and then tried to arrange a professional boxing bout with Hack Wilson in Chicago Stadium. Courtesy National Baseball Hall of Fame Library Cooperstown NY.

19. Rogers Hornsby, still number 2 on the all-time career batting list, joined the Cubs in 1929. His costly acquisition transformed the team into instant pennant favorites, but the downside of his presence became apparent only more gradually. Courtesy National Baseball Hall of Fame Library Cooperstown NY.

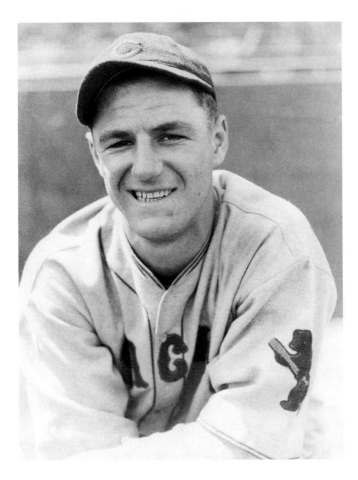

20. *(opposite top)* Rogers Hornsby, Hack Wilson, Kiki Cuyler, and Riggs Stephenson made up the core of "Murderers' Row," the chosen term of 1929 for this intimidating aggregation. Just above Stephenson's shoulder, note the "jury box"—the remaining stub of Wrigley Field's left-field bleachers—and the old ground-level scoreboard. The ballpark's current outfield configuration, with its curving, ivy-clad walls and towering scoreboard, did not materialize until the late 1930s. Courtesy National Baseball Hall of Fame Library Coopers-town NY.

21. *(opposite bottom)* Uhhh! Hack Wilson demonstrates his blue-collar grit by hitting his 46th home run, August 30, 1930. He would hit 10 more on the year to establish a National League record that lasted nearly seven decades. Note a Wilson trademark—the perpetually dirty uniform. Courtesy National Baseball Hall of Fame Library Cooperstown NY.

22. *(above)* Only months after Bill Jurges cracked the Cubs' starting lineup in 1932, an ex-girlfriend shot the young defensive wizard under murky circumstances. Soon Mark Koenig, who had played with Babe Ruth on the 1927 Yankees, took over Jurges's shortstop position and sparked the Cubs' pennant surge. The resulting sequence of events roused Babe Ruth's ire. Courtesy National Baseball Hall of Fame Library Cooperstown NY.

23. *(top)* Gabby Hartnett's famous pose with Al Capone and son at Comiskey Park symbolized the Chicago zeitgeist and created a sensation, but it was the least of the controversies that dogged the Cub franchise in the early 1930s. Courtesy National Baseball Hall of Fame Library Cooperstown NY.

24. *(bottom)* The really manic Ladies Day demonstrations were history by 1934, when this photo was taken, but the enthusiasm that female fans added to the surroundings was still unmistakable. Courtesy National Baseball Hall of Fame Library Cooperstown NY.

at the "temple of the sun dodgers," as the popular Frolics was known around town; now, with the sun about to come up, Malone wanted the bill. He had to be at the ballpark for practice later that morning.[15]

Malone and his guests had wandered into a neighborhood once known as part of "the Levee." For decades it had been notorious for providing one kind of illicit nightlife or another. A bordello named Freiberg's had originally occupied the Frolics' building, employing some of the thousands of prostitutes who worked in the Levee. Two famously corrupt pols, the First Ward's alderman, "Bathhouse John" Coughlin, and "Hinky Dink" Kenna, a precinct captain, oversaw the Levee's graft and payoffs under the benevolent eye of the Chicago police force.[16]

A reform crusade before the war shut down the area's most open vice. Its best-known madams, the Everleigh sisters, retired on their riches to New York. The neighborhood was no longer "the Levee," but old habits lingered on. Coughlin and Kenna maintained their political control of the ward, which included the Loop on its north end. Near Freiberg's, on Wabash Avenue, Jim Colosimo started running Chicago's first large-scale racketeering operation from an eponymous restaurant. In 1920 he was murdered there, probably by a newcomer from Brooklyn named Alphonse Caponi.[17]

Colosimo's restaurant outlived its founder by many years, partly due to good food and Italian music, partly due to management's skill at outwitting revenue agents. The best the Feds could do in the 1920s was to shut the restaurant down for a year. Meanwhile, the Frolics started up in Freiberg's old location, around the corner. A couple of doors down, at 2222 South Wabash, Al Capone opened the Four Deuces nightclub. He liked to visit the Frolics, too, and act as though he owned it.[18]

For the rest of the decade similar speakeasies and night spots operated south of the Frolics on "the Stroll," all the way to 47th and State, deep into Bronzeville, the city's booming, overcrowded ghetto. In the famed "black and tan" cafés—the Dreamland, the Sunset, the Plantation—the races could mix freely, listening and dancing to the music of Jelly Roll Morton, Louis Armstrong, and scores of other talents. For a few years in the mid-twenties their uptempo improvising transformed the South Side of Chicago into the world's jazz capital. Aspiring white players—Benny Goodman, Artie Shaw, and Eddie Condon from Austin High on the West

Side, Gene Krupa from the South Side, Bix Beiderbecke and Hoagy Carmichael from the small-town Midwest—crowded into black-and-tans to hear Armstrong play with King Oliver's band. The near South Side, remembered Condon, was "so full of music that if you held up an instrument the breeze would play it." The horns wailed above the smoke and the clinking glasses and the Charleston-dancing crowds. A police raid could be the signal for the shattering of hundreds of glasses and bottles on the floor, or a panicked rush for the exits. Capone, they said, would occasionally show up somewhere unannounced, order the patrons out, and commandeer the club and its musicians for himself and the boys.[19]

The Frolics, standing closer to the Loop, at the northern fringe of this Jazz Age hotbed, was a more conventional venue—a cabaret with more dance girls than jazz innovators. From dusk to dawn in the club's well-appointed environs, a cross-section of influential sun dodgers—mobsters, gamblers, prominent businessmen, lawyers, journalists, stage folk—could take in four nightly floor shows, dozens of chorus girls, and standup comics like Joe E. Lewis, a young man from the Lower East Side of New York. Beginning in 1925, Lewis had appeared in four shows a night, joking and singing current favorites like "Eddy Steady," "Yes, We Have No Bananas," "Ain't We Got Fun?" and "Oogie Oogie Wa Wa."[20]

Two years before Pat Malone's visit, the Frolics had been one of the main targets of the celebrated citywide "hip flask" raid, aimed at establishments that encouraged their customers to bring their own liquor. It was said that the raid put more than two hundred musicians out of work and accelerated the exodus of such talents as Benny Goodman and Louis Armstrong to New York. In 1927, a year before that, the Frolics' co-owners, Jakie Adler and Frank Lawro, had been kidnapped and held for one hundred thousand dollars. After Adler reemerged unharmed, telling the police of eight men armed with sawed-off shotguns blindfolding and chaining him, Lieutenant Michael Grady muttered, "They must think we were born yesterday." Later that year, just before Christmas, one of Adler's dancers, Mrs. Allen Munn Prevo, killed herself on her third try after coming under suspicion in the "bathtub murder" of a Mrs. Carl Wood. Prevo's suicide note took care to wish everyone a merry Christmas, but true to the gangland code, she left the identity of Mrs. Wood's murderer a mystery.

She was survived by Mr. Prevo, an accused bigamist who had beaten the murder rap by questioning the validity of his wife's first marriage.[21]

The Frolics was just around the corner from not only the Four Deuces but Al Capone's headquarters, the Metropole Hotel. On one of his visits to the Frolics, Capone first caught Joe Lewis's act before hiring him to work at a North Side nightclub (for perhaps a fivefold raise), and a rivalry over control of Lewis's contract led to a horrific knife slashing that left the young man mutilated and near death in his hotel room. In the immediate wake of the assault, Lewis, his vocal cords severed, could communicate only through nods. After partially recovering from his wounds, he returned to the Frolics carrying a pistol in his pocket, searching for the man he believed responsible, Capone's lieutenant "Machine Gun Jack" McGurn. The Frolics, where Chicago's legitimate and illegitimate worlds met, was the likeliest place in the huge city to find McGurn. As it was, a couple of patrolmen intercepted Lewis on the sidewalk just outside and arrested him for carrying a concealed weapon. Eventually Lewis regained his stage voice and staged a heroic comeback. By the Eisenhower era, he was a national celebrity, the subject of a best-selling biography and a movie starring Frank Sinatra.[22]

Around 1950 Lewis's biographer, Art Cohn, visited South Wabash Avenue in search of the Jazz Age. Cohn spied a fire-scarred façade on which he could still make out the Four Deuces' blistered "2222." Around the corner, on 22nd Street, Cohn found a building he thought might have housed the Frolics. The sign on the building read "Bungalow Beefburgers."

Sleek postwar automobiles rushed by the sidewalks that had once teemed with bobbed haircuts and raccoon coats. The jazz babies were all dead and gone: McGurn and Capone; Bix Beiderbecke; Pat Malone and his running mate, Hack Wilson, too. If Cohn heard the sounds of hot live jazz wafting about the corner of 22nd and Wabash, he forgot to mention it.[23]

The evening of May 8 and into the morning of May 9, 1930, Malone and company took in the floor show at the Frolics and ordered a continual flow of ginger ale—the usual preparation for mixing a drink, Prohibition-style. With dawn approaching, Malone began asking for his bill. Finally it came,

$35.40, a goodly total for 1930-vintage ginger ale, and presented in person by one of the Frolics' current owners, Herman Griffin.

Malone glanced at the slip of paper. He told Griffin, "Say, this is on the house. I'm a professional artist and I don't pay anywhere."[24] Griffin was unimpressed. Besides being on the edge of White Sox country, Malone was also speaking rudely to a man who may not have been entirely unfamiliar with the underworld—unless he somehow possessed a background much different from that of his predecessors, the alleged victims of the hundred-thousand-dollar "kidnapping" just three years earlier. "You'll pay here or go to jail," Griffin told the pitcher. Two detectives materialized with unnatural speed to haul Malone to the South State Street Station, where he was booked for disturbing the peace and defrauding an innkeeper. Joe McCarthy's ace, Chicago's lone twenty-game winner of 1929, found himself locked up with a half a dozen moaning drunks.[25]

Reporters showed up to pepper Malone with questions. "Write what you please," he snapped. "I refuse to say anything." McCarthy got the news later in the morning. Asked what he was going to do, he replied with a crisp, unheroic, "Going to get Pat out of this jam as fast as possible." Then he paused. "But first I'm going to telephone Bill Veeck. I want to share the worry." By midmorning, Malone's wife, Marion, had arrived at the jail to post the two-hundred-dollar bond. Before the morning was out, Malone appeared before Joseph McCarthy—Judge Joseph L. McCarthy, an avowed Cub fan. Like the Cubs' Joseph V., this McCarthy seemed more concerned about preserving the pitching rotation than enforcing the rules too strictly. The thin, balding judge invited Malone into his chambers for a discussion. A few minutes later the two emerged to report that all charges would be dropped in return for an apology to Griffin and payment of the bill.[26]

Judge McCarthy posed genially next to the hulking Malone as the flash-bulbs popped. "It was all a misunderstanding," Griffin purred. Malone made sure one thing was clear. "I want it understood that I hadn't been drinking. I had just taken my friends to the Frolics to see the show there." And drink $35.40 worth of ginger ale. Mrs. Malone made sure that her bail cash was returned. Clad in a lavender spring suit, she created at least one comparison to Greta Garbo.[27]

By the time Malone got back to the North Side, the ballpark had begun to fill up with women—nothing to do with Pat's heroics, but the second Ladies Day of the year. A couple of days before, a line of female fans a block long had formed at 9:00 a.m. to snap up free advance tickets for Friday's ballgame. By 4:00 p.m. the Cubs had given away twenty thousand. On Friday afternoon, joined by fifteen thousand paying customers, the women shrieked and hollered while the stalwart Hal Carlson improved on his complete game, 15-hit win of May 2 by tossing a 14-hitter. The Cubs, suddenly on a seven-game winning streak after their 8-8 start, grabbed the league lead for the first time since the previous September. The next day McCarthy put Malone back on the mound. He was knocked out in the third inning, and the Cubs fell back in the pack once again.[28]

McCarthy's pitching staff was unprepared for the Year of the Hitter. Bush, underweight, sore-armed, and fighting boils on his arm, yielded 30 runs in his first 45 innings; Fred Blake, 41 in 55. McCarthy was using Malone as a reliever since he couldn't finish his starts. None of it was enhancing McCarthy's job security.[29]

The Cub pilot wasn't alone in worrying about his job in the summer of 1930, as the Great Depression settled over the land. The stock market, rallying from the depths it had sounded shortly after the World Series, recovered more than half the lost ground by spring, then drifted uncertainly through the summer. Real economic data were at least six months slow and inaccurate to boot, so official statistics were poor guides to what was really happening. False optimism filled the void. Almost daily, President Hoover and business pundits delivered predictions about turning the economic corner. On the street corners of Chicago, it was hard for the ordinary citizen to understand what was happening.[30]

A late spring cold snap had struck the city, and the lowest temperatures, with a dash of wind chill, registered near the lakefront; the afternoon of May 26, fewer than 3,500 shivering souls turned out to watch the Reds beat the Cubs, 6–2, in fifty-degree weather.

"Carlson Cub Hope against Frey" had read a headline in the *Daily Times* the afternoon of Tuesday the 27th, but the game was rained out. Carlson had volunteered to start that afternoon even though he had been struck on his pitching hand by a batted ball just days earlier. After dinner, Carlson settled into an armchair and chatted with Ki Cuyler in the lobby of the Hotel Carlos, a small residential hotel on the second block of Shef-field Avenue north of Wrigley Field. Both Carlson, whose wife, Eva, was pregnant, and Cuyler left their families at home all summer—Cuyler's in Michigan, Carlson's in Rockford, forty-five miles northwest of Chicago; the two men stayed at the Carlos during the Cubs' home stands. Several of the franchise's bachelors also lived there: Stephenson, Heathcote, and the team's clubhouse attendant, Ed Froelich, a young man who had cajoled Joe McCarthy into hiring him several years earlier much as Andy Frain had done with Mr. Wrigley.[31]

In contrast with the temperamental Pat Malone and the theatrical, ailing Guy Bush (who was winless for the year), Carlson had developed into one of McCarthy's reliables, the bellwether of a contender. He led the staff, which had only one complete game to its credit in the past two weeks, with a 4-2 record. The Cubs and Joe McCarthy, their record so far a mere 19-19, losers of 11 of 15, would need him to withstand the onslaught of the National League's offenses in 1930. Another game with Cincinnati was scheduled the next day, and McCarthy might call on Carlson again. Around ten o'clock Carlson excused himself and turned in for the night.

About 2:15 Ed Froelich's phone rang. It was Carlson, who told the youngster, "I feel pretty bad. You better get a doctor." Froelich hurried down to Carlson's room, where Carlson told him that although he was still in pain, he might only be suffering another attack of the stomach ulcers that had laid him up before. He might not need any help after all.[32]

Froelich stayed with Carlson anyway. Before 3:00 a.m. the pitcher began bleeding from his mouth. Froelich hastily roused Cuyler, Stephenson, and Heathcote. The three entered Carlson's room to find that their teammate could barely recognize them. They rang the team physician, Dr. John Davis, who lived just up Sheffield Avenue. Davis arrived quickly and looked at Carlson, who revived long enough to tell Davis, "It feels like that trouble I had on the coast two years ago." Davis immediately called Illinois Masonic Hospital for an ambulance, but as Davis, the three Cubs, and Froelich looked on helplessly, Carlson went into a coma, and before the ambulance could arrive his breathing stopped. Dr. Davis attributed the death to a stomach hemorrhage.[33]

In spite of their awful night, the Carlos residents all made it to the park for that afternoon's game with Cincinnati, and McCarthy wrote Cuyler and Stephenson into the starting lineup as usual. The Cubs wore black armbands. Carlson's road roomie, Hartnett, caught Guy Bush and then Pat Malone in the relief role that might have gone to Carlson. "Give 'em the old pepper, kid," Hartnett yelled at his teammates, but no one was fooled.[34]

After the Cubs survived a Cincinnati comeback, 6–5, the ballplayers showered and dressed, then headed to Linn's Chapel, not far away on Clark Street. Bill Veeck delivered the eulogy at a short memorial service for Carlson: "The man who came back," he called Carlson: "an example to the world," "a man of unquestioned courage." The Cubs, followed by hundreds of fans, filed by the flag-draped casket, where two members of the VFW stood guard. Hartnett sobbed. The silent Carlson seldom dwelt on his problems. Few teammates realized that he had been gassed in the Argonne in 1918, when several of them had still been kids.[35]

After the memorial service several teammates escorted the body to Rockford, where the funeral would be held at the Carlson home. Pregnancy and childbirth were still extra-hazardous in those days, so the news had been kept from Mrs. Carlson at first. Veeck quietly put out the word that the Cubs would pay her the rest of Carlson's 1930 salary. He also announced that the next day's game would be postponed to allow the rest of the Cubs to travel to Rockford for the funeral.[36]

After the day off, the Cardinals arrived in town for a Memorial Day double-header, a morning-afternoon affair. The first game began at 10:15: Root versus the Cardinals' Syl Johnson before just twelve thousand early risers. The Cubs pushed one run across in the second, and then in the third Hornsby came up after a single by English.

Hornsby, bad heel and all, had returned to the lineup several weeks before, still limping, but kept his batting average over .300. He singled once in the first inning on Memorial Day morning; in the third he scorched Johnson's delivery into right center for a double that scored English. He was still on second when Cuyler flied out to the right fielder, whose return throw to the infield went awry. Hornsby lit out for third, but Frank Frisch retrieved the ball quickly and fired to Johnson, coming over to cover the bag. Still favoring his sore right foot, Hornsby slid awkwardly. Years later, he recalled trying to stop his slide with his left leg; he didn't mention the presence of Johnson, with whom he evidently collided. There was an audible snap. Hornsby collapsed in a heap by the bag while McCarthy and the other Cubs came running.[37]

Hornsby's left ankle was broken. Before the shocked crowd, his teammates carried him to the clubhouse. After a trip to the hospital, Hornsby was back on the Cubs' bench for the afternoon contest, his leg in a cast. The Cubs won both games to push themselves three games over .500.

The next day, Hornsby hobbled out to home plate on crutches to receive the 1929 Most Valuable Player award—a thousand dollars in gold coins handed over by John Heydler, the league president, and a gold medal from the Baseball Writers' Association of America. Then he returned to his home in St. Louis. No one knew when the Greatest Right-Handed Hitter could return to action, if ever.[38]

While Veeck hunted for replacements for Carlson and Hornsby, it was time for the club to head east for the first of three long trips. McCarthy, his active roster stripped of its two most seasoned veterans, was dependent more than ever on Wilson's and Malone's contributions.

The pair, talented as they were, never threatened anybody with their leadership qualities. Once, during a game of pinochle, Doc Lotshaw looked at Wilson and said with a sigh, "If a blackbird had your brains he'd fly backwards." At that, Wilson, the bigger star and two years older, dominated his partnership with Malone. Malone, who could overpower the batters when things went well—faster than Vance in his prime, some said—lost his concentration easily and even berated errant teammates, as he had the hapless Zack Taylor in game 5 against the Athletics. An error afield could reduce Malone to a bellowing incompetent, a patsy for other ball clubs to knock out of the box. As for Wilson, a called third strike was an excuse to carp at the umpire or hurl his bat. Without the umpire to blame when he struck out swinging, he might turn on the pitcher and yell, "Why doncha warm up, ya bum?"[39]

Wilson and Malone's idea of pregame fun was to roll up their shirtsleeves and compare biceps, which may have been their most harmless recreation. For seven decades, the deeds of the two have defined baseball decadence. The stories are legion, from a cross-section of reports: hotel rooms wrecked, passersby beaten up on a whim, innocents dangled from hotel windows.[40]

Urban legends, embellished with each retelling? Perhaps, but even Charlie Grimm, McCarthy's friend and captain, and himself a bon vivant of note, conceded that McCarthy had lost control of the situation. McCarthy tried appealing to his stars' reason and common sense, as in the famous worm demonstration. See what happens to the worm? asked McCarthy, dropping a worm in a glass of gin. Sure, Wilson answered—if you drink, you don't get worms. McCarthy did not give up. Time and again, Bob Lewis, the Cubs' traveling secretary, watched McCarthy call Wilson and Malone to his office: "He'd give them the routine. . . . 'Don't you like me anymore? . . . Haven't I been treating you fairly? . . . You guys are letting me down.'" The two would leave the office tearfully, resolved to do better for their boss—their friend. Of course, it never lasted.[41]

Eight more pennants and seven world championships lay in Joe McCarthy's future, and he didn't get them by coddling his charges. But the McCarthy of 1930 was only four years removed from Louisville, a one-time career minor leaguer who might never get another chance at Wrigley's kind of money. "What am I supposed to do?" McCarthy asked plaintively. "Tell [Wilson] to live a clean life and he'll hit better?"[42]

He had a point. Sober or not, Wilson would outhomer Babe Ruth in 1930 and set records destined to last for decades. Malone tied for the league lead in victories and complete games, winning 20 for the second straight year with one of the best fastballs in the business. And there was no guarantee at all that they could have saved McCarthy's job by taking the pledge.

After McCarthy was gone, the *Tribune*'s Irving Vaughan, who enjoyed William Wrigley's favor for any number of exclusive stories and interviews, repeatedly mentioned the breakdown in discipline in 1930 as deciding McCarthy's fate—even though he, Vaughan, had been in the elevator of the Ben Franklin Hotel after game 5 in October 1929 when Wrigley vowed to replace McCarthy. Yet not only the Cub owner was down on McCarthy this intensely warm summer.[43] The success of Murderers' Row seemed to prove to many that McCarthy didn't understand "inside baseball," the traditional yardstick of a manager's baseball IQ. Forgotten were McCarthy's original role in turning a tail-ender into contenders in little more than a year and his plucky stand against the great, drunken Alexander. No, he was a mere pencil pusher who only had to write the names of English, Wilson, Cuyler, Hartnett, and Stephenson onto the lineup card to carry the day (a foreshadowing of the "push-button manager" charge that Jimmy Dykes leveled at McCarthy years later). And there was the way Mac handled his pitching staff during the offensive onslaught of 1930. Even in those relief-shy days, McCarthy was notorious for staying with his starter as long as practicable, and then some. Perhaps he was nothing but a "busher" after all, one who had naively spoiled his boys on their way to stardom.[44]

Inevitably, perhaps, thoughts of a managerial Hornsby, dormant for a year and a half, returned. The Rajah was at home in St. Louis, rehabilitating his ankle, yet thoughts of Hornsby dominated the ball club. Once, in mid-June, rumors flew that he was in Chicago without McCarthy's knowledge. Even as the team fought its way back into first place, the talk about Hornsby continued. Was he loyal to McCarthy or not? Was his playing career over (additional fodder for managerial speculation)? Would the Cubs deal him to resolve the situation? Veeck was as unflappable as ever when asked about the last point: "There's nothing to it. We haven't reached the point where we are trying to get rid of .375 hitters."[45]

On June 3 the Philadelphia Phillies let Grover Alexander go. He had been unable to add a single victory to his career total of 373 after hooking on with his old ball club in spring training. The Phillies were well on their way to a worst-ever staff ERA of 6.71, but Alex's dwarfed that at 9.14. He had stayed too long. Alex was the worst pitcher on the worst staff in history. The two months following his release were a confusion of minor league tryouts and firings. By the end of the summer he was out of organized baseball for good.[46]

Alexander's career crashed amid a historic offensive outpouring. The first week of June signaled, if anyone needed it, that 1930 would bring all the trends of the last decade to a climax. First the Cubs closed out their home stand by thumping Pittsburgh, 16–4. Then they headed to Braves Field, so long a sepulcher for ambitious hitters. But the Cubs scored 43 runs in three victories there: 15–2, 18–10, and 10–7. At their next stop, Ebbets Field in Brooklyn, they started off by routing the first-place Dodgers 13–0. That made it nine straight victories and 56 runs in four days, before the winning streak ended when they slumped to 9 runs the next day against the Dodgers, who scored 12 times against the struggling Guy Bush and a host of relievers.

During the barrage Wilson pulled even with Babe Ruth for the major league home run lead, 16. A few weeks later Ruth edged back in front, 22–19. Wilson kept pace. On June 23 he hit for the cycle, cracking five of the Cubs' 24 hits and his 22nd home run, while the Cubs dismantled the Phils, 21–8.

Hartnett had 13 home runs himself; Stephenson was hitting .391; Cuyler was at .350 with the usual flock of stolen bases. "Folks, what a ballplayer!" exclaimed one sportswriter after watching Cuyler for a few days in early July. With a club like this, who needed the Greatest Right-Handed Hitter, anyway? It was high summer, a time, the last for years to come, when people could still believe that things were going to turn around. With a fresh lake breeze, a cumulus-dotted sky, and wise men telling you that confidence and psychology were the keys to a rebound, what harm was there in spending the afternoon at the ballpark?[47]

On Friday, June 27, the first-place Dodgers entered Wrigley Field to encounter a horde of thirty thousand female fans—assuredly the most women anyone had ever seen at one time in a major league ballpark. Veeck found that he had only ten thousand seats or so left for the paying clientele of twenty thousand who had turned out, itself a notable weekday count regardless of the freeloading women. This must have been the day Veeck's son described thirty years later in *Veeck—As in Wreck*: a mob of women surging in the streets; a plea from Veeck Sr. for patience; and the final assault on the gates, sweeping aside Veeck and all organized opposition.[48]

Veeck Jr. may have exaggerated the violence of the takeover. At least once the women were inside the walls, they respected their surroundings. Thousands of them massed eight to ten deep before the left-field wall, behind a rope held by a few bemused Andy Frains and policemen. A scattering of straw-hatted men stood gallantly to the rear. Almost every woman wore a cloche hat. That symbol of the Roaring Twenties, the above-the-knee skirt, had fallen with the stock market: every hemline now hung below the knee.[49]

The ball club's official attendance figure for 1930 was 1,467,881, a drop of barely 1 percent from 1929's glittering mark. Mere figures couldn't do justice to the phenomenon. After his traumatic June 27, Bill Veeck continued wrestling with ways to keep the women coming while leaving enough room for the paying customers. The Wednesday-advance-ticket policy evolved by midsummer into a mail-in system, two tickets per application with a maximum distribution of 17,500. To Veeck's dismay, the new scheme produced 35,000 applications in its first week.[50]

For another struggle with first-place Brooklyn, in the first week of August, the Cub president tried limiting the tickets to one per applicant (still with a maximum of 17,500 total), apparently reasoning that fewer women would want to attend if a friend wasn't lucky enough to get a ticket too. Quite the contrary. In response, a hundred thousand requests descended upon Mr. Wrigley's overburdened executive.[51]

Veeck nonetheless held firm to his 17,500 ceiling, even when he had to climb over sacks of mail to enter his office. His perseverance was rewarded. Many women upgraded their free passes by paying a small extra amount for a box seat. And having visited the ballpark and liked it, they turned into long-term cash customers, just as Veeck and Wrigley had planned. Radio, which had sparked the boom, kept it going, explained Mrs. Herbert Barth and Miss Catherine O'Connor to the *Tribune*'s roving reporter that August.[52]

Veeck was selling out the ballpark regularly in spite of the giveaways. Before 1930 the National League attendance record for a single series was 110,000 paid admissions. Brooklyn's visit in late June topped that mark by pulling in 115,000 (not including the 30,000 women who turned out for Ladies Day). When the Dodgers returned in August, 129,000 paid admissions established another new mark, which lasted only ten days, until 163,000 turned out to watch four games with the Giants.[53]

At 2:30 p.m. on Sunday, August 24, Veeck had sold 45,000 tickets for the finale of the New York series. Cecil B. DeMille might have staged the scene outside the windows of Veeck's Wrigley Field offices. Would-be patrons thronged the streets in every direction. Automobiles and streetcars were stranded in their midst. Box holders resorted to police escorts to make their way to the entrance gates.

Looking out at the panorama before him, Veeck concluded that there were more people outside the park than he had already admitted. Knowing that nearly five thousand people were already overcrowding the outfield, he ordered the ticket windows closed for the afternoon.[54]

One main attraction was drawing the unheard-of crowds, of course. Motherless, deformed, unschooled, alcoholic, banished, ridiculed, jeered, sued, and maligned, Hack Wilson had made himself peerless, not just among the Cubs, but throughout the league, and perhaps baseball. He was outdistancing the entire National League, the veterans and the youngsters too, like Ott of the Giants and Klein of the Phils, both of whom had outhomered him the summer before. Their own 1930 performances would have set records a few years before, but in the year of the hitter, no one was the equal of the Hacker.

With the National League as good as conquered, Wilson's last slugging rival was the Bambino himself. Since becoming an everyday player and virtually revolutionizing the game a decade earlier, the Yankee superstar had led the major league in home runs ten times. Only a serious illness one year, and a suspension another, had prevented his going 12 for 12.

Ruth maintained a narrow home run margin over Wilson throughout July. But Wilson achieved another milestone at Ebbets Field on the 19th. In the sixth inning he homered again against Vance, this time on an 0-2 pitch. In the eighth, with a Cub rally brewing, Wilson came up again, swinging three bats menacingly. The Dodger manager, Wilbert Robinson, quickly signaled Vance to depart. Without a murmur the Dazzler stuck his glove in his pocket and walked off the field, a hunted hunter. The Cubs hung on to win, 5–4.[55]

On July 24, Ruth's 36th homer pushed his margin to seven, well ahead of his 1927 pace. The Cubs won 19–15 at Philadelphia's tiny Baker Bowl, but Wilson went homerless. Before the game of the 26th he marched about the sidelines to the beat of a military band, resting his long, narrow-handled bat on his shoulder like a rifle. When the game began he aimed the bat at the offerings of the sorry Philadelphia pitching staff. Thrice he homered, in the first, second, and ninth innings, to close the gap on Ruth. The score that day was 16–2.[56]

By August 2 Wilson had hit two more homers to bring his total to 34. Though he still trailed Ruth (and barely led Gehrig), Wilson felt confident enough to make a public prediction: he was going to break the National League season mark of 43 Chuck Klein had set just the year before. In fact, Wilson was on a pace to hit 53. Only one other human being had ever hit that many in a major league season.[57]

The following week Wilson staged another three-homer day, this time in a doubleheader. Veeck Jr. immortalized the scene in his first book:

Lotshaw patiently dunking a very hungover Wilson in a huge tub of ice water, desperately trying to make him fit for major league baseball that afternoon.[58] Veeck's memoir places the ice bath in the Cub clubhouse in full view of Joe McCarthy and the entire ball club. The episode may have seemed comical enough to a teenager, but his dad's boss had a different take on such matters. Wilson apparently showed up unavailable for work more than once that season. Once he was pulled from a game for "miseries of the stomach"; a month later, he complained about the same trouble, but two days later he was taking Lotshaw's ice water bath. "I guess I'll have to have my appendix taken out someday," he would tell the long-suffering trainer. On August 29, Wilson excused himself from the game with a muscle pain in his side; perhaps so, but twenty-four hours later, back in the lineup, he was good for two more home runs.[59]

"Bonded in bourbon and bottled in rye," Veeck Jr. would famously brand Wilson and his buddy Malone. The epic fecklessness of it, in the midst of such extraordinary achievement, at once built the legend of Hack Wilson for posterity and delayed his election to the Hall of Fame by decades. Hack's famous boast about never visiting his hotel room until 11:00 a.m. game day was nothing that would change William Wrigley's mind about Joe McCarthy, nor was the Cubs' 13-4 August home stand. They took six of eight from their closest competition, the Dodgers and the Giants, but all Wrigley could do was grouse to a friend, "They should be ten games ahead." He had perhaps forgotten that for two years running, a major part of the Cubs' offense had been *hors de combat*, not to mention Guy Bush's astronomical ERA increase in the current season—a rate some 16 times steeper than the league's 0.20 ERA increase above 1929 levels—or the sore-armed Charlie Root's periodic absences from the rotation. Injuries virtually ended Grimm's and Stephenson's seasons by August. To fill the gaps, Veeck shuttled a patchwork of youth, including the former minor league batting champion Danny Taylor, and veterans, most notably Grimm's fill-in, the well-traveled (and future Hall of Fame electee) George "High Pockets" Kelly.[60]

It made little difference to Hack whom McCarthy put in the lineup. During the August drive, Wilson smashed 13 homers and drove in an almost superhuman 53 runs—an annual rate close to 300. Years later, someone asked Stephenson how in the world he had accumulated just 68

RBI in the mad, mad world of 1930. Passing over his prolonged absences from the lineup—382 plate appearances after averaging well over 500 for 1927–29—the ever-modest Stephenson is supposed to have explained, "Hack didn't leave anybody out there for me to drive in." Wilson was inspiring his teammates by sheer force of talent. When he went to the plate against the Dodgers in mid-August, a Cub yelled from the bench to Wilbert Robinson: "Hey, Robbie! Don't you see who's at bat? You better move back those infielders or next thing you'll have to pry one of your boys off the fence with a putty knife!"[61]

On August 18, in a 17–3 demolition of the Phillies, Wilson crashed his 42nd home run, just one shy of Chuck Klein's year-old NL mark. That night—doubtless on a tour of the nightspots—he offered another prediction: he would break the record the next day. For once in 1930, Wilson failed to deliver: he hit only one home run, tying Klein's mark. But Klein, playing right field for the Phils, acknowledged Wilson with a little wave as the Cub slugger toured the bases.[62]

Six homerless days went by, until August 26. Wilson, trying for one of his belly-dive catches, let Lloyd Waner's seventh-inning drive off Sheriff Blake sail past for an inside-the-park homer. After Blake finally got the side out, Wilson returned to the bench and sought out his fellow West Virginian. He would atone for his error, Wilson swore to Blake, with a home run "for your sake and the pride of West Virginia"—and he meant that inning. He promptly stepped up and slammed a solo shot to set the new National League mark of 44. In one stroke, he had called his shot, fulfilled his August 2 prediction, and tied Ruth for the major league lead.[63]

It seemed that the Cubs could do little wrong. On August 24 Danny Taylor, substituting for the ailing Riggs Stephenson, stole home in the bottom of the ninth to beat the Giants. Hartnett had replaced much of Hornsby's offense with 28 homers of his own through late August. Cuyler, leading the league in runs scored and stolen bases, was as brilliant as ever. On August 24, he took off after a long drive into right field, leaped, snared the ball, and sent one of the overflow police sprawling with a clean block. From foul territory, Cuyler maintained his footing, whirled, and fired a strike to the infield to hold the base runner. "Almost miraculous," pronounced an out-of-town correspondent witnessing the act. The same day Cuyler also snared a blooper one-handed while sliding on the seat of his pants; a few days later he delivered "one of his famous throws" to cut down a Cardinal who had dared to presume third base.[64]

The Cubs lost in twenty innings to St. Louis on the 28th, then erased a 5–0 lead in the bottom of the ninth the next day and retied the score with three more runs in the eleventh. Stephenson, back in the lineup for the first time in three weeks, tripled to lead off the bottom of the thirteenth and eventually scored the winning run.

On the 30th, a gorgeous day in the mid-seventies with a nip of fall in the air, Wilson slugged his 45th and 46th home runs in a 16–4 trouncing that put the Cubs 7½ ahead of the fourth-place Cardinals. That summer the *Tribune* was perfecting dramatic stop-action photography taken at ground level from somewhere near the on-deck circle. The shots, spread across the first page of the sport section, captured the players in startling action closeups, silhouetted against the unfocused background of stands and white-shirted crowd. This day the *Tribune*'s anonymous photographer highlighted Wilson against the packed first-base grandstand while he follows through in the fourth inning on home run number 46. Gus Mancuso, the St. Louis catcher, still has his glove out for the pitch that never reaches him. The force of Wilson's swing has already turned his massive torso to the third-base side. His extra-long bat, having finished the full circle of the swing, points directly behind the plate. Wilson's eyes are half-shut from the exertion; he looks down at a spot just in front of the plate. His expression, not quite a grimace, is one of intense concentration and effort. He is the toolmaker, butcher, stacker of wheat made sporting flesh.[65]

In the stands the men and women cheered. In the traditional farewell to summer, straw hats sailed from the stands onto the field. Another photographer caught two stylish young women huddled under an umbrella, gazing rapturously at the scene. "Names, please?" the cameraman asked after snapping them. "Just Hack Wilson's public," one gushed.[66]

Wilson was now a week ahead of Ruth's 1927 pace; Ruth himself was still stuck on 44. Three days earlier, Wilson had also passed Lou Gehrig for the major league lead in a less-publicized category: runs batted in. It was a statistic the local dailies didn't even include in their Sunday averages, even though Ruth and Gehrig (and in 1929, Hornsby and Wilson) had been piling up outsize RBI totals for years.

Wilson's 6 RBI on August 30 put him at 157 for the season—18 short of Gehrig's 1927 record with a full month still to go. September 1930 would be the last time the Sunday averages would omit the RBI. Hack Wilson would see to that.

The shower of straw for numbers 45 and 46 was the high point. For the second straight year the Cubs had pulled away from the league with an August drive. In just three weeks, more than six hundred thousand souls, paying and complimentary, had visited Mr. Wrigley's ball yard—a hundred thousand or so more customers than the pennant-winning Cardinals would attract all year.[67]

As the Yankees slipped to another second-place finish behind the A's, William Wrigley was acknowledged by acclamation as owner of the best, the most popular, the most lucrative franchise in baseball. Even McCarthy seemed to have his good name back. When the lead reached five games, the dour little man succumbed to enthusiasm. "They can't stop us from winning a second consecutive pennant," he blurted out. No less an authority than Connie Mack, on his way to his own second consecutive pennant, agreed.[68]

McCarthy was known to be a cautious, even close-mouthed, man, and the schedule seemed to back him up. There were only three games apiece left against the nearest runners-up, Brooklyn and New York. The Cardinals, in an utter roller coaster of a season, had roared into fourth place with a brilliant August, but they were still eight games back.

Besides, a reinforcement was on the way: the Rajah himself, whose playing days were not over after all. Quietly returning to Chicago at the beginning of the August home stand, he began working out with the ball club. "The old bones feel all right," he said after his first session. "I feel like a fellow reporting for spring training."[69] On August 19 he made his first official appearance in nearly three months, rolling out to the infield as a pinch hitter. Another nine days went by before he appeared again, drawing a walk in another pinch-hitting appearance. On August 31 he pinch hit in the fifth inning. The Cards' Bill Hallahan needed just nine pitches to strike out the Rajah and two other Cubs.

While Hornsby rehabilitated himself, McCarthy juggled the lackluster pitching staff and the latest version of the American Association infield.

Woody English, the only member of the 1929 infield not ailing or slumping, shifted between short and third. Since 1901 only three men had crossed the plate 150 times in a season. In 1930, they were joined by four others, one of them the slight, twenty-three-year-old English, thanks to a .335 batting average, 17 triples, and Hack Wilson.

English moved back to shortstop when Les Bell finally began contributing at third base in August, and "High Pockets" Kelly, a star of McGraw's great teams of the early twenties, spelled the injured Charlie Grimm at first. On the mound, McCarthy was holding daily auditions for a motley collection of youngsters and castoffs, with unfamiliar names like Teachout, Nelson, and Osborn. Malone and Root were the only two productive pitchers left from 1929's triumphal march. Bush, who had never shaken off an attack of boils followed by a freak arm injury, both sustained that spring, was usually ineffective. After he butchered one start during the August home stand, one newspaper recap began, "Guy Bush went into combat . . . with nothing much but a pleasing Southern drawl, an affable nature, his uniform, and a drug store glove."[70]

By the end of the year Bush would allow nearly four hundred men on base in 225 innings, staggering to an outlandish 6.20 ERA that belied his 15-10 record. Bush's ineffectiveness affected not only the starting rotation—he had always been McCarthy's favorite reliever—but now the manager could no longer count on Bush's rubber arm on days between starts. The staff as a whole would deliver only 67 complete games in 1930, after finishing 83 and 75 the previous two seasons.

Somehow McCarthy parlayed his patched-up roster, a prolonged absence from Stephenson, and Wilson's occasional day off into the 16-4 August home stand. Near the end of the month, though, two starters, Root and Blake, came up lame within days of each other. McCarthy used an extravagant five pitchers in one doubleheader, and the 28th's action-filled twenty-inning game against the Cardinals took its toll too. On the 31st, St. Louis captured the last game of the series, 8–3. The next day the Cubs scored only one run in a doubleheader disaster in Cincinnati. Their lead was four. After several more days of alternating victories and defeats, the margin had shrunk to 2½. Both Brooklyn and St. Louis, healthy again and playing brilliant ball, were closing in.

There had been an undercurrent in the ballpark that hadn't been heard for years. McCarthy's habitual presence in the third-base coaching box made him a lightning rod for booing. His tendency to leave his starters in was attracting more criticism than ever, not surprising considering the inflated batting averages of 1930. A downside of encouraging female attendance materialized when a Miss E. E. S. wrote the *Chicago Daily Times* to revive a hardy perennial: benching Wilson to get Cliff Heathcote's inspirational presence back into the lineup. (It was true that even Heathie was slugging a career-high .523, but that figure paled next to Wilson's titanic .723.) Rumors about McCarthy's shaky standing with Wrigley revived; when asked about the talk, Veeck issued only an ominous "There will be no discussion of McCarthy's contract until the season is finished." Fueling the widespread unease, unfairly or not, was the impression created by Hornsby's brooding presence on the bench as McCarthy juggled lineups of rookies and journeymen.[71]

After the first few losses in early September, McCarthy finally threw Hornsby into the breach on the 4th. The Rajah started the next three ballgames, managing three hits in eleven official plate appearances and committing three errors afield. Ed Burns of the *Tribune* thought Hornsby's game on September 6 was the worst one of his career.

Burns was in earshot about a half hour before game time on September 7 when Hornsby went up to McCarthy and told him that a charley horse in each leg was making it difficult for him to move. McCarthy asked Hornsby to use his best judgment about whether he should play; Hornsby replied that sitting down would be the best thing, adding that he would play if McCarthy wanted him to. His brief 1930 comeback was over. As Hornsby walked off, McCarthy turned to Burns. "I'm glad you were here to hear that," the Cub manager said wearily, "because in a couple of days I'll be reading stories that I kept him on the bench to embarrass him." His prediction was off by only a few days.[72]

It was time for the Cubs to head east again. Usually the eastern trip went down the coast, starting with Boston; this time it began in Brooklyn. After that the team would play in Philadelphia, New York, and finally Boston.

Malone lost a decently pitched game in the opener at Ebbets Field on September 9, 3–0. With the lead down to 2½ games, it would be up to Root, McCarthy's mainstay ever since Alexander's departure. Hartnett once said of his stocky battery mate, "[I]f it were possible to cut Charlie Root's heart up into 25 chunks and transplant them into that many other pitchers, I'd have 25 great pitchers in no time." Root had been in and out of the rotation with arm trouble, but McCarthy's dependable, poker-faced lieutenant wouldn't even admit that there was a problem with his arm. That showed an awful lot of heart, but a healthy arm was what Root really needed at the moment. The Dodgers routed him almost before he had finished his warmups. He had, in fact, thrown his last pitch for the year, and for that matter, for Joe McCarthy. The rout was on. For the second straight day the Gowanus Goofs shut down Murderers' Row as the Cub bench looked on morosely. (Even in the general disaster, though, Wilson managed to blast a line drive so vicious that it broke a finger on the glove hand of Rube Bressler, Brooklyn's left fielder.) The next day Vance took over, striking out thirteen Cubs, including Wilson twice. By the seventh inning Murderers' Row had accumulated twenty-six consecutive scoreless innings over the past three days. Then Wilson proved again that no man alive, even his former nemesis, could thwart him in 1930: he crashed his 48th homer of the year—the Cubs' first run of the entire series. But Vance already had the runs he needed for a 2–1 victory.[73]

With the Dodgers and the Cardinals winning relentlessly each day, the once-comfortable lead had shrunk to a mere half game. Back in Chicago, the entire city seemed transfixed by the drama. The fate of Hack and the team seemed to be on every tongue. Four stations were airing the games live, probably a new high in road game re-creations. Traffic stopped in the Loop while passersby craned for a look at impromptu scoreboards in department store and barbershop windows. Before the third game in Brooklyn, a telegram of support signed by 3,600 fans arrived in the Cub clubhouse. McCarthy and the ballplayers stared at the huge list of names when it arrived at the visitors' clubhouse. Try as they might, they seemed helpless to turn things around. They had now lost nine of their last twelve games. In the three victories they had scored 37 runs; in nine defeats, just 25.[74]

The next day the Cubs were scheduled to open in Philadelphia. Before the game, a cluster had already formed before the *Herald and Examiner*'s electronic Pictograph at State and Washington. One man said hopefully, "They say it's raining in Philadelphia. Maybe it's all off." Nearby someone else was overheard telling his companion, "I hate to tell you what I think . . . the Cubs are through. It's tough, but it's all in a lifetime." Contrary to such negativism, the game got under way and the Cubs thrashed the Phillies, 17–4. English was 4 for 6, Cuyler 4 for 5, Wilson 4 for 5 with his 49th home run.

The next day Pat Malone, though hit hard in a park that did not favor right-handed pitching, gutted it out into the bottom of the eighth with a 5–5 tie. He had two outs and a man on base when a specter from McCarthy's earliest days with the Cubs materialized: it was Lefty O'Doul, hobbling to the plate as a pinch hitter. This was the converted pitcher Wrigley had signed before McCarthy's first spring in Catalina. McCarthy had cut him for his defensive deficiencies, but O'Doul, far from sinking from view, had batted .378 for San Francisco of the Pacific Coast League in 1926. That feat earned the thirty-year-old one more shot in the bigs, where he not only stuck but prospered mightily, hitting .398 to win the 1929 batting title.

By mid-September 1930 O'Doul had cooled off to .380, a full 20 points behind the Giants' Bill Terry, and he had missed several games with a shin splint. Nonetheless, he was more than ready to spite McCarthy any way possible. With Wrigley looking on from a box seat, Pat Malone tried to sneak a 2-1 curve past O'Doul. The slugger stepped up in the box and lofted the ball high over Baker Bowl's towering, but close-in, right-field fence. Wrigley moaned, "O'Doul, my O'Doul," as the gimpy Phillie circled the bases. In the Loop, a great groan went up from the throng watching the *Herald and Examiner*'s Pictograph. In the top of the ninth Footsie Blair, English, and Cuyler went down, and the Cubs were out of first place for good.[75]

The follies continued on Monday, after a Sunday hiatus to observe Philadelphia's blue laws. Heathcote and Wilson twice crossed signals and let fly balls drop safely. The Phillies took a five-run lead, which the Cubs erased with a seven-run fifth, but the Phillies, aided by a pinch-single from O'Doul, exploded for six in the eighth to retake the lead, 11–10. Undaunted, the Cubs tied the game in the top of the ninth. The Phillies' bench was so short that they had to let Hal Elliott, their reliever, lead off the bottom of the inning. Elliott singled, but in such unfamiliar territory the .111 hitter was picked off base. O'Doul, limping to the plate, passed by the crestfallen Elliott. "Never mind, kid," the thirty-three-year-old O'Doul assured the thirty-one-year-old Elliott, loudly enough to be heard in the grandstands. Then he stepped up and slammed another homer to end the game.[76]

This time Wrigley was not around for the coup de grâce. He had ducked out during the Phillies' big eighth. The inimitable Philadelphia fans had been on him all afternoon, asking how much he would give for O'Doul now, and telling him that the Phillies were saving his ball club another embarrassment against the Athletics. "They made me think I was friendless. And Philadelphia is my home town," Wrigley remembered later.[77]

The Cubs took the second game with the help of a landmark contribution from Wilson, his 50th home run, but Wrigley's intuition was correct: O'Doul's two homers had decided the 1930 pennant race, which the Cubs eventually lost by two games. Then it was off to New York for three games with the Giants. The main attraction, however, was a showdown just across the river between the two clubs that had just vaulted over the Cubs in the standings—Brooklyn and St. Louis. The Cubs' one hope was that some Dodger-Cardinal attrition would open them a back door into first place. The borough was agog with anticipation after thirty years with just one Dodger pennant. In a preview of the mania that would erupt when the franchise revived in the 1940s, fans armed with bells, whistles, and dishpans jammed the ballpark. Between innings a saxophone, a drum, and a sliphorn provided inspiration as Vance squared off against Wild Bill Hallahan. Even the Chicago writers had to admit that Dodger fans, presented with a winner, could outroot anybody.[78]

Across the East River at the Polo Grounds, Carl Hubbell, not yet the mound legend he would become, upset those desperate calculations, three-hitting the Cubs' right-handed hitters with ten strikeouts. To face the gifted Hubbell, McCarthy had only a shopworn lefty named Jess Petty, who was driven to cover early. The Giants won 7–0. Although Wrigley was in Manhattan, he did not bother to make the trip to the stadium. His absence was noted.[79]

At Ebbets, Vance fanned eleven Cardinals himself before the wildly excited Brooklyn crowd. But St. Louis pushed across the only run of the game in the tenth. The Cardinals had finally reached first place after winning 30 of 38 games in five weeks.

On Wednesday the Cardinals took another thriller from the Dodgers, wiping out a Dodger lead to win by a run and take a one-game lead over the Dodgers. Across the river, Wilson hammered his 51st and 52nd home runs out of the Polo Grounds. His 176th RBI surpassed Lou Gehrig's single-season runs-batted-in record of 175, set only three years earlier, and the Cubs had a desperately needed 5–2 victory. Of course, each home run had represented a new league record, and now each Wilson RBI would likewise set a major league record. Hack had blazed into territory few had tread before, or would again.

The deficit was 1½ with nine to play. The club needed just one win from the Dodgers across the river, the same team that had seemed invincible against them the week before. The next day, Thursday, September 18, ended that daydream. While the Giants dropped the Cubs 6–2 behind Fred Fitzsimmons, the doughty Cardinals took another squeaker in the packed, but noticeably quieter, Ebbets Field, 4–3. Suddenly, they were two up on the Dodgers and 2½ on the Cubs.

Rather than overnight in New York, McCarthy ordered his men to leave New York on the evening train to Boston. It was surely a downhearted group making its way northward that evening. In the "hyena car," the newcomers and reserves—Blair, Beck, Teachout, both Taylors—were openly upset at missing the chance for a World Series check. But Cuyler and Hartnett were the only higher-salaried veterans on the best-paid club in the league who seemed to share the subs' disappointment. Wilson was a lone, diehard optimist, backing up a defiant pennant prediction he had given Grantland Rice in a radio interview the night before. But in the main, defeatism was in the air. One of Wilson's less-enthusiastic teammates complained that the team would have to lower itself by playing the lowly White Sox in the City Series.[80]

Nonchalance aside, the injuries, the weeks of uncertainty about their manager, and the long slide had sapped the once-swashbuckling Murderers' Row, or what was left of it. There had been Wrigley and Veeck's mysterious comings and goings, and the even stranger behavior of the Rajah. Hornsby, who was on the train and the team but not of it, had designated himself a bullpen catcher in addition to his occasional pinch-hitting duties.[81] At times Hornsby barely acknowledged McCarthy's authority. He and Ray Schalk had skipped a team meeting before one of the games at the Polo Grounds; they strolled out on the field while the rest of the team huddled.[82] It was the "busher" treatment all over again; all that was missing was for Old Alex to materialize in the bullpen.

After the Cubs' train arrived in Boston, newspapermen began bird-dogging the players for a scoop on the McCarthy-Hornsby drama. McCarthy came upon a player and a writer huddling in the hotel lobby and berated them. Another writer managed to spirit a Cub player to the movies for his side of the story.[83] McCarthy and Hornsby themselves couldn't insist often enough that they got along just fine. McCarthy would add, "My contract does not expire until January 1. The future will take care of itself."[84]

The future—and William Wrigley. He and Veeck had both returned to Chicago, where Wrigley summoned the *Tribune*'s Irving Vaughan to his office across the street from the Tribune Tower on a sun-splashed Friday afternoon. To meet with Wrigley, Vaughan had to skip one of the season's more interesting assignments at Comiskey Park—Babe Ruth and the Yanks were in town.

At Comiskey Park, the Bronx Bombers were manhandling the Sox's 21-game winner, Ted Lyons. By the third inning the Yanks turned the contest into a 12–0 laugher. That game was of no concern as Vaughan entered Wrigley's office, though: he found the Cubs' owner shuttling between his desk and the ticker tape machine he kept in his office. After updating Vaughan on the score at Braves Field (the Cubs were winning), he mentioned that he wanted to discuss other matters. He opened by confiding that he had feared from the start of the road trip that it would come to a bad end. "I felt they were at the end of their rope," he said.

Vaughan suggested a cause of the team's downfall—an "accumulation of evil," he called it: Carlson's passing, Hornsby's injury, the sore arms on the pitching staff, the absences of other regulars. "You've hit the nail squarely on the head," Wrigley exclaimed. Baseball wasn't like any other business, he said, recalling that rainy Saturday in the Baker Bowl when he had been trapped in his box among the abusive Phillie fans. "I still refer to him as 'my Mr. O'Doul,'" he said wistfully.

Wrigley kept checking the tape every few minutes for news of the Cubs' game. Vaughan saw his chance to ask the question that was on millions of minds. What was going to happen to McCarthy, anyway?

Wrigley was coy. "I will not say that McCarthy will not be manager next year," Wrigley began. "Neither will I say he will not be offered a new contract."

"We have no way of knowing what McCarthy might demand in salary," he went on. "He might ask $100,000 in salary. Or maybe McCarthy might not want the job any longer. *He might feel that by not winning he had placed me in an embarrassing position.*

"Why don't you go down and ask Bill Veeck about it?" Wrigley added as an afterthought. "Whatever he says or does I will second. I regard Veeck's baseball judgment as perfect. He's running the job." Then he excused himself for a weekend at Lake Geneva, Wisconsin.[85]

The next day another reporter took Wrigley's suggestion and tracked Veeck down at the suburban Hinsdale Golf Club. Veeck wasn't much more enlightening than his boss. No decision on McCarthy would be made during the season, he said.

The reporter pressed. "The action will be taken sometime in October?" he asked.

"Why, yes," Veeck replied.[86]

In Boston, someone relayed Wrigley's comments to McCarthy. McCarthy quickly changed the subject to lighter topics. Hornsby, though, was in a fouler mood than usual, complaining about "propaganda." The only reason he was spending his time in the bullpen, he had explained, was for the exercise. "Why can't they leave me out of this?" he wondered out loud to another reporter.[87]

The Cubs dropped their Saturday afternoon ballgame to the Braves. This, their last loss of 1930, virtually foreclosed any pennant hopes: three down with six to go. The next day the team rallied to beat the Braves, and they followed up with another win on Monday. Wilson swatted his 53rd home run for yet another National League record.

Warren Brown, the sports editor of the *Chicago Herald and Examiner*, had been covering the Cubs while they played in New York, but he was eager to get back to Chicago. All the speculation on McCarthy's fate had Brown worried—he might lose the biggest story of the year, maybe of his career. Brown was, in fact, the friend in whom Joe McCarthy had confided on the way to Catalina that spring, predicting that 1930 would be his last with the

Cubs. For months, Brown harbored his secret while Murderers' Row struggled to retain its championship.

By midsummer, even though the Cubs were in the thick of the race, the scuttlebutt convinced Brown that McCarthy's prediction had been dead on. He made a crucial decision. His friendship with McCarthy, Brown decided, outweighed his technical journalistic obligations. Warren Brown, department head and columnist, began moonlighting as an unpaid sports agent.

Lanky and debonair, a former college first baseman who had actually played a few innings of minor league ball in the Bay Area, Brown knew sports figures great and small over the country. His column in the *Herald and Examiner*, "So They Tell Me," covered the general sports scene—golf, boxing, and football—as much as baseball. In mid-September the Cardinals-Dodgers showdown in Brooklyn gave Brown a good excuse to send Wayne Otto, his regular Cub correspondent, over to Ebbets Field while he reported on the Cubs-Giants battle of also-rans at the Polo Grounds— and to see for himself what was happening with McCarthy's situation.

Brown had visited New York at least once earlier that summer. On his own initiative he dropped in on a friend of the Yankees' owner, Colonel Jacob Ruppert. What would be McCarthy's chances of hooking on with the Yanks? the Chicagoan inquired. According to the account Brown published more than fifteen years later, his contact went to see Ruppert and reported back that the Yankee owner had brushed him off. Ruppert was skeptical that a successful manager fighting for his second straight pennant could be fearing for his job.

But Ruppert hadn't said no. Back in Chicago, Brown cornered McCarthy in the dugout. Brown tossed the skipper a hypothetical: "Would you like to manage the Yankees?"

"Who wouldn't?" McCarthy answered. "Why?"

Brown replied evasively and went about his duties. Soon he was on the phone to Ruppert's friend. McCarthy hadn't said no, either, he said.[88]

An irresistible process was under way. The Yankees were finishing behind the Athletics for the second year in a row; the team was in transition; they were dissatisfied with their rookie manager, Bob Shawkey. Eventually Ruppert arranged a meeting with Wrigley. The two most powerful owners in baseball agreed, in effect, to transfer Joe McCarthy from the second city to the first, not much differently than they would swap a utility shortstop from Reading.

By the middle of September, rumors about McCarthy and the Cubs were frequent enough that reporters were pressing Wrigley, Veeck, McCarthy, and even Hornsby with questions. What was McCarthy's status? Would he be offered a new contract? When? Was there bad blood between him and Hornsby? The only formal interview any of the four men granted was Wrigley's sit-down with the *Tribune*'s Irving Vaughan. Although Wrigley ruminated and philosophized, saying nothing of any real substance and avoiding direct answers, the story was a banner headline on the *Tribune*'s first page, outweighing any other national or international news. For Brown, it was a near-miss: he could plausibly guess that Wrigley had told Vaughan the truth but asked him to sit on the story for a day or two while everything was worked out.

Brown had no time to lose if he wanted to save his scoop. He had returned to Chicago after the Giants series ended, probably arriving about the time that Vaughan and Wrigley sat down in the Wrigley Building. All weekend Brown worked feverishly to write up his Big Story. The front-page thunderbolt hit Madison Street late Sunday night. "Win, lose, or draw, Joe McCarthy will not be manager of the Chicago Cubs next season," Brown began. In several thousand words of background, analysis, and forecasting that followed, he kept his main source secret. Nor did he bring up Colonel Ruppert and the Yankee job, or his own freelance efforts on behalf of McCarthy.[89]

That evening, a WGN announcer hastened to call Brown's scoop "a lot of hooey." WGN attacked Brown's story again on Monday night: "False rumors continue to circulate about a change in the management of the Cubs. There is no foundation in fact for these rumors." Vance didn't reveal his source or his reasoning, but in the meantime the *Tribune*'s Irving Vaughan had been called again to meet with William Wrigley, this time somewhere in the tycoon's twenty-two-room apartment on Lake Shore Drive. Afterward Vaughan hurried back to the Tribune Tower to file his own exclusive for Tuesday morning's edition.[90]

The Cubs' train had left Boston Monday night for Chicago and chugged to Albany, New York, where it stopped Tuesday morning. Vaughan's fellow baseball correspondent, Ed Burns, stepped off the train to call the office. After hanging up, he quickly bustled back to the Pullman car and sought out McCarthy. William Wrigley had talked to Vaughan the night before, Burns told McCarthy, and announced that Hornsby was his choice for 1931. It was on the front page of the *Trib*. Warren Brown's brilliant, unconventional reportage had turned out to be true.

McCarthy might as well have learned that a utility infielder had cracked his favorite bat. Showing no surprise, McCarthy replied evenly, "I am merely the latest in a long line of Cub managers. [Frank] Chance is the only one who lasted as long as I have." Then he added, "In my 24 years in baseball I have never asked for a job and I don't intend to start now." That was as close as he came to letting on that he had another job in the works.[91]

It was like no other baseball firing before or since, a smooth, corporate-style reshuffling. Wrigley had decided to break up the combination that had rebuilt the Cubs—his ambitions and fantastic financial resources, Jack Doyle's repeated scouting coups, Veeck's cool judgment, and McCarthy's amply demonstrated abilities. Having made his fortune relying on energy and determination, he was allowing the tantalizing disappointments of the past year, short-term thought, and the nearness of baseball glamour to guide his judgment. McCarthy, however splendid the services rendered, didn't seem to be a finisher; his résumé read "minor league champion" and "World Series loser."

Hornsby, on the other hand, had already won the title Mac hadn't, and that the aging Wrigley desired so desperately. He was a cowboy come east, or at least midwest, taller and leaner than the pudgy Mac, and never shy about expressing his expert baseball opinion. Mingling with Hornsby at Catalina, posing with him at the train station, Wrigley was yet the fellow who had missed out on the fun in boyhood; even his closest associates referred approvingly to his "boyish enthusiasm." Wrigley was clearly not going to brook any opposition to his enthusiasm for Rogers Hornsby. Even Wrigley's flesh and blood were secondary. Sometime after the Rajah's hiring, Phil Wrigley, an aviation buff, proposed flying his dad and Hornsby across the San Pedro Channel to Catalina. The elder Wrigley was game, but he turned to Hornsby and said, "Rog, you can't go." "Why not?" Hornsby asked. "You're too valuable," Mr. Wrigley informed him and everyone else within earshot.[92]

McCarthy, not quite so important. "Joe is taking a manly attitude toward the whole thing," Wrigley noted once news of the dismissal was out. "He assured me that he wasn't going to complain after five years in which there was never a cross word between us." (Wrigley also hinted that he knew just what was up with the Yankees' interest in McCarthy's services.) Veeck, too, waxed positive. "[Hornsby] hasn't sought the job. It is being offered to him," he offered. "It is possible because of the many rumors flying around for the last month that a slight chill may have developed between the pair," he added, "but I have McCarthy's word that when it was a matter of playing the game that Hornsby never balked or refused orders."[93]

Veeck was still waiting for Harry Grabiner of the White Sox to issue the City Series challenge, which by tradition had to come from the first team to fall out of the pennant race. The expectation was McCarthy would manage those games as well as the last four games of the regular season. The carefully planned transition soon foundered. McCarthy left the team train in Buffalo, as he often did, to see Mrs. McCarthy, then returned to Chicago early Thursday armed with his own agenda. He headed to Wrigley Building, where he went into conference with Veeck and Wrigley. An hour later the three emerged and issued a statement. "We realized that it might prove embarrassing for [McCarthy and Hornsby] if we had a 1930 manager and a 1931 manager in the dugout and on the field at the same time. So we granted his request"—that is, to leave Wrigley's employ forthwith. McCarthy would be paid through the end of the calendar year, Veeck said, in accordance with his contract.[94]

And that was the end of it. McCarthy visited the ballpark to say farewell in the clubhouse he had overseen for five memorable years. Then Hornsby took charge while McCarthy headed to a seat in the left-field grandstand, where he joined two other ex-managers, Pants Rowland and none other than Jack Hendricks, late of the Cincinnati Reds. McCarthy and Hendricks, foes from the days of Kolp and Donohue, watched as Hornsby strolled over to William Wrigley's box to pose for photographers. Booing, vociferous, prolonged, broke out nearby. Far off in the bleachers, men in shirtsleeves and open collars cupped their hands to their mouths to "throw" their protests to Mr. Wrigley's ears. A smattering of cheers was audible.[95]

For the first time since 1926, no Cub manager stalked the third-base coaching box when the Cubs came to bat: Ray Schalk took up the post instead. English and Hartnett both homered in the early innings, but the crowd barely reacted. In the dugout the Cubs seemed quiet and uneasy. Guy Bush had probably spoken for most of them when he was flagged down the day before at the Lincoln Fields racetrack. "No, no, you mustn't talk about that," he drawled politely when someone brought up the subject of the big change. No one could blame the fellows for feeling anxious if they had seen a headline on the front page of that morning's *Herald and Examiner*:

"Hornsby Will Put 12 of Cubs Up for Auction."[96]

The Cubs eked out a 4–3 win with Hornsby hunkered down in the dugout; when the Reds threatened in the top of the ninth, the new manager had Captain Grimm go to the mound to make the first pitching change of the new regime. The win was the Cubs' fourth straight, but they lost half a game in the standings: three out with three to go, and the next day the Cardinals clinched their pennant before ten thousand in St. Louis. In Chicago, the summer of 1930 was suddenly over. The weather had turned autumnal, windy and cold. Twenty-two thousand fans were still willing to turn out for the season's last Ladies Day, even though many of them had to use blankets like Bears' fans in November. Pat Malone pitched his 20th victory. The minority of men on hand seemed to think the women were as giddy as ever, the loss of the pennant and McCarthy notwithstanding.

Wilson capped a four-run rally in the seventh with a wind-blown home run, his 54th, into the bleachers. There were not enough men or skimmers left, either one, so the women tore their scorecards into confetti and tossed them from the upper deck. Wilson and Cuyler, who had scored ahead of him, had to step around the piles to get back to the dugout.[97]

Wilson followed up Saturday with two more home runs, numbers 55 and 56, in the Cubs' fifth straight win. Hartnett added two homers of his own, his 36th and 37th. No two teammates, save Ruth and Gehrig, had ever accumulated 93 home runs in one year. Indeed, with one day left Wilson had a chance to tie or surpass Ruth's magic mark of 60. After all, he had already homered three times in one game that year, that long hot summer of 1930.

It was not to be. Wilson managed only two RBI singles the last day of the year, though they made history of their own—the season RBI mark of 191 that has stood through all the decades since. It was another 1930 slug-fest, a 13–11 Cub comeback after spotting the Reds a nine-run lead. Hack and the rest of the runners-up crew still had enough appeal to draw another turnout of 22,000. Wilson's historic final RBI scored English on an infield single in the eighth inning.

Earlier in the day, another farewell performance had taken place before a smaller group gathered at the Chicago Board of Trade's splendid new skyscraper, an Art Deco masterpiece topped by a statue of Ceres. It was Joe McCarthy Day, planned in happier times as a season-ending ceremony held before an adoring crowd at Cubs Park. Instead, several dozen loyal-ists crowded into an office at the new Board of Trade tower to present McCarthy with a 194-piece silver service. McCarthy muttered his thanks while the others looked on awkwardly. Charlie Grimm, solemn for once, was at his old skipper's side, the only Cub in attendance. A telegram for McCarthy arrived from Connie Mack. It read, "I would rather lose a World Series to you than play anyone else."[98]

McCarthy left town later in the day. The leaves were already falling and the air was raw for late September. Lawns and shrubbery were dormant after the long drought. In the prairies stretching to the west, brushfire alerts were the order of the day—conditions not unlike those before the Great Fire, fifty-nine years earlier to the week.

Another manmade disaster was in progress, though, and there was no denying it now. To avoid the thirty-seven-degree temperatures and a cutting north wind, two thousand unemployed men ate and slept in a converted warehouse at 850 North Union, a shelter funded by William Wrigley. Al Capone, too, opened a South Side soup kitchen that fed twenty thousand a week. Just down Randolph Street from the Oriental Theater, what they dubbed a "Hooverville" had arisen, criss-crossed by Prosperity Road, Hard Times Avenue, and Easy Street.[99]

Much of Chicago was trying to ignore the signs of disaster, or honestly thought the worst was over. All the authorities and the smart-money men were still confident that things were going to turn around. "GOOD TIMES COMING: HOOVER" read the *Tribune*'s page 1 headline on October 3.

The fans still could not get enough baseball. One hundred sixty-two thousand fans, the second-best attendance ever for the autumn event, turned out to see the Cubs take a six-game City Series from the Sox. Wilson clubbed his 57th and 58th home runs since Opening Day and drove in six more runs—197! Malone beaned Johnny Watwood; Cuyler ignited the winning rally in the sixth game with a real Cuyler rarity—a bunt. The last game set new Comiskey Park records for fruit throwing, with Wilson, as always, the target. It would be the Sox fans' last opportunity to abuse the man they loved to hate.

Meanwhile, more baseball was available each evening at the American Giants' park. For the second straight year, Art Shires and Earle Mack's "American League All-Stars" were squaring off against the Giants in a postseason exhibition series.[100]

The Giants had begun night games (and even a ladies night) at Schorling's Park during their regular season; in an apparent effort to attract wider patronage, they also advertised the Mack all-star games in the *Tribune*. It was innovation by desperation. The Bronzeville community had been the first and hardest-hit by the economic collapse. The Giants' attendance was declining; all the NNL clubs were losing money. Hope for Rube Foster's recovery had long since disappeared; in fact, he had only two more months to live. One Sunday night in August, the novelty of playing under the lights plus a starting assignment for Satchel Paige of the Birmingham Black Barons drew a sizable number of newcomers to the park— "more white fans . . . than our own people," noted the *Chicago Defender*. But after Paige repeatedly tried to bean the Giants' shortstop, one Miller, the incensed Chicago player charged the mound, bat in hand. Paige ran for his life with Miller in pursuit. The Birmingham catcher headed to the dugout to get a bat of his own before plainclothes policemen stopped him. By the time order was restored, the stands were half empty, the departing fans muttering that they would never return.[101]

By early October Paige was back at Schorling's Park to throw for the Giants, not at them. The Chicagoans had invited Paige, Oscar Charleston, Sanford Jackson, and other Negro League stalwarts to join them for a multigame set—all but one scheduled under the lights—against Earle Mack's barnstormers. The roster of Mack's All-Stars could claim none other than Mr. Wrigley's O'Doul—just weeks removed from battering the Cubs' pennant hopes—Charlie Gehringer, and Harry Heilmann. Shires went 5 for 6 in a Saturday night game, his club's only victory; the next afternoon he and the Giants' "Steel Arm" Davis enjoyed themselves hamming it up before the crowd at Schorling's Park. Monday night Mack's club dropped its third of four, despite driving Paige to the showers with a vigorous ninth-inning rally. The last game of the series was canceled, and then the Great One was off for Hollywood, where, he announced, he planned to enter that town's principal industry.[102]

Shires's would-be rival from his boxing days a year before had entered show business, too. After the City Series ended, Wilson made a short visit to Martinsburg, where a victory parade down King Street and the keys to a new Buick greeted him. A band was playing, and the streets were festooned with signs reading "Hack." A few days later, he was back in Chicago, where the newspapers' movie sections had been announcing that Wilson, Cuyler, Heathcote, and Hartnett were going to open in a variety act, "Rarin' to Go," at the Oriental Theater on October 9. A last-minute hitch developed at the first rehearsal, days before opening: the Balaban & Katz theater people—the same folks who had narrowly avoided putting Cuyler, Heathcote, and Grimm on stage at the Oriental the year before—learned that Wilson and Hartnett, unlike last year's cast, could not sing.[103]

But the show had to go on. A backup team of singers was improvised, and at eleven o'clock the morning of October 9, the Oriental Theater's stage rose and whirled to reveal the four Cubs. The overwhelmingly female audience cheered as eagerly as at Ladies Day in August. The ballplayers answered an emcee's questions about their trade and then Cuyler, Heathcote, and a couple of off-stage voices broke into "I've Been Blue, Just Thinking of You" while Wilson and Hartnett lip-synched. At the show's climax, the ballplayers hurled baseballs into the balcony seats, where the ballpark rules of ownership evidently applied.[104]

Pat Malone attended the performance one day and visited backstage afterward. There he learned that Wilson and Hartnett, earning $2,000 and $1,250 a week respectively for their vaudeville stint, were faking it. The man who had never grown up guffawed.[105]

Life was a party for Pat Malone and Hack Wilson, but all parties end. After spending each week in a different Balaban & Katz theater, the act wound up at the end of October. Wilson returned to West Virginia, Heathcote and Malone to Pennsylvania, Cuyler to Michigan. Joe McCarthy was back in Buffalo, sure that his new house would be paid for. He had just signed a contract to manage the New York Yankees.

The party lights were going out for Art Shires, too. In Hollywood he tried to reinvent himself once more, insulting stars on the set, eloping with a Chicago flapper in early December, and getting charged with carrying concealed brass knuckles after an arrest for public drunkenness. By January, he was back in Milwaukee to sign a contract with the minor league Brewers.[106]

A Chicago girl named Mafalda Capone, Al's baby sister, also got married in December. Mingling with the guests at St. Mary's Church in Cicero were state's attorney agents Patrick Roche and his men Louis Capparelli and Mike Casey. They arrested five ushers for carrying concealed weapons. Al was a no-show.[107]

The Capone gathering had been huge, but not as large as the crowd that gathered the next day at a church on the South Side. It was a leaden Sunday afternoon, but despite the weather and the woes of the time, the church was packed; another three thousand people who remembered Rube Foster's life and works lined up outside in the sleet and snow for a chance to say good-bye. The *Tribune* recognized the "Hero of Negro League Baseball" with greater eloquence than it had allowed his championships, concluding: "Foster was buried as he lived—the hero of thousands on the south side. . . . The auditorium was packed, while outside 3,000 stood in the snow and rain. . . . [M]en and women from all walks of life attended the services."[108]

Foster's crowds would no doubt have been larger over the years if the *Tribune* had paid him such attention in his prime. The NNL, an early victim of the Depression, had finished its last season as a full-fledged league with an established schedule, rosters, and franchises. The Giants themselves would be held together by Dave Malarcher, but many of the league's franchises in smaller cities weren't so solid. In 1931 the Giants would be forced to barnstorm to make a living, and Schorling's Park soon fell into disrepair.

Elsewhere the 1920s were dying hard. The Cubs' new manager was busy leveraging his new status into a long line of credit at bookmaking establishments. Earl Carroll, a New York theatrical producer, was making plans to bring Chicago his "Vanities," which had been prosecuted for obscenity in New York. An aspiring showgirl, a West Sider named Violet Popovich, might have attended "Rarin' to Go." The idea of working for a show like Earl Carroll's would have appealed to an attractive brunette who had suffered a turbulent home life, and so might the idea of meeting ballplayers.[109]

By mid-February, Earl Carroll's revue, costarring William Demarest some thirty years before his role as the uncle in *My Three Sons*, had opened in and run three weeks without incident at a Loop theater. Then, during the first act on February 13, as Don Howard once again warbled "Song of the Moonbeams" with lights low and bare-limbed women cavorting about the stage, a policeman stepped from the wings and announced, "There will be no more show tonight." The patrons stirred in their seats. Was this part of the act? Their answer came quickly when policemen ordered the women off the stage. The curtain dropped, the house lights came on, and a spokesman told the astonished patrons that they could get refunds at the box office.[110]

At the South State Street station—the same venue that Pat Malone had visited the previous May—the group was bundled into the "bullpen," and the cast, including twenty-eight showgirls—one named Violet—was booked for participating in an obscene play. From the beginning, though, the raid had only added elements of comic opera. The *Tribune* noted one scene in particular said to have galvanized the authorities. In the sketch, entitled "The Noble Experiment," two men meet in a New York speakeasy; each recognizes the other as a Chicagoan, pulls out a gun, and shoots him dead.[111]

The show's promoters obtained an injunction to allow the show to go on, and the farce within the farce proceeded. The troupers soon enough found themselves in court, where the prosecution's star witness, one Effie Sigler of the city's motion picture censorship board, proved her own ability to entertain audiences. She claimed the performers were "seemingly nude" and "apparently bare." Asked to be more specific, she described the "back dance": "[The girls'] backs were exposed, and I don't mean from the waist up." Tittering rippled through the courtroom. After the bailiff's gavel restored order, Sigler's testimony turned to a bedroom scene involving the mention of pink draperies. More giggling. Flustered, Sigler rebuked the bench: "I think that that word 'pink' is simply insulting. I don't think it's a giggling matter and I think you ought to keep those girls quiet." Later, a deputy police commissioner called in to salvage the prosecution's case could only resort to "I know vulgarity when I see it." Just where the judge stood on the case became obvious when he lightheartedly served as the straight man while the defense attorney delivered a punch line from the scene. The jury speedily decided in favor of Violet and her cohorts, who went back to work before sellout houses.[112]

By then it was clear that Mayor Thompson, still clinging to office three years after the Pineapple Primary, had decided to order the raid and prosecution because it was satirizing his administration. Clearly, the gravity of the city's and the country's crisis had not yet quenched the spirit of the Jazz Age. Certainly, the Hack Wilson boom, founded 1926, showed no signs of abating. Earlier, the Hacker had met with William Veeck at Pittsburgh, where the Cubs' president stopped on his way to the annual baseball meetings in New York. The main stumbling block seemed to be that Veeck wanted to sign the slugger to a two-year contract, but without apparent haggling, the two agreed that Wilson deserved a one-year contract for $33,000, an amount that boosted the little slugger's pay to the levels of Gehrig and Hornsby, if still somewhat shy of the Bambino's $70,000 figure. And he would pay only 14 percent federal income tax on the last $2,000, and less overall—another 1920s phenomenon due for a radical change.

Wilson's contract completed the club's annual re-signings with Veeck's usual efficiency. Soon the boys, no longer McCarthymen, would be riding the Santa Fe Railway special to Los Angeles for another spring training in paradise, then on to another contending season. This time, Murderers' Row could finally appear in its full strength: English, Cuyler, Hornsby, Wilson, Hartnett, Stephenson. If Veeck thought anything might go wrong with his plan, or if he knew anything about the intense dislike several of this veterans felt for their new manager, it was a point he failed to address.[113]

11 | "A Lousy Outfield"

I go to his place of business. Why shouldn't he come to mine?

If you don't want me to talk to the big fellow, Judge, why don't you tell him yourself? —*Statements attributed to Gabby Hartnett after being photographed with Al Capone*

Sirens screaming, a caravan of police vehicles careened into the Loop just after 10:00 the evening of May 3, 1932. The five cars raced past the Federal Building at Jackson and Clark and pulled up to the entrance of the Dearborn Street Station. Plainclothesmen burst from their vehicles and surrounded the second car in the convoy. Two prisoners stepped out into a sea of police, reporters, cameramen, and onlookers. Klieg lights bathed the area while dozens of smaller flashbulbs went off with the pop-pop-pop of a small-arms firefight.[1]

The first prisoner, an accused auto thief named Morici, was of no interest to the bystanders. They had come to see the big, well-dressed man who was almost arm in arm with Morici. In fact, the two had been handcuffed together, although at the request of the larger man, sheriff's deputies were trying to hide the arrangement from the photographers. Only once did the ruse fail. In all the jostling, a coat sleeve was pulled up on one man's arm. For a few seconds, the cuffs lay exposed for the photographers, and the rest of the world, to see. "Damn it, come on. Let's get out of this," growled Al Capone.

After a decade in virtual control of Chicago, or large swatches of it, the Big Fella was on his way to the federal penitentiary in Atlanta. All appeals had been lost, all attempts to fix the jury, plea bargain with the judge, manipulate popular opinion, and bribe public officials had come to naught. Capone tried to keep up a jaunty front in the last days before leaving Chicago for good, dressing in his usual natty style and humoring the newsmen who hounded him. But he couldn't hide his underlying bitterness at the idea of going to prison for income tax evasion. "My sentence would have been 2½ years, but just because I went to a few baseball games they made it 11 years," he blurted out at one point in the final days.[2]

Less than two weeks after Capone's leavetaking, temperatures near the lake finally reached the seventies consistently for the first time that spring. But even though the afternoon of Sunday, May 15, 1932, brought sunshine and blue skies, just 26,000 customers found their way to Wrigley Field to watch the first-place Cubs play the Phils. Only a couple of years before, Bill Veeck would have sold out the ballpark on such a day, the Andy Frains stretching ropes across the outfield and disgruntled latecomers jostling outside the ticket windows on Addison.[3]

Those had been the days of Wilson's slugging surge and madcap sellouts. Much had changed at the ballpark since. The Depression was humbling the city of the big shoulders: nearly 750,000 residents—half the city's workforce and a staggering 10 percent of the nation's total—were unemployed, and many more were not working full time. Thousands of men gathered listlessly in Wacker Drive's lower level every evening. Many Chicagoans had left the city to try their luck on abandoned farms downstate at five dollars a month. The empty seats at the ballpark reflected these realities, and others. Capone, for one, was off to the Atlanta pen; he had made his last visit to Wrigley Field or anywhere else in the town he had dominated. His erstwhile ally, Big Bill Thompson, had been an ex-mayor for nearly a year, the last Republican mayor Chicago would elect in the twentieth century. Yet another titan of Chicago's 1920s, Samuel Insull, had sunk into utter bankruptcy, stripped of control over the utilities complex that had once delivered one-eighth of the electric power in the United States. Soon he would leave town for Europe, a fugitive from justice.[4]

There was also, each home game, the vacant seat in the owner's box behind third base. William Wrigley would never again join a Wrigley Field crowd, large or small. Near the end of January (and just months after the passing of the White Sox's Charles Comiskey), he had died in his sleep after a short, severe illness, just weeks before he was due at Catalina to greet the lads debarking from the *Avalon*. After a funeral service in Pasadena, Wrigley's body was taken to Catalina for eventual placement in a mausoleum on the heights overlooking Avalon Harbor. His fellow Chicagoan of nearly identical age, Insull, had virtually created an industry that supplied something tangible and crucial to the U.S. economy; Wrigley had spent his life delivering an unnutritious product that rotted teeth, and then marketed the spectacle of grown men playing an escapist fantasy. Yet it was Wrigley who had kept his corporation private and debt-free while Insull floundered and ruined himself in the turbulent financial markets following the Crash. Insull and his son faced years of litigation and struggle, while control of the Wrigley Company, and Wrigley's separate holding, the Chicago National League Ball Club, passed smoothly to Philip Wrigley, who had been running the gum business for his father since 1925. The new owner was a quiet man who had never shown much interest in baseball. It would be nearly a month into the season before he even occupied the owner's box at Wrigley Field.[5]

The most obvious change, though, was in neither the bleachers nor the box seats, but on the field. Every home date Riggs Stephenson trotted out to his post in left field, and the peerless Ki Cuyler to his in right, but the burly, sweaty fellow they had flanked was gone. One of baseball's greatest, longest-running outfield trios had been broken up, and Hack Wilson was a Cub no more.

Training camp somehow began at Santa Catalina in February 1932, even without any Wrigley waiting on the dock or Hack Wilson strolling down the *Avalon*'s gangplank. A monsoon poured down on the Magic Isle for the first few days while the players waited in the St. Catherine's Hotel. Finally the clouds parted and work began under the gimlet eye of Rogers Hornsby, beginning his second year at the helm of the Cubs. Grover Alexander, Hornsby's old buddy from the championship year in St. Louis, was on hand to get into shape for his semipro season and lend Hornsby a hand with the pitchers. It was Alex's first spring training on Catalina since 1926, which had been Joe McCarthy and Hack Wilson's first year on the Cubs.[6]

For 1932 Hornsby had altered the routine: the rookies now accompanied the early contingent of pitchers and catchers. They arrived, dazzled by the long Pullman trip across the continent, the three-hour cruise across the channel, and their sudden appearance in paradise. In the troubled world of 1932, the dreams and aspirations of youth and the ageless hopefuls of

Catalina, still soared as they always had. The Cubs were rebuilding, so the youngsters were more numerous than ever: Bill Herman, a ballyhooed second baseman from the American Association; Stanley Hack, a third baseman from the Pacific Coast League notorious for his $75,000 price tag; and a host of now-forgotten hopefuls fated to brief careers in the majors, or none at all—Harry Taylor, first base; Vince Barton, outfielder; Bud Tinning, Leroy Herrmann, and Red MacKenzie, pitchers. Dogging the Cubs on the eastern seaboard the previous summer, MacKenzie had talked Hornsby into giving him a tryout, and Hornsby had the Cubs' Los Angeles farm club sign the youngster. Pat Flanagan, wbbm's baseball broadcaster, singled out the youngster as a comer, and Irving Vaughan of the *Tribune* added, "Red is the kid they think might develop into another Bob Grove."[7]

Hornsby did nothing to dampen such talk; he was probably the "they" who saw in MacKenzie another Grove. The dour man who had fired Wilson was talking constantly, touting the wares, hustling to sell his new program after a third-place finish. At the batting cage, next to the sliding pit, wherever two or three Cubs gathered together, he was a man in his element, an extrovert scrutinizing, evaluating, dispensing tips, touting the youngsters as representatives of a new era that would feature the deadball virtues instead of the long-range bombardments of Murderers' Row. Among the holdovers, only Cuyler, Stephenson, and English had guaranteed jobs, and Stephenson's only if he recovered from the broken ankle that had cut short his 1931 season. To augment the plan for the post-Wilson era, Hornsby and Veeck had stockpiled the league's deepest and most veteran pitching staff, a "Big Five" that fortified the dependable trio of Root, Malone, and Bush with Bob Smith and especially the renowned National League veteran Burleigh Grimes, the exchange for Wilson after the 1931 season.

"Pep" and "spirit" were the watchwords. After a year of experimentation and turmoil, Hornsby the manager had turned McCarthy's approach inside out: pitching, fielding, and "the uncanny knack Hornsby seems to have for guessing right," one observer would call it after watching the Cubs grab the league lead for much of the spring.[8] An afterthought among all the prospects was Bill Jurges, a quiet, slick-fielding infield reserve who had hit just .201 in 1931 for the Cubs before ending the year at the Reading farm club, where he was slated to work further on his batting stroke if he weren't first packaged in a trade. After the veterans arrived in camp and intrasquad games began, Jurges was relegated to the "Goof" (or "Yannigan") squad rather than the "Regulars." He did not even make an appearance when the New York Giants sailed over for a series of practice games, and he was still a reserve when the Cubs traveled to the mainland in midmonth to play a series of exhibitions against several PCL clubs. By late March Jurges had accumulated only thirteen plate appearances. Then, on March 27, Woody English tore a fingernail in a game with the Missions of San Francisco. Jurges, filling in, startled everyone by going 5 for 8 in his first two starts, including a home run and five RBI in the second game against the Detroit Tigers in Los Angeles's version of Wrigley Field, where he went 3 for 4 against two bona fide major league pitchers, Tommy Bridges and Earl Whitehill of the Detroit Tigers. His fielding and throwing were as bravura as ever.[9] Soon the Cubs' train began the long journey to Opening Day at Cincinnati, stopping at Fort Worth, Dallas, and Kansas City to play the local minor league clubs. At Kansas City the Cubs announced that English's bothersome finger was actually broken; he would be laid up six weeks. The opener was four days off, and that meant Jurges would be the Cubs' shortstop.[10]

Like the understudy in a hackneyed Broadway plot, the youngster was ready for his main chance. He was a whirlwind of action in Cincinnati, crossing over the bag to knock down the second baseman, Herman, and take a short fly, and the next day victimizing the reserve rightfielder, Marvin Gudat, on a similar mission. In St. Louis, Jurges knifed between Kiki Cuyler and Johnny Moore, the new centerfielder, while those two were circling beneath a high fly in shallow right center. Then he abruptly ended a close game by flinging himself headlong at Pepper Martin's hard shot and turning it into a rapid-fire double play.[11]

All this activity had its result. When English was finally ready to return to the lineup, Hornsby benched his high-priced rookie third baseman, Stanley Hack, moved English to third in his place, and kept Jurges at short. Jurges had become the centerpiece of the nimble Cub defense as the club took the league lead in the season's early weeks. Once Charlie Grimm raced to the hole for a ground ball, bounced off the stationary Bill Klem, and reversed his course back to first base for the putout. Another time

Jurges slipped in the April mud after gloving a grounder; from the seat of his pants he nailed a perfect throw to Herman to get a force at second. The young catcher Rollie Hemsley outdid them all by gobbling up a sacrifice bunt, running down the batter for the tag out, and then whirling and throwing to second to catch the base runner sliding in. Men who had watched decades of big league play agreed: they had never seen a catcher do that.[12]

Hornsby seemed to have a spare part for every breakdown. When the thirty-eight-year-old Grimes missed his first start of the year with the flu, Hornsby trotted out Lon Warneke, another obscure reserve who had spent most of 1931 on the bench. The lanky youngster, stuffing an enormous wad of tobacco in his cheek, calmly threw a complete game, and when Grimes had to back out of his next start with a toothache, Warneke went twelve innings for another complete game. Warneke had yielded just three runs in twenty innings. He finished his third start, and a fourth and a fifth. Tall, and quiet like Jurges, unflappable, a hard thrower with excellent control, and a fast worker like Grover Alexander, Warneke seemed to be a reincarnation of Alex—who had, in fact, tutored the youth at Catalina as a guest of Hornsby that spring. Warneke's complete game against the Giants on May 10 took just and an hour and forty-eight minutes to finish, despite the Cubs' nine runs and eleven hits in support. Only six of the Giants' putouts had left the infield. By the end of May, when Warneke's streak reached nine straight complete games, he had upstaged the league's better-touted newcomers: the Cardinals' Dizzy Dean, Brooklyn's hard-throwing Van Lingle Mungo, and the Cubs' own Bud Tinning, who had received far more attention at Catalina. As for Grimes, he was on his way to taking Warneke's place as Hornsby's mop-up man; in fact, his storied career as the scowling, stubble-bearded terror of the National League was all but finished.[13]

Woody English's eclipse was not as swift as Grimes's, but big league ball would never be the same for him, either. Jurges and his fellow rookie, Bill Herman, were teaming superbly around second base. Herman, a deft, wide-ranging fielder, also settled in as a steady .300 hitter, going 12 for 20 in one stretch in May. In early June, with the Cardinals' Dizzy Dean on second, he contributed his own dazzler by streaking behind the bag to grab Ernie Orsatti's smash, then whirling 360 degrees to get enough on the throw to cut down an astonished Dean. It was a play "you might see in the big leagues once in ten years if you're lucky," Irving Vaughan told the baseball world in the *Sporting News*. The English-Hornsby keystone combination that the Cubs had taken to the World Series in 1929 seemed as dated as Tinker to Evers.[14]

Hornsby had indeed put together one of the tightest defensive infields the major leagues had seen in many years. The upshot was that English—the *Sporting News* all-star shortstop for 1931, the leadoff man for the memorable high summers of Murderers' Row—was being recycled. He had lost his leadoff spot to Herman after averaging 133 runs scored from 1928 through 1931. Never again would he score more than 70 runs in a season or hit .300. English had peaked at the tender age of twenty-five—though within a few months he would once again play shortstop for the Chicago Cubs, this time as an emergency replacement.

And then there was Red MacKenzie, whose spring hadn't gone as well as Bill Jurges's or Lon Warneke's. In February, MacKenzie and Bill Veeck, shaking hands, had occupied the center of the rookie's group photo taken in the Wrigley Building. Once on Catalina, he fell and hurt his elbow. He convalesced, he came back and struggled; the Cubs ticketed him for Los Angeles, and finally they sent him to Fort Wayne, Indiana. No more comparisons to Lefty Grove were heard. Downtown Fort Wayne was a little less than 150 miles from the Wrigley Building, but MacKenzie would never close the gap again.[15]

Bill Jurges had spent much of 1931 warming the Cub bench alongside an unlikely companion. For 1931 marked the crash of Hack Wilson. That sudden fall, like the memorable batting explosion in 1930, had been colossal, precipitous, unprecedented. Pushed by some combination of physical decline, low morale, and the deadened baseball, Wilson's home run total dropped by the same amount—43—that had constituted the league home run record only two years before.

From the Cub bench, the young reserve Jurges had a front-row seat for Wilson's long benchings, his pouts, his mammoth drunken spells and the suspensions that followed, the apologies and the tearful promises to reform. The carefree days under McCarthy were over. The Rajah dictated where in the count his batters could hit—a crippling restriction for the free-swinging Wilson—and called the pitches for every pitcher as well. The big three of the staff, Root, Bush, and Malone, by now had years of experience working with Hartnett, but Hornsby drove a wedge into that relationship by platooning Hartnett with the agile, much-younger Hemsley. Hemsley promptly joined Wilson and Malone in a spectacular bender that got them all suspended.[16]

Even with a depression in full swing, an unproductive alcoholic earning four hundred dollars a game could still generate support if he had accumulated a huge storehouse of popularity and a nemesis named Hornsby. Though Wilson had only ten home runs by midseason and a batting average under .300, his public still ruled the ballpark. On the last day of June 1931, William Wrigley had to summon the *Tribune*'s Irving Vaughan for another exclusive interview, this time to let Chicagoans know that he alone owned the Cubs and that Hornsby was his manager for life—as it turned out, a time frame much shorter than Hornsby or anyone else could anticipate.[17]

The second half of 1931 turned ugly as the Cubs fell far from the league lead and Wilson and Hornsby feuded. Wilson's dissipation intensified even as his slugging slowed from subpar to abysmal: the terror of 1930 managed to hit exactly three home runs in the second half of 1931. In early September, Wilson capped his dismal season by inciting Malone to attack two newspapermen in a railroad car. Wilson, not Malone, took the fall. Suspended indefinitely and banned from the clubhouse, he watched his teammates from the grandstand, where the ushers had to shoo crowds of admirers away.[18]

Before Wilson left town for good in mid-September, the Cubs and the White Sox staged a benefit game for the unemployed in Comiskey Park. It was the memorable day that Hartnett, who himself had struggled through a difficult year, strolled over to Al Capone's box and autographed Sonny Capone's baseball, with a platoon of photographers on hand to record the moment.

Both Hartnett and especially Capone probably regretted the pose, which attracted attention all over the country—and more important, it was not the center of attention for the people in the house, for the fans had their own public enemy: Rogers Hornsby. Cub and Sox fans, united at last, tossed lemons at the Rajah and booed him at every turn, with special gusto when he found himself trapped off second base in the sixth inning.[19]

Charlie Root, unfazed by Hornsby's baserunning, finished with a six-hit shutout to beat the Sox. The next day, the Cubs were back at Wrigley Field to continue their home stand, and the Cub fans refused to let up on Hornsby. That weekend, Hornsby silenced his critics with a majestic, game-ending grand slam off the Braves' Bruce Cunningham.

Hornsby's bravura grand slam was a reminder of the defunct Murderers' Row. Its members were all past thirty now; Wilson was off the squad, and Cuyler was the only survivor with the physical ability and good health to dominate over a stretch of weeks or months. Hartnett's playing days would outlast all of them—seven years later he would launch one of baseball's most celebrated home runs—but in September 1931 he seemed to be a fading catcher whose biggest headline had been shaking hands with a mobster. Hornsby himself, his feet and legs troubling him, had played his last stretch as a regular. At the start of September, he turned his second-base job over to the newly acquired Bill Herman for an extended look-see. Herman, like Hornsby, would one day earn election to the Hall of Fame as a second baseman, but Hornsby carefully hid any enthusiasm he felt about the youngster's potential. "So many humpty-dumpty players come up in the majors now that you can't take a chance on waiting to look them over in spring camp," he remarked while writing the talented youngster's name into the lineup for the first time.[20]

The Cubs spent the rest of the 1931 season at home. They swept easily through the rest of their schedule and took firm hold of third place, but no one thought that anything had been solved. That December, Wilson was officially dispatched to St. Louis for Burleigh Grimes. The old gang was breaking up. Sheriff Blake, once a reliable part of McCarthy's rotation, the timid infield reserve Clyde Beck, and even Cliff Heathcote had already been cut loose. After disposing of Wilson at the baseball meetings in early December, Veeck began shopping even those two old faithfuls, Grimm and Hartnett. Barney Dreyfuss had once rid himself of his banjo players, and now Rogers Hornsby was dismantling the Cubs' vaudevillians.[21]

Hornsby's youth corps won steadily in the first weeks of 1932. They forged ahead the first week of the season and then defeated the champion Cardinals the first five times the clubs met. In late April, though, injury struck the roster again: Ki Cuyler broke a bone in his foot while running the bases. On crutches, he went home to Michigan.[22]

The outfield, shorn of Wilson, had already figured to be the weak spot in Hornsby's rebuilding project. Stephenson, the old reliable, was himself trying to come back from an ankle break that had cut short his 1931 season—or, in view of his thirty-four years, perhaps his career. With Cuyler out, the Rajah would have to make do with Stevie and a collection of journeymen, whose chances for the Hall of Fame were substantially less than Bill Herman's. Hornsby, though, proved himself to be an equal-opportunity curmudgeon, barking, "I'm going to stick [Johnny] Moore in center and he'll have to make good. Then there's Dan Taylor. He's another that will have to show me."[23]

Dan Taylor was a McCarthy-era holdover, a lusty hitter and fearless base runner who had subbed spectacularly for Stephenson during the long August home stand in 1930, temporarily upstaging the prime of Hack Wilson with a memorable, game-winning steal of home against the Giants. Taylor was a dependable bench jockey in the bargain. But there was a good reason he had been kept in the minor leagues until his late twenties. He was thoroughly ungraceful afield, poor enough to draw comparison to the Sox's lumbering slugger Smead Jolley.[24]

In early May, Taylor personally settled the problem for Hornsby, beyond all doubt. The Cubs invaded Forbes Field in Pittsburgh. In the fourth inning of the first game Pie Traynor, the Pirates' star third baseman, drove a line drive to right field. Taylor dived for the ball, but it hit the ground first. No error was charged on the play.

Two innings later, with two out, Taylor again tried to trap a line drive, this time one off the bat of Gus Dugas. As the ball bounced away from Taylor's grasp, Dugas raced all the way to third base to earn one of his his 3 triples among 45 lifetime hits. Floyd Vaughan came up next. A youngster who had only recently cracked the regular lineup, he would be good for 2,103 hits and a spot in the Hall of Fame as "Arky." Vaughan's blow likewise scooted past the befuddled Taylor for a triple, Vaughan's third of the 128 he would accumulate in the big leagues. Next up was Bill Brenzel, destined to solve major league pitching 2,060 times less often than Vaughan. Based on the afternoon's result so far, he too drove the ball toward Taylor, who this time got a glove on it but couldn't hang on. Vaughan scored and Brenzel pulled into second. The play was scored a double, Brenzel's first of nine for his career.

Strangely, Taylor was yet to be called for an error, but in the visitors' dugout, Hornsby was seething. In the sparsely populated stands, the mid-week turnout of some two thousand badgered the Cubs unmercifully with shrill jeers that could be heard and understood individually. The Rajah called for time as a reserve, Marv Gudat, donned a glove and trotted toward right field.

The raucous fans hushed at the unusual turn of events. They watched intently as Gudat made his way to right field, and Taylor, head down, walked slowly off. A murmur passed through the stands. Gudat took up his fielding stance and Taylor disappeared from view. The Pirate fans stared after him briefly; then they resumed their heckling. Hornsby's harsh intervention had its short-term benefits, for Gudat played an errorless right field and drove in three runs to help the Cubs overtake the Pirates, 8–6. They beat the Pirates the next day, too, before returning to Chicago. They remained tied for first with St. Louis, and they would remain first or tied for first through this unusually chilly spring—a "blackberry winter," as they called it in the rural Midwest—until the last week of June.[25]

Danny Taylor never appeared in a Cub uniform again. Within days of his public humiliation, Bill Veeck sold him to Brooklyn, where the Dodgers needed a backup for Hack Wilson. In Wilson, Taylor, and Lefty O'Doul, the Dodgers had stocked a complete outfield of disgruntled, hard-hitting ex-Cubs.

The question was whether that threesome was any more disgruntled than the veterans who remained in Hornsby's clubhouse—or doghouse.

Francis Joseph "Lefty" O'Doul and, more important, Lewis Robert "Hack" Wilson, late of the Chicago Cubs and now of the Brooklyn Dodgers, arrived in Chicago, forty-eight hours after Danny Taylor's banishment, for a four-game set Wilson's new club would play in Wrigley Field. The fans mobbed the grinning little big man as he stepped off the train and the air crackled with their welcoming cries. "Hack!" "How you feelin', Hack?" "Hit one for us!" Nearby an onlooker scowled. "My old lady says she's goin' to quit goin' over there, just because they traded old Hack," he muttered.

Wilson, smiling broadly, made his way slowly to his cab. When he reached the Belmont Hotel, a crush of Dazzy Vance and various taller teammates obscured the view of Wilson from the front desk. The ex-Cub finally decided he would have to speak up to get some service. "I'm Wilson. Where's my room?"

"So you're Wilson," answered the desk clerk. Then he brought up the subject that was on everyone's mind: "Does Hornsby know you're here?"

"He will," Wilson replied.[26]

Bold words considering the uncertain winter and spring Wilson had spent after his failures in 1931. After he balked at St. Louis's plan to cut his pay from $33,000 to $7,000, Branch Rickey quickly passed him on to the Dodgers, where Wilson salvaged perhaps half of his old Cub salary. Brooklyn seemed like a more congenial destination for one of Hack's sensibility; the fans, if less numerous than those in Chicago, were noted even then as true enthusiasts. The Brooklyns had their new outfielders and an optimistic outlook on the new season; they had a new manager and a lineup strong enough with Wilson's acquisition that they had traded their own bellwether, Babe Herman, to bolster their defense. Wilson was the center of attention in spring training at Florida, where even his dieting was closely scrutinized by the large and energetic New York press. But Wilson hurt his leg in the early days of the season, and he was in and out of the lineup. When he returned to Chicago on May 5,he had only two home runs and few runs batted in, and no reprise of 1930 looked in sight.

At Wrigley Field, though, hundreds of cloth-capped youngsters, on a school day, packed the fifty-cent bleachers in right field, behind the mesh barrier that had been Wilson's favorite home run target. Wilson, now a right fielder, ignored the league's rule against mingling with the fans—an artifact of the previous September's Hartnett-Capone encounter—and greeted dozens of climbing, reaching boys pressed against the wire and stretching their arms through the mesh, a fortunate few able to shake Wilson's hand.[27]

Except for the strange uniform now stretched on Wilson's frame, it might have been old times. Lemons bounded out near the batter's box when he first came to the plate. There were boos when Wilson struck out his first time up, and cheers when he got his one hit for the day, a single. For extra déjà vu, Wilson, hampered by his bad knee, also botched two attempts at sliding catches in a 2–1 Dodger victory.[28] Wilson went hitless in game 2. He had to sit out game 3. Even with Wilson on the bench, though, the Hornsby-Wilson tension lingered. Lefty O'Doul upended Stan Hack with a hard slide, Joe Stripp slid into Jurges, Woody English retaliated against Tony Cuccinello. On Sunday, Danny Taylor appeared in the final game of the series—in a Dodger uniform. Brooklyn had purchased him the day before. In his first appearance as a Dodger, he pinch-hit unsuccessfully against Burleigh Grimes.[29]

The Cubs maintained their lead in the weeks after the Dodger series. Adding Warneke to the already formidable rotation of Root, Bush, and Malone created arguably the deepest staff in the National League, if not the majors. Hornsby's starters were knocked out of the box only three times through May 10, and the Cubs were stranding only 20 percent of their base runners. Youth and inexperience produced the inevitable breakdowns, to be sure: Herman's four errors and Jurges's two made up six of a startling seven errors the Cubs committed on May 12, and on the 15th Warneke suffered his first loss when the Phillies poured six runs across the plate from the seventh inning on. He lost his next start, too, although giving up just three runs in 10⅔ stalwart innings. Hornsby had donned a summer skimmer ten days ahead of the traditional beginning of summer, Decoration Day, and he didn't try to hide his smile in public. But the insiders' consensus held that the day-to-day strain of low-scoring games, scratching for every hit and run, would wear Hornsby's low-powered outfit down.[30]

No doubt about it, the Cubs had played above expectations with two of their stars laid up for long stretches, but they were hardly dominating the league. The new-era lineup had produced exactly seven home runs in the season's first thousand at-bats; the team batting average stood at .247, last in the league. Late May brought four quick losses in six road games, and the Rajah began dwelling loudly on the lineup's lack of power.

Cuyler was still on crutches, nearly a month after hurting his foot. From his home in Michigan, far north on the Lake Huron shoreline, he paid regular visits to a specialist in Chicago, but even as the doctors applied successively lighter casts to the injured foot, Cuyler complained that it still hurt.[31]

Clearly, Veeck needed to swing a deal for another hitter before the June 15 trading deadline if Cuyler were not 100 percent anytime soon. The Cub president's Pullman car hooked up to the team train on its trip to the East Coast in early June. Veeck customarily accompanied "the boys" on their first long road trip anyway. This year, though, Veeck would find himself riding along with the ball club right into August.[32]

Hornsby had a backup plan in case Veeck couldn't obtain a power hitter by June 15. On the Cub bench sat a little-used but serviceable utility man, in fact, one who currently held the highest current lifetime batting average in the major leagues: the Rajah himself. The year before, playing part time on his bad legs, he had still tied for seventh place in league home runs and hit .331. After Taylor's forced departure, Hornsby spent the rest of May getting himself back into shape and trying to acquire the necessary skills for a spot he had played only briefly a decade before: right field. On May 29, he debuted in the first game of a doubleheader to mixed applause and boos at Wrigley Field. By the fourth inning of the next day's second game, the new right fielder was 2 for 12 at the plate. With the boobirds now in full cry, the unflappable Rajah stroked a first-pitch home run off Tex Carleton to help gain a split for the day with St. Louis. A "hitting heart"— that the man had.[33]

Then it was off on a road trip, first to Pittsburgh, where the fans roared with laughter to see the Rajah, their bitter enemy of so many years and so many bitterly fought campaigns, gamboling in the very right-field spot where he had made Danny Taylor walk the plank a few weeks before. The next stop was Bill Jurges's hometown of Brooklyn. By this time the Dodgers were a team on the upswing. Wilson, his leg healed, had hit five home runs in two weeks, and next to Wilson in the outfield was the Bums' new center fielder, none other than Danny Taylor, rescued from oblivion less than a month after judgment day in Forbes Field. Now he was batting leadoff for a contender.[34]

The fans tossed lemons at the Cubs while the clubs were splitting the first two games of the series amid increasing tension. The Brooklyn pitchers hit Hornsby hit twice, and Guy Bush answered by hitting two Dodgers. The real hostilities began when Malone started the third game. In the bottom of the first, he loaded the bases, setting the stage for the inaugural Malone-Wilson confrontation. Wilson crushed a drive that stuck freakishly in the right-field screen for a grand slam. Malone, galvanized, began aiming his mighty fastball straight at Dodger uniforms; even his erstwhile pal Wilson had to hit the deck twice. Van Lingle Mungo answered in kind for the Dodgers; Jurges was spiked by Al Lopez in a collision at second that left him knocked out, and in the ninth Hartnett, who had homered for the only two Cub runs of the day, went down writhing with a fastball to the elbow. The dugouts emptied again. "Just like the Argonne," muttered Lefty O'Doul. When it was all done, the Dodgers had a 5–2 victory.[35]

Trouble followed the next day. In the first inning Mickey Finn upended Jurges at second base. The two tumbled into the dust, swinging and gouging, soon joined by English. O'Doul led a Dodger charge from the dugout, followed by the Cubs from theirs. Police had to intervene. The umpires ejected both Finn and Jurges, and as they trudged off into the tunnel that led to the clubhouses, the membership of both clubs followed en masse, eager to see another bout under the stands. The umpires finally shooed the ballplayers back to work, their heads hanging.[36]

There were more collisions, and one more spiking. In the ninth inning Danny Taylor's dazzling running catch started a double play that ended the game and the series—take that, Rogers Hornsby! The Dodgers had grabbed three of four from the Cubs. They had also shown Bill Veeck, who taken in the whole series, what kind of effect William Wrigley's favorite manager had on the opposition, just by being himself.

The losses to the Dodgers seemed to rattle Hornsby's youngsters. Jurges was out several days with his spike wounds, and the defense began to buckle. Even Kiki Cuyler's return to the lineup on June 15 failed to improve matters. Hornsby applied more negative motivation, forbidding his players to make the short trip from New York to Philadelphia for the Schmeling-Sharkey prizefight, then scheduling a rugged workout on a day off, but the Cubs' grip on first place continued to loosen.[37]

Hornsby had made one more enemy in New York—one he would regret. Hornsby had not been able to hide his disappointment when the June 15 deadline passed without the hoped-for reinforcement. The Cubs' problem, he told a New York reporter, was the club's "lousy outfield." Unfortunately for Rogers Hornsby's future with the Chicago Cubs, Bill Veeck was in New York to read about what his manager thought of his efforts.[38]

If Hornsby was trying to force the issue, he had chosen a poor moment for it. Going to the press with a complaint about Veeck's policies was reckless to begin with, but more than that, it had been barely a month since Hornsby had insisted that Veeck cut an outfielder—Danny Taylor, the man Veeck had just watched for several days patrolling centerfield and batting leadoff for a winning ball club. And there had been other tensions between the two men. During the Brooklyn series Veeck ordered Hornsby to remove himself from the lineup and, discovering (or pretending to discover) that Hornsby called the pitches for even veterans like Grimes and Hartnett, he told Hornsby that the batteries should handle pitch selection themselves. Hornsby relented on both counts, reserving only his right to dictate to the youthful Warneke. The whole process was palpably different from the days of William Wrigley.[39]

Veeck had also witnessed the breakdown of discipline and the animosities on display at Ebbets, and he probably learned of Hornsby's determination that Cuyler, who had rejoined the team in New York, play center field as soon as feasible, even though his injury had slowed him up and Johnny Moore was playing capably in the position. Cuyler, in fact, had balked at returning to the lineup so soon. The only dependable run producer left on the roster was the faithful Stephenson.

Hornsby was also at odds with another holdover from the McCarthy era. Although Gabby Hartnett had more power than anyone left on the roster, Hornsby was platooning him and the nimble, light-hitting Rollie Hemsley. In one game Hartnett, curious why his pitcher was shaking off his signals, went out to the mound to find out. "Hornsby told me to," came the answer. Hartnett—Grover Alexander's protégé, Hal Carlson's roommate, tutor of Bush, Root, and Malone—stalked to the dugout and threw his gear at Hornsby's feet. "You catch," he snarled.[40]

After his outburst Hartnett bided his time and said no more. Beneath the bluster he had always been a guarded man. "That's right, that's right" had always been the way he fended off unsolicited observations and comments, while inwardly maintaining his own counsel. He had been anything but cocksure while sitting on the bench in 1929, when his shoulder problem had coincided almost exactly with his wife's pregnancy, and he had been the one who collapsed at Carlson's bier. Now he was a thirty-one-year-old platoon player whose manager saw him as a pal of the old boss.[41]

Hartnett was out of action for several days after Mungo's fastball to his forearm. About the same time Cuyler, still favoring his foot, returned unwillingly to the lineup. Although Hornsby seemed to counting on Cuyler as the Cubs' main power source, Cuyler had always been a streak hitter, not an RBI machine like Hornsby or Stephenson. His strengths were asymmetric, rattling the enemy with athleticism and unpredictable feats.[42]

A much-younger Cuyler had famously ended up at loggerheads with another manager, Donie Bush, who among other issues had insisted Cuyler play hurt and attempted to play Cuyler at a new position. Bush had not won another pennant after trading Cuyler away; his last major league job was managing two futile seasons with the Sox while Cuyler starred across town for the Wrigleys. Bush lost that job too. It was the fate of all managers, a thought that may have occurred to Cuyler as he trudged out to work each day on his sore foot.[43]

The Bruins returned to Chicago at the end of June with eight wins to show for their twenty-one-game trip. The team had scored just 92 runs in the twenty-one road games. Hornsby had moved Cuyler to center field June 30 even though he was still limping, and he was hitting poorly. (This was also the date that the Cubs began wearing numbered jerseys; Cuyler became the Cubs' first number 3, his spot in the lineup.) The trading deadline had passed without the appearance of any reinforcements. Meanwhile, the Pirates had been on a tear. Under .500 a month before, they slipped past the Cubs into first place by the end of June.[44]

Hornsby chose this point to do what he had been planning for weeks: bench Johnny Moore, the default center fielder since Danny Taylor's firing, and install Kiki Cuyler there—a position he hadn't played since early 1927. The Cubs and the Pirates fought over first place for several days until the two clubs met for a doubleheader in Pittsburgh on July 4. The Pirates quickly knocked Grimes out in the first game and went on to win, 9–6. In the second game, Cuyler homered in the fourth inning to give the Cubs the early lead. In the seventh inning Herman's dash into the outfield spooked Vince Barton and Cuyler into letting Pie Traynor's pop fly fall among the three. That kept a three-run Pirate rally alive. Cuyler misplayed balls in both the eighth and the ninth to help the Bucs score the tying run and send the game into extra innings. In the tenth Arky Vaughan's infield hit plated the winning run. The Cubs' prolonged stay in first place was over, and Hornsby's outfield looked lousier than ever—no small thanks to him.[45]

Hornsby was fighting a personal losing streak, too. The latest blow had arrived just as the Cubs returned to Chicago from their trip to the eastern seaboard. The U.S. Appeals Board ruled that Hornsby's ownership of Texas real estate did not allow him to claim residence there on his 1926 and 1927 federal tax returns, when he actually resided in Missouri. The decision left Hornsby $8,653 in debt to Uncle Sam.[46]

At first blush, Hornsby was one major leaguer who should have been unfazed by such a bill. But Hornsby's forty-thousand-dollar annual player-manager salary, three or four times the pay of most stars, did not mean he had the wherewithal to repay Uncle Sam. The problem had been building for years, and in fact, his attempted tax chiseling was only a symptom of his financial troubles. Hornsby's financial dealings first attracted public interest in the late twenties, when a bookmaker sued him for $92,000 of unpaid gambling debts—more than a million dollars in twenty-first-century money. The suit was dismissed on the grounds that a gambling debt was unenforceable in Missouri, the state of filing. Hornsby's supporters spoke of his "vindication," a generous conclusion considering that Hornsby had admitted to breaking the law and welshing on his debts. Later that year the C. E. Allen affair underscored Hornsby's continuing addiction to playing the horses.[47]

Joe McCarthy, though, had never uttered a discouraging word about Hornsby's betting after the Rajah joined his baseball family; quite the opposite. It was McCarthy's departure in the fall of 1930 that seemed to reopen the floodgates. In Chicago's multitude of illegal bookmaking joints—"handbooks"—it became common knowledge that Hornsby was using his new position to get in on the gambling action.

During spring training in 1931 the new manager's wife contacted Bill Veeck. Mrs. Hornsby told Veeck she had moved from the Hornsbys' home in St. Louis and returned to their farm out in the county for lack of funds. She gave Veeck the name of a Chicago bookmaker who was dunning Hornsby for $5,400. Hornsby had stopped payment on checks made out to the bookmaker for that amount.

Veeck met with the bookie, and then reached Hornsby long distance at

Catalina. Soon thereafter, the $5,400 was paid, and Veeck made arrangements to send part of Hornsby's salary directly to his wife each month. The episode left little doubt about where the Rajah's paychecks disappeared. He was said to be laying down $2,000 at a time, a far cry from the $2 bet of the everyday bettor. One big problem, it seemed, was that Hornsby wasn't very good at his hobby. He always bet on the "top" horse—bets so expensive by definition that winning didn't always pay off. That's just how the bookies wanted it, naturally enough. The system worked as long as the customer could keep raising enough cash, and what better mark than William Wrigley's favorite manager?[48]

Hornsby couldn't, the Cubs and the rest of baseball would learn.

12 ‖ Room 509

Velma: No sense of—honor, reporters. Broke into my apartment the night I—
  left, and stole a whole suit-case of letters—valuable letters—letters from
  men who have loved me . . .
Roxie: And a "Diagram of the Apartment"—my God! See the spot marked *X*.
  [Points with satisfaction.] That's where he fell—the dirty piker!"
—Maurine Watkins, "Chicago" (1927)

In the summer of 1932, the minor league franchises of many small cities
across the country could no longer make a go of it. In midsummer, two
familiar minor leagues, the Three-I and the Eastern, suspended operations
for want of fans and revenues. A couple of weeks later, a Cub affiliate, the
Reading Keys of the International League, also found itself in trouble.
The Wrigleys' seemingly bottomless reserves, though, provided the Reading Keys with a lifeline. The club simply arranged to shift from Pennsylvania to New York and become the Albany Senators.[1]

At the opening game in Albany, a hearty crowd of seven thousand
greeted the team, including Vince Barton and several other former Cubs.
Les Bell, who had been cut from the major league club at Catalina that
spring, and Harry Taylor, a first baseman who had stuck with the Cubs
for several weeks early in the year, both went 0 for 4. Barton homered in
the ninth to beat Buffalo, 2–1.

It was a bittersweet accomplishment for the tall Canadian. One of the
minor leagues' leading power hitters of the early 1930s, he had hit 32 home
runs to Joe Hauser's 63 for the Baltimore Orioles two years before, then
another 17 with the Cubs' Los Angeles affiliate in 1931 when Hornsby
called him up to replace Hack Wilson in the lineup. In late August 1931,
it was his temporary absence to attend his brother's funeral in Ontario
that precipitated Hornsby's decision to send the pitcher Bud Teachout into

the outfield instead of Wilson. Barton ended up his rookie season with 13 home runs and 50 RBI in just 230 at-bats, and the next spring Hornsby patiently tutored Barton to change from slugging to hitting, to keep his shoulder up instead of dropping it to golf the ball out of the park. But as the 1932 season progressed, Barton's strikeouts mounted. Danny Taylor's downfall provided another opportunity, but Barton looked as overmatched as ever against major league pitching.[2]

Regardless, the last weeks of Vince Barton, major leaguer, had been eventful. He had been in the lineup for several showdowns with the league-leading Pirates, during which he, Cuyler, and Herman had flubbed the ninth-inning fly ball. At one point in July he had wrecked a borrowed automobile, and as a result he and manager Hornsby had to visit a judge to explain things—not any old Chicago magistrate, but the baseball commissioner on Michigan Avenue. Landis was evidently satisfied with Barton's explanation, because no more was heard of the matter.

Above all there had been the turmoil at the Hotel Carlos in early July. There Barton had been surrounded by police and reporters who wanted to hear everything he knew about the incredible scene he had just witnessed.[3]

Even after Hal Carlson's death in 1930, several Cubs, notably Ki Cuyler, had continued to summer at the Carlos, just north of the ballpark. Bill Jurges had lived there during his on-and-off service with the club in 1931, and he had moved back in for 1932 along with his fellow bachelors Barton and Marv Gudat. They were all in residence the morning of Wednesday, July 6, when the Cubs were scheduled to start the second half of their season. The day dawned sunny and warm after the damp chill of the past few days, weather that had typified so much of the low-scoring, sparsely attended games of spring and early summer.

Barton, Gudat, and their teammates prepared to meet in the lobby and head down to the park. The laggard was Bill Jurges, who had been detained in room 509 by a phone call about a quarter of ten. It was a girlfriend he had met when he lived in the Carlos the summer before. She had just moved back into the hotel that weekend, and she wanted to see him. "C'mon up," Jurges told her.[4]

It was not something he was looking forward to. There had been tears and angry scenes already since Violet's divorce became final in May: she had waited outside the clubhouse after a game and tried to grab his arm as he left; during the Cubs' visit to New York in June, she showed up and started another row. While registering at the Carlos again earlier that week, she told the desk clerks that she was going to "get Bill, and maybe Kiki, too." The Carlos personnel evidently didn't pass the information along to either Cub. Nor had Jurges heard that the night before, a guest at the hotel had seen Violet taking some sort of target practice with a friend from the New York trip.[5]

Bill had met Violet in 1931 when the Wilson-Malone partnership was still leading the league in most consecutive nights on the town. While Hornsby dealt with that problem, some of the Cub veterans began dating the young woman, and eventually she and Jurges, only three years apart in age, became involved. A native West Sider, born Violet Popovich, she had spent much of her childhood in an orphanage, run away from home at fifteen, joined Earl Carroll's chorus line at age seventeen, taken the stage name Violet Valli, and married at eighteen. Her husband had deserted her two months after their wedding; she obtained her divorce three years later, in May 1932. Now Violet Popovich Valli was free to press her suit upon the young shortstop.[6]

Jurges was a bigger catch than he had been the summer before. Near the end of 1931 the Cubs returned him to the minors to make room for Bill Herman, a better-regarded, high-priced prospect, and whether Bill would ever return to Chicago as a Cub had become problematic. Then came spring 1932 at Catalina: English's injury, Jurges's sudden emergence as a dependable hitter to go along with his always superior glovework, and perhaps even more remarkable, praise from Hornsby. The Bill Jurges who returned to Chicago was no longer a struggling utility player, but a key member of a contending team. His mentors, Hornsby and Ki Cuyler, were fitness buffs who both stressed turning in early every night. Cuyler had even provided Jurges advice about dating, and Valli in particular.

About 10:15 there was a knock on the door of room 509. Jurges pulled it open and Valli stepped unsteadily through the doorway.

Marv Gudat, the extra outfielder who had replaced Danny Taylor at Forbes Field in May, slouched in a chair in the lobby of the Carlos. Gudat had stuck with the club for the entire first half of the season, his best performance so far in the major leagues, further than most under Rogers Hornsby. And he had done it in a way few big leaguers could. After originally breaking in as a pitcher with Cincinnati, where his 3.38 ERA in 26 innings was somehow not good enough for the sorry Reds, he returned to the minors and reinvented himself as a reserve outfielder–first baseman. Washing ashore at Catalina in the spring of 1932, he hit and fielded well enough to satisfy Hornsby. In the worst year of the Depression, Gudat was now making more money as an outfield reserve than he could have commanded as a starting pitcher in Cincinnati.

Along with Gudat and the other Cub players, several other folks had gathered in the lobby. When Jurges showed up, the group would head for the ballpark two blocks south and prepare for batting practice. In the group, providentially, was Dr. John Davis, the team physician, who lived not far away on Sheffield Avenue. Dr. Davis was the physician who had reached Hal Carlson's side that awful night two years before. On this bright morning, the doctor had no inkling that another Cub's life would soon be in his hands.

The men halted their small talk and banter for a moment at the sound of three rapid pops—perhaps a few leftover firecrackers from the Fourth, or the backfire of a truck passing by on Sheffield. Then they heard Bill Jurges's voice, shouting for help. Gudat was the first to head for the stairwell. Racing up the five floors to Jurges's room, he came upon an astonishing scene in room 509: Jurges sprawled across a chair, holding his side, blood everywhere, Violet Valli standing nearby. She was bleeding herself, much less heavily, from her forearm.[7]

"I've been shot," Jurges gasped. "Get a doctor." Gudat rushed out to find Dr. Davis just as Barton arrived. Valli was holding her arms out to Jurges. He pushed her away. "Get the gun in the other room there," he ordered Barton. "Don't let her get it." Barton picked up the weapon, a small-caliber handgun. Soon a team from the Illinois Masonic Hospital arrived, led by an intern who quickly examined Jurges. "Doc, how am I?" Jurges asked him. "I'll give you 20 minutes to live. You've got it bad," the young doctor replied.

At Jurges's request, Dr. Davis conducted his own examination of the wounded ballplayer. The main trauma was a wound in Jurges's right side near the lower rib; there was also a slight flesh wound in his left hand. The rib had prevented the bullet from reaching Jurges's liver. "What do you think?" Jurges asked. Davis told him he would be all right. "That doctor over there gave me 20 minutes," Jurges told him, more relieved than angry. Davis also examined Violet, who appeared to have suffered only a flesh wound to her left wrist.[8]

As soon as the medical crew had taken Jurges and Valli away, police and reporters headed for the young woman's room on the first floor, where they began prowling through her possessions. "Valli" was a stage name, they learned. Several empty bottles of gin turned up, plus a note addressed to her brother. That afternoon the tabloids published what the police had given them:

> To me life without Billy isn't worth living, but why should I leave this earth alone? I'm going to take Billy with me. We were getting along just famously, just as everything should go, but a few people like Ki-Ki Cuyler and Lew Steadman forgot that there might be anything fine and beautiful in our love for each other and dragged it in the mud. I know what I'm doing is best for me and I hate to do it—but???[9]

Cuyler's name came up again when Hotel Carlos employees were interviewed. It was after reading a telegram at the front desk the night before that Valli was supposed to have declared that she would "get Bill, and maybe Kiki, too."[10]

The investigation also continued at the hospital, where Valli announced, "I wanted to marry him. I went to his room to commit suicide." That confused Lieutenant O'Brien of the Chicago police force, who demanded: "What were you doing in Jurges's room?"

"I went there to kill myself," Valli repeated.

"Why didn't you do the job in your own room?"

"I won't say."

"What's your reason for suicide?"

"Private reasons," Valli snapped.[11]

When the hubbub had died down, Valli repeated within a reporter's earshot that her only plan had been to kill herself. Had she and Jurges had been engaged? "No, but we were going together for a year. . . .

"I want to live now."

By the next day Valli had been moved to the Bridewell jail, where she had been confined on a preliminary charge of assault with intent to kill. Virginia Gardner of the *Chicago Tribune* found Valli on a cot in the jail's hospital unit, where the doctors had found a broken bone in her wrist. Valli confirmed for Gardner that she had chosen Jurges's room for a suicide attempt because "I wanted to see him once more." She repeated that meant to kill herself, not Jurges: "He [Jurges] knows that." The note to her brother? "Too much gin," she said, and she proclaimed her love for Jurges (who, she added, had sent her a note that said "he'd do anything he could to help me"). She also volunteered, "Kiki Cuyler is the only other baseball player I've ever known, and I'm certainly not wild about him."[12]

Despite Valli's protests, a Chicago paper had already reported that before meeting Jurges, Valli had been "friendly" with at least one other major leaguer, the Cincinnati Reds' Leo Durocher. Then and now, someone reading that is entitled to think "unfounded gossip," but in the twenty-first century we know that Durocher was a notorious and boastful lecher. It doesn't help Valli's credibility that Durocher's name had popped up from the four-hundred-plus men who wore a big league uniform each year, or that decades later Jurges and Al Lopez (then a catcher with the Brooklyn Dodgers) both remembered Valli as essentially a camp-follower with numerous liaisons among the ballplayers.[13]

Cuyler sounded puzzled when he heard that Valli was talking about him: he had just been providing a young ballplayer with advice, he said—his counsel was to avoid a commitment at this point in his career. That seemed consistent with the wording of Valli's note—"a few people like Ki-Ki Cuyler and Lew Steadman forgot that there might be anything fine and beautiful in our love for each other"—but several of Valli's contemporaries thought otherwise. George Brace, then a young photographer's assistant, thought another Cub besides Jurges and Cuyler was directly involved. In the 1960s Bill Veeck Jr. suggested that Valli had tracked a married lover to Jurges's room, Jurges taking the bullets when he tried to intervene: "Billy, being single, kept the intended victim's name out of it, leaving everybody to believe that he had got shot on his own merits." In retirement Jurges himself endorsed the married-man theory and named him: Kiki Cuyler (while admitting that he, Jurges, was also sleeping with

Popovich). According to Jurges, Valli had a key to Cuyler's room and left a note on his mirror that Tuesday morning: "I'M GOING TO KILL YOU!"[14]

Valli already had a detailed biography for a twenty-one-year-old—chorus girl, divorcée, and model. After spending much of her childhood in an orphanage, Valli, in fact, had first made the pages of the *Tribune* back in July 1926:

WHIPPED FOR STAYING OUT LATE, GIRL RUNS AWAY

Violet Popovich, 15 years old, 4516 East Harrison Street, was whipped for going to a movie with a boy and staying out late last Sunday night. Monday she ran away from home and yesterday the Fillmore Street police were asked to find her.[15]

When or whether Violet was found was never reported; likewise her years in an orphanage, which may have resulted from the runaway episode. Her mother's name in 1932 was Heindel, so a stepfather, not Mr. Popovich, might have been the one whipping her in 1926. It was no wonder that a woman of Valli's physical attractiveness would seek out the company of ballplayers, some of the best-paid young men of similar education and backgrounds that the city had to offer. Woody English had found his bride among the throngs of ladies day, and Sheriff Blake, the now-departed pitcher of the McCarthy era, had married a showgirl. Why not Bill Jurges? Ballplayers made many multiples the income of an ordinary working man. To have known ballplayers and actually lived among them, even become involved with one, might have seemed like the main chance, the only chance, to an attractive twenty-one-year-old without education, social connections, or a reliable income.

Within hours, Jurges managed to sit up slightly in bed and smile for a photographer. Still, he had suffered a major trauma; as the night wore on, he had to ask repeatedly for painkillers. The next day he told police he would not file a complaint against Valli or appear as a witness against her. The police department went ahead and filed assault charges anyway.[16]

The case was assigned to Judge John J. Sbarbaro, the doughty survivor of the Pineapple Primary in 1928 and before that, the undertaker for Dion

O'Banion and his various departed allies. Sbarbaro, officially a Republican, had continued his remarkable talent for adapting, and even flourishing, in unpromising circumstances. Big Bill Thompson, and the Republican Party in general, had been routed in the municipal elections of 1931, but in a countywide judgeship Sbarbaro had so far survived the stranglehold the Democrats had developed within the city limits. So it was that, long after O'Banion, the Pineapple Primary, and Bill Jurges's wounding, an Italian Catholic Republican from the heart of the Near North Side's Little Italy survived and prospered through the New Deal, the Fair Deal, several Democratic mayors, and almost to the New Frontier—another twenty-eight years of office holding. He was seventy years old and still a sitting judge in March 1960 when the commercial airliner he was taking to Florida exploded in a clear blue sky over Tell City, Indiana, with no survivors.

As a proven survivor, a North Sider from birth, and thus a Cub fan, Sbarbaro was the ideal fixer to keep the Valli-Jurges case from getting out of hand. The frequent mention of Cuyler's name was itself a warning signal. Sbarbaro, himself a former prosecutor, quickly granted a motion from the state's attorney's office to subpoena Jurges as a witness as soon as his condition allowed. In Chicago, of course, stern words and the show of action were one way to look good to the public while placating various private interests.

This was the same the judge, though, who, with his departed colleague Bill McSwiggin, had questioned Al Capone about Dion O'Banion's murder eight years earlier. On the morning of July 15, Sbarbaro's courtroom was packed from wall to wall, a predominantly female crowd that included several of Valli's fellow showgirls. Valli, flanked by her attorneys, one a former judge, looked stunning in a white crepe dress and cape trimmed in red, red earrings and pumps, heavy red lipstick, and a white felt hat. Her lower left arm was bandaged above the wrist. The photographers pushed through the crowd trying to get the best angle on the lovers. Each time they did, there was a pop not unlike the sounds of Valli's .22.

The only sign of injury on Jurges was a bandage on his hand. Although he cut a good figure in a gray suit set off by a colorful tie, he was the nervous one. Dr. Davis and Pat Malone accompanied him. When Sbarbaro called him, he said, "Your Honor, I have no desire to testify against this woman." He was twisting a handkerchief in his hands. The dazzling Valli stood only a few feet away, but neither glanced at the other.

"You don't want to prosecute?" Sbarbaro asked.

"No," Jurges answered.

"But you've been subpoenaed," protested a prosecutor.

"You've no reason to expect any more trouble from this woman?" Sbarbaro continued.

"No," said Jurges again.

"Let it be recorded that this case is dismissed for want of prosecution," Sbarbaro pronounced. Then, after a pause, he added, "Let's hope no more ballplayers are shot."[17]

Jurges, a smile breaking his usually deadpan expression, left the courtroom accompanied by Malone and Dr. Davis. The press crowded around Valli in a nearby room. "I owe it to my self-respect to forget it, to leave it all behind," she told them, repeating the phrases like a mantra. Several days later Valli announced that she had signed a twenty-two-week contract to appear on neighborhood vaudeville stages as "Violet Valli—the Most Talked-of Girl in Chicago." Within a week the show had been upgraded, or downgraded, depending on one's point of view, to the State-Congress theater, near the Loop, where she would appear as "Violet Valli . . . 'The Girl Who Shot for Love' . . . Stars in 'Bare Cub Follies' . . . A Screamingly Funny Burlesque Production." She would take to the stage with her arm still bandaged and in a splint.[18]

The Cub organization tried to ignore the more lurid implications that critics and cynics might draw from the Valli incident. Hornsby confined his remarks to possible effects on the Cubs' pennant hopes; once again he praised Jurges: "unquestionably . . . one of the finest shortstops in the league." Veeck, in what a later age would call damage control, announced: "The stories we have about the affair sound truthful," he said, in case anyone thought they didn't. "It is just one of those things. Today is a nice day for a ballgame and the sooner Jurges gets back the better."[19]

Veeck was either bluffing or dangerously ill informed. His management regime was making the Wilson-Malone rampages look like fraternity pranks. Rumors about the shooting and the Cubs in general were racing through the jail, the courthouse, and the ballpark, and from there into the papers. A couple of days later, with Jurges still in the hospital, Valli's mother, attorney, and bail bondsman trooped into his room for short visit. After a stay of some ten minutes, they left without disclosing their mission. Jurges told reporters that they only wanted to know if he would press charges, but a few days after that, news came from New York that the NYPD had located a possible witness to the shooting: Valli's mysterious companion, "Betty." Further, the New Yorkers learned, Valli had sent Cuyler's wife a letter that "threatened" her if she refused to divorce Cuyler. Betty and a Joe Cardella were in on the scheme.[20]

Veeck already knew that Hornsby was borrowing heavily and leaving gambling IOUs around town, but now other Cubs were supposed to be involved. Hornsby was even said to be placing bets during home games, using club personnel to run out to the bookies. The Cub players had noticed a mysterious figure lurking near them at Wrigley Field and in hotel lobbies on the road. "Mr. M———", as the would-be undercover agent was known, liked to use disguises, which, plainly, were not working.[21]

In the old days, Veeck might have conducted his investigation and sent the result to Mr. Wrigley in an executive summary, with perhaps his recommendations, and waited for Wrigley's advice. But that option was no longer available, and Hornsby, no Joe McCarthy to begin with, was looking more and more like part of the problem, not the solution. Bill Veeck was going to have to handle this mess all on his own.

13 | Informants

You and your ideas. Once you lay aside your bat, you're a detriment to any club. —Fred Lindstrom to Rogers Hornsby, 1927

Woody English had a lot of thinking to do as he headed his new Packard convertible the few blocks south from the ballpark to his apartment at the Surf Hotel. The Cubs had won that afternoon and he was playing shortstop again, but something had just come up that would be hard to explain to his wife.

English had done more than his share of explaining to her already that year. In February, just as he was getting ready to leave for Catalina, a young woman in his hometown of Newark, Ohio, filed a breach of promise suit against him. Emily Evans Haag had hard evidence: a ring and several letters from English. Her attorney told the newspapers that his client had been engaged to English for three years.[1]

English had already tried at least once to settle things with Haag. A few weeks after he eloped with Helen Golan in December 1930, he had made his ex-fiancée a settlement offer of $1,500, which she declined. Woody and Helen, the newlyweds, had known each other for five months before suddenly visiting the justice of the peace in Crown Point, Indiana, just over the state line. Helen and Woody had been introduced by friends after a ballgame in July 1930.

Hometown Emily might have made a better match for English than a blonde Chicago flapper. English didn't seem the big-city type, aside from the typical ballplayer's taste for flashy cars and expensive suits. Immediately after the elopement, he took Helen back to Ohio, where he introduced the Chicago-reared twenty-year-old to rural midwestern culture by spending the winter hunting. At home his main entertainment was curling up with a detective mystery, and he enjoyed playing bridge. He didn't care for going to the movies, listening to the radio, or dancing. During the season, Helen said, she treated herself to a movie or a show when Woody went on the road.[2]

If the household atmosphere was a bit strained after Emily's suit, English had several other worries that spring. His broken finger that spring had been his first major layoff since he had joined the Cubs in 1927. Then, by the time he was ready to play again, Bill Jurges had won his old job. English found himself shunted off to the position where Jurges had filled in the year before—third base, a spot for slick-fielding but slowing veterans. English, though, was a mere twenty-five despite all his experience. Hornsby also assigned English, the leadoff man for some of the highest-scoring teams in baseball history, to hit second in the lineup. It was still nice work that Woody was getting, just not quite as nice.[3]

During the Cubs' May home stand, English bought a brand-new Packard coupe worth $2,200, parked it for the night outside his apartment building at Surf and Pine avenues, and found it missing the next morning. Upsetting as that was, the Packard was easily replaced. All things considered, English was still a young man to be envied, a veteran starter on a perennial major league contender, widely respected throughout the circuit as a deft fielder, a pesky hitter, a cunning tactician, and an umpire baiter of note.[4]

On Sunday, July 10, English had been back at shortstop for just four days. The team seemed to be rallying: 4 of 4 starting out the season's second half, all four complete games from the staff with no lineup changes. For all the surprises of the past few months, English was not prepared for an old roommate to pay him a visit that Sunday. Woody had always been on good terms with this generally unpopular teammate, a veteran who had worked with English on his hitting, moving him farther back in the batter's box and showing him how to step into the pitch and use his wrists. The result of his teammate's help had been two wonderful seasons: 1930, when English hit .335 with 67 extra-base hits, a .430 on-base percentage, and a .511 slugging percentage; in the diminished offensive world of 1931, he had hit with less power but managed a .319 batting average, good for ninth place in the league, and a .391 on-base percentage. All the time he had maintained his superb defensive work, even starting more than a hundred games at third base when needed. After his remarkable two-year run, he had been the runner-up to Chuck Klein in the *Sporting News* sportswriters' poll for the National League's most valuable player.[5]

English's old roomie wanted to borrow some money. It wasn't just a few hundred dollars that the man was requesting with some urgency, but close to $2,000—some $25,000 in contemporary money. Although Emily Haag's lawsuit had already strained English's finances, he gulped hard and agreed to advance his teammate the money. He had little choice.[6]

The same veteran also paid a visit to Guy Bush, whose complete-game victory that afternoon represented a proud moment in the big leagues: "Pitcher Makes Two Hits; That Stuns Braves," a headline told its astonished readers the next day. Bush may not have been surprised to hear that his teammate needed money: the two of them had been through this before in 1929, when Bush had co-signed a note for five thousand dollars. The note was paid up in due course. This new request, to guarantee two thousand dollars, was for less than half the 1929 sum. Bush, the owner of several small businesses, had to wonder whether he would be called on again, but his teammate wasn't the sort of fellow it was easy to turn down. Bush too agreed to help.[7]

Warneke followed up Bush's victory with his twelfth win the next day. The Cubs had had themselves a five-game winning streak since Jurges's shooting. Warneke's ERA dipped to 2.11 for 136 innings pitched. Hartnett delivered three hits, more than making up for the absence of Rollie Hemsley, who had ludicrously foreshadowed Jurges's injury by hurting his eye with a firecracker on July 4.

On the 11th Jurges appeared at the ballpark in a box seat with Dr. Davis and Red Grange, the great Bears' halfback. Jurges, hatless, pointed out diamond intricacies to Grange, also hatless and noticeably heavier than in his collegiate days. Two days later Jurges was back in uniform, working out with his teammates while they prepared for Hack Wilson and the Dodgers. Two days later, he made his court appearance before Judge Sbarbaro.[8]

Wilson's May–June hot streak had continued into July: he had hit in seventeen of his last eighteen ballgames. For the year now he had 15 homers, 63 RBI, and a .300-plus batting average—a modest output compared to his numbers in midseason 1930, but in this new era, no Cub came close to those numbers. In fact, in the entire league only Klein and Hurst of the Phillies, maximizing their tiny ballpark, were outslugging Wilson. Cub fans would also get their first look at Danny Taylor in a Brooklyn uniform. Bill Veeck could be forgiven if he wondered exactly what constituted a "lousy outfield."

Beginning with batting practice, Wilson drew ovations each time he stepped into the batter's box. By the fifth the Dodgers built a 3–0 lead, but the Cubs tied things with two in the fifth and one in the sixth. Danny Taylor crashed a seventh-inning double with two out to give the Dodgers their fifth and ultimately decisive run; Wilson was 1 for 4, but he had provided the fans a trademark strikeout. Before the game Jurges had worked out in uniform for the first time, and the next day, Violet Valli was among the spectators in the stands behind first base. Hornsby tried generating more offense by rejoining the lineup. He had two hits and an RBI and followed up with two hits and two RBI the next day. Wilson had managed only one scratch single in eleven at-bats; the Rajah had raised his season batting average 40 points, and his team had beaten the Dodgers two straight without a single fight or beanball. After the game, Hornsby's mood was expansive. "[Stan] Hack can field 'em faster than I can, but if I can do a little hittin' I think it will count more right now," he said. "Even if it is pretty tough on the old puppies."[9]

But the next day the Cubs' new third baseman committed two errors, and his 1 for 2 wasn't enough to overcome the Dodgers. The New York Giants were next for a five-game series, the club's first Chicago appearance in nearly thirty years without John McGraw. The first day, in a Sunday doubleheader, Hornsby went hitless in seven trips to the plate. On Monday, with the Giants ahead 2–1 in the fifth inning, Jo-Jo Moore and then Hughie Critz aimed bunts Hornsby's way at third. He couldn't finish either play. The Giants eventually scored two runs on Fred Lindstrom's double.

In the eighth, six more hits ballooned the Giants' lead to 13–1. With the bases loaded and one out, Hornsby's fellow playing manager, Bill Terry, slapped a ball down to Hornsby, who threw it away. Two more runs came across. After another double and Johnny Vergez's fourth hit of the day, Doc Marshall grounded to Hornsby, who threw the ball away again. The score was now 13–1.

Danny Taylor had seldom looked any more futile with a glove in hand.

The crowd of just fifteen thousand, much of it female, aimed a steady barrage of catcalls at Hornsby. In the bottom of the ninth he banged in the final Cub run of the day with a single, but the ladies would have none of it. They raised a derisive cheer as the scoreboard registered the Cubs' 13–3 deficit.[10]

Hornsby's hit had broken an 0-for-11 stretch. Before the next day's game he received an ultimatum from Veeck: bench that third baseman immediately. It was the latest in the series of start-and-stop orders Veeck had issued to Hornsby: run a youth movement; insert himself in right field; bench himself; let the batteries call the pitches. But the essential Hornsby hadn't changed. Before one of the Dodger games the week before, Hornsby overheard a Cub regular greet one of the Bums with a friendly jibe. "Cut it out," Hornsby growled. "We're out here to beat these guys, not kid with them." The rest of the Cubs stared straight ahead, saying nothing to their teammates or the newspapermen nearby. No chatter rang across the diamond. Hornsby, looking around, seemed satisfied with the result.[11]

Veeck wasn't. After Hornsby's final benching, a New York sportswriter sounded out Veeck. "Too bad Rog just can't go and get 'em anymore," he remarked.

Veeck replied evenly, "Yes, it is too bad. We all hate to admit when we get too old to do the things we used to do."

"But I guess Rog needn't worry," the reporter continued. "He still has a swell career as manager ahead."

Veeck did not answer. Instead, he whistled quietly to himself.[12]

Rogers Hornsby, for his part, had planned a surprise for the boss.

After finishing the homestand, the Cubs hopped on the train for Pittsburgh to meet the Pirates, whom they now trailed by 3½ games. The next day Bill Jurges finally reappeared in the lineup, playing third to conserve his strength while English remained at short. Pat Malone allowed the Pirates three runs in the second, but otherwise he battled his opponents to a standstill through eight innings with his high, inside fastball. The Pirates' early scoring continued to stand, and with two out in the ninth and the Cubs trailing 3–1, Hornsby sent up a pinch hitter for Malone: Frank Demaree, just up from the Pacific Coast League. The youngster popped up for the final out.

Back at the Hotel Schenley, Veeck cornered Hornsby. True, Jurges had just played a full game less than three weeks after taking bullets, but that didn't concern Veeck, according to later accounts. Instead, Veeck took issue with Frank Demaree's ninth-inning plate appearance. Why had Hornsby given a rookie his first major league at-bat with an important game on the line? And, Veeck went on, why hadn't Hornsby called a team meeting before the game the day before?

Hornsby retorted that he had met with Malone: the rest of the team hardly needed another meeting for their twelfth game of the year with the Pirates. As for Demaree's appearance, it was the manager's business to use his players as he saw fit. If Veeck didn't like it, Hornsby said with typical bluntness, he could find himself another manager.

"That's a good idea, Rog. I may give that some thought," Veeck shot back before leaving.[13]

Veeck's attitude might have hardened further the next morning if he glanced at one of the Pittsburgh papers. In bold lettering on the front page was an editorial, two columns wide, urging retaliation against the headhunting Cubs. Andy Lotshaw had already boasted to Pittsburgh sportswriters that the Cub pitchers had the Pittsburgh lineup "intimidated." The makings of a showdown were becoming unmistakable.[14]

Matters were quiet until the bottom of the second, when the home plate umpire called a potential third strike a ball. Charlie Root stalked off the mound gesturing and shouting homeward. The *Tribune*'s Ed Burns, a veteran Root watcher, looked on with apprehension. "Calm, Charley is a great pitcher. Mad, he pitches like your old Aunt Kate," concluded Burns. Within minutes, four Pirates had scored; two more had to be thrown out at the plate. Zack Taylor got up slowly from the second play; Adam Comorosky's spikes had slashed him on his right hand and thigh. Hartnett replaced him. When Hornsby pulled Root the next inning after another Pirate outbreak, the little pitcher traded insults with the fans in the box seats as he headed for the dugout.

The rest of the day was touch and go. The Cubs surrounded Cy Rigler in the seventh after a close play at third. Even the Pittsburgh writers thought the runner was out. Pat Malone, sent in to relieve on less than twenty-four hours' rest, faced, and hit, Comorosky. Comorosky charged the mound before being intercepted, and English squared off with the

Pirates' Tony Piet before an umpire stepped between them. The final score of 11–7 increased the Pirates' lead to 4½ games.[15]

The two teams had to leave quickly for a Sunday doubleheader in Wrigley Field. The Cubs were at risk of dropping 6½ games behind the Pirates with a three-week road trip just ahead. Still, despite the urgency of returning to Chicago before the wee hours, Hornsby decided it was time for one of those clubhouse meetings Veeck had been urging.

Hornsby began by addressing Malone. "Pat," he began, "what would you think of a fellow who informed your office that you hadn't called a meeting?"

Not much, Malone replied.

Then Hornsby turned to Hartnett. "Gabby," he asked the veteran, "what would *you* think of a fellow who was an informer?"

This time Hornsby's question lingered in the dank air of the visitors' clubhouse. Hartnett said nothing in reply.

Hornsby quickly put the same question to Charlie Grimm, with the same result.

Hornsby, satisfied that he had his answer, cut loose with an oath. Then he turned to yet another distinguished holdover from the McCarthy days, Ki Cuyler. How in the world, Hornsby asked, had Cuyler misplayed Earl Grace's double during the second inning rally?

Hornsby had picked on the wrong man at the wrong time. Cuyler had been playing on his bad foot for six weeks. That was why the proud and talented one was still hobbling around and butchering chances. Nor was Cuyler, the Cubs' marquee player since Wilson's removal, accustomed to managerial criticism, and he was a fellow who didn't back down; it was in Forbes Field, in fact, where he and Donnie Bush had clashed over the center-field question five years before. What was more, Hornsby was a manager on thin ice—anyone could sense that. Coolly, Cuyler informed Hornsby that it was none of his business.[16]

Now it was in the open. Three veterans of Murderers' Row, one way or another, were undermining the boss. And he seemed helpless to do anything about it.

"Player War On!" screamed one headline back in Chicago the next morning. Lured by the publicity, only the second overflow crowd of the Depression-wracked year turned out. Lon Warneke spoiled the day for those who came out to the park hoping to see more mayhem, scattering seven Pirate hits in the first game. In the second game, the Cubs took an early 5–0 lead, but the Pirates overtook the Cubs, who managed just one single over the last five innings. The final score was 7–5.[17]

The Cubs headed for Boston, not to see Wrigley Field for another three weeks, with the prospect of returning much further than 4½ back. The only starter who was holding up was the one whose pitches Hornsby was still calling—Warneke. Malone, Root, and Bush, all freed by Veeck six weeks earlier, were looking whipped—a "used-up bunch," the *Tribune*'s Ed Burns thought. It must have been an unhappy caravan headed for Boston: Hornsby, the weary pitching rotation, dissident veterans—and Veeck. Hornsby was no longer assigned his usual drawing room on the team Pullman.[18]

The Cubs got in only four of their five scheduled games in Boston before the rains came. Even winning three of them was no help, for the Pirates had taken 6 of 7 since leaving Chicago the Sunday before. The Bucs, who had won 26 of their last 37, now owned a six-game lead over the Cubs.

At the start of the trip Hornsby had issued his final decree as a Cub manager. All pitchers would henceforth be classified "at arms"; that is, he now considered every game so crucial that even the frontline starters would be on call at any moment, Malone's back-to-back failures at Pittsburgh notwithstanding.[19] Even in an era when all pitchers, from the rotation leader on down, were expected to lend a hand from time to time, Hornsby's proclamation was notable. Perhaps it was another "McGraw tactic," a throwback to the old days of Iron Joes and Big Eds whose arms were ruined by overwork before they turned thirty. Or was "at arms" another inspiration from Veeck? On July 26 he and Hornsby sat at separate tables on opposite sides of the hotel dining room in Boston.[20]

When the final game of the Boston series was rained out, the Cubs hopped the noon train to Brooklyn, heading down the coast through a steady downpour. In Flatbush the rain let up the next day long enough to allow them to play the Dodgers. Hack Wilson was waiting for Hornsby and the Cubs. Stouts drove in four runs as the Dodgers shelled Malone from the mound in the fifth inning of a 7–2 victory.

"At arms" was put to its first real test in a doubleheader against Brooklyn

July 31. Root threw a complete game victory in the first game, but with the score tied 4–4 in the seventh inning of the second game, Cuyler, still laboring on his bad foot, had trouble running down a long drive, which went for a triple. Hornsby abruptly removed Burleigh Grimes and called in the next day's scheduled starter, Lon Warneke. The youngster was going to make his first relief appearance facing Lefty O'Doul, not only the league's leading hitter at nearly .370 but no doubt crushing right-handed pitching somewhere above .400.

Warneke had lost just three times for the year, but in only minutes he earned his fourth loss. O'Doul banged a single through the box to tie the score. The thirty-five-year-old O'Doul stole second while Warneke was striking out Wilson, then scored on a single by Tony Cuccinello.

The Dodgers' 5–4 lead stood up into the top of the ninth, when the Greatest Right-handed Hitter pinch-hit for Warneke leading off, his last at-bat in a Cub uniform. He flied out. The Cubs were still able to get the tying run in scoring position twice, but base-running blunders and a sensational stop by the Dodgers' shortstop ended the game.

The two teams had the next day off. Bush, lobby sitting at the Commodore in midtown Manhattan, researched the Cubs' remaining schedule and discovered that the Pirates and the Cubs would close the season with a four-game series at Wrigley Field in late September. Bush forecast that Pittsburgh would arrive three games ahead of the Cubs. Guy would beat them in the first game, followed by victories from Root, Warneke, and then himself redux in a showdown on the last day of the season.[21]

In Philadelphia, the Pirates were dropping their third game in a row after their long, winning surge, yet their lead remained a discouraging five games. Few in Bush's tiny audience believed any longer that the September series would make any difference.

The Mudcat had also dropped Pat Malone's name from the rotation. Perhaps the Irishman would be at arms, or perhaps that would be one beanball pitcher too many. Then again, "at arms" and beanballs and most things associated with Rogers Hornsby might be on their way out before late September.

14 | "Nothing to It"

Any manager who doesn't win a pennant in Chi, of course, is regarded as so much extra baggage. That's how it is in the baseball business. —Daniel M. Daniel, *The Sporting News*, August 11, 1932

While Guy Bush spent his off day conjuring an unlikely September surge, Veeck and Hornsby conferred about the discouraging realities of early August. The club had just released Vince Barton to Reading, the great hopes once placed in his slugging prowess finally abandoned. He would never return to the big leagues.[1]

The club's weaknesses were no secret: Moore couldn't hit lefties, Cuyler was still off form, English was hitting well below .300. Grimes's main contribution had been to provide Warneke his big chance with frequent illnesses. The sore-armed Root seemed to be over the hill. Malone still threw as fast and competed as hard as he had in his twenty-victory seasons, but repeatedly the least setback—a bad call, an error—ignited his temper and led to complete collapse. With Hornsby's encouragement, he often seemed to be more interested in throwing at the batters than in getting them out. He had become a .500 pitcher.

Hornsby brought up his latest scheme: using the new flyhawk Demaree, whose pinch-hit appearance had provoked the confrontation with Veeck in Pittsburgh, in the lineup. Veeck demurred—no more rookies with the race on the line. The next afternoon, though, the lineup card showed Demaree penciled in for his first major league start as the Cubs and Dodgers squared off again for the final game of their series. Fittingly, it was Danny Taylor and Hack Wilson who engineered Rogers Hornsby's farewell loss. Warneke took a 2–1 lead into the bottom of the eighth, but doubles by Taylor and Wilson sandwiched around a sacrifice by Stripp tied the score.[2]

Other ghosts of the Cub past rose up to finish off Warneke and Hornsby. Lefty O'Doul contributed a sacrifice fly for a 3–2 Dodger lead, and Johnny Frederick, who had crushed the Cub pennant hopes in September 1930, crashed a double off the right-field wall to pad the lead. The seven thousand Dodger fans roared without letup from the moment Taylor doubled until Bud Clancy grounded into the inning's third out. Just two afternoons of "at arms" had reduced Warneke's record from 16-3 to 16-5. Three of the five defeats had come in Brooklyn at the hands of the Dodgers.

The Cubs had to leave immediately for Philadelphia, site of the week's only good news: the Phillies had just smashed the Pirates four straight. After five doubleheaders in six days, the team's pitching had collapsed. It was the Pirates' first real stumble since their surge began in June. The Cubs had actually picked up a game on first while dropping three of four in Brooklyn.

Veeck went into conference with Hornsby again on the train to Philadelphia. The accounts of what they discussed conflict, but the discouraging series in Brooklyn had generated all sorts of possibilities: "at arms" and Hornsby's use of Warneke; Demaree's appearance in the lineup that afternoon; Hornsby's choice of himself as a pinch hitter in the second game of the doubleheader.[3]

If Bill Veeck's continued presence on road trips had been a novelty for the Cubs of 1932, so was the absence of direct involvement by the owner. Unlike Wrigley *père*, Philip Wrigley, or P. K., as he was known even then, did not visit Catalina for spring training. He finally dropped by to watch a game on the Cubs' post–training camp tour of the Bay Area. After skipping both Opening Day in Cincinnati and the Cubs' home opener in Chicago, he was first spotted in the owner's box at Wrigley Field in early May; after that, the press fell silent about his attendance. The smaller crowds, the empty box behind the Cub dugout, the low-scoring games, the rookies playing where superstars used to tread: it seemed unlikely that the uproarious days of Murderers' Row, the packed street scenes, outfields filled with fans would return anytime soon.[4]

In fairness, Phil Wrigley was busy running a major corporation, a job he'd taken on when he was just thirty. It was his maturity and competence that had allowed his father to ease into retirement as chairman of the board, his appointment book usually empty enough to take in that afternoon's Cub game. Phil, now thirty-seven, also had an entirely different personality from his father's: methodical, cautious, low key. He frankly admitted that his real motivation for retaining ownership of the ball club was filial respect.[5]

Wrigley left the Wrigley Building the evening of August 2 with no particular focus on his sporting subsidiary. After dinner the phone rang in his North Shore home. It was the *Daily News*'s John Carmichael, calling from the paper's headquarters, just around the bend of the Chicago River from the Wrigley Building. Big news about the Cubs, said Carmichael. His paper had just received an emergency bulletin from Philadelphia, where the Cubs had detrained earlier that evening. Hornsby and Veeck had called an impromptu press conference at the hotel, where Veeck announced Hornsby's resignation as Cub manager. Veeck had introduced Charlie Grimm as the new manager.

There was a pause on the line. "So it happened," Wrigley finally said into the phone, almost to himself. Then, remembering that he had a news-man on the line, he continued, "Well, this is the first I've heard of it—from you. I guess Bill forgot to call me up, or maybe he couldn't get me."

Wrigley's transparent surprise might have puzzled Carmichael in turn. What corporate head was this unguarded with the press? Carmichael was newsman enough to keep boring in. Had there been any warning that the blockbuster story was in the offing? "Did I know anything about it?" Wrigley repeated. "Well, yes and no. I knew that Bill was dissatisfied with the way things were going and I rather suspected that he planned some change. But until now I didn't know that it had been effected."

Then Wrigley charged ahead without prompting. "In regard to any personal habits, such as gambling, having any effect on his dismissal, I know nothing about it, but I would say, 'Nothing to it.' What he or anyone else does off the ball field, I don't know. That's Veeck's business."[6]

While Carmichael wrote up a sidebar on his interview, full of revelations about Phil Wrigley's commitment to the Chicago National League Ball Cub, the *Daily News* had its main news story to assemble.

President Veeck, after the team arrived from New York, called Hornsby to his suite in the Benjamin Franklin Hotel.

"Well, Rog," he said, "I've decided to make a change."

To which Hornsby replied: "That's all right with me so long as I get my money."[7]

The two men had then begun their final argument. Hornsby, whose contract ran through December 31, asked for one lump sum. Veeck, however, insisted that the Cubs pay him semimonthly through the contract's termination date. Bob Lewis, the Cubs' traveling secretary, gathered the press corps to announce the change. Soon Veeck and Hornsby, both apparently composed, appeared to meet the newspapermen.

"Rog and I have just concluded a conference," Veeck announced. "The outcome is that Rog is leaving the club but will be paid his full salary, his contract running through December 31, 1932. We have asked waivers on Hornsby as a ballplayer and they have been given. He is a free agent.

"Charlie Grimm is now manager of the Cubs. He will be in full charge when the players take the field against Philadelphia tomorrow."

A reporter asked if any specific incident had brought on the change. Veeck turned to Hornsby. "There has been no quarrel, has there, Rog?"

Hornsby laughed nervously. "I guess we won't call it a quarrel. Only big differences of opinion about the ball club and the way it should be handled."[8]

With the formalities concluded, Veeck and Hornsby went back behind closed doors to continue negotiations. Soon some of the Cub players were called in to join the discussion. Loud voices could be heard through the thick doors, far into the night.[9]

Hundreds of telegrams and phone calls poured into the Benjamin Franklin Hotel as the word of the big change got around. Grimm and Riggs Stephenson, who were rooming together on the road, stayed up late to handle the crush. Stephenson turned in at midnight, but Grimm kept at it until 2:00. Just after he had dozed off, Grimm was awakened by shouting. He saw Stephenson standing up in bed and pulling on the bed sheets. Stevie had been dreaming that his relatives had all fallen down an open well back in Alabama, and he had to pull them out with a rope.[10]

Grimm never got back to sleep. The next morning Grimm was still exuberant despite his sleepless night. First he called the Cubs together. While

"Nothing to It"

a steady rain drummed on the windowpanes, he told the men that he had served under good managers who had taught him what he had to do to help the club. His success, and theirs, he said, would come down to one thing: "Hustle. We're facing a fight and we have a fine chance to win this pennant. I'm depending on every fellow on the club to give his best. And I know he will." He also announced that English would replace him as captain.[11]

It was a stirring talk, but his players didn't seem to need much convincing that things were going to improve. They heard the new boss out in a low-key fashion; then nearly everyone filed down to the lobby. The casual air evaporated at the sight of Hornsby sitting forlornly, his bags packed and wearing a full day's growth of beard. All but two of the twenty-two men left on the squad lined up to shake the Rajah's hand, muttering commonplaces: "Good-bye, Rog"; "Good luck to you." The reporters could hear the catch in some throats, the finality of the hero's departure sinking in. Who among them could ever accomplish what he had; when in their lives would they again live and work day to day with one of the baseball divinities?[12]

Hornsby was contemplative about his abrupt termination from the late Mr. Wrigley's ball club. "Whatever my shortcomings may have been as a manager, I gave the team all I had, and no man can do more than that," he told no one in particular. "When I am made manager I intend to be the manager. I don't pass the buck. Right or wrong, I'm responsible for my actions. If credit is due to me, I want it; and if condemnation, I'll take that. I can take it, you know, either way. I never was a crybaby." He and "the office staff" had argued in recent weeks, Hornsby admitted. "There were times when things were said in heat, but I thought they had been forgotten," he said plaintively.

"Well, I'm 36 years old now," Hornsby told the group. "I'll rest the remainder of the season and draw my pay. But you can say I'll be in the running next year."[13]

Back in the Windy City, the female fans seemed to support Veeck's move, some applying nonstandard criteria. Claire Brehm of Kenmore Avenue told the *Daily News*, "I like Charlie Grimm lots better than Hornsby and I think most other girls do too." Marcella Eddington, who lived in the same North Side neighborhood, agreed: "I think the change is swell. I like Grimm much better. Why? Just because."

Bernice Studzinski, yet another Kenmore Avenue resident, proved a rare female Hornsby fan: "I think they gave Hornsby a bad break. He's better looking than Grimm any day in the week." May Morrisey of East 41st Street offered a South Sider's view: "I'm a Sox fan but I think the Cubs will do better with Grimm as manager. Hornsby looks nice in his pictures, though."

The men, avoiding the question of how well either man photographed, lined up with Veeck too. "Hornsby never was very popular on the North Side. . . . The boys will work for Charlie," said T. R. Cruttenden of North Paulina. Spencer King of East 47th Place echoed, "Grimm suits me to a T. I think he should have been made manager long ago." Henry Wright, a YMCA resident, agreed: "[I] always thought Hornsby was a great player but a poor manager. Charlie Grimm is the most popular man on the team." "Hornsby's not friendly enough," added D. J. Peterson of Ridge Avenue on the North Side.[14]

An ex-Cub fan read about the big news at a local hotel. Joe McCarthy, in Chicago with his front-running Yankees, said cautiously, "Well, we all get it sooner or later. A manager just can't go on and on with any club. If things don't break right, he just has to get out."

McCarthy said he didn't care that he wouldn't be able to face Hornsby in the World Series. "Hornsby and I haven't anything against each other. We always were friends and we still speak to each other." Charlie Grimm? He had "a knack for handling men and has a winning personality. When I was with the Cubs, Grimm was the most popular boy on the club."[15]

In Brooklyn, Hack Wilson was asked for his reactions, too. "Jobs are too scarce nowadays to be glad anybody got fired, even if it was somebody you don't get along with," he said. "Besides, I don't hold any grudge against Hornsby. We had a lot of trouble when I was playing under him, but that doesn't mean he isn't a good manager and a great ball player." Hornsby was "the greatest right-handed hitter baseball ever saw," Wilson added. "He's still a pretty good player, despite his age. It shouldn't be much trouble for him to get another job."[16]

Meanwhile, Veeck and Wrigley were busy explaining the decision. Wrigley was asked about his role in the firing. "I'm a 'gum man.' Veeck is a 'baseball man.' Everything he does is all right with me." He told another reporter, "We have had no trouble with Hornsby. He did a pretty good job. We believe he got as far as he could, however, and Grimm can go a little further."

The night before Wrigley had referenced Hornsby's gambling problems, so one reporter asked Veeck if that had played a role in his dismissal. "There is positively nothing to it," Veeck replied. "The only reason Hornsby was discharged as manager is because we disagreed over his handling of the team."[17]

But the rumors wouldn't go away. The subject came up again when Hornsby was interviewed back home in Missouri a few days later. Hornsby chuckled at the suggestion that he had been fired for betting on horses. He had made a visit to the commissioner's office recently, Hornsby explained, but it had nothing to do with horse racing. He, Vince Barton, and Judge Landis had merely been conferring about a borrowed auto that Barton had wrecked.[18]

Arch Ward, the sports editor of the *Tribune*, furrowed his brow over these puzzlements and sat down before his typewriter. "There probably were deeper reasons for [the] changes. It is unlikely that the owners of the club measure a manager's worth entirely by the standings of the teams."[19]

Ward seemed to be saying, very cautiously, that something other than "standings" were involved in Hornsby's departure. The next day his counterpart and chief rival, Warren Brown of the *Herald and Examiner*, went him one better. After recounting the saga that had led to the dismissal of his friend Joe McCarthy, he examined Hornsby's management, and though players had been frank about their dislike for the Rajah, there had to be more to the dismissal. Had Hornsby been fired for nonperformance? "That this is the real reason I very much doubt," Brown concluded.[20]

Warren Brown was well connected, knowledgeable, and smart. When he publicly doubted something very much, it was time to take stock.

Jolly Cholly seemed to be the cure for the Chicago National League Ball Club's long nightmare. Grimm bustled about, talking pennant, exhorting, and in general trying to undo nearly two years of mistrust and miscommunication. At infield practice the next day, the Cubs' infielders whipped the ball around with such spirit that the famously jaded Philadelphia fans broke into applause.[21]

Hornsby and everything to do with him were being wiped off the books like an outdated entry in a Soviet encyclopedia. "Duster Ball Out," read one headline soon after Grimm took over. Hornsby's beanball strategy had only alienated the players and aroused the populace in both Pittsburgh and Brooklyn. Grimm said simply: "It's foolish to think a good hitter will back away after being 'dusted.' It makes him all the more determined to hit the next one."[22]

Tobacco smoke swirled around the locker room as Grimm spoke. Smoking in the clubhouse, empathy for opponents—where would it end? On August 4 the public address man at the Baker Bowl called Grimm out of the dugout minutes before his debut as a major league manager. Grimm found himself eyeball to eyeball with a huge floral horseshoe. "Who's it from?" asked Grimm with a puzzled look. "From the Cubs," the announcer told him.[23]

The players had pooled their own money for the flowers. "My gosh," Grimm stammered. "The boys must like me." No one, at least in the Cubs' entourage, could remember ballplayers getting so sentimental short of injury or death.[24]

The flowers were carted off and the post-Hornsby era officially began. The Cubs exploded for eight runs in the second inning, Grimm himself hitting a single and then a double off the top of the right-field scoreboard. He also electrified the crowd with several sensational defensive stops, once knocking down Chuck Klein's hot smash down the line and converting it into an out; then, in the ninth Grimm defended the Cubs' eleven-run lead by grabbing one of Hartnett's bullet throws with his bare hand. The crowd gasped.[25]

After the last out Malone, the starting and winning pitcher, swaggered over and gave Grimm a hearty clap on the back. "How'd yuh like it, you big Dutchman? I can't think of anybody else I'd rather win one for," he proclaimed before heading off to the clubhouse, whistling. The ugly clubhouse scene in Forbes Field less than two weeks before seemed forgotten.[26]

Hornsby's leavetaking meant a spot on the twenty-three-man roster was open, and the lobby of the Ben Franklin buzzed with talk about who might be included in some sort of deal. Veeck finally announced that he had found the twenty-third man to replace Hornsby: Mark Koenig, the still-young shortstop of the fabled 1927 Yankees. Since that epic season,

"Nothing to It"

Koenig's effectiveness had gradually declined, and the Yankees and then the Tigers had both moved him along because of the problem. Jack Doyle spotted Koenig playing for Sacramento of the Pacific Coast League earlier in the summer and recommended his acquisition by the Cubs.[27]

All the same, Veeck sounded apologetic that he hadn't found Grimm a better player for the stretch drive. The new man was assigned Hornsby's old number, 9.[28]

The Phils were enjoying, for them, a good year—three games above .500 in August. Chuck Klein and Don Hurst headed a group of Philadelphia sluggers who were bashing Baker Bowl's tin right-field Lifebuoy sign at a league-leading rate. Their recent four-game dismantling of the Pirates featured such scores as 18–5 and 11–6. After the opening loss to Malone and the Cubs, the Phils quickly drove Charlie Root to cover the next day and handed Jolly Cholly his first managerial defeat, 9–2.

Phillie fans were on fire: five of six from the league's two front-running teams! For the series-concluding Saturday afternoon doubleheader, the turnout overwhelmed the Phils' decaying arena. By the time the fire marshals had finished turning people away, there were twenty thousand in the stands—two thousand over the seating capacity—and five thousand on their way back home.[29]

There might never be another day like it in Baker Bowl, a ramshackle structure with less than a decade left of major league life: 70 base hits, 19 walks, 9 errors, 14 doubles, 3 home runs, and 37 runs. The Cubs came out for the showdown with just twenty-one able bodies on hand. Koenig was in transit from the West Coast, and early that morning Grimm had suspended Hemsley after an arrest for drunken driving. Thanks to Hemsley's escapade, the manager and his roommate, Stephenson, the cleanup hitter, were once again short of sleep.

The Cubs blew leads of 6–1 in the first game and 5–1 in the second. The pride of the Cub staff, Bush, Malone, and Root, staggered through a six-run seventh inning. One Phillie pitcher pinch hit for another and homered. Grimm grabbed a pop foul out of the stands with his bare hand. With the bases loaded, Herman booted a ground ball, but Jurges ran it down, whirled, and fired home to catch Pinky Whitney trying to score. Riggs Stephenson threw a man out at the plate to end the first game.

In the second game, the Phillies scored two runs in the ninth to tie the score at 8–8, leaving the winning run in scoring position. But in the top of the eleventh the Cubs retook the lead. In the bottom of the inning the Phils loaded the bases with two out for their cleanup man, Don Hurst. The Philadelphia fans leaped to their feet, yelling and screaming. Jakie May, the only rested pitcher besides Warneke that Grimm had, came in to face Don Hurst. "Jakie, do you feel hot?" Grimm asked the ancient lefty above the din. "Sir, I am hotter than a firecracker," the South Carolinian replied. Hurst looked at two of May's pitches before slamming the third offering to center field, where young Demaree hauled in the drive to end the game.[30]

The Cubs had to head immediately to New York, where Grimm needed a "stop" from Lon Warneke to prevent his overworked staff from collapsing like that of the Pirates. Warneke had never thrown a pitch that Rogers Hornsby hadn't chosen.

The Cubs showed up on time at a very wet Polo Grounds, and the Warneke-Hartnett experiment got under way. Starting for the first time without pitch-by-pitch guidance from the dugout, Warneke tossed a methodical five-hitter, shutting the Giants out for the first seven innings. Yet another tenet of the Hornsby book had been refuted, right where McGraw tactics had been born. Hartnett celebrated the occasion with a four for five afternoon, including a home run and three RBI. Pat Malone and three other pitchers were hammered in the second game, an 8–1 Giants' triumph, but Monday would be a day off, and the Pirates had just dropped another doubleheader.[31]

That made nine losses in a row for the Pirates; the Cubs had closed to within a game and a half. After a day off on Monday, August 8, the Pirates lost again on Tuesday, a 4–0 shutout at Boston. The same afternoon the Cubs returned to action before a mere three thousand customers at the Polo Grounds. For eight innings Chicago's predominantly right-handed lineup struggled futilely against Carl Hubbell's renowned screwball. With two outs in the ninth the Giants were up 3–2, and the Cubs' chances of closing the gap with the Pirates looked hopeless.

Hartnett slapped a weak bouncer down the third-base line. Before Fred Lindstrom, the Giants' third baseman, could pick it up and fire on to first for the game-ender, the ball clipped third base and rocketed crazily into the infield for a gift single. Hartnett being one of the slowest men in baseball, Grimm called on Stan Hack, the almost-forgotten rookie sensation of spring training, and one of the few men in the league who could match Cuyler's speed, to pinch run. Bill Herman, the next hitter, topped another roller, this one headed to Bill Terry at first base. Terry picked up the ball cleanly and eased a lob over to Hubbell, coming off the mound to cover the bag for the third out.

Hubbell dropped the ball.

The fleet-footed Hack dashed for third and beyond while Hubbell frantically tracked the ball down. As Hack tore home, Hubbell heaved the ball desperately into the Cub dugout. The game was tied.[32]

Hubbell stalked back to the mound. Woody English banged the first real hit of the inning, a single into left center that scored Herman from second, and the opportunist Cubs had a 4–3 lead that stood up through the bottom of the ninth. With Hubbell disposed of for the time being, their chances of taking the series with the Giants looked good for the morrow. Then they would leave town for their next stop, Pittsburgh, where with luck a win would put them in first place.

The ascension of the popular Grimm and the team's unexpected success on the road had turned the whole season around. Back in Chicago the *Daily News* was working up a huge front-page story on the Cubs that would run Thursday, the day the Cubs reached Pittsburgh. Meanwhile, Commissioner Landis consulted the schedule and decided that Pittsburgh would be a fine place to take in a Cub game.

15 || "No Particular Pal of Mine"

No player who throws a ballgame, no player that undertakes or promises to throw a ballgame, no player that sits in conference with a bunch of crooked players and gamblers where the ways and means of throwing a game are discussed and does not promptly tell his club about it, will ever play professional baseball. —Kenesaw Mountain Landis, barring the Black Sox from organized baseball, 1921

Rain washed out the final Cubs-Giants game in the second inning Wednesday afternoon, August 10. The Cubs, full of animal spirits after the ninth-inning lightning against Hubbell, were chafing. They had championship bravado, the brawler's desire to take on all comers. Bob Lewis shepherded the Cubs to the station to leave for Pittsburgh, where they would play just one game on their way back to Chicago. Circumstances had suddenly made this scheduling whim a showdown.

Statisticians were consulting the record books to find the case of a front-runner losing ten straight ballgames this late in the season. The Bucs had spent most of July sweeping all before them while the Cubs struggled with their internal problems and talent shortages. Then four doubleheaders in six days punished the Pirates at their weakest point, their pitching staff. No Pirate pitcher had thrown a complete game for almost two weeks, a real crisis in the early 1930s. Pittsburgh's rookie double-play combination, Piet at second and Vaughan at short, came unglued in the losing streak, committing disastrous errors. The Bucs finally broke the streak on the last day of their eastern trip, but it was only the first game of another doubleheader; Boston took the second game, squeezing the winning run home to win 3–2. Pittsburgh's lead remained a half game over the idle Cubs.[1]

The Pirates quickly left Boston for home, arriving in Pittsburgh after the Cubs had already checked into the Hotel Schenley. The two clubs would meet for only one game the next afternoon.

The usual mix of ballplayers, newspapermen, and hangers-on had populated the lobby of the Schenley the next morning when the short, rumpled figure of Kenesaw Mountain Landis strode through the front door and up to the desk. After checking in, he bustled up to his room for a shower and a room-service breakfast. (He had just arrived on the overnight train from Chicago.) When he emerged, at least two representatives of the Chicago press confronted him.[2]

"Why are you here, Commissioner?" the *Daily News* correspondent demanded.

"I just came to see the two top teams play for the National League lead," Landis replied with studied nonchalance.

"Are you here to investigate charges of gambling by members of the Cub team?" the newsman pressed.

"You can draw your own conclusions," Landis replied curtly. "I won't say anything now. See me in a couple of hours."[3]

Charlie Grimm approached the scene. "Why is Landis here?" the *Daily News* man asked him.

"I don't know," replied Grimm, honestly enough, since Landis had just now summoned him.

"Do you think he's here about gambling charges?" pressed the reporter.

"If he is, it's news to me," Grimm answered. "I haven't had any information about such a matter." That wasn't so believable.

The reporters waited outside while Landis and Grimm conferred. The writers dogged the Cub manager once again when he reemerged. What had he and Landis discussed?

"Oh, we just talked about the crowds at the baseball parks and things like that," Grimm told the newsmen. Landis had asked him how the ball club was doing and how he liked his new job, Grimm continued. "He did not bring up the subject of gambling at any time," Grimm volunteered, and then the rookie manager blurted something the reporters could use: "You can say that pitcher Guy Bush is not guilty of gambling. Bush's ticket has been bought for St. Louis and he will accompany the club there tonight to pitch a game of the series.

"If there was anything to this sensation Bush would have been ordered back to Chicago," Grimm said emphatically.[4]

Who had said anything about Bush? Either Landis or someone else—Bill Veeck?—must have. The reporters next caught up with Bush, who claimed, depending on which paper one read, either that he hadn't talked to Landis at all, or that he had spoken to Landis briefly about the condition of his pitching arm and baseball in general.[5]

Bush stressed one point: he didn't know why his name was being brought up with Hornsby's. "He was no particular pal of mine. I talked with him when I met him at the ballpark. I never went out with him otherwise. I wouldn't know how to place a bet with a bookie. I've made an occasional bet on the horses at the track during the off season."[6]

The *Daily News* reporter went back to Landis. "I'm always investigating—everywhere," the commissioner told him. "I'm going to Cleveland tonight, but not in connection with this investigation."

The reporter pounced. "What investigation?"

"Well . . ." The hunter had become the hunted, and caught.

"Gambling?"

"Yes."

Now that formed a basis for an investigation, and a scandal. Oddly enough, the name of Rogers Hornsby had not yet been mentioned by anyone involved.[7]

In Chicago the afternoon tabloids were running war-size headlines about the Cubs' problems.

The *Daily News* linked Landis's Pittsburgh visit to a mass of sordid but unsubstantiated detail: one Cub with bad gambling credit recruiting another to "front" for him; two Cubs (not necessarily the first two mentioned) making daily trips to a handbook (an off-track betting site) at Broadway and Belmont, not far from the ballpark; two "blondes [laying] the dough" for unnamed Cubs; four Cub employees, again unnamed, relaying information from bookies to Cub ballplayers during games; and one Cub incurring gambling debts of $38,000 he couldn't repay. The latter's creditors, the *Daily News* said, had threatened to sue.

Guy Bush was being recalled to Chicago for a conference with Bill Veeck. Bush's picture appeared next to the story, in between Veeck's and

Rogers Hornsby's. The caption under Hornsby's picture was the only place his name appeared in the article.[8]

Veeck spoke up from 936 Wrigley Building. "Let Landis dig down into this thing. Let him uncover every detail, and then let him give us a statement. All these undermining rumors about gambling *and such* have got to stop. It is up to Judge Landis." Veeck said he had not ordered Guy Bush back to Chicago. "Bush is not coming home," Veeck said in his best clipped tones, "and there will be no conference."[9]

Veeck in Chicago and Grimm and Bush in Pittsburgh had presented a united front: gambling was not involved. They had not said that the Cubs weren't involved in something, that Rogers Hornsby wasn't involved in something, or that they didn't have a big problem on their hands.

In any event, Judge Landis would have the final word. Along with the *Daily News* charges, the wire service dispatches in that afternoon's Pittsburgh papers carried Landis's remarks made in Chicago nearly twenty-four hours earlier. He and the owners were going to stamp out gambling, he said, *"even if it means the wrecking of valuable ball clubs. . . .* One scandal such as we had in 1919 is enough."[10]

If any of the 22,000 Pittsburgh fans who had turned out for the midweek game noticed Landis's white-haired head in the box seats, few of them could yet have learned what had hit the streets in Chicago. They were out to watch a midseason drama, one that everyone expected to be a turning point of the pennant race.[11]

Both managers sent out their aces, Warneke (17-5) and Steve Swetonic (11-4). The two pitchers dueled scorelessly into the seventh inning. The Pirates loaded the bases without scoring in the first inning and threatened a couple of other times, but a Moore–Jurges–English relay and a running catch on Paul Waner's long drive to right field snuffed both rallies.

The Pirates finally broke out with two runs off Warneke in the seventh. Warneke was due to lead off the top of the eighth for the Cubs, but Grimm called on Marv Gudat, Jurges's rescuer at the Carlos and the contributor of a big pinch hit in the previous Saturday's doubleheader.

Gudat doubled, Herman followed with a single to right, and English took an outside pitch into the right-field corner for a triple that tied things at 2–2. Somehow Swetonic coaxed the next three Cubs into stranding

English at third, even though with one out, he had to knock down Stephenson's line drive to get the out and hold English.

Then Warneke's replacement came in from the bullpen. Landis, from his front-row vantage point, watched in surprise. Grimm had bypassed the club's most-used relievers and singled out Guy Bush to relieve Warneke. He was not returning to Chicago for a conference. Veeck was in Chicago; Grimm may have been acting on his own or in consultation with his boss.

Swetonic and the Pirates had six outs left to break the tie; the Cubs had three. The gangly Bush began his usual routine, pawing the ground before each pitch, falling off toward third base afterward. He set down the heart of the Pittsburgh order—Paul Waner, Adam Comorosky, and Pie Traynor—on a fly ball and two ground balls to Jurges.

That was good enough that in the top of the ninth, Grimm let the notoriously weak-hitting Bush bat for himself. Bush amazed everyone with a rare single, but the Cubs couldn't move him around, and he was stranded. Bush returned to the mound and disposed of the Pirates in the ninth with only a bunt single by Vaughan. In the Cubs' tenth, the team manufactured a run on an error, a single, and a sacrifice fly.

Bush would be the winning pitcher if he could hold on to the new 3–2 lead. With one out, Lloyd Waner blasted his offering deep into right field. Cuyler ran desperately toward the distant wall, reached up, and hauled in the ball for out two. Paul Waner followed with an easy fly to Moore in center for the third out.

"I guess that shows whether Bush has his heart in the game!" Grimm crowed in the clubhouse. In just nine days, Grimm's men had overtaken the Pirates. The Cubs were back in first place for the first time since before Jurges was shot. Grimm had placed his own bet and won. He had proved that he could protect his men and inspire them under the glare of the most powerful figure in baseball. Landis, upstaged by the swift turn of events, departed for an evening arrangement in Cleveland, and the Cubs left for St. Louis that night in a state of euphoria.[12]

The Cubs rolled into St. Louis Friday as if the flag was theirs for the asking. Several Cub spouses had taken the train from Chicago to meet their menfolk after three long and eventful weeks. Mrs. Grimm and her daughter came in from Normandy to join them. The happy group headed to the Park Plaza Hotel. There Guy Bush sifted through a pile of messages from supportive fans in Chicago.

Bush felt safe talking. "I can't make head nor tail of those charts showing the history of horses, and I wouldn't know how to make a bet with a bookie if somebody asked me to," he exclaimed. "Now that someone appears to be trying to ruin me, I've decided never to go near a race track as long as I'm in baseball."[13]

Only a few miles away, a gentleman farmer was giving a reporter his own thoughts on the subject. In between questions, Rogers Hornsby gazed from the porch of his Missouri farmhouse to a rain-drenched landscape of bluegrass, corn, and maples that stretched beyond. A bird dog lay at his side. If any Cubs bet on races, it was without his knowledge, and vice versa, he assured his listener. But when the reporter asked if gambling had had gotten him fired, Hornsby's expression changed: "Say, don't think for a minute that Judge Landis is crazy enough to start banishing players or managers because they bet on race horses."[14]

Then Hornsby calmed down. The Cubs would have revived under him, too, he claimed. After all, he had developed and built the whole team— Warneke was his special project. And he'd kept them in the running through the extended absences of Cuyler, English, and Jurges.

Good points, and well made. But soon Hornsby would be explaining himself to a tougher audience. Judge Landis had decided to visit St. Louis, too.

Two days into the uproar, it was becoming difficult to remember exactly who was being accused of what. Hornsby's picture ran next to articles that talked about "Cub players." Landis's staff at the 333 North Michigan building seemed uninformed about just what was going on, although one reporter noted that Landis's number 2 man, Leslie O'Connor, was also out of the office. National League President John Heydler, contacted in New York, knew nothing: "I have been trying all night to find out just what it is all about and how it started. I am confident that the Chicago club officials are competent to handle their own affairs." On Friday, with Landis due back in town, the main club official, Bill Veeck, had still not heard from the commissioner.[15]

Landis headed back to Chicago (with a possible stopover in Cleveland) after the Cubs-Pirates game Thursday afternoon. A crowd of reporters met him at the station the next morning. The judge hurried off as if he had a pressing appointment, but the newsmen followed him to his residence at the Chicago Beach Hotel, then to his downtown offices, all the while peppering him with questions that he ignored.[16]

Finally the Lord High Commissioner decided to share his thoughts. "About this alleged investigation, now. The only statement I'll make about it is this—that it does not involve the playing of any ballgames."

The mob of reporters shouted at the commissioner for an explanation. Twenty-four hours earlier, Landis had been alluding to the Black Sox scandal, which, whatever it was, had involved the playing of ballgames. Now he seemed to be backpedaling. "Young man, young man," he told one of his interrogators, "I'm just a young, verdant person and I cannot be cross-examined successfully because I'll get myself all tangled up."[17]

Another reporter tried his luck: "What are we to understand by this 'alleged investigation'?"

"I don't react successfully to cross-examination," Landis growled. He rose from his desk and walked over to the windows that overlooked the enormous blue lake. Out loud, he mused, "I think I shall go out and play a round of golf."[18]

A horse named Wrigley Field ran in the seventh race at Hawthorne that afternoon, but no one paid any mind. Cub fans, buoyed by the road trip and the thriller in Pittsburgh, fired off hundreds more telegrams of support to Bush.

By Friday afternoon the *Daily News* was blaming the commissioner for reading too much into its investigation. "If [Landis] is investigating gambling," the paper quoted a "fan" who sounded suspiciously like the *Daily News* editors, "why doesn't he say so? If he has investigated gambling and hasn't found any substantiation for the charges, why doesn't he give the team a clean bill of health? His present stand is doing more harm than good."[19]

Good questions, although perhaps the editors might have been better advised to ask them before running the exposé. The judge meant to answer them.

16 | "That Story Is Terrible, Judge"

I guess that'll learn Ban Johnson that he can't frame an honest bunch of ballplayers. —Chick Gandil, former Chicago White Sox player, 1921

With his wife, Lillian, and his seven-year-old, Mae Jean, Charlie Grimm settled into the familiar surroundings of his home in suburban Normandy. Lillian had been busy rounding up the relatives and friends for a Saturday night bash following the Cubs-Cardinals game. The Grimm family orchestra would provide the entertainment: Charlie's sister and brother alternating on the piano, his mother on the harmonica, one uncle on the guitar, another on the mandolin, and of course, Karl Johann strumming his fabulous banjo. All performers being bilingual, the audience would hear German folk songs and no doubt some material in English; Charlie might perform some magic tricks during the breaks. His brother, an accomplished piano player, vowed that the keyboard would be occupied until midnight.[1]

Charlie didn't know it, but Judge Landis had planned his own get-together with a few of Charlie's pals at the Park Plaza on Saturday morning—and Charlie wasn't invited. Landis arrived in St. Louis on the overnight train and showed up at the hotel early in the morning. This time the commissioner was flanked by his executive secretary, Leslie O'Connor, carrying a fat notebook under his arm. While reporters jostled frantically for position and shouted questions, Landis and O'Connor marched to their suite.

Landis appeared well rested and eager for a good round of cross-examination, even though the sixty-five-year-old had traveled more than a thousand miles since Wednesday night, stopped in four cities, talked to dozens of ballplayers and reporters, and possibly squeezed in some golf Friday afternoon. At each stop—Pittsburgh, Cleveland, Chicago, and now St. Louis—he was able to alight from his comfortable Pullman compartment and reach his local destination in a few minutes. Nor was it necessary to be a corporate chieftain or some other potentate to obtain such service in the world of 1932, although it surely took considerable means. Landis, who had voluntarily taken a significant pay cut in consideration of the Depression, would have had a sizeable expense account to maintain such a lifestyle.

At the doorway a collection of baseball men was waiting: Woody English, Pat Malone, Guy Bush, Coach Charley O'Leary, and Rogers Hornsby. They followed Landis and O'Connor into the room. At the door Landis took a look at the circus in the hallway. "See me later," he told them before banging the door shut.

Inside the room the six men and a stenographer sat down in front of the individual who had made his name by banishing the eight Black Sox for life—after they had been acquitted in a court of law. What the stenographer took down would go into O'Connor's notebook and affect their lives forever. Bush was most visibly on edge. Even after his wife had met him at the station the day before and proclaimed her faith in him, Bush was still protesting his innocence to anyone who would listen.[2]

Bush wasn't the only one feeling the stress. "I'm getting sick and tired of all this bunk that's going around about me," Hornsby had complained to a newsman before Landis arrived. "Just a little more and some individuals are likely to find themselves with trouble on their hands.

"They're starting stories now that I owed money to the Cub ballclub and also members of the team. That's an out-and-out lie."[3]

It was precisely such stories that Judge Landis wanted to discuss with the group; for weeks, O'Connor had been filling his notebook with information on the off-field doings of the Chicago National League Ball Club. Landis began by turning to Bush. "Did you ever have any financial dealings with Mr. Hornsby?"

The question had nothing to do with anything the papers had reported, but Bush replied evenly, "I signed a note for him—that is all. It was just before we went east."[4]

"Just what was the transaction?" Landis asked.

"I signed a note for Mr. Hornsby to borrow $2,000."

"Did he give you any reason why he wanted the money?"

"Yes, sir. He said he wanted to pay back income tax."

The judge asked Bush about other dealings he might have had with Hornsby. Bush told Landis that there was only one: a $5,000 note he had signed for Hornsby in 1929. "It has been repaid," Bush said.

Landis then questioned O'Leary and English, who confirmed that Hornsby had approached both of them for cash loans. Hornsby owed O'Leary the entire $2,000 he had borrowed and English about $1,200 of a $2,000 loan. Hornsby had assured O'Leary he would repay the loan when he "got straightened out."

Landis turned now to Pat Malone. Again, the questions revolved around loans to Hornsby. Malone said Hornsby had borrowed $250 from him in Pittsburgh on July 22, and he had repaid it before leaving the club.

Landis turned to the last man in the room he hadn't questioned. "Well, Hornsby," Landis began unceremoniously, "you told English alone and Bush why you wanted the money?"[5]

"Yes," replied Hornsby.

"Was it paid on taxes?"

"It was applied on taxes and on interest on my place."

After some further fencing, Landis trapped Hornsby into admitting that he had used the money for "other bills" besides his tax arrears, contrary to what he had told his teammates.

Landis had heard enough about the loans. "Now, there has been a considerable amount of rumor and gossip and publication, among other things, to the effect that Guy Bush was interested with you in betting on horses."

"Guy Bush never made a bet with me," Hornsby replied.

Landis acted as though he hadn't heard him. "Is it true that you were interested together?" he asked.

"No, it is not true."

Landis did not let up. "Did you ever know of him [Bush] doing anything of the sort?"

"No, I did not know of him doing anything like that. I don't know what they do. I never asked them."

Bush broke in. "I don't even know what one of those damn places look like where you go to make a bet. Don't you think this attack has been unfair to me?"

"If you are innocent, yes," Landis replied, apparently unperturbed by the interruption.[6]

"I am innocent," Bush protested.

"But I am trying to find out. You know why I am here, don't you?" asked Landis.

"Yes, but you know it is bad for them to accuse me of something I am not guilty of," Bush cried.

"Well, Guy, they have been accusing me for sixty years," Landis explained in a fatherly tone. "No matter what anybody accuses you of, or ever accused you of, or may accuse you of hereafter, if the whole world believes this accusation but you know it is not true, that will carry you along, won't it?"

"It will carry me along, but I am in the public eye, that is it," Bush responded.

Landis still had unfinished business with the Rajah. Had Hornsby bet with any other Cubs besides the gentlemen present? he asked. Hornsby replied no.

Landis was unsatisfied. "There has been some sort of activity that has resulted in a lot of talk and a lot of accusations and publicity, all revolving around racetrack bets. Now, have you made any racetrack bets this summer?"[7]

"No."

"None this summer. None of this money that you borrowed from these players had any relation to bets on races?"

"No."

"When did you make your last bet on a race?"

"Oh, I don't know the dates; I don't keep the dates on them."

"Well, what about when? What year?"

Hornsby misstepped. "Well, about, a long time ago, about '29, I guess '30, something like that."

It was a lie, and a clumsy lie. Everyone knew that Hornsby could hardly go a day without placing a bet.

Landis had obviously rattled Hornsby. The judge kept on. "Have you made a bet on a horse race since 1930? This is 1932. Have you made a bet on a horse race this year?" he pressed.

Just in time, Hornsby's trial court experience came back to him. "Well, I am not going to say whether I have or not."

"Or last year?" Landis continued.

"Put in my position, I am not going to say. I refuse to answer that question," Hornsby snapped.

Landis's voice rose for the first time. "I will say that I am not so much interested in an answer to that question from our standpoint as I am from the standpoint of these boys here, Guy Bush and Charles O'Leary and Woody English and Pat Malone, some of whose names have been badgered about in the last few weeks as having been interested with you in betting on the races."

Landis had offered Hornsby a way out. If exonerating the Cubs was the objective here, Hornsby was willing to help out; hell, the guys might remember him when they divvied up the World Series shares. It was no secret that a Cubs-Yankees series could break all existing attendance records.

"Those fellows, Judge, as I said before, never have been interested with me in any way in betting."

"As far as these four men, Pat Malone, Woody English, Charley O'Leary, and Guy Bush, are concerned, they never had a thing to do with any bet you made, if you ever made a bet? They never had anything to do with it?"

"They had nothing to do with it."

Now it was Leslie O'Connor's turn, with some follow-up questions about the loans. He came on strong, like a reliever coming in with fresh stuff. He phrased his first question to Hornsby in the negative. "This money was not used to pay income taxes, was it, Mr. Hornsby?"

"Sir?" Hornsby was understandably confused. After some more badgering, Hornsby decided he wasn't going to let an aide-de-camp trap him. "That does not make any difference," he snapped. "I asked them to loan it to me personally. I am not on the witness stand for you. I will protect myself in that respect. If you are going to be the lawyer, I will bring up mine."[8]

O'Connor countered, "You got these boys into this, in a way."

"I never got them into anything. I will talk to the judge, not you, about anything like that."

Landis took over the questioning again. He still had issues left to explore. This time he wanted to know the details of the note Bush had signed for him. The two thrashed about a bit, defining what a "note" was versus an "installment loan."

Finally Hornsby produced a sheet of paper and handed it to Landis. With a note of triumph, he said, "If you want to read this, you can read this, and then you can see how these business deals were arranged, with Mr. Veeck and I, with these three gentlemen."[9]

Landis, puzzled, looked it over the sheet. "'August 3, 1932,'" he began to read. He glanced at Hornsby. "Where was this, Philadelphia?" he asked.

"Yes, sir," Hornsby replied.

Hornsby had just handed Landis a formal agreement with the Cubs that he had signed late the night he was fired. It held the gist of what Landis had just spent half the morning establishing, but it had taken the commissioner of baseball ten days to track it down.

Landis continued: "'William L. Veeck, president, Chicago National League Ball Club. Dear Sir . . .'"

Hornsby broke in. "I do not want that thing read for that thing there," he said, gesturing toward O'Connor's notebook, or possibly the stenographer. "That is for you; that is personal, between him and I. I just showed you that. He [Veeck] will show you the same one, the original, if you want it. These gentlemen were all present when it was drawn up."

For confirmation Hornsby turned to English, always known for his ability to get along with Hornsby. "Is that right or wrong?" Hornsby demanded.

"Right," said English.

Landis had to be irked. Bill Veeck had neatly solved the problem of repaying the loans weeks ago, so tidily that the commissioner had not been requested or needed. Landis had taken three overnight train journeys, fielded dozens of questions, and suffered through a barrage of criticism—all in the hopes that he would finally corner Hornsby. Yet the answers had been in Hornsby's breast pocket all the time.

There was nothing left for Landis to do but to carry on with the rest of his agenda. He and O'Connor had uncovered a few other unresolved issues that might yet trip Hornsby up. One was the matter of a bad check a bookmaker named Smith had made out to Hornsby for one of his rare wins. Hornsby established that the check was bad because the savings and loan upon which it was drawn "went busted." "It closed up the morning I tried to cash it." Another bookmaker, Schwartz, now held the check, according to Hornsby. Landis asked if "some barber out there in the neighborhood of the ball park" was involved in the transaction. Hornsby explained that "John the barber" had only put him in touch with Smith: "I was in there getting a haircut." Hornsby's explanation satisfied Landis that John the barber was not Schwartz, not Smith, and not a party with whom Hornsby had placed bets.[10]

Landis then asked Hornsby why everyone had smiled when Andy Lotshaw's name came up a few minutes earlier. "If you bet any money on a horse race, did Andy have part of it?" asked Landis.

"Hell, no," Hornsby flared up. "I should say not—no sir, no, no, none of these fellows, Judge, had anything to do with it, as I said before. At any time whatsoever, Andy Lotshaw or nobody else had anything to do with it. If I wanted to bet on a horse, I did."

Hornsby's flare-up did not annoy Landis, who explained, "What I mean is this: is it also in this thing that an usher or two ushers at the ballpark, at your request, went out and placed bets for you during a ball game?"

"No, not me, no sir. I don't know anything about that. That is something new. I never had anybody make any bets for me. If I made them, I made them before I went to the ball game."

"Is it also part of the story that these bets were placed by you either through the ushers or otherwise from time to time during the progress of a ball game?"

"No."

"That you would go out from the dugout, out back behind someplace to—"

"That is not so," Hornsby interrupted.

"—to place your orders for bets?"

"That is not so," Hornsby repeated. "I don't know anything about that. That is not so."

"That is not true?"

"That is not true."

"As far as you know, no employee, usher or otherwise, at the ball park, or around the ball park there, had any contact with anything you did, if you had anything to do in placing bets?"

"No."

Landis had reached a dead end. Time to try a friendly face.

"Guy," Landis said cordially, returning to his first witness, "when did you first hear that anyone was using your name around [*sic*] as having been in on bets on races? When did you first hear that there was talk of that sort?"

Bush stammered, "Well, they told me about it in the newspapers in Chicago, when I was in Pittsburgh the other morning."

"That is, just last week?"

"Yes, sir; the day before yesterday."

"Up until that time you had never heard anybody say—"

"No, sir."

"Guy, there is a part of that story that you and Rogers went together up in the neighborhood of the Broadway territory and that you contacted a couple of ladies known as blondes. Is this story—"

"I'm glad you mentioned that," said Bush, his voice rising. "That is some—"

"I want you to listen to this; this is part of the story," Landis cautioned. He could have added that it was taken almost verbatim from the *Daily News* story of two long days ago.

"Yes, sir, I know it."

"No matter how you laugh about the stories, or how silly—"

"I am not laughing, because it is serious with me," Bush replied with some heat.

"I am telling you, I have got to find out about these things."

"Yes, sir."

"Now, is there any basis whatever for these stories?"

"None whatever. No, sir."

It was Hornsby's turn to interrupt. "What is that supposed to be?" he demanded, meaning the mention of blondes. "That is news to me. I never heard of it." Hornsby, it seemed, really didn't read anything but racing forms.

Landis set about filling him in. "That is part of it, that you and Bush contacted with a couple of blonde ladies and that they went and got you what is called a scratch sheet in some place up there on Broadway, or in that neighborhood—"

"You can get scratch sheets at any corner you want them," Hornsby said.

"—that they came back and gave you these scratch sheets and that you or Guy Bush delivered to one or both of these blondes a substantial sum of money and they went out and turned this money over to a bookmaker or betting commissioner or somebody else to be wagered on a horse race."

Hornsby snorted. "This is a lot of bunk for these guys."

Bush blurted out, "That is a hell of a story to be telling about a man that is married, I will tell you that."

Landis tried to press on. "Rogers, did you and Joe [Bush] have social relations, outside of the ball game?"

"No, sir."

"Did you ever go places together?"

Bush jumped in again. "Never been no place," he averred.

"No," said Hornsby, ignoring the interruption.

Bush wasn't finished, although the hearing just about was. "I think that story, Judge, is terrible," he cried out. "They put under my picture that some club player owed $38,000. Why would they pick out my name and my picture to put in the paper and then say some Cub player owed $38,000?"

Landis tried to get back on point. "Do you know anything about any Cub player owing $38,000?"

"No," replied Bush. Then he went back to the point he wanted to make. "It is funny they would pick out my picture."

"Do you, O'Leary?" Landis asked.

"No, sir."

"Do you, Malone?"

Malone joined in the rebellious spirit gathering in the room. "I don't know anybody that has got $38,000," he said brightly. True enough—even Malone, one of the best-paid pitchers in the league, would need nearly two years to earn thirty-eight grand.

In case anyone had missed his drift, Bush continued, "That is terrible. The public will naturally think that I owe the money, it being printed under my picture. I think that story is terrible, Judge. I don't give a damn what anybody says, it is lousy."

There was no reply from the judge. The stenographer's work for the day was over. The meeting began to break up.

After the transcript was distributed, Landis had the text distributed to the press, with a curt "The testimony speaks for itself." All he had to show for four days of maneuvering was the news that Veeck had wrapped up the problem without help from the commissioner's office.

Veeck himself had not been heard from all day. The Cub president normally spent his weekends on Park Street in Hinsdale, near his family and the Hinsdale Golf Club, where he was president. Veeck was such a golfing enthusiast that he had once tried to downplay Hornsby's gambling habit with his own little confession: "I play golf."

The past few days, Veeck had monitored the crisis from downtown, where he could quickly obtain each special edition the afternoon papers brought out for successive bombshell reports. We can imagine newsboys, just like those in the black-and-white movies, standing on street corners in the Loop and hollering "Extra! Extra!—Judge Landis accuses the Cubs of gambling!" Veeck could keep up with the breaking news in near "real time," use long-distance and telegraph services, and issue frequent rebuttals and analysis.

On a Saturday in serene Hinsdale, though, Veeck was no better off than a twenty-first-century executive without a smartphone or laptop. Though within an hour or so summaries of Landis's transcript were running in special editions of the *Daily News* and the *Evening American*, Veeck was virtually incommunicado. For economic reasons, the newspapers didn't take the extra time and expense to expedite special editions out to the far-off, less-populous suburbs.

That left the telephone as a quick and easy way to reach the Cub president, but evidently no one in Chicago connected with the club, such as Dr. Davis, rang up Veeck to say something like, "Bill, there's been hell to pay in St. Louis today"; likewise in St. Louis, neither the Cubs' traveling secretary, Bob Lewis, nor Charlie Grimm called. It was Saturday; the

"That Story Is Terrible, Judge"

office at the Wrigley Building was closed, and the ballpark was shuttered.

Warren Brown of the a.m. *Herald and Examiner* sensed his opportunity. At the time of Hornsby's firing, Brown had stated flatly that something other than the Cubs' won-loss record was involved, and the news from St. Louis made it clear he had been right. Brown should have felt vindicated and happy, but the timing of events meant that in the morning, when his paper's Sunday edition came out, the hearing would be old news thanks to intensive coverage in the afternoon papers, such as the headline screaming from the *Daily News*'s sports section: LANDIS BARES 'ROG' LOANS.

Brown, then, needed an angle to freshen the story for the Sunday readership, and he knew where Veeck spent his Saturday afternoons. An excellent athlete himself, he may have even played golf with Veeck. Thus, Warren Brown, the classiest sports journalist in Chicago, probable fellow golfer, and Joe McCarthy ally, sought out Bill Veeck at the Hinsdale Golf Club. As Brown had hoped, he was the first to tell Veeck about Landis's foray to St. Louis.[11]

The fifty-four-year-old Veeck, serious weekend golfer that he was, had probably played eighteen holes that morning: a five-mile walk in the August sun. By the time Brown caught up with him, he would have been relaxing in the clubhouse, which despite Prohibition may have served its members alcohol, or at least looked the other way.

Hot, tired, in late-middle age, knowledgeable and possibly the slightest bit tipsy: what else could an inquiring reporter ask for in an interview subject? Brown's stature in the field, aided by his role in the McCarthy episode, made him a familiar and trusted character. Perhaps for the first time in Veeck's long career, he lowered his guard and decided to explain his actions from the start.

Veeck repeated, as he had all week, that Hornsby's performance as manager had been the key to letting him go—but before making a decision, he had interviewed "some of the veterans on the team," probably meaning the holdover McCarthyites: Hartnett, Grimm, Stephenson, Root, Cuyler. Whomever Veeck spoke to, they passed along what they knew about the loans and the loan guarantees. "That clinched the matter," Veeck told Brown. "I was determined then to go through." The night of the firing, he and Hornsby's creditors on the ball club worked out the repayment agreement with Hornsby. Then, he said, he notified Landis and John Heydler, the National League president about what they had decided. It was a plausible account, sufficient to give Brown a scoop the next morning.

And yet . . . in St. Louis, Landis had acted thunderstruck to learn about the Philadelphia agreement. All the parties, not just Veeck, seemed to be having trouble with their stories. Hornsby had threatened to sue anyone who would suggest he had borrowed money from his players, even though he was carrying a copy of the repayment agreement in his pocket. Landis launched his investigation without consulting Veeck or John Heydler, and when he finally held a hearing, he spent half the morning rehashing the newspaper charges before blundering into another area where he had not done his homework. Before day's end, Veeck was back to denying that the loans ever had anything to do with firing Hornsby.[12]

A thousand miles away, in New York, a waspish columnist named Westbrook Pegler mulled over the reports from St. Louis and Chicago. Was this how the commissioner justified his massive annual salary and guaranteed the integrity of baseball? As Pegler saw it, Landis had obviously known all about the loans—"an old domestic custom of the baseball business . . . deemed to be unethical now that it has been brought to official attention"—before he even started. Investigating the loans had unearthed the gambling rumors. But even though nothing substantive had turned up, said Pegler, Landis had left matters hanging:

> Having created the scandal by his mysterious and spectacular demeanor, [Landis] would not admit that he had overdramatized his job and attempted to close the incident with a noncommittal report which leaves the Cubs still under a suspicion which apparently is unjust.
>
> So although the players have done nothing that anybody has heard of to discredit their club and the national pastime of which the judge is the guarantor, the judge himself, by his reticence and mysteriousness, has tended to aggravate the suspicion.[13]

Pegler's analysis was correct in terms of the players' psychology; no Cub would soon forget the front-page photograph of Guy Bush near the

"$38,000" figure. That said, and regardless of the judge's propensity for grandstanding, dismissing the issue as "the old domestic custom" of manager-ballplayer loans was myopic. Hornsby's gambling, enabled by his position as baseball's highest-paid manager, had clearly placed him in unmanageable financial straits and brought him perilously close to the underworld of hypercompounding interest, knee cappings, and worse. Veeck, acting decisively to protect his ball club from a situation that he had allowed to fester too long, and Landis, a step or two behind but empowered to protect the game with drastic measures if warranted, had formed a formidable if clumsy defensive alliance in depth. The system had worked, however imperfectly.

Pegler, who knew Ben Hecht and Charles MacArthur from his Chicago days, also ignored the newspapers' role in provoking the furor. The *Daily News* alone had provided enough yellow journalism for a sequel to *The Front Page*. (Hecht had in fact once worked for the *Daily News*.) Chicago's other papers had hardly distinguished themselves. Once the *News* libeled Guy Bush and rushed to publication without any modicum of evidence, its rivals either recirculated the charges mindlessly (probably rationalizing that they were now "news") or prematurely declared the end of the "alleged scandal" and mocked the *Daily News*—which then preened itself in print when Landis finally pried some hard facts loose at the Park Plaza. Gossip, rumor, cowardice, contradictions, rank speculation, premature celebration, and hypocrisy had crammed Chicago's sports sections for days on end—and that was only the journalists' end of it. The editors and sportswriters involved—Brown, Ward, Vaughan, Burns, Marvin McCarthy, Simons, Carmichael, Munzel, Prell—would work in the Windy City for decades to come, at least one of them, McCarthy, in a high management position until 1974. They wrote histories and reminiscences galore about the great days and the good old boys of Mr. Wrigley's ball club, but not one would talk or write of those days in August 1932 when a baseball abyss had seemed to open and close with each revelation, and they flailed in ignorance and eagerness for a scoop.

Landis's actions, on the other hand, were much more than the useless exercise Pegler derided. The commissioner had just conducted a whirlwind operation that harked back to the German general staff's use of railroads and prefigured Henry Kissinger's "shuttle diplomacy." From his midcontinental base, Landis had struck without warning, roaming across nearly two thousand miles of the vast Midwest in three days, moving incommunicado, leaving dazed targets in his wake. The element of surprise, the ease of train service, and the rapidity of modern communications meant that millions could be informed within hours, even minutes, of the commissioner's next foray, and all the less prepared for the next blow and where it would fall. Was a "noncommittal report" all he could point to as a result? Not exactly. First, Landis's publicity had guaranteed that Rogers Hornsby would never manage anything but hopeless second-division entities again. NO BIG CITY BIG MONEY. More than that, Landis had reminded everyone that he was not to be trifled with; even the densest baseball people great and small could imagine how bad a day it could be when the judge dropped by unannounced. Was this process fair? Not at all, as Guy Bush had been quick to point out, but then the Black Sox scandal had been uncovered by a grand jury sifting through unsubstantiated gossip and hearsay and stumbling across revelations, exactly as Landis had just done.

In Chicago, these episodes had come and gone in flashes over ten days. When the excitement subsided, the local favorites were in first place, commanded by the affable Kaptink, a link to the great McCarthy and even the great Alexander, a friend of all. The 1932 Cubs now seemed safe from the hanging judge of the 1919 White Sox, all at the cost of one surly misfit.

McCarthy's right-hand man was in place; might the heady days before the Crash yet return? Might not Chicagoans fill the ballpark again, day after day, the way it had been not so long ago, and blaze their way to another delirious, nonsensical winning streak?

Yes, that was a possibility. Still, Westbrook Pegler had sensed the situation's underlying dynamic: a group of unsophisticated young men had been through an unnerving ordeal, and putting things right wouldn't be easy, Charlie Grimm's ebullient reassurances aside.

17 ‖ The Natural

The ball . . . sailed through the light and up into the dark, like a white star
seeking an old constellation. . . . The Knights poured out of their dugout to
pound [Hobbs's] back, and hundreds of their rooters hopped about in the field.
He stood on the home base, lifting his cap to the lady's empty seat. —Bernard
Malamud, *The Natural*

While Judge Landis convened his meeting at the Park Plaza Hotel, Pat
Roche and Louis Capparelli of the Illinois state's attorney's office delved
into another investigation related to the Chicago Cubs. Their target was
a less-renowned figure than Rogers Hornsby; their target was Lucius
Barnett, a small businessman and hustler whose principal occupation
seemed to be looking for the main chance.[1]

Hustlers and racketeers were no strangers to Chief Investigator Roche
and his assistant. Roche had raided a warehouse of Al Capone's long before
Eliot Ness tried it, and he was the one chosen to pick up Capone when the
big fellow finally decided to turn himself in after the McSwiggin shooting.
In December 1930, Roche and Capparelli, with another detective, invaded
the wedding of Capone's younger sister and arrested several ushers.
(Capone was not present.) A rumor later spread that Big Al wanted to
assassinate Roche; it was probably untrue, but the rumor itself confirmed
Roche's stature. Capparelli, for his part, had turned down a thousand-
dollar bribe while arresting Murray "The Hump" Humphreys, a Capone
protégé and extortionist said to have contributed "vote early and vote
often" to our familiar quotations.[2]

The thirty-two-year-old Capparelli was known as merciless on law-
breakers; in eight years on the force, he had already shot several men. In
early June, Roche had sent Capparelli and two other officers to corner
three hoodlums who had been shaking down Morris Schachter, a gambler.

With the victim's cooperation, Capparelli and his men concealed themselves before the criminals arrived for their latest payment. "We're police officers—stick up your hands," ordered Capparelli, stepping from the shadows. One outlaw dropped his moneybag and pulled a gun; Capparelli dispatched him with a shotgun blast to the chest. The dead man's associates were no luckier; one of Capparelli's companions gunned down the last of the crew as he tried to flee. In 1932 police who shot to kill were more often than not regarded as heroes. Roche proudly said of his men's action: "Three desperate characters have been removed from the streets of Chicago and undoubtedly numerous kidnappings and extortions have been prevented." The *Tribune* recognized the officers with its monthly hundred-dollar hero award.[3]

Capparelli stayed shooting-free through most of the summer, and in mid-August Roche called him in to investigate a different sort of extortion. This time the suspect seemed less dangerous, but the complainant was much better known: it was Bill Jurges's old girlfriend, Violet Valli, most recently a headliner in local burlesque venues as "The Girl Who Shot for Love." She claimed that Barnett, her bail bondsman, had refused to return some personal belongings she had given him to safeguard during her legal troubles in July.

On Friday, August 12, Valli had made an appearance in Chicago Avenue Court, where the inevitable Judge John Sbarbaro presided. Unless the judge had taken in one of Valli's burlesque performances, it was probably the first time he had seen the young woman since she had appeared in his court a month before. Valli explained that while she was jailed, she had entrusted Barnett with some two dozen letters that Bill Jurges had written her. The problem, it seemed, went far beyond her own desire to regain her materials. Barnett was proposing to publish Jurges's messages as a booklet that he would market in all the major league cities. He would pay Valli five thousand dollars up front and up to twenty thousand later.[4]

On the face of it, Barnett's numbers sounded unrealistic—more than a quarter of a million dollars in 2013 terms to exploit a scandal that had dissipated like a brief summer squall. Who outside Chicago would even be interested in reading Jurges's letters to Valli?

Judge Sbarbaro, that wily veteran of Chicago's streets, expressed skepticism about the situation. "This looks like a publicity scheme," he told

Valli, and tried to give his reelection chances a boost: "Besides, I'm a Cub fan myself." This particular Republican judge needed all the good publicity he could get. He was up for reelection in November, and 1932 was definitely looking like a Democratic year. After some back and forth about the merits of a warrant for disorderly conduct versus one for larceny, the judge and Valli disappeared into his chambers for a conference. Whatever the young woman told him, Sbarbaro emerged a few minutes later with a changed outlook: "I hold no brief for Miss Valli, but publication of letters that would hurt Jurges or the Cubs must be prevented. I advised Miss Valli how to proceed to prevent that, if she is sincere."[5]

Judge Sbarbaro seemed to be saying that however weak Valli's legal case may have been, the case to protect the Cubs was strong. The letters held something—at least Valli had convinced Sbarbaro that they held something—that had put some fairly grandiose ideas into Barnett's head and changed a savvy judge's mind.

Valli's hearing was on Friday, August 12. The next morning Sergeant Capparelli, probably driving one of the powerful, stripped-down Lincolns that the Chicago lawmen of the era favored, headed out to pick up Barnett for questioning. He found the suspect, a well-tailored fellow who wore glasses, at 2434 Burling Street, his residence several blocks south of Wrigley Field. Capparelli took Barnett to his vehicle and transported him downtown to Pat Roche's office in the Metropolitan Building.[6]

Capparelli pulled up to the front door and led Barnett into the lobby without handcuffs. Later, Barnett would explain that he feared he was being kidnapped—but then false police uniforms and badges had facilitated the Massacre, and all poor Barnett knew was that an Italian-named gentleman who no doubt packed a gun had taken him for a ride.

Entering the semidarkness of the lobby, Barnett saw his chance. He whirled and kicked the lawman below the belt. As Capparelli doubled over in pain, Barnett bolted for the door. Capparelli managed to give chase and catch Barnett on the sidewalk outside. While the men struggled, two policemen who had been waiting with Violet Valli in a nearby restaurant rushed over to help. Three traffic cops quickly joined the melée, and combined the six law enforcers finally overwhelmed Barnett. Roche, arriving from his office upstairs, ordered his men to lock Barnett up at the detective bureau, where he was booked for assault, extortion, larceny, resisting a policeman, and disorderly conduct. Considering the profile of the policeman he had just attacked, he was lucky to be alive.[7]

Valli must have watched the scuffle or its aftermath after her restaurant companions joined in. At any rate, when things had settled down, Roche took her up to his office to interview her. The figures she provided for Barnett's offer were now $2,500 cash, $5,000 total, much lower than the amounts she had given Judge Sbarbaro the day before, but she gave Roche a more detailed history of Barnett's schemes. His first idea, Valli said, had been that she sue not only Jurges but also Kiki Cuyler for $50,000 apiece. After that, she continued, Barnett had proposed publishing the letters as "The Love Letters of a Shortstop." "I wouldn't let him do that. I think too much of Bill," proclaimed Violet Popovich Valli—glossing over the phone call she had placed to Jurges at Barnett's prompting when the Cubs had visited New York. Barnett had done the talking, threatening to file suit against Jurges if he did not come up with $20,000 immediately.[8]

After hearing Valli out, Roche gave the press his professional opinion. Barnett, he thought, had no intention of filing a lawsuit or publishing the letters; he was running a blackmailing operation. That explained the new extortion charge against Barnett: the state's attorney now considered Barnett's schemes as felonious, in contrast to Valli's original low-level complaints. Barnett might now find himself more susceptible to some sort of plea-bargaining.

Beyond the illegalities, Barnett had managed to reopen a topic that almost everyone north of Comiskey Park wanted to go away: Ki Cuyler's connection to the Bill Jurges shooting. The news narrative once again trotted out the explanation for Cuyler's involvement: he had "objected" to Jurges's involvement with Valli. For that a blackmailer saw a hundred-thousand-dollar payday? Streetwise characters like Sbarbaro, Roche, and Barnett all knew that was bunkum. Besides, any relatively up-to-date Bill Jurges scrapbook would have an entry from July 15 concerning a letter Valli had written Mrs. Cuyler from New York with the help of "Betty" and a Joe Cardella. Barnett, then, was not the only con artist trying to exploit Cuyler's predicament—and just what did Cuyler's wife have to do with advising a young shortstop?[9]

Monday morning, Barnett appeared in John Sbarbaro's court for arraignment on his rapidly expanding portfolio of charges. Sbarbaro raised Bar-

The Natural

nett's bail from $2,500 to $10,000. The extortion charge might have justified the fourfold increase, but to make sure that everyone understood his reasoning, the judge announced: "I'm doing this to protect the Cubs from unjust scandal." He put the case over until the 22nd.[10]

Barnett protested to a reporter that Valli had it all wrong: he had posted Valli's bond and endorsed her hospital bills at the request of his pastor, whose church ran an orphanage where Valli grew up. When he took Valli home from the hospital, Barnett said, she pulled the letters out of a trunk and told him to take them. Later, "I offered to burn them up in her presence as soon as she had paid her hospital bills," he said in a hurt tone. But some time later Valli showed up with a policeman to retrieve them.[11]

"These letters refer to scandals," Barnett said ominously. "Their publication would wreck a ballclub. . . . I have it in black and white that Miss Valli has previously embarrassed both Jurges and Kiki Cuyler." Some of the letters were from Cuyler, he added, and dated back two years.[12]

Barnett may have been in contempt of court, since keeping such details out of the papers was Sbarbaro's expressed goal. The news outlet for his interview was itself interesting: the *Daily Times*, a three-year-old afternoon tabloid, forerunner of the eventual *Sun-Times*. A tabloid, by definition, was the voice of the masses, the working class—blue-collar folks less likely to be taken in by the "Victorian gent"—the respectable press that had peddled Cuyler's involvement in the matter as that of a kindly mentor with a young teammate.[13]

Barnett's extortion scheme might have gone awry; he might even be facing the penitentiary, but he had effectively countered the combined forces of the Cubs, a judge, and a prosecutor by virtue of the overriding fact that he still had possession of the incriminating letters and direct knowledge of their contents. Lucius Barnett, small-time hustler, was playing bluff with the powers that be.

Bill Jurges and the Cubs had just returned to Chicago that morning from their St. Louis series, where they finished by dropping a doubleheader, 2–0 and 2–1, losing one game when Ripper Collins grabbed a long two-out drive to right field bare-handed with two Cubs on base in the ninth. The lead over the Pirates shrank to a half game.[14]

The unfazed squad detrained at the Illinois Central station laughing and joking. "Forget about St. Louis," said Charlie Grimm to hundreds of supporters jamming the concourse. "We got to lose some of 'em, don't we? The boys told me they'd bring me home on top, and they did. That's all that matters." Grimm took a look at the adoring crowd and cried out, "What a town!" Then, skipping breakfast, he took off for the Cub offices in the Wrigley Building for his first official visit as manager.[15]

Five hundred fans were already in line for Charlie Grimm Day when the ballpark gates swung open at 11:45 the next morning. By 1:15 thousands were crowding the stands, applauding Grimm as he took batting practice. Two bands ran through sometimes-clashing versions of "I Love You Truly," "Charley, My Boy," and "Happy Days Are Here Again" while the customers streamed in. At 2:45, just before game time, ten Andy Frain ushers began lugging Grimm's presents to the plate: five foot high baskets of roses, bouquets, and a platinum watch. Kiwanians, Rotarians, and Elks crowded round. Hartnett's business associate, Ed Kavanaugh, directed ceremonies. It was the most elaborate "day" the ballpark had seen since Grover Alexander received his new Lincoln all those years ago. Alex was, in fact, due in town in a few days with the House of David, a barnstorming team he had been with the past two seasons.[16]

Grimm, abashed by the cheers, pulled off his cap and swung it around his head in acknowledgment like a little boy. The crowd cheered louder. Here was a regular guy you could root for, and McCarthy's handpicked lieutenant, at that.[17]

Finally the game got under way. The first seven innings were scoreless, with Warneke allowing only five harmless hits. But in the top of the eighth, two one-out singles, a triple, and two more quick singles brought in three quick runs. Grimm pulled Warneke, the first time all year he had been relieved in mid-inning.

The customers were making for the exits when the Cubs came up for their last at-bat in the ninth, still trailing 3–0. With one out, Herman, English, and Cuyler all doubled. The half-empty park came alive. With each hit, a few more straw hats sailed onto the field; soon there were small piles here and there in foul territory. Stephenson followed Cuyler's double by pulling a one-strike pitch into left field to score Cuyler with the tying run. The umpires had to call time while ushers and groundskeepers scooped up the latest shower of hats.[18]

A single and an error sandwiched around a popup loaded the bases for Bill Jurges, who was finishing his first day of work at Mr. Wrigley's park since July 4. Jurges stepped up and drove the ball over Wally Berger's head in center field, and Stephenson strolled in from third with the winning run. A final shower of straw hats sailed from the stands to the roar of the crowd and the glee of the Cubs.[19]

The second and third games of the series with the Braves were excruciating—34 mostly futile innings, 19 one day and 15 the next, with a remarkable 12-inning scoreless relief job by Bud Tinning, a rookie who had lived in Hornsby's doghouse, and two more thrilling, last-inning rallies. Guy Bush, slipping into the old relief role he had enjoyed under McCarthy, threw fewer than two innings total and picked up both wins.

Bush's teammates were needling him about his windfall victories, a decided change from such recent locker room wit as "Why don't you pay the bookie that $38,000?" Bush himself was back to his old bravado. It was true that his relief outings allowed him regrettably few opportunities to bat, he allowed, but "[T]here would have been less strain on everybody if I could have come to bat with men on base," he cracked. "Wants to Bat," read the caption under his picture in the *Tribune* the next morning.[20]

Bush bragging about his hitting, straw hats piled near home plate: it harked back to the days of Wilson–Hornsby, but Murderers' Row had left town with Capone. The surge since Grimm took over had been powered by come-from-behind heroics, opposition lapses, and just plain luck. The Cubs were fifth in team hitting and sixth in runs scored. Hornsby had rebuilt the roster around pitching and defense; the staff ace was a gangling twenty-four-year-old in his first pennant race. One of the team's remaining superstars, Cuyler, was still struggling. His double on Charlie Grimm Day had been his first hit in six days.

Fortunately, the Cubs' traditional rivals, the Cardinals and the Giants, were in even worse straits—both stuck in the second division, with only a half-dozen games or so separating the first six teams in the league. The league's usual also-rans were getting a shot at the prize money—most notably Hack Wilson–led Brooklyn, which had suddenly leaped over the Pirates in the standings and closed in on the Cubs by winning 20 of its last 25 ballgames.

Grimm had learned from his mentor, Joe McCarthy, to sacrifice a little defense for another good bat. Grimm began experimenting with Mark Koenig, Hornsby's replacement on the roster. First he batted the switch-hitter in place of Jurges in the third game of the Braves series. Koenig rewarded his new skipper by blasting a rocket that bounced off the second-base umpire; the base runner from second had to be held at third.

The next day Grimm sat Jurges and wrote in Koenig's name at shortstop. Bill was having a little problem with his stomach, the press was told. With Jurges out of the lineup and twenty thousand women, but just ten thousand men, watching, the Cubs once again fell behind and tried another ninth-inning rally. Koenig beat out a bunt single with one out, but his teammates stranded him to end the game. The loss dropped the Cubs' lead over Brooklyn to two games.[21]

The next day, a Saturday, a mere thirteen thousand Chicagoans showed up for the first of four games with the Phillies. For perhaps the first time Bill Veeck must have realized what a million other businessmen had felt, one by one, as their livelihoods dried up. There was no bad-weather excuse, no unpopular manager, no lament for Hack Wilson. On the contrary, it was the Cubs' first weekend at home in a month, they had stormed into first and grabbed headlines for every imaginable reason, and one of the most popular men in the history of the franchise was making out the lineup every day.

Still, there it was, a crowd of only thirteen thousand diehards at 3:00 on a gorgeous Saturday afternoon. The problem certainly wasn't that the Sox were playing at 35th and Shields—the schedule makers made sure that the Cubs and the Sox were seldom in town the same day. Not far from Sox Park, though, the American Giants were still in business at Cole's 39th Street Park, formerly Schorling's Park, newly renamed and spruced up for 1932. Though Rube Foster's Negro National League had passed out of existence, this Saturday night the Giants would have a local celebrity, still beloved of many Cub fans, opposing them, and they had placed an advance item in the *Tribune* in a place that a lot of people were likely to see—right under the latest update on Violet Valli's struggle with Lucius Barnett:

Grover Cleveland Alexander, former National League pitching star, will face Cole's American Giants for the House of David team in a night game at the American Giants' ballpark tomorrow.[22]

The House of David, a religious community headquartered in Benton Harbor, Michigan, had hired the forty-five-year-old Grover Alexander as a player-manager for its barnstorming semipro team. Everyone on the roster except Alex wore a beard, one of the sect's requirements. Besides making out the lineup card, Alexander's only requirement was to pitch an inning or two each game. As Alexander remembered it, "I always picked the eighth or ninth inning and prayed for rain."[23]

The night game format at Cole's Park might have allowed Alex to venture up to the North Side and watch the club he had tutored at the Magic Isle six months before; he could drop by the clubhouse to see his protégés and the old mates: Bush, whom he had taught the screwball; Hartnett; and young Warneke, who had obviously internalized keeping the ball knee-high on the outside corner. The warm-hearted Grimm had already named one friend of Hornsby's, Woody English, as captain; in the same spirit he would welcome the great Alexander, throw his arm around him, and later break into song if the day brought victory.

Or perhaps not. It was no carefree Kaptink at the old ballpark that afternoon. Grimm and the Cubs seemed determined to goad the umpires, as if they were the second-division Sox looking for someone to blame for their failures. One dispute became so heated that Grimm and the Cubs forgot to call time with a Phillie runner loose on the bases. The next inning, Grimm and his starter, Bush, were both tossed for disputing an interference call. Next Burleigh Grimes, who had been haranguing the umpires from the bench, was ordered to leave. Finally, with the Cubs down 5–2 and two outs in the ninth, Captain English managed to get thrown out of the dugout.[24]

There was still one out left for the suddenly listless club. Johnny Moore's single to center barely drew a reaction from the stands. Grimm's replacement, Marv Gudat, drew a walk, and the afternoon was prolonged a few minutes more. Hartnett stepped in and blasted a sizzling grounder that ricocheted off the second baseman's shin and into center field. Moore came around to score; Gudat legged it to third. It was 5–3, with the tying runs on base.

Everyone on the Cubs' depleted bench climbed to the front step of the dugout. Jurges trotted out to pinch run for the leaden-footed Hartnett, while Koenig came to the plate, coolly swinging three bats around his shoulders and over his head, Bronx-bomber style.[25]

Koenig, a switch-hitter, stepped into the left-handed batter's box. Four of his five hits in a Cub uniform so far had come on the first pitch. He waited, and the first offering came in on the inner portion of the plate. Koenig pulled it on a line toward right field. The ball climbed higher and higher, above Chuck Klein's head and then over the tall fence that screened the right-field bleachers, 321 feet from home plate.

The Cub bench swarmed out to the plate to mob Koenig as he rounded third behind Gudat and Jurges, just ahead of hundreds of fans, each intent on reaching their new hero. Too late, the Andy Frains tried to restore order, but the celebration continued, all over the field as well as the stands, for another half hour.[26]

Koenig homered at 4:48 p.m. If Grover Alexander was still in the grandstand to witness the finale, someone might have sought him out and invited him to a speakeasy, or Pat Pieper's restaurant on Clark; after all, there were three hours yet until the game with the Giants. Grover Alexander may well have partied too long that evening. The Giants started their own master, Willie Foster, but when the home team came to bat a Davidian named Lefty Tolles took the mound. Alexander was a no-show in the box score as Foster struck out 14 visitors; the Giants prevailed 3–0.[27]

Sunday afternoon, Alexander did manage to start against the semipro Duffy Florals at Shrewbridge Field on the South Side. This time the old master removed himself after the first inning per his contractual arrangement, and someone recorded only as "Grant" pitched the rest of the way for the Davidians, who were no-hit by Johnny Brice of the Florals. By that time any continuing interest Chicagoans might have had in their distinguished visitor had been overtaken by the unrelenting excitement at Cubs Park.[28]

Koenig's home run was an August thunderclap that startled the city from its many cares. Mr. Wrigley was no longer cheerleading from his box, the

Hacker and the Rajah were no longer crushing drives to all points of the park, but beginning the next afternoon, a classic Sunday turnout, the fans once again began straining the seating capacity of the ballpark, at thirty- or even forty-thousand-plus in the middle of the work week. The applications for the twenty thousand Ladies Day admissions, which had been dwindling earlier in the summer, surged so heavily that Veeck began running two Ladies Days a week. As of August 26, 55,000 women had applied for the September 2 contest scheduled with the Cardinals.[29]

In all, nearly four hundred thousand cheering Chicagoans would come out to Mr. Wrigley's ballyard for the three-week August home stand—a figure every bit the equal of the 1929 or 1930 turnouts, and a season's worth of business in Philadelphia, Pittsburgh, or St. Louis. Even in Brooklyn, the borough's best season since 1925 attracted just 681,827 of the faithful to Ebbets Field—the league's second-best showing to Wrigley Field's eventual 974,688.[30]

The Cubs' renaissance, a balm for the Depression-wracked city, looked even better compared to the fate of the Bruins' South Side neighbors. The woebegone White Sox had taken center stage only once all season, in late May, when their manager and three players beat up an umpire, George Moriarty, in the dugout runway at Cleveland. Moriarty wound up hospitalized with cuts, bruises, and a broken hand. Even so, the four Sox hadn't been able to deliver a knockout punch. After several of the Indians came to the umpire's rescue, the forty-seven-year-old Moriarty, a teammate of Ty Cobb's rough-and-ready Tigers in the early years of the century, staggered to his feet. Mouth bleeding, he asked, "Now, who else is there among you who think I'm yellow?"[31]

Sox manager Lew Fonseca told the league president that he hadn't actually hit anyone, but he was fined a substantial five hundred dollars anyway. Fonseca didn't seem like the bully type. A past American League batting champion, he had played every position but catcher. "A scholarly man and a magician of no mean talent," Ed Burns of the *Tribune* called him. Fonseca was the first White Sox manager not hired by Charles Comiskey (the Sox founder had died the previous autumn, a few months before Wrigley), and it showed. The new man announced in spring training that since his pitchers needed to conserve their strength for the long season ahead, they didn't need to train especially hard. For the position players, Fonseca stressed learning to hit to the opposite field, a difficult enough chore for the typical ballplayer, but that was only the beginning. Their eager new manager also taught them a complex new system of signals that changed each day, with alternate and auxiliary signals as well as special codes for the pitchers and catchers. The Sox, alas, muffed the complicated system game after game, and the club remained sunk in the second division, lack of talent still constituting the real problem.[32]

With the season a virtual loss by July, Fonseca began leaving the team on short scouting trips. Reporting in from Montreal on the 23rd, he explained that although the Sox roster was basically all right, the team could still use a hard-hitting outfielder or two, a good third baseman, a first baseman, and a couple of pitchers. Who couldn't?[33]

Unfruitful as these scouting jaunts proved for the franchise, they may have inadvertently jump-started Fonseca's second career. Sometime his first season the new manager had embarked on yet another innovation: filming to analyze ballplayers' skills and techniques. Applying this new technique in the bushes, to record for the Sox brass exactly what he liked or disliked about various prospects, should have proved irresistible for a trailblazer like Fonseca. Whether or not he actually wielded a camera as he scouted the hinterlands in July 1932, Fonseca was unwittingly preparing a career change—a good thing for managers in general, and Sox managers in particular. After the 1933 season (in which the Sox improved significantly, to 67 victories from 49 in Fonseca's inaugural season), the Sox skipper persuaded the American League to hire him as its first official filmmaker, a role that eventually expanded to include instructional films, player highlights, and World Series features. When the Sox finally cut him loose after a 4-11 start in 1934, Fonseca's second career was well under way. Fonseca did not, however, produce the first or even the best-known World Series footage filmed in the 1930s. A couple of other Chicago camera buffs had already done that for an event that had a greater impact on Charlie Grimm than it did Fonseca: Babe Ruth's at-bat, Wrigley Field, fifth inning, October 1, 1932.[34]

In early August 1932, Fonseca, returning discouraged from his nine-day exploration of the American Association, threatened to quit if management didn't provide better material. Other clubs, it seemed, had already signed the players he was interested in. Evidently, winning organizations targeted and signed the most talented prospects weeks or even months ahead of time, rather than dispatch midseason moonlighters.[35]

Even a noncomformist like Fonseca didn't consider walking down the street to 39th and Wentworth and scouting the talent that had been on display there for years. In 1931 the Negro National League had collapsed, and for the second half of the season the club, now styled the "Columbia Giants," was reduced to barnstorming against independent teams. By 1932, though, new ownership had dramatically faced down the recession by transforming Schorling's Park from a rickety firetrap into a modern stadium with a public address system and brand-new press box. Many of the old gang were back on the field, including the profoundly excellent Willie Foster on the mound and the sophisticated Dave Malarcher juggling his lineup superbly. While plans went forward to launch a new league in 1933, the Giants played in an eastern league, often at night, curbed destructive wrangling with umpires, and supplemented their income with contests against barnstormers like the House of David.[36]

Fonseca soldiered on without any such reinforcements. His Pale Hose hit bottom on August 26 at Boston. While the Cubs were scoring nine runs in one inning for their seventh straight win, the White Sox absorbed their fifteenth loss in seventeen games, 11–8. Chicago pitchers yielded 13 hits, a sorry performance at any time, and outdid that by issuing no fewer than 14 walks.

Charlie Grimm lacked an elaborate signaling system to compare to Fonseca's, as the comedic episode with the forgotten Philadelphia baserunner had indicated. But Fonseca's player-manager counterpart had recently proven himself a standout at haranguing umpires (fisticuffs not included), and he too was an amateur magician and an excellent singer—a baritone to Fonseca's tenor. There's no record that the two ever teamed up on the stage, but by decade's end the two former managers would find themselves sharing the broadcasting booth as announcing partners, a short but memorable stint that gave birth, among other drollery, to the now-familiar game of guessing each day's attendance.[37]

If the Joker Wild wasn't necessarily Fonseca's intellectual equal, he was better at winning the affections of the fans and the press. A few days after the Phillie game in which four Cubs, including Grimm, had been ejected, National League President John Heydler rendered his decision on the

Cubs' misdeeds. He fined Grimm, Bush, and English a hundred dollars apiece, but Grimes went scot-free, though he too had been ejected.

Reporters asked Grimm why he thought Grimes wasn't fined. "Burleigh talked back, too," Grimm assured his questioners with a grin. "But he didn't use any of his $100 words."[38]

Despite the almost-daily celebrating at Clark and Addison, Kiki Cuyler was finding it hard to join the fun. Deep into August, he had accumulated just four home runs and his batting average was stalled in the .260s, an order of magnitude below his lifetime average of .335. At one stretch he went nearly a week without a hit.

The broken bone in Cuyler's foot had healed, but the cast he had worn all spring left him with a pinched nerve. He still couldn't put weight on his big toe, he said. Grimm had him back in right field, the spot Cuyler liked best, but his hitting was still subpar; he went weeks at a time without a multi-hit game. With Hornsby gone, no one was whispering any longer that Cuyler might be "soldiering," but some of the sportswriters suggested that a long rest might be the best thing for Cuyler.[39]

Unmentioned as a cause of Cuyler's woes was the Valli story, which just wouldn't go away. Judge Sbarbaro and Lucius Barnett were playing a cat-and-mouse game, and the mouse was holding his own. At the next hearing the public learned that Barnett had released some, but not all, of the purloined notes. The judge assured the citizens of Chicago that he would not let up on Lucius Barnett in an election year: "I want to keep this case under my jurisdiction to prevent embarrassment to the Cubs so that their chances of winning the pennant will not be harmed. I don't want this thing to worry Jurges."[40]

A few days later Barnett was back in Sbarbaro's court for a third hearing: Valli had apparently told authorities that the more sensational items were still missing from what Barnett had turned over. Barnett produced no more letters for the court.

It was high-stakes defiance of the system, and shrewd bargaining. Sbarbaro had a couple of choices: he could throw the book at Barnett, perhaps add charges of contempt or withholding evidence, but convicting Barnett wasn't the object: ensuring that the letters were safely out of circulation and reelecting the judge were, and there Barnett had the advantage. It would accomplish little to put Barnett away if another avalanche of bad publicity fell upon the Cubs.

Sbarbaro had seen much of more of life than most forty-two-year-olds—he had interrogated Richard Loeb and Al Capone, he had been an undertaker for mobster clients, and he had risen in the ranks of Big Bill Thompson's organization. Sbarbaro decided to fine Barnett one hundred dollars for each of the resisting arrest, assault, and disorderly conduct charges. The fines were stiff, but Barnett would face no extra jail time, a hint that Barnett might avoid doing hard time for the larceny and extortion counts. All the while, Valli looked on silently from the rear of the courtroom.

Then, without further ceremony, Sbarbaro announced that he was sending the larceny and extortion charges to a felony court for a hearing September 7. There, Lucius Barnett might encounter a judge who might be, say, a White Sox fan not facing reelection.[41]

We don't know how quickly Barnett gave in, except that it occurred sometime before the September court date. That day, felony court judge Frank Padden learned from Sergeant Capparelli that the letters had indeed been returned to Valli (who did not even appear). Judge Padden then dismissed the remaining counts against Barnett. After two months of criminalities and sensationalism, the episode had ended with a whimper.[42]

We do know that when Judge Sbarbaro sent Barnett's case to felony court, Kiki Cuyler was 7 for his last 50 at-bats. That afternoon he collected two hits to begin a hitting streak that continued into September. As the days went by his power output began to surge.

Koenig's heroic ninth-inning home run on August 20 earned him his third straight start at shortstop. He contributed no hits but a sensational play afield to Lon Warneke's 18th victory, a four-hit shutout over the Phillies. Koenig's agility afield was surprising people who remembered him as a stout-hitting but a less-than-nimble Yankee shortstop.[43]

Koenig, in fact, was a baseball Lazarus, a supposedly washed-up remnant of the 1927 Yankees, the original Murderers' Row, already considered the team by which all others were measured. Koenig improved his offensive statistics the next two years, but in 1930 his career went into a puzzling tailspin. The Yankees dealt Koenig and his declining batting average to Detroit, where he even tried pitching at one point as a possible way to stay in the big leagues. That experiment failed, and in spring 1932 the Tigers released him. The rest of the American League passed on him. Koenig, the man who had tripled and then scored on Babe Ruth's 60th home run, was out of the majors before reaching twenty-eight.[44]

Koenig's eyesight, they said, was deteriorating; not only was his batting suffering, but he had begun to miss routine balls in the field. He had tried eyeglasses, but they hadn't helped matters either. Finally, stranded on the West Coast as a prematurely retired big leaguer, he decided to undergo surgery on his sinuses. The effect on his play was almost immediate. Catching on at short for the San Francisco Missions of the Pacific Coast League, he hit near .400. His fielding improved too. By midseason the Cubs' head scout, Jack Doyle, was reporting back to Bill Veeck that the Cubs could use this fallen star. Veeck was unenthusiastic: aside from the health problems, the Cub boss might have heard about Koenig's reputation from his Yankee days as a moody, streaky player. Nonetheless, on that August 5, Veeck purchased Koenig to replace the incorrigible thirty-six-year-old utility infielder he had just cut loose.[45]

The Cubs won the final two games of the Philadelphia series, 8–4 and 5–1, with Koenig turning in more sparkling defensive plays. Both days he scored a run, but in each game it took late-inning doubles from more unexpected sources—Burleigh Grimes and Pat Malone—to nail down the wins. The record for the home stand was 7–1, thanks largely to Koenig's efforts, but for all the improvement the Cubs still resembled the scrappy, underpowered team Hornsby had guided to first place in the chilly spring weather.[46]

New York, at least in one part of the city, was undergoing its own baseball revival. Though the Yanks were in first, it wasn't Babe Ruth, Lou Gehrig, or Joe McCarthy rousing the masses. Instead, it seemed that an old Chicago hero was inspiring the borough of Brooklyn. On August 22, more than a thousand Dodger fans poured across the East River to give Hack Wilson and his mates a send-off at Grand Central Station. They cheered wildly; a band played; Wilson, O'Doul, Stripp, Cuccinello, and the rest of the squad dashed from taxis to the gates to board the Lake Shore Limited.

The Natural

Confidence was running so high that Dodger management okayed printing World Series tickets.[47]

The destination was Chicago, where the Dodgers could overtake the Cubs with a three-game sweep. The Daffiness Boys, the Flatbushers, the Gowanus Goofs, the Robins (for former manager Wilbert Robinson)—there was many an epithet for this squad to live down in its first year without either Wilbert Robinson or slugging Babe Herman available, and they had done a good job of it with a 24-7 record since late July. They sported the league's top hitter (O'Doul, at .370, working on a 20-game hitting streak); several other .300 hitters; the league's number 3 RBI man (Wilson, with 107 to Stephenson's Cub-leading 68); and a pitcher on his way to a 20-victory season (Watty Clark). These were the same Brooklyns who had been thrown at by the Cubs and had thrown back; they had spiked them and fought them; they were a team of batting champions and home run record holders, deep and confident.

August had been Wilson's best month since the heroic days of 1930. On the 2nd he had put the final touches on the Hornsby era with a few well-timed hits at Ebbets Field. Then Rogers Hornsby fell, and fell hard, exposed as just as bad a boy as Wilson had ever been. Ever since, Wilson had been demonstrating that he could still propel a team into contention with his slugging. The Brooklyn fans, ever hungry for a hero, jacked his bulk on their shoulders after one Wilsonian performance. Wilson seemed to have come back, all the way back.[48]

Stouts was keeping the same hours he ever had, though. On arriving in Chicago, he promptly headed for the old North Side locations that had been his undoing as a Cub. He was out late the night before the series opened, boasting that his drives would "tear down Wrigley's right-field wall." Wilson still managed to show up at the ballpark in time for batting practice the next day. While he waited his turn, a familiar voice piped up nearby: "Hey there, old Hans und Fritz." It was Charlie Grimm, using the pet nickname he had given Wilson in the glory days. "Don't think you'll hit one today, do you?" Jolly Cholly asked.[49]

Wilson grinned, remembering the halcyon days of the '20s. Because of Hornsby, the two had barely been able to speak to each other for the past year. Now they were friends again—or still. The other players took up the cue from the two veterans. Laughter and banter rang out throughout the rest of the pregame session. Besides, Wilson and Danny Taylor had already confirmed to reporters that any hard feelings over leaving Chicago had vanished with Hornsby's firing.[50]

Yet another bustling midweek crowd filled the stands as the Cubs met their last serious competition for the title. The old Cub nemeses—Wilson, with two key strikeouts, O'Doul, Johnny Frederick—found themselves unable to deliver in key spots. In the eighth, down three, the Bums put two on with two out, and O'Doul, Mr. Wrigley's O'Doul, smashed a long drive to deepest right center. A groan went up from the grandstands, but Moore caught up with the ball just feet short of the screen. That ended the last Dodger threat, and the Cubs hung on for a 7–4 triumph and a 4½ game lead.[51]

Now the Dodgers had to win the last two games to gain any ground before leaving town, but in the third inning of game 2 the home team scored three runs, followed quickly by six in the fourth. Cuyler had the big blow, a bases-loaded double that cleared the bases. It was all the Cubs and Guy Bush needed to win 9–3. The Cubs' lead mounted to 5½ games.[52]

The final game of the series was a mercy killing. Koenig led a nine-run outburst in the third inning with two singles; Cuyler added a two-run single. The rally went on interminably until Koenig was cut down trying to steal with two outs. Out in the stands, some of the merry Ladies Day crowd of 35,000 began chanting for World Series tickets.

The final score was 10–4. The Cubs' quick and brutal destruction of the Robins had been total: 26 runs and 38 hits in three games. The Bums made four errors in the three games; the Cubs only one, a throw that Koenig dropped in game 3 to end a club errorless streak of 45 innings. Brooklyn left town 6½ down, their pennant hopes in virtual ruins.

Hack Wilson, still perspiring and trying to make the Cubs regret him, was the Dodgers' only bright spot of the final day, with two singles and a homer. The gals took time out from their pennant celebrations to applaud him enthusiastically.[53]

Suddenly the Cubs bestrode the league. "The only way these guys can lose is by being in a train wreck," observed the Giants' Fred Lindstrom after a few days' exposure to the bedlam at Wrigley Field. With four days to go in August, the Cubs' lead swelled to seven games over the Dodgers

The Natural

and 7½ over the Pirates, nearly as large as the 10-plus games that Yankees had on Connie Mack's A's. But the Yanks were nearly 50 games above break-even, at 86-37. The A's were themselves some 30 games above .500. The Cubs, although 17-5 since Hornsby's firing, were still only 19 over.[54]

Koenig's recent success in Chicago underscored the Yankees' seemingly boundless depth and strength. His old club, unquestionably weaker at shortstop without him, was still humming to a 107-victory season, just three wins worse than the all-conquering '27 club. The 1932 Yankees sported eight future Hall of Famers and merely superb mortals at most other roster spots. Koenig was missed but not regretted in New York.

In the National League, the Yankee spare tire was a vital Cub part, an instant National League star. "We wouldn't be in first place if it wasn't for Mark," Grimm admitted after the pennant was clinched. The Yankees, too, were keeping an eye on their ex-mate's contributions. The day after Koenig's homer against the Phils, his old roommate and double-play partner, Tony Lazzeri, telegrammed his congratulations. Koenig and Lazzeri went all the way back to their boyhood days in Oakland, where they had starred as amateur teammates.[55]

The Yankees were having their last great year with Babe Ruth on the roster, and their first great year under McCarthy. McCarthy, taking over the year before, had issued the same edict he had at Catalina in 1926, except to go one step further: he simply banned card playing in the Yankee clubhouse. The second time around, we know, McCarthy never let up, not in '32 or any year thereafter. He enforced and intensified the rules for off-field dress and bearing that he had introduced in Chicago. McCarthy was making it in a real world city now, not a gawky midwestern adolescent pretender like Chicago. New Yorkers expected to be top drawer in everything. Excellence could gain their respect, but not the love they gave Ruth and later DiMaggio.

McCarthy set about supplying New York with winning that even Ruth had never dreamed of. The faster the championships came, the more remote he became. His alcoholism, already noticeable in Chicago, worsened as the years went by, and the New York press, soon deprived of Ruth's colorful headlines and relegated to the coolness of the McCarthy–DiMaggio era, retreated to a respectful distance. A sure way to end an interview with him was to ask what the real story about Hornsby was. In New York he never coached third base as he had during the halcyon days in Mr. Wrigley's ballyard, his owner cheering just feet away in the boxes, the park filled with giddy, grateful fans. With the new ball club the owner kept a regal distance, and McCarthy's championships would be won in the cold surroundings of a huge stadium.[56]

Supposedly, Ruth wanted Joe McCarthy's job, but that subplot, with Ruth taking on the Hornsby role, had hardly impeded the stately progress of the Yank flagship. The lineup had not been shut out in more than a year. The Yanks would score 1,002 runs by season's end, nearly matching St. Louis's major league record (1,004 in 1930), and four more than McCarthy's last Cub ball club (998 the same year). New York had the league's best ERA, too. Much as he had in Chicago in 1929–30, McCarthy melded the relentless offense with deep, consistent pitching—six pitchers with 121 innings or more, four of them with 16 or more wins. The club won a remarkable 62 of 77 home games and lost no more than three in a row all year.

Only once in 1932 had the Yanks faced anything like the Cubs' troubles. That came when Bill Dickey threw a blind punch at Washington's Carl Reynolds after a play at the plate in early July. The blow broke Reynolds's jaw—a few weeks later, his jaws still wired shut, he nearly choked to death—and Dickey was suspended for a month.[57]

A few weeks later, Babe Ruth pulled a hamstring going after a fly ball and had to leave the lineup for a spell. The injury set off a spate of "Is Ruth through?" commentary, and by the time the Yanks got both Dickey and Ruth back in the lineup in early August, their lead over the A's had dwindled to 7½ games. The mighty Yanks seemed unconcerned. August 4 was Dickey's first game back from the suspended list. He went 4 for 6 in a 15–3 rout of—who else?—Fonseca's White Sox, and the Yanks' onward march resumed.

Saturday the 27th's scheduled doubleheader with the New York Giants brought out an overflow crowd of 41,000. The Andy Frain ushers dragged out the ropes to handle the surplus.

Like the rest of the National League, the Giants had no book on Koenig. They knew a bit more about his rookie keystone partner, Billy Herman, who had been matching Koenig base hit for base hit on the home stand

and gobbling up balls all over his side of the diamond. Cuyler's .260-something batting average and his four-game hitting streak didn't look like much of a concern to the Giants.

Cuyler, though, opened the doubleheader with a three-run homer, just his fifth of the year, high over the right-field screen, in a 6–1 triumph. In the second game Cuyler started the scoring again with a single in the fourth on the way to a 5–0 win. The Cubs' streak had grown to nine.

The next day, rain came down steadily until just before the usual starting time of 3:00 p.m. The Cubs passed the time watching Bob Smith clog dance in the Cub clubhouse. Just before game time, the sun peeked through, and the Cubs took the field while Judge Landis and Bill Veeck watched together on the third-base side. Cuyler drove in two runs in the third with a bad-hop single, then homered in the eighth, a monstrous shot halfway across Waveland Avenue behind the left-field wall. With the bases loaded and the score tied in the ninth, his sacrifice fly to Mel Ott in right plated the game-winning run.[58]

In the series' next contest, Hubbell and Root dueled scorelessly for five innings. Then Ott homered; Cuyler answered with his third homer in three days, a three-run shot. The score was tied when the Cubs filled the bases in the ninth. There was an inevitability to the way that Hughie Critz, the New York second baseman, fumbled a ground ball. Herman scampered in from third with the winning run. The latest ninth-inning win was the least heroic of the home stand, but the Cubs' streak grew to eleven.

The next afternoon Commissioner Landis again joined Bill Veeck, this time with Bill Jr. and a high school classmate of Bill's from Hinsdale in the front-row company box. An 80 percent eclipse of the sun took place just minutes after the game began at 3:00. Players in the dugout and fans alike, unwisely, peered at the sun through bits of smoked glass. By that time the Giants had driven Warneke from the mound before he could get anybody out.

After homering on three consecutive days, Cuyler had 21 RBI and 10 runs scored for the home stand. In the bottom of the third, with dark storm clouds racing across the sky, he launched one of the mightiest drives seen since Charlie Weeghman had opened the ballpark for business. The ball crashed off the scoreboard in deepest center and bounced back into the playing field, limiting Kiki to a triple. Within seconds a deluge, complete with thunder and lightning, drove the ballplayers to cover. Cuyler had anticipated the novelist Bernard Malamud by twenty years, and Hollywood and Robert Redford by fifty, but he had only just begun.

Twenty-seven minutes later, the downpour had let up enough to resume play, and the Old Hoss banged Cuyler home with a double. The rain returned in a steady but playable drizzle in the seventh inning while the Giants opened up a 5–3 lead. In the eighth, still in the rain, the Cubs scored to close to 5–4. Bob Smith held the Giants in the top of the ninth.

The rain continued. In the bottom of the ninth the Cubs launched a barrage of singles off "Fat Freddie" Fitzsimmons, who had pitched all 8⅔ innings. One run came in, and then, with two outs and two strikes, English's single sent the potential tying run slogging through the mud to third.

Cuyler came up with two outs and two on. He singled to center, and the game was tied.

The rain had become the Giants' best hope. In slow motion, they went about a pitching change and a leisurely intentional walk to Stephenson to load the bases. Now the Giants had to work Johnny Moore in the strike zone. Moore grounded to Hughie Critz, who slipped and fell in the mud with English pounding in from third toward the plate. Critz, still seated in the mud, desperately aimed the ball to Bill Terry at first in time to catch Moore, stumbling toward the bag.

Although it was the last game of the series and the Giants had a train to catch, the home plate umpire George Magerkurth decreed extra innings in the rain. In the quagmire, the Cubs' new pitcher, Guy Bush, quickly gave up a walk, two hit batsmen, a single, and a wild pitch. Soon the Giants had themselves a handsome 9–5 lead and were on their way to a win that would make their trip back to the East Coast a pleasant one.

To that end, the first two Cub batters in the bottom of the tenth went down meekly with a ground out and a foul fly. The rain was still falling. The Giants' taxis were idling just outside the park, ready to take them to the train station and the ride home. Koenig came up. Fifteen thousand fans or so were still huddled under the canopy of the main grandstand. Their damp spirits were hardly raised, especially seeing Zack Taylor, the third-string catcher, kneeling in the on-deck circle in case Koenig got on.

The fans barely stirred when the unstoppable Koenig delivered again—this time crashing a home run to right field. It was 9–6.

After a long afternoon of substitutions, there was no one left to hit for Taylor, who had been to the plate exactly 16 times on the year. Taylor delivered an improbable single to center. Now the top of the order was coming up. As Bill Herman took his place in the batter's box, Bill Terry ran up excitedly to the plate from his first-base position. Just a minute, he screamed. Taylor shouldn't have batted—it had been the pitcher's turn to hit. Taylor is out! The game is over!

Basically, Grimm had made so many substitutions in the eighth and ninth innings that he had lost track of his roster—even though he had been safe and dry in the dugout watching the game for the past two innings. Terry had figured it out seconds too late. Under the rules, Magerkurth explained, the protest had to be made before the next hitter had received a pitch. Since Herman had already looked over the first offering, Taylor's single was in the books, as official a safety as a box score had ever recorded.

Herman singled, too, as he had been doing all week. Then English followed suit to drive in Taylor. Now everyone still huddled underneath the giant canopy of the upper deck was watching. Cuyler was up.

It was 9–7, Giants. Two on, two out, the tying runs on base. Cuyler slowly worked the count to 2-2 while the rain came down. The Giants edged up in the mud on their toes, one strike, one pitch from the ride home.

Cuyler swung at the fifth pitch and connected. It was a high, deep drive through the raindrops, soaring out to right center. Up it climbed into the bleacher seats, not far from where his earlier triple had beaten the thunderburst. But this time the ball sailed into the stands. The game was over, the series was over, and probably the pennant race.

The Cubs, paying no heed to the downpour, surged from the dugout while Herman, English, and Cuyler splashed around the bases. Pat Malone led the way, waving his cap like a cowboy; Grimm and Zack Taylor stumbled behind him joyfully, their arms wrapped around one another. President Veeck bellowed what his son took to be a rebel yell and catapulted his three-piece-clad figure over the railing; Bill Jr. and his classmate somehow got past Landis to follow him. When last glimpsed by the youngsters, the Cub president was engulfed by hundreds of cheering, drenched partisans who had deserted the haven of the grandstand and closed in on Cuyler. The ushers fought their way through the hordes to rescue the franchise player.[59]

With Cuyler safe and on his way to the clubhouse, the ushers began to clear the field, by now a mess of cleat marks and civilian shoe prints. In the Cub clubhouse, the celebration continued without letup. While the batboy hugged Grimm, the Cubs made Cuyler stand on a table and cried something like "Speech, speech." All about, clenched fists pumped up and down. Lon Warneke, already showered and in street clothes after his first-inning exit, a hand-rolled cigarette in his left hand, beamed as if he had actually won his twentieth victory.[60]

The players hooted at Cuyler's stuttering remarks, pulled him down from his perch on the table, stripped him of his uniform, and scoured him with shower brushes. Koenig received the same treatment. The happy troupe presumably dragged them off to the showers, where the ensemble sang their mindless, designated victory ditty, over and over:

> Keep on smiling
> And don't get sore.
> Keep on smiling
> And don't get sore.[61]

Three decades later, Bill Veeck Jr. still remembered the game as the greatest he had ever seen. Cuyler's dramatics were hardly on the order of Merkle missing second base (written up by Veeck Sr. himself), or Hartnett's "Homer in the Gloamin'" six years hence; it was just one grand incident closing the Cubs' 11th consecutive victory in a string that would reach 14, yet it had the feel of a pennant clincher, crystallizing Cuyler's comeback, Grimm's inspirational abilities, the definitive closure of the Hornsby era, the end of Bartnett's blackmail scheme and the bad feelings of the past two years. Said the next day's *Daily News*:

> There are no words left in our vocabulary to describe [the Cubs] any more, and [as] far as we know, there are none left in the dictionary. ... It was a five-run revolution in the tenth inning that they pulled, a wild and maniacal uprising, topped by a booming homer by the one

and only Kiki Cuyler. . . . [It] sent some 15,000 more of the populace away as candidates for that booby hatch that is going to be over-crowded if this thing doesn't let up soon.[62]

It was difficult to imagine so dramatic a home run struck again anytime soon in Wrigley Field, if ever.

18 | "Mugs . . . Chiselers"

Wilson: Everyone's getting this New York bug. It's just a rube town.
Schwartz: I was on a New York paper once—the *Times*. Jese! You might as well
work in a bank.
—Ben Hecht and Charles MacArthur, *The Front Page*

Nor will you ever see an artist call his shot before hitting one of the longest
drives ever made on the ground in a World Series game, laughing at and
mocking the enemy, two strikes gone. —Westbrook Pegler, *Chicago Tribune*,
October 2, 1932

Early in the evening of September 7, 1932, Mr. and Mrs. Babe Ruth stepped
out of an elevator and into the lobby of Detroit's Book-Cadillac Hotel,
where the New York Yankees had checked in that morning. The Ruths
checked out, then headed out the door for the train station. Soon they were
aboard the 8:30 Michigan Central for New York.[1]

An hour went by before the rest of the Yankees learned from the press
that their most famous player had been spotted skipping town on the overnight train. No one had even seen him since check-in. As far as anyone
knew, the Babe and his wife had been holed up in their suite all day, order-
ing room service meals.

A mild panic broke out. Mark Roth, the Yankees' traveling secretary,
put through a long-distance call to Joe McCarthy at his home near Buffalo,
where he was spending the day off. McCarthy was unfazed. He told Roth
that Ruth had already called him and asked permission to return to New
York. It seemed that Ruth, a notorious hypochondriac, thought he was
coming down with appendicitis, and he wanted to see the team doctor in
New York.[2]

While the Michigan Central chugged east into the sunrise, the news
that the Bambino might be ill enough to miss the World Series reached

Manhattan. Could it be another "bellyache heard round the world," like the hot dog episode that had ruined Ruth's 1925 season? Early in the afternoon, the baseball writers scurried from the Polo Grounds, where the seventh-place Giants' contest with the eighth-place Reds had been rained out, and headed for midtown to cover the Bambino's return. There they joined a crowd of 1,500 waiting when the train pulled into Grand Central Station. In the newsrooms, rewrite men chain-smoked and readied themselves for their colleagues to phone in the news from the station, dispatches that could dwarf World Series copy.[3]

Ruth stayed in his berth after the train pulled in, an hour or so late. Then he dressed and, with Mrs. Ruth at his side, made his way through the knots of newsmen and onlookers. He winced occasionally. He felt better than the night before, he said, "but still not so good. . . . I don't want no strange doctors tinkering with me," he added.

"Just one more shot, Babe. One more shot," the cameramen were begging.

"Say, this isn't making me feel any better," Ruth admonished amiably while the shutters continued to click. He waved off a wheelchair that the redcaps offered him; then he and Mrs. Ruth entered a taxi and left for their home on West 88th Street for observation by the Yankees' team physician, Dr. Edward King.[4]

The world waited impatiently for updates on the Ruth crisis. Dr. King, appraising the most valuable single body in the world, took a full hour at the apartment before he stepped out to report to the Yankee office. Ruth was running a temperature, the waiting world learned, but Dr. King had stopped short of diagnosing full-blown appendicitis. He had some other concerns that he did not share with his patient. Ruth was confined to his apartment for several days.

The weather in New York was prematurely cool, and that much chillier in Boston, where the Cubs were playing the Braves. In their long-sleeved jerseys, they no longer looked or played like the invincible conquerors of the sultry August–September home stand, with its 18 victories in 20 games capped by Cuyler's five home runs in five days. Koenig aggravated an old wrist injury after making two errors in a doubleheader loss. Warneke, who had won his 20th the last day in Chicago, struggled with a sore back;

Grimm and Cuyler both came up lame. Andy Lotshaw dragged out his lotions and sunlamps and began working on the invalids.[5]

The National League leaders dropped three of five in Boston, including one inning that Ed Burns considered their worst since Hack Wilson had lost the fly balls in Philadelphia. Then they moved on to New York, where bulletins on Ruth's current temperature overshadowed their arrival. But the New York sportswriters, remembering the Dodgers' and Giants' disastrous visits to Wrigley Field not long before, were taking notes on the subtle change in the Cubs. The bench was still boisterous, perhaps overly so, and they won two of three at Ebbets Field, losing in the ninth inning of the final game on a Johnny Frederick pinch home run. Then they went to extra innings in three of their four games at the Polo Grounds. Cuyler, back in the lineup, salvaged the finale by throwing out the winning run at the plate in the tenth and then homering in the eleventh. These were the kinds of games the Cubs had won all year, but now they were just an ordinary, scrappy National League team with slick fielders, a lively bench, and a .500 road record. The oddsmakers in New York duly revised their series odds from 5:3 to 2:1.[6]

Some of the Cubs claimed Ruth had been scouting them at the Polo Grounds, but Ruth laughed when confronted about it—after all, he had been confined to quarters for a week, holding ice bags to his side. It was true that his temperature was back to normal; he would begin working out at Yankee Stadium in a few days and rejoin the Yanks in plenty of time for the series. He had the look of a man who had been given a second chance.[7]

Ruth agreed with the sportswriting consensus: at best, the Cubs were third placers in the American League, he told Dan Daniel of the *New York World-Telegraph*. In his opinion, the Cubs would have won the pennant even with Hornsby still in charge. And he scoffed at those rumors that the Cubs had soldiered on the Rajah.[8]

Ruth was rubbing down a new bat, long and thin-handled. "Yes, I am experimenting with the Hack Wilson model. If you meet the ball squarely with it, that leather sails plenty, but if you don't get the meat of the bat on the ball the stick cracks. I'm willing to try anything," Ruth said. "You never stop learning."[9]

The Depression had unquestionably wounded Chicago with greater intensity than it had any other major metropolitan area. The city's unemployment rate, at nearly 50 percent, easily doubled the national average, estimated at 20 to 25 percent; June's Loop banking crisis, one of the most devastating in U.S. history since the beginnings of the Republic, had closed dozens of banks and financially ruined tens of thousands of citizens. The morning of the Cubs' pennant-celebrating parade, the Cook County state's attorney released a list of Samuel Insull's 205 closest insider-trading colleagues; the city's teachers had gone for weeks and months on end without paychecks. One man lost his house for lack of $341 although the city owed him $850 in salary. The problems seemed catastrophic, unending, insoluble.

Nonetheless, the afternoon of September 22 Charlie Grimm rode down LaSalle Street past more people than he had seen at one time in his life—oceans of them, roaring and cheering. Bits of ticker tape and torn-up phone books showered the limestone canyon of LaSalle Street, which in June had been filled with the panic's victims, besieging bank offices for their vanished savings. On this sunny September morning, a friendly figure leaned out from nearly every window.

Murderers' Row, Charles Lindbergh, Marshal Foch, Knute Rockne's triumphant Notre Dame teams: none of them had drawn such a crowd in Chicago—perhaps 150,000 people lining the route down Clark, west on Jackson Boulevard, and up LaSalle. Ki Cuyler's bases-loaded triple against the Pirates had clinched the pennant two days before, and the Loop was having a party. Stretching behind Grimm were eleven more touring cars filled with Cubs, followed by innumerable autos that had joined the procession back at Wrigley Field. In the big cream-colored lead Buick with Grimm were the city's official greeter, George Gaw, and Thomas Bowler, the politician who had unhesitatingly put his career on the line for Hack Wilson in July 1929. Every horn blared; when the lead car passed by Lincoln Park, the yachts in the marina added their sirens, joined by tugboats and then factory whistles all over town. The animals in the nearby zoo stirred restlessly at the disturbance.

The scene in the Loop was surreal—joy and celebration not a mile from Hooverville across the river, 150,000 delirious midday celebrants massed in the center of the staggering, bankrupt, scandal-wracked city. They stood fifteen and twenty deep throughout, the pretty faces of secretaries peered from windows, clusters of men stood silhouetted on rooftops, and daredevils crawled out on the cornices of City Hall, where a wedge of police opened a path for the ballplayers to reach the rostrum.

Mayor Anton Cermak, who had unseated Big Bill Thompson the year before, spoke words of praise for the Cubs, remembrance of William Wrigley, and a general sense of thankfulness for a pennant gained so early in his first term. Necks craned as the onlookers tried to make out the individual players, so different in appearance with their civilian suits and ties.

The ruling party's candidate for state's attorney in the November elections presented each player with a bat as he was introduced. Then the ballplayers had to speak a very few words. "Bring on those Yanks," Hartnett cried. It was the bashful English who unleashed a veritable barrage of words: "I'm plenty scared right now, but I won't be when we meet the Yankees next week," he promised. The Old Hoss set off the loudest cheer of the afternoon when he croaked, "Hello, folks," into the microphone and then stepped away.[10]

Finally the police led Veeck, twenty players, and two coaches through the crowd and back to their vehicles for the return trip to Wrigley Field. It had been an unprecedented scene: the more-glamorous, dominant group of 1929 had received no such celebration. But then few ball clubs had ever been roiled quite the way the 1932 Cubs had. Violet Valli had been seen among the well-wishers at the caravan's beginnings that morning; exactly what team could claim that distinction? Perhaps the city had abandoned Mr. Wrigley's grandiose vision of the 1920s for the reality of a harsh new decade. These Cubs, short on power, constantly embattled, the remaining stars now in their thirties, several married to Chicago women, were more like Everymen, friends and neighbors who went out each day and did the best they could—"old neighborhood guys" who weren't above picking up their own groceries. The communitarian spirit, however, could dissipate quickly when a Depression-era Chicagoan faced a tight spot. The day before the parade, twenty-four hours after Cuyler tripled to clinch the pennant, Grimm's men met in the clubhouse and planned how to divide the World Series money: full shares to themselves; full shares to the two coaches; half shares to Koenig and the players' two faithful road aides,

Bob Lewis and Andy Lotshaw; and quarter shares to Frank Demaree and another rookie, Leroy Herrmann. Rogers Hornsby, a member of the club for its first ninety-nine games, was ignored, as was Vince Barton.[11]

Charlie had recused himself from the meeting because he was the manager; he left Woody English, the captain, in charge. It was the players' money to do with as they saw fit, he said. Some guessed that the winning shares might be worth nine thousand dollars per player—much greater than the size of the tax bill that Hornsby had received earlier in the summer. A deputy collector of revenue had formally filed the complaint in U.S. district court in St. Louis the week before.[12]

In '29—Grimm would have been presiding then, as captain—each of the Cubs had chipped in five hundred apiece for Mr. Wrigley's other employees. Back then the world was full of money. Five hundred dollars was something you could make in a day on the stock market. Even in 1930, with the Depression closing in, the players had remembered Hal Carlson's widow with a full share of both their second place and City Series money— more than a thousand dollars.[13]

As the sounds of celebration subsided in the Loop, people around the country were questioning whether the Cubs had dealt fairly with Hornsby, the man who had constructed the team over a two-year period, still a preeminent figure in the game, and a man in desperate financial trouble. In St. Louis, a National League manager told a newsman, "No team could have any luck after doing what the Cubs did. . . . I hope the Yankees win four straight." The next day the Yankees voted twenty-six full and thirteen partial shares, including the clubhouse boy and several players who hadn't worn a Yankee uniform in months.[14]

Once Hornsby had been the bad guy who had betrayed McCarthy; now McCarthy's ball club championed his cause. In Missouri Hornsby announced he would appeal to Landis for a cut of the series share. The youngsters he developed, Hornsby said, ignoring Mark Koenig, had made the difference for the Cubs. "I don't even know what the rules on the subject say—I did not even read them," he told reporters. But Hornsby thought he was more deserving than some of those who were cut in for full shares. "If the judge views the situation from my standpoint, I will be happy. If he doesn't, well, that's all right too."[15]

Charlie's fellows seemed dry-eyed about Hornsby's predicament. A few of them, after all, were still being repaid from Hornsby's garnished paychecks, and they didn't believe for a minute that anything but Veeck's intervention had rescued them. One source said that Hornsby's name had simply been ignored; another said the veterans had pushed the rookies into cutting Hornsby out. Herman and Jurges had supposedly lobbied to keep Koenig's share at one-half.[16]

The Yankees heard the stories. Ruth was back with the team now, although he had looked out of shape in his first few games. But the last day of the season he rocketed a ball into the seats.

The Cubs' season ended Sunday, September 25, three days after the parade, a 5–3 Cincinnati victory. Since the close of the decisive home stand in early September, they had played twenty-four games, winning just twelve. The press took notice. Although most commentators gave the Cubs an edge over the Yankees in pitching and defense, the team had hit a composite 69 home runs in 1932 (a decline from 171 in 1930) and slugged .392 (compared to 1930's .481); the 1932 Yankees figures were 160 homers and a .454 slugging percentage. Overall, the Bombers had won 107 games, 17 better than the Cubs, and they had won 62 of 77 home games, compared to the Cubs' 53 at Wrigley Field, even with the fabulous 18-2 home stand of August and early September.

What was more, Ruth was back in the lineup. Even with his layoff, and four months shy of his thirty-eighth birthday, he had finished second in the league in home runs, fifth in batting average, and first in on-base percentage. He and Lou Gehrig alone had outhomered the Cubs by six.

With August's momentum clearly history, the Cubs' remaining hopes centered on their formidable pitching staff. "Cubs Hold Pitching Edge in World Series," the *Tribune* pre-series examination of the situation began hopefully. "There is an old belief, and it is a good one when it works, that pitching decides a short baseball series." The *New York Times* didn't disagree, noting: "Stellar Pitching Staff Gives Cubs Edge on Defense over the Yankees." Any Cub advantage, though, was problematic: it was no secret that Ruth and Gehrig batted left-handed, and the Cubs had just one southpaw pitcher, the thirty-six-year-old Jakie May.[17]

The team would board the train for New York Tuesday morning, but in the meantime Stevie would need to cook a few meals. He put on his suit and hat and went to market, trudging home with two overflowing bags of groceries.

Manhattan was a gray and forbidding isle, closed in by fog and rain. Its mighty civilization appeared indifferent to the coming showdown or the puny challengers who had stepped ashore. Grimm's National Leaguers wandered almost unnoticed among the potted plants of the Commodore Hotel lobby and the pulsating neon of Broadway. There they took in dinner and entertainment, untroubled by the boastings of the few New Yorkers who recognized them. Grimm had a date with an old admirer of his, the man who had seen his potential and kept him on as Cub captain when most of the world considered him nothing more than a zany banjo player. He took a taxi to a local radio station, where, inside the studio, Joe McCarthy greeted him, and then, as arranged, the friendly rivals went on the air to discuss the World Series. Afterward pupil and mentor would have clapped each other on the back and headed into the fog-laden Manhattan night. The scene may have spoiled the picture of McCarthy plotting vengeance against the Cubs, but the implacable McCarthy would still insist on taking the championship, heedless of his old friends in Chicago.[18]

It was still misting Wednesday morning, drizzly topcoat weather, when the ballplayers finally arrived in Yankee Stadium, bedecked in red, white, and blue for the first time since 1928. The white-haired Judge Landis, a battered hat in his hands, decreed ten minutes before noon that the show should go on despite the rain and a cavernously empty stadium. More rain arrived by the 1:30 starting time, but twenty minutes late, Grimm and McCarthy shook hands, the band played the new national anthem, and Red Ruffing threw the first pitch to Billy Herman.[19]

Herman singled on Ruffing's fourth pitch. Before the inning was out the Cubs had a 2–0 lead, and overconfidence. With Lotshaw in full cry, they began riding their old coach Jimmy Burke. Grimm mocked Red Ruffing after striking out. Ruth was incredulous to hear the Cubs' trainer—a busher—carrying on as if he were a real major leaguer. The Bam took up the Yankees' answer, calling hoarsely to the upholstered visitors bench about the half share of Mark Koenig.[20]

Soon the sun began breaking through and Gehrig launched a home run when Bush got a fastball up on a 2-2 count. The Yankees had the lead,

3–2, and the Cubs looked suddenly spent as they tried to whip the new ball around the infield. Bush collapsed in a welter of bases on balls. One Yankee after another paraded across the plate before a subdued crowd. The score finally lurched to 12–6, New York. The New Yorkers filed out as if they had just watched the Yanks crush some tail-enders in midseason.[21]

The skies remained clear the next day for Warneke versus Lefty Gomez, a duel of youngsters who had been adolescents the last time their teams had reached the World Series. For the second straight day the Cub starter overthrew his fastball, filled the bases with walks, gave up scratch hits when an out was needed. As the Yankees once again forged ahead, the dugouts rang with insults. Lotshaw led the Cubs' counterattack against Ruth. The Bambino ignored him. Instead, he called out to an old teammate who was out of the series after reinjuring his wrist in the first game. "So they're going to give you a half share, are they, Mark? Well, you better collect that five bucks right now."[22]

Warneke regained his control after his early wild spell, but it was too late. Gomez stayed ahead with a lethal strikeout pitch, and the Yanks had another victory, 5–2, although outhitting the Cubs only 10–9. Ruth, who had contributed only rhetoric, two singles, and some shoddy fielding in two days, was the loudest person in the stadium. "Sure, I'm on 'em. I hope we beat 'em four straight," he boomed. "They gave Hornsby and Koenig a sour deal in their player cut. They're chiselers and I tell 'em so.

"Haw, hah. You ought to see Grimm burn when I round first and holler, 'Big-hearted Charlie.' Imagine those guys moaning about the small crowds."[23]

Then it was off to the train station for a journey past the inland seas. By midmorning, an hour apart, the teams' trains roared by the fiery furnaces of the Calumet, past the bedlam of the stockyards, the hopelessness of the Black Belt, the squalor of the Hoovervilles in the vacant lots that dotted the landscape, once the home of the Cubs, and on to the LaSalle Street station in the midst of the Loop.

In spite of the pall of Depression, the teams entered an entirely different city and atmosphere from the blasé metropolis the two clubs had just left. The Cubs arrived first to find ten thousand fans packed in the head house to welcome their wounded heroes. Grimm, smiling, sporting a white fedora with a black band, made his way with his wife through the well-wishers. His players followed, their faces lighting up at the sound of the cheers. Cuyler yelled to the crowd, "We'll get 'em, boys. It's not over yet."[24]

Many in the throng, sensing otherwise, stayed to pay homage to the Yankees. Outside, the Loop streets filled with the curious, eager to catch a lunchtime glimpse of Ruth and the rest of what they knew to be the world's best ball club.

The crowds returned to their stores and their offices, if they still had them to return to. But another group of visitors from New York was coming into town, and that evening they would be greeted by twice the onlookers times ten, a welcome that would dwarf Charlie Grimm's victory parade a week before, the greatest crowd in the history of the city and no doubt the greatest gathering anywhere in that year of Depression and presidential campaigning.[25]

While the baseball Yankees settled into the Edgewater Beach Hotel on the north shore, the new visitors, a man named Roosevelt and his party, arrived at the Congress Hotel overlooking the sweep of Grant Park. The streets once more filled with cheering onlookers. This Roosevelt, the favored candidate for President of the United States, drove slowly through a human ocean in the same touring car that had borne Charlie Grimm the week before. A thousand torchlights waved before the candidate, exhorting him to help the city where half the people had no work. Prostrate Chicago wanted its baseball champion, but it wanted its life and its work back even more desperately, and so its cries and its cheers wafted into the autumn night and across the great glassy surface of the lake.[26]

Whether or not Babe Ruth attended the parade for his fellow New Yorker, the Bambino found time after the Yanks arrived to visit a hospital bed, where there lay a young man without sight, his eyeballs blown away by a gangland bomb, the eighty-fourth of the year in Chicago, a dollar's worth of dynamite with a price beyond any measure. The youth was a Cub fan, and he, like the other boys of '29 and '32, still believed that the New Yorkers could be turned back, that Chicago could be first, that the hard times would end, and that he would see again. But he was wrong; none of it would be. The Babe, who within hours would crush his favorites, lingered in the room as he traded boasts with a Chicagoan once more, ever so gently this time, telling the only truth he could tell the young man,

"Mugs . . . Chiselers" 367

who, full of the brashness of the young city, told the world's greatest ballplayer that he must lose that day. Babe, who knew the true answer and more, gave the lad an autographed baseball and bade him the best. He threatened no home runs, though he was confident that they would come very soon.[27]

Bill Veeck had doubled the size of the bleachers, just as in 1929, by extending them beyond the park walls and over the city streets. While the teams warmed up these enlarged bleachers filled up in a rush, the green seats of the grandstands remained mostly empty. The Babe muffed the first batting-practice ball hit to him in left field, and the bleachers, always the first to fill, erupted in lemon throwing, an activity dormant since Hornsby's departure two months earlier. Ruth, laughing and roaring at the new challenge from the upstart city, threw the fruit back, and although the boos turned to cheers, the bleacher dwellers and Ruth tossed the lemons this way, then that, for half an hour.[28]

A warm west wind, the old friend of Wilson and Hornsby and Cuyler, blew lakeward beneath a cloudless sky. Ruth, who three years before had wished aloud for the chance to bat at Wrigley Field, lifted his practice pitches into the bleachers again and again, to the awe of the bleacherites and the more genteel grandstand and box seat folk, now straggling in in their more fashionable way. One surreal clout caught the wind and sailed over the regular bleachers and the temporary bleachers that stood taller and behind them, across Sheffield, and on toward the El track that ran through the next block. Between swings the Yankees' Hercules became an orator, a vengeful god casting judgment on the Cubs huddled in their dugout. "Cheap chiselers!" he cried again and again, and he added other language so vivid that the newsreel people had to shut down their equipment.[29]

His turn at bat complete, the prophet of doom stalked before the Cub dugout: "Hey, mugs! . . . You mugs are not going to see the Yankee Stadium any more this year. . . . This World Series is going to be over Sunday afternoon. Four straight." He turned to the customers in the third-base box seats and asked, "Did you hear what I told them over there? I told them they ain't going back to New York. We lick 'em here, today and tomorrow."[30]

It was a bright, breezy day, contrasting with the gloomy starts in New York. Acres of red, white, and blue bunting greeted the arrivals outside the park, and inside it draped from the upper deck. Four hundred of Andy Frain's men bustled about in their blue-and-gold regalia, and the Board of Trade Legion Band marched in, horns blaring, through an outfield gate. The grandstand began to fill. Some thirty minutes before game time, Governor Roosevelt, his own growing popularity confirmed by the huge demonstration the night before, made his way to box 76, midway between the screen and the first-base dugout, with Mayor Cermak, Mrs. Roosevelt, and her son James. McCarthy and Grimm were brought before the politicians. McCarthy wore a relaxed smile; the Joker Wild showed the photographers a different side. Looking ill at ease, he was the first to slip away, muttering, "Sorry, I got to work now."[31]

A gigantic American flag was paraded around the field by the assembled rosters of both clubs and then somehow mounted on the centerfield flagpole. After it rose to a level with the crowded apartment rooftops across Waveland and Sheffield, the band played the national anthem. Governor Roosevelt threw out the first ball, and play began. A din started up as soon as Ruth came to the plate in the first inning. It took only two pitches, two balls, for Root to lose control, and a third for Ruth to initiate Wrigley Field with a drive that arced far into the temporary bleachers behind right-center field, high above Sheffield Avenue and outside the outer wall of the ballpark. The air rang with both praise and boos as Ruth circled the bases. The Yankees were ahead 3–0 before making an out.

Both teams homered, ran the basepaths wildly, and surrendered bases and runs with maladroit defense. Cuyler leaped and stabbed Ruth's long drive at the fence; Gehrig homered; Cuyler answered in his turn at bat. The left-field bleacherites roared when Ruth missed a shoe-top catch; after the batter pulled into second with a double, the Babe turned and doffed his cap. Soon Ruth's gift developed into a run that tied the game at 4–4.

It was rollicking baseball as the Cubs had played it during the stretch drive. The crowd believed in their team of destiny again, the remnant of Murderers' Row that had met every test. When Ruth came up with one out in the top of the fifth, a roar exploded from the grandstand, rocking the temporary bleachers and the huge Old Glory waving majestically toward the lake. A single lemon bounded toward the plate. From the steps of the dugout, a trio of Cub furies—Bush, Lotshaw, and Grimes—leveled all the invective that seasoned big leaguers could muster. They respected nothing of their foe: his heritage, his achievements, his appearance. But Ruth, only moments before the pot-bellied blunderer of the outfield, met their challenge defiantly. More intent on the dugout than the problem of Root's pitching, Ruth watched Root throw a strike, a ball, a ball, and another strike; he was busy taking up the Cubs' dare, mocking them and holding up his fingers to remind them how many strikes he had left. The park was a bedlam. After the second strike, Bush crawled out from the dugout onto the field in his frenzy to bait the legendary creature before him, who seemed to reply with some gesture toward Bush, or Root, or a much farther point of the park.[32]

In the low post-equinox sun, the shadow of the grandstand had advanced past the third-base line and home plate. Ruth stood in shadow while Root delivered from full sunlight. The governor of New York watched from box 76 with his wife and son and the mayor as Ruth pointed—some thought at Bush and the Cubs, others at the bleachers. Root's fifth pitch bored in from sun to shade, a fastball on the outside part of the plate, and Ruth swung for the first and last time in his at-bat.

The ball soared for some distant spot to the right of the scoreboard, high over the temporary stands, crashing into a zone that some later claimed no Wrigley Field batsman had ever reached. Boys who had perched in a tree chased the ball while Ruth gamboled joyfully around first base. Every few feet he punched the air with the joyous air of a conqueror. Ruth jeered the crowd, jeered the Cub infielders as he passed them, jeered the dugout as he rounded third base. In box 76, the governor of New York threw his head back and laughed his soon-to-be-famous laugh. The crowd, abruptly about-facing, cheered wildly in tribute to the mastery it had just witnessed.[33]

Ruth's bat lay on the ground where he had tossed it. The batboy retrieved it and returned with Ruth to the dugout while the din continued—a yellow model, definitely not the black Hack Wilson model Ruth had recently considered. Then Gehrig stepped in and drove Root's next pitch down the right-field line and into the temporary stands above the park's exterior wall for a two-run Yankee lead, 6–4.[34]

The miracle rally that had always materialized in August tried to make its appearance for the Cubs, but the talisman of Koenig, who had reinjured his wrist in New York, was absent. Malone relieved Root effectively, and the Cubs put multiple base runners on several more times. But by the time Hartnett led off the ninth scattered booing, the result of his misadventures in the field at the top of the inning, broke out—probably the first booing aimed at a Cub since Hornsby's final appearance in July. Hartnett hushed the malcontents with a majestic home run far above Ruth's head in left field, but after English rolled weakly to Gehrig with two outs in the ninth, the final score read 7–5, and the series numbers an insurmountable 3-0.[35]

The crowd filed out underneath the grandstand as Grimm and his men trudged up the ramp to the clubhouse. The booing was finished; the fans swarmed close to their beaten heroes, touching, clasping hands, slapping backs. Cuyler and Stephenson choked out thanks to them; Grimm cried bitter tears. "Can you beat that?" he asked when he finally reached the clubhouse. "Don't it make you sick that we can't even win one game for a bunch of folks like that? They ought to throw us in the lake, and just look at them."[36]

In the visitors' locker room Ruth's voice rose in guttural joy. "Did Mr. Ruth chase those Cubs back into the dugout?" he crowed. Not hearing an answer, he boomed, "I'll say Mr. Ruth did." Nearby, Bill "Bojangles" Robinson, a vaudevillian of fame, sprang atop a trunk and danced while the players clapped and cheered. Bojangles had a huge bet down on the Yankees, and there wasn't much doubt left that he was going to collect. McCarthy gave an unusually long address to his men: "Get your bags packed tomorrow, fellows. I think we'll be leaving right after the game."[37]

The record books say that the Yanks and the Cubs played another 54 outs in the 1932 World Series. Bush, finger bleeding, had to leave the game in the first inning; Warneke's arm began to throb, and he left in the fourth. Like an army in collapse, the Cubs sent out the old, the young, the halt—Grimes, May, Tinning—to meet the enemy. In midrout a blimp appeared overhead without warning, and later a swarm of what were described as flying ants descended on the grandstands. Old Jakie May struck Ruth out twice, and the Cubs tied the score at 5–5. But after May loaded the bases in the seventh, three Yankee singles brought in four runs. With three on and two out in the bottom of the Cubs' eighth, Herb Pennock struck Rollie Hemsley out with a slow, grand sweep of a curve. In the ninth inning the Yankees thrashed Burleigh Grimes, last winter's barter for Wilson, until they had accumulated the largest run total in series history. The booing returned, stronger than ever. "Bring Hornsby back," came the despairing cry from the stands. The score was 13–5.[38]

Bill Herman led off the Cub ninth with a single. The Yankees ignored him, but not the fans, who jeered while he took second, then third, and scored on English's ground out. The fans jeered again. Then Cuyler struck out. Stephenson lifted a fly ball to Ben Chapman in right field, who took it in just ahead of several boys who had just hiked themselves over the screen.[39]

The excited Yankees dashed to their locker room. One wild yell soared over the bedlam—that of the "divine comedian" Ruth, ecstatic in spite of a swollen forearm where Bush had hit him with a pitch. "Boy, what a victory. My hat's off to you, Mac . . . but while I seem to have the floor, how about us fixing up the clubhouse boy? In the series I've been with this team before we always each gave him two bucks. I don't see why we shouldn't do likewise." Gomez forthwith pulled out his wallet and two dollars, and the clubhouse attendant was on his way to an extra five hundred in our inflated dollars.

Soon the divine comedian was in the showers, where he led an ensemble in a ragged "Sidewalks of New York": "East side, west side, all around the town." Then the Yanks' red, white, and blue trunks were carried to the station, where the traveling secretary had sent the remainder of their luggage that morning. As McCarthy had told them the night before, they wouldn't be going back to the Edgewater Beach.[40]

In the Cubs' clubhouse the only noise was Burleigh Grimes bellowing at some of the baseball writers. No one paid him much mind; Ol' Stubblebeard, the mastermind of the voting on Hornsby's and Koenig's shares, had been of little help most of the season, and not at all in the series. Charlie Grimm tossed his glove down and said, "Well, that's that. Give credit where credit is due. They've got more power than I ever saw before in one place. You fellows gave me all you had, you're damn right you did and you know it."[41]

He pointed to his ribs, sticking through his shirt. "I've lost 22 pounds since taking the manager's job, and if anyone thinks it's been easy they can guess again." He yelled over to some of the longer faces in the room. "We won together and we lost together. It's not a disgrace to lose to a ballclub like that." Then he turned back to the reporters. "Now for my fishing rod," he told them. "Back to the farm and nothing to do for weeks but fish and fish."[42]

The other Cubs readied themselves for their own postseason journeys. Pat Malone and Zack Taylor would go hunting together. Riggs Stephenson was going to hunt squirrels back home in Alabama. Lon Warneke loaded his coupe for the return drive to the Arkansas farm, where his dad had forgone the series to spend the week rounding up the family's three hundred head of cattle. The elder Warneke allowed that the Warnekes might be "stuck," prices being as low as they were, but at least Lon would be back home, where he could live all winter for the cost of a month up North. Charlie Root was going to take his family on a tour of the South Seas, just about as far from Babe Ruth as it was possible to get.[43]

The Yankees, still singing "East side, west side," boarded a bus and headed for the station, surrounded by a motorcycle-police squad with their sirens screaming. The special steamed from Union Station and, gaining speed, streaked across the pancake-flat farmland of northern Indiana and Ohio, while the sounds of revelry and celebration floated into the rural night. In the morning the train roared down the Hudson Valley into the city. A crowd of satisfied New Yorkers was at Grand Central Station to greet their conquering champions, but only two players appeared on the deck. Everyone else, including Ruth and Gehrig, had slipped off the train at earlier stops.[44]

Once back at his apartment, the heart of the world's champions learned how the Yankees planned to reward him. Heroics or not, said the morning paper, the Yankees planned to cut his pay again. The great Bam would be thirty-eight in February; he and his manager were not close; and the word around town was that that September episode was no mere attack of appendicitis: the Babe had been diagnosed with a bad heart. None of that diminished Ruth's spirits. "Boy, I wish I'd known that," he cried upon learning from a reporter about Frank Demaree's quarter share. "I'd have *really* let 'em have it."[45]

Ruth and McCarthy had at least managed to take a world championship. Rogers Hornsby had no championship ring, job, or even a loser's share of the series money, and within days he needed to make a nine hundred dollar interest payment on his farm mortgage. After spending the series pretending that he wasn't paying attention, he confided that he knew just what the Cubs had done wrong: they'd pitched the Yanks' big guns inside, especially Gehrig, who had led both teams with a .529 batting average. Hornsby didn't explain how he came by this information from several hundred miles away, but Hornsby had every incentive to savor the mauling as it unfolded near the shores of Lake Michigan, probably tuning in to the CBS broadcast (Bob Elson and Pat Flanagan with the play-by-play) rather than NBC's (an odd coupling of Graham McNamee and Hal Totten).[46]

There was still a chance that Landis would force the Cubs to give Hornsby some series money. After all, in 1928 Landis had ordered the White Sox to give Art Shires a full share of the City Series money, even though Shires was an August call-up. The losers' shares for the '32 Series, according to the Cubs' twenty-four-share logic, would come to nearly $4,250. (A full Yanks' share was $5,010.) A full share for Hornsby would lower each Cub's take by $180—enough perhaps make his interest payment and help with his back taxes. Landis, dogged by a heavy cold, put off making a decision for more than a week. On October 14, nearly three weeks after Hornsby's appeal, the lord most high handed down his decision: the Cubs owed Hornsby none of the series pot. Landis cited a specific rule governing players who had left the club before September 1.[47]

Rogers Hornsby finished his thirtieth lap around the track at the downtown St. Louis YMCA. He was twenty laps a day better than before his workouts had begun a couple of weeks before, and he didn't have to walk every third or fourth time around the track. His color was back, and he was breathing easily and deeply again, a well-conditioned athlete, if one in the autumn of his career.[48]

Hornsby planned to keep this up, along with medicine ball, weights, and a rowing machine, every morning at eleven o'clock. Even though his contract with the Chicago Cubs had only eleven more days to run, through December 31, he was going to be a big leaguer again in 1933; Branch Rickey of the Cardinals had already signed him to a contract. If his legs were good, he might even get the chance to start at second base for Rickey's ball club, with Frankie Frisch moving over to third to make room for him. No one

"Mugs . . . Chiselers"

on the Cardinals seemed concerned that the Rajah would undermine Gabby Street, the manager, or squander his salary on parimutuel bets.

The morning of December 20 Hornsby had an errand to run before his gymnasium session. He drove out to the courthouse in Clayton, the St. Louis County seat. It was a typical December day in the lower Midwest, raining and chilly. At the courthouse there was a small group of men in suits—lawyers, businessmen, a few journalists.

Everyone gathered in the courtroom, where the business of the day got under way. An agent of the Mississippi Valley Trust Co., who said he represented Colonel J. A. Ware of California, put in a bid of fifteen thousand dollars for Mr. and Mrs. Hornsby's farm on Bridgeton Station Road. The Hornsbys owed nine hundred dollars in interest as well as an unspecified amount in county taxes. That had been only days after Judge Landis had rejected Hornsby's bid for a share of the series money.

The Hornsbys had already resigned themselves to the blow—Mrs. Hornsby called the foreclosure "just another hard knock"; the farmhouse had been too big to keep up, anyway. The gavel came down, and one more reminder of the decade that had roared so loud changed hands—eighty-six acres, the fourteen-room house, the outbuildings, the Hornsbys' down payment, four years of payments on the mortgage, the little business selling sod to Mr. Wrigley. Hornsby showed up at the Y by 11:00, ready to continue his comeback. "No, I ain't going into any of my troubles," Hornsby said, but before beginning his workout, he ran through his speech about yes-men and baseball politics and doing things his way, the same points he had made many times before.[49]

Forty-two hundred dollars might have covered the shortfall nicely, $4,200 that Grimm and Judge Landis had done nothing to obtain for Hornsby, but Hornsby said nothing about it. He plunged into his workout routine.

Come spring Rogers Hornsby would have a job, a place on a major league roster, one of 368 in the world, and in December 1932 finding any work had never been more difficult. For once Hornsby had beaten the odds. In a few days he and his family would celebrate Christmas at their city apartment, just as the Grimms would a few miles away in Normandy, and all the rest of the Cubs who had kept their jobs.

And that was cause enough for cheer.

NOTES

I. THE CAPITAL OF BASEBALL

1. 33,000: *Tribune* and *Herald and Examiner,* both September 14, 1931. In Boston, the Boston Braves' 1931 attendance was 515,005 (about 6,700 per game); see Thorn and Palmer, *Total Baseball,* 145. Radio stations: five is the number most frequently given for stations broadcasting Cub games in the era; see *Tribune,* August 31, 1930. But in two successive summers the *Daily Times* listed six stations broadcasting Cub games: July 30, 1931 (WBBM, WCFL, WGN, WIBO, WJJD, WMAQ), and August 15, 1932 (same lineup with the exception of WJKS taking the place of WJJD). *Sporting News,* August 4, 1932, listed only three of those stations in an article analyzing the most popular broadcasters but added WENR as a fifth station. Whatever the exact number, it was difficult to hear anything but baseball on a home game day; see "The Times Talkies," *Daily Times,* June 30, 1931, for the opinions the paper solicited from several Chicago residents: Helene Roberts, Harvey Johnson, Coral Sandage, Y. P. Harnden, Anne MacIntyre, and F. A. Farrell.

2. Parlors: Schmidt, *The Mayor Who Cleaned Up Chicago,* 86. Tongues: Zorbaugh, *The Gold Coast and the Slum,* 45.

3. "House That Ruth Built": the Cubs outdrew the Yankees each year from 1928 through 1932; see Thorn and Palmer, *Total Baseball,* 144–45. Single-season attendance mark: The Cubs' 1929 attendance of 1.485 million was not exceeded until the totals recorded in 1946 by the New York Yankees (2.265 million) and Detroit Tigers (1.722 million), both of the American League.

4. Storm the gates: Ed Froelich interview in Golenbock, *Wrigleyville,* 203; Veeck, *Veeck—as in Wreck,* 27; *Saturday Evening Post,* September 13, 1930, 25.

5. Kingpin: several reminiscences mention Al Capone as a Wrigley Field regular. His main gangland rivals, however, were headquartered much more conveniently on the North Side; of them, only "Schemer" Drucci seems to have been a documented visitor (to a Bears game; see chapter 3). Bergreen, *Capone,* 227 (based on an interview with an anonymous source); see also Veeck, *Veeck—as in Wreck,* 35–36; Grimm, *Jolly Cholly's Story,* 48–49; *Tribune,* August 2, 1988 (reminiscence of Billy Herman: "Capone was a big

377

baseball fan. He'd walk into the ballpark like the president walking in today, with bodyguards all around him"). Woody English, in Golenbock, *Wrigleyville*, 219–20, remembers that "one day [Capone] came to see us play," but his details involve Gabby Hartnett being photographed shaking hands with Capone, publication in the newspapers, and Judge Kenesaw Mountain Landis's reaction, which all correspond to an incident before the Cubs-Sox benefit game at Comiskey Park, September 9, 1931.

6. Three or four days: *Time*, September 19, 1932, 29. "Bill": Zimmerman, *William Wrigley, Jr.*, 280, 282. Monitored: Ed Froelich interview in Golenbock, *Wrigleyville*, 202. Pride of the major leagues: *Herald and Examiner*, June 3, 1932 ("[The Cubs] have been written up as the 'Beau Brummels' of the league."). Leaping: for an example on the road, see *Tribune*, July 30, 1928. Up close: *Tribune*, and "So They Tell Me," *Herald and Examiner*, both January 27, 1932. Cigars: Jack Hendrickson, untitled article, *Sun-Times Midwest Magazine*, March 6, 1977, in Chicago Historical Museum Archives, "Biography, Wrigley, William Jr." file. Island visits: *Tribune*, July 25, 1929 ("William Wrigley . . . has returned from his annual summer jaunt to Catalina Island"); *Daily News*, July 25, 1929; *New York Times*, September 22, 1929; Linton, "A History of Chicago Radio," 178 (1927 stay).

7. Payroll: Seymour, *Baseball: The Golden Age*, 346. According to Creamer, *Babe*, 351, Lou Gehrig made only $8,000 in 1930, when Ruth earned $80,000. In 1931 Rogers Hornsby reportedly earned $40,000 and Hack Wilson, $33,000 (*Daily Times*, February 1, 1932; *Tribune*, February 2, 1932).

8. Megaphone: *Daily News*, May 26, 1926; Casey, "Casey at the Bat, Writes of Players, Fans and Thrills," *Daily News*, October 1, 1932 ("large green megaphone"); *Tribune*, October 23, 1974. Pieper continued as the Cubs' announcer until his death in 1974. A loudspeaker system was installed in Wrigley Field in 1934 (*Tribune*, April 8, 1934). Assistant: *New York Times*, June 6, 1925. Foul line: *Tribune*, February 18, 1971. See also Golenbock, *Wrigleyville*, 183. Numbered jerseys: *Tribune*, July 1, 1932.

9. Swaggering: *Herald and Examiner*, September 14, 1931.

10. Jeering: *Tribune*, September 14, 1931; *Herald and Examiner*, September 14, 1931; *Sporting News*, September 24, 1931; *Daily News*, May 31, 1932; *Saturday Evening Post*, September 11, 1943. See also Additional Source Comments, "Jeering."

11. "Wintry-souled": Honig, *Baseball America*, 140. Never overswung: *Tribune*, May 1, 1930; *New York Times*, May 14, 1931; Hornsby and Surface, *My War with Baseball*, 79.

12. Diverse: Gems, *Windy City Wars*, 17. Twenty-five percent: "City Gains 700,000 Population," *Daily Times*, May 9, 1930. "Largest Lithuanian":

Spinney, *City of Big Shoulders*, 141. Knife and fork: Schoenberg, *Mr. Capone*, 149. Bathing: Ehrgott, "Chicago in the '20s," 5.

13. Chicagoans: see "Rajah's Greeting from the Bleachers" (photo and caption), *Daily Times*, September 26, 1930 ("The most rabid Cub fans hold down the plain plank seats in the bleachers every time the North Side team plays at home."); Kelly, "No Covered Yawns in This Series Crowd," *Herald and Examiner*, October 2, 1932 ("the cross-section of Chicago that included everyone from the social luminary to the politician to the truck driver"). See also *New York Times*, June 7, 1925 ("[B]ig hand from bleacherites [at Cubs' Park]. Tony folks in shaded seats may root for a ballplayer when they see one."), and Seymour, *Baseball: The Golden Age*, 5. Doublemint twins: *Tribune*, April 25, 1924. 50 cents: *Tribune*, August 4, 1925. Major league bleacher prices were set at 50 cents beginning with the 1920 season. See *Tribune*, December 9 and 22, 1919; *New York Times*, December 9, 1919, and February 12, 1920. Streetcar: Whittingham, *Chicago Bears*, 12–13, and Ehrgott, "Chicago in the '20s," 2. See also Heuer, "Neighbors," 32.

14. First forty years: Fans from the west and south sides spoke in "What Do You Like about the Cubs?" *Tribune*, August 11, 1929; "Cubs, Cards Are Nice Boys, Lady Fans Say," *Tribune*, August 30, 1930; "Cubs Owe Their Success to Good Subs, Fan Says," *Tribune*, August 30, 1930; "5 out of 6 Favor Grimm as Hornsby Successor," *Daily News*, August 3, 1932. But Riess, *Touching Base*, 115–16 n.38, cites a *Sporting News* report of September 13, 1917, that "West Side fans" (probably meaning fans of the immediate West Side, where the Cubs had played) no longer followed the team after its move to the North Side. Lardner: *Tribune*, April 23, 1914. A North Side resident of the 1920s recalled that a south wind could bring the stockyard smell to the North Side (Ehrgott, "Chicago in the '20s," 3).

15. "City of the Future": "Chicago: City of Superlatives," *New York Times*, February 23, 1930. "Chicagoans grow weary": Sherwood Anderson, *Horses and Men* (1923), qtd. in C. Andrews, *Chicago in Story*, 202. The *New York Times* echoed these observations on February 23, 1930.

16. Bleacher betting: Cataneo, *Hornsby Hit One*, 69. See also Burt Shotton's remarks, AP in *Tribune*, April 15, 1932; Seymour, *Baseball: The Golden Age*, 388–89. For details of professional sports and ethnic groups in Chicago at the time, see Gems, *Windy City Wars*, passim.; Lindberg, *Chicago by Gaslight*, 208.

17. Bookmaking: Stuart, *20 Incredible Years*, 425, cited a 1935 estimate that five thousand handbooks were operating within the city limits.

18. Volstead Act: Gems, *Windy City Wars*, 141; Gottfried, *Boss Cermak of Chicago*, 102. Speakeasies: Gottfried, *Boss Cermak of Chicago*, 139 ("15,000 to 20,000

retail outlets [for breweries]" circa 1924); Kenney, *Chicago Jazz*, 153 ("16,000 beer flats" in the late 1920s [quoting *Variety* magazine]). Tended bar: Gleason, "Legends with Pat Pieper."

19. Spokesman: "Old Gold Bats 1000% as Hornsby Takes the Blindfold Cigarette Test" (advertisement), *Tribune*, August 22, 1928. Welshed: Doutrich, *Cardinals and the Yankees*, 16.

20. Working-class idol: UP in *Indianapolis Times*, June 29, 1931; Gems, *Windy City Wars*, 178.

21. Hard-drinking: two eyewitness accounts were given by George Brace (interview) and Pat Pieper (in Gleason, "Legends with Pat Pieper").

22. Met the ball: *Tribune*, July 11, 1928; *St. Louis Post-Dispatch*, October 14, 1929; Hornsby and Surface, *My War with Baseball*, 79 ("I just tried to meet the ball, and didn't try to get fancy."). Grand slam: *Tribune*, September 14, 1931; "Herman Fills Holes for Cubs at Second," *Sporting News*, September 24, 1931; Hornsby and Surface, *My War with Baseball*, 92. Hornsby placed the incident in 1932 and named "Frank House"—evidently Fred Frankhouse—as the pitcher who gave up the homer, but Frankhouse appeared in the second game of the doubleheader in September 1931. The other details of the anecdote parallel the events of September 13, 1932.

23. Hornsby faction: *Tribune*, September 14, 1931; *Daily Times*, September 14, 1931. Straw hats: *Tribune*, *Herald and Examiner*; "That Famous Homer" (photo), *Daily Times*, September 14, 1931.

24. Handshakes: *Tribune*, September 14, 1931.

25. "Smartest": *Daily Times*, August 3, 1932.

26. Excesses: see chapter 10.

27. Restructuring: *Sporting News*, January 21, 1932.

28. Polo Grounds: *Daily News*, September 8, 1931; UP in *Indianapolis Times*, September 7, 1931; "Wilson and Malone Break Their Slates," *Sporting News*, September 17, 1931. "In advance": *Daily Times*, August 31, 1931. "A sport at night": *Tribune*, September 1, 1931.

29. "Through": *Tribune*, September 5, 1931. See also "Cubs Eliminate Chief Nemesis in Obtaining Burleigh Grimes, *Sporting News*, December 17, 1931.

30. "Hello, Pat": *Evening American*, September 8, 1931 (by 1932 the paper's masthead read simply *"Chicago American,"* but for much of the period covered in this work, the paper styled itself the *"Chicago Evening American"*). For another report on the Malone-Johnson fracas, see also United Press dispatch (George Kirksey byline), dateline September 9, 1931, in HOF files. "Everything": *Daily News*, August 19, 1938.

31. "Mr. Veeck": *Herald and Examiner*, September 7, 1931. Most popular player: apparently that very much held true despite Wilson's poor season. *Herald and*

Examiner, August 31, 1931 ("Hack Wilson is still the big favorite with the North Side addicts. The boys and girls haven't forgotten that he gave them the major portion of their thrills in 1930"). See also photo of Wilson and youthful admirers in September 1931, in Lane, "Crash of a Popular Idol," 388.

32. Detectives: UP in *Indianapolis Times,* September 7, 1931; *Herald and Examiner,* September 7, 1931. "Liar": *Daily News,* August 19, 1938.

33. Well-wishers: *Herald and Examiner* and *Daily Times,* September 8, 1931.

34. Ward: *Tribune,* August 14, 1931. Out of work: Mayer and Wade, *Chicago,* 358–60. Parks, Michigan Avenue bridge: Mayer and Wade, *Chicago,* 358. Shantytowns: Spinney, *City of Big Shoulders,* 192. Condemned buildings: Farr, *Chicago,* 375.

35. Politicians: *Herald and Examiner,* September 10, 1931. Landis: "Baseball Czar and Granddaughter See Game," *Tribune,* September 10, 1931. Wilson and wife: *Herald and Examiner,* September 10, 1931 (photo, "Smiling Through"). Cheers: *Herald and Examiner,* September 10, 1931. Lemons and tomatoes: *Herald and Examiner,* September 10, 1931; "In the Wake of the News," *Tribune,* September 10, 1931. Booed: *Tribune,* September 10, 1931.

36. Walked over: *Herald and Examiner,* September 10, 1931. According to an Internet item posted in September 2011 ("80 Years Later, Infamous Capone Photo Debunked," http://www.free-press-release.com, accessed April 7, 2012), the Hartnett-Capone pose was initiated by a third party, a young Chicago newsman named Frank Zak. The basis for the claim is a "lost interview" with Zak, although neither the date of the interview nor the interviewer is identified. It's not clear exactly what this elaborate account, if true, debunks, since newspapers frequently ran posed photos in this era, but it would at least confirm Capone's reputation as a sports buff. Capone: untitled photo caption in *Daily Times,* September 10, 1931. McGurn: "Gang Chief and His Son among Those Who See Charity Game" (photo), *Tribune,* September 10, 1931. Several sources mention that Capone used a stand-in for his son.

37. Banish him: that winter, Hartnett was reportedly concerned that he would be traded ("Blasts from the Windy City," *Sporting News,* December 17, 1931).

38. Nation's eye: *Sporting News,* June 2, 1932 (photo, "The Cause of the 'Gag' Rule"—"printed in many papers throughout the country"); Spink, *Judge Landis,* 201 (the photo ran "in newspapers from coast-to-coast"). Several different shots ran in the various Chicago newspapers.

39. "His place of business": Mead, *Two Spectacular Seasons,* 74. Another oft-repeated version is along the lines of "If you don't want me talking to the Big Fella, you tell him, Judge." Player-fan interaction: *Sporting News,* February 11, 1932 (rule adopted by NL), and May 26, 1932 (rule rescinded by NL but not AL). The National League's decision to overturn the rule came shortly after

Gabby Street of the St. Louis Cardinals was fined five dollars for speaking to an uncle he hadn't seen since childhood (*Tribune*, April 29, 1932), or a "judge" (*New York Times*, April 28, 1932). Both accounts agree that the veteran umpire Beans Reardon reported Street's infraction to the league office. According to the *Sporting News* of May 26, 1932, the AL had the rule on the books before the National League. The *Daily Times* of August 13, 1931, had depicted the umpire Roy Van Graflan enforcing the rule in the Comiskey Park grandstand.

40. In between: *Tribune*, September 12, 1931. Buick: Boone and Grunska, *Hack*, 100.

41. Little gym: "Wilson, Buffeted by Cubs and Cards, Striving Hard for Comeback," *Sporting News*, January 21, 1932.

42. Double figures: the National League's home run leaders in Wilson's peak years, 1926 to 1930, were Wilson, 177, Jim Bottomley, 113, Chick Hafey, 104, and Rogers Hornsby, 99. Draw: *Daily Times*, March 20, 1931 ("Hack is almost a big a gate attraction in strange places now as Babe Ruth was a few years ago."); *Sporting News*, August 25, 1932, 5. Most-booed: see, for instance, *Tribune*, September 14, 1928, and July 22, August 26, and October 5, 1929; *Daily News*, July 22, 1929; *Daily Times*, May 28, September 2, 1930; *New York Times*, July 21, 1929, and July 23, 1930; and "The Babe Ruth of the National League," *Baseball Magazine* (February 1931), 425. Neck reddening: "Speaking of Sports," *Tribune*, April 18, 1928; "Scribbled by Scribes," *Sporting News*, February 11, 1932. Bat slamming: *Sporting News*, January 21, 1932. Lemon shower: "Scribbled by Scribes," *Sporting News*, February 11, 1932. Police escort: *Tribune*, July 26, 1929; *Daily Times*, September 12, 1929.

43. Sought after: Grimm, *Jolly Cholly's Story*, 60.

44. Fade: Farr, *Chicago*, 381. "Second City": Liebling, *Chicago*, 29, 44, 66.

2. SAMPLES OF BASEBALL

1. Illegitimate: Boone and Grunska, *Hack*, 5. The material is based on interviews the authors, two educators from the Chicago area, held in Martinsburg with several of Wilson's friends and acquaintances. During Wilson's playing days, Wilson or his ghostwriter mentioned that his father was sixty-eight years old at that time (1931) and living with one of his sisters, but made no mention of whether his parents had ever married (*Daily Times*, January 28, 1931). The article named two older "sisters," Sadie and Emmie—most likely half-sisters if Wilson's mother, Jennie Caldwell, was sixteen at the time of his birth, as Boone and Grunska state. Partin, who visited Martinsburg in the 1980s, corroborates Jennie's age without mentioning the legitimacy question ("Lewis Robert 'Hack' Wilson," 2). Orphaned son: Partin, "Lewis Robert 'Hack' Wilson," 2, and Boone and Grunska, *Hack*, 4–9. 200 pounds: although

often listed at 190 or 195 pounds, Wilson himself gave his year-round weight as 210 (*Daily Times*, February 23, 1931).

2. "I'll be back": *Daily Times*, February 7, 1931. "The best outfielder": *Sporting News*, June 24, 1978.

3. Ill: *Daily News*, May 8, 1926; but see "Corcoran's Close Ups," *Evening American*, May 24, 1926, suggesting that McGraw considered Wilson susceptible to fan abuse. "Tris Speaker": *Herald and Examiner*, October 9, 1925. In 1931 Wilson recalled how McGraw had more than once praised his outfielding skills to the press (*Daily Times*, February 9, 1931). More than fifty years later, Al Lopez, another famed manager and Wilson's teammate in 1932–33), praised Wilson's outfielding skills (*Philadelphia Inquirer*, March 11, 1979). That said, Wilson's fielding percentage was one of the lowest among full-time National League outfielders of the era.

4. Sized up: Wilson indicated that the pair's "paths first crossed" at Louisville in 1925 (*Daily Times*, February 7, 1931).

5. October 7: *Tribune*, October 8, 1925.

6. Pitching giants: See one contemporary sportswriter, Ed Wray, who listed the "big four pitchers of all time—Cy Young, Christy Mathewson, Walter Johnson, and Alex himself" (*St. Louis Post-Dispatch*, August 20, 1929).

7. A thousand dollars: The 1925 winner's payoff was $561 (*Tribune*, October 14, 1925), on some seventy thousand total attendance. In 1926 the winning Sox team's shares were nine hundred dollars each (*Tribune*, October 4, 1926). That amount was probably equaled in 1928, the best-attended City Series, with more than 168,000 attendance through the first six games (*Tribune*, October 9, 1928). Incentive: *Tribune*, August 28, 1934, in Lindberg, *White Sox Encyclopedia*, 472.

8. Schorling's Park: Lowry, *Green Cathedrals*, 51.

9. Foster: Shatzkin, *The Ballplayers*, 352–53; Light, *Cultural Encyclopedia of Baseball*, 275. Schorling: Tygiel, *Past Time*, 130.

10. Special market: *Chicago Defender*, September 17, 1927. Neighborhood population: Spinney, *City of Big Shoulders*, 167–68.

11. 12,000: *Chicago Defender*, June 5, 1926. Earle Mack's ball clubs, night games, Ladies Nights: *Chicago Defender*, various issues, September and October 1930. Lending players: *Chicago Defender*, December 13, 1930.

12. Buckner: Lanctot, *Fair Dealing*, 184; *Chicago Defender*, July 9, 1932 (photo), March 4, 1933, and November 26, 1938. Dozens of workers: *Chicago Defender*, October 31, 1931. Yancey: Keepnews, notes for *Classic Jazz Piano*, 3. Editorial: *Chicago Defender*, October 31, 1931.

13. Boycotting: see "Geiger Says" in *Evening American*, October 1, 1932, and "Talking It Over" in *Tribune*, August 22, 1932; a discussion of American

League politics is found in Stout and Johnson, *Red Sox Century*, 151–52. Pacific Coast League shortstop: *Pittsburgh Press*, August 8, 1927. $125,000: *Tribune*, February 28, 1928.

14. Favorite saying: Zimmerman, *William Wrigley, Jr.*, 282. See also *Herald and Examiner*, January 27, 1932: "Be enthusiastic, keep your mind occupied, and work hard." Empires: Zimmerman, *William Wrigley, Jr.*, passim. Residences: "Wrigley Plants in Many Lands to Close Today," *Tribune*, January 28, 1932; *Sporting News*, February 4, 1932. Duplex: Mayer and Wade, *Chicago*, 322.

15. Playing: Crowell, "The Wonder of Wrigley," 195. "How was your game?": P. K. Wrigley, interview, 112. "The hell with it": *Sun-Times Midwest Magazine*, March 6, 1977.

16. Sixteenth of seventeen: dateline March 26, 1964, in *Sun-Times* clipping file. Usher characteristics: *Tribune*, March 28, 1945; *Daily News*, April 21, 1941; dateline June 16, 1946, in *Sun-Times* clipping file, May 2001; Brace, interview; and Ed Froelich, interview in Golenbock, *Wrigleyville*, 202.

17. "Mr. Wrigley isn't in": *Tribune*, March 28, 1945. "My name's Frain": *Daily News*, April 21, 1941. "Those ushers of yours": dateline December 28, 1937, in *Sun-Times* clipping file. See also Froelich interview in Golenbock, *Wrigleyville*, 202–3.

18. "Dirty shirts": [*Daily News*?], mid-1930s, in *Sun-Times* clipping files. Fisticuffs: Barnett and Cook, "King of the Ushers," 47; and Froelich, interview in Golenbock, *Wrigleyville*, 203. Loan: Barnett and Cook, "King of the Ushers," 48; *Tribune*, March 28, 1945; *Daily News*, March 25, 1964; Froelich, interview in Golenbock, *Wrigleyville*, 203. Height, school: dateline June 16, 1946, in *Sun-Times* clipping file; *Tribune*, January 11, 1948; Ernest Tucker, untitled article, *Chicago American Magazine*, February 14, 1960. Derby, conventions: Barnett and Cook, "King of the Ushers," 43, 47; "Want Andy Frain? Look for a Crowd," *Herald*-Examiner (previously *Herald and Examiner*), ca. 1942, in *Sun-Times* clipping file. Military discipline: dateline June 16, 1946, in *Sun-Times* clipping file; Paul Galloway, "The Frain Gang—Our Man in the 'House of Usher,'" *Sun-Times* May 7, 1978.

19. Nominations: "Refused Nomination That Made Coolidge President," *Herald and Examiner*, January 27, 1932; "Wm. Wrigley Dies in Arizona," *Tribune*, January 27, 1932; "Life of Wrigley," chapter 4; *Los Angeles Examiner*, February 17, 1932. Hospitality: *Tribune*, February 21, 22, 23, and 24, 1930; and Zimmerman, *William Wrigley, Jr.*, 200. See "Coolidge and Wrigley Vacationing," *Herald and Examiner*, January 27, 1932, for a photo of Mr. and Mrs. Wrigley, Mr. and Mrs. Coolidge, and Mr. and Mrs. George H. Reynolds at the Wrigley estate in Catalina.

20. "Faith": Zimmerman, *William Wrigley, Jr.*, 154. According to "Chewing-Gum

King's Rise a Modern Business Romance," *New York Times,* March 1, 1925,
Philip Wrigley supervised the construction of the building. Floodlights:
Evening American, May 22, 1926.

21. The city held: Drury, *Chicago in Seven Days,* 62, 116, 104. Zoo: *Tribune,*
    October 4, 1923. Traffic: Zorbaugh, *The Gold Coast and the Slum,* 43. State
    and Madison: *Tribune,* October 15, 1926.

22. Saarinen: Stamper, *North Michigan Avenue,* 30.

23. Flags unfurled: "672,048 Census Gain Gives Chicago 3,373,753,'" *New York
    Times,* June 12, 1930.

24. "Too much of a sport": Wrigley and Crissey, "Owning a Big League Team,"
    24. Greatest baseball team: see Rogers Hornsby's remarks in *Baseball
    Magazine,* October 1932, 488. Control: "Young Wrigley Slated to Head Big
    Gum Concern," *Tribune,* January 22, 1925. Dissenting shareholder: *New York
    Times,* June 7, 1925. Lasker was said to advocate stricter training methods, a
    probable euphemism for discipline. It may be coincidental that WMAQ's radio
    coverage began just days before the sale. Any dissension between Lasker and
    Wrigley seems to have dissipated by September 1926, when the two took the
    train to Philadelphia to see the first Dempsey-Tunney fight *(Tribune,*
    September 24, 1926).

25. Collateral: *Herald and Examiner,* January 27, 1932, mentions "an air of
    mystery about the transaction," with Wrigley, J. Ogden Armour, A. D.
    Lasker, and "several others" involved (Weeghman unmentioned).
    Contemporary newspaper reports and later reminiscences provide incomplete
    and often contradictory accounts (*Tribune,* January 16, 1916, and Vaughan,
    Tribune, January 27, 1932); Zimmerman, *William Wrigley, Jr.,* 209, 210, 213;
    Cruikshank and Schultz, *Man Who Sold America,* 158–60; Gunther, 118.
    Warren Brown (*Chicago Cubs,* 78–82) provides the most complete version,
    with Wrigley gradually buying out Weeghman and then the other partners.
    Exactly how much stock Lasker owned at any one point, and when Wrigley
    bought him out, is unclear. By June 1925, though, Wrigley held undisputed
    control of the franchise ("Wrigley Gets Cubs Stock," *New York Times,* June 7,
    1925). Whatever the exact arrangements, from 1918 on Wrigley's name was
    most frequently mentioned as the owner of the franchise.

26. Frequently and unsuccessfully: Otto, "Wrigley, Always a Fan, Spent Millions
    to Win," *Herald and Examiner,* January 27, 1932. Enhancements: the park
    underwent significant changes over the winter of 1923, boosting capacity
    from around 17,000 to more than 31,000, which included 5,000 bleacher seats
    and 9,300 box/reserved seats (*Tribune,* February 4, April 5 and 17, 1923).
    Removing 1,500 seats in the left-field bleachers left capacity at approximately
    28,000 (*Tribune,* August 4, 1925, and April 24, 1926); double-decking the

western grandstand increased capacity to 35,000 (*Tribune*, April 14, 1927); and completing the upper deck increased capacity, at least temporarily, to 45,000 (*Tribune*, April 18, 1928). In addition, the ladies' restrooms were said to be the first in the big leagues (*Daily News*, January 31, 1927), and the glass-enclosed press box was touted as the best in baseball when it opened (*Tribune*, April 22, 1928). "In All the World": Cubs' and Sox's advertisements, various editions of the *Tribune*, mid-1920s.

27. Pickpockets: *Tribune*, March 28, 1945. Uncouth, wandered: Riess, *Touching Base*, 59. Pop bottles: Wrigley, "Owning a Big League Team," 25; *Tribune*, September 10 and 13, 1927. The pop bottle insurrection of September 1927 may have been one catalyst in the decision to deploy the Andy Frain ushers the next year (see chapter 4). Epileptic: Shatzkin, *Ballplayers*, 9; Levy, *Joe McCarthy*, 108; and Sher, "Ups and Downs of Old Pete," *Sport*, April 1950, in Gallen, *Baseball Chronicles*, 143.

28. Toppled: *Tribune*, May 29, 1926; *Daily News*, May 28, 1926.

29. Left field bleachers: *Tribune*, August 4, 1925. Chilled spectators: *Tribune*, October 5, 1925; *Herald and Examiner*, October 5, 1925. Team-record: Jack Clements's seventeen home runs in 1893 had been the previous single season high by a catcher (see "Progression of Season Catcher Homerun Record [Playing Catcher Position Only]," at Encyclopedia of Baseball Catchers website, http://bb_catchers.tripod.com/catchers/hr_record_sea.htm, accessed June 8, 2012).

30. Kaney: *Tribune*, April 26, 1924; "Today's Radio Programs," *Tribune*, October 1–6, 1924.

31. KDKA: "Year In Review: 1921 National League." Cincinnati: "1924—Gene Mittendorf broadcast the Opening Day game (Apr. 15) over WMH," per fact sheet from Cincinnati Reds media file, 1989, via John Kiesewetter, *Cincinnati Enquirer* columnist, June 16, 1999. Many websites list Mittendorf and the year 1924 without specifying Opening Day. World Series: "Radio Broadcasting Started at KDKA Four Years Ago Today," *New York Times*, November 2, 1924 ("In 1921 radio was used to broadcast results of the world series of baseball games from the original WJZ station at Newark, N.J."); Archer, *History of Radio to 1926*, 280, 321–22. See also appendixes, "World Series." Press box: Ryan was stationed in "the press coop" (*Tribune*, October 12, 1925). Information on exactly where the early baseball announcers stationed themselves at Cubs Park is scarce; Kaney (October 1924) and Ryan (April 1925) definitely used the Comiskey Park and Cubs Park rooftops; by late May 1926, the WMAQ team is documented as occupying the press box at Cubs Park (*Daily News*, May 26, 1926). "Asking too much": Brown, *Chicago Cubs*, 108–9.

32. Ryan and technician: *Tribune*, April 14, 1925. Hofman: *Daily News*, April 13

and 14, 1925; Linton, "A History of Chicago Radio," 117. Baseball histories commonly mention 1924 as the year of WMAQ's first baseball broadcast. Efforts to locate evidence of 1924 baseball broadcasts by WMAQ proved fruitless. By June 1924, WMAQ was reporting baseball scores every fifteen minutes, starting at 4:00 p.m. ("Today's Radio Programs," *Tribune*). Assist: *Tribune*, September 24, 1908.

33. Northwestern University: Dierks, "Ryan at the Mike," G10. Kentucky Derby and Indianapolis 500: Ryan was the Derby's first broadcaster (*Tribune*, May 10, 1925), but Sen Kaney announced the first radio broadcast of the 500 (*Tribune*, May 25, 1924). See also *Tribune*, October 8, 1978. "After midnight": *Tribune*, September 15, 1929.

34. Grange, "gee whiz": Fink, WGN, 18–19.

35. Phone lines: Fink, WGN *Radio Timeline*, 18–19. Scopes trial: *Tribune*, coverage beginning July 5, 1925. Mencken: Rodgers, *Mencken*, 283.

36. WGN signal: Fink's WGN: *A Pictorial History* is silent on the size and scope of the audience for the Scopes broadcast, as are several more recent broadcast histories; and the *Tribune* itself the summer of the trial. (The paper carried standard news accounts filed by reporters, with Ryan devoting his regular Sunday column to the subject ["Inside the Loud Speaker," July 19 and 26, and August 2, 1925].) A clue may lie in the *Tribune*'s statement (October 6, 1925) that Ryan's 1925 World Series broadcasts would be carried on "a chain of coast to coast stations": i.e., WGN would link up with the developing AT&T/WEAF network. That network, the predecessor of NBC, had already linked twenty or more permanent and temporary members at one time for special events, including a "permanent network" for the 1924 presidential campaign, in which WGN had participated (Archer, *History of Radio to 1926*, 345). If WGN used such a network for the Scopes trial, it was not mentioned in the *Tribune* or in 1961's WGN: *A Pictorial History*.

37. 1925 World Series: *Tribune*, October 6–14, 1925. According to these editions of the *Tribune*, Ryan (odd) and McNamee (even) had alternated their duties game by game. However, the *Tribune* did not specify an announcer the morning of game 7, which would have been Ryan's turn. Patterson, *Golden Voices of Baseball*, 29, states that "McNamee sat in the rain describing the Pirates' 9–7 win over Walter Johnson and the Senators at soggy Forbes Field. Rain was pouring down his neck while he covered his microphone with his jacket."

38. "Stick to music": Patterson, *Golden Voices of Baseball*, 29. Open letter: *Tribune*, October 2, 1927.

39. Oldfield, Rickenbacker: *Tribune*, May 31, 1926. De Valera: *Tribune*, April 18, 1927. The Irish leader was then "between jobs." Ederle: *Tribune*, February 13, 1927. Swanson: *Tribune*, April 21 and June 21, 1925.

40. WGN mail: *Tribune,* April 18, 1925. For the second broadcast, Saturday, April 18, WGN mentioned adding a second microphone to pick up crowd noise.

41. Horodesky, etc.: *Daily News,* April 18, 1925. A Google search on Ms. Horodesky, with or without her middle name, conducted October 23, 2011, produced no results, nor did her name appear in any *New York Times Index* of that era. Recitals, etc.: *Tribune,* "Today's Radio Programs," various editions, 1924 to 1926.

42. Last game: *Daily News,* April 21, 1925.

43. "Frequency partners": Linton, "A History of Chicago Radio," 107.

44. Pratt and Daw: Linton, "A History of Chicago Radio," 107.

45. Petite: "Judith Waller—First Lady of Radio," 1. "We don't know either": Williamson, "Judith Carey Waller," 111. This article draws heavily on an interview Waller gave in 1951. The assertion in the article that "WMAQ broadcast the first baseball play-by-play from a home ball park" (112) is only partially correct, since WGN and WMAQ both made their first regular-season broadcasts from the 1925 home opener (*Tribune* and *Daily News,* both April 14, 1925). In addition, WGN had broadcast the postseason 1924 City Series from both Cubs and Comiskey parks.

46. Filled in: "Judith Waller—First Lady of Radio." This web page draws on the April 1947 edition of *Chainbreak,* a WMAQ newsletter. Sir Gilbert Parker: "Frightened Stars, Silent Nights," 1. Lawson forbade: "Frightened Stars, Silent Nights," 1.

47. Mother wrote: Williamson, "Judith Carey Waller," 112. Several hundred thousand sets: In January 1924, a *Chicago Tribune* survey estimated that the Chicago area contained more than a hundred thousand radio receivers ("WGN Radio Timeline"). If radio ownership increased tenfold nationally from 1922 to 1925 (DeFleur, *Theories of Mass Communication,* 20), a doubling or tripling of the *Tribune*'s figure by the time Waller and Wrigley met before the 1925 season is conceivable.

48. Gained entrance: Williamson, "Judith Carey Waller," 112, and *Daily News,* September 17, 1932.

49. Cigar: see an account of Wrigley's in-office press conference the next year, *Herald and Examiner,* October 13, 1925 ("between cigar puffs . . . flicking the ashes from the cigar"). Thunderstorm: see, for instance, estimates of the losses from a heavy rain in *Tribune,* July 4, 1932.

50. "Intrigued"; "you know nothing": Williamson, "Judith Carey Waller," 112.

51. Edifice in Los Angeles: Gershman, *Diamonds,* 185.

52. Billboards, gum samples: Wharton, "Case of the Moving Jaws," December 1947, 61.

53. Russell Pratt and "Hal": *Daily News,* June 1 and June 19, 1925. Rewrite man:

Battistella, first page of photocopy. uc football: *Daily News,* June 1, 1925, and Caton, "Radio Station wmaq," 163. Phobias: Ham, *Broadcasting Baseball,* 52. This information seems consistent with the *Daily News* announcements: Hofman's announced appearance at the home opener (April 14, 1925), the subsequent absence of wmaq baseball broadcasts for the next week, despite a pledge on April 14 that Hofman would be reporting from the park "each afternoon this week"; and the belated announcement, with no mention of Hofman, of another broadcast on the last day of the Cubs' home stand (*Daily News,* April 20, 1925).

54. Guest shots: *Daily News,* June 15, 16, and 19, 1925. For the latter, Richard Taber of *Is Zat So?,* a comedy playing at the Adelphi, appeared with Hal Totten. Display advertising: *Tribune,* June 5 and 12, 1925. "Escort": e.g., *Tribune,* August 20, 1926. The *New York Times,* August 4, 1929, said that "20 years earlier" male escorts were mandatory at a major league ladies days in general.

55. "Announcer": in early August, "an announcer," unidentified, delivered the broadcast; on September 3, the *Daily News* specified Russell Pratt as the broadcaster for that day's game, but the next day, the broadcaster was simply "a wmaq announcer," followed on September 5 with the bare announcement that the game would be reported, with no announcer mentioned (*Daily News,* August 1, and September 4 and 5, 1925). Pratt was in Chicago September 5 for his regular Saturday night musical program.

56. "Dean": *Daily News,* October 7, 1929. Note that a month earlier, wgn had dubbed its own Quin Ryan as "dean of baseball announcers" (wgn display ad, *Tribune,* September 1, 1929).

57. Comiskey declined: *Daily News,* June 24, 1925 ("wmaq had sought permission to broadcast the Sox games, but was refused"). The White Sox were probably adhering to the current American League policy. Scores: "In the Air Today," various editions, *Chicago Daily News,* June–September 1925. It can be assumed that such duties were assigned to Totten, he being the only *Daily News* staffer mentioned as a sportscaster. (Regular updates on scores were broadcast as early as 1922 by kyw in Chicago: Sterling and Kittross, *Stay Tuned,* 77.)

58. uc football: *Daily News,* June 1, 1925, and Caton, "Radio Station wmaq," 163. Baritone: Battistella, untitled, 1.

59. Farmer: *Daily News,* September 17, 1932. Battery-powered: see Sterling and Kittross, *Stay Tuned,* 81.

60. Haircuts: *Tribune,* September 23, 1927. Lunch counter: *Tribune,* September 14, 1929.

61. "They keep coming": *Tribune,* April 14, 1927. Yankee attendance: Thorn and Palmer, *Total Baseball,* 144–45.

62. Gosden and Correll: *Tribune,* April 25, 1926 (Sam 'n' Henry to appear on three Cubs' broadcasts in May), and July 4, 1926; Ryan mentioned his on-the-air interaction with the comedy act in his weekly column, *Tribune,* June 6, 1926. Bill Hay: "Radio Programs for Today," *Tribune,* various editions, August and September 1926.

63. White Sox: *Tribune,* various editions from the summers of 1926 and 1927. Five stations: *Daily News,* various editions from the summers of 1928 and 1929; apparently, 1929 was the year the number first reached five. At least six stations might carry the Cubs' games at any one time: see, for instance, the *Daily Times,* July 30, 1931, and August 15, 1932, listing six stations. In all, at least nine stations were listed in the *Daily News* and the *Daily Times* at one time or another: KYW, WBBM, WCFL, WENR, WGN, WIBO, WJJD, WJKS, and WMAQ. (After January 1, 1928, when WGN began selling its airtime, the *Tribune* no longer systematically listed programs of stations that competed with WGN, its affiliate.) See also Chase, *Sound and Fury,* 179–81.

64. "Cola Coki": "Baseball Broadcasts Are No Longer Banned," *New York Times,* September 14, 1930.

65. Less "inspirational," etc.: Crepeau, *Baseball,* 185. Other cities: *Tribune,* August 31, 1930. Conventional consensus: Seymour, *Baseball: The Golden Age,* 345–46, and "Support of Chicago May Save the Radio," *Sporting News,* November 17, 1932.

66. "Ladies' Day Today": *Tribune,* June 12, 1925 (advertisement).

67. Before the turn of the century: Seymour, *Baseball: The Early Years,* 328. See also Riess, *Touching Base,* 28, regarding the National League's 1909 discontinuance and eventual reinstatement of the practice during World War I. See also the *Tribune,* April 26, 1918: "Ladies Day will be observed at the Cubs park every Friday from now on unless some of the National League magnates succeed again in stopping it." For several years: e.g., *Tribune,* April 26, 1918, several dates in 1922 and 1923, and April 25, 1924; *Daily News,* April 14, 1925. A few thousand women: a 1922 Ladies Day attracted a total crowd of about ten thousand (*Tribune,* July 8, 1922). In 1925 the *Daily News* mentioned that "sometimes 5,000 women have assembled at the park on Friday" (April 14, 1925). In July 1926 the ballpark held "about 6,000 paying customers and almost as many women and kids who spent nothing more than the afternoon" (Tribune, July 10, 1926). For announcements of the White Sox's ladies days, see advertisements under the "Amusements" section banner of the *Tribune,* most Fridays in throughout the 1920s.

68. 17,000: *Herald and Examiner,* February 23, 1929. 25,000 women: *Tribune,* August 7, 1929. 240,000: *Herald and Examiner,* January 27, 1932. ("Last Summer, on twelve Ladies Days, it was estimated that 240,000 were Friday

guests." The paper estimated that the Ladies Day average for the two previous seasons was around 20,000 per game.)

69. Fill the streets: *Saturday Evening Post*, September 13, 1930, 25, and *Daily News*, September 20, 1932. Mrs. Lumpp: *Tribune*, August 30, 1930.

70. Foul ball: *Tribune*, August 4, 1931 (photo). Parasols: *Herald and Examiner*, September 3, 1928. Hand clapping: "Ladies' Days at Ball Games Found Successful in West," *New York Times*, August 4, 1929, section 8. Savvy: *Daily News*, January 31, 1927; *Tribune*, August 17, 1930, and August 27, 1932. Veeck estimated: *Daily News*, January 31, 1927, and September 20, 1932.

71. Besieged: Grosklos, telephone interview, corroborated by *Tribune*, August 27, 1932—"[T]here are still too many [ladies day guests] who stand under the clubhouse runway and gape at the perspiring athletes as they rush to and from their baths."

72. Restrooms: *Daily News*, January 31, 1927. "Samples of baseball": Heuer, "Neighbors," 26. Upgrade: *Tribune*, August 20, 1930.

73. Oak Street Beach: *Daily News*, June 6, 1925 (photo).

74. Comiskey Park boxes: *Tribune*, October 14, 1925.

75. Twenty summers: *Tribune*, September 16, 1929. McCarthy evidently wintered in his hometown of Germantown, Pennsylvania, until he joined Buffalo of the International League in 1914 (Levy, *Joe McCarthy*, 26, 33, 37, 40). Busher: *Tribune*, May 19, 1926; Brown, *Chicago Cubs*, 94; and Seymour, *Baseball: The Golden Age*, 449.

76. $12,000: *Tribune*, October 13, 1925. See also *Daily News*, October 10, 1925. Rumors regarding McCarthy's status had circulated throughout summer 1925. Well established: *Tribune*, October 10, 1925.

77. Unspecified "stockholders" (Wrigley?) may have forced Veeck's hand in the Maranville hiring. See AP in *Indianapolis Star*, July 8, 1925. Cabdriver: *Tribune*, July 11, 1925.

78. Unwritten rules: Levy, 100–101.

79. Telegram: *Tribune*, October 13, 1925.

80. "Shoot a million": *Herald and Examiner*, October 13, 1925. "Get in the lineup ourselves": *Daily News*, October 13, 1925.

81. Valuable information: O'Neal, *American Association*, 55.

82. Lewis Wilson: *Tribune*, October 10, 1925.

3. THE AGE OF WILSON BEGINS

1. "It's nothing": *Tribune*, May 9, 1926.

2. "Take him out!": *Tribune*, May 3, 1926.

3. Mobbed: see *Tribune*, April 26, and May 12, 1926. Waved: Boone and Grunska, *Hack*, 61. It's possible, of course, that the radio coverage had caused the

increased interest and attendance, but the fact that the first recorded incident occurred on April 26, i.e., before WMAQ resumed Cub broadcasting, indicates the contrary. Tended bar: "Legends with Pat Pieper," *Sun-Times*, July 23, 1972.

4. Teammates: *Tribune*, May 9, 1926. Swing around: *Tribune*, May 10, 1926.

5. Alexander Day: *Tribune* and *Herald and Examiner*, both May 23, 1926. Lincoln: *Daily News*, May 22, 1926.

6. Thunderbolt: *Evening American* and *Tribune*, both May 24, 1926.

7. Speakeasies: Stuart (*20 Incredible Years*, 190) estimates that Chicago's total number of alcohol-related "retail outlets," speakeasies included, ranged from fifteen to twenty thousand. From that number must be subtracted six thousand soda parlors serving beer (Schmidt, *Mayor Who Cleaned Up Chicago*, 86). Enforce the law: Schmidt, *Mayor Who Cleaned Up Chicago*, 139.

8. Thompson machine gun: *Literary Digest*, May 15, 1926, 12; Lewis and Smith, *Chicago*, 452. Murder rate: Lewis and Smith, *Chicago*, 467. Lewis and Smith refer to "shoulder guns" that could fire 100 rounds per minute.

9. McSwiggin: *Tribune*, April 28, 1926.

10. Modifying or dropping: Lewis and Smith, *Chicago*, 467. Crowe: "Ask Congress Check on Crime in Chicago," *New York Times*, February 28, 1926.

11. O'Banion: *Tribune*, November 11 and 12, 1924. Rooftops: *Tribune*, November 15, 1924.

12. Standard Oil Building: *Tribune*, August 11, 1926, Funerals: *Tribune*, October 15 and 16, 1926; and *New York Times*, October 16, 1926. The *Tribune*, February 18, 1928, indicates that Sbarbaro's partner, Thomas Brizzolara, had been had been the on-site manager of the firm's operations since the early 1920s, but Sbarbaro was actively involved in the Weiss funeral. "Sbarbaro for Judge": Kobler, *Capone*, 191.

13. "Liked the kid": Bergreen, *Capone*, 194.

14. Austrian: Seymour, *Baseball: The Golden Age*, 312, 328; and "Wrigley Files Libel Suit for Ku Klux Label," *Tribune*, February 4, 1923. Triggered: See Seymour, *Baseball: The Golden Age*, 297–98, for a nutshell account of Veeck's actions and their immediate effects.

15. Lingle: R. Smith, *Colonel*, 291–93.

16. Private army: W. Andrews, *Battle for Chicago*, 232. Small talk: Stuart, *20 Incredible Years*, 463–64.

17. Acquainted with Capone: Veeck, *Veeck—as in Wreck*, 35–36, says that the teenage Veeck Jr. (b. 1914) had met Capone at Wrigley Field; the club president's contact with the famous visitor was likely. Cars: according to Veeck's grandson, Veeck liked big cars and bought a Duesenberg for his aunt (Krehbiel, telephone conversation).

18. Rowdies: *Saturday Evening Post*, September 13, 1930, 25.

19. Union dues: *Daily News*, March 28, 1929; *Tribune*, August 21, 1931; and *Daily News*, July 28, 1934.

20. Siege: Lewis and Smith, *Chicago*, 452–53.

21. Erupted: *Daily News*, May 24, 1926; *Tribune*, May 24 and 25, 1926. No relation between the Frains and the ushering entrepreneur Andy Frain was mentioned. Andy Frain himself grew up on the South Side. Rear window: "'Hack' Wilson was seized as he made a dash for the rear window" ("'Hack' Wilson Seized in Raid," dateline May 24, 1926, in *Sun-Times* clipping files), which may be the origin of the oft-repeated story that the police found him "stuck" or "wedged" in the window (Golenbock, *Wrigleyville*, 222; Levy, *Joe McCarthy*, 114). The *Daily News*, May 24, 1926, said only that Wilson "attempted to slide home through the rear door."

22. Suggested: *Tribune*, September 24, 1929. This account was written by Edward Burns, who was not covering the Cubs in May 1926 but interviewed Wilson frequently during the ballplayer's Cub years.

23. Give orders: *Tribune*, February 15 and 22, 1926. "Pretty good": *Tribune*, March 31, 1926.

24. April Fool's: *Daily News*, April 1, 1925. Kidding: *Tribune*, February 15 and 22, 1926, and March 4, 1927. See also *Herald and Examiner*, September 24, 1930: "Joe took a card-playing, drinking crew of supposed misfits five years ago . . . and overnight transformed it." Poker: *Daily News*, April 6, 1925, and *Tribune*, February 13, 1926; see also "Leaves from a Fan's Scrapbook: Guy T. (Joe) Bush," *Sporting News*, December 29, 1932.

25. "High hat": *Tribune*, March 4, 1927. Sprain, fracture: *Tribune*, March 4 and 11, 1926. Second opinion: *Tribune*, March 12, 1926. Crutches: Sher, in Gallen, *Baseball Chronicles*, 144.

26. Acquired O'Doul's contract: Zimmerman, *William Wrigley, Jr.*, 222; *Los Angeles Times*, January 27, 1932; and *Tribune*, September 11, 1932. The latter characterizes the O'Doul transaction as a one-time violation of Wrigley's strict "hands-off" player policy, but the *New York Times*, September 22, 1929, indicated that Wrigley made offers for both Frank Frisch and Fred Lindstrom after the 1928 season. Additionally, in both 1927 and 1928 Wrigley appears to have directly sought Lyn Lary of the PCL, and in 1928, Jimmy Reese as well (*Tribune*, August 17, 1927, and August 29, 1928). Glovework: *Tribune*, March 12, 1926 ("[O'Doul] has shown some glaring defects as a fielder and hasn't lived up to his hitting reputation.").

27. Hollywood: "What's the Matter with Lefty O'Doul?" *Evening American*, May 21, 1926 ("'Lefty' was given every opportunity in the face of the keenest of competition."), and "Cub Owner Still Covets Robin Slugger, 'Tis Said," *Daily Times*, September 14, 1931 ("In fact, O'Doul looked pretty terrible the

spring he was with the Cubs."). In an early report from Catalina in 1926 ("Cubs Bailiwick Crowded with Center Fielders: Lefty O'Doul Most Promising Recruit," *Tribune,* February 18, 1926), Irving Vaughan devoted his first three paragraphs to O'Doul and followed up with a two-sentence paragraph on Wilson. "My O'Doul": "Cubs: As Wrigley Sees Them," *Tribune,* September 20, 1930; Zimmerman, *William Wrigley, Jr.,* 222.

28. Grumbling: *Tribune,* April 6 and September 29, 1926, and August 18, 1929; Brown, *Chicago Cubs,* 94. Sore elbow: *Tribune,* February 26, March 12 and 17, 1926.

29. Impertinence: Enright, *Chicago Cubs,* 98. Enright, a Chicago sportswriter beginning in the late 1920s, specifically mentions Kansas City. See also Golenbock, *Wrigleyville,* 193 (Ed Froelich interview: Maranville the subject of the discussion), and Sher, in Gallen, *Baseball Chronicles,* 144–45 (McCarthy discussing former Cub traded to Pittsburgh, apparently Maranville). Airplane: *Tribune,* April 13, 1926.

30. Pitching arm: *Tribune,* May 19, 20, and 22, 1926.

31. Commotion: *Daily News,* May 28, 1926; *Tribune,* May 29, 1926. Treatment: *Tribune,* May 30 ("taking treatments for his arm"), June 3 (Alexander's "lame arm is improving") and 4, 1926 ("have his arm treated a little longer").

32. Cooper: *Tribune,* June 9, 1926, and August 18, 1929 ("Cooper had complained about Killefer's tactics. When he started the same about McCarthy he was tossed overboard"). Duels: *Pittsburgh Sun-Telegraph,* October 13, 1927.

33. No hurry: *Tribune,* June 16, 1926; Brown, *Chicago Cubs,* 95.

34. "Suspended": *Tribune,* June 27, 1926.

35. His case: *Tribune,* June 18, 1926. Working out daily: *Tribune,* June 23, 1926.

36. Final announcement: *Tribune,* June 23, 1926. Outfielders: "Cubs Drop Moore and Brooks," *Evening American,* June 22, 1926. Telegram: Light, *Cultural Encyclopedia of Baseball,* 747. According to Irving Vaughan, *Tribune,* January 27, 1932, Wrigley made the decision to cut Alexander.

37. Rooming house: Heuer, "Neighbors," 32. Teared up: Sher, in Gallen, *Baseball Chronicles,* 145; see also Westbrook Pegler, *Tribune,* October 11, 1926: "[Alexander] sat alone in his room that night last summer when Joe McCarthy of the Cubs decided that old man Alexander was no good for [*sic*] any more and let him go."

38. Lincoln: automobile advertisements in Chicago newspapers, May 1926. Four- and five-passenger 1925 and 1926 Lincoln sedans apparently ranged in value between $4,500 and $6,000.

39. Positive words: Hornsby 1962, 152.

40. "Bat boy": *Tribune,* June 28, 1926. Tipped: Sher, in Gallen, *Baseball Chronicles,* 145.

41. Without justification: *Tribune,* April 18, 1928.

42. Luque: *Evening American*, June 23, 1926; *Tribune*, June 24, 1926. Hit the dirt: Ed Froelich interview in Golenbock, *Wrigleyville*, 237–38. Froelich has Luque pitching for New York, where he did not play until 1932.

43. Exhibit A: *Daily News*, May 16, 1926. Mistakes: *Tribune*, April 25, 1926, and March 4, 1927. Rare speech: *Tribune*, April 18, 1928. The incident dates from 1927; the unnamed outfielder was a "newer star," either Wilson or possibly Earl Webb.

44. "Strong puss": Brown, "Gabby Likes 'Em Hot," 15.

45. Catalina: the Cubs trained one week on Catalina in 1921, then spent the remainder of spring training based at Pasadena (*Tribune*, February 25, 1921). Catalina became the permanent spring-training base the following year (*Tribune*, February 20, 1922). "Gabby": *Daily News*, May 31, 1933 (naming Ed Smith, evidently an L.A. newspaperman); *Sporting News*, February 27, 1936; Murphy, *Gabby Hartnett Story*, 18; McNeil, *Gabby Hartnett*, 36–37 (naming Dean Sullivan of the *Herald and Examiner*); Hornof, telephone interview. Irving Vaughan, however, claimed that Hartnett earned the nickname when he "jabbered continually" on the train to California (*Tribune*, September 17, 1932).

46. "All right": Warren Brown in *Herald and Examiner*, July 24, 1938; Jim Enright in *Chicago American*, November 9, 1958 (placing the incident in Cincinnati on Opening Day 1922). Irving Vaughan (*Tribune*, September 17, 1932) has Killefer referring to the rookie Hartnett as "a great catcher" during an exhibition series; "Leaves from a Fan's Scrapbook, *Sporting News*, December 8, 1932, quotes Killefer as saying, "Boys, there's a catcher." "First big-league game": Reynolds, "Hartnett Catching," 50. Game ball: Brown 1939, "Gabby Likes 'Em Hot," 85, and *Chicago American*, November 9, 1958.

47. Matinee idol: *Daily News*, April 14, 1925. High-living: AP in *Indianapolis Star*, September 23, 1932. Autos: *Tribune*, September 29, 1928. Hotel lobby: *Daily News*, April 1, 1925. $200: Murphy, *Gabby Hartnett Story*, 66.

48. "Old neighborhood guy": Murphy, *Gabby Hartnett Story*, 63. Dinners: Murphy, *Gabby Hartnett Story*, 24, and reminiscence of author's father, ca. 1965.

49. Hitting flies; prom: Farrell, *My Baseball Diary*, 242–43. Gleason: *Sun-Times*, February 17, 1970.

50. Bleachers: *Daily News*, April 21, 1925 (batters "aiming" at left-field bleachers for easy homers); *Evening American*, June 22, 1926 (Mandy Brooks another Cub "homer hero" affected by the removal of the bleachers).

51. Two Hartnetts: *Daily News*, July 15, 1937. Directed: *Pittsburgh Sun-Telegraph*, August 19, 1927; *Tribune*, September 14, 1928; "Cub Fans Praise Hartnett, Wrigley for Team's Work," *Tribune*, September 2, 1930; and *Baseball Magazine*, March 1931, 470. Pitches, etc.: Brown, "Gabby Likes 'Em Hot," 88.

52. Quick: *Daily News*, August 5, 1927 (McCarthy quote), and June 1, 1933. "Let 'em run": *Tribune*, August 2, 1988. Contemporaries agreed: see, for instance, *Tribune*, July 22, 1928, and *Daily News*, June 1, 1933. Killefer: *Daily News*, August 5, 1927. McGraw: *Pittsburgh Sun-Telegraph*, August 19, 1927. Hooper: Murphy, *Gabby Hartnett Story*, 25.

53. "Hartnett don't miss": *Herald and Examiner*, August 3, 1928.

54. Throw: *Tribune*, July 2, 1927. Irving Vaughan observed, "Hack must have thought it was a fly ball," a kind of foreshadowing of the "Boom-Boom" Beck incident some years later. Here there was no mention of disciplinary action by McCarthy.

55. "Greatest catcher": *Daily News*, August 5, 1927, and June 1, 1933; *Time*, August 1, 1938, 31. See also Shatzkin, *Ballplayers*, 451.

56. Paderewski: J. G. Taylor Spink in *Sporting News*, September 6, 1945.

57. "Banjo players": Lieb, *Pittsburgh Pirates*, 202. See also *Tribune*, September 25, 1932.

58. Malcontent: see *Pittsburgh Post-Gazette*, August 9, 1927 ("[Emil] Yde's speech in Freeport, Ill., after the Cozy Dolan–Jimmy O'Connell affair that 'that is not all that was wrong,' paved the way for the release of Lefty Grimm, Rabbit Maranville, and Wilbur Cooper"); *Tribune*, April 18, 1945. See also "Leaves from a Fan's Scrapbook," *Sporting News*, September 22, 1932.

59. Taxi: *Tribune*, July 11, 1925. Captain: *Tribune*, July 10, 1925.

60. Still captain: *Tribune*, June 22, 1926.

61. "Der Kaptink": see, for instance, *Daily News*, July 29, 1929; *Daily Times*, September 26, 1929; *Daily Times*, March 2 and October 4, 1932. Mimic: Descriptions of the younger Grimm's on-field antics, if any, would most likely have appeared in the Pittsburgh papers of the early 1920s, which this writer has not pored over. Typical of later comments about those days is this from Wayne Otto, *Herald and Examiner*, August 5, 1932: "Grimm, erstwhile master of diamond pantomimes and the comedian of the majors whose clowning made him famous not so many years ago." Ashes: *Sporting News*, November 28, 1983, 69.

62. Early morning: *Tribune*, September 25, 1932. Impromptu concerts: *Tribune*, September 25, 1932; *Daily News*, August 10, 1932. $450 banjo: *Tribune*, September 18, 1929; *Daily News*, August 3, 1932 ("good one . . . cost $450); *Sporting News*, September 22, 1932 ($425). The latter two stories differ on whether Grimm took the instrument on the road during the season. Auditioning teammates: *Tribune*, February 27, 1927. 4/4 time; good days: *Tribune*, September 18, 1929. Soothe morale: *Sporting News*, November 28, 1983, 69. Airwaves: *Tribune*, February 22, 1926. Orphaned banjos: *Tribune*, October 1, 1928. Without modification: *Sporting News*, September 22, 1932.

63. Oil portrait: *Tribune*, October 1, 1928, and *New York Times*, August 22, 1931. Rendition of Wrigley Field: *Tribune*, April 28 and September 18, 1929; *Daily News*, August 3, 1932. Woodworking shop, custom furniture: *Tribune*, April 28, 1929, and Daily *News*, August 3, 1932. Magician's equipment: *Tribune*, April 28, 1929; and *Daily News*, August 3, 1932. Not Mac's equal: "So They Tell Me," *Herald and Examiner*, September 27, 1932.

64. "Entertainer": Aaron, *I Had a Hammer*, 96. A member of Grimm's 1954 Milwaukee Braves club, Danny O'Connell, criticized Grimm's "easygoing" ways in the *Sporting News*, February 2, 1955. "Over to us": Augie Galan, in Phalen, *Our Chicago Cubs*, 5. See also Brown, *Chicago Cubs*, 141, which observes that an "every man for himself basis" prevailed on Grimm's 1935 Cubs (for whom Galan played). In 1937, Quentin Reynolds noted: "Manager Charley Grimm of Chicago has such confidence in Gabby [Hartnett] that he allows him to handle the pitchers with no managerial help" (Reynolds, "Hartnett Catching," 50). X's and O's: Pafko, telephone interview. Pafko and O'Connell were teammates on the Braves in the 1950s.

65. German: *Tribune*, April 26, 1928. Balk: *Tribune*, July 17, 1932. Grimm was at bat when he began his pantomime. After George Barr, the home plate umpire, called the balk on Watty Clark, two Cub runners advanced, and Max Carey, the Brooklyn manager, was ejected from the game for arguing the call. Grimm then struck out, but Hartnett singled the runners home. "Happy Warrior": *New York Times*, August 11, 1932. Brandish two bats: *New York Times*, August 22, 1931. "Cocky": *Tribune*, April 18, 1928. "Double-jointed": *Tribune*, September 14, 1928. Burnout: Art ["Butch"] Weis, quoted in Murphy, *Gabby Hartnett Story*, 59. Mimicking: *Sporting News*, September 6, 1945.

66. Unchanged: *Time*, August 27, 1945.

67. Somersault: *New York Times*, October 10, 1929; "Foxx Loses Decision" (photo caption), *Herald and Examiner*, October 10, 1929.

68. "Family": *Tribune*, October 15, 1925. Delegation: *Tribune*, June 26, 1926. See also *Chicago Defender*, August 31, 1929, citing 2,300 seats reserved in Cincinnati by Louisvillians to "honor " McCarthy (5,000 applied for the tickets).

69. Rigler: *Tribune*, July 1, 1926.

70. Dead run: *Tribune*, July 2, 1926 (photo, "Hack and His Gang").

71. A blow: *Tribune*, July 8, 1926.

72. Sweat: *Tribune*, August 17, 1926 (Wilson "perpetually perspiring"), and *Daily Times*, February 19, 1931. Uniform: *Tribune*, April 18, 1928, and September 14, 1928; *Daily Times*, April 14, 1931; Veeck, *Hustler's Handbook*, 165; and Seymour, *Baseball: Golden Age*, 451.

73. Bat: *Daily Times*, February 16, 1931; Grimm, *Jolly Cholly's Story*, 52; and *Baseball Digest*, July 1989, 79.

74. Swing: "Aye! Eyes Count Most in Slugging, Hack Says," *Daily Times*, February 16, 1931 ("[Wilson] is a free swinger, and his vicious 'cutting' at the ball is the reason for his many strikeouts, as well as homers."). Flushed: "Wilson, Lewis Robert (Hack)," undated, typewritten sheet in HOF file; *Tribune*, September 14, 1928. Bat flying: *Tribune*, August 1, 1928, and May 26, 1929; *New York Times*, July 21, 1929. Reardon: Gerlach, *Men in Blue*, 16; Grimm, *Jolly Cholly's Story*, 53, repeats the story with Bill Klem as the umpire.

75. "High ball," bat, shin guards: *Tribune*, July 6, 1926. Profanely: *Tribune*, July 7, 1926.

76. Wobbled: *Tribune*, September 15, 1926.

77. Lemons: *Daily Times*, January 27, 1931.

78. Gesture: *Tribune*, September 3, 1926.

79. Disgust: AP in *Tribune*, October 4, 1926.

80. "Yeah, Alec!": Westbrook Pegler, *Tribune*, October 11, 1926.

81. Gardner: *Chicago Defender*, October 23, 1926.

82. Vacation: *Chicago Defender*, July 17, 1926. Directors: *Chicago Defender*, September 11, 1926.

83. Kankakee: Shatzkin, *Ballplayers*, 353.

84. Complimentary pass: Whittingham, *Chicago Bears*, 62.

85. Drucci: *Tribune*, October 18, 1926.

86. "Wrigley Field": *Tribune*, December 4, 1926.

4. THE MCCARTHYMEN TAKE THE STAGE

1. Overachieving: "Wilson, Webb and Stephenson Big Factors in Chicago's Fight for Pennant," *Pittsburgh Press*, August 6, 1927.

2. Odd-looking: *Tribune*, October 3, 1929. In command: *Tribune*, July 19, 1926 ("working corners to perfection"); *New York Times*, June 7, 1930 ("seeming nonchalance, superb skill and control"). No peering: *Daily News*, November 7, 1970. Inside: *Sun-Times*, November 15, 1966.

3. "Calm": *Tribune*, October 1, 1932. Uncomplainingly: *Tribune*, October 10, 1928 ("Ed Walsh Sr., Charlie Root and others who became imbued with the 'I'd die for dear old Rutgers' spirit to their ultimate sorrow").

4. Underdog: *Tribune*, September 11, 1927. "Cubs are in": *Tribune*, August 9, 1927. Renamed: *Tribune*, December 4, 1926 ("Wrigley Field . . . now is the official moniker of the north side lot."). 200,000: Thorn and Palmer, *Total Baseball*, 145.

5. Press box: Ryan, "Inside the Loud Speaker," *Tribune*, April 25, 1926. WMAQ apparently also had entree to the press box by May 1926, judging from a photograph in "They Aid in Getting Baseball News over Air to Fans," *Daily News*, May 26, 1926.

6. On-the-field interview: in 1971, Hal Totten claimed credit for originating such interviews (*Daily News,* August 30, 1971). A year earlier, Bob Elson had taken credit for conducting the first on-the-field interview (with Connie Mack) as part of his 1930 World Series broadcast (C. Smith, "Voices of Cub Broadcasters," 136). Essanay extra: "Inside the Loud Speaker," *Tribune,* July 12, 1925; Dierks, "Ryan at the Mike," G10 (interview with Ryan).

7. Grandma: "Inside the Loud Speaker," *Tribune,* June 12, 1927.

8. "The father of sportscasting": Patterson, *Golden Voices of Baseball,* 21. 1935 World Series: Barber, *Broadcasters,* 91. Ryan's replacement was Bob Elson, whom he supervised as station manager at WGN, making it likely that Ryan was at least consulted on the decision.

9. Totten: "Hal Totten's Broadcast of World Series Opener," *Daily News,* October 8, 1929. This excerpt is taken from a transcript of Totten's broadcast of the first game of the 1929 World Series. If any banter filled the dead time between pitches, no mention was made of it.

10. Flanagan re-creations: Patterson, *Golden Voices of Baseball,* 40, and C. Smith, "Voices of Cub Broadcasters," 135. O'Hara and White Sox: Patterson, *Golden Voices of Baseball,* 41.

11. American League franchises: in 1927 Ban Johnson evidently lifted a non-broadcasting edict he had issued in 1925. Crepeau, *Baseball,* 185. See also *New York Times,* September 14, 1930 (Comiskey's role). Telegraphed updates: Caton, "Radio Station WMAQ,"243 (WMAQ, Totten); "Radio Programs for Today," *Tribune,* various editions, August and September 1927 (WGN, Ryan). The updates were given between innings; WGN, at least, was commercial-free to that point, providing ample airtime for the updates.

12. "Mr. Radio": *Cleveland Plain Dealer,* ca. April 1942, in Poindexter, *Golden Throats,* 196.

13. Seating capacity: A random sampling of figures the press supplied for the park's seating capacity from 1926 to 1932 suggests that the figures varied almost season by season. See Additional Sources, "Seating Capacity." Ropes: there are several easily accessible photographs that illustrated where the outfield standees were placed. For URLs and discussion, see Additional Sources, "Ropes." Mounted police: Ed Froelich interview in Golenbock, *Wrigleyville,* 203.

14. "Rope": *Sports Illustrated,* July 7, 1980, 54.

15. Deep center: *Tribune,* October 5, 1929. Bill Veeck Jr.: Veeck, *Hustler's Handbook,* 165; *Tribune,* October 5, 1929, and May 19, 1928 ("[W]ith one out in the ninth, Wilson made a diving catch to get Moore's drive two inches off the grass. He got his eyebrows full of sod, but the hand he got from the Ladies' day crowd of some 20,000 was worth the effort"). Any way

necessary: *Herald and Examiner,* July 7, 1928. Magerkurth: *Tribune,* May 31, 1932. Stephenson's arm: Brace, interview. Wilson's arm: *Tribune,* October 5, 1929; Grimm, *Jolly Cholly's Story,* 55. Stephenson evidently made a more favorable impression upon his arrival in Chicago, according to two different observers in the *Tribune,* June 17, and July 28, 1926.

16. Big inning: *Indianapolis Star,* September 15, 1929; *Herald and Examiner,* October 6, 1929. Sacrifice bunt: *Indianapolis Star,* September 15, 1929; *Tribune,* September 26, 1930.

17. Offensive rewards: *Tribune,* April 25, 1926.

18. Autograph signer: *Daily News,* October 8, 1929. Stepped out: Brace, interview. "Stevie": *Times,* October 3, 1932; *Tribune,* May 9, and October 2, 1928. $100,000: Stephenson II, telephone interview. $450 check: *Sun-Times,* February 22, 1955.

19. Waved huge bat: *Tribune,* April 18, 1928. Judge of strike zone: Grimm, *Jolly Cholly's Story,* 52. Dreaded: *Tribune,* September 14, 1928. Crowd-pleasing strikeouts: *Daily News,* October 8, 1929. Two-strike hitting: see McCarthy's comments, *New York World Telegram,* September 26, 1932. Consensus: *Tribune,* September 14, 1928; *New York Times,* September 26, 1932; *Daily Times,* September 27, 1929. Tantrums: see, for instance, *New York Times,* July 21, 1929 (Wilson throws bat "viciously" after striking out). "Outside?": Murdock, 233. See also *Tribune,* September 16, 1932: "When [Stephenson] is feeling real mad about an umpire, he might give him a mean look." "Never booed": *Daily News,* July 13, 1932; *New York Times,* September 23, 1932; *Baseball Magazine,* November 1932, 301. However, Stephenson was booed at Forbes Field in 1932 when he bunted on Steve Swetonic, who was laboring on a sore foot ("Mirrors of Sport," *Pittsburgh Post-Gazette,* July 23, 1932). The paper quickly added that Stephenson was "one of the most popular players in the league."

20. "Gol darn it," fruit, pop bottles: *Tribune,* September 13, 1927.

21. "Hello, brother": *Tribune,* May 13, 1928.

22. Fraternal organizations: *Daily Times,* February 23, 1931. "Roly-poly": *Tribune,* August 16, 1931. Collection: *Tribune,* March 31, 1927. "He does it": *Tribune,* August 27, 1930, probably referring to a visit Wilson made to the Municipal Tuberculosis Hospital after the Cubs beat the Phillies, 17–3. Wilson visited with children at the institution until "nearly 10:00 p.m. (Mead, *Two Spectacular Seasons,* 85).

23. "Stick it out": *Sporting News,* July 26, 1980, in Gifford, *Neighborhood of Baseball,* 163.

24. "Oh, hell": *Tribune,* September 16, 1932.

25. Polo Grounds: *Tribune,* September 23, 1929.

26. "Rubberhead": Karst and Jones, *Who's Who*, 423.

27. "Wrong uniform": *Tribune*, October 3, 1929.

28. Fast, strong-armed: *Tribune*, October 5, 1929.

29. "John Gilbert": *Tribune*, July 7, 1929. Restoration: *Tribune*, May 23, June 2, and October 3, 1929; *Daily Times*, September 3, 1930. "Heathie fan": *Tribune*, June 16, 1929; *Times*, September 3, 1930.

30. Second-guessing: *Tribune*, October 3, 1929.

31. Threesome: *Tribune*, March 16 and April 21, 1929. Wilson sang tenor for Grimm and Heathcote's group in spring 1927 (*Tribune*, February 28, 1927). Road roommates: *Tribune*, September 7, 1930.

32. "Silent Swede": *Tribune*, August 20, 1929. Great War: *Tribune*, August 25, 1929, and May 29, 1930; *Daily Times*, May 28, 1930. Distinguished Service Cross, Croix de Guerre: *Daily Times*, May 29, 1930. Concealed: *Tribune*, May 29, 1930.

33. Pitches, delivery: *Tribune*, August 14 and 25, 1929; AP dispatch in *Indianapolis Star*, May 29, 1930 ("remarkable control and a good change of pace"). Spitter ban: *Tribune*, August 25, 1929, and May 29, 1930 (Bill Veeck says he "learned to pitch without the spitter"); AP dispatch in *Indianapolis Star*, May 29, 1930. Forgot, or declined: Faber and Faber, *Spitballers*, 5, say that "Barney Dreyfuss refused to certify any of his hurlers as spitballers," leaving open the question of why he had hired Carlson in the first place. On the background of the spitball ban, see *New York Times*, December 15, 1920; Faber and Faber, *Spitballers*, 10–11. Ball down: *New York Times*, July 14, 1929.

34. Baker Bowl collapse: *New York Times*, May 15, 1927; and Westcott, *Philadelphia's Old Ballparks*, 78. Westcott quotes the head umpire as saying he called the game "on account of panic," not rain. It's unclear how many of the displaced fans were still in the affected section before the collapse. In the *Tribune*, August 25, 1929, Irving Vaughan suggested that the Phillies' need for repair funds precipitated the deal for Carlson.

35. Prewar style: *Tribune*, August 25, 1929 ("His pose on the mound looks like a woodcut from the playing days of A. G. Spaulding").

36. "Shrine," road roommates: *Daily Times*, May 29, 1930.

37. Alexander's first game: *Sun-Times*, October 21, 1952. Federal League, Cleveland: *Sun-Times*, February 23, 1953; *Daily News*, September 11, 1937, and May 7, 1945. Halas: *Sun-Times*, October 21, 1952. Halas played briefly for the New York Yankees in 1919. Millwright, first baseman, experience, medical volumes: Roberts, *Chicago Bears*, 14, 15.

38. Helping Alexander: "Lotshaw, Former Trainer for Cubs and Bears, Dies," *Tribune*, February 24, 1953. "Lotshaw, Retired Cubs, Bears Trainer, Dies," *American*, ca. February 1953, in HOF files, ties Lotshaw's services to

Alexander's nineteen-inning game in the 1922 City Series, three years ahead of the actual game. Alexander did start two games in the 1922 City Series, including a seventh-game shutout. Loud tie: *Tribune*, February 12, 1926. Liniment: H. G. Lotshaw, June 24, 1999; see also Hornsby and Surface, *My War with Baseball*, 65.

39. Lelivelt: [John C.] Hoffman, ca. 1938, *Sun-Times* clipping files. Up in the air: *Tribune*, March 1, 1932. Batting practice duel: "Lotshaw, 30 Years with Cubs, Quits," *Tribune*, ca. October 1952, and "Lotshaw Called Malone's Bluff with Over-Fence Rap," July 28, 1962, in HOF.

40. "You are out!": *Tribune*, March 10, 1931. Ruby was 0-2 with an error at second base as the Cubs beat the movie folk, 19–1. Brown also went hitless with an error. Hornsby, Cuyler, Stephenson all hit at least twice; Bud Teachout, was the winning pitcher. "Banana cart": *Sun-Times*, April 25, 1943. "Embalming fluid": *Tribune*, July 10, 1931.

41. "In the nude": *Sun-Times*, March 1, 1946. "Remember the face," "Nagurski": *Sun-Times*, February 10, 1953.

42. Coca Cola: Brown, *Chicago Cubs*, 102–3.

43. Hurley: "Voice of the People," *Tribune*, September 5, 1927.

44. Choking: *Tribune*, September 1, 1927, August 8, 1929.

45. Restrained Alex: *Tribune*, September 5, 1927. Pop bottles: *Tribune*, September 10 and 13, 1927.

46. "Build that ballpark bigger": *Tribune*, September 12, 1927.

47. Thompson: *Chicago Defender*, October 8, 1927.

48. Umpire baiting: *Chicago Defender*, April 30, and October 22, 1927; Peterson, *Only the Ball Was White*, 90–91.

49. Contract: *Tribune*, September 21, 1927. Ringside seats: *Tribune*, September 15 and 22, 1927; Woody English interview in Golenbock, *Wrigleyville*, 202.

50. Fedoras: see Carlson posed in street clothes with six other Cubs, *Herald and Examiner*, October 8, 1929 ("All's Quiet").

51. "Move along": *New York Times*, September 23, 1927.

52. Celebrities: *New York Times* and *Tribune*, September 23, 1927. "Kid": Randy Roberts, *Jack Dempsey*, 257, quoted in Littlewood, *Arch*, 43.

53. "Tunney Is DOWN!": Poindexter, *Golden Throats*, 62.

5 . MY DAD THE SPORTSWRITER

1. Getz: *Tribune*, April 19, 1928; Pegler, "Chicago First! Wrigley Was a Home Towner," *Tribune*, January 28, 1932.

2. Rodeo: "Big Bill Day at the Rodeo" (advertisement for the Cook County Republican Central Committee), *Tribune*, August 22, 1927. Rats: Stuart, *20 Incredible Years*, 269; see also Bukowski, *Big Bill Thompson*, 166. Cheering

crowds: Lewis and Smith, *Chicago,* 488. Succeeding Coolidge: R. Smith, *The Colonel,* 274–75. Seven-thousand-mile trip: Stuart, *20 Incredible Years,* 336–37.

3. Prince of Wales: Spinney, *City of Big Shoulders,* 186. The king's two sons visited Canada in 1927, the year Thompson issued his threat (see "Royal Visits from 1786 to 1951," on the Canadian Heritage website, http://www.pch.gc.ca/pgm/ceem-cced/fr-rf/1786–1951-eng.cfm, accessed June 16, 2012). Ethnic appeals: Spinney, *City of Big Shoulders,* 181–87. Tacit ally: Stuart, *20 Incredible Years,* 317; Gottfried, *Boss Cermak of Chicago,* 213; R. Smith, *Colonel,* 271–72.

4. "Hands of Death": *Chicago Tribune,* various editions, mid-1920s. More than sixty: Lewis and Smith, *Chicago,* 478.

5. Bombings: "Chicago Bombers Wreck Judge's Home," *New York Times,* February 18, 1928; "Three Bombings, One a Judge," *Tribune,* February 18, 1928.

6. "Carcass": Lewis and Smith, *Chicago,* 479. Hundred thousand votes: *Tribune,* April 11, 1928.

7. Withdraw: Stuart, *20 Incredible Years,* 379. Good-government group: *Tribune,* September 24, 1928. A 1924 *Daily News* photo ("[Prince of Wales and William Wrigley, Jr., chewing gum magnate and owner of Chicago Cubs]," http://memory.loc.gov/ammem/ndlpcoop/ichihtml/cdnhome.html) of Wrigley hosting the Prince of Wales (the future Edward VIII) at the Wrigley Building indicates that Wrigley might not have endorsed Thompson's campaign of abuse toward all things British, especially the royal family.

8. Slipped: *Tribune,* June 22, 1928. Midsummer's afternoon: *Daily News,* June 21, 1928; *Herald and Examiner,* June 22, 1928; *Evening Post,* June 22, 1928.

9. Thumbs: the author's paternal grandmother, who lived just a few blocks from Young across Broadway, was one such mother (Ehrgott, "Chicago in the '20s").

10. Milk wagon drivers' union: *Collier's,* May 12, 1928, 11.

11. Scrutiny: *Daily Times,* February 12, 1931.

12. Vaulted: *Herald and Examiner,* June 22, 1928. Hartnett and Kelly: *Tribune,* June 22, 1928. Commentary: *Herald and Examiner,* June 23, 1928.

13. Surged: *Herald and Examiner,* June 22, 1928.

14. Lewis, shouted: *Herald and Examiner,* June 22, 1928.

15. Wilson noticed: *Evening Post,* June 22, 1928.

16. "Sportsman": *Tribune* and *Herald and Examiner,* June 23, 1928. (Veeck, *Hustler's Handbook,* 167, mentions Wilson using a bat to attack Young, but none of the contemporary accounts mention the bat.) $1 and costs, $100: *Herald and Examiner,* June 23, 1928.

17. Hammered: *Tribune,* June 24, 1928. Stands shook: *Herald and Examiner,* June 25, 1928.

18. Young's suit: *Tribune*, July 26, 1928.

19. Quick to boo: *Tribune*, May 14, 1928 ("The razz [Cuyler] got when he struck out in the first turned to plaudits after his play on Roush").

20. Ebbets Field: "KiKi Cuyler Staging Brilliant Comeback," dateline April 15, 1938; Dave Camerer, "Cuyler Starring as Regular," *New York World-Telegram* [?], dateline June 23, 1938, in HOF files. McGill: Ralph McGill, "A Memory of Ki Ki Cuyler" (no dateline, ca. 1950, HOF files). Monroe: "What Say," *Chicago Defender*, April 16, 1932.

21. Augmented: *Baseball Magazine*, March 1932, 446. Cobb comparison: Lane, "Has Ty Cobb a Rival in This Man?" *Baseball Magazine*, May 1927; Lane, "Where a Brilliant Career Fell Short," *Baseball Magazine*, September 1929; "Cub Scout Says Cuyler Was 'Righthanded Cobb'" (reminiscences of Jack Doyle), *Daily News*, ca. 1950, in HOF files. Doyle was the scout who signed Gabby Hartnett and several other Cub players.

22. Worrywart: Lane, "Where a Brilliant Career Fell Short," *Baseball Magazine*, September 1929 ("rather high strung and sensitive"); *Tribune*, October 5, 1929 ("inclined to be fretful"), September 21, 1932 ("easily upset by little things"), and June 2, 1935 ("admits he is rather sensitive"); *Herald and Examiner*, September 13, 1932 ("fretting over something or another"). Vainglorious: *Herald and Examiner*, September 21, 1932 ("always a theatrical sort"), and Woody English interview in Golenbock, *Wrigleyville*, 206. "Batting average player": *Daily Times*, July 3, 1935; Woody English interview in Golenbock, *Wrigleyville*, 206. "Yellow": *Pittsburgh Post-Gazette*, August 9, 1927. Hitless: *Daily News*, July 22, 1968 (quoting Paul Waner). Trouble: *Pittsburgh Sun-Telegraph*, August 9, 1927. Waner, in the *Daily News* article, July 22, 1968, referenced above, said Bush benched Cuyler after he griped about going hitless; however, Cuyler was 1 for 3 in the game that triggered his fine and benching, August 6, 1927. The incident at second base occurred in the fourth inning after he drew a walk.

After the World Series, Cuyler provided a lengthy and detailed interview to the Associated Press: see "Cuyler Case Overshadows Series Comment: 'Ki' Makes Statement; Bush Remains Silent," *Pittsburgh Post-Gazette*, October 10, 1927; "Cuyler Discusses Banishment Case," *Sporting News*, October 13, 1927. See also Brundidge, "Cuyler, Leading Base Stealer, Was Traded for Not Sliding," *Sporting News*, February 5, 1931.

23. Pirate management tired: *Pittsburgh Sun-Telegraph*, August 9, 1927. Regis M. Welsh made the point twice in his article. Photo: *Pittsburgh Sun-Telegraph*, August 13, 1927. Chanting: *Pittsburgh Press*, October 3, 1927.

24. Defeatism: see "Sports of the Times," *New York Times*, September 28, 1932; Creamer, *Babe*, 309. Many fans: *Pittsburgh Post-Gazette*, October 10, 1927.

Banner: *Pittsburgh Press*, October 6, 1927. Pinch hitting: *Pittsburgh Post-Gazette*, October 6, 1927.

25. Demonstrations continued: *Pittsburgh Post-Gazette*, October 10, 1927 ("demonstrations against Bush in the two games here"). Yankee Stadium crowds: *Pittsburgh Post-Gazette*, October 10, 1927.

26. "Well, Barney": *Daily News*, September 19, 1932.

27. Brickell: The outfielder did help his career slugging percentage with a total of 23 triples.

28. Executive: *Tribune*, February 24, 1928.

29. Different: *Tribune*, September 25, 1929; *Sporting News*, August 4, 1932, 4. West Point: *Tribune*, June 23, 1929; *Indianapolis Times*, August 26, 1929; Thomas J. Connery, "Cuyler Turns down Football for Career on the Diamond," dateline August 11, 1933, in HOF files; Brundidge, "Cuyler, Leading Base Stealer, Was Traded for Not Sliding," *Sporting News*, February 5, 1931; "Cuyler, Hazen S. 'Kiki'," typewritten biographical information sheet in HOF files. Cotillions: *Tribune*, September 25, 1929, and June 2, 1935.

30. Black Knight and Malone's background: *Tribune*, May 12, 1929; "Perce Lay (Pat) Malone," February 9, 1933 (HOF); Hillman, "Pat Malone," 170. McGraw: Graham, *McGraw of the Giants*, 178. Ramona: *Tribune*, September 30, 1928.

31. Few interested: *Tribune*, February 23, 1928.

32. McCarthy, curveball: *Tribune*, March 2, 1928. 46,000: *Tribune*, April 19, 1928 ("dazzled" the Reds with his speed). "A fellow like McGraw": *Tribune*, September 28, 1929.

33. Flu: *Tribune*, August 25, 1929. Examining physician: *Daily Times*, May 29, 1930 ("Two years ago a physician gave [Carlson] but months to live."). The *Tribune*, same date, said that in 1928 the "best physicians in Los Angeles" thought Carlson had "pitched his last ballgame." In uniform: *Tribune*, April 19, 1928.

34. Hand: *Tribune*, April 22, 1928. Booing: *Daily Times*, September 30, 1929 (re: 1928 season—"didn't live up to expectations . . . no few boos from Chicago fans"). Leaps, throws: *Tribune*, May 14 and September 15, 1928, and *Herald and Examiner*, August 17, 1928. Speed: *Tribune*, August 1, 1928.

35. Platoon: *Tribune*, June 5, 1928. Benching: *Tribune*, June 24, 1928.

36. Klem: *Tribune* and *New York Times*, both August 1, 1928.

37. Pfirman: *Tribune*, August 21, 1928. Fine: *Tribune*, August 22, 1928.

38. 46,000: Tribune, September 10, 1928.

39. Planning meeting: *New York Times*, September 18, 1928. "No foolin'!": *Tribune*, September 15, 1928.

40. Veeck: Details of Veeck's early life and career come mainly from John Carmichael's six-part series that ran in the *Daily News* from September 15 to

20, 1932. Other points were supplied by Frederick Krehbiel on various dates, 1998 and 1999. See also Linn, *Great Connection*, 61–63.

41. Police: *Tribune*, April 19, 1928. Andy Frain: *Daily News*, April 21, 1941; *Tribune*, March 28, 1945; dateline June 16, 1946, in *Sun-Times* clipping file.

42. 125 ushers: *Sporting News*, December 8, 1932. The 1946 account specifies "a tough Sunday in 1928." In this and all other accounts, Frain approached William Wrigley directly.

43. Sports reporting: Noverr and Ziewacz, *Games They Played*, 71. One example the authors provide originates in Muncie, Indiana, a small city in Veeck's home state. From 1890 to 1923—approximately embracing the years of Veeck's journalistic career—one newspaper's coverage devoted to sports increased fourfold. "Bill Bailey": *Evening American*, December 9, 1918. For Bill Bailey's report on the Merkle donnybrook, see *Evening American*, September 24, 1908 ("'Cubs' Game,' Is O'Day's Ruling against Giants"), bylined "Bill Bailey." According to the *American*, October 7, 1933, 1908 was Veeck's first year as a baseball writer for the *American*, although according to a much earlier version, he started with the paper in 1905 (*Evening American*, December 9, 1918). Poker: *Tribune*, April 11, 1926, and August 18, 1929.

44. Minor league franchise: *American*, October 7, 1933. Baseball Writers Association: *Evening American*, December 9, 1918.

45. More involved: Cruikshank and Schultz, *Man Who Sold America*, 159–60, based mainly on Albert Lasker's dictated memoirs; Lasker indicated he was actually the majority shareholder of the Cubs until into the 1920s.

46. Dinner: Brown, *Chicago Cubs*, 80.

47. Vice president: *Tribune*, December 8 and 9, 1918; *Evening American*, December 9, 1918; *New York Times*, December 8, 1918. League meeting: *Tribune* and *New York Times*, December 11, 1918.

48. President: *Tribune*, July 7, 1919. "High kind": Cruikshank and Schultz, *Man Who Sold America*, 161. However, Zimmerman, *William Wrigley, Jr.*, 213, says that Lasker opposed Veeck's appointment.

49. Magee: *New York Times*, June 9, 1920; Seymour, *Baseball: The Golden Age*, 291–92.

50. Telegrams: *Tribune*, September 5, 1920. Cooperation: Veeck "offered to assist the prosecutor and the grand jury in every way during the impending grand jury investigation." See "Hoyne and Veeck Plan Cub Inquiry," *Tribune*, September 9, 1920.

51. Lasker Plan: Seymour *Baseball: The Golden Age*, 311–14, and Cruikshank and Schultz, *Man Who Sold America*, 163–67.

52. Just the man: Seymour *Baseball: The Golden Age*, 314. "BASEBALL": Voigt, *American Baseball*, 143.

53. "Bill": *Tribune* (?), dateline January 21(?), 1926, in *Sun-Times* clipping files. "Not a chance": *Tribune*, October 7, 1925. "I didn't know": *Tribune*, April 11, 1926.

54. Holdouts: *Daily News*, January 21, 1931; *Tribune*, October 6, 1933. "In a minute": P. K. Wrigley, interview, 195. "A sportswriter": Eskenazi, *Bill Veeck*, 32. Bronzeville often blamed: *Chicago Defender*, September 4, 1932, September 24, 1932, and September 16, 1933. Hero worship: Veeck, *Veeck—as in Wreck*, 23–36.

55. "Great": *Tribune*, October 6, 1933. See also Littlewood, *Arch*, 70 (but n.b. that on page 68, Littlewood reverses the chronology of the Negro League versus the major league all-star game). Interleague play: *Daily News*, August 22, 1933; *American*, October 6, 1933; AP dispatch in *Tribune*, October 6, 1933.

56. "Fifteen percent": Whittingham, *Chicago Bears*, 21–22.

57. Grange: Roberts, *Chicago Bears*, 64–65.

58. "That's plenty": UP dispatch in *Indianapolis Times*, August 10, 1929.

59. C. E. Allen: "Phone Bills Reveal Race Tip Scandal," *Tribune*, September 14, 1928; "Turf Scandal's 'Jockey Allen' Is Identified," *Tribune*, September 15, 1928. See also AP in *St. Louis Post-Dispatch*, September 14, 1928.

60. "Look it up," "Don't know Jockey Allen": AP in *St. Louis Post-Dispatch*, September 14, 1928.

61. Stock market: Hornsby and Surface, *My War with Baseball*, 25, and Crepeau, *Baseball*, 135.

62. Conduct detrimental: *Tribune*, September 14, 1928. Seymour, *Baseball: The Golden Age*, 387, locates Landis's powers in the phrase "for the best interests of the game."

63. Gypsy star: contemporary retrospectives of Hornsby's wanderings were provided by John Kieran in "Hornsby, the Vanishing American," in "Sports of the Times," *New York Times*, August 5, 1932; Dick Farrington, "Farming with Farrington," *Sporting News*, August 11, 1932; George Kirksey, "Gambling Plays Heavy Role in Decline of 'The Rajah,'" UP dispatch in *Indianapolis Times*, August 14, 1929. See also Seymour, *Baseball: The Golden Age*, 393–95. String of scandals: Seymour, *Baseball: The Golden Age*, 374–79. The specific affairs involved Phil Douglas, Jimmy O'Connell, and Benny Kauff, all New York Giants whom Commissioner Landis banished from organized baseball from 1921 to 1924.

64. Nips: "Wrigley Not Always a 'King'; Piloted 'Nips'—Prairie Team," *Evening American*, May 22, 1926; "Dad Would Have Loved It, Says Bill Wrigley," undated clipping, ca. late 1970s, in HOF files; Otto, *Herald and Examiner*, January 27, 1932. See also Additional Sources, "Nips."

65. "Released": *Tribune*, September 20, 1930. Telescope: Vitti, *Chicago Cubs*, 32.

66. Easy mark: Otto, *Herald and Examiner*, January 27, 1932.

67. PCL shortstop: *Pittsburgh Press*, August 8, 1927; *Tribune*, February 28, 1928. Offer: *Tribune*, August 17, 1927.

68. Boater: *Evening American*, May 22, 1926. Nearly every home game: *New York Times*, September 22, 1929. Box seat: "Cubs Start East," *Tribune*, April 30, 1928. Cigars: Linton, "A History of Chicago Radio," 178. Hook-up: *New York Times*, September 22, 1929; Linton, "A History of Chicago Radio," 178. Polo Grounds: *Tribune*, July 30, 1928.

69. Contract: *Tribune*, August 31, 1928.

70. Planning meeting: *Tribune*, November 8, 2011. See also *New York Times*, September 18, 1928.

71. Row: Veeck, *Veeck—as in Wreck*, 25.

72. Hankering: *Tribune*, December 16, 1926, and February 9, 1928.

73. To greet Veeck: *Tribune*, November 8, 1928; Kaese, *Boston Braves*, 208. Irving Vaughn, who contributed the *Tribune*'s November 8 piece, had mentioned Veeck's presence at Braves Field in his game wrap-up (*Tribune*, September 19, 1928), and he repeated the point the next month (*Tribune*, October 16, 1928). For a nearly contemporaneous instance, see also *Tribune*, March 15, 1932: "[U]nder the rule which prevents tampering with players, Veeck was unable to say anything more then 'Howdy!' to [Babe Herman]."

74. Pop fly: *Herald and Examiner*, September 19, 1928.

75. Photograph: Graham, *McGraw of the Giants*, 234.

76. "Detriment": Daley, 157, in Golenbock, *Wrigleyville*, 209. Another chance: *Tribune* ("no disgrace" to be let out from New York) and *Indianapolis Times* ("servility, self-abasement," and toadying to the front office necessary at Polo Grounds), August 20, 1929.

77. "Terrible": *Daily News*, September 17, 1932. "Lose my job": Kaese, *Boston Braves*, 208.

78. "Let's get him": *Daily News*, September 17, 1932.

79. $150,000, $137,000: *Tribune*, November 8, 1928.

80. Judged, bluegrass: *Tribune*, November 14, 1928.

81. Sheer depth: The Cubs' "row" at full strength numbered five. The Bronx Bombers' 1927 roster posted a better slugging percentage than did either the 1929 or the 1930 Cubs, although only Ruth, Gehrig, and Lazzeri among the 1927 Yankees hit more than eleven home runs. The Yanks' greatest advantage came via triples (103 versus the Cubs' totals of 46 and 72 in their best years). The 1930 Cubs, helped by the extra-lively ball, outhomered the 1927 Yanks, 171–158 (gaining 37 home runs from Hartnett but losing exactly the same number through Hornsby's drop from 39 to 2). In 1929, too, a healthy Hartnett could have greatly closed the '27 Yanks' 158–131 home run margin. Overall, the 1929 and 1930 Chicago clubs both outscored the 1927 Yankees.

1. Murderers' row: for one early instance of the phrase applied to the Cubs, see *Tribune*, April 14, 1929. Later that year, the *Cincinnati Enquirer*, July 3, 1929, and the *St. Louis Star*, July 19, 1929 ("the Chewing Gum King's famous 'Four Horsemen,' who are frequently referred to as Murderers' Row"), both used the phrase. "Gangsters": "Russia Willing to Let Chicago Keep Few Machine Guns," *Tribune*, February 23, 1928. For an American perspective, see the lead paragraph of Samuel Merwin, "Chicago, the American Paradox," *Saturday Evening Post*, October 26, 1929, 8.

2. Honeymoon: Murphy, *Gabby Hartnett Story*, 29; McNeil, *Gabby Hartnett*, 125. Isle with a smile: Hendrickson, *Sun-Times Midwest Magazine*.

3. Downstate: *Tribune*, February 15, 1929.

4. Mobbed: *Tribune*, February 23, 1929.

5. Kansas City: *Herald and Examiner*, February 23, 1929. See also *Tribune*, February 12, 1926. Alkali: *Tribune*, February 13, 1926. Purple cloud: Frant-Walsh, "St. Catherine's Isle," 363. "Winds never blow": Wyler, "William Wrigley, Jr.," 241.

6. Evers: *Tribune*, February 25, 1921. Ships: Brown, *Chicago Cubs*, 85, and Pedersen, *Catalina Island*, 65; see also *Tribune*, February 17, 1932. Bowling alley: *Tribune*, February 15, 1926. "Shoot me": *Tribune*, March 12, 1929.

7. One of the first: "Hartnett Suffers as Usual on Trip to Avalon," *Tribune*, February 22, 1930. Dead or alive: *Tribune*, February 15, 1926. "Horse and buggy": *Tribune*, March 12, 1929. Flight: *Daily News*, February 17, 1932; *Tribune*, February 27 and March 1, 1932.

8. The bridge: Brown, *Chicago Cubs*, 106. Brown was at Catalina when the main troupe of Cubs arrived and filed a story (*Herald and Examiner*, February 27, 1929), but that report did not provide any details of the journey or mention Wrigley's presence on board the *Catalina*.

9. McGraw first: Light, *Cultural Encyclopedia of Baseball*, 686. See also Alexander, *John McGraw*, 129–30.

10. Ada Wrigley: Zimmerman, *William Wrigley, Jr.*, 238. Before visiting: Brown, *Chicago Cubs*, 83; Pettey, *Tribune*, January 27, 1932 (interview with John Hertz, founder of Yellow Cab and Hertz Auto Rental); and Hendrickson, *Sun-Times Midwest Magazine*, 13 in Chicago Historical Society Archives, "Biography, Wrigley, William Jr." file. According to Irving Vaughan ("Wrigley's Son to Carry On Dream of a Winner," *Tribune*, January 27, 1932), however, Wrigley's agent purchased an option to purchase Catalina, evidently without consulting Wrigley, and Wrigley then visited the island before making his offer.

11. Shortages: Zimmerman, *William Wrigley, Jr.*, 241; Brown, *Chicago Cubs*, 84. Musical ensembles: *Tribune*, February 22, 1930, and February 17, 1931; *Herald and Examiner*, February 16, 1932. Most of these accounts referred to a "fife-and-drum corps"; a photo in the *1997 Spring Training Baseball Yearbook* ("Greetings from Catalina Island," 23), plainly shows a brass band leading the Cubs to practice in 1932.

12. 1929 arrival: *Herald and Examiner* and *Tribune*, February 27, 1929. Spanish style: Federal Writers' Project, *California*, 369. Wrigley *père* initiated the style, although Philip later launched a downtown modernization project (Pedersen, *Catalina Island*, 100).

13. "Great": *Herald and Examiner*, February 27, 1929.

14. Conspicuous volunteer: *Tribune*, February 27 and March 6, 1929. Attractions and excursions: Federal Writers' Project, *California*, 367–79.

15. Outside Avalon: Frant-Walsh, "St. Catherine's Island," 363–64. Bison: Pedersen, *Catalina Island*, 89. "Snipe": Vitti, *Chicago Cubs*, 63.

16. Goat hunts, etc.: "Greetings from Catalina Island," 21; *Tribune*, March 5, 1932. Such efforts continued after spring training. Mrs. Veeck held a tea each year for the players' wives, and Mrs. Wrigley periodically hosted get-togethers at the Wrigley compound near Lake Geneva, Wisconsin. Frederick Krehbiel, September 10, 1999. Honeymoon: *Tribune*, January 29 and February 15, 1929; *Herald and Examiner*, February 19, 1932; *Daily News*, February 20, 1932; Hornof interview, June 26, 1999; Stephenson III, telephone interview. Dead fish: *Tribune*, February 14, 1927. Butter, rock: *Daily Times*, February 18, 1932.

17. Silent films: Pedersen, "Catalina Island History." Movie birds: Federal Writers' Project, *California*, 376. Joe E. Brown: *Tribune*, March 10, 1931, February 27, 1932 (game in Los Angeles). Starlets: Boone and Grunska, *Hack*, 104; *Daily Times*, March 7, 1931 (photo of Rogers Hornsby signing a baseball for Rochelle Hudson and Arline Judge). See also *Tribune*, March 13, 1937. Reagan: Reagan, *Reagan*, 29–31; *1997 Spring Training Yearbook*, 22–23; Vitti, *Chicago Cubs* 77.

18. Santa Catalina economy: *Business Week*, May 21, 1930, 28; Zimmerman, *William Wrigley, Jr.*, 262; P. K. Wrigley, interview, 116–17, 120.

19. Phil arrived: P. K. Wrigley, interview, 116.

20. Mountainside: Vaughan, *Tribune*, January 27, 1932; Brown, *Chicago Cubs*, 85. Clubhouse: "Greetings from Catalina Island," 21, and Federal Writers' Project, *California*, 375. "Tell 'em quick": "Story of How Gum Became a Big Business," *Tribune*, January 27, 1932.

21. "Impossible": *New York Times*, January 15, 1927. Ederle: "Offers Prize to Miss Ederle," *New York Times*, August 12, 1926. Sweetened the purse: *New York Times*, December 11, 1926.

22. "Mrs. Schoemmell": "Foreign Leaders Enter Catalina Race," AP dispatch in *New York Times*, December 17, 1926. Thousands watched: "Colors Blend in Sea Race," *Los Angeles Times*, January 16, 1927. *Avalon*: "153 to Swim Today for Catalina Prize," *New York Times*, January 15, 1927. Not all 153 who registered showed up to take the plunge. "Knotted and twisted": "Colors Blend in Sea Race," *Los Angeles Times*, January 16, 1927. Only Young: "Lad Wins Catalina Swim," *New York Times*, January 17, 1927. Five pounds: "Youth Staked All for Love of His Mother," *Los Angeles Times*, January 17, 1927; *Time*, January 24, 1927, gave Young's weight loss as twenty-five pounds.

23. $75,000: "Women Bother Catalina Hero," *Los Angeles Times*, January 23, 1927. *Time*: *Time*, January 24, 1927. Screen tests: "Young Riding Tide of Fame," *Los Angeles Times*, January 18, 1927; "Young Avoids Dotted Lines," *Los Angeles Times*, January 19, 1927. Lawyer: "Wrigley Takes Channel Victor under His Wing," *Tribune*, January 19, 1927.

24. Women only: "Wrigley Plans Women's Race," *Los Angeles Times*, January 18, 1927. Concluded Brown: Brown, *Win, Lose, or Draw*, 255–56.

25. Blockade: "Swimmers Will Have Protection," *Los Angeles Times*, January 9, 1927. "Overtown": Vitti, *Chicago Cubs* 83.

26. "Camera operators": *Tribune*, February 19, 1929. See also *Herald and Examiner*, February 19, 1929 ("five or six rows of photographers"); *Tribune*, February 27, 1929.

27. Real news: *Tribune*, March 1, 5, and 8, 1929.

28. Strode about: *Tribune*, March 6, 1929. Gonzalez: *Tribune*, March 6, 1929. "Cousin": *Tribune*, February 27, 1929.

29. Every conversation: *Tribune*, April 7, 1929. Emcee: *Daily News*, March 27, 1944. "Great gawd!": *Tribune*, June 23, 1929, corroborating the report of Hornsby's refusal to dance at Catalina (*Tribune*, March 2, 1929).

30. Roommate: *Tribune*, February 28, 1929.

31. "Aloha Oe": *Tribune*, March 11, 1932. Los Angeles: *Tribune*, March 9, 1929. Steak: Brown 1946, 107. Contemporary reports often mentioned Hornsby's steak diet: see *Tribune*, September 19, 1929; and *Sporting News*, June 30, 1932.

32. Berg: Dawidoff, *Catcher Was a Spy*, 56–57. Bicycle: *Tribune*, September 28, 1928.

33. Falk: *Tribune*, July 21, 1929. Kamm: *Tribune*, August 2, 1930; Lindberg, *White Sox Encyclopedia*, 112. Clean Sox: *Tribune*, September 15, 1929 ("The Sox have had three 'I Knew Him When' managers in a row.").

34. "The great American League": *Tribune*, March 10, 1929. City Series shares: *Tribune*, October 10, and November 1, 1928.

35. Rubbing mud: Andres, CNN, October 28, 2009. Shires: *Tribune*, March 6 (named captain), March 31 (suspended), and May 16, 1929 (fistfight).

36. Wardrobe: "You Don't Tell Me!" undated, in HOF files ca. spring 1929; *St. Louis Star-Chronicle*, December 12, 1929. Durocher: UP in HOF files, June 3, 1929. "Squawking": Frank Graham, "A Close-Up of Art Shires," dateline March 25, 1929, in HOF files. Ruth comparison: *Daily News*, June 22, 1929.

37. Chaw: *New York Telegram*, July 12, 1929; *St. Louis Star-Chronicle*, December 12, 1929; *Tribune*, June 17, 1930. Regaled: *Tribune*, November 3, 1928, and June 30, 1929 (colleges); Frank Graham, "A Close-Up of Art Shires," dateline March 25, 1929, in HOF files; James S. Collins, "Almost the Naked Truth," New York World News Service, dateline March 25, 1929, in HOF files; *New York Times*, August 1, 1929; and *St. Louis Star-Chronicle*, December 12, 1929. Concocting: *New York News*, April 10, 1930.

38. Rivalry: *Tribune*, April 7 (demotion from the cleanup spot "has furnished a challenge that will be interesting to watch. Instead of sulking Wilson has turned on the steam.") and April 14, 1929 ("It's a friendly rivalry, but Hack is out to show the world that Rogers can't steal his fan following on the basis of slugging"). St. Patrick's Day: *Tribune*, March 18, 1929. "A riot": *Tribune*, April 13, 1929.

39. Hyena car, etc.: *Tribune*, April 21, 1929. The article referred to the players' "talking machines"—portable record players. See Tim Gracyk, "A History of Portable Talking Machines," Tim's Phonographs and Old Records, http://www.gracyk.com/portable.shtml. Air-conditioning: "Pullman Richmond California Shops."

40. Uniform: *Tribune*, April 16, 1929.

7. "A SORT OF FRENZY"

1. Grand opening: advertisement, *Tribune*, July 1, 1929.

2. Smart money: *Tribune*, July 26, 1929 ("The Cubs were not supposed to be game, and some of the boys on the other teams remarked as much and more"). Dejected: *Daily News*, April 17 ("forced smile . . . unhappy"), October 3, 1929 ("quieter . . . wistful"); *Tribune*, February 21 ("depressed"), and July 30, 1930 ("panicky manner . . . bordering on paranoia"), September 17, 1932 ("slid up and down the bench").

3. Pretzel-like: *Chicago Herald-American*, April 3, 1945. See also *Daily News*, October 12, 1929 ("Fell down only once"); *Tribune*, October 12, 1929 ("[O]ne of the joke batsmen of the game . . . flippancy of the young man while facing Earnshaw"). Dressed flamboyantly: *Tribune* August 6, and September 26, 1929; "Blasts from the Windy City as Majors Held Their Confabs," *Sporting News*, December 17, 1931.

4. Taxi: *Tribune*, June 9, 1929. First road trip: *Tribune*, August 6, 1929.

5. Miniature golf: *Tribune*, September 14, 1932. Gas stations: *Tribune*, September

14, 1932; *Daily Times*, August 30, 1932; *Daily News*, December 12, 1932, and July 3, 1934; *Sporting News*, December 29, 1932.

6. Spectacle: *Tribune*, September 16, 1929; *Time*, September 5, 1932; *New York Daily News*, September 12, 1932; Williams, *New York World-Telegram*, September 28, 1932; Hunt, *New York Daily News*, September 29, 1932; "Suh?": *Daily News*, April 26, 1945.

7. Deliveries: *Tribune*, April 6 and September 11, 1927, and April 7, 1929; *Daily Times*, March 24, 1932; *Daily News*, July 2, 1934; *Tribune*, April 6, 1945. Screwball: *Tribune*, September 14, 1932; *Daily News*, July 2, 1934. On Alexander's role in teaching Bush the scroogie, see *Daily News*, January 16, 1934 (There y'are—that's the way old Alexander taught me to hold it"). See also *Tribune*, February 25, 1932.

8. Starters: *Tribune*, July 6, 1929.

9. "A. Suarez": Figueredo, *Cuban Baseball*, 174.

10. "Mississip": *Tribune*, September 29, 1928. "Self-consh": *Tribune*, May 26, 1929.

11. "Good field": Dawidoff, *Catcher Was a Spy*, 50; Hood, *Gashouse Gang*, 69; and Echevarría, *Pride of Havana*, 144.

12. Sports pages: *Tribune*, May 26, 1929.

13. Dissidents: *Tribune*, May 23, and June 2, 1929.

14. Declined: *Tribune*, July 10, 1929; see also *New York Times*, May 8, 1929, for a sample of Hendrick's analysis of the Cubs.

15. Pinch-hit: *Tribune*, July 3, 1929.

16. Critz: *Cincinnati Enquirer* and *Tribune*, both July 3, 1929.

17. "Fathead": "Scribbled by Scribes," *Sporting News*, July 14, 1932.

18. Bolted: *Tribune*, July 5, 1929; see also *Daily News*, July 5, 1929; *Cincinnati Enquirer*, July 5, 1929. Howled: *Tribune*, July 12, 1929.

19. Union Station: *Tribune*, *Daily News*, and *Cincinnati Enquirer*, all July 5, 1929.

20. "No Dempsey": *Tribune*, July 6, 1929. "Something doing": AP in *Indianapolis Star*, July 7, 1929.

21. "Cracks": *Tribune*, July 8, 1929.

22. "Vilest words": *Daily News*, July 6, 1929. In a bylined series published in early 1931, Wilson said that Kolp had made "aspersions upon my ancestors" and that Donahue had made "filthy accusations" (*Daily Times*, February 13, 1931). "Riot": AP in *Indianapolis Star*, July 7, 1929.

23. Reds grumbled: *Cincinnati Enquirer*, July 7, 1929.

24. Bowler: *Tribune*, July 10, 1929.

25. Chatterbox: *Tribune*, July 8 and 11, 1929.

26. "Tea wagon": *Tribune*, July 12, 1929.

27. "Just joking": *Tribune*, July 10, 1929.

28. Statement: *Tribune*, July 13, 1929.

29. Joyfully: *Daily News*, July 13, 1929.

30. Taylor: *Evening American*, July 6, 1929; *Tribune*, September 17, 1929.

31. McMillan: *New York Times*, July 14, 1929.

32. Boxing gloves: *New York Times*, July 14, 1929.

33. Tossing: *New York Times*, July 21, 1929.

34. Vance: *Daily News*, *Tribune*, July 22, 1929.

35. Pittsburgh: "Mr. Dreyfuss Is Embarrassed by His Pirates Again," *Tribune*, August 30, 1929.

36. Wrigley: *Daily News* and *Tribune*, both July 25, 1929. Cable: *Tribune*, July 10, 1929. Police escort: *Tribune*, July 26, 1929. The escort arrangement evidently continued for some time: see *Daily Times*, September 12, 1929.

37. "Snipers": Heuer, "Neighbors," 24. Lampposts: *Tribune*, August 7, 1929.

38. Freely admitted: AP dateline June 22, 1929, in HOF files. Roommate: *New York Telegram*, July 12, 1929; *New York Times*, August 1, 1929. Umpires: *Daily News*, July 9, 1929.

39. Wrongful death: "Shires, White Sox Captain, Sued for 'Beaning,'" AP dispatch, dateline March 27, 1929, in HOF clipping file; "Art Shires Sued for $25,411 in "Death of Negro Baseball Fan," *Sporting News*, April 4, 1929, in HOF clipping file; *Tribune*, May 21, 1929.

40. Fines: "Art's Ring Earnings Top Baseball Pay," AP dispatch, January 9, 1930, in HOF file.

41. Poetry: *Tribune*, July 30, August 1, and August 5, 1929.

42. Vaudeville: *Tribune*, August 2, 1929.

43. "The Jedge": *Tribune*, August 4, 1929.

44. Announcer: *Tribune*, August 4, 1929.

45. Fungo record: *New York Times*, August 1, 1929.

46. *Scientific American*: *Tribune*, August 28, 1929.

47. "Throats": *Tribune*, August 9, 1929.

48. Fussell: *Tribune*, August 14, 1929.

49. Resignation: *Tribune*, August 29, 1929.

50. Lumbago: AP dispatch in *Washington Post*, July 10, 1929.

51. Mathewson's record: Mathewson's victory total was later revised to 373. No-show: Kavanagh, 130. Home to Nebraska: *New York Times*, August 22, 1929. Divorce: *Tribune*, October 4, 1929.

52. Ticker tape: *Tribune*, August 14, 1929.

53. Shires and Wilson: *Tribune*, August 27, 1929.

54. Sox: *Tribune*, September 1, 1929.

55. Last kiss: "Dever Rites Set for Friday," *Times*, September 4, 1929.

56. Out-of-towners: UP dispatch in *Indianapolis Times*, August 27, 1929.

57. Municipal parks: *Tribune*, August 14, 1929. Rosenberg: Cataneo, *Hornsby Hit One*, 67.

58. "Boys, Do You Like the Cubs?": *Tribune*, August 9, 11, 12, 15, and 18, 1929.

59. Radio hookup: *Tribune*, August 26, 1929.

60. Hats, ovation: *Herald and Examiner*, September 1, 1929; *Tribune*, September 2, 1929.

61. Applications: *Tribune*, September 10 and 13, 1929.

62. Cahill: *Herald and Examiner*, September 13, 1929. Opportunities: *Tribune*, September 23, 1930 ("summoned almost nightly to dinners or entertainment" [September 1929]); *Herald and Examiner*, September 9, 1929; *Daily Times*, September 26, 1929; *Tribune*, October 11, 1929. Boy Scout: *Tribune*, September 13, 1929.

63. WENR: *Times*, September 3 and 16, 1929.

64. Acting captain: *Tribune*, September 1, 1929. Bonus: *Tribune*, September 20, 1929.

65. Stockton: *St. Louis Post-Dispatch*, August 20, 1929. For more McCarthy remarks in the same vein, see *Daily Times*, September 11, 1929.

66. Pupils: *New York Times*, July 14, 1929; *Indianapolis Times*, October 1, 1929; *Daily News*, August 2, 1934. Burke: AP in *Indianapolis Star*, September 15, 1929.

67. Ben Franklin Hotel: *Tribune* and *Daily Times*, both September 14, 1929, and Shires's account in *Tribune*, September 15, 1929, all place a house detective on the scene before Blackburne's arrival, without further explanation.

68. "Stool pigeons," "dicks": *Tribune*, September 15, 1929; *Daily Times*, September 14, 1929.

69. Mack: *Herald and Examiner*, September 15, 1929.

70. Banjo: *Tribune*, February 22, 1926. Broadcasting home games: *Daily Times*, September 3, 1929. Grimm would return to broadcasting for the Cubs over the decades.

71. Hornsby captain: *Tribune*, September 1, 1929.

72. Ankles: *Tribune*, August 13, 1929; *Herald and Examiner*, September 7, 1929. According to Al Lopez, a teammate of Wilson's in 1932–33, "He had his ankles taped before every game, the only player I ever knew of at that time who did." Lopez added that adhesive tape, not a wrap, was used (*Philadelphia Inquirer*, March 11, 1979). See also *Tribune*, July 10, 1931 (small ankles, years of wrapping with adhesive tape before every game). Heel: Hornsby, *My Kind of Baseball*, 1953, 108: "It began to bother me in the late weeks of the 1929 season."

8. MCCARTHY'S DEBACLE

1. Tinee's review: "Oriental Opens with Gay Comedy," *Tribune*, May 9, 1926. 3,216: "Balaban and Katz Open New Loop Movie Theater," *Tribune*, May 9, 1926. See David Balaban, *The Chicago Movie Palaces of Balaban and Katz* (Chicago: Arcadia Publishing, 2006), 40 (3,217 as of 1934), and an advertisement for the Heywood-Wakefield company ("over 2,800 chairs" supplied to the theater ["Oriental Theater," 25]). Presentation acts: See, for instance, Crafton, *Talkies*, 75, and Koszarski, *Evening's Entertainment*, 47–48 (a review of the program at the Oriental's sister Loop theater, the Chicago Theater, in August 1926), and 53. *Tramp:* the IMDB.com website, accessed April 18, 2012, lists Frank Capra as an uncredited scriptwriter for the movie.

2. Decorations: "Oriental Theater," most pages. Colors: *Tribune*, May 9, 1926. Glass ceiling: Bushnell, "Chicago's Magnificent Movie Palaces," 101. Turbaned: *Tribune*, May 9, 1926.

3. "Today!": *Herald and Examiner*, October 8, 1929.

4. Images: *Tribune*, September 14, 1930.

5. Rosenberg: Cataneo, *Hornsby Hit One*, 69. Playograph: "Seeing the Game by Proxy" (photo), *Herald and Examiner*, October 9, 1929. Sidearming, underhanding: Vaughan, Burns, *Tribune*, October 9, 1929; Brandt, *New York Times*, October 9, 1929.

6. Flabbergasted: Pegler, and "Athletics, Too, Have Word of Praise for Root" (no byline), *Tribune*, October 9, 1929; Williams, *Indianapolis Times*, October 9, 1929; and Lieb, *Connie Mack*, 1945, 224. Late-arriving: "Disappointed" (photo), *Herald and Examiner*, October 9, 1929.

7. Simmons asked Mack: Lieb, *Connie Mack*, 224.

8. 12,000: *Tribune*, October 9, 1929. Rooftops, telescope: Keys, *Daily News*, and Avery, *Herald and Examiner*, both October 9, 1929. Eugene May: photo caption, *Herald and Examiner*, October 9, 1929.

9. Seat prices: *Herald and Examiner*, September 11, 1929; *Tribune*, September 13, 1929. 200,000: *Tribune*, September 18, 1929. Bleacher lines: *Daily News*, October 8, 1929.

10. Mrs. Field: *Daily News* and *Herald and Examiner*, both October 9, 1929.

11. Genteel: *Tribune* and special to *New York Times*, both October 9, 1929.

12. Jury box: Brandt, *New York Times*, October 9 and 15, 1929; Williams, *Indianapolis Times*, October 9, 1929. Hand: Totten broadcast transcript, *Daily News*, October 8, 1929. Totten was the CBS "anchor" for the Wrigley Field series games.

13. Ambled: Joe Williams, *Indianapolis Times*, October 9, 1929.

14. Longest hit: Totten broadcast transcript, *Daily News*, October 8, 1929.

15. Left behind: UP in *Indianapolis Times*, August 10, 1929 (Mack—Ehmke gets players "riled and dissatisfied"); Kiernan, *New York Times*, October 11, 1929; Pegler, *Tribune*, October 9, 1929; and Lieb, *Connie Mack*, 223. Six days' rest, fight: UP in *Indianapolis Times*, August 10, 1929.

16. Slipped into: Kieran, *New York Times*, October 11, 1929; Crusinberry, *Daily News*, October 11, 1929; *Indianapolis Times*, September 20, 1929; and Lieb, *Connie Mack*, 223.

17. Fruits of experience: Crusinberry, *Daily News*, October 11, 1929.

18. Tinker: *Daily Times*, September 12, 1929; *Herald and Examiner*, September 18 and September 24, 1929. See also Charlie Root's and Woody English's versions told to Carmichael, *Daily News*, September 14 and 27, 1932. Pantomime: *Herald and Examiner*, October 12, 1929.

19. Cobb: Woltz, *Herald and Examiner*, October 8, 1929. See also Brandt, *New York Times*, October 8, 1929 ("whispers around the lobby," and interview with unnamed Athletic regarding Ehmke).

20. Ruth: Stanton, *Daily News*, October 9, 1929; the actual quote is "How I would love to play in this ballpark a couple of years!" The quote, with "dump" in place of "ballpark," is usually attributed to Ruth in 1932.

21. Blankets: photos in *Daily News*, October 9, 1929.

22. Jockeying: Maxwell ("D.M."), *Tribune*, October 10, 1929; Totten broadcast transcript, *Daily News*, October 8 ("You can hear a chorus of catcalls from the Athletics") and 9, 1929 ("The Athletic jockeying is working pretty hard down there on Malone."). Redirected: Totten broadcast transcript, *Daily News*, October 8, 1929 ("The crowds yell back at the Philadelphia bench. This is the noisiest bench I have ever seen here, and they yell back at the crowd").

23. Outright boos: Brown, *Herald and Examiner*, October 10, 1929; Ward, *Tribune*, October 10, 1929.

24. Booed: Brown, *Herald and Examiner*, October 10, 1929.

25. Buttonholed: Vaughan, *Tribune*, October 10, 1929, and September 23, 1930. Three years later Charlie Root, a staunch supporter of McCarthy, endorsed Hornsby's analysis: "That first game I pitched, wasn't a bad ball game, but a home run by Foxx settled it in their favor. And we were pitching all wrong to 'em at that. We got the wrong dope" (Carmichael, *Daily News*, September 14, 1932). In the 1932 series, of course, Hornsby once again said the Cubs pitchers were misinformed—that time after the fact—and Root was once again hit hard: see chapter 18.

26. Cub bench: Otto, *Herald and Examiner*, October 13, 1929.

27. Blanket: Totten simulated broadcast, *Daily News*, October 12, 1929. Although not the CBS announcer for the Philadelphia games, Totten covered the three games "in the style in which he broadcast the Chicago games over WMAQ."

28. High-spirited and laughing: Vaughan, Burns, Maxwell, *Tribune*, October 12, 1929.

29. Banjo: Burns, *Tribune*, October 12, 1929. Smiling: Otto, *Herald and Examiner*, October 12, 1929. Indigestion: Maxwell (D.M.), *Tribune*, October 10, 1929. "Can't lose": Zimmerman, *William Wrigley, Jr.*, 234.

30. "Give you plenty": Kieran, *New York Times*, October 13, 1929.

31. Cub bench: Totten simulated broadcast transcript, *Daily News*, October 12, 1929.

32. Otto: *Herald and Examiner*, October 13, 1929.

33. "Won't be shut out": Lieb, *Connie Mack*, 227.

34. Consensus: Drebinger, *New York Times*, and Cobb, *St. Louis Post-Dispatch*, both October 12, 1929.

35. Taylor's tosses: Stockton and McGraw, *St. Louis Post-Dispatch*, October 12, 1929.

36. Moaned: *Saturday Evening Post*, February 11, 1938, 86.

37. Collins's slide: special dispatch, *Tribune*, October 13, 1929. Scoreboard: Kieran, *New York Times*, October 13, 1929.

38. Stockyard cheer: *Tribune*, September 14, 1930.

39. Rare visit: AP in *Tribune*, October 13, 1929.

40. "Breaks": McGowen, *New York Times*, October 13, 1929. Lotshaw: *Daily Times*, February 21, 1937.

41. "Couldn't see": Vaughan, *Tribune*, October 13, 1929.

42. Press corps: Brown, *Herald and Examiner*, October 14, 1929. "Terrific flop": Burns, *Tribune*, October 13, 1929. "Jangled mass": *New York Times*, October 13, 1929.

43. Evers and Cobb: AP in *Tribune*, October 14, 1929.

44. Other fingers: UP and Williams in *Indianapolis Times*, October 14, 1929; Otto, *Herald and Examiner*, October 16, 1929; Keys, *Daily News*, October 17, 1929.

45. "Baloney": Vaughan, *Tribune*, and Brandt, *New York Times*, both October 14, 1929.

46. "Moaning": Brown, Otto, *Herald and Examiner*, October 14, 1929.

47. Venison: Brandt, *New York Times*, October 14, 1929. Hunting trip: Otto, *Herald and Examiner*, October 14, 1929.

48. Language: Otto, *Herald and Examiner*, October 16, 1929; AP, *Tribune*, October 23, 1929.

49. Vaudeville: Burns, *Tribune*, October 11 and 14, 1929, and October 15, 1932; Carmichael, *Daily News*, August 9, 1932.

50. Generally friendly: *New York Times*, October 15, 1929. "Beer!": Kashatus, *Philadelphia Athletics*, 56, and Lieb, *Connie Mack*, 228. Bouquet: Otto, *Herald and Examiner*, October 15, 1929.

51. Hat twitched: Runyon, *Herald and Examiner,* October 15, 1929.

52. Grim-faced: Otto, *Herald and Examiner,* October 15, 1929.

53. Seventh-inning stretch: Runyon, *Herald and Examiner,* October 15, 1929.

54. Shadows: Vaughan, *Tribune,* October 15, 1929. Smiling broadly: Williams, *Indianapolis Times,* October 15, 1929.

55. Unconcerned: Joe Williams, "Talking It Over," *Indianapolis Times,* October 15, 1929.

56. "Helpful": Stockton, *St. Louis Post-Dispatch,* October 14, 1929. Berated: Joe Williams, "Talking It Over," *Indianapolis Times,* October 15, 1929.

57. Dumbfounded: Runyon, *Herald and Examiner,* October 15, 1929.

58. "Crazy": Totten, *Daily News,* October 14, 1929.

59. Tracked: Vaughan, *Tribune,* October 15, 1929. "Hoover Kept Neutral at Game, He Tells Philadelphia Mayor," AP in *New York Times,* October 15, 1929. See also photo caption in "War Ended," *Herald and Examiner,* October 15, 1929 ("The Cubs were ahead when the picture was taken, which might explain [Hoover's] smile."). Fans remained seated: Runyon, *Herald and Examiner,* October 15, 1929.

60. "Funeral Train": Corcoran, "McCarthy Happy as Yanks Win Title," *Evening American,* October 3, 1932.

61. Half a day's wages: Heuer, "Neighbors," 26. The average workman's wage was $1,500 per annum in the 1920s—less than seven dollars a day for a laborer (Schlesinger, *The Crisis of the Old Order,* 111).

62. Consensus: Keys, *Daily News,* October 17, 1929.

63. "I'll be damned": *Tribune,* October 15, 1929.

64. Elevator: Vaughan, *Tribune,* January 27, 1932.

65. Union Station: *Tribune,* October 16, 1929.

66. Brokers: *Herald and Examiner,* October 29, 1930.

9. "I WANTED WILSON"

1. Ragen's Colts: Lindberg, *Chicago by Gaslight,* 208–9. Humiliating: Farrell, *Young Lonigan,* 74.

2. White City: Sawyers, *Chicago Sketches,* 234. Hunt: see Farrell, *Studs Lonigan,* 158, 193. Despite being a fervent White Sox fan (as well as an acquaintance of Gabby Hartnett) who was deeply affected by the Black Sox affair, Farrell put little baseball into his trilogy. Studs's father, however, was portrayed as a devoted Sox fan.

3. Daly-Shires bout: *Tribune,* December 10, 1929. Face forward: *Tribune,* January 5, 1930. "Get me Tunney": AP dispatch, dateline December 10, 1929, in HOF files.

4. Clothes: Boone and Grunska, *Hack,* plate 20.

5. Hunting: Wilson, "Lewis R. (Hack) Wilson."

6. Telegram: Boone and Grunska, *Hack* 86.

7. Agreed to fight: *Tribune*, December 14, 1929. $200,000: Soderman, "Major League Ballplayer," 6.

8. Veeck: *Tribune*, December 15, 1929; and "Shires May Meet Hack Wilson Next," dateline December 19, 1929, in HOF files.

9. Bank, lodge, residence: *Tribune*, December 17, 1929.

10. Quandary solved: *Tribune*, December 17, 1929. "Hit him!": Roberts, *Chicago Bears,* 57. Flanagan: "Radio Announcer Socked in Eye by Irate Fan," AP dispatch, dateline December 17, 1929, in HOF files; Roberts, *Chicago Bears,* 57.

11. McGurn: Roberts, *Chicago Bears,* 55.

12. "Battleship": "The 'Not So Great' Shires Is Deluged by Challenges," AP dispatch, dateline December 17, 1929, in HOF files.

13. "Quarter of a million": *Tribune*, December 20, 1929.

14. Lowdown: United News dispatch in HOF files, December 20, 1929.

15. Christmas cards: *Tribune*, December 23 and 24, 1929.

16. Bailey: *Tribune*, December 27, 1929. Criss: *Pittsburgh Post-Gazette*, January 1, 1930; *Tribune*, January 3, 1930.

17. Gerry: AP dispatch, dateline January 5, 1930, in HOF files, and *Tribune*, January 5, 1930.

18. Faeth: "Shires Knocks Out Faeth; Clouds Disappear," AP dispatch, dateline January 8, 1930, and [*Sporting News* ?], dateline January 16, 1930, both in HOF files.

19. Cleared: "Clouds Hovering over Shires Disappearing," AP dispatch, dateline January 7, 1930, in HOF files. Michigan authority: "Shires Will Escape Ban," *Pittsburgh Post-Gazette*, January 3, 1930.

20. Spohrer: AP dispatch in *Tribune*, January 11, 1930, and "Shires Kayoes Spohrer in 4th," United News dispatch in HOF files, dateline January 10, 1930. The AP dispatch placed the knockdown in the "opening round."

21. Payday: "Art's Ring Earnings Top Baseball Pay," AP dispatch, dateline January 9, 1930, in HOF files; *Tribune*, January 12, 1930. The *Tribune* directly quoted Shires saying that the five fights had earned him $10,500, whereas the AP report put Shires's take from the Spohrer bout alone at $10,000. "Razz the Babe": *Tribune*, January 12, 1930.

22. Mrs. Lawson: "Judgment Given against Shires," dateline January 11, 1930; unattributed dispatch, dateline January 16, 1930, in HOF files. Larkin: *Tribune*, January 13, 1930.

23. Inner sanctum: Bert Demby, UP dispatch, dateline January 18, 1930, in HOF files; "Landis Outpoints Shires in Oratory," *Sporting News*, January 23, 1930.

24. Comiskey: *Tribune*, March 20, 1930.

25. New Shires: Jimmy Powers, *New York News*, April 10, 1930.

26. "I'm human": *Tribune*, July 11, 1930. Number 13: H. G. Salsinger, "The Sidelines," dateline July 15, 1930, in HOF files. Milwaukee: "Griffs' Trade Hope Faded with Shires," *Sporting News*, December 11, 1930.

27. Beer: *Evening Post*, February 11, 1930; *Tribune* and *Herald and Examiner*, both February 12, 1930; UP dispatch in *Indianapolis Times*, February 12, 1930. Physician's testimony: *Evening Post*, February 11, 1930. "Thumping," "slapped": *Tribune*, June 22 and 23, 1928. "Punched": *St. Louis Post-Dispatch*, June 22, 1928. "Swipes": *Evening Post*, June 22, 1928.

28. Wilson's version: *Daily News*, February 11, 1930, and *Tribune* and *Herald and Examiner*, February 12, 1930.

29. Argumentative: *Tribune*, February 12, 1930. "A name": *Daily News*, February 11, 1930. Herbert Simons's article in the *Daily Times*, February 11, 1930, said: "Hack's attorneys said that Young came charging down the aisle, making reference to Wilson's ancestors in a loud voice." In a minibiography published a year and a day after the trial, Wilson said that Young was "libeling my ancestors in a raucous voice" (*Daily Times*, February 12, 1931). Opening remarks: *Daily Times*, February 11, 1930.

30. Parade: *Evening American*, February 11, 1930. Grinning: *Evening American*, February 11, 1930.

10. THE PRIME OF MR. HACK WILSON

1. "Happy Days Are Here Again": *Tribune*, February 22, 1930. "Happy Days Have Come Again" was the title provided by the reporter. Glass-bottomed boat: *New York Times*, February 21, 1930.

2. Lindbergh: *New York Times*, February 22, 1930. Assassination warning: *New York Times*, February 25, 1930.

3. Disappointment: *Tribune*, January 27, 1932. See also McCarthy's remarks in *Sporting News*, December 3, 1931, 3.

4. Tonsils: *Tribune*, November 21, 1929. Grabbed a mitt: *Tribune*, February 25, 1930.

5. "Settle it": *Tribune*, March 2, 1930. Schalk: *Herald and Examiner*, September 22, 1930.

6. Longtime friend: Brown, *Chicago Cubs*, 118. "Must have a winner": *Herald and Examiner*, January 27, 1932.

7. Slowed down: *Tribune*, March 2 and 25, and April 15, 1930. Operation: Hornsby, *My Kind of Baseball*, 108–9, and *Tribune*, April 9, 1930 ("Dr. Hyland . . . removed a growth from Hornsby's heel last winter."). Tiptoe: *Tribune*, March 30, 1930. Returned to Chicago: *Tribune*, April 5, 1930. Beaming: *Tribune*, September 24, 1930. Hornsby made a trip to Chicago April

4 and rejoined the team in Kansas City a few days later; the Cubs began play at St. Louis April 15, and opened at home the 22nd.

8. Specialist: *Tribune*, April 7, 1930. Surgeon: *Tribune*, April 9, 1930. Electric treatment: *Tribune*, May 6, 1930.

9. Soft drink parlors: *Tribune*, May 2, 1930. Boils: *Tribune*, May 2 and 6, 1930; *Daily Times*, May 28, 1930.

10. Tinker: *New York Times*, July 22, 1930.

11. "Sunny Boy": *Daily Times*, May 5, 1930.

12. Sunglasses: *Tribune*, February 11 and March 1, 1930. Shades: Golenbock, *Wrigleyville*, 220.

13. Humiliating: *Tribune*, September 27, 1926, July 22, 1929, and August 6, 1929. Beck: *Saturday Evening Post*, February 11, 1939, 89.

14. Smile: "Wilson Ends Vance's Spell; Cubs Win, 3–1," *Tribune*, May 7, 1930.

15. "Temple of the sun dodgers": Drury, *Chicago in Seven Days*, 148.

16. Levee: Lindberg, *Chicago by Gaslight*, 111–12; and Drury, *Chicago in Seven Days*, 148–49. Freiberg's: Lindberg, *Chicago by Gaslight*, 150; Kenney, *Chicago Jazz*, 63.

17. Colosimo: Drury, *Chicago in Seven Days*, 147.

18. Four Deuces: Drury, *Chicago in Seven Days*, 147. By the time Drury's book came out in 1930, the Four Deuces was evidently closed, or at least Capone was no longer the visible owner-operator. Capone visits: "Cooney Closes Cafe; Mystery Stirs First Ward," *Tribune*, November 26, 1939 (article concerning a successor establishment, the Royal Frolics).

19. The "Stroll," Armstrong, Morton: Spinney, *City of Big Shoulders*, 170. Races could mix: Kenney, *Chicago Jazz*, 17. Jazz capital: Bushnell, "When Jazz Came to Chicago," 141 (after 1928, "Harlem was becoming the new national center for jazz . . . but the Windy City had been the friendly home for jazz for a dozen glorious years"); A. Smith, *Chicago's Left Bank*, 93 ("In the late 1920s Chicago-style jazz . . . swept across the country" to Hollywood and New York). See also "Chicago Theatrical News," *Chicago Defender*, September 11, 1926; Carmichael and Longstreet, *Sometimes I Wonder*, 103; Kenney, *Chicago Jazz*, xiv–xv; and Ogren, *Jazz Revolution*, 61. Lincoln Gardens: Carmichael and Longstreet, *Sometimes I Wonder*, 101. Police raid: "U.S. Raids Big Night Clubs," *Tribune*, December 31, 1930. Commandeer: A. Smith, *Chicago's Left Bank*, 92.

20. Cabaret: Drury, *Chicago in Seven Days*, 148. Dance girls: Kenney, *Chicago Jazz*, 63. However, Kenney (154) places at least one noted jazzman, the clarinetist Jimmie Noone, at the Midnight Club as of 1931, Joking and singing: Cohn, *Joker Is Wild*, 340.

21. "Hip flask" raid, Goodman, Armstrong: Kenney, *Chicago Jazz*, 155.

Kidnapped: "Kidnapped Café Owners and Driver Freed," *Tribune*, April 19, 1927. Adler: *Tribune*, April 18 and 19, 1927. Mrs. Prevo: *Tribune*, December 21, 1927.

22. Capone: Cohn, *Joker Is Wild*, 42. Cohn names a Ralph Gillette as one of the Frolic's co-owners when Lewis played there. Kenney, *Chicago Jazz*, 63, says Ike Bloom opened the venue after the First World War. Lewis: "Cabaret Man's Fears Told as Stabbing Clew," *Tribune*, November 9, 1927; Cohn, *Joker Is Wild*, 41.

23. Dead and gone: Cohn, *Joker Is Wild*, 341.

24. "Artist": *Evening American*, May 9, 1930.

25. South State Street Station, drunks, "refuse to say": *Daily Times*, May 9, 1930.

26. "Get Pat out," Marion Malone: *Daily Times*, May 9, 1930. Cub fan: *Evening American*, May 9, 1930.

27. "A misunderstanding," "hadn't been drinking": *Evening American*, May 9, 1930. Garbo: *Daily Times*, May 9, 1930.

28. 20,000: *Tribune*, May 8, 1930.

29. Boils: *Daily Times*, May 28, 1930.

30. Predictions: see various article titles listed in 1930 *New York Times Index*, "Business—General Conditions."

31. "Carlson Cub Hope": *Daily Times*, May 27, 1930. Froelich: *Daily Times*, May 28, 1930 ("bat boy"); *Tribune*, May 29,1930 ("clubhouse boy"); Froelich interview in Golenbock, 183.

32. Excused himself: *Tribune*, May 29, 1930. "Feel pretty bad": *Daily Times*, May 28, 1930.

33. Dr. Davis: *Tribune*, May 29, 1930. "Feels like that trouble": *Daily Times*, May 28, 1930. Death: *Daily Times*, May 28, 1930; *Tribune*, May 29, 1930; AP dispatch in *Indianapolis Star*, May 29, 1930.

34. Armbands, "pepper": "On with the Show" (photo caption), *Daily Times*, May 29, 1930.

35. Eulogy: *Tribune*, May 29, 1930. Sobbed: *Daily Times*, May 29, 1930.

36. Few realized: *Tribune*, May 29, 1930. News had been kept: *Daily Times*, May 28, 1930. Salary, postponement: *Tribune*, May 30, 1930.

37. Slid: Hornsby, *My Kind of Baseball*, 110; *Tribune*, May 31, 1930; and AP dispatch in *Indianapolis Star*, May 31, 1930 ("[Hornsby's] leg crashed against Pitcher Sylvester Johnson, covering the bag, and was fractured").

38. Most Valuable Player: AP dispatch in *Indianapolis Star*, May 31, 1930.

39. "Blackbird": *Chicago Sun-Times*, February 22, 1955. Dominated: Grimm, *Jolly Cholly's Story*, 61. Lose concentration: *Tribune*, October 3, 1929, October 1, 1930, and April 10, 1932; *Herald and Examiner*, April 19, 1932. For a spectacular instance, see Joe Williams's account of Malone's behavior in the

fifth game of the 1929 World Series (*Indianapolis Times*, October 15, 1929). "Ya bum": *Sun-Times*, February 22, 1955.

40. Biceps: *Tribune*, August 19, 1930. Legion: The press provided few specifics during the pair's heyday. After Hornsby's crackdown began, euphemistic phrases about their fondness for "banquets" and references to curfew violations came into use. Specific accounts became more common after Wilson's death in late 1948. See John Carmichael, *Daily News*, November 26, 1948; John Carmichael, *Sporting News*, December 8, 1948, 19; Bob Lewis, *Sun-Times*, February 22, 1955; Boone and Grunska, *Hack*, 135–36; Golenbock, *Wrigleyville*, 198 (Ed Froelich); *Baseball Digest*, June 1996, 81; Brace, interview.

41. Lost control: Grimm, *Jolly Cholly's Story*, 56–57. Worm: "Wilson Hit Everything Hard, Including Gin," *Sporting News*, June 24, 1978, 12. Lewis watched: *Sun-Times*, February 22, 1955. See also *Tribune*, November 24, 1948; Grimm, *Jolly Cholly's Story*, 56.

42. "Clean life?": Mead, *Two Spectacular Seasons*, 85.

43. Vaughan repeatedly mentioned: "Hornsby Gets Job," *Tribune*, September 23, 1930. See also Vaughan in *Tribune*, July 1, 1931, and January 27, 1932 ("Wrigley's Son to Carry on Dream of a Winner"). See also comments in *Tribune*, September 24, 1930, and January 2, 1931 (corroboration from Ed Burns, who alternated with Vaughan on Cubs and Sox coverage); UP quoting Wrigley in the *Indianapolis Times*, September 13, 1930 ("I haven't forgotten last year, when there was a letdown after the pennant was won").

44. Pencil pusher: *Tribune*, August 27 and September 5, 1930. Pitching staff: see Crackerjack ad, *Tribune*, May 26, 1930; *Daily Times*, May 27, and September 3, 1930; *Tribune*, June 1 and July 9, 1930; UP in *Indianapolis Times*, August 22, 1930.

45. Dominated the ball club: *Tribune*, June 19, July 10 and 30, 1930; *New York Times*, July 16, 1930.

46. Alexander: *Tribune*, June 4, July 17, and August 6, 1930.

47. "What a ballplayer!": *Tribune*, July 9, 1930.

48. Horde: *Tribune*, June 28, 1930. Plea: Veeck, *Veeck—as in Wreck*, 27. This event was possibly described in the *Saturday Evening Post*, September 13, 1930, 25.

49. Massed: *Tribune*, June 28, 1930.

50. Official attendance: the *Herald and Examiner*, September 1, 1930, noted: "The following figures are unofficial, since it is not the custom to give out official statistics on paid attendance at box offices nowadays, but it may be said that they are as nearly correct as any unofficial estimate can be." Note, however, the *Tribune*, August 17, 1930: "President Veeck yesterday announced the

actual [emphasis added] attendance figures for the Brooklyn series."
Regardless of whether the figures were official or unofficial, no newspaper of
the time reported attendance regularly. Newspaper accounts frequently noted
"paid attendance," as opposed to Ladies Day, youth attendance, and paid and
unpaid admissions: compare *Herald and Examiner*, September 1, 1930, and
Tribune, September 5, 1932, which detailed figures on the 1932 season. Mail-in
system: see Cubs' display ad in *Tribune*, July 25, 1930. 35,000: *Tribune*, July 30,
1930.

51. 100,000: *Tribune*, August 9, 1930.

52. Sacks: Mead, *Two Spectacular Seasons*, 29. Upgraded: *Tribune*, August 20
    (McCarthy—"[N]early half the women passing through the gates had bought
    tickets"). Cash customers: *Tribune*, August 30, 1930 (Catherine O'Connor—
    "[I]f I haven't a pass I buy a ticket").

53. Single series records: *Tribune*, June 30 and August 25, 1930; UP in *Indianapolis
    Times*, August 25, 1930.

54. Ticket windows: *Tribune*, August 25, 1930. See also *Herald and Examiner*,
    September 1, 1930. (For the August 24 game, "it was estimated by President
    Bill Veeck that he turned away nearly as many persons as were in the
    park—approximately 47,000.")

55. Swinging three bats: *Tribune*, July 20, 1930.

56. Marched: *Tribune*, July 27, 1930.

57. Prediction: *Tribune*, August 3, 1930.

58. Ice water: Veeck, *Veeck—as in Wreck*, 32. Note that Wilson hit three homers
    in the doubleheader—not in one game; Veeck understandably confused it
    with the three-homer single game of July 26.

59. Different take: *Tribune*, July 1, 1931. "Miseries of the stomach": *Tribune*, July
    9 and August 9, 1930. The three-homer doubleheader took place August 10.
    "Appendix": Grimm, *Jolly Cholly's Story*, 53. Muscle: *Tribune*, August 30,
    1930.

60. "Bonded in bourbon": Veeck, *Hustler's Handbook*, 167. Hotel room: *Tribune*,
    August 21, 1938. "Ten games ahead": Boone and Grunska, *Hack*, 99.

61. "Putty knife": NEA Service in *Indianapolis Times*, August 25, 1930.

62. Prediction: *Tribune*, August 19, 1930.

63. "West Virginia": *Tribune*, August 27, 1930.

64. Clean block: *Tribune*, August 25, 1930. "Miraculous": UP in *Indianapolis
    Times*, August 25, 1920. "Famous throws": *Tribune*, August 29, 1930.

65. Stop-action: *Tribune*, August 31, 1930.

66. "Hack Wilson's public": *Daily Times*, September 2, 1930. The caption to the
    photograph indicates that was probably taken several days earlier, which
    would have involved home runs number 45 or 46.

67. Six hundred thousand: *Herald and Examiner*, September 1, 1930 ("unofficial" figures).

68. "Can't stop us": UP in *Indianapolis Times*, August 25, 1930.

69. Working out: *Tribune*, July 30, 1930. See also *Tribune*, August 15, 1930.

70. Boils, freak injury: *Tribune* and *Daily Times*, both May 28, 1930. "Drug store glove": *Tribune*, August 14, 1930.

71. Booing, criticism: *Tribune*, September 26, 1930; *Herald and Examiner*, September 22, 25, and 26, 1930 ("the cries of the wolves"). Miss E. E. S.: *Daily Times*, September 3, 1930 (reply by Harold Shade). Rumors: *Tribune*, September 7, 21, and 23, 1930; UP dispatch in *Indianapolis Times*, September 22, 1930; *St. Louis Post-Dispatch*, September 24, 1930. Impression: *Tribune*, September 23, 1930.

72. Charley horse: *Tribune*, September 8 and 23, 1930. Vaughan reported the full incident two weeks later, but Burns made the original, less detailed, report. Prediction was off: see *Daily Times*, September 23, 1930 (benching Hornsby as a malcontent—one in a list of perceived McCarthy negatives).

73. Root: *Saturday Evening Post*, February 11, 1939, 86; *Tribune*, September 11, 1930. Cub bench, Bressler: *Herald and Examiner*, September 11, 1930.

74. Transfixed: *Tribune*, September 12 ("every score board in the city drew spectators.") and 13, 1930 ("Crain Necks to See Board").

75. Sneak a curve: *Tribune*, September 14, 1930. "My O'Doul": W. Brown, *Chicago Cubs*, 99. See also *Tribune*, September 20, 1930. Pictograph: *Herald and Examiner*, September 16, 1930.

76. "Never mind, kid": *Tribune*, September 16, 1930.

77. Wrigley was not around: "Owner Wrigley Plays Hide and Seek at Cub Game," *Tribune*, September 16, 1930. See also "Frederick Sets Pinch Home Run Record at Five," *Tribune*, September 11, 1932. ("It so happened that Mr. Wrigley was present when Lefty socked that first pinch homer"—i.e., he was not present for O'Doul's second home run on Monday the 15th. Wrigley definitely skipped the first game at the Polo Grounds on Tuesday the 16th ["Owner Wrigley Absent as Club Loses," *Tribune*, September 17, 1930].) "Friendless": *Tribune*, September 20, 1930.

78. Brooklyn: UP in *Indianapolis Times*, September 16, 1930; Westbrook Pegler, *Tribune*, September 19, 1930.

79. Wrigley's absence: *Tribune*, September 17, 1930.

80. Veterans: *Tribune*, September 21, 1930 (Cub stars "smiling"—Wilson, Hornsby, Malone, Root, Stephenson, Grimm; "melancholy"—Cuyler, Bush, Hartnett). City Series: *Tribune*, September 22, 1930. Better paid: see *Tribune*, January 19, 1931. "Whether Wilson finally gets $30,000 or $40,000, the Cubs probably will be the highest priced ball club in existence." Hartnett was listed

at $18,000 for the past season, with one pitcher also paid that amount and another (unnamed) player's salary estimated at $22,000. Rice interview: *Herald and Examiner*, September 19, 1930. Wilson predicted: *Tribune*, September 28, 1930 ("One of the greatest Wrigley stars"—Wilson's interview with Rice would point to his fitting this description, rather than the other better-known Cubs—Hornsby, Malone, Root, Cuyler, and Hartnett). Note also *Tribune*, September 21, 1930, referenced above.

81. Uncertainty: *Tribune*, September 7 and 21, 1930; *St. Louis Post-Dispatch*, September 24, 1930. Bullpen catcher: *Tribune*, September 10 and 13, 1930; *Herald and Examiner*, September 22, 1930.

82. Team meeting: *Herald and Examiner*, September 22, 1930.

83. Boston newspapermen: *Tribune*, September 22, 1930.

84. "Take care of itself": *Tribune*, September 21, 1930.

85. "My Mr. O'Doul": "Cubs: As Wrigley Sees Them," *Tribune*, September 20, 1930 (emphasis added).

86. Hinsdale: *Daily Times*, September 20, 1930.

87. "Propaganda," exercise: *Herald and Examiner*, September 22, 1930. "Why can't they?": *Daily Times*, September 22, 1930.

88. Brown's mission: Barrow and Kahn, *My Fifty Years*, 165, places Brown at Madison Square Garden and names Barrow as the intermediary between Brown and Ruppert. Brown mentions a "George Perry," perhaps for diplomatic reasons, and other details differ. But the essential story is similar. See Brown, *Chicago Cubs*, 119–20. Ruppert arranged: Brown, *Chicago Cubs*, 119–20. But see also *Tribune*, September 24, 1930, where Ruppert said he had had no contact yet with Wrigley: "'I have seen McCarthy one once in my life ... and that was a great many years ago. I know absolutely nothing about his being through as manager of the Cubs except what I have read in the papers."

89. "Win, lose, or draw": *Herald and Examiner*, September 22, 1930.

90. Vance: *Herald and Examiner*, September 24, 1930.

91. Albany: *Tribune*, September 23, 1930.

92. "Too valuable": P. K. Wrigley, interview.

93. "Manly attitude": *Tribune*, September 24, 1930. Wrigley hinted: *Herald and Examiner*, September 25, 1930 ("The teams that want [McCarthy] will have to go to him. And there will be several that will go, too, unless I'm altogether wrong.")

94. Conference: *Daily Times*, September 25, 1930; *Tribune*, September 25, 1930.

95. Booing broke out: compare *Tribune* ("a salvo of boos, balanced by applause") versus *Herald and Examiner* ("[A] tidal wave of booing. ... The crowd blasted forth its disapproval in no uncertain manner."), both September 26, 1930. Shirtsleeves: *Daily Times*, September 26, 1930.

96. Subdued and uneasy: *Tribune,* September 26, 1930. Lincoln Fields: *Daily Times,* September 26, 1930. "Auction": *Herald and Examiner,* September 25, 1930. See also "May Be Changes—Hornsby," *Daily Times,* September 24, 1930.

97. Confetti: *Herald and Examiner* and *Tribune,* both September 27, 1930.

98. Silver service: *Daily Times,* September 27, 1930; *Herald and Examiner,* September 28, 1930.

99. Warehouse: *Tribune,* October 14, 18, and 27, 1930; "Gives Shelter and Meals to 2,000 Homeless Men," *Herald and Examiner,* January 27, 1932. Soup kitchen: Bergreen, *Capone,* 400–401. Hooverville: "Chicago Jobless Colonize," *New York Times,* November 12, 1930, in Paul Dickson and Thomas B. Allen, *The Bonus Army: An American Epic* (New York: Walker & Co., 2004), 308–9 n.31.

100. Shires: *Chicago Defender,* October 4, 1930.

101. Advertised: *Tribune,* October 3, 1930. NNL: *Chicago Defender,* August 23, 1930. Peterson, *Only the Ball Was White,* 89–91, records the breakup of the first NNL.

102. Shires, "Steel Arm" Davis: *Chicago Defender,* October 11, 1930.

103. King Street, Buick: Boone and Grunska, *Hack,* 100. Band, signs: Partin, "Lewis Robert 'Hack' Wilson," 19.

104. Oriental: advertisement in movie section, *Tribune,* October 11, 1930; "Cub Stars in Stage Debut," *American,* October 11, 1930; *Tribune,* June 2, 1935; Fitzgerald, interview.

105. Malone discovered: *New York Times,* June 20, 1932.

106. Brass knuckles: *Tribune,* December 31, 1930, untitled clipping in HOF files, dateline January 8, 1931.

107. St. Mary's Church: *Tribune,* December 15, 1930.

108. Funeral: "Foster, Hero of Negro Baseball League, Buried," *Tribune,* December 16, 1930.

109. Prosecuted for obscenity: *New York Times,* July 18, 1930. A grand jury refused to indict Carroll and his co-defendants, *New York Times,* August 13, 1930.

110. "No more show tonight": *Tribune,* February 14, 1931.

111. "The Noble Experiment": *Tribune,* February 15, 1931.

112. Court: *Tribune,* February 22, 1931.

113. Wilson's contract: "Wilson Accepts Cub Terms; Best Paid Man in League?" *Tribune,* February 3, 1931. Intense dislike: Warren Brown, "McCarthy Offered Post as Manager of N.Y. Yankees," *Herald and Examiner,* September 24, 1930. Brown wrote: "[A]t least four members of the present cast, three of them stars . . . have neither friendship for, nor sympathy with[,] Hornsby."

Brown had visited the team at the Polo Grounds just before McCarthy's firing. A few days earlier, the *Tribune* (September 21, 1930) had mentioned that "Root is one of the closest personal friends of Manager McCarthy on the team," and Grimm was soon to attend McCarthy's farewell party (*Daily Times*, September 27, 1930).

11. "A LOUSY OUTFIELD"

1. Caravan: "Capone Speeds to Atlanta," *Tribune*, May 4, 1932.

2. Blurted out: *Herald and Examiner,* May 3, 1932.

3. 26,000: *Tribune*, May 16, 1932. For other indications of the spring attendance decline, see also *Tribune*, April 7 and 14, 1932 ("slim attendance at some of the openers yesterday"); *Daily News*, March 21 and 27, 1932; *Herald and Examiner*, May 29, 1932 (Babe Ruth column).

4. Unemployed: Gottfried, *Boss Cermak of Chicago,* 241. Wacker Drive: Mayer and Wade, 360. Abandoned farms: "Quit Chicago for Farms," *New York Times*, April 15, 1932. Insull: Forrest McDonald's *Insull* (Chicago: University of Chicago Press, 1962) provides a sympathetic account of Insull's financial troubles. For a different viewpoint, see Raymond B. Vickers's *Panic in the Loop: Chicago's Banking Crisis of 1932* (Lanham, Md.: Lexington Books, 2011).

5. Wrigley: "Wm. Wrigley Dies in Arizona," *Herald and Examiner*, January 27, 1932. Funeral: "Wrigley Rites Are Held in Pasadena Home," *Tribune*, January 29, 1932. Philip Wrigley: Vaughan, *Tribune*, February 1 ("There is no basis for the whisperings, already going on, that the youthful magnate, because of a supposed lack of interest in baseball, may dispose of the controlling interest and thus open the way for a wholesale shifting of the official personnel"), and May 9, 1932 (P. K. Wrigley attends his first game of the season at Wrigley Field).

6. Alexander: *Daily News*, February 24, 1932; *Tribune*, February 23, February 25, 1932.

7. Rookies first: *Herald and Examiner*, February 12, 1932. MacKenzie: *Tribune*, February 14 and 20, 1932; *Daily Times*, February 15, 1932 ("Keep your eye peeled for Red MacKenzie. He is a left hander you are going to hear things from.").

8. Novices: *Daily News*, February 13, 1932; *Tribune*, February 14, 1932; *Herald and Examiner*, February 14, 1932. Deadened ball: see, for instance, "Pendulum Swinging Back from Swat and Primitive Punch to Skill on Paths, More Subtle Strategy," *Sporting News*, November 19, 1931; *Daily News*, March 1, April 12 and 18, 1932; *Tribune*, April 12, 1932. "Uncanny knack": *Tribune*, June 14, 1932. See also *Tribune*, April 30, 1932.

9. Slick-fielding, etc.: see *Tribune*, February 14 and 24, May 24, 1932 ("has

repeatedly come up with batted balls which with other shortstops would have gone for hits"). Slated: *Tribune*, February 24 ("Jurges might go to the Braves"), March 8 (possibly bound for the L.A. Angels) and March 15, 1932 (to stay in L.A. after exhibition season); *Herald and Examiner*, March 9, 1932 ("Kreevich to Get Infield Trial as Jurges, Blair Fade "). First starts: *Tribune*, March 30, March 31, 1932.

10. English's finger: *Tribune*, March 31 and April 9, 1932; *Daily News*, April 9, 1932.

11. Hustling: *Tribune*, April 15 and 19, 1932.

12. Grimm, seat of his pants: *Herald and Examiner* and *Tribune*, both May 9, 1932. Hemsley sprang: *Herald and Examiner*, May 7, 1932. (For another one of Hemsley's defensive feats, see *Tribune*, May 2, 1932.)

13. Warneke's first start: *Daily News*, April 15, 1932; *Tribune*, April 15, 1932. Reincarnation: *Tribune*, May 11, 1932.

14. Herman: *Daily News*, July 5, 1932.

15. Shaking hands: *Daily News*, February 13, 1932. Convalesced: *Tribune*, May 5 and 7, 1932. Fort Wayne: *Tribune*, May 19, 1932. The Fort Wayne club soon returned MacKenzie to the Cubs, who then released him unconditionally *(Tribune*, June 2, 1932).

16. Called the pitches: see *Herald and Examiner*, August 6, 1932; *Daily Times*, August 3, 1932. Dictated: *Sporting News*, January 21, 1932, 3. Bender: Alexander, *Rogers Hornsby*, 168.

17. Sympathy: *Tribune*, July 19, 1931 (photo, "Wilson Gets Boys' Vote "); *Herald and Examiner*, August 21 (Boy Scouts in center-field stands cheered Cuyler and Wilson), August 31 ("Wilson is still the big favorite with the North Side addicts."), September 7 (surrounded at ballpark by fans demanding autograph), September 8 (crowd storms Wilson's box at Wrigley Field), and September 10, 1931 (cheering breaks out when Wilson takes his seat at Comiskey Park); *Daily Times*, September 5 ("roundly cheered each at-bat" the previous Sunday), September 8, 1931 (besieged by "thousands" of admirers); *Baseball Magazine*, February 1932, 388 ("suffered no apparent decline in popularity" in 1931—photo, Wilson surrounded by happy boys). Summon Vaughan: *Tribune*, July 1, 1931.

18. Inciting: *Tribune* and *Daily Times*, both September 8, 1931. Ushers, clubhouse: *Herald and Examiner*, September 8, 1931.

19. Public enemy: *Herald and Examiner*, September 10, 1931.

20. "Humpty-dumpty": *Tribune*, August 28, 1931.

21. Shopped: Hartnett, see "Blasts from the Windy City," *Sporting News* December, 1931; Grimm, see *New York Times*, August 4, 1932.

22. Cuyler's foot: *Tribune* and *Daily News*, both April 25, 1932.

23. Hornsby barked: *Herald and Examiner*, May 12, 1932.

24. Jolley: *Tribune*, September 5, 1931 (fan letter—Danny Taylor "clumsier fielder than Smead Jolley, and that going some ").

25. Gus Dugas et al.: *Herald and Examiner* and *Tribune*, both May 4, 1932.

26. Stepped off: *Daily News*, May 5, 1932.

27. Cloth-capped: *Herald and Examiner*, May 6, 1932.

28. Lemons: *Tribune*, May 6, 1932.

29. Strain: *New York Times*, May 8, 1932.

30. Skimmer: *Tribune*, May 20, 1932. Smile: *Herald and Examiner*, May 22, 1932.

31. Cuyler's recovery: *Tribune*, May 13 and 16, 1932; *Daily News*, May 17, 1932.

32. Veeck accompanied: *Tribune*, June 11, 13, 14, and 22, 1932; *Daily News*, June 13, 1932. See also *Tribune*, *Daily News*, and *Daily Times*, August 3, 1932.

33. In shape: *Herald and Examiner*, May 27, 1932. Debuted: *Tribune*, May 30, 1932. Silenced: *Tribune*, May 31, 1932.

34. Fans roared: *Herald and Examiner*, June 3, 1932.

35. Lemons: *Tribune*, June 8, 1932. First-ever: the pair's only possible overlap in the minor leagues was in 1925, when Malone appeared in four games for the Minneapolis Millers of the American Association and Wilson spent half the season with Toledo. On May 7, 1932, Wilson was on the bench when Malone pitched a complete game against the Dodgers in Chicago. Brushbacks, collisions: *Tribune*, *Herald and Examiner*, and *New York Times*, all June 10, 1932; "Alleged Dusting Lead to Cub-Dodger Scraps," *Sporting News*, June 16, 1932.

36. Jurges-Finn fight: *Herald and Examiner* and *Tribune*, both June 11, 1932; "Alleged Dusting Lead to Cub-Dodger Scraps," *Sporting News*, June 16, 1932.

37. Prizefight: *Herald and Examiner*, June 22, 1932. Workout: *Tribune* and *Herald and Examiner*, both June 29, 1932.

38. "Lousy outfield": *Tribune*, August 6, 1932 (Hornsby, New York, June 1932: a "lousy" outfield without Cuyler; byline Irving Vaughan); see also, among others, *Daily Times*, August 3, 1932 (Hornsby quoted as saying Cubs' outfield "lamentably weak"; byline Herbert Simons).

39. Benched: *Tribune*, August 6, 1932 ("request" from the front office); *Daily Times*, August 3, 1932 ("Veeck is understood to have ordered Hornsby to bench himself "); *Herald and Examiner*, August 6, 1932 ("order sent out for Hornsby to stay out of the lineup"; "the front office order that Hornsby get into the lineup"); *Baseball Magazine*, October 1932, 488 ("They" [front office?] don't want me there [in the lineup]"; interview given in late July 1932). Pitch selection: *Herald and Examiner*, August 3 and 6, 1932 (Veeck objected to pitch calling as "McGraw tactics"; byline Wayne Otto); *Daily Times* (p.m. paper using "McGraw tactics" etc. wording almost identical to the a.m. *H&E*'s; byline Herbert Simons), August 3, 1932; *Daily News*, August 4, 1932 (Hornsby:

"For the first six weeks of the season I did call every pitch"; byline William H. Fort). See also AP in *Daily Times*, August 24, 1932 ("At Chicago Hornsby is said to have attempted to imitate many of McGraw's methods, including the detailed direction of every player's activities at bat and in the field.")

40. "You catch": Fitzgerald, interview.

41. Bided: "So They Tell Me," *Herald and Examiner*, August 13, 1932. "That's right": *Daily News*, July 15, 1937.

42. Cuyler's foot: *Tribune*, June 4, 8, 9, and 14 ("Cuyler Says He Isn't Ready"), 1932, *Herald and Examiner*, July 26 ("Cuyler seems to be favoring his foot") and August 3, 1932 ("Cuyler's speed has been impaired by his broken toe-bone"); *Daily News* ("[O]nly the insistence of Hornsby brought [Cuyler] back into action at an early date."), *Daily Times* ("[F]ollowing a broken toe bone," Cuyler was "unable to function as he did previously"), August 3, 1932. Streaky: Warren Brown, *Herald and Examiner*, October 4, 1932 ("Cuyler had his usual streak of success and his equally usual streak of docility").

43. New position: *Pittsburgh Post Gazette*, October 10, 1927 ("[P]laying left field is about the worst thing I do").

44. Numbered jerseys: "10th Victory Is Warneke's Goal Today," *Tribune*, July 1, 1932.

45. Pirate victories: *Tribune*, July 5, 1932.

46. Appeals Board: "Hornsby Bats .000 in Tax Tilt with U.S. Appeals Board," *Daily News*, June 30, 1932; *New York Times*, July 1, 1932; "Board Decides Hornsby Must Pay $8,653 Tax," *Sporting News*, July 7, 1932. For a summary, see Alexander, *Rogers Hornsby*, 326 n.34.

47. Salary: *Sporting News*, August 11, 1932 ("Hornsby had two contracts with the Chicago Cubs—one as a player at a nominal sum and another as a manager, the two paying him approximately $40,000 a year.").

48. Mrs. Hornsby's story: *Sunday Times*, August 14, 1932. The day after this story ran, however, Veeck was asked, "Is it true that a bookmaker came to you with a rubber check he had received from Hornsby and asked the club to make it good?" Veeck replied, "It is positively untrue. I have never received a rubber check issued by Hornsby from anybody" (*Tribune*, August 15, 1932).

12. ROOM 509

1. Two familiar minor leagues: *Tribune*, July 16 and 18, 1932. Reading Keys: *New York Times*, August 4, 1932.

2. Tutored: *Daily News*, March 8, 1932. Awkward swing: "Linn's Lines," *Daily Times*, July 14, 1932.

3. Borrowed auto: *Tribune*, August 6, 1932 (Landis "summoned both Barton and Hornsby" regarding a damaged auto).

4. Phone call: *Daily News*, July 6, 1932; but see *Herald and Examiner*, July 7, 1932: "Hotel officials said she had phoned Jurges several times during the morning, but that he had refused to see her." "C'mon up": Holtzman and Vass, *Baseball, Chicago Style*, 53.

5. Divorced: "I Didn't Want to Kill Bill—Just Myself," *Sun-Times* clipping file, date stamp July 7, 1932. Clubhouse: *Herald and Examiner*, July 7, 1932. New York: *Tribune*, July 7, 1932. "Get Bill": *Herald and Examiner*, July 7, 1932; AP in *St. Louis Post-Dispatch*, July 6, 1932 ("get Jurges"). Target practice: "Player Wounded in Side, Hand by Spurned Sweetheart," date stamp July 6, 1932, *Sun-Times* clipping file.

6. Earl Carroll: *Tribune*, July 7, 1932 ("*Scandals*" that day, but "*Vanities*" in "Jurges' Girl Friend Blames Shooting on 'Too Much Gin,'" *Tribune*, July 8, 1932).

7. Gudat, Barton: *Daily News*, July 6, 1932.

8. Intern: Holtzman and Vass, *Baseball, Chicago Style*, 54. Davis's examination: *Daily News*, July 6, 1932; *Tribune* and *Herald and Examiner*, both July 7, 1932.

9. Bottles: *Tribune*, July 7, 1932. Note: *Tribune*, July 7, 1932; *Herald and Examiner*, July 7, 1932.

10. Telegram: *Herald and Examiner*, July 7, 1932.

11. O'Brien's questions: *Herald and Examiner*, July 7, 1932.

12. "I want to live now": AP in *Evansville Courier*, July 7, 1932. "Too much gin": *Tribune*, July 8, 1932.

13. "Friendly": "Player Wounded in Side, Hand by Spurned Sweetheart," *Sun-Times* clipping file, date stamp July 6, 1932. Jurges and Lopez: Holtzman and Vass, *Baseball, Chicago Style*, 54.

14. Another Cub: Brace, interview. Bill Veeck Jr., suggested: Veeck, *Hustler's Handbook*, 164; Linn, telephone interview; Linn, letter. "I'M GOING TO KILL YOU!": Holtzman and Vass, *Baseball, Chicago Style*, 54.

15. Runaway: *Tribune*, July 21, 1926.

16. Sit up: *Tribune*, July 7, 1932. Complaint: *Tribune*, July 8, 1932.

17. Subpoena: *Daily News*, July 12, 1932. Courtroom: *Daily News*, July 15, 1932; "Cub Player Forgives Girl for Shooting," *Sun-Times* clipping file, date stamp July 15, 1932.

18. "The Most Talked of Girl in Chicago": "Jurges O.K.'s Stage Contract for His 'Gungirl,'" *Sun-Times* clipping file, date stamp July 19, 1932; "The Girl Who Shot for Love": *Tribune*, July 26, 1932, 11. The advertisement ran immediately above the daily White Sox billing. According to "Five Wild Weeks Give the Cubs a Succession of Varied Thrills," *Sporting News*, August 18, 1932, thousands of handbills promoting Valli's act were distributed in Wrigley Field

on July 24. The *Evening Post*, August 12, 1932, referred to Valli's burlesque show in the past tense.

19. Hornsby: AP in *Indianapolis Star*, July 7, 1932. Veeck: "Girl Who Shot Jurges Held on Police Charge," *Daily News*, July 7, 1932.

20. Visit: "Girl in Jurges Shooting Gives Bond; Praises Billy; 'Good Friends,' She Says," *Sun-Times* clipping file, date stamp July 9, 1932; "2 Bullets and Out for Her, He Says; Might Prosecute," *Sun-Times* clipping file, date stamp July 10, 1932. NYPD: "Girl Who Shot Bill Jurges Set Free by Court," *Daily News*, July 15, 1932.

21. "Mr. M——": *Pittsburgh Post-Gazette*, August 15, 1932.

13. INFORMANTS

1. Breach of promise: "Woody English Sued; Girl Claims He Promised to Wed," *Tribune*, February 24, 1932; see also "Ohio Girl Claims Shortstop Did 'Runout' on Her" and "by Ex-Fiancée," fragment in *Chicago Sun-Times* clipping file, date stamp February 24, 1932.

2. Hunting: *Tribune*, December 17, 1930. Curling up: *New York World Telegram*, March 27, 1937.

3. Injury: *Tribune*, April 9, 1932.

4. Coupe: *Daily News*, May 18, 1932, which identified the automobile a "coupe," no make indicated. In 1994 English recalled owning a Packard convertible in 1932—perhaps the replacement for the stolen coupe (*Baseball Digest*, September 1994, 86). Both articles, six decades apart, cite the same purchase price. Tactician: *New York World Telegram*, September 22, 1937. Umpire baiter: *Daily News*, December 5, 1936.

5. Helped: *Daily News*, August 2, 1934; Keller, *Sports Collector's Digest*, July 27, 1990, 150 (English interview). MVP voting: "Lou Gehrig and Chuck Klein Are Named Most Valuable in Majors," *Sporting News*, October 22, 1931.

6. $2,000: *Tribune*, August 14, 1932.

7. Small business: *Tribune*, September 14, 1932; *Daily Times*, August 30, 1932; *Daily News*, December 12, 1932, and July 3, 1934; *Sporting News*, December 29, 1932.

8. Grange: *Tribune*, July 12, 1932. Working out: *Tribune* and *Herald and Examiner*, both July 14, 1932.

9. Ovations: *Tribune*, July 14, 1932. Valli: *Tribune*, July 15, 1932. "Old puppies": *Tribune*, July 16, 1932.

10. Catcalls: *Herald and Examiner* and *New York Times*, both July 19, 1932.

11. Ultimatum: *Daily Times*, August 3, 1932. "Cut it out": *Daily Times*, August 30, 1932.

12. Whistled: *Daily Times*, August 3, 1932.

13. Demaree: *Daily Times,* August 3, 1932, refers explicitly to the row over Demaree's first major league appearance; Hornsby, *My Kind of Baseball,* 105–6, roughly corroborates that version and ties the incident to his firing. As Hornsby remembered it, though, the game was not close and the pennant not "at stake": "It was a perfect setting for a trial of Demaree." "Good idea": *Tribune,* August 6, 1932 ("I simply told him [Veeck] that he need not consider me if he wanted to make a change"); *Daily Times,* August 12, 1932 ("If he thought the club could do better under another manager—why, go ahead and make the change.")
14. Retaliation: *Tribune,* July 24, 1932. Lotshaw: *Pittsburgh Press,* July 25, 1932.
15. Taylor, Comorosky: *Tribune* and *Herald and Examiner,* both July 24, 1932. Root stalked: *Tribune,* July 24, 1932.
16. "Pat": the *St. Louis Post-Dispatch,* January 14, 1933, corroborated this account, based on a report in a Philadelphia newspaper (see Alexander, *Rogers Hornsby,* 177), with Hornsby. Besides Hornsby, Malone, Hartnett, and Cuyler, the article mentioned "a veteran infielder" as a figure in the incident. Of the Cub roster at the time, only Grimm and Woody English fit the latter description. See also UP dispatch in *Tribune,* January 15, 1933 and Warren Brown's comments after Hornsby's firing, *Herald and Examiner,* August 5, 1932: "Hornsby undoubtedly antagonized several of his players. It is no secret that at least three of them, one a newcomer this season, expressed themselves openly on the subject." Cuyler told: *Tribune* ("Cuyler apparently knew of Hornsby's waning authority, for he is reported to have returned an impertinent answer") and *Daily News* ("[N]or has [Cuyler], it is alleged, taken the Rajah's questioning kindly"), both August 3, 1932; "Rambling around the Circuit with Pitcher Snorter Casey," *Sporting News,* August 11, 1932 ("Kiki tells Rog to go jump in the lake").
17. "Player War": *Tribune,* July 24, 1932.
18. Used-up bunch: *Tribune,* July 26, 1932. Drawing room: *Tribune,* August 6, 1932.
19. "At arms": *Herald and Examiner,* July 26, 1932.
20. Separate tables: *Daily News* and *Tribune,* both August 3, 1932.
21. Lobby sitting: *Tribune,* August 2, 1932.

14. "NOTHING TO IT"

1. Veeck and Hornsby conferred: *Herald and Examiner,* August 2, 1932. Barton released: *Daily News,* July 30, 1932.
2. Veeck demurred: *Daily Times,* August 3, 1932.
3. Conference: *New York Times,* August 3, 1932.
4. Dropped in: *Tribune* (P. K. "visiting them for the first time") and *Daily News,* April 1, 1932. First spotted: *Tribune,* May 9, 1932.

5. Philip Wrigley: Angle, *P. K. Wrigley*, 58–60; Veeck, *Veeck—as in Wreck*, 38–39.

6. Phone: *Daily News*, August 3, 1932.

7. "Well, Rog": William Fort, special dispatch, *Daily News*, August 3, 1932; see also *Herald and Examiner*, August 3, 1932.

8. "Rog and I": *Tribune*, August 3, 1932.

9. Behind closed doors: "Five Wild Weeks Give the Cubs a Succession of Varied Thrills," *Sporting News*, August 18, 1932.

10. Stayed up: *Tribune*, August 4, 1932.

11. New captain: *Tribune* and *Herald and Examiner*, both August 4, 1932.

12. Low-key: *Herald and Examiner*, August 4, 1932. Commonplaces: *Daily News*, August 4, 1932.

13. Contemplative: *Daily News*, August 4, 1932; AP dispatch in *Indianapolis Star*, August 3, 1932; AP in *New York Times*, August 4, 1932.

14. Fan reaction: *Daily News*, August 3, 1932.

15. McCarthy in Chicago: *Daily News*, August 3, 1932; *Daily Times*, August 3, 1932.

16. Wilson's reactions: *Daily News*, August 3, 1932.

17. "Nothing to it": *Tribune*, August 4, 1932.

18. Back home: *Tribune*, August 6, 1932.

19. "Deeper reasons": "Talking It Over," *Tribune*, August 4, 1932.

20. "I very much doubt": "So They Tell Me," *Herald and Examiner*, August 5, 1932.

21. Infield practice: *Herald and Examiner*, August 5, 1932. The *Tribune*, June 24, 1932, had noted the jaded Philadelphia fans "praised no one. When there was no opportunity for abuse they kept quiet and hoped." See also *Daily Times*, February 18, 1931, for the remarks of Hack Wilson or his ghostwriter ("Say, all those jokes you hear about [Phillie fans] are correct. Absolutely the zero [*sic*] in enthusiasm").

22. Duster ball: *Herald and Examiner*, August 11, 1932.

23. Tobacco smoke: *Daily Times*, August 11, 1932.

24. Horseshoe: *Herald and Examiner* and *Tribune*, both August 5, 1932.

25. Barehanded: *Herald and Examiner*, August 5, 1932.

26. "Dutchman": *Daily News*, August 9, 1932.

27. Lobby buzzed: *Daily News*, August 4, 1932. Twenty-third man: *Tribune*, August 6, 1932. The major leagues had reduced the player limit for each team from twenty-five to twenty-three; *Daily Times*, August 31, 1932, and Crepeau, *Baseball*, 177.

28. Apologetic: *New York World-Telegram*, September 24, 1932. No. 9: *Daily Times*, August 16, 1932.

29. Phillie fans: *Tribune*, August 7, 1932.
30. Doubleheader: *Tribune* and *Herald and Examiner*, both August 7, 1932. Firecracker: *Tribune*, August 8, 1932.
31. Experiment: *Tribune* and *Daily Times*, both August 8, 1932.
32. Hubbell: *Tribune*, August 10, 1932.

15. "NO PARTICULAR PAL OF MINE"

1. Historians: *Tribune*, August 10, 1932.
2. Schenley: *Daily News*, *Daily Times*, and *Pittsburgh Sun-Telegraph*, August 11, 1932.
3. "Top teams": *Daily Times*, August 11, 1932.
4. Grimm remarks: *Daily News* and *Daily Times*, both August 11, 1932.
5. Bush claimed: *Herald and Examiner*, August 12, 1932.
6. "No particular pal": *Daily News*, August 11, 1932.
7. "Always investigating": *Daily Times*, August 11, 1932; *Tribune*, August 12, 1932. The *Tribune* places Landis's statement at the ballpark, rather than the hotel.
8. *Daily News* charges: *Daily News*, August 11, 1932.
9. "Let Landis": *Daily Times*, August 11, 1932 (emphasis added). 936 Wrigley Building: see Veeck, *Hustler's Handbook*, 124.
10. "Wrecking": *Pittsburgh Sun-Telegraph*, August 11, 1932 (emphasis added).
11. Showdown: *Daily News*, August 11, 1932; *Tribune*, August 12, 1932.
12. "Guess that shows": *Daily News*, August 12, 1932. Euphoria: *Tribune*, August 12, 1932.
13. Mrs. Grimm, "Ruin me": "Cubs Parade into St. Louis Like Champions," *Tribune*, August 13, 1932.
14. "Crazy enough": *Daily Times*, August 12, 1932.
15. O'Connor: "Landis' Aids [*sic*] Surprised," *Tribune*, August 12, 1932. Heydler: "It's News to Heydler," *Tribune*, August 12, 1932. Veeck: "Landis Keeps Up His Loud Silence on Gambling Rumors," *Tribune*, August 13, 1932.
16. Station: "Landis Keeps Up His Loud Silence on Gambling Rumors," *Tribune*, August 13, 1932. Chicago Beach: "Baseball Not under Investigation—Landis," *Herald and Examiner*, August 13, 1932.
17. "Young man": "Thrown Games Not Involved," *Daily News*, August 12, 1932.
18. "Golf": "Baseball Not under Investigation—Landis," *Herald and Examiner*, August 13, 1932.
19. "Fan": "Thrown Games Not Involved," *Daily News*, August 12, 1932.

16. "THAT STORY IS TERRIBLE, JUDGE"

1. Saturday night: *Tribune*, August 13, 1932. Orchestra members: see *Tribune*, September 18, 1929; *Daily News*, August 3, 1932.

2. Notebook: *Daily Times*, August 14, 1932. Ed Burns mentioned the stenographer in his dispatch for the *Sporting News*, August 18, 1932. The use of a mimeograph machine seems to have been a prerequisite to the operation, since Landis distributed several thirty-eight-page copies of the testimony soon after the close of the hearing. Protest: *Tribune*, August 15, 1932 ("[Bush] has been boiling over ever since Landis arrived in Pittsburgh last week").

3. "Sick and tired": "Landis Grills Cubs, Hornsby," *Daily Times*, August 14, 1932.

4. "Signed a note": "Finds No Proof of Betting By Cubs' Players," jump head "Landis Quiz of Gambling Rumors Reveals Hornsby Borrowed Large Sums from Five Cub Players," *Tribune*, August 14, 1932 (hereafter "Landis Quiz"), column 2. The *Tribune*'s dialogue-rich summary of Landis's hearing twice mentions a conclusion to the affair ("at the close of the hearing" in column 2 and, several thousand words later in column 5, "Landis then closed the hearing," followed by dialogue entirely different from that used in column 2). The *Herald and Examiner*'s summary of the hearing ("Bare Hornsby's $11,350 Debts to Cub Players," August 14, 1932) contains considerably less direct quotation but includes a Bush-Landis exchange that the *Tribune* uses only partially at the very beginning of its own, more-complete transcript quotations. In the absence of further explanation, the location of this exchange has been surmised (see n.6), and the hearing's adjournment is taken from column 1 of the *Tribune*. The notes indicate when the resequenced version, following the *Herald and Examiner*'s guidelines, jumps to a different column in the *Tribune* story. The testimony ran in section 2, page 2, of that day's *Tribune* sports section.

5. "You told English alone": "Landis Quiz," column 3.

6. "If you are innocent": "Landis Quiz," column 2. The *Herald and Examiner* account places Bush's outburst after this group of Landis's questions.

7. "Some sort of activity": "Landis Quiz," column 3.

8. "Sir?": "Landis Quiz," column 4.

9. "Read this": "Landis Quiz," column 4.

10. "John the barber: "Landis Quiz," column 5.

11. Hinsdale Golf Club: *Herald and Examiner*, August 14, 1932 ("The news of the hearing in St. Louis was given to Veeck at the Hinsdale Golf Club"). "A reporter" interviewed Veeck; the byline was that of Warren Brown, the sports editor of the Hearst chain's *Herald and Examiner*. Although Brown might have traveled to St. Louis that day, that's doubtful, considering the secrecy surrounding Landis's comings and goings. Another factor could be that Veeck had worked for the Hearst's *Evening American* before Brown arrived in Chicago in the early 1920s.

12. Back to denying: *Tribune*, August 15, 1932. See also *Pittsburgh Press*, August

13, 1932—"If we had known about [the borrowing] before we decided to let him out it probably would have played a part in his removal."

13. Pegler: "Czar Business in Baseball, Boxing Fades," *Tribune*, August 22, 1932.

17. THE NATURAL

1. State's attorney's office: "Police Hold Chief of Jurges Blackmail Plot," *Tribune*, August 14, 1932.

2. Warehouse: *Tribune*, August 6, 1927. See Schoenberg, *Mr. Capone*, 174. Assassination rumor: Schoenberg, *Mr. Capone*, 296. Humphreys: Murray, 223–224.

3. Extortionists: *Tribune*, July 17, 1932.

4. Two dozen letters: *Evening Post*, August 12, 1932.

5. Reelection: *Tribune*, December 26, 1932.

6. 2434 Burling Street: *Tribune*, August 14, 1932. Well-tailored: "Alleged Blackmailer of Cub Player Seized" (photo with caption), *Tribune*, August 14, 1932.

7. Kicked, out the door: *Tribune*, August 14, 1932. Barnett "kicked" Capparelli, leaving him "painfully injured." Booked: *Tribune*, August 16, 1932. This report included "impersonating a police officer" as one charge; "resisting" was the term used in "Girl Regains Jurges Notes; Continue Case," *Tribune*, August 19, 1932.

8. "Back to Brooklyn": *Evening Post*, August 12, 1932. Phone call: *Tribune*, August 14, 1932.

9. Mrs. Cuyler: "Girl Who Shot Bill Jurges Set Free by Court," *Daily News*, July 15, 1932.

10. Arraignment: *Tribune*, August 16, 1932.

11. Barnett protested: *Daily Times*, August 16, 1932.

12. "Wreck a ballclub": *Daily Times*, August 16, 1932.

13. "Victorian gent": see discussion in Tom Wolfe's *The Right Stuff*, chap. 5, "In Single Combat."

14. Barehanded: *Tribune*, August 15, 1932.

15. "What a town!": *Daily Times*, August 15, 1932.

16. Five hundred fans: *Daily Times*, August 16, 1932.

17. Swung his cap: *Herald and Examiner*, August 17, 1932.

18. Making for the exits: *Evening Post*, August 17, 1932.

19. Hats: *Daily Times*, August 17, 1932.

20. "Wants to bat": *Tribune*, August 19, 1932.

21. Stomach problem: *Tribune*, August 20, 1932.

22. Cole's Park: *Chicago Defender*, July 16, 1932. Advance item: *Tribune*, August 19, 1932.

23. Alexander's requirements: Hawkins and Bertolino, *House of David Baseball Team,* 34, 76.

24. Goad the umpires: *Tribune,* August 21, 1932.

25. Swinging three bats: *Herald and Examiner,* August 21, 1932.

26. Hundreds of fans: *Tribune,* August 21, 1932. Continued . . . up in the stands: *Herald and Examiner,* August 21, 1932.

27. Tolles: *Chicago Defender,* August 27, 1932.

28. Florals: *Tribune,* August 22, 1932.

29. 55,000 applications: *Tribune,* August 27, 1932.

30. Season's worth: Thorn and Palmer, *Total Baseball,* 145.

31. Brawl: *Tribune,* May 31, 1932; *Sporting News,* June 2, 1932. "Yellow?": Williams, *New York World-Telegram,* August 18, 1932.

32. Conserve strength: *Tribune,* July 3, 1932. Signals: *Tribune,* June 12, 1932.

33. Scouting trips: *Herald and Examiner,* July 22, 1932.

34. Sometime in 1932: *Tribune,* December 17, 1933 ("During the last two seasons Fonseca has been busy with his own camera").

35. Quit: *Tribune,* August 2, 1932. Exploration: *Tribune,* August 9 and 22, 1932.

36. Barnstorming: *Chicago Defender,* July 4, 1931 ("[The Giants] . . . will play independent ball for the remainder of the season"). Renovated park: *Chicago Defender,* March 6 ("new stands, bleachers, and field boxes with safety concrete base"), and July 9, 1932.

37. Fonseca's tenor: *Tribune,* August 9, 1932. At other times Fonseca's voice was described as a baritone. Guessing attendance: Brown, *Chicago Cubs,* 170.

38. "$100 words": *Daily Times,* August 23, 1932.

39. Soldiering: see, for instance, Babe Ruth's comments in *Herald and Examiner,* September 8, 1932, and Burleigh Grimes's (a denial) in the *Pittsburgh Post-Gazette,* August 11, 1932. Sportswriters: *Tribune* and *Daily Times,* both August 23, 1932.

40. "Prevent embarrassment: "Girl Regains Jurges Notes; Continue Case," *Tribune,* August 19, 1932.

41. Valli looked on: "Jurges Letter Suspect Fined on 3 Charges," *Tribune,* August 24, 1932.

42. Judge Padden: "Dismiss Extortion Charges in Jurges Shooting Case," *Tribune,* September 9, 1932.

43. Agility afield: *Herald and Examiner,* September 1, 1932 ("goes all over the place and comes up with the ball, handling it with effortless style").

44. Tried pitching: "Mighty Smack His Big Thrill," *Daily News,* August 24, 1932; "Kid Kumbak: Koenig!" *Daily Times,* September 12, 1932; and "They Don't Come Back? How About Case of Mark Koenig?" *Tribune,* September 19, 1932.

45. Surgery: *Herald and Examiner,* August 21, 1932; *Tribune,* September 19, 1932.

According to "Kid Kumbak," *Daily Times*, September 12, 1932, "regular muscle exercise provided by an oculist" solved Koenig's eye problems. Doyle: *Daily News*, August 24, 1932. Koenig's acquisition is often mistakenly connected to Jurges's shooting. Unenthusiastic: *New York World-Telegram*, September 24, 1932 ("He was the best we could get. All the better men in the minors are owned by major league clubs"). Moody: "Cubs' Infield Excels on Defense, but Yankee Quartet Hits Harder," *New York Herald-Tribune*, September 25, 1932. See also remarks by Tony Lazzeri, Koenig's roommate in New York, in Daniel, *New York World-Telegram*, August 17, 1932 ("When he was blue, I'd tell [Koenig] how good he was").

46. Sparkling: *Tribune*, August 22 ("a whale of a game at shortstop") and August 23, 1932 ("four brilliant plays").

47. Grand Central: *New York Times*, August 23, 1932.

48. Jacked: "Carey's Cares Lighter as Team Wades into Pennant Scramble," *Sporting News*, August 25, 1932.

49. Out late: *Tribune*, August 25, 1932. "Hans und Fritz": *Daily Times*, August 30, 1932 ("Hans and Fritz" in the newspaper's copy).

50. Hard feelings: *Daily News*, August 25, 1932.

51. Groan: *Tribune*, August 25, 1932.

52. Brooklyn series: *Tribune*, August 26 and 27, 1932; *Herald and Examiner*, August 27, 1932.

53. Applause, pennant celebrations: *Herald and Examiner*, August 27, 1932.

54. Lindstrom: *Herald and Examiner*, August 31, 1932.

55. Grimm admitted: *Daily Times*, September 12, 1932. Telegram: *Daily News*, August 24, 1932. Boyhood days: *Sunday Times*, September 18, 1932.

56. Card playing: Levy, *Joe McCarthy*, 157. Alcoholism: Brace, interview. A sure way: "McCarthy Gives Chicago Second Loser in Big Way," AP in *New York Herald Tribune*, October 3, 1932.

57. Dickey threw: *Tribune*, July 5, 1932. Almost choked: AP dispatch in *Washington Post*, July 21, 1932.

58. Clog dance: *Herald and Examiner*, August 29, 1932. Peered: *Tribune* and *Herald and Examiner*, September 1, 1932.

59. Cubs surged: "The Old College Spirit" (photo caption), *Daily Times*, September 1, 1932. Ushers: *Tribune*, September 1, 1932.

60. Celebration continued: *Daily Times*, September 1, 1932; *Tribune*, September 4, 1932. Warneke, in street clothes: "The Old College Spirit" (photo caption), *Daily Times*, September 1, 1932. Warneke, not identified in the caption, is clearly recognizable.

61. Ditty: *Tribune*, September 4, 1932.

62. Greatest game: Veeck, *Veeck—as in Wreck*, 28. Veeck placed the game in "the

year we finally won our first pennant," with several added inaccuracies, but his narrative leaves little doubt that he was recalling the game of August 31, 1932. A more accurate reminiscence came from Charlie Grimm in John Carmichael's classic *My Greatest Day in Baseball*, 31 (based on "My Biggest Baseball Day: Aug. 31, '32, When Kiki Hit a Homer," *Daily News*, March 10, 1943). "There are no words left": *Daily News*, September 1, 1932.

18. "MUGS . . . CHISELERS"

1. Book-Cadillac: *New York Times*, September 8, 1932.
2. "Marse Joe": Kieran, "Sports of the Times: Ten for the Babe," *New York Times*, September 27, 1932. This nickname, a reference to McCarthy's long American Association tenure in Louisville, was vastly outnumbered in the Chicago press by "Mac." Third-base coaching box: "So They Tell Me," *Herald and Examiner*, September 27, 1932.
3. Crowd: *New York Daily News*, September 9, 1932. Rewrite men: *Tribune*, September 9, 1932.
4. "One more shot": *New York Herald-Tribune*, September 9, 1932. Wheelchair: *New York Daily News*, September 9, 1932.
5. Sunlamps: *Tribune*, September 8, 1932.
6. Taking notes: *New York World-Telegram* and *New York Herald Tribune*, both September 16, 1932. Ordinary team: *Herald and Examiner*, September 8, 1932. Lively bench: *Daily Times*, September 14, 1932.
7. Scouting: *Daily News*, September 16, 1932; *New York World-Telegram*, September 19, 1932.
8. Hornsby in charge: *Herald and Examiner*, September 8, 1932 (Ruth's syndicated, ghostwritten column). "Wray's Column," *St. Louis Post-Dispatch*, September 23, 1932, cited that particular column as valid evidence of Ruth's point of view.
9. Wilson's bat: *New York World-Telegram*, September 19, 1932. In a series of articles published in the *Daily Times* after Wilson's great 1930 season, he and his ghostwriter mentioned: "As for the bat, I have stuck to the same model ever since I broke in with Martinsburg. It's a special build, with a real thin handle and most of the 40 to 42 ounce weight at the damaging end" (*Daily Times*, February 16, 1931).
10. Horns, limousine, yachts, whistles: *Daily News*, September 22, 1932. Wrigley, Lindbergh: for a particularly good photo of the crowd, see *Daily Times*, September 22, 1932. Windows, bat: *Herald and Examiner*, September 23, 1932. A *Tribune* photo of the same date shows Mayor Cermak handing a bat to Grimm. Civilian suits: *Tribune*, September 23, 1932. Paper, "plenty scared," "Hello, folks": *New York Times*, September 23, 1932. The *Daily Times* noted on September 22 that Violet Valli was among the crowd at the parade's starting line.

11. Groceries: for a photo of Riggs Stephenson with two baskets of groceries in hand, see "Complete Relaxation—Not a Mind on Baseball" (photo caption), *Tribune*, September 24, 1932. Shares: *Tribune* and *New York Times*, both September 22, 1932.

12. Nine thousand dollars per player: *Herald and Examiner*, September 22, 1932. Tax bill: "Rajah in $8,412 U.S. Tax Suit," *Herald and Examiner*, September 14, 1932; "$8,412 Plaster Hung on Hornsby," *New York Daily News*, September 14, 1932.

13. Five hundred dollars apiece: "M'Carthy Hits Trail Today for Winter Quarters," *Tribune*, October 17, 1929. The '29 Cubs, with a roster of twenty-five, included enough extra parties in the payoff that their loser's share, which would have been four thousand dollars, was reduced to about thirty-five hundred. Widow's share: *Tribune*, October 17, 1930.

14. Questioning: Daniel, *New York World-Telegram*, September 23, 1932 (New Yorkers "somewhat surprised at the wallop the Cubs took at Hornsby"); Brown, *Herald and Examiner*, September 29, 1932 (Cub vote "caused a lot of discussion" around the country); and McCarthy, *Daily Times*, October 2, 1932. "No team": *St. Louis Post-Dispatch*, September 26, 1932. The Pirates were playing the Cardinals that weekend in St. Louis, so the unnamed manager was probably George Gibson, the current Pittsburgh manager (and an interim Cub manager in September 1925). Yankees: *New York Times*, September 24, 1932.

15. Appeal: "Rajah Demands Series Cash," *Daily Times*, September 24, 1932; "Hornsby Protests to Landis Cubs' Failure to Vote Him a Share," *St. Louis Post-Dispatch*, September 24, 1932.

16. Charlie's fellows: *Daily Times*, September 21, 1932; *Daily News*, September 23, 1932; see also "Hornsby Will Haunt Cubs' Peace of Mind," *Sporting News*, November 3, 1932, and Woody English interview in Golenbock, *Wrigleyville*, 232–33. Didn't believe: Prell, "Await Landis Verdict on Series Split," *Evening American*, October 3, 1932.

17. "Cubs Hold Pitching Edge": *Tribune*, September 24, 1932. "Stellar Pitching Staff": *New York Times*, September 24, 1932.

18. Indifferent: Brandt, *New York Times*, September 27, 1932; Runyon (Universal Services), *Herald and Examiner*, September 28, 1932; Simons, *Sunday Times*, October 2, 1932. Potted plants: UP in *Indianapolis Star*, September 28, 1932. Entertainment: Brandt, *New York Times*, September 28, 1932. Studio: *New York Times*, September 28, 1932.

19. Landis decreed: Daniel, *New York World-Telegram*, September 28, 1932.

20. Burke: Meany, *New York World-Telegram*, September 29, 1932. Full cry: *Herald and Examiner*, October 6, 1932; see also Bill Klem's remarks in Daniel,

New York World-Telegram, October 6, 1932. Mocked: Williams, *New York World-Telegram*, September 29, 1932. Ruth: Cross, *New York Herald Tribune*, September 29, 1932.

21. Looked spent: *Baseball Magazine*, November 1932, 303. Filed out: Nicolet, *New York World-Telegram*, September 28, 1932; Hunt, *New York Daily News*, September 29, 1932.

22. Lotshaw led: Tynan, *New York Herald Tribune*, September 30, 1932; "Cubs Jittery as Play Starts," *Tribune*, September 30, 1932; Cross, *New York Herald Tribune*, September 30, 1932. "Are they, Mark?": Vaughan, *Tribune*, October 1, 1932. See also "Grimm Praises Gomez as Greater Than Grove and Picks Root to Face Pipgras in 3rd Game," *New York Herald-Tribune*, September 30, 1932 ("You can bet I told them plenty about cutting in Mark Koenig for only a half share").

23. "Big-hearted Charlie": Powers, *New York Daily News*, September 30, 1932; see also Tynan, *New York Herald Tribune*, October 2, 1932 (seventh inning, "Ruth had some more fun with the bench warmers in the Chicago dugout").

24. "We'll get 'em": Carmichael, *Daily News*, September 30, 1932.

25. Twice, times ten: "'Forgotten Men' of Chicago Cheer Gov. Roosevelt," *Evening American*, October 1, 1932.

26. Touring car: "'Forgotten Men' of Chicago Cheer Gov. Roosevelt," *Evening American*, October 1, 1932. City Greeter George Gaw's car had transported Charlie Grimm in the Cubs' pennant celebration the week before (*Daily Times*, September 22, 1932).

27. Young man without sight: "Ruth Visits Youth Injured in Bombing," *New York Times*, October 2, 1932; "Boy Blinded by Bomb Gets Visit from Babe Ruth," *Tribune*, October 2, 1932. Dollar's worth: "Police Expert Reveals Inside of Bomb Racket," *Tribune*, September 22, 1932. Chief Investigator Patrick Roche was one of the first upon the scene, according to "Bomb Injures 2 before Judge's Home," *Tribune*, September 21, 1932.

28. Lemon throwing: Casey, *Daily News*, October 1, 1932; Otto, *Herald and Examiner*, October 2, 1932; "Yanks' Homers Owe Much to West Wind," special to *New York Times*, October 2, 1932.

29. West wind: "Yanks Homers," *New York Times*, and Ward, *Tribune*, both October 2, 1932. "Cheap chiselers!": Casey, *Daily News*, October 1, 1932.

30. "Hey, mugs!": Pegler, *Chicago Tribune*, October 2, 1932.

31. Ushers, band: Corcoran, *American*, October 1, 1932. Box 76: *Tribune*, October 2, 1932. See also Kelly, *Herald and Examiner*, same date (FDR in "front box, behind and slightly to the right of home plate"). Ill at ease: see photo in *New York Daily News*, October 2, 1932. "Got to work": Hall, *Daily Times*, October 2, 1932.

32. Single lemon: Corcoran, "Cork Tips," *Evening American*, October 1, 1932; Baer, "Babe Friendly, but Fan Throws Lemon and Slugger Cracks Homer," *Herald and Examiner*, October 2, 1932. Some gesture: see Additional Sources, "Some Gesture."

33. Scoreboard: Ruth's shot, which passed close by the scoreboard's extreme right corner or edge, was hit virtually to dead center field: the pre-1937 scoreboard stood at an oblique angle almost entirely to the left of dead center, with only a small portion extending to the right of a direct line running from home plate through second base. After the 1937 reconfiguration, a similar drive would probably have reached high into the present center-field bleachers. No Wrigley Field batsman: Keys, *Daily News*, October 1, 1932 ("a place where no man has ever hit a baseball before. It was without question the longest home run ever driven out at Wrigley Field"); Brown, *Herald and Examiner*, October 2, 1932 ("perhaps the longest wallop ever [at Wrigley Field]"). President Veeck, however, told Marvin McCarthy in the *Daily Times*, October 4, 1932: "The farthest and most powerful drive ever hit in Wrigley Field was, I believe, one made by Hack Wilson in 1929. He hit the scoreboard up high and slightly to the left, about where the 'out' shot [*sic*; slot?] is located." The *Daily Times* added that when Hack struck the scoreboard, "the figures on the board did crazy little sidesteps, like the figures in a Ziegfeld chorus sometimes do." Veeck said that Rogers Hornsby, as a Cardinal, had struck the lower edge of the scoreboard with the park's second-longest home run. Threw his head: Runyon, *Herald and Examiner*, October 2, 1932. Cheering in tribute: Drebinger, *New York Times*, October 2, 1932; Williams, "Ruth Calls Shot as He Puts Homer No. 2 in Side Pocket," *New York World-Telegram*, October 1, 1932; Corcoran, "Cork Tips," *Evening American*, October 1, 1932; Povich, *Washington Post*, October 2, 1932 ("Ruth and Gehrig "transformed a booing, hostile stadium populace into an admiring, adulating mob").

34. Hack Wilson model: Hunt, *New York Daily News*, October 2, 1932, noticed Ruth's "yellow truncheon" lying on the ground after the fifth-inning homer.

35. Booing: Williams, *New York World-Telegram*, October 1, 1932; special dispatch, *New York Times*, and Burns, *Tribune*, both October 2, 1932.

36. "Beat that?": Brandt, *New York Times*, October 2, 1932.

37. "Mr. Ruth": "Yanks Going Home Tonight, They Declare," *Tribune*, October 2, 1932. Robinson's bet: according to "Ruth, Mates on Rampage," *New York World-Telegram*, October 3, 1932, the bet was for ten thousand dollars. "Get your bags packed": Brandt, *New York Times*, October 2, 1932.

38. Booing: Baer, *Herald and Examiner*, and Burns, *Tribune*, both October 3, 1932. "Bring Hornsby back": Williams, *New York World-Telegram*, October 3, 1932.

39. Jeered: Drebinger, *New York Times*, October 3, 1932.

40. "Divine comedian": Gallico, "Clown and Hero," *New York Daily News,*
October 3, 1932. Clubhouse attendant: Munzel, *Herald and Examiner*, October
3, 1932. "East side, west side": Sewell, *Daily News*, October 3, 1932 (column
by Joe Sewell of the Yankees); AP in *New York Herald Tribune*, October 3,
1932; "Ruth, Mates on Rampage," *New York World-Telegram*, October 3, 1932.
Trunks: UP in *Indianapolis Star*, October 3, 1932. Luggage: Pegler, *Tribune*,
October 3, 1932.

41. Grimes bellowing: Vaughan, *Tribune*, October 3, 1932. Vaughan predicted
that Grimes would not be back next year. A later *Sporting News* wrap-up of
the World Series, presumably contributed by Vaughan, used the same phrase
in mentioning that "the man supposed to have fought hardest to keep
Hornsby out will not be present next season" ("Hornsby Will Haunt Cubs'
Peace of Mind," *Sporting News*, November 3, 1932).

42. Ribs: Vaughan, *Tribune*, October 3, 1932; MacNamara, *Herald and Examiner*,
October 3, 1932; Margolis, *Daily Times*, October 3, 1932.

43. Player destinations: Simons, "Weary of Baseball, Cubs Players Scatter,"
Daily Times, October 3, 1932. Warneke Sr.: "Warneke Sr. Misses Series,"
Sporting News, October 6, 1932.

44. Grand Central: Daniel, *New York World-Telegram*, October 3, 1932.

45. Pay cut, bad heart: Hunt, *New York Daily News*, October 5, 1932; "Ruth to
Get Salary Slash; Too Big a Risk for $75,000," *Tribune*, October 5, 1932.
"Wish I'd known": Meany, *New York World-Telegram*, October 4, 1932.

46. Hornsby pretending; "Hornsby Not Interested" (AP dispatch), *New York
Times*, September 30, 1932. Hornsby analysis: "Gossip of Fourth Game,"
Sporting News, October 6, 1932.

47. Series shares: "Yank Share $5,010; Cubs $4,244" (sidebar), *Daily Times*,
October 3, 1932. See also the attendance summaries that ran in various
Chicago and New York newspapers, October 2 and 3, 1932. Landis's cold:
Tribune and *Daily Times*, October 5, 1932. Lord most high: *Herald and
Examiner*, October 15, 1932. Woody English (in Golenbock, *Wrigleyville*,
233) remembers Landis interviewing him about Mark Koenig's World Series
share. Since the public appeal was Hornsby's, Ruth's showmanship must
probably be credited with altering English's recollection.

48. YMCA: *Tribune*, December 2, 1932; *St. Louis Post-Dispatch*, December 22, 1932;
Dick Farrington, *Sporting News*, December 29, 1932.

49. Clayton courthouse: "Rogers Hornsby Farm Sold for $15,000 at Foreclosure,"
St. Louis Post-Dispatch, December 20, 1932; *Tribune*, December 18 and 21, 1932.

ADDITIONAL SOURCE COMMENTS

6   JEERING: The immediate reportage on the Hornsby at-bat mentioned, but deemphasized, anti-Hornsby sentiment among the crowd. For instance, the *Tribune*, September 14, 1931, tilted toward the Hornsby faction ("Those who wanted to boo . . . were vastly outnumbered"), although the reporter, Irving Vaughan, did acknowledge that after the first strike there was renewed booing. The *Herald and Examiner*, September 14, 1931, only alluded to the anti-Hornsbyites ("Hornsby's courage . . . facing the *possible wrath* [emphasis added] of the 33,000 fans"—whom it also referred to as "the Romans") and dwelt on the favorable demonstrations that transpired after Hornsby's grand slam. The United Press, however, saw the struggle in starker terms, without qualification: "boos greeted [Hornsby]" when he came to bat in the tenth, before he was able to win them over with his grand slam. Ten days later (September 24, 1931), the *Sporting News* more forthrightly referred to the general situation and tied it to the game of September 13: "[T]he [razzing?] campaign against [Hornsby] is still on and there is an inclination . . . to boo him whenever he appears" (followed by a section referring to the September 13 game and subtitled "Hornsby Stills His Critics"). Early in the next season Ralph Cannon, in the *Daily News*, May 31, 1932, recalled the hostility to Hornsby as he came to bat: "a crowd that was grumbling and hostile over the Hack Wilson episode," and a full twelve years later (almost to the day) Stanley Frank, a prominent national sports journalist, quoted "old inhabitants of Wrigley Field" who remembered a "violent demonstration" of 1931 in which "the wolves attacked Rogers Hornsby. . . . [He] crushed the mob by hitting a pinch home run with the bases loaded to beat the Braves" ("The Decline and Fall of the Cubs," *Saturday Evening Post*, September 11, 1943).

A twelve-year delay is ordinarily considered a negative factor in the trustworthiness of reports: a thirty-five-year-old who spoke to Frank in 1943 could have remembered his twenty-three-year-old self participating in a glorious struggle against the man in the black hat (Hornsby) and "misremembered" the rest. However, several other factors mitigate that problem:

1) Hornsby's booing at the Cubs-Sox benefit game a few days earlier had attracted more attention nationally than would the usual game of a third-place team out of the running, establishing a precondition for the September 13 confrontation; 2) William Wrigley was still alive in September 1931 and Rogers Hornsby was his man, a fact that must have carried weight, consciously or unconsciously, with the Chicago-based press, toward de-emphasizing the discontent; 3) the authors of the two most complete accounts (quoted above) of the incident had direct personal ties to Cub management: Irving Vaughan of the *Tribune* was Wrigley's designated interviewer, called in several times in recent years for exclusive, front-page interviews, and as for the *Herald and Examiner*'s Wayne Otto, Hornsby had personally rescued him from a physical assault by a Cub player just two weeks earlier; 4) Frank's observation of twelve years later was an aside by an out-of-town writer comparing the 1931 incident to a fan demonstration of 1943, so he had no apparent motive to bring up the 1931 incident. Frank was an accomplished journalist who had more than enough material on hand about the 1943 incident to make his case, so his treatment of the Hornsby affair had more of the historical treatment about it.

CHAPTER 2

25 WORLD SERIES: "Radio Broadcasting Began Four Years Ago Today," *New York Times*, November 2, 1924, says, "In 1921 radio was used to broadcast results of the world series of baseball games from the original WJZ station at Newark, N.J.," confirmed in Archer, *History of Radio to 1926*, 280, 321–22. The efforts mentioned by the *Times* and Archer involved broadcasts that originated with station WEAF in New York. There were, however, evidently non-WEAF attempts to carry the World Series over the airwaves. Linton, "A History of Chicago Radio," 74, quotes WMAQ's log of October 9, 1923, naming Roy E. Garrison, a *Daily News* correspondent, as the broadcaster of a "play-by-play description, a technique developed the previous year in the east"—evidently a long-range re-creation of the 1923 World Series for WMAQ. In addition, "KYW Will Broadcast World Series Again by New Method" (*Evening American*, October 6, 1925), began, "For the fourth consecutive year, the Chicago Evening American–Westinghouse KYW sports service will broadcast the world series baseball games play by play, beginning with the opening game at Pittsburgh tomorrow." KYW was affiliated with the Westinghouse KDKA station in Pittsburgh, neither of which had been listed as part of any network organized by WEAF. As with the *Daily News* effort, these broadcasts may have involved studio re-creations (*Evening American*, October 12, 1925): "Most fans preferred the running story of the game that came in by

telegraph. It was just as fast, clear, and without the background of noises and shouts present from the field."

CHAPTER 4

98   SEATING CAPACITY: Reports on the seating capacity of the park at Addison and Clark were sporadic and unmonitored. Nonetheless, taken as a whole they provide a rough picture of how seating increased and then fluctuated.

Tribune, April 17, 1923: "more than 31,000" ("[Cubs Park] now is the largest single deck baseball park in the country, the seating capacity having been boosted from 16,500 to more than 31,000").

Tribune, April 24, 1926: 28,000.

Tribune, April 14, 1927: 35,000 ("[The] park now seats 35,000 persons." The Clark Street side of the upper deck had been completed during the off season).

Tribune, April 16, 1928: 45,000 after adding 7,000 seats for completion of the upper deck. (The 7,000 figure implies that the park contained 38,000 seats at the end of the 1927 season, rather than the 35,000 reported on April 14, 1927, above.)

Herald and Examiner, October 6, 1929: 43,000 (report that addition of 8,000 temporary seats for the World Series would boost park seating capacity to 51,000).

UP dispatch of August 25, 1930: less than 43,000 (crowd of 43,000; Kiki Cuyler ran into a policeman in foul territory, indicating an overflow crowd).

Tribune, April 15, 1931: less than 43,000 (crowd figure given as 43,000; sizable overflow section plainly visible in a photograph; hence, seating capacity was less than 43,000).

Tribune, August 28, 1932: crowd of 41,000 "overflowed on the field" (park seating, then, less than 41,000).

Daily News, September 19, 1932: 42,000 (item said addition of 12,000 temporary seats for World Series would bring capacity to 54,000).

The best generalization to draw from these varying reports may be that the park's "moving average" descended from the mid-40,000s to the low 40,000s by 1932, probably as the ballclub utilized larger, more comfortable seats.

98   ROPES: The maximum possible number of overflow standees is difficult to gauge due to the repeated fluctuations in reported seating capacity, inconsistencies in reporting crowd figures, and the inevitable variations in the extra number of people who showed up on any given day. Usually, news reports for overflow days provided only an overall crowd figure, but the *Tribune*, July 2, 1926, mentioned a specific overflow attendance figure of 4,000, with an overall attendance figure that day of 35,000; two months later, the Cubs again

drew 35,000 (*Tribune*, August 30, 1926), which logically means another overflow figure of 4,000 (although that point wasn't raised for the second date). Then again, the standees at the next year's home opener may have exceeded 4,000: "[The] park now seats 35,000 persons. It was inadequate Tuesday by 10,000" (*Tribune*, April 14, 1927). The 10,000 figure, of course, could have included not only overflow tickets sold but some number of fans standing in the aisles. For photography of SRO/overflow crowds, see *Tribune*, August 30, 1926; July 27, 1929 (available online at http://www.loc.gov/ pictures/resource/pan.6a28670/, accessed October 11, 2011); June 28, 1930 ("When the Cubs Entertained Wrigley Field's Largest Crowd"); August 16, 1930 ("When Ladies' Day Crowd Helped to Set New Attendance Record at Cubs Park,"); and April 15, 1931 ("When 43,000 Wished the Cubs Good Luck on a New Pennant Chase"). See also a Chicago Historical Society photograph (http://hdl.loc.gov/loc.ndlpcoop/ichicdn.s069126, accessed September 5, 2011), identified as from "a 1929 World Series game," although the fans are wearing summer clothing and Chicago's 1929 series games were played in early October.

CHAPTER 5

140 NIPS: "Wrigley Not Always a 'King'; Piloted 'Nips'—Prairie Team," *Evening American*, May 23, 1926. The byline for the story of Wrigley's Nips was that of the veteran Chicago sportswriter Jimmy Corcoran, who later moved to the *Herald and Examiner* (see obituary posted at Baseball Fever website, http://www.baseball-fever.com/showthread.php?57538-Meet-The-Sports-Writers/page8, accessed June 17, 2012). Wrigley's erstwhile co-owner, Albert Lasker, later claimed that before investing in the Cubs, "[Wrigley] had no interest in baseball. I don't think Mr. Wrigley even knew that there were three strikes for an out. I mean that seriously. I'm *sure* he didn't know what a squeeze play would mean" (Cruikshank and Schultz, *Man Who Sold America*, 180 [emphasis in original]). Some sixty years after Corcoran wrote about Wrigley's Nips, AP's special correspondent, Will Grimsley, brought up the Nips in a column following the death of William's son, Philip Wrigley ("Dad Would Have Loved It, Says Bill Wrigley," undated clipping, ca. late 1970s, in HOF files). Grimsley provided extra details not present in Corcoran's lengthy account of 1926: "[William Wrigley] formed a semi-pro baseball team of bookkeepers and salesmen called the 'Wrigley Nips,' who played only on weekends. Pay ranged from $5 to $25 a game." (Grimsley was the National Sportscasters and Sportswriters Association's Sports Writer of the Year for 1978, 1980, 1981, and 1983; see "Grimsley Covered Sports for AP for 40 Years," AP obituary posted at ESPN Classic website, November 12, 2002, http://espn

.go.com/classic/obit/s/2002/1104/1455843.html, accessed June 17, 2012.) In 1905 (a date that corresponds to Corcoran's time frame) the *Tribune* listed the Wrigley Nips twice under reports for "Prairie Teams" (May 31 and July 31, 1905), and another item in 1910 mentioned "the former Wrigley Nips" (May 24, 1910). See also Otto, *Herald and Examiner*, January 27, 1932: "Wrigley became intensely interested in the old Cub team . . . under the leadership of the immortal Frank Chance. . . . 'Someday I'll own a ball club and it probably will be the Cubs,' Wrigley declared then." Lasker's description of the pre-ownership Wrigley as a baseball ignoramus perhaps reflects a complicated relationship between two aggressive and extraordinarily successful men.

CHAPTER 18

370 SOME GESTURE: Authorities differ on the proof provided by the films that Matt Kandle and Harold Warp shot at Wrigley Field during the third game of the 1932 World Series. For instance, in 2007, Stout and Johnson pronounced the Warp film definitive: "[W]hen the footage came to light, the evidence was irrefutable: Ruth clearly didn't point to center field, he merely gestured toward the Cub bench" (*The Cubs*, 150). A year earlier, however, Bill Deane, a former senior research associate at the National Baseball Hall of Fame Library, cited the Kandle film to support a contrary conclusion: Ruth, Deane believed, had pointed toward Root or the outfield, but "definitely not" at the Cubs dugout (Dickson, *Dickson Baseball Dictionary*, 158). Ruth's most recent biographer, Leigh Montville, favors Stout and Johnson's interpretation: "A pair of 16mm home movies discovered more than a half-century later seemed to indicate that Ruth might have pointed at the Cubs bench and at Bush rather than center field . . , but both films were taken from angles that left room for doubt" (Montville, *Big Bam*, 311). See Glenn Stout and Richard A. Johnson, *The Cubs: The Complete Story of the Chicago Cubs* [Boston: Houghton Mifflin Harcourt, 2007]; Paul Dickson, *The Dickson Baseball Dictionary*, 3rd ed. [New York: W. W. Norton, 2011]; and Leigh Montville, *The Big Bam: The Life and Times of Babe Ruth* [New York: Broadway Books, 2006].) Perhaps more telling, Tom Manning, in his play-by-play call for NBC, clearly uttered the words "Babe Ruth is pointing out to center field and he's yelling at the Cubs that the next pitch over is going out into center field!" (Joe Garner, *And the Crowd Goes Wild: Relive the Most Celebrated Sporting Events Ever Broadcast* [Naperville IL: Sourcebooks, 1999], disc 1, track 2, "Babe Ruth Calls His Shot" [Bob Costas narrates the Manning call]). In the majority of reports published in Chicago and New York newspapers after game 3, the predominant theme was Ruth's use of his fingers to point at the Cubs' dugout. Only two articles reporting on the game mentioned a gesture toward the outfield,

one of them using the word "pointing" (as well as "called his shot").
"Pointed" was then repeated in following days. John Walsh (*Sports Illustrated*,
October 18, 1965) seems to have begun the practice of combing through
microfilms for clues about Ruth's shot. Robert Creamer (*Babe*) and Jerome
Holtzman (*Chicago Tribune*, November 1, 1987) both reviewed a substantial
cross-section of the reports listed below; this collection adds several observers
and their exact phrasings. While Walsh displayed the fervor of an explorer
discovering treasure in the old vaults, Creamer and Holtzman both concluded
more dispassionately that Joe Williams of the *New York World-Telegram*,
overcome by the drama he had witnessed, had kick-started the legend. Yet
John Drebinger of the Newspaper of Record immediately and independently
corroborated Williams. It's also difficult to believe that the radio man on the
spot, Tom Manning, could have come up with almost the same fabrication—
at the moment it occurred. Finally, Charlie Grimm himself used the words
"called his shot" before the end of the year—Grimm thus becoming the first
player on either side who positively affirmed the incident (and of course, he
was playing first base at the time). Against those witnesses must be held the
many recorded observers, obviously watching intently, who simply didn't
bring the matter up.

Among the reports and commentary filed on game day and soon thereafter, the descriptions (and just as important, the omitted descriptions) of
Ruth's fifth-inning at-bat in game 3 can be loosely divided into: 1) no report;
2) Ruth's use of fingers; and 3) Ruth pointing and using "gestures" (which
variously specify the dugout, the outfield, and points beyond), or nothing in
particular.

1. No Report (Reporter-Observer Described Ruth's Fifth-Inning Home Run Minus Finger-Pointing or Gestures)

J. Roy Stockton, *St. Louis Post-Dispatch* (October 1, 1932), simply said that Ruth's
fifth inning home run was "one of the longest homers ever hit in the park."

Shirley Povich (*Washington Post*, October 2, 1932): "[W]ith one out in the fifth . . .
[t]he count was two-and-two on the Babe. . . . Ruth rapped [the ball] on a
direct extremity to the farthest extremity of [center] field."

Alan Gould (Associated Press dispatch in *Los Angeles Times*, October 2, 1932):
"Babe and Larrupin' Lou ripped off home runs in the fifth to put the final
crusher on Root. Ruth's second drive, the longest of the day, cleared the wire
fence just in front of the bleachers in extreme center field."

Damon Runyon (syndicated column for Universal Service, *Herald and Examiner*,
October 2, 1932): "[I]n the fifth inning when the score is a tie and Babe Ruth
busts his second long homer, one of the longest drives ever seen in these parts,

Governor Franklin Delano Roosevelt of New York forgets himself. 'Haw-haw-haw' he roars." (Runyon later mentioned that Ruth had made "gestures with his hands" but did not specify a specific at-bat.)

Arthur "Bugs" Baer ("Bugs Baer Says: Babe Friendly, but Fan Throws Lemon and Slugger Cracks Homer," syndicated column for Universal Service, *Herald and Examiner,* October 2, 1932). Baer described Ruth's first-inning at-bat and home run in detail, then added, "There were more home runs after that, but this one [i.e., in the first inning] was the kingpin."

Babe Ruth ("Ruth Asserts Fine Pitching Turned Trend of Series toward Yankees," *Herald and Examiner,* October 2, 1932; no copyright information available, although his column of the next day in the same newspaper was credited to the Christy Walsh Syndicate). The closest Ruth's ghostwriter came to mentioning Ruth's fifth-inning experience was to say (getting the number of the inning wrong): "The Cubs were crushed when Lou Gehrig knocked Charley Root out of the box with that second homer of his in the sixth [*sic*] inning. That was our sixth run, the run which won the game because it was one more than the Cubs could match." The ghost also mentioned "boos and the stray lemons and the razzing which they gave me" without specifying a context.

Gordon Cobbledick (*Cleveland Plain Dealer*) and Jimmy Isaminger (*Philadelphia Inquirer*): These two reporters "didn't see" Ruth's call, according to Jerome Holtzman in "The Yankees' Babe Ruth Gestures toward Wrigley Fields Bleachers" (*Tribune,* November 1, 1987). Holtzman served as the official historian for Major League Baseball from 1999 until his death in 2008.

Edgar Munzel ("Here Is Detailed Account of Yanks 7-5 Win Over Cubs," *Herald and Examiner,* October 2, 1932): "After some lengthy jockeying with the Cubs in the dugout, Ruth hit a tremendous home run into the extreme corner of the right field bleachers where the . . . bleachers join the center field scoreboard. . . . Gehrig followed with a home run down the right field line into the temporary bleachers." (Munzel also wrote a feature article, below, that mentioned Ruth's raising his fingers.)

John Drebinger wrote one story crediting Ruth with a gesture, but his paper's play-by-play account did not mention it: "Ruth held a spirited debate with the Cubs substitutes on their bench while Root was serving three balls and two strikes [the count was actually 2-2], then swung at the sixth pitch and hit a tremendous drive which sailed over the bleachers' screen and came down at the base of the flagpole beside the scoreboard in deepest center for his second home run of the game. Gehrig wasted no time but swung on Root's first pitch" ("Yankees Beat Cubs, 7-5, for Third Straight in World's Series Before 51,000," *New York Times,* October 2, 1932).

Ruth's Use of Fingers

Game-Day Stories of Ruth Raising Fingers but Not Pointing

"Held up a couple more fingers" (Jimmy Corcoran, *Evening American,* October 1).

"Stuck up two fingers" (*Sunday Times,* October 2).

"Holding up two fingers" (Irving Vaughan, *Chicago Tribune,* October 2).

"Held up two fingers" (Ed Burns, *Chicago Tribune,* October 2).

"Held up two fingers" (Paul Gallico, *New York Daily News,* October 2).

"Held up two fingers" (Richards Vidmer, *New York Herald-Tribune,* October 2;
earlier, Vidmer remarked that Ruth "pointed to the right-field bleachers," but
in the first inning).

"Very dramatically raised one finger, and then two" (Edgar Munzel, *Herald and
Examiner,* October 2: feature article on Ruth, but Munzel also wrote a full
play-by-play account).

"[T]he Cub players, yelling from their dugout, were making uncomplimentary
remarks. The Babe, [*sic*] waved them back to their dugout, raising his two
fingers to tell them that there were two strikes on him and to watch out"
(Charles Dunkley, AP in *Indianapolis Star,* October 2).

"The Babe held up one finger and finally two on each hand with the count two and
two. Then wham! He caught Root's next pitch and they never got the ball
back. . . . As [Ruth] trotted around the bags, he held up four fingers, signify-
ing a home run" ("Series Highlights," Associated Press in *Washington Post,*
October 2; this unattributed article may have been written by Alan Gould, the
AP correspondent referenced in the "No report" section above for his game
summary).

Ruth Gesturing

Toward the Dugout without Mention of the Outfield

"Put up two fingers. . . . Then, with a warning gesture of his hand to Bush, he sent
him the signal for the customers to see" (Westbrook Pegler, *Chicago Tribune,*
October 2).

"Called his shot . . . with derisive gestures towards the Cubs' dugout" (Warren
Brown, *Herald and Examiner,* October 2: no details of pointing, raising
fingers, etc.).

Referencing the Outfield without Gesturing

"Peered out there at the score board" (John Carmichael, *Daily News,* October 1).

Gesturing or Motioning toward the Outfield

"Called his shot . . . pointed to centre [*sic*] field" (Joe Williams, *New York*

World-Telegram, October 1); also "held up one finger" (Williams, returning
to the fifth inning later in his write-up).

"[I]n no mistaken motions the Babe notified the crowd that the nature of his
retaliation would be a wallop right out [*sic*] the confines of the park (John
Drebinger, *New York Times*, October 2; Ruth also "signaled with his fingers
after each pitch").

Post–Game Day Reports that Ruth "Pointed"

"Pointed like a duelist to the spot" (Paul Gallico, *New York Daily News*, October
3). Note that Gallico's original report of October 2 mentioned no pointing by
Ruth but did mention that he "held up two fingers."

"Pointed out the spot" (Tom Meany, *New York World-Telegram*, October 4).

"Pointed out where he was going to hit the next one" (Bill Corum, *New York
Journal-American*—"a day after" Gallico, per Creamer, *Babe*, 364).

"Two balls, and up went two fingers on the left hand. And now he wiped his hands
on his trousers and pointed toward the distant bleachers. Root wound up and
pegged a fast ball—and the Babe hit it out of the park" ("McCarthy Fulfills
Rupert Prophecy," Joe Vila, *Sporting News*, October 6, 1932).

Post-October 1932

"And that Ruth. Calling his shot and hitting one over the center fence. When he
calls his shot I say to the other players, 'This guy is a sucker after all.' When
he hits that ball I begin to suspect that we are licked" (Charlie Grimm, quoted
by Dan Daniel in "Rambling 'Round the Circuit with Pitcher Snorter Casey,"
Sporting News, December 22, 1932). Grimm's is the oldest direct confirmation
by a ballplayer of the shot. Many more of the participants in the infield and
the dugouts spoke out over the decades, just as inconclusively as the journalists who wrote things down that day. One thing is certain in this fog of
confusion: Babe Ruth gave the people in the ballpark that day (including the
future president) their money's worth of entertainment.

BIBLIOGRAPHY

NEWSPAPERS AND MAGAZINES

The majority of newspaper citations come from those listed below, taken from issues dated 1918 to 1934. To avoid repetition, Chicago papers are listed in the notes without the name of the city: *Tribune, Daily News,* etc.

Chicago Daily News
Chicago Daily Times
Chicago Defender
Chicago Evening American
Chicago Evening Post
Chicago Herald and Examiner, Chicago Herald-Examiner
Chicago Tribune
Chicago Sun-Times clipping file (items from various Chicago newspapers)
Cincinnati Enquirer
Indianapolis Star
Indianapolis Times
New York Times
New York Herald Tribune
New York Daily News
Pittsburgh Post-Gazette
Pittsburgh Press
Pittsburgh Sun-Telegraph
Sporting News
St. Louis Post-Dispatch
Time Magazine

BOOKS

Chicago National League Ball Club

Angle, Paul M. *P. K. Wrigley: A Memoir of a Modest Man.* Skokie IL: Rand McNally, 1975.

Boone, Robert S., and Gerald S. Grunska, *Hack: The Meteoric Life of One of Baseball's First Superstars, Hack Wilson*. Highland Park IL: Highland Press, 1978.

Brown, Warren. *The Chicago Cubs*. New York: G.P. Putnam's Sons, 1946.

Enright, James. *Chicago Cubs*. New York: Collier, 1975.

Gifford, Barry. *The Neighborhood of Baseball: A Personal History of the Chicago Cubs*. New York: Dutton, 1981.

Golenbock, Peter. *Wrigleyville: A Magical History Tour of the Chicago Cubs*. New York: St. Martin's, 1996.

Grimm, Charlie, with Ed Prell. *Jolly Cholly's Story: Baseball, I Love You*. Chicago: Regnery, 1968.

Holtzman, Jerome, and George Vass. *Baseball Chicago Style: A Tale of Two Teams, One City*. Chicago: Bonus Books, 2001.

————. *The Chicago Cubs Encyclopedia*. Philadelphia: Temple University Press, 1997.

McNeil, William F. *Gabby Hartnett: The Life and Times of the Cubs' Greatest Catcher*. Jefferson NC: McFarland, 2004.

Murphy, James M. *The Gabby Hartnett Story*. Smithtown NY: Exposition Press, 1983.

Smith, Curt. "The Voices of Cub Broadcasters." In *Northsiders: Essays on the History and Culture of the Chicago Cubs*. Edited by Gerald C. Wood and Andrew Hazucha, 134–41. Jefferson NC: McFarland, 2008.

Vitti, Jim. *Chicago Cubs: Baseball on Catalina Island*. Charleston SC: Arcadia Publishing, 2010.

Zimmerman, William. *William Wrigley, Jr.: The Man and His Business, 1861–1932*. Chicago: private edition printed by R. R. Donnelly and Sons at the Lakeside Press, 1935.

General Baseball

Aaron, Henry, with Lonnie Wheeler. *I Had a Hammer: The Hank Aaron Story*. New York: Harper Collins, 1991.

Barber, Red. *The Broadcasters*. New York: Dial Press, 1970.

Barrow, Edward G., with James M. Kahn. *My Fifty Years in Baseball*. New York: Coward-McCann, 1951.

Brown, Warren. *The Chicago White Sox*. New York: G. P. Putnam's Sons, 1952.

Alexander, Charles C. *John McGraw*. New York: Viking, 1988.

————. *Rogers Hornsby*. New York: Henry Holt, 1995.

Carmichael, John. *My Greatest Day in Baseball*. Lincoln: University of Nebraska Press, 1996.

Cataneo, David. *Hornsby Hit One over My Head: A Fans' Oral History of Baseball*. New York: Harvest, 1997.

Creamer, Robert W. *Babe: The Legend Comes to Life*. New York: Simon and Schuster, 1974.

Crepeau, Richard C. *Baseball: America's Diamond Mind, 1919–1941*. Gainesville: University Presses of Florida, 1980.

Dawidoff, Nicholas. *The Catcher Was a Spy: The Mysterious Life of Moe Berg*. New York: Pantheon Books, 1994.

Doutrich, Paul E. *The Cardinals and the Yankees: A Classic Season and St. Louis in Seven*. Jefferson NC: McFarland, 2011.

Echevarría, Roberto González. *The Pride of Havana: The History of Cuban Baseball*. New York: Oxford University Press, 1999.

Eskenazi, Gerald. *Bill Veeck: A Baseball Legend*. New York: McGraw-Hill, 1988.

Faber, Charles F., and Richard B. Faber. *Spitballers: The Last Legal Hurlers of the Wet One*. Jefferson NC: McFarland, 2006.

Farrell, James T. *My Baseball Diary*. New York: A. S. Barnes, 1957.

Figueredo, Jorge S. *Cuban Baseball: A Statistical History, 1878–1961*. Jefferson NC: McFarland, 2003.

Fleming, Gordon H. *The Dizziest Season: The Gashouse Gang Chases the Pennant*. New York: William Morrow, 1984.

Gallen, David, ed. *The Baseball Chronicles*. New York: Carroll and Graf, 1991.

Gerlach, Larry R. *The Men in Blue: Conversations with Umpires*. New York, Viking, 1980.

Gershman, Michael. *Diamonds: The Evolution of the Ballpark*. Boston: Houghton Mifflin, 1993.

Graham, Frank. *McGraw of the Giants: An Informal Biography*. New York: G.P. Putman's Sons, 1944.

Ham, Eldon L. *Broadcasting Baseball: A History of the National Pastime on Radio and Television*. Jefferson NC: McFarland, 2011.

Hawkins, Joel, and Terry Bertolino. *The House of David Baseball Team*. Chicago: Arcadia, 2000.

Honig, Donald. *Baseball America: The Heroes of the Game and the Times of Their Glory*. New York: Macmillan, 1985.

Hood, Robert E. *The Gashouse Gang*. New York: William Morrow, 1976.

Hornsby, Rogers. *My Kind of Baseball*. Edited by J. Roy Stockton. New York: David McKay, 1953.

Hornsby, Rogers, and Bill Surface. *My War with Baseball*. New York: Coward-McCann, 1962.

Kaese, Harold. *The Boston Braves*. New York: G. P. Putnam's Sons, 1948.

Karst, Gene, and Martin J. Jones Jr. *Who's Who in Professional Baseball*. New Rochelle NY: Arlington House, 1973.

Kashatus, William. *The Philadelphia Athletics*. Portsmouth NH: Arcardia Publishing, 2002.

Kavanagh, Jack. *Ol' Pete: The Grover Alexander Story*. South Bend IN: Diamond Communications, 1996.

Lanctot, Neil. *Fair Dealing and Clean Playing: The Hilldale Club and the Development of Black Professional Baseball, 1910–1932*. Syracuse: Syracuse University Press, 2007.

Levy, Alan H. *Joe McCarthy: Architect of the Yankee Dynasty*. Jefferson NC: McFarland and Co., 2005.

Lieb, Fred. *Connie Mack: Grand Old Man of Baseball*. New York: G. P. Putnam's Sons, 1945.

———. *The Pittsburgh Pirates*. New York: G. P. Putnam's Sons, 1948.

Light, Jonathan Fraser. *The Cultural Encyclopedia of Baseball*. Jefferson NC: McFarland, 1997.

Lindberg, Richard. *The White Sox Encyclopedia*. Philadelphia: Temple University Press, 1997.

Lowry, Philip J. *Green Cathedrals: The Ultimate Celebration of Major League and Negro League Ballparks*. New York: Walker, 2006.

Mead, William. *Two Spectacular Seasons*. New York: Macmillan, 1990.

Murdock, Eugene. *Baseball between the Wars: Memories of the Game by the Men Who Played It*. Westport CT: Meckler, 1992.

Okrent Daniel, and Steve Wulf. *Baseball Anecdotes*. New York: Oxford University Press, 1989.

O'Neal, Bill. *The American Association: A Baseball History, 1902–1991*. Austin TX: Eakin Press, 1992.

Peterson, Robert. *Only the Ball Was White: A History of the Legendary Black Players and All-Black Professional Teams*. Englewood Cliffs NJ: Prentice-Hall, 1970.

Phalen, Richard C. *Our Chicago Cubs: Inside the History and the Mystery of Baseball's Favorite Franchise*. South Bend IN: Diamond Communications, 1992.

Riess, Steven A. *Touching Base: Professional Baseball and American Culture in the Progressive Era*. Westport CT: Greenwood Press, 1980.

Ritter, Lawrence S. *The Babe: A Life in Pictures*. New York: Ticknor and Fields, 1988.

Seymour, Harold. *Baseball: The Early Years*. New York: Oxford University Press, 1960.

———. *Baseball: The Golden Age*. New York: Oxford University Press, 1989.

———. *Baseball: The People's Game*. New York: Oxford University Press, 1990.

Shatzkin, Mike, ed. *The Ballplayers: Baseball's Ultimate Biographical Reference*. New York: Arbor House/William Morrow, 1990.

Spink, J. G. Taylor. *Judge Landis and Twenty-five Years of Baseball*. New York: T. Y. Crowell Co., 1947.

Stout, Glenn, and Richard A. Johnson. *Red Sox Century: One Hundred Years of Red Sox Baseball*. Boston: Houghton Mifflin, 2000.

Thorn, John, and Pete Palmer, eds. *Total Baseball: The Ultimate Encyclopedia of Baseball*. 3rd ed. New York: HarperCollins, 1993.

Tygiel, Jules. *Past Time: Baseball as History*. New York: Oxford University Press, 2000.

Veeck, Bill, with Ed Linn. *Veeck—as in Wreck: The Autobiography of Bill Veeck*. New York: G. P. Putnam's Sons, 1962.

———. *The Hustler's Handbook*. New York: G. P. Putnam's Sons, 1965.

Voigt, David Q. *American Baseball*. Vol. 2. University Park: Pennsylvania State University Press, 1983.

Westcott, Rich. *Philadelphia's Old Ballparks*. Philadelphia: Temple University Press, 1996.

"Year in Review: 1921 National League." Baseball Almanac, http://www.baseball-almanac.com/yearly/yr1921n.shtml.

Chicago-Related

Andrews, Clarence A. *Chicago in Story: A Literary History*. Iowa City: Midwest Heritage Publishing, 1982.

Andrews, Wayne. *Battle for Chicago*. New York: Harcourt, 1946.

Bergreen, Laurence. *Capone: The Man and the Era*. New York: Simon and Schuster, 1994.

Boone, Robert S. *Inside Job: A Life of Teaching*. Chicago: Puddin'Head Press: 2003.

Bukowski, Douglas. *Big Bill Thompson, Chicago, and the Politics of Image*. Urbana: University of Illinois Press, 1998.

Cruikshank, Jeffrey L., and Arthur W. Schultz. *The Man Who Sold America: Albert D. Lasker and the Creation of the Advertising Century*. Boston: Harvard Business Review Press: 2010.

Dierks, Jack. "Ryan at the Mike." *Chicago Tribune Magazine*, December 24, 1972.

Douglass, Harlan Paul. *The Suburban Trend*. New York: Arno Press, 1970.

Drury, John. *Chicago in Seven Days*. New York: Robert M. McBride and Sons, 1930.

Farr, Finis. *Chicago: A Personal History of America's Most American City*. New Rochelle NY: Arlington House, 1973.

Farrell, James T. *Studs Lonigan*. New York: Modern Library, 1938.

Fink, John. WGN: *A Pictorial History*. Chicago: WGN, Inc., 1961.

Gems, Gerald R. *Windy City Wars: Labor, Leisure, and Sport in the Making of Chicago*. Lanham MD: Scarecrow Press, 1997.

Gottfried, Alex. *Boss Cermak of Chicago: A Study of Political Leadership*. Seattle: University of Washington Press, 1962.

Kenney, William Howland. *Chicago Jazz: A Cultural History, 1904–1930*. New York: Oxford University Press, 1993.

Kobler, John. *Capone: The Life and World of Al Capone*. New York: Da Capo Press, 1971.

Lewis, Lloyd, and Henry Justin Smith. *Chicago: The History of Its Reputation*. New York: Harcourt, Brace, 1929.

Liebling, A. J. *Chicago: The Second City*. New York: Knopf, 1952.

Linn, Ed. *A Great Connection*. 2nd ed. Washington DC: Regnery Publishing, 1998.

Littlewood, Thomas B. *Arch—A Promoter, Not a Poet: The Story of Arch Ward*. Ames: Iowa State University Press, 1990.

Lindberg, Richard. *Chicago by Gaslight: A History of Chicago's Netherworld, 1880–1920*. Chicago: Academy Chicago Publishers, 1996.

Mayer, Harold M., and Richard C. Wade. *Chicago: Growth of a Metropolis*. Chicago: University of Chicago Press, 1969.

Murray, George. *The Legacy of Al Capone: Portraits and Annals of America's Public Enemies*. New York: G.P. Putnam's Sons, 1975.

Noverr, Douglas A., and Lawrence E. Ziewacz. *The Games They Played: Sports in American History, 1865–1980*. Chicago: Nelson-Hall, 1983.

Roberts, Howard. *The Chicago Bears*. New York: G. P. Putnam's Sons, 1947.

Sawyers, June Skinner. *Chicago Sketches: Urban Tales, Stories, and Legends from Chicago History*. Chicago: Wild Onion Books, 1995.

Schmidt, John R. *"The Mayor Who Cleaned Up Chicago": A Political Biography of William E. Dever*. DeKalb: Northern Illinois University Press, 1989.

Schoenberg, Robert J. *Mr. Capone: The Real—and Complete—Story of Al Capone*. New York: William Morrow, 1993.

Smith, Alson J. *Chicago's Left Bank*. Chicago: Regnery, 1953.

Smith, Richard Norton. *The Colonel: The Life and Legend of Robert R. McCormick, 1880–1955*. Boston: Houghton Mifflin, 1997.

Spinney, Robert G. *City of Big Shoulders: A History of Chicago*. DeKalb: Northern Illinois University Press, 2000.

Stamper, John W. *North Michigan Avenue: A Building Book from the Chicago Historical Society*. Petaluma CA: Pomegranate Communications, 2005.

Stuart, William H. *The 20 Incredible Years, as "Heard and Seen."* Chicago: M. A. Donohue, 1935.

Whittingham, Richard. *The Chicago Bears from George Halas to Super Bowl XX: An Illustrated History*. New York: Simon and Schuster, 1986.

Zorbaugh, Harvey W. *The Gold Coast and the Slum: A Sociological Study of Chicago's Near North Side*. Chicago: University of Chicago Press, 1929.

General Interest

Archer, Gleason L. *History of Radio to 1926.* New York: Arno Press and the New York Times, 1971.

Brown, Warren. *Win, Lose, or Draw.* New York: G. P. Putnam's Sons, 1947.

Carmichael, Hoagy, with Stephen Longstreet. *Sometimes I Wonder: The Story of Hoagy Carmichael.* New York: Farrar, Straus and Giroux, 1965.

Chase, Francis S. *Sound and Fury: an Informal History of Broadcasting.* New York: Harper and Brothers, 1942.

Cohn, Art. *The Joker Is Wild: The Story of Joe E. Lewis.* New York: Random House, 1955.

Crafton, Donald. *The Talkies: American's Transition to Sound, 1926–1931.* Berkeley: University of California Press, 1997.

DeFleur, Melvin. *Theories of Mass Communication.* 2nd ed. New York: David McKay, 1970.

Federal Writers' Project of the Works Progress Administration of Northern California. *California: A Guide to the Golden State.* New York: Hastings House, 1939.

Frederick Lewis Allen, Only Yesterday: An Informal History of the 1920s. New York: Harper and Row, 1931/1964.

Gunther, John. *Taken at the Flood: The Story of Albert D. Lasker.* New York: Harper, 1960.

Koszarski, Richard. *An Evening's Entertainment: The Age of the Silent Feature Picture, 1915–1918.* Berkeley: University of California Press, 1990.

Ogren, Kathy J. *The Jazz Revolution: Twenties America and the Meaning of Jazz.* New York: Oxford University Press, 1989.

Patterson, Ted. *The Golden Voices of Baseball.* Champaign IL: Sports Publishing, 2002.

Pedersen, Jeannine L. *Catalina Island.* Charleston SC: Arcadia Publishing, 2004.

Poindexter, Ray. *Golden Throats and Silver Tongues.* Conway AR: River Road Press, 1978.

Reagan, Ronald. *Reagan: A Life in Letters.* Edited by Kiron K. Skinner, Annelise Anderson, and Martin Anderson. New York: Free Press, 2004.

Rodgers, Marion Elizabeth. *Mencken: The American Iconoclast.* New York: Oxford University Press, 2005.

Schlesinger, Arthur M. *The Crisis of the Old Order.* Boston: Houghton Mifflin, 1957.

Sterling, Christopher H., and John M. Kittross. *Stay Tuned: A Concise History of American Broadcasting.* Belmont CA: Wadsworth, 1978.

JOURNALS, MAGAZINES, AND WEB SOURCES
Baseball

Andres, Thomas. "Harvesting Baseball's 'Magic Mud.'" CNN U.S., October 28, 2009, http://articles.cnn.com/2009-10-28/us/baseball. mud_1_major-league-baseball-mud-new-ball?_s=PM:US.

Battistella, John B. Untitled and undated article, ca. 1968. Chicago Historical Society files.

Brown, Warren. "Gabby Likes 'Em Hot." *Saturday Evening Post*, February 11, 1939.

Castle, George. "Cubs Glory Days in 1930s Recalled by Woody English." *Baseball Digest*, September 1994.

Crowell, Merle. "The Wonder Story of Wrigley." *American Magazine*, March 1920.

"50 Years Ago." *Chicago History*, Summer 1976.

Frank, Stanley. "The Decline and Fall of the Cubs." *Saturday Evening Post*, September 11, 1943.

Gleason, Dan. "Legends with Pat Pieper." *Chicago Sun-Times Today Magazine*, July 23, 1972.

"Greetings from Catalina Island." *1997 Spring Training Baseball Yearbook* 10 (Spring 1997).

Heuer, Robert. "Neighbors: The Cubs and the Community." *Reader*, April 12, 1985.

Hillman, J. R. "Pat Malone: Threw Hard and Played Harder." *Sports Collectors Digest*, February 7, 1997.

Hubbard, Celia. "Rent Reasonable to Right Parties: Gold Coast Apartments 1906–1929." *Chicago History*, Summer 1979, 76.

Keller, Brent. "Former Cubs Shortstop Woody English Interviewed." *Sports Collectors Digest*, July 27, 1990, 150–51.

Lane, F. C. "The Crash of a Popular Idol." *Baseball Magazine*, February 1932.

———. "McCarthy's Right-Hand Man." *Baseball Magazine*, March 1932.

———. "The Most Colorful Team in Baseball." *Baseball Magazine*, March 1932.

———. "The Passing of Rogers Hornsby." *Baseball Magazine*, October 1932.

———. "Riggs Stephenson, Who Led the Cubs' Offense." *Baseball Magazine*, November 1932.

Library of Congress. "American Memory Collection: Photographs from the *Chicago Daily News*, 1902–1933." http://memory.loc.gov/ammem/ ndlpcoop/ichihtml/cdnhome.html.

Nardinelli, Clark. "Judge Landis and the Art of Cartel Enforcement." In *Baseball History: An Annual of Original Baseball Research*. Edited by Peter Levine. New York: Stadium Books, 1990.

Pedersen, Jeannine. "Catalina Island History: Catalina Island's Hollywood History." Catalina Island Chamber of Commerce and Visitors Bureau. http://www.catalinachamber.com/catalina/history.

"President Hoover's Trials at the World Series." *Literary Digest*, November 2, 1929.

Reynolds, Quentin. "Hartnett Catching." *Collier's*, August 21, 1937.

"Selling Catalina by the Ton." *Business Week*, May 21, 1930.

Soderman, Bob. "Major League Ballplayer Turns Fighter." *Official Boxing Record*, ca. 1955.

Swift, E. M. "One Place That Hasn't Seen the Lights." *Sports Illustrated*, July 7, 1980.

Towers, Wayne M. "World Series Coverage in New York City in the 1920s." *Journalism Monographs* 73 (August 1981).

Wharton, Don. "The Case of the Moving Jaws." *Reader's Digest*, December 1947.

Wrigley, William, as told to Forest Crissey. "Owning a Big League Team." *Saturday Evening Post*, September 13, 1930.

Chicago-Related

Barnett, Lincoln, and Gene Cook. "King of the Ushers: Andy Frain, World's No. 1 Crowd Engineer, Bosses the Delegates at Chicago Conventions." *Reader's Digest*, October 1944, 43 et seq.

Bushnell, D. "Chicago's Magnificent Movie Palaces." *Chicago History*, Winter 1978.

———. "When Jazz Came to Chicago." *Chicago History*, Spring 1971.

"Frightened Stars, Silent Nights All in 25 Year Story." Originally in *The Chainbreak*, April 1947. *Broadcasting in Chicago: 1921–1989 (and Thereafter)*. http://www.richsamuels.com/nbcmm/wmaq/waller/waller2.html.

"Judith Waller—First Lady of Radio." Originally in *The Chainbreak*, April 1947. *Broadcasting in Chicago: 1921–1989 (and Thereafter)*. http://www.richsamuels.com/nbcmm/wmaq/waller/waller1.html.

Keepnews, Orrin. Notes for *Classic Jazz Piano, 1927–1957* (music CD). New York: BMG Music, 1988.

Merwyn, Samuel. "Chicago: The American Paradox." *Saturday Evening Post*, October 26, 1929.

"The Oriental Theater: Remaking a Legend." *Theatre Historical Society of America Annual*, No. 24 (1997).

"WGN Radio Timeline." WGNGOLD.COM, http://www.wgngold.com/timeline/1920s1930s.htm.

White, P. "Looting the Loop." *Collier's*, May 12, 1928.

Williamson, Mary E. "Judith Carey Waller: Chicago Broadcasting Pioneer." *Journalism History* 3, no. 4 (1976–77).

General

Frant-Walsh, Joseph. "St. Catherine's Isle." *The Commonweal,* January 29, 1930.

"Machine Guns Now—What Next?" *Literary Digest,* May 15, 1926.

"Richmond Pullman: Air Conditioning Program." Pullman Richmond California Shops, http://www.pullmanshops.com/1934_AC.htm.

Wyler, Lorraine. "William Wrigley, Jr.—Bird Lover." *Nature Magazine,* April 1931.

UNPUBLISHED WORKS

Caton, Chester F. "Radio Station WMAQ: A History of Its Independent Years (1922–1931)." Ph.D. diss., Northwestern University, 1951.

Ehrgott, Roberts, Sr. "Chicago in the '20s." Unpublished manuscript, ca. 1994.

Linton, Bruce A. "A History of Chicago Radio Station Programming, 1921–1931." Ph.D. diss., Northwestern University, 1953.

Partin, Clyde. "Lewis Robert 'Hack' Wilson, 1900–1948." Paper presented at the annual meeting of the North American Society for Sport History, University of British Columbia, Vancouver, May 23–26, 1986.

Wilson, Robert. "Lewis R. (Hack) Wilson: 'The Forgotten Man of Baseball.'" National Baseball Hall of Fame Library and Museum files, 1979.

Wrigley, Philip K. Interview with Paul Angle, May 9, 1965. Transcript. Chicago Historical Society Manuscripts and Archives Collection.

INTERVIEWS

Brace, George. Interview with author. Chicago, October 30, 1998.

Fitzgerald, John P. Interview with author. Des Plaines IL, September 13, 1999.

Groskloss, Dr. H. Howard. Telephone interview with author. January 17, 1999.

Hornof, Sheila Hartnett. Telephone interview with author. June 26, 1999.

Krehbiel, Frederick. Interview with author. Hinsdale IL, September 10, 1999.

———. Telephone interview with author. November 18, 1998.

Linn, Edward. Telephone interview with author. February 2, 1999.

Moore, Joseph Gregg. Telephone interview with author. January 19, 1999.

Pafko, Andrew. Telephone interview with author. April 21, 1995.

Root, Robert C. Telephone interview with author. July 25, 1999.

Sayers, Marla L. (née Stephenson). Telephone interview with author. July 28, 1999.

Stephenson, Riggs, II. Telephone interview with author. July 27, 1999.

Stephenson, Riggs, III. Telephone interview with author. July 5, 1999.

CORRESPONDENCE

Krehbiel, Frederick. Letter to author. November 24, 1998.

Linn, Edward. Letter to author. March 31, 1999.

INDEX

467

Barsotti, Louis, 117

Barth, Mrs. Herbert, 54, 238

Barton, Vince, 266, 279, 282–83, 285, 301, 307, 363

baseball, 141, 178; batting upsurge in, 178–79; and Black Sox scandal, 29; "busher" as term in, 56; changes in, 22–23; and gambling, 68, 132–33; Golden Age of, 7, 176; and interleague play, 135; and minor league franchises, 282; minor league teams, 137; as modern corporations, 137; as national institution, 46; as national pastime 51; popularity of, 46, 51; and racetrack betting, 9, 139; and radio, 2–3, 37–39, 41–43, 46–52, 61–62, 94–95, 97, 238, 391–92n3; and "rubbing mud," 160; scouts of, 137; ban on spitball in, 104; and straw hats, 242; transformation of, 24; and year of hitter, 225, 231

Baseball Writers Association, 130–31

Battling Criss, 216–17

Beck, Clyde, 226, 249, 271

Beiderbecke, Bix, 228–29

Bell, Les, 2, 225, 244, 282

Benas, Milton, 181

Bender, Chief, 201

Berg, Moe, 159, 168, 193

Berger, Wally, 225, 339

Birmingham Black Barons, 258

Bishop, Max, 204

Blackburne, Lena, 176, 219; and fistfights with Shires, 160, 184–85

Black Sox scandal, 17, 24, 29–30, 66–68, 133, 159, 161, 312, 320, 332, 419n2

Blackstone Hotel, 33

Blair, Footsie, 247, 249

Blake, Fred "Sheriff," 106, 119, 126, 148, 167, 231, 241, 271, 288

Blankenship, Ted, 25, 37, 58, 87, 158–59; Alexander's duel with, 78

Boston Braves, 1, 6, 11, 18, 64, 72, 128, 138, 140, 142, 145, 173, 176, 183, 236, 251, 271, 294, 299, 312, 339, 359, 360; attendance numbers of, 377n1

Boston Red Sox, 131, 145, 178

Bottomley, Jim, 43, 120–21, 382n42

Bowler, Thomas, 172–73, 181, 361

Brabbets, Lefty, 141

Brace, George, 287

Bramhall, Jack, 63

Breadon, Sam, 137

Brebner, Charles, 64

Brehm, Claire, 305

Brenzel, Bill, 272–73

Bressler, Rube, 246

Brickell, Fred, 124–25

Bridges, Tommy, 267

Bridwell, Al, 38

Brief, Bunny, 24

Brizzolara, Thomas, 392n12

Bronzeville (neighborhood), 15, 28–29, 134, 227, 258

Brooklyn Dodgers, 73, 174–76, 236–38, 241, 246, 248–49, 252, 273–77, 294–95, 299–300, 302, 339–40, 348–51

Brown, Joe E., 108, 153

Brown, Mordecai "Three-Finger," 13, 27, 74, 162, 180, 402n40

Brown, Warren, 156, 307, 329–31, 385n25, 438n11, 454; scoop of, 251–54; "So They Tell Me" column of, 252

Brunke, Mrs. Gustav, 54

Bryan, William Jennings, 39–40

Buckner, Bill, 28–29

Buckner, Harry, 28

Burke, Jimmy, 24, 59, 141, 184, 365

Burke, Patrick, 69

Burns, Ed, 156–57, 201, 213–15, 245, 253–54, 297, 299, 331, 343, 360, 426n72, 454

Bush, Donie, 123–24, 127, 179, 219–20, 279, 298, 404n22

Bush, Guy, 48, 70, 106, 112–13, 148, 157,

O'Connell, Jimmy, 407n63
O'Connor, Catherine, 238
O'Connor, Leslie, 317, 319–20, 323–24
O'Doul, Frank "Lefty," 70–71, 73,
    141–42, 247–48, 250, 258, 273, 275,
    277, 300, 302, 348–50, 393n26, 426n77
O'Farrell, Bob, 77
O'Hara, Johnny, 97
Oldfield, Barney, 41
The Old Man and the Sea (Hemingway),
    168
O'Leary, Charley: gambling investiga-
    tion of, 320–21, 323, 327
Oliver, Joe "King," 228
Oriental Theater, 187–89, 199, 203, 259
Orsatti, Ernie, 173, 268
Osborn, Bob, 72, 244
Ott, Mel, 239, 353
Otto, Wayne, 13, 198, 239, 252, 353, 448,
    451
Overall, Orval, 27

Pacific Coast League, 107
Padden, Frank, 347
Paderewski, Ignace, 81
Paige, Leroy "Satchel," 258–59
Parker, Sir Gilbert, 45
Pasadena CA: spring training at, 77,
    395n45
Pegler, Westbrook, 330–32, 358, 454
Pennock, Herb, 89, 372
Pestka, Betty, 182
Peterson, D. J., 306
Petty, Jess, 121–22, 248
Pfirman, Cy, 110, 128
Philadelphia PA: blue laws in, 202, 247
Philadelphia A's. *See* Philadelphia
    Athletics
Philadelphia Athletics, 84, 184–85, 189,
    192, 196, 202, 243, 252, 351; scouting
    against Cubs by, 193; and World
    Series, 194–95, 199–207

Philadelphia Phillies, 18, 63, 105–6, 131,
    178, 180, 186, 236, 241, 247–48, 264,
    275, 302, 309–10, 340, 347–48, 401n34
Pieper, Pat, 5–6, 10, 62, 169, 178, 224,
    342, 378n8
Piet, Tony, 298, 312
Pilsen (neighborhood), 9
"Pineapple Primary," 118, 262, 288–89
Pinelli, Babe, 78
Pittsburgh Pirates, 25, 38, 41–42, 47, 54,
    81, 94, 104, 123–25, 165, 175–76, 179,
    186, 236, 272–73, 276, 279, 296–97,
    298–300, 302, 309–12, 315–16, 337,
    339, 351, 361
Plantation (nightclub), 227
Polo Grounds, 12, 23, 84, 86, 102–3,
    127–28, 142, 174, 180, 186, 193,
    248–50, 252, 310, 359–60
Popovich, Violet. *See* Valli, Violet
Povich, Shirley, 452
Powers, Jimmy, 219
Pratt, Russell, 44, 47–48, 389n55
Prell, Ed, 331
Prevo, Allen Munn, 229
Prevo, Mrs. Allen Munn, 228–29
Prohibition, 19, 116, 139

Quigley, Ernie, 109
Quinn, Jack, 194, 196–97

race riots, 9, 209
radio broadcasting, 45–49, 388n47; and
    advertising, 43–44; and attendance,
    61, 95; of baseball games, 37–39, 62,
    94–95, 238, 391–92n3; and emer-
    gence of play-by-play, 95; and
    Scopes trial, 39–40; and women, 96.
    See also sports broadcasting
Ragen Colts, 9, 209
Randolph, Robert, 34
Reading Keys, 282. *See also* Albany
    Senators

Waller, Judith, 44–50, 52–53, 61, 95–96

Walsh, Ed, 178

Walsh, John, 452

Waner, Lloyd, 124, 241, 316

Waner, Paul, 315–16

Ward, Arch, 15, 135, 307, 331

Ware, J. A., 375

Warneke, Lon, 269, 275, 294, 300–302, 310, 315–17, 338, 347, 353, 356, 359, 366, 371, 373; Grimes's substitutes for, 268; Hornsby callingpitches for, 278, 299

Warp, Harold, 451

Washington Senators, 220

Watkins, Maurine, 282

Watwood, Johnny, 258

WEAF (radio station), 40

Webb, Earl, 98, 104, 112, 142, 395n43

Weeghman, Charles, 35, 130–31, 353, 385n25

Weiss, Hymie, 17, 66, 91–92

WENR (radio station), 183, 186

West Side Grounds, 8

WGN (radio station), 37, 40, 42, 43, 47–48, 51, 61, 95–97, 113, 387n36

White City, 210–11, 216

Whitehill, Earl, 267

Whitney, Pinky, 309

Williams, Cy, 79

Williams, Joe, 452, 454–55

William Wrigley Co., 30, 265, 282

Wilson, Bobby, 18, 211

Wilson, Lewis "Hack," 16, 17, 21, 26, 54, 68, 71, 80, 85, 94, 96, 98, 103–4, 109–10, 112–13, 122, 124, 126–27, 141, 144, 146, 148–49, 158, 161, 163–64, 175–76, 179–84, 186–87, 191, 194, 199–202, 208, 211, 222, 225–26, 229, 234, 244, 246–47, 249, 260, 265, 272, 282–83, 298–301, 339, 348, 358, 360–61, 368, 370, 372, 382n42, 395n43, 399–400n15, 400n22, 401n31, 412n38, 425n58, 426–27n80, 431n35, 445n33; ankle sprain of, 60–61, 63; ankles' taping of, 415n72; arrest of, 69; background of, 22, 382–83n1; bat of, 86; batting style of, 12; benching of, 168–69; booing at, 121; as blue-collar hero, 10; boxing career of, 214–18; and boxing match against Shires, 212–13; as box office draw, 239; comeback of, 18; coming out of, 62; contract signing of, 262; controvery surrounding, 101; crash of, 269; as Cubs' superstar, 76; as Cuyler's rival, 125; as Dodger, 349–50; downfall of, 20; drinking of, 22, 240; extraordinary life of, 19; fans' mingling with, 274; fighting of, 119–20, 170–71; fining of, 121, 128, 172; firing of, 266; first home run of, 72; Foxx catch of, 197–98; fruit throwing at, 87–88, 258; generosity of, 101–2; and Hall of Fame election, 240; historicRBI of, 257; hits scoreboard, 64; hitting streak of, 19, 87, 174, 237, 241, 248, 294–95; home runs of, 251; Hornsby's feud with, 270, 275; on Hornsby's resignation, 306; as hot-head, 19, 171–72; hustling of, 99; joins Cubs, 59; and Kolp brawl, 170–72; legend of, 63; and Malone, 128, 270, 276–77; Martinsburg victory parade for, 259; in minors, 23–24; and Murderers' Row, 174; with New York Giants, 23–24; and NL home run crown, 86; 1930 season of, 19; notoriety of, 87; outfielding of, 383n3; persona of, 69; physique of, 22; popularity of, 14, 18; prosecution of, 173; rage of, 86; records set by, 235; reputation of, 86; and Ruth, 239, 241–42, 256; salary of, 20, 64; slump of, 128; and Sox

attendance at, 2–3, 98, 106, 188, 343; betting at, 9; and bleachers, 7–10, 68, 190, 368, 379n13; Chicago population at, 4; culture of, 191; customer base of, 36; Depression's effect on attendance, 264; enhancements at, 36, 92, 385–86n26; fans at, 1; female fans of, 3, 237; football at, 136; and gambling, 68; Joe McCarthy Day at, 257; jury box at, 7; Ladies Day at, 3–4, 190, 231, 343; and name change, 92; as place to be seen, 190; pop bottle insurrection at, 75, 109–10, 386n27; rowdies at, 36; seating capacity of, 449–50; skimmers at, 3; and World Series (1932), 451–55. *See also* Cubs Park

"Wrigley Nips," 140–41, 450–51

Xenia, Princess, 112

Yancey, Jimmy, 29
Yankee Stadium, 2, 23, 29, 84, 112, 365
Young, Cy, 25
Young, Edward, 118–20, 215, 220–21, 225; arrest of, 121; lawsuit of, 122; and Wilson incident, 118–19, 120–21, 421n29
Young, George, 155
Young Lonigan (Farrell), 209
Youngs, Ross, 23–24, 102

Zak, Frank, 381n36
Zimmerman, Heinie, 86